Publishing and Multimedia Law

Publishing and Multimedia Law

Michael Henry
Solicitor

Butterworths
London, Dublin, Edinburgh
1994

United Kingdom	Butterworth & Co (Publishers) Ltd, 88 Kingsway, LONDON WC2B 6AB and 4 Hill Street, EDINBURGH EH2 3JZ
Australia	Butterworths, SYDNEY, MELBOURNE, BRISBANE, ADELAIDE, PERTH, CANBERRA and HOBART
Canada	Butterworths Canada Ltd, TORONTO and VANCOUVER
Ireland	Butterworth (Ireland) Ltd, DUBLIN
Malaysia	Malayan Law Journal Sdn Bhd, KUALA LUMPUR
New Zealand	Butterworths of New Zealand Ltd, WELLINGTON and AUCKLAND
Puerto Rico	Butterworths of Puerto Rico, Inc, SAN JUAN
Singapore	Butterworths Asia, SINGAPORE
South Africa	Butterworths Publishers (Pty) Ltd, DURBAN
USA	Butterworth Legal Publishers, CARLSBAD, California and SALEM, New Hampshire

A CIP Catalogue record for this book is available from the British Library.

ISBN 0 406 03768 X

This book is produced on paper produced from timber harvested from sustainable forest

Typeset by Create Publishing Services Ltd, Bath, Avon
Printed and bound by William Clowes Ltd Beccles & London

About this book

About the text

The text is aimed at two different readerships: at professionals who are active in the world of publishing and multimedia; and also at the legal profession. Some parts of the text may, therefore, be of limited interest to the publishing or multimedia professional, whilst others may be of limited interest to lawyers.

The book is intended to be a general guide to the law, and cannot be a substitute for legal advice. Neither the author nor the publisher accept any responsibility for loss occasioned to any person acting or refraining from acting as a result of material contained in this publication.

Where legislation is summarised, the text aims to provide a précis of the legislation using, wherever possible, the words and phrases of the original Act. Although this may, occasionally, result in certain infelicities of style, the words and sense of the legislation are retained.

The law in the text is correct as at 1 January 1994.

About the documents

The documents contained in this book are precedent documents which may be suitable for use in certain transactions in the publishing and multimedia business. All documents need to be amended to suit appropriate circumstances.

The difficulty of amending documents should not be under-estimated. In many cases, the level of skill required to amend a document may be equal to that required to draft it.

A non-exclusive licence to use and reproduce the documents contained in this book (other than document 37) exists in favour of all purchasers of the book. The documents may be freely copied and used, but it is a condition of the licence that neither the author nor the publisher accepts any responsibility for loss occasioned to any person using the documents or acting or refraining from acting as a result of material contained in them.

About the disk

The disk accompanying this book contain the full text of all documents (except document 37) and the full text of all accompanying notes.

A non-exclusive licence exists in favour of all purchasers of the book, permitting the free copying and use of the disk subject to the same conditions as those which apply to the use of the documents (see "About The Documents" above).

Acknowledgments

The author would like to acknowledge the assistance of:

Amanda Eveleigh and Amanda Bridge for 110 wpm and 100% accuracy;

Neil Baker, Nicola Gillespie, Christine Mathisen, Simon Paolo and Tim Robinson for research assistance;

Peter Bond for assistance on competition law matters;

Julian Hemming for assistance on employment law matters;

Susan Oake for advice in relation to newspapers and the press;

Jeffrey Boloten for his laconic observations; and

Jenny Cottrell for contributing the sections on taxation in Chapters 11 and 12.

All royalties from this book will be applied by Actionaid towards the relief of famine and poverty in the developing countries.

Giving
People
Choices

ACTIONAID

Contents

H. Agents, personal representatives and executors

I. General principles of the law of agency

3. Creation, existence and transfer of copyrights and trade marks   37

A. Introduction

B. Definition of copyright

C. Copyright works

D. Requirements for copyright protection in the United Kingdom

E. Originality

5. Moral rights and rights of privacy and personality   75

B. General matters relating to authors' agreements

C. Copyright and moral rights

D. Specific provisions in authors' agreements

E. Minimum terms agreements

8. Permissions, fair dealing, rights, clearances, permitted acts and Crown and Parliamentary copyright   117

A. Introduction

B. Permissions and fair dealing

C. Reporting events, incidental inclusion, use of notes, public reading

9. Liability for content   138

E. Motion picture and television rights

F. Remuneration provisions in rights agreements

G. Participations in receipts and profits

H. Taxation

12. Distribution agreements – the commercial terms   209

A. Introduction

B. Principal terms

C. Delivery and risk

D. Retention of title

E. Sale or return

F. Undertakings and obligations

G. Value Added Tax

H. Distribution and sale of goods

13. Infringement and enforcement   235

A. Introduction

B. Infringement of copyright

16. Competition law   260

A. Introduction

B. United Kingdom competition law

C. European Union competition law

D. Distribution agreements

E. Purchasing agreements

F. Licensing agreements

G. Agency agreements

H. European Free Trade Association

E. Collective licensing schemes

F. Copyright ownership, rental rights, subsidiary rights and patents

G. Development and production of multimedia works

H. Licensing distribution and joint ventures

I. Databases and telecommunications

J. Computer misuse

20. Publishing and multimedia – the future   339

List of documents

Table of Statutes

Table of cases

1. Ideas and rights

[IMPORTANT NOTE: Please read the section "About this book" on page v, before referring to any of the matters in this chapter]

A. Introduction

1.1 Purpose of this chapter

The period between the first moment a publisher or multimedia company has an idea for a work (or is first approached by an author) and the moment the author signs the commissioning agreement, is of crucial importance.

During this period a number of fundamental decisions are made, some by default, others through constraint, and a number of issues will arise both directly and indirectly.

The aim of this chapter is to examine the legal and commercial implications of these issues, beginning with an analysis of the protection of ideas and the law relating to confidentiality. The different types of publication rights and various subsidiary rights which might be acquired by a publisher or multimedia company are then examined, before the chapter lists some of the matters which need to be considered before a work is commissioned.

The question of whether copyright should be assigned or licensed is frequently raised by authors. The differences between assignments and licences of copyrights and the multiplicity of copyright are examined. The chapter concludes with practical advice on commissioning works.

B. Ideas and confidentiality

1.2 Are ideas protected by copyright?

The first stage in the creative process of any work is the conception of the idea behind the work itself. The idea for a work may occur either to publisher/multimedia company or to an author. When a literary work is at the idea stage, and nothing about it has been written down, or discussed, the work will not be protected by the laws of copyright (see paragraphs 3.2 to 3.20).

1

Although ideas may not be protected by copyright, there are circumstances where they may be protected by other laws. The use of the ideas in these circumstances may be unlawful. It is therefore important for publishers and multimedia companies to be aware of and to recognise the circumstances in which they may not make free use of the ideas of others.

1.3 How can ideas be protected?

How do you obtain protection for ideas? The law recognises that some types of information are confidential, and protects the owner of confidential information from its unauthorised use or disclosure. Protection is available at common law and in order to qualify for this kind of protection it must be shown that:

(a) the information was capable of having the necessary quality of confidence[1] (see paragraph 1.4); and
(b) the information was imparted in confidence either under an express condition of confidentiality, or in circumstances where confidentiality would be implied[2].

1 See *Coco v A N Clark (Engineers) Ltd* [1969] RPC 41; *Jarman & Platt Ltd v I Barget Ltd* [1977] FSR 260, CA.
2 *G D Searle & Co Ltd v Celltech Ltd* [1982] FSR 92, CA.

1.4 What material has the "necessary quality of confidence"?

There is no requirement for the information to be in tangible form[3], and although the information must not be common knowledge, it may have had some circulation[4]. Where artistic and literary confidences are concerned, even if the confidential details have been given circulation previously, the courts have, in the past, been prepared to restrain the further circulation of information which has been made available in a confidential context[5].

A number of different categories of information are capable of being protected by the laws relating to confidentiality. These include technical secrets[6], know-how[7], recipes[8], and business secrets including matters such as management or accountants reports[9]. In order to qualify, however, the material must have the necessary quality of confidence or secrecy about it.

It is difficult to provide universally applicable guidelines as to what the necessary quality of confidence or secrecy might be in any given situation, but readily available material of a mundane nature will not generally be capable of protection. The courts will not permit the law of confidentiality to be used in such a way as to permit individuals to create monopoly no-go areas over whole subject areas; this would clearly be against the public interest.

It will follow, therefore, that if an author approaches a company with an idea for a history of Wellington's military campaign in Spain, the idea, of itself, will not have the necessary quality of confidence, and will not prevent the company from subsequently commissioning another author to write a book on the subject.

If, however, the original author had discovered in an archive in Lisbon certain "lost" military papers whose existence was unknown to all but the author, and which dramatically changed the historians' view of the Peninsular War, the existence of these papers would clearly be confidential information. The company could not subsequently commission another author to write a book or screenplay or other work using the "lost" papers, without breaking the confidence of the first author.

3 See, for example, *Cranleigh Precision Engineering Ltd v Bryant* [1964] 3 All ER 289, [1965] 1 WLR 1293.
4 *McNichol v Sportsman's Book Stores* [1930] MacG Cop Cos [1928–35] 116; *Nichrotherm Electrical Company Ltd v Percy* [1957] RPC 207, CA.
5 *Gilbert v Star Newspaper Company* (1894) 11 TLR 4.
6 *Amber Size & Chemical Company Ltd v Menzel* [1913] 2 Ch 239.
7 *Stevenson Jordan & Harrison Ltd v MacDonald & Evans* [1952] ITLR 101, CA.
8 *Yovatt v Winyard* (1820) 1 JAC & W 394; *Morison v Moat* (1851) 9 Hare 241.
9 *Jarman & Platt Ltd v I Barget Ltd* [1977] FSR 260, CA.

C. Confidentiality

1.5 Relevance of confidentiality laws

There are three principal areas of the law relating to confidentiality which are relevant to the business of publishing and multimedia companies:

(a) between the company and its authors;
(b) between the company's authors and third parties;
(c) between the company and its employees.

1.6 Confidentiality between company and author

Where an author submits unsolicited material to a company, it will not be a breach of confidentiality if the company uses the material solely to determine whether or not it wishes to enter into an agreement with the author in relation to the material[10]. The company may also submit the material, on a confidential basis, to independent third parties for evaluation, without being in breach of any confidentiality obligation.

In fact it is in this area that the company may find the greatest risk. How can the company make sure that its author has not plagiarised other people's material or broken their confidence?

There may be occasions where a company receives submissions involving near identical or similar material from two different authors. The company will not be in breach of its confidentiality obligations towards Author 1 if it commissions Author 2 to write a work. The company should, however, ensure that no material provided by Author 1 is made available to Author 2 and will also need to enquire as to the existence of any links between Author 1 and Author 2 so as to eliminate any problem.

10 *Johnson v Heat & Air Systems Ltd* (1941) 58 RPC 229; *Talbot v General Television Corporation Pty Ltd* [1981] RPC 1 (Vict SC).

1.7 Confidentiality between authors and third parties

If, in the example given in paragraph 1.6, Author 2 has "borrowed" his or her material from Author 1, then the company will have a problem. It is in the interests of the company to flush out any potential problems of this nature at the earliest possible stage, and although the author's contract should always contain a warranty dealing with breach of confidentiality, there is no substitute or short-cut for common sense.

In certain types of publication, it is unlikely that there could be any risk. In others, there are obvious risk factors. For example, a work about a member of the Royal Family written by a former employee and containing details of their personal life would obviously be a potential problem. Similarly, a work in which a spouse (or former spouse) revealed matters of marital confidence might also cause difficulties.

Where a work does breach confidence, the company's position will not be improved if the company is unaware of the breach. The wounded third party can still seek an injunction to restrain publication of other exploitation of the work.

1.8 Confidentiality between company and employee

Persons who are employed have certain good faith obligations towards their employers. One of these obligations is not to disclose confidential information.

Companies may experience difficulties when employees leave employment and use information which they obtained from the company in order to compete against the company.

Where the information consists of trade secrets, a company may prevent its use or disclosure by former employees. Where the information is of a trivial character or is easily available from public sources, its use cannot be prevented.

There is, however, a further category of information which is of a confidential nature (such as sales information) but which, once learned, forms part of the employee's own knowledge and experience. Once the employment is at an end the law permits a former employee to use their skill and knowledge for their own benefit, and to trade in competition with their former employer.

If a company wishes to protect itself from former employees using skill and knowledge which they have acquired from the company to compete against it, a specific restriction (known as a restrictive covenant) needs to be inserted into an employee's contract of employment. The restriction should be no wider than that necessary to protect the company's business interests and should relate to a stated area, geographic location and type of business, if it is to be enforceable.

1.9 Court procedures for breach of confidentiality

In order for companies to bring court proceedings for a breach of confidentiality, it is not necessary to show that an employee deliberately broke their duty of confidentiality. The unauthorised, or even subconscious, use of materials which have been submitted in confidence may form the basis of legal proceedings[11]. Even only a partial disclosure of confidential material will be actionable if a material part of the confidential information is disclosed[12].

11 *Seager v Copydex Ltd* [1967] 2 All ER 415, [1967] 1 WLR 923, CA; *Terrapin Ltd v Builders Supply Company (Hayes) Ltd* [1967] RPC 375.
12 *Amber Size & Chemical Company Ltd v Menzel* [1913] 2 Ch 239.

1.10 How to impose confidentiality obligations

Where it is desired to impose obligations of confidentiality upon a person, it is advisable, where possible, to create some written record that the material has been disclosed in confidence. A form of confidentiality agreement is contained in Document 1. This document will create a relationship of confidentiality, but many companies, authors or other persons may be reluctant to sign it, because it implies mistrust.

A more practical way of establishing an obligation of confidentiality is to make an initial telephone call to the person to whom the information is going to be disclosed and to say that you intend to make available certain material on a confidential basis. If they accept this, then you can send the materials to them under cover of a letter which states that they have been submitted on a confidential basis. It is, of course, open to the recipient to return the materials unread, or to return them to you with a submission agreement (see paragraph 1.11).

1.11 Unsolicited manuscripts

When an author sends the manuscript of a book to a company, this amounts to an offer to enter into negotiations, and does not constitute a contractual offer. Acceptance by the company of the manuscript will therefore not form a binding contract to publish the book. (For an explanation of the importance of the concepts of offer and acceptance in the law of contract, see paragraphs 2.5 and 2.6.)

The company will have a duty to look after any manuscript received by the company (unsolicited or not) and will be liable to the author for its loss, where such loss is due to the negligence of the company or its employees.

Some companies return all unsolicited material unread. The material is returned under cover of a standard letter which invites the person who submitted the material to return it, accompanied by an executed submission agreement. The purpose of the submission agreement is to reduce the risk of legal proceedings being brought against a company by persons who may claim direct, indirect, or subconscious infringement of copyright, or breach of confidence or passing off (see paragraph 3.19). A form of submission letter is contained in Document 2. It should be noted that the use of a submission agreement will not give a company carte blanche to infringe copyright and other rights. It will merely prevent persons whose material has been rejected by the company from making frivolous claims.

1.12 Disclosure of contents of manuscripts and confidential information

A company can submit a manuscript to a third party for an opinion. Although the company will remain liable for loss or destruction of the manuscript, there is no obligation on the company to prevent the manuscript, or copies of it, falling into the possession of persons who might then use or exploit the work without the author's consent. Unauthorised use of copyright material can, of course, be prevented by an author where that author's right of copyright is infringed (see paragraphs 13.1 to 13.17).

Companies may in some cases disclose information to professional advisers (lawyers, accountants etc) who are themselves bound by confidentiality obligations. The courts can also make orders requiring the disclosure of information and failure to comply with those orders may constitute contempt of court (see paragraphs 10.2 to 10.6).

D. Acquiring rights generally

1.13 Types of rights a company may acquire

There are three key points of information which a company needs to identify in acquiring rights (whether from an author or another company). These are:

(a) *The type of rights being acquired:* Is the company acquiring publication rights alone? Or are subsidiary rights also being acquired?
(b) *The territory:* Over what geographical area may the rights be exercised?
(c) *The term:* For what period may the rights be exercised?

1.14 Publication rights and subsidiary rights

Where a company acquires publication rights in a work the company will normally obtain the right to print and publish the work, or cause it to be published, in volume or sheet form. The publication rights will normally include all forms of exploitation that the company intends to undertake. They may also in some cases include forms of exploitation which the company does not intend to undertake, but intends to license to third parties (such as United States paperback rights for example). Rights which the company does not intend or is not capable itself of exploiting, but intends to sub-license to third parties are frequently dealt with as subsidiary rights.

It will be appreciated that the distinction is frequently blurred. In some cases a company may acquire both hardback and paperback publication rights and may license the paperback rights onwards to an associated imprint, or a third party. In other cases, the publication rights acquired by a company may include only hardback rights but the company might still retain the paperback rights as a subsidiary right (ie a right which the company itself will not exercise but will authorise others to exercise).

1.15 Payment for publication rights and subsidiary rights

The payment provisions which publishers offer authors normally differ slightly, depending on the types of rights being acquired.

A publisher will generally offer to pay an author from whom publication rights are being acquired, a royalty. The royalty will normally be a percentage of the cover price of each copy of the book which is printed by the publisher and is sold.

There are occasions, however, when a publisher licenses publication rights to third parties, and on these occasions a publisher has a choice. It may either pay the author a royalty for each copy of the book sold by the publisher's licensee or, alternatively, it may pay the author a percentage of the sums it receives from its licensees.

The disadvantage to the publisher of the former course, is that it will be liable to pay the author even if the publisher never receives the money from its licensees. In practice this liability may be difficult for an author to prove. If the sub-licensee does not pay the publisher, it may not even provide the publisher with sales figures. If the publisher has no sales figures, it will be even harder for an author to get these to establish that a debt is payable by the publisher. If the second option is chosen the publisher will only be liable to pay the author a percentage of what it actually receives.

Where a publisher authorises the exploitation of subsidiary rights, the publisher will normally pay to the author a percentage of the income which has been received by the publisher (as opposed to a specific sum for each copy of the book which is sold). This will mean that the author's receipts will be reduced if the publisher's sub-licensees sell books at less than the recommended price, or if the publisher or the sub-licensees have bad debts.

1.16 Types of subsidiary rights

It is normal for a specific clause in publishing contracts to deal with granting subsidiary rights to the publisher. A number of separate rights can be grouped together, under the generic heading of subsidiary rights. The definition is somewhat loose, since it will, in each case, depend on the precise terms of the contract. The following are all subsidiary rights.

(a) Anthology and quotation rights

These rights permit the publisher to authorise the reproduction of extracts from a work (including illustrations and maps) in other publications. Where a publisher acquires anthology and quotation rights, the publisher will be able to give permissions (see paragraph 8.2).

(b) Book Club rights

Book Club rights are sometimes acquired by a publisher in the grant of publication rights (see paragraph 1.14).

(c) Braille

Sometimes a provision giving the publisher the right to authorise the use of a book in braille form, or in talking book form, is included within subsidiary rights clause. Alternatively, a separate clause may be included, which deals specifically with braille, and gives the publisher the right to make such use available free of charge.

(d) Computer game rights

Computer game rights permit the publisher to authorise the making and exploitation of computer games based on the book.

(e) Digest rights

Digest rights permit the publisher to authorise an abridgement, or condensation, of the book in magazines, journals, periodicals, newspapers or other works.

(f) Educational rights

Educational rights permit the publisher to authorise the publication of a special edition of the book, which may contain additional material which makes it suitable for school use.

(g) First serial rights

The first serial right is the right to publish extracts from the book in one issue, or more than one successive, or non-successive, issue of newspapers, magazines or periodicals. First issue rights are normally exercised before publication of the book. It is normal also for them to be limited in scope, so as to avoid damaging the sales prospects of the book. The first serial rights are intended to stimulate demand for the book, not to provide a substitute for it.

(h) Information storage and retrieval system rights

These rights are sometimes (misleadingly) referred to as the mechanical reproduction rights. They permit the publisher to use, and authorise the book to be used, in electronic databases by means of storage and retrieval systems, microfilm, magnetic tape or disk or reprography.

(i) Merchandising rights

Merchandising rights permit the publisher to authorise the use of characters or illustrations from the book in, or on, articles other than books.

(j) Motion picture and television rights

These are the rights to authorise the making of any film or television production based on the book. Occasionally the rights covered by this category may extend to videograms, records and computer games.

(k) Paperback rights

Frequently paperback rights will be obtained by the publisher in the publication rights clause (see paragraph 1.14), but these will depend on the circumstances.

(l) Reading rights

Reading rights permit the publisher to authorise the straight, or non-dramatic, reading of the book on radio or television, or the live stage, and also may extend to include the making of videograms or records.

(m) Reprint rights

Reprint rights permit the publisher to authorise the reprinting of the book. Sometimes this may be done by foreign publishers using materials which have been produced by other foreign publishers.

(n) Second and subsequent serial rights

These rights are normally defined as the right to authorise the issue, or publication, of the book in newspapers, or periodicals which appear subsequent to those in which the book was first serialised. A person acquiring second or subsequent serial rights before the first serial rights have been exercised, will normally wish to specify a date from which the second serial rights may be exercised. Without such a provision, if the purchaser of the first serial rights goes into liquidation, or decides not to exercise them, the second serial rights cannot be exploited.

(o) Single issue rights

These rights are sometimes referred to as "one-shot" newspaper or periodical rights. They comprise the right to authorise the publication of the book (sometimes in condensed form) in a single issue of a periodical or newspaper.

(p) Sound recording rights

These rights permit the publisher to authorise the making and exploitation of sound recordings incorporating the book.

(q) Translation rights

Depending on the territory for which the publisher acquires printed publication rights, the translation rights may be treated as publication rights, rather than subsidiary rights. In other words, if the publisher acquires the

9

right to publish the book in Spain, it will need at the same time to acquire the right to translate the book into Spanish.

(r) US rights

Rights for the territory of the United States of America (or in some cases United States of America and Canada which are often treated as the same market) are generally subject to different financial provisions. Normally a publisher will wish to apply a lower royalty for sales in the North American market.

E. Factors to be considered in relation to acquiring rights

1.17 What matters need to be considered before commissioning or acquiring a book?

Before a book is commissioned, a number of matters need to be considered, so that appropriate provision may be made in the commissioning agreement. The publisher and the author need to identify exactly what role the author is to play. Will the author be involved as author, or co-author, or adaptor, or editor?

If the book is to include or be based on copyright material (see paragraph 3.2), what authorisations, permissions or releases (see paragraph 8.2) need to be obtained from copyright owners, in order to clear the use of the underlying rights in the work?

Where a book is to contain interviews given by living persons, their consent in writing will need to be obtained in order to avoid infringement of rights of privacy or rights of publicity (see paragraphs 5.20 and 5.21).

Additionally, all interview subjects will need to assign the copyright in their interviews because, even though the author may have written them down, (s)he may not be the sole author for copyright purposes (see paragraph 3.10). This is particularly important where a book is "ghosted".

Before the 1988 Copyright, Designs and Patents Act, the subject of a "ghosted" autobiography did not have any copyright in the words, but, where any interview has been given on or after 1 August 1989, the interview subject may, in many cases, own or co-own the copyright in what is written down (see paragraph 3.10). It should be noted that this does not prevent use by a journalist of information obtained in an interview, for the purpose of reporting current events (see paragraph 8.8).

Where a book is neither written, nor adapted, by the person offering it to the publisher, the publisher will normally wish to check the history of ownership of the book (often referred to as its "chain of title") to ensure that the person offering it has good title to it (actually owns it). The publisher will also need to verify matters relating to the book's authorship, and in some cases obtain warranties from the authors of the book (if these are not the persons selling it).

A checklist to be followed by publishers before issuing commissioning agreements is contained in Document 3. This contains details of the principal factors which will need to be included in an offer letter. Great care should be taken by the publisher to avoid creating a contract when issuing an offer letter, and for this reason all such correspondence should be headed "subject to contract". Care should also be taken not to create any contractual commitment to publish the work when it is delivered (see paragraph 1.23).

1.18   Should copyright be assigned or licensed?

Should publishers require authors to assign copyright, or should the copyright simply be licensed? Many authors feel strongly that they should not assign rights to publishers, but should only license them. They feel that the copyright in the book should remain at all times vested in them. This fact has been recognised by publishers who are prepared in many cases to be granted exclusive licences in a book. Multimedia companies will, in many cases, need to acquire assignments of copyright, rather than licences.

What is the difference between an assignment and a licence? (See paragraphs 3.38 to 3.40 and paragraph 11.3.) In general terms it can be compared to the difference between freehold property and leasehold property. When rights in a book are assigned to a publisher, the territory in which the publisher can exercise those rights will be specified. The publisher will be the owner of those rights in that territory, for all time, and is free to exploit or dispose of them in the publisher's absolute discretion, in exactly the same way as the owner of a freehold in a house. There is one small difference between houses and books. At the end of the copyright period in a book, the copyright owner cannot stop anyone else exploiting it, although (s)he may continue to exploit the book.

Where a publisher is granted a licence of rights, the period in which the rights can be exercised and the territory will again be specified, but the publisher will only have the right to sub-licence the rights to third parties, if the publishing agreement permits the publisher to do so. If the publisher commits a serious breach of the publisher's obligations, then the author will generally be able to terminate the licence, which will bring to an end the publisher's rights and leave the author free to make new arrangements for the exploitation of the book.

Outright assignments of copyright are not generally capable of termination. In some cases, a document may give the author the right to have the copyright in a book reassigned, following any serious breach by the publisher. It is, however, possible for an author to assign a copyright to a publisher for a designated period which will end on the expiry of a number of years, or the occurrence of any serious breach of the agreement by the publisher, whichever happens first. While there is no legal difficulty in effecting such an assignment, it is not yet common practice in the publishing industry.

1.19   Rights and exclusivity

Where copyright in a work is assigned, the person who acquires it (or the "assignee") will generally have the exclusive right to do and/or authorise the doing of the various acts which are restricted by copyright (see paragraph 3.2).

Where copyright in a work is licensed, the licensee (or person to whom the licence is granted) will have the right to do the specific acts which are authorised in the licence. The licensee will not generally have the right to authorise other persons to exploit the licensed rights, unless the licence agreement contains an express provision allowing the licensee to grant sub-licences. When the rights of a licensee terminate, the rights of sub-licensees will also terminate, unless the contract provides that they will continue. When a licence terminates either at the end of the licence period, or when the licensor (the person granting the rights) exercises a termination right, the author or licensor will be free to make new arrangements for the exploitation of the work.

The rights granted under a licence may be exclusive or non-exclusive, or a combination. Generally, a publisher will acquire exclusive rights, and it is most important that the contract should specify that the rights have been granted on an exclusive basis. If the licence is exclusive, this means that the author cannot grant rights in the work to anyone else. If the licence is non-exclusive the author is free to grant rights in the work to third parties. Failure to specify that the licence is exclusive will not only expose the publisher to potential competition from other non-exclusive licensees, but it will mean that the publisher may have serious difficulties in preventing infringement of copyright by third parties, because a non-exclusive licensee cannot start court proceedings without the consent of the copyright owner.

An exclusive licensee has the right to start court proceedings without the consent of the copyright owner, although certain formalities need to be observed (see paragraph 13.11). Where the rights of a copyright owner and an exclusive licensee overlap, the courts have the power to divide up any damages awarded for copyright infringement, and share them between the owner and the licensee.

1.20 Multiplicity of copyright

One of the most difficult concepts to grasp, is that of the multiple nature of copyright. Frequently an author will express the desire to "keep the copyright" in a work. This can cause misunderstandings, since it is perfectly possible for an author to make literally dozens of assignments or licences of copyright to different companies, for different territories, each dealing with a different type of right.

An author may be reluctant to assign rights of copyright to a publisher, in case the publisher becomes insolvent. From a publisher's point of view, a licence, as opposed to an assignment, may give the publisher certain difficulties in enforcing rights of copyright, since the author may have to be made a party to proceedings to prevent infringement of copyright. It may also raise difficulties in sub-licensing, because if the publisher's rights end, for any reason, the rights of the publisher's sub-licensees will also terminate (see paragraph 1.19) unless specific provision is made (see Document 4 Clause 16.3).

In deciding whether an assignment or a licence is appropriate, certain external factors will also be relevant. For example, where a publisher engages a translator to make a translation of a work, the publisher will normally wish to obtain an assignment of the copyright in the translation. The reason for this is that the publisher will wish to make use of the translation in as many territories as possible. When a publisher sells book rights to Spain the publisher may wish the Spanish publisher to commission a Spanish language translation, obtain the copyright in the Spanish translation and assign that copyright to the English publisher. This will then permit the English publisher to sell both the book rights and the Spanish translation rights in South America.

From the translator's point of view, there is little point in retaining the copyright in a translation of a work which is still in copyright, since the translation cannot be exploited in other territories without the consent of the original author or the original publisher.

Where a general editor of a work is engaged by a publisher, the publisher will generally require the copyright to be assigned, and normally a general editor will have little reason to object since their work cannot be exploited without the consent of the copyright owner or licensee of all other contributions to the work.

Multimedia companies will, in many cases, need rights to be assigned, rather than licensed.

1.21   Moral rights

Moral rights are examined in detail in paragraphs 5.1 to 5.22. Their relevance to an author's agreement is that publishers frequently wish authors to waive their moral rights. The strength of feeling of authors on this issue runs extremely high, but the issue may be placed in clearer perspective when the basic facts surrounding it are examined.

Moral rights under United Kingdom law are statutory rights. In other words, they have been created by statute, or Act of Parliament. The Act in this case is the Copyright, Designs and Patents Act 1988[13]. Statutory moral rights are enjoyed by all individuals whose works are protected by copyright in the United Kingdom, including foreign authors.

In addition to having moral rights, all authors who sign contracts will also acquire contractual rights (or rights under their contracts). It is possible, therefore, for an author to enjoy both statutory moral rights and contractual rights which are of a similar nature. Where an author is expressly given the contractual right to be identified on copies of a book, and has absolute control over the text, the author will not be unfairly prejudiced by giving up the author's statutory rights. The implications of moral rights for publishers and multimedia companies are more fully examined in paragraphs 5.22 and paragraphs 19.10 to 19.12.

13 Copyright, Designs and Patents Act 1988 Chapter IV SS77–89.

F.   Commercial terms of commissioning agreements

1.22   What payment terms should be offered?

Payment arrangements which may be entered into by publishing or multimedia companies can be divided into three basic types.

(a) Outright fee

Where a flat fee is paid an author or owner will accept payment of the fee in return for assigning the copyright in the work to a publishing or multimedia company. The company will not be obliged to make any further payments by way of royalties to the author or owner.

(b) Advance and royalty

As an alternative to receiving a flat fee, the company may agree to pay an advance against a royalty. The advance is usually payable partly on signature of the contract, partly on delivery of the completed manuscript or typescript and partly on first publication or other exploitation of the work.

Additionally the company will agree to pay the author or owner a royalty. The advance is normally recoupable from the royalty. This means that the company will recover out of the first royalties, a sum equal to the advance. In practice this means that the author or owner will only receive royalty income from the work when the advance has been recouped. Whether the advance is recoupable solely from royalties payable in respect of sales of the work, or whether the author's share of income derived from exploitation of subsidiary rights is also be applied towards recoupment of the advance, will depend on the terms of the contract. From the company's point of view it is preferable if the advance is recouped from all money payable to the author. And again from the company's point of view, it is better if only the author's share of income derived from the exploitation of subsidiary rights is applied towards recoupment of the author's advance.

In many cases it will be preferable for an author or owner to negotiate a high advance. It is not normal for companies to recover interest on their advance, and the effect is, therefore, that the author or owner will have the use of the advance money without payment of any interest from the date the advance is paid until the date royalties become payable to the author or owner. There is no reason, however, why a company should not insert into an author's or owner's contract a provision permitting the company to recover interest on the advance. Although this is common practice in the film and television and music and recording industries, it is not yet widespread practice in the publishing world.

With some types of works, such as translations, or compilations, the company may pay the translator or the editor an outright fee. It is becoming increasingly common, however, for persons such as translators or editors to require the payment of royalties for their work. The percentages of the royalties will, of course, be significantly lower than those which are normally payable to an author.

(c) Percentage of receipts

In some cases a company may wish to offer to pay an author a percentage of the company's gross receipts, or net receipts. Explanations of these terms are provided in paragraph 11.24. Where a company wishes to offer such payment terms to an author, it is important that the expressions gross receipts and net receipts (or whatever other terms are chosen) are defined carefully, since there is no single prevailing meaning.

1.23 What form should the offer take?

A company must exercise extreme caution in making any offer because even a verbal offer can, when accepted by the person to whom it is made, constitute a binding contract.

For this reason it is prudent business practice for companies to ensure that all offers are made in writing and are clearly stated to be "subject to contract". This means that acceptance by the author (or other person) will not of itself create a contract. The contract will generally not be created until both parties sign an agreement. If there are other matters which need to be determined before a contract can be entered into, the offer letter should also state what these are.

The inadvertent creation of a contract can not only be embarrassing, but can also cause financial loss to companies. Since a contract can be created verbally (see paragraphs 2.2 to 2.8), it is possible for a company to enter into a contract in a telephone conversation with an author. If the author can produce sufficient evidence to prove the conversation took place, the author will be able to sue to enforce the contract, to require either payment of compensation or publication or other exploitation of the work.

If the work, in the opinion of the company, is not of acceptable quality, then the company may wish to require rewrites, or to reject the work altogether. A written contract will usually give the company the right to require these things (see Document 4) but it is unlikely that an oral (or verbal) contract will contain so much detail.

In a recent case[14] the court found after considering the relevant evidence (principally tape recordings of the author's telephone conversations which had been made by the author) that an oral contract had been entered into between a company and an author, which contained an absolute obligation on the part of the company to publish the author's work. Even though the company did not regard the work as satisfactory, non-publication was considered by the court to be a breach of contract which entitled the author to damages.

It is also a prudent step for all companies to ensure that whenever they sign any contract, or issue any written instruction which might form the basis of a contract (see Chapter 2), their signature is clearly stated to be "for and on behalf of [A Company Limited]". There have been occasions where the courts have held that representatives or employees of companies have unwittingly created contracts in their own right, which were not binding on their companies but could be enforced against them personally.

The risk of personal liability can easily be avoided. The main danger to the individual arises when they operate outside the ambit of their authority. If their job description, or the rules of their company, require them to obtain the consent of the board of directors of the company, or the approval of the Managing Director, or of a committee, before entering into any contract, then they must ensure that they comply with these directions. If they do so, and ensure that all offers which are made are in writing and are stated to be subject to contract, and are signed for and on behalf of the company, then they ought in most circumstances to be perfectly safe.

A further matter for a company to consider, is whether the company wishes to create a binding commitment to publish or otherwise exploit the work when delivered. There may be occasions when the work delivered to the company does not meet the expectations which the company originally had when the work was commissioned. Although the author's contract might include a provision outlining what would happen in such circumstances, there may be occasions where a commissioning letter ought also to deal with this situation, should the work be delivered following the despatch of the commissioning letter, and before the issue of the author's contract.

14 *Malcolm v Chancellor, Masters and Scholars of University of Oxford* (1990) *Times,* 19 December, CA.

2. The law of contract and the law of agency

[IMPORTANT NOTE: Please read the section "About this book" on page v, before referring to any of the matters in this chapter]

A. Introduction

2.1 Purpose of this chapter

The purpose of this chapter is to examine the basic legal principles which apply to the creation and enforceability of contracts.

An understanding of the basic principles of contract law will assist publishers and multimedia professionals from inadvertently creating contractual relationships, or entering into contracts which are voidable or unenforceable.

Appreciating the consequences of misrepresentation (even where it is innocent) and the complexities which result where the parties to a contract are mistaken in certain matters, may assist in reinforcing the importance of clarity and accuracy – unattainable ideals towards which we all aspire.

The business dealings of publishers and multimedia professionals bring them into contact with a wide circle of people, some of whom have extremely interesting characteristics, when viewed in a legal context. That is why this chapter also examines the capacity of agents, personal representatives and executors, to enter into contracts on behalf of living or dead authors.

All of us are aware that contracts frequently go wrong, and the overriding concern of all prudent businessmen must be to eliminate risk and to limit liability in such situations. The law relating to agency provides companies with the means of excluding liability to third parties when exploiting subsidiary, and other, rights. Very few agreements take advantage of this means of eliminating risk, but the brief summary of the law relating to agency at the end of this chapter may assist publishers and multimedia professionals to appreciate its significance.

B.   Formation and enforceability of contracts

2.2   What is a contract?[1]

A contract is a legally enforceable agreement. For most practical purposes there is little distinction between the word "contract" and the word "agreement".

There is no requirement for contracts to be in writing unless the contract involves land. An oral contract (ie a verbal contract made between two people talking) is just as binding as a contract in writing.

A number of elements are, however, required to be satisfied before a contract can be brought into existence. These elements are set out in paragraphs 2.3 to 2.8. The persons involved must also have the capacity to enter into a contract.

1 For a more detailed analysis see *Chitty on Contracts* (Sweet & Maxwell, 26th Edition, Vol 1, General Principles, Chapter 1, or *Cheshire Fifoot and Furmston's Law of Contract* (Butterworths, 12th Edition) Chapters 1 to 8.

2.3   Capacity of persons[2]

A valid contract may be made by any person whom the law recognises as having legal personality, such as individuals, limited liability companies, partnerships, corporations and the Crown.

There must be at least two separate and definite parties to a contract, so, for example, an organisation cannot enter into a contract with itself. The parties to the contract must be definite persons which exist at the time the contract was made. It is not possible to contract on behalf of a proposed company, which is not in existence. Any such attempt will result either in a void contract which cannot be ratified by the company even when it is formed, or in a contract which will not bind the proposed company but which will bind the unfortunate individual who attempted to enter into the arrangements on behalf of the proposed company.

A contract between two divisions of a company, or two branch offices, will also be void, since these are not two separate legal entities. A contract between a company and its main shareholder is, however, enforceable since they are two separate legal entities.

It is important to be aware that a number of classes of person do not have the capacity to enter into contracts or are capable of contracting only to a limited extent. These classes of person include bankrupts (whose property, with effect from the declaration of bankruptcy, belongs to their trustee in bankruptcy), minors (who are persons under the age of 18, although in some cases minors will be liable for contracts for goods suitable to the condition in life of the minor, and the minor's actual requirements), persons of unsound mind, alien enemies and drunkards. There are additional circumstances in which corporations, or companies, and their receivers, and partnerships, are not capable of entering into binding contracts, particularly in relation to insolvency.

2 See *Chitty*, Chapter 8; *Cheshire Fifoot & Furmston* Chapter 13.

2.4 Limited liability companies[3]

Under United Kingdom law, limited liability companies may be either private companies or public companies. Private companies are prohibited from offering their shares or debentures to the public, and their company names include the word "limited" which distinguishes them from public companies, which are permitted to offer their shares or debentures to the public, and to include in their company name the words "public limited company" or "plc".

Every public and private company is required by law to adopt and file at the Companies Registry a Memorandum of Association and Articles of Association which controls the future activities of the company, in the same way as a constitution. The Memorandum of Association sets out the company's objects and powers. The Articles of Association contain the provisions which govern the relationship between the company's members (or shareholders).

A company has a totally separate and distinct legal identity from its members (or shareholders) and its directors. In principle neither shareholders nor directors are liable for the acts or debts of the company, although there are exceptions where individuals may be liable in the case of wrongful or fraudulent trading (see paragraphs 15.7 and 15.8) and misrepresentation (see paragraph 2.17), for example.

The liability of the company is generally limited to the value of the company's share capital plus the sum of its assets – hence the term limited liability company – and the company's creditors do not have recourse to the assets of the directors or shareholders except in the case of wrongful trading or misrepresentation. This contrasts greatly with the position where an individual enters into a contract. In such circumstances, his or her liability is unlimited. The protection which limited liability offers individuals from the uncertainties of unlimited liability, and the risk of bankruptcy, is one of the most persuasive factors in support of trading through a limited liability company, rather than in one's own name. This protection is, of course, surrendered where personal guarantees are provided by owners of companies. There are circumstances where entities who find themselves committed to significant expenditure in reliance on a contractual commitment with a company whose share capital (and therefore maximum liability) is £100, should seek the additional protection offered by personal guarantees.

Although a person cannot enter into a contract with himself or herself, a company can enter into a contract with a director or a shareholder. Where directors have interests in contracts which are entered into by their companies, they are required by law to declare their interests.

The relations of public or private limited liability companies both between their members, and within themselves, are governed by legislation – principally the Companies Acts 1985 to 1989 and the Insolvency Act 1986. The Companies Acts contain provisions which, amongst other things, specify the duties owed by directors, rights of shareholders (minority or otherwise), accounting and record keeping formalities, procedures for changing a company's Memorandum of Association or Articles of Association, and also the circumstances in which a company can be dissolved (or wound up) or put into liquidation (solvent or insolvent).

Any contract which is outside the scope of the powers of a company, as set out in its Memorandum of Association, is void, even if the contract is subsequently ratified by every member of the company. In the case, however, of a person dealing with the company in good faith, any transaction decided on by the directors of the company is deemed to be one which it is within the capacity of the company to enter into, and the power of the directors to bind the company is deemed to be free of any limitation under the Memorandum or Articles of Association of the company. The provisions of the Companies Act 1989, which came into force from 1 March 1990, further protect third parties from any lack of capacity on the part of the directors of a company. They provide that the validity of any acts done by a company shall not be called into question by reason of anything in its Memorandum of Association.

3 See *Chitty,* Chapter 9; *Cheshire Fifoot & Furmston* Chapter 13.

2.5   Elements of a contract[4]

The parties must be in agreement. Normally a consensus (or agreement) is reached by the process of offer and acceptance. The law requires that an offer, on identifiable terms, receives unqualified acceptance from the person to whom the offer was made.

(a)   Offer[5]

The offer may come from the person who intends to buy (eg I will buy your book for £500) or it may come from the person who intends to sell (eg I will sell you my book for £500). It is important, however, to distinguish between an offer and what is known as an invitation to treat. An invitation to treat consists of a statement or conduct which invites a party to make an offer, such as an author sending an unsolicited manuscript to a company (see paragraph 1.11). For example, the display of goods for sale in a shop window with their prices attached is not an offer made by the seller, but an invitation to treat. Other examples of invitations to treat, include menus in restaurants (the offer is made only when the customer has selected what the customer wishes to eat, and, if the dish is off the menu, there will be no acceptance), and the display of goods in a shop (the offer arises when the prospective buyer asks for an item in the shop, or presents it at a till).

Normally a business offer will be slightly more complicated than "I offer to buy your book for £500". It may, in practice, contain a number of detailed terms and provisions, and may require acceptance within a certain time or in a certain manner.

(b)   Acceptance[6]

Acceptance of an offer does not have to be in writing. In some cases acceptance does not even have to be oral, since it can be implied by the conduct of the person to whom the offer was made. Silence cannot, however, constitute acceptance. Acceptance must, however, be unconditional and unqualified, and must be in the same terms as the original offer.

If the purported acceptance seeks to introduce new terms, or seeks to vary the terms of the original offer, a contract will not be created, and the purported acceptance will be merely a counter-offer, which will not create a contract unless it is accepted.

Difficulties may arise where two parties try and create a contract by using (say) their standard purchase orders or standard sales forms. Where a buyer issues a purchase order on its standard terms of trading and the seller, on receipt of the order, then issues the seller's own terms, it is sometimes difficult to establish what the contractual position is. Difficulties may also arise where only one party issues a standard form document, which the other party returns with amendments. The contractual position will depend on the circumstances in each case, but great care should be taken to avoid, if at all possible, the "battle of the forms" situation.

4 See *Chitty*, Chapter 2; *Cheshire Fifoot & Furmston* Chapter 3.
5 See *Chitty*, paras 42–53; *Cheshire Fifoot & Furmston* Chapter 3.
6 See *Chitty*, paras 54–89; *Cheshire Fifoot & Furmston* Chapter 3.

2.6 Withdrawal and acceptance of offers[7]

An offer can be withdrawn at any time, until it is accepted. Where valid acceptance has occurred, a binding contract will have been created. An offer may, however, stipulate a time within which acceptance must be made. If this is the case, there is, generally speaking, nothing to prevent the person making the offer from withdrawing the offer before the end of such time, provided withdrawal of the offer is communicated to the person to whom the offer was made.

If the withdrawal of the offer is not communicated, then the person to whom the offer is made will be free to accept the offer, and a binding contract will be created. There are some exceptions to this rule, such as the situation where the person to whom the offer was made, has moved address without telling the person making the offer.

In order for the acceptance of an offer to complete the formation of a contract, the acceptance must be communicated to the person who made the offer. Where there is no requirement for notice of the acceptance to be in writing, acceptance may be communicated orally.

Where acceptance is made by post, the acceptance takes effect the moment the letter is posted. The court regards the letter as being posted when it is put in the control of the Post Office, or one of the employees of the Post Office who is authorised to receive letters. This rule applies only, however, where it was reasonable to expect the offer to be accepted by post.

7 See *Chitty*, paras 90–107; *Cheshire Fifoot & Furmston* Chapter 3.

2.7 Legal relations and consideration[8]

An agreement will not be contractually enforceable unless it evinces an intention to create legal relations. Certain arrangements (such as arrange-

ments between members of the same family) are never intended to be contracts, and have been held by the courts to lack the necessary intention to
create legally enforceable contractual arrangements. As a general rule, all a
company's dealings are likely to be intended to create legal relations, so this
requirement is unlikely to cause difficulties[9].

A contract must also be supported by consideration. The legal definition of
consideration is some right, interest, profit, or benefit accrues to one party, or
some forbearance, detriment, loss, or responsibility is given, suffered, or
undertaken, by the other party.

In layman's terms, consideration normally means either the payment of
money or an agreement to pay money. The payment of an advance by a
company when an author signs a contract is consideration. The agreement by
a company to pay an advance on delivery of a completed work is consideration. A publisher's agreement to pay a royalty following publication of a
book is consideration. Even a publisher's agreement to publish a book is
capable of being consideration.

Money which has already been paid is not consideration, and if a contract
contains an undertaking (ie agreement) from a company to pay an author a
sum of money which has already been paid, there will not be sufficient
consideration, and (in the absence of other matters which might amount to
consideration) a binding contract will not be created.

A further pitfall to avoid is the payment of the consideration to a person
who is not a party to the contract. If, for example, an author agrees to write
and deliver to a company a work in consideration of the company agreeing to
pay the author's friend £500, that will not constitute valid consideration,
since the money is being paid to a third party.

The rule relating to third party consideration may appear curious, when
account is taken of the fact that payment of the consideration cannot in some
circumstances be made to a third party. Payment to third parties happens
frequently, where authors direct that payments are to be made to their agents.
Such directions are perfectly acceptable, and do not mean that the consideration of the contract is payable to the agent, since the agent is not a party to
the contract. Although the author may have directed that all payments are
made to the agent, the author can in many cases revoke, at any time, the
direction, and receive payment direct. It is also possible for an author to
assign his or her right to receive royalties from a particular contract to a third
party.

The courts do not concern themselves whether the bargain made by
someone who enters into a contract is a fair one or not. The payment by one
party of too much money or too little money may, however, be evidence of
duress, or mistake, or may induce the court to imply a breach of warranty,
and may, therefore, give the court grounds for setting aside a bargain on the
basis of fraud, undue influence, or unconscionability (see paragraph 2.23).

The consideration necessary to support a contract must be of some value,
although it may be nominal. There is no legal requirement for consideration
to be paid for an assignment or licence of copyright, and it is theoretically
possible for a company to obtain all its rights authorisations (by way of
assignment or licence) with no payments to third parties. There would be
practical disadvantages to a company conducting business in this manner,
since there are certain obligations which companies need to be able to impose

on authors and other parties (such as the obligation to deliver text) and warranties (see paragraph 7.15) which need to be contractually enforceable. For this reason many documents, notably releases and permissions, contain nominal consideration of £1.

A contractual relationship may, however, be created even where no consideration is payable. Where a document is executed as a deed, it will create a contract even if no consideration is payable. Individuals are sometimes nervous, however, when asked to sign deeds, although they may be perfectly happy to sign a letter which contains a reference to nominal consideration.

Where a contract is not supported by any consideration, it may still be enforceable if entered into by way of deed. Certain statutes require contractual documents to be under seal where they relate to conveyances of land, or conveyances of any interest in land, or where they relate to transfers of shares in certain companies, and transfers of suretyships. Some contracts must, by law, be made by deed, and some are required to be made or evidenced in writing.

8 See *Chitty*, Chapter 3; *Cheshire Fifoot & Furmston* Chapters 4 and 5.
9 See *Chitty*, Chapter 9, paras 129–151; *Cheshire Fifoot & Furmston* Chapters 4 and 5.

2.8 Implied terms and custom and practice[10]

Although the courts will not make a contract where none exists, the courts will uphold bargains made between businessmen wherever possible, and will recognise that such agreements frequently record only the most important elements in a crude and summary fashion. A contract will not be defective simply because it is open to more than one construction, if the courts can establish the meaning intended.

If satisfied that there was an ascertainable and determinable intention to contract, the courts will try to give effect to the intention, and will look at the substance of the agreement which was intended to be made between the parties. This approach is particularly important for parties who have acted in the belief that certain terms have created a contract between them.

As a general rule, the courts will not make or improve contracts if the express terms are clear. The express terms will be applied even if the courts think some other term might have been more suitable. However, the courts will imply terms where the parties must have intended the term to form part of the contract ("something so obvious it goes without saying")[11] or where the term is necessary in the business sense to give efficacy to the contract.

In the absence of any contrary intention, the courts may imply into a contract any local custom or usage which normally governs the particular type of contract in question, as representing the presumed intention of the parties. It may also be possible to import a term into a contract on the basis of a previous course of dealing between the parties.

10 See *Chitty*, Chapter 13; *Cheshire Fifoot & Furmston* Chapter 6.
11 *Shirlaw v Southern Foundries* (1926) Ltd [1939] 2 KB 206.

C. Performance of contractual obligations

2.9 Performance[12]

The general rule, in contract law, is that a party to a contract is required to perform exactly what that party undertook to do, and is not entitled to substitute for the promised obligations other obligations which may be equally advantageous for the other party.

As a rule, a party to a contract cannot transfer its liability under the contract without the consent of the other party, although the benefit of a contract may, however, be assigned. There is no objection to the substitution of the performance by a third party of duties that are not connected with the skilled character or other qualifications of the original party of the contract. Liability under a contract may also be transferred with the consent of all parties, so as to discharge the original contract, and to novate (or create a new contract).

Rights and liabilities of parties to a contract may, in some circumstances, be assigned by operation of law when, for example, a party dies or becomes bankrupt. No right or liability of a purely personal nature (ie one which is dependent on skill or qualification of the party) can be assigned by operation of law.

12 See *Chitty*, Chapter 21, paras 149 ff; *Cheshire Fifoot & Furmston* Chapter 18.

2.10 Time for performance[13]

Where a contract does not provide a time by which obligations are to be performed, the law implies an undertaking by each party to perform their part of the agreement within a reasonable time. Where a contract provides for a certain action to be performed by a certain date, failure to perform by that date will not be considered a breach of the contract, unless time is expressly stipulated by the parties to be "of the essence", or unless the subject matter of the contract, or the surrounding circumstances, show that time should be considered to be of the essence. Failure by an author to deliver a manuscript by a stated date will not be a contractual breach unless the contract provided that time was of the essence.

Where time is not initially of the essence, a party who has been subjected to unreasonable delay may give notice to the party in default, fixing a reasonable time for performance, and stating that in the event of non-performance within the fixed time, the contract will be treated as being broken.

13 See *Chitty*, Chapter 21, paras 1500–1509; *Cheshire Fifoot & Furmston* Chapter 18.

2.11 Payment[14]

Payment may be proved to have been made either by production of a receipt, or by any other evidence from which the fact of payment may be inferred. In some circumstances, payment may even be presumed, from the length of time which has elapsed since the debt became due.

A receipt is not conclusive evidence of payment, merely an admission, and evidence may be considered by a court to prove the intention with which the receipt was given, and whether any payment was in fact made and, if so, on what terms and in respect of what matter.

The posting of a cheque which is lost will not constitute payment, unless the person making the payment was requested to make it in such manner, in which case the person requesting this may have been taken to have run the risk of a cheque being lost.

14 See *Chitty*, Chapter 21, paras 1518–1554; *Cheshire Fifoot & Furmston* Chapter 18.

D. Exclusion clauses and unfair contractual terms

2.12 Exclusion clauses generally[15]

An exclusion clause is a clause to exclude or limit one party's liability for breach of contract or misrepresentation. Exclusion clauses fall into two basic categories. One type seeks to exclude or cut down the primary obligation of the contract. (A provision in a distribution agreement which states that the distributor will have no liability to the publisher if the distributor fails to perform certain obligations would fall into this category.) The second type seeks to restrict the rights of the other party in the event of breach of some primary obligation by, for example, limiting the amount of damages which can be recovered.

An exclusion clause which excludes all liability in relation to the performance of the primary obligation, may have the effect of rendering the agreement unilateral, and removing all contractual force from the agreement, making it unenforceable. For example, a provision in a book distribution agreement which stated that the distributor had no liability for any breach whatever would make performance of the agreement by the distributor optional, and the court might find such a provision unenforceable.

15 See *Chitty*, Chapter 14, paras 964 ff.

2.13 Sale of goods

Some obligations cannot be excluded. For example, in any contract for the sale of goods, there are certain implied undertakings as to the title (or ownership of the goods) being free from incumbrances (such as security interests or other rights of third parties)[16]. In some contracts there are also implied undertakings as to compliance with description, merchantable quality, fitness for purpose, and correspondence with samples[17]. These undertakings cannot be excluded in the case of any person dealing as a consumer, and may be excluded in other cases only so far as reasonable[18].

Any term which attempts to exclude any of the above implied undertakings and warranties is therefore void, if it is contained in a contract with a consumer (see paragraph 2.14 for the definition), and in any other cases will be enforceable only to the extent that it is fair and reasonable[19] (see paragraph 2.15 for the test of reasonableness). The above restrictions on the validity of exclusions do not apply to international supply contracts, or to agreements the proper law of which is the law of the United Kingdom, but which, apart from the choice of United Kingdom law, would be governed by the laws of another country.

16 Sale of Goods Act 1979 S12.
17 Ibid S14.
18 Unfair Contract Terms Act 1977 SS6(2) and 7(2).
19 Ibid SS6(3) and 7(3).

2.14 Exclusion of liability

Any provision of an agreement which would exclude or restrict liability of one party for any misrepresentation made before the contract was made is unenforceable, except to the extent that a court may allow reliance on the representation as being fair and reasonable in the circumstances[20].

A person deals as a consumer if they do not make the contract in the course of business, or hold themselves out as doing so, and the other party to the contract does make it in the course of the business, and the goods passing under the contract are of a type ordinarily supplied for private use or consumption[21].

Liability for death or personal injury resulting from negligence cannot be excluded or restricted in any contract[22]. In the case of other loss or damage, liability for negligence may be excluded or restricted only so far as may be reasonable.[23]

20 Unfair Contract Terms Act 1977 S8(1), substituting S3 of the Misrepresentation Act 1967.
21 Ibid S12(1).
22 Ibid S2(1).
23 Ibid S2(2).

2.15 Reasonableness

The test of reasonableness, applied to any contractual term is whether or not the term was a fair and reasonable one to be included in the contract, having regard to circumstances which were, or ought reasonably to have been known to, or in the contemplation of, the parties at the time the contract was made[24].

Where a person wishes to rely on an exclusion clause, the court will consider the resources which that person could expect to have available for the purpose of meeting the liability which is sought to be excluded, and how far it was open to such person to obtain insurance cover in respect of the risk[25].

In determining whether or not a provision satisfies the test of reasonableness the courts will consider a number of provisions including the following:

(a) the relative strength of bargaining positions of the parties taking into account (amongst other things) alternative means by which the customer's requirements could have been met[26];

(b) whether the customer received an inducement to agree to the relevant term, or whether the customer had an opportunity of entering into a similar contract with other persons without having to accept a similar term[27];

(c) whether the customer knew, or ought reasonably to have known, of the existence and extent of the term, having regard, amongst other things, to the custom of the trade and any previous course of dealing of the parties[28];

(d) where the term excludes, or restricts, any relevant liability if some condition is not complied with, whether it was reasonable at the time of the contract to expect that compliance with that condition would be practicable[29];

(e) whether the goods were manufactured, processed or adapted, to the special order of the customer[30].

24 Unfair Contract Terms Act 1977 S11(1).
25 Ibid S11(4).
26 Ibid Sch 2(a).
27 Ibid Sch 2(b).
28 Ibid Sch 2(c).
29 Ibid Sch 2(d).
30 Ibid Sch 2(e).

2.16 Construction of exclusion clauses

Exclusion clauses are construed strictly by the courts, and hidden meanings cannot, therefore, be read into them. Exclusion clauses require clear wording, since any ambiguity in them will be construed by the courts against the party which seeks to rely on them. General words of exclusion will not normally be construed so as to cover fundamental breaches, which go to the very root of the contract; they may also be construed as having no application to liability for negligence.

Exclusion clauses will be construed in such a way that they do not afford protection to a party who is acting outside the scope of the contract, or to a party whose performance is different in kind from that contemplated by the contract, and will not normally be interpreted in such a way as to deprive an agreement of contractual content and to turn it merely into a declaration of intent.

Where an exclusion clause appears in a printed standard form of contract, and there is a conflict between that clause and another clause which is written or typed in, or otherwise added to the printed form, then the latter will generally prevail, since the courts will give greater weight to what the parties have expressly agreed in detail, rather than to what appears in standard forms. The courts may also refuse to give effect to an exclusion clause which might wholly nullify another positive clause of the contract.

In those circumstances where companies wish to exclude liability, they should pay particular attention to the matters set out above, in order to ensure that the exclusion may be contractually enforceable.

E. Misrepresentation and mistake

2.17 Misrepresentation generally[31]

There are many occasions where persons enter into contracts as a result of statements or representations which have been made to them. Where the representations are included in the contract they will very often take the form of warranties (see paragraph 7.15) and any untrue representation may be a breach of the warranty and may entitle the person to whom it was made to rescind or terminate the contract (see paragraphs 14.1 to 14.10).

But what is the position where the representation is not incorporated in the contract? The person to whom it was made may be entitled to rescind the contract, recover any money they have paid and may also be entitled to recover damages in respect of any loss they have suffered.

What if the contract contains an exclusion clause (see paragraph 2.12) which excludes or restricts liability in the event of misrepresentation? Any such clause will be of no force or effect unless it satisfies the test of reasonableness referred to in paragraph 2.15.

What does a company have to prove to recover damages for misrepresentation? A company will have to show that the representation:

(a)   was not only false but fraudulent; or
(b)   was negligent; or
(c)   cannot be proved to have been believed to be true by the person who made it.

A statement will be fraudulent if the person making it did not know it to be true, or knew or believed that it was false, or did not actually and honestly believe it to be true. A statement which is made with indifference or recklessness will be fraudulent unless the person making it can show that they actually and honestly believed that it was true.

There are, however, occasions where a person makes a statement which in objective terms has a meaning different from the one intended, but this will not amount to misrepresentation if that person can show the statement was true in the sense the statement was intended, and that this sense was one which might reasonably be attached to the statement.

It is not necessary for a person who makes a fraudulent misrepresentation to intend to defraud. Caprice, mischievousness or stupidity will be sufficient for a person to be liable, if they cannot demonstrate they actually and honestly believed the statement and there is no requirement to prove wickedness or intent to deceive or injure.

31 See *Chitty*, Chapter 6; *Cheshire Fifoot & Furmston* Chapter 9.

2.18   Mistake and impossibility[32]

If two parties reach an agreement that is based on a fundamental mistake, that mistake will negate their consensus (see paragraph 2.5) and prevent a binding contract from coming into existence. Where the mistake is not fundamental to the formation of an agreement, it will not negate the contract[33].

A mistake is fundamental if the mistaken party would not have entered into the contract had they realised the mistake. Mistakes may be categorised into three types:

(a)   mistake as to person;

(b) mistake as to subject matter; and
(c) mistake as to terms.

Where a promise is, at the time when it was made, manifestly incapable of performance, either by fact or by law, then a binding contract cannot exist, either because there can have been no intention to create legal relations, or because there was no consideration.

For example, where, unknown to the parties, the buyer is already the owner of what the seller purports to sell, any intended transfer of ownership is clearly impossible and the sale is void. Alternatively, if both parties are mistaken in relation to the existence of some quality which the subject of the contract is thought to have, whose absence makes the subject matter essentially different from what it was believed to be, then the contract will be void. Mistake as to quality by one party alone will not render the contract void, whether or not the other party is aware of it, unless the mistake is fundamental, and is actively caused by the other party.

32 See *Chitty,* Chapter 5; *Cheshire Fifoot & Furmston* Chapter 8.
33 *Hartog v Colin & Shields* [1939] 3 All ER 566.

F. Frustration and force majeure[34]

2.19 Impossibility and frustration

A contract which is incapable of performance at the time when it is made, is, generally void from the very beginning. A perfectly valid contract may, however, be rendered incapable of performance by subsequent impossibility. This will normally bring the contract to an end from the moment of impossibility. In some cases, however, a contracting party may have made an absolute promise to perform certain obligations and will not be excused by non-performance even if this is subsequently rendered impossible.

Where an agreement has been entered into on the assumption that some fundamental state of affairs should continue to exist, and an event occurs which renders performance of the contract impossible, or only possible in a very different way from that originally contemplated by the parties, all further performance of their obligations may be excused as a result of the application of the doctrine of frustration.

In order for the doctrine to apply, the frustrating event must arise without fault of either party. Deliberate choice not to perform the contract, or to put performance out of the power of the parties, will constitute default. An act of negligence will not necessarily, however, deprive a party of the possibility of using the doctrine of frustration, as a defence for any claim.

Frustration may be caused by a number of different types of event, including physical destruction of the subject matter of the contract, cancellation of an expected event, delay, subsequent legal changes, death or incapacity.

A contract will not be discharged by the doctrine of frustration simply because it becomes more difficult to perform or becomes more onerous. The doctrine cannot generally be used to excuse performance of a contract, on account of rises or falls in price, depreciation of currency or unexpected obstacles to the execution of the contract. These are the ordinary risks of business, and will not excuse inability of performance by any party, unless otherwise agreed.

Companies should avoid entering into contractual arrangements which require them to perform obligations which are outside their control. The normal method chosen to limit liability in such circumstances is to agree upon provisions which apply in the event of force majeure. Such provisions frequently provide for the return of sums paid under the contract.

34 See *Chitty*, Chapter 23; *Cheshire Fifoot & Furmston* Chapter 20.

2.20   Force majeure and act of God[35]

Many contracts contain provisions which provide that their performance may be excused, if they are rendered impossible by the occurrence of an act of God, or an event of force majeure. These provisions are effective so long as they are not uncertain. They may even allow the courts to take account of a party's obligations under other contracts, despite the normal rule that it is generally no excuse that contracts with third parties prevent the fulfilment of the contract in question. Where, however, a contract excuses a party from delay due to unavoidable causes, they may not be able to rely on the law relating to force majeure if they fail, before making the contract, to enquire whether such unavoidable causes exist and to inform the other party.

An Act of God may be defined as being an extraordinary occurrence or circumstance, which could not have been foreseen, and which could not have been guarded against. An alternative definition is that it is an accident, due to natural causes, directly and exclusively without human intervention, which could not by any amount of ability have been foreseen or, if foreseen, could not by any amount of human care and skill have been resisted. An Act of God need not be unique, nor need it have happened for the first time. It is enough for it to have been extraordinary and not reasonably capable of having been anticipated.

While there are circumstances where the inclusion of force majeure provisions in a contract will be in a company's interest, there will equally be occasions when it is not – where, for example, the company wishes to impose an absolute obligation on a third party.

When force majeure provisions are included in a contract, they are normally inserted towards the end, amongst the so-called "boiler plate", and occasionally force majeure provisions may be found which, on a close reading, can be seen to excuse performance for less than compelling reasons.

35 See *Chitty*, Chapter 14, paras 1035–1045.

G.   Illegal, void and voidable contracts[36]

2.21   Illegal and void contracts

Even where a contract is not defective by reason of form, or of lack of agreement, or for want of consideration, the contract may still be illegal, void or voidable. This may be the case either where the contract involves the commission of an unlawful act (whether the act is unlawful by statute or by common law), or because the contract offends against the principles of order or morality.

Any contract entered into with the object of committing an illegal act is unenforceable and may not be enforced by any party to the contract or by the courts. The fact that one or both parties were ignorant that the contract involved a breach of law, or that their purpose of entering into the contract was unlawful, is irrelevant.

Generally the courts will refuse to enforce a contract for the commission of an unlawful act. Various different categories of illegal or void contracts have been developed by the courts including agreements which tend to be injurious to the public or against the public good; contracts made with the enemy in time of war; agreements which oust the jurisdiction of the courts, or interfere with the course of justice; agreements which are in unreasonable restraint of trade.

Other categories exist, such as contracts for the sale of public offices or titles, agreements which interfere with the free exercise of votes, contracts which are made upon consideration for a sexually immoral purpose, and contracts which are prejudicial to family life.

Contracts of the last two categories are not illegal but are void because they offend public policy. Void contracts are unenforceable, but unlike illegal contracts, a method of giving effect to the contract may be found through the application of the doctrine of severance.

36 See *Chitty*, Chapter 1, paras 16–19; *Cheshire Fifoot & Furmston* Chapters 10 to 12.

2.22 Severance[37]

Severance is a process by which the void, or illegal parts, are cut away from a contract which may otherwise be entirely lawful, leaving the valid parts of the contract to be enforced, without the void or illegal parts. Where the objects of a contract involve illegal, rather than simply void, provisions, severance is generally not possible.

In the instances where severance is permitted, it must be possible simply to strike out the offending parts of the contract, since the courts will not rewrite or rearrange the contract. A court may not be prepared to sever a provision if to do so would entirely alter the scope and intention of the agreement. Once the void (or in exceptional cases, illegal) provisions have been deleted from a contract, what is left must contain all the characteristics of a valid contract. It will follow that if the severed part contains the only consideration clause, the contract will be unenforceable (see paragraph 2.7).

37 See *Chitty*, Chapter 16, paras 1281–1293.

2.23 Voidable contracts

A contract may be voidable by any party who has entered into it under duress, or undue influence, or whilst drunk, or insane.

Duress means compulsion, under which a person acts through fear of personal suffering from actual, or threatened, injury to the body, or confinement. A threat of criminal prosecution or civil or bankruptcy proceedings will not, of itself, amount to duress, but may do so if it is intended, and calculated, to cause terror. A contract obtained by duress is voidable or, in some cases, void. If, however, the party entitled to avoid such a contract acts on it, then it will become binding on that party.

Undue influence is the unconscionable use by one person of power possessed by that person over another, in order to induce the other to enter into a contract. If the parties were, at the time of a transaction, or shortly before it, in a particular confidential relationship to each other (such as that of parent and child, trustee and beneficiary, adviser and client) undue influence will, in some cases, be presumed unless it can be shown that it did not exist. It can be proved that undue influence did not exist by showing that the transaction appeared fair, and that the party who might have been subject to undue influence received competent independent advice.

The fact that a person was drunk when entering into an agreement may be a defence to an action brought to enforce the agreement, if the drunkenness was so extreme as to deprive that person of the ability to reason. The courts will not, however, avoid a contract if the extent of drunkenness merely deprived the person of business sense. Relief may, however, be granted by the courts to a drunken person, if it can be shown that the person's condition was known to the other party at the time the contract was made, and that some unfair advantage was taken of it. The drunken person will, however, become liable under any contract made under the influence of drink if, after becoming sober, such person ratifies the contract or enters into a new contract. A contract for the reasonable price of necessities (ie goods suitable to a person's condition in life, and to such person's actual requirements at the time of sale and delivery), which are sold and delivered to a drunk person, will be binding.

H.   Agents, personal representatives and executors

Normally the persons with whom a publisher or multimedia professional enters into contracts will be acting in their own capacity but there are three common situations where a publisher or multimedia professional will have dealings with persons who act in a special capacity, as agent, or personal representative, or literary executor.

2.24   Agents

Many authors are represented by agents who negotiate the terms of contracts on the author's behalf.

In the eyes of the law, the acts of the agent are considered to be the acts of the person the agent represents (or principal). The powers and duties of the agent, including the agent's powers to sign agreements on behalf of its principals will, however, depend on whatever agreement exists between agent/author. The general principles of the law of agency are considered in paragraphs 2.26 to 2.29.

It would appear that very few agents require the authors they represent to execute agency agreements and this might cause difficulties to a publisher or multimedia company. If a contract is executed by an agent on behalf of an author it is possible that, unless the agent had express written authority, an author (or more likely an author's estate) could maintain that the contract was not binding on the author, either because the agent had no authority to sign, or because the author had not consented, or because the consent of the author had been given on grounds of mistake, or had been induced by a misrepresentation.

Contracts with authors form part of the tools of a media company's trade and are the source of all rights which the company exploits in its business. Any uncertainty which might affect them is, from the company's point of view, highly undesirable. Companies should, therefore, as a matter of routine, require all contracts to be executed by the relevant author and, if possible, witnessed. Where there is any doubt as to the mental capacity of the author, a company will need to seek specific legal advice, and failure to attend to this matter could invalidate any contract entered into.

From the point of view of an agent, any claim that the agent has exceeded his or her authority is similarly undesirable and should be eliminated. An agent will, however, wish to safeguard their right to receive remuneration, and it would, therefore, be appropriate, in suitable cases, for the contract to contain an irrevocable payment direction in the agent's favour directing the company to pay to the author's agent all sums due to the author under the contract.

2.25 Personal representatives and executors

Death is an inevitable fact of life, and all publishers and multimedia companies will, from time to time, have to deal with deceased authors or their estates. The effect of an author's death after a contract has been signed is examined in paragraph 7.3. This paragraph, however, examines how a company can enter into a contract when an author has already died.

On the death of a person, their property passes by what is known as "operation of law" to the person's personal representatives. The time of transmission of the property is the moment of death. In order, however, to be able to prove that they have the legal right to deal with the deceased's property, the personal representatives have to obtain a grant of probate of the author's will or letters of administration from the court.

They will then be able to transfer any copyrights in accordance with the directions contained in the deceased author's will or, if the author died without a valid will (intestate), in accordance with the intestacy rules.

A company acquiring rights from an author's estate should therefore normally ask to see the following original (or certified copy) documents: the will, the grant of probate (or if no will, the grant of letters of administration of the estate, which takes the place of the grant of probate) together with any vesting assent executed by the personal representatives. A vesting assent is a document which will transfer the copyright in a work to the beneficiary named in the will or, where there was no will, the person entitled under the intestacy rules.

The company will need to check that the details of the above documents comply with the provisions of the will. Wills may contain provisions which deal with manuscripts (or typescripts) separately from their copyrights. Where a will bequeaths documents or other material things incorporating unpublished original literary, dramatic, musical or artistic works or films or sound recordings to a person, the copyright in those works will pass to the person entitled to those documents or other material things, unless the will (or any codicil to it) contains a contrary intention.

It is also possible for an author to appoint a literary executor by will, and, once the will has been admitted to probate, the literary executor will be able to deal with the relevant copyrights on the terms stated in the will (or codicil).

I. General principles of the law of agency[38]

2.26 Agency generally

The concept of the agency relationship is that the acts of the agent are considered to be binding on the person whom the agent represents (the principal).

Agency has been described as the relationship which arises whenever one person has authority to act on behalf of another, and consents to act in such a way.

An agent may be a sole agent, or an exclusive agent, and be appointed for a particular purpose or for a particular territory. The appointment of the agent may be oral or in writing.

If the agreement between agent and principal is oral, the terms and scope of the agent's authority will be questions of fact, and will depend on the circumstances of the particular case. The extent of an agent's authority, will, in such cases, be determined by inference from all the circumstances (but see also paragraph 2.30).

The primary duty of the commercial agent is to perform what the agent has undertaken to do and not to exceed its authority. In performing its obligations, the agent has a duty to show proper skill and care in accordance with the terms of the contract and the principal's instructions.

38 See *Chitty*, Vol 2, Chapter 1; *Cheshire Fifoot & Furmston* Chapter 15.

2.27 Agent's fiduciary duties

Fiduciary duties (or duties of good faith) are implied into all agency relationships, unless they are excluded by contract. They could, broadly speaking, be described as duties to act in the utmost good faith towards the principal.

The most important of the agent's fiduciary duties to the principal are:
(a)   an agent has a duty not to place itself in a position where the agent's duties conflict with its own interests;
(b)   an agent is usually not entitled, although there are exceptions, to delegate its duties and generally is required to carry out its principal's instructions personally;

(c) an agent should not place itself in a position where it has to balance the agent's own interests against those of the principal. This duty is closely associated with the agent's duty not to take advantage of its principal, or make a secret profit, by exploiting its position;

(d) an agent has a duty not to accept bribes or secret commissions.

(e) an agent has a duty to hand over money it is holding for the principal. Sometimes an agent will be under a duty to keep the principal's money separate and will be treated as trustee of the principal. The agent also has a duty to keep accurate accounts and to produce them to the principal, if so required.

2.28 Rights of agent against principal

The agent is entitled to be indemnified by the principal for losses suffered and reimbursement for all expenses and liabilities reasonably incurred in the performance of the agent's duties.

An agent possesses the right against its principal to be remunerated for the agent's services if the contract so provides (see paragraphs 2.30 and 16.27).

The agent's entitlement to receive commission will normally end on the expiry of the agency relationship, unless the contract contains express provision to the contrary.

2.29 Liability and contractual rights

In what circumstances can an agent become personally liable under a contract the agent made with a third party on behalf of its principal? The general rule is that an agent simply establishes contractual relations between the principal and third party and then "drops out of the transaction". The agent is not a separate party to the contract and does not therefore become personally liable under it. The agent may not sue a third party on the contracts. The only person who may sue is the principal, and the only person who can be sued is the principal.

However, the general rule is always subject to the correct inference to be drawn from all the circumstances, and there are a number of instances where the agent may be liable on the contract, the most obvious being where the agent makes some misrepresentation, or where the agent acts on behalf of an undisclosed principal. Until the third party discovers the existence of the undisclosed principal, the third party's contract is with the agent, who is liable under the contract. Once the principal's existence is established, the third party will have the choice of whether to sue the agent or the principal.

Where an agent contracts with a third party on behalf of its principal, the agent is not a party to the contract and cannot sue the third party on it. However, where the parties intended that the agent should have rights, as well as liabilities, under the contract, the agent will be entitled to sue the third party. Furthermore, the agent's agreement with its principal may give the agent exclusive rights to collect income, and may appoint the agent as the principal's attorney for the purpose of commencing legal proceedings and collecting income.

An agent's authority may expressly permit it to enforce contracts on behalf of the principal, authorising it under a power of attorney or other express provision, to enforce, sue upon, and collect money arising under pre-specified agreements.

2.30 Significance of the law of agency for publishers

The law of agency offers publishers the opportunity of licensing the exploitation of rights in relation to literary works in such a way as to avoid liability if there is any infringement of copyright in certain circumstances. There are significant European Union reforms to the law relating to commercial agents, but these reforms are considered elsewhere in this work (see paragraph 16.27).

Most standard publishing contracts do not make use of this opportunity and provide that both publication rights and subsidiary rights are licensed to the publisher. In many cases, the publisher will not wish to exploit the subsidiary rights, but will intend to license these to third parties. If there is any defect in the rights, the publisher will incur liability.

If, however, a publisher acquires publication rights only in those countries and in those media where it will itself publish, and is appointed as the exclusive agent of the author to sell the subsidiary rights, the publisher will be able to license the subsidiary rights in other media and territories (and those publication rights which the publisher itself does not wish to exploit) as the agent of the author. The publisher will then be able to collect the proceeds from those transactions, apply them to recoup any advance previously paid to the author and, provided that the publisher discloses that it is acting as the agent of the author, the publisher will remain free from any liability to the licensee if there is any claim for infringement of copyright or other contractual claim.

It is also possible for use to be made of the agency rules by multimedia companies. Clearly there are circumstances where there could be advantages.

With effect from 1 January 1994 statutory regulations governing the rights of commercial agents came into force in the United Kingdom. These arrangements are summarised in paragraph 16.27. In view of their wide scope it would be prudent for all companies to review their existing contractual arrangements in the light of such regulations.

3. Creation, existence and transfer of copyrights and trade marks

[IMPORTANT NOTE: Please read the section "About this book" on page v, before referring to any of the matters in this chapter].

[*In this chapter all statutory references are to the Copyright, Designs and Patents Act 1988 unless otherwise specified.*]

A. Introduction

3.1 Purpose of this chapter

The entire business of a publisher or multimedia company consists of exploiting rights which are protected by copyright. A basic understanding of the law relating to copyright is therefore a fundamental requirement for any publisher or multimedia professional.

A basic understanding of copyright law will enable a publisher or multimedia professional not only to identify potential problems which affect their business, or the value of rights acquired by them, but will also enable them to identify business opportunities.

B. Definition of copyright

3.2 What is copyright?

Copyright is, quite literally, the right to copy a work. The law relating to copyright in the United Kingdom is set out in the Copyright, Designs and Patents Act 1988 which repealed and replaced the Copyright Act 1956 which in turn repealed the Copyright Act 1911. The provisions originally contained in these Acts will, however, still apply, with some modifications, to works created or published whilst they were in force. International copyright protection is governed by two international treaties, the Berne Convention and the Universal Copyright Convention (see paragraphs 4.3 and 4.4).

Under United Kingdom law, the owner of a copyright has the exclusive right to do, or authorise the doing of, certain acts in relation to his or her work. In the United Kingdom, the acts which are restricted by copyright are[1]:

(a) copying a copyright work[2];
(b) issuing copies of a copyright work to the public[3];
(c) performing, showing or playing a copyright work in public[4];
(d) broadcasting a copyright work or including it in a cable programme service[5];
(e) making an adaptation of a copyright work or doing in respect of any adaptation any of the acts specified in (a) to (d) above[6].

If a person does any of the acts listed above without the consent or licence of a copyright owner, then (s)he is committing a primary infringement of copyright. Both primary infringement and secondary infringement are dealt with later in this work (paragraphs 13.2 to 13.8).

1 Copyright, Designs and Patents Act 1988 S16.
2 S17.
3 S18.
4 S19.
5 S20.
6 S21.

3.3 International copyright

Although United Kingdom law gives copyright protection solely in the United Kingdom of England, Wales, Scotland, Northern Ireland and Hong Kong, because this country has signed various international copyright conventions, other countries will give their own copyright protection to works protected under United Kingdom law. This foreign copyright protection will obviously vary from country to country, and will be subject to different legal principles, rules of evidence etc.

Because, however, the copyright conventions impose various minimum standards on each country which has signed them, it is possible, in practice (at least initially), to assume that the types of copyright protection granted by most countries will be similar to those granted in the United Kingdom. International copyright protection is examined in paragraphs 4.2 to 4.8.

3.4 Types of copyright works

Under United Kingdom law, copyright subsists in the following types of works:

(a) original literary, dramatic, musical, or artistic works[7];
(b) sound recordings, films, broadcasts, or cable programmes[8];
(c) typographical arrangements of published editions[9].

Copyright will only subsist in a work if the requirements for copyright protection (referred to in paragraphs 3.11 to 3.21) are met.

7 S1(1)(a).
8 S1(1)(b).
9 S1(1)(c).

C. Copyright works

3.5 Literary, dramatic and musical works

A literary work is any work, other than a dramatic, or musical, work which is written, spoken, or sung. Tables, computations, computer programs and preparatory design material for computer programs[10], novels and plays are all literary works[11].

A dramatic work will include a work of dance or mime. Certain aspects of stage "business" may now be protected by the laws of copyright.

A musical work is a work which consists of music, exclusive of any words, or action intended to be sung, spoken or performed, with the music[12]. In the case of a song which contains both words and music, the musical elements are therefore protected as a musical work, and the lyrics are protected as a literary work.

An opera involves a number of separate copyrights. The music in an opera will be classified as musical works, the words of the songs in the opera will be literary works and the libretto of the opera will be a literary work as well as a dramatic work.

10 The Copyright (Computer Programs) Regulations 1992.
11 S3(1).
12 S3(1).

3.6 Artistic works

There are three basic types of artistic work which qualify for copyright protection, being:

(a) A graphic work, photograph, sculpture or collage[13]:
    – a graphic work includes any painting, drawing, diagram, map, chart, plan, engraving, etching, lithograph, woodcut, or similar work;
    – a photograph means a recording of light, or other radiation, on any medium on which an image is produced, or from which an image may be produced, provided the photograph is not part of a film;
    – a sculpture includes a cast or model which is made for the purposes of sculpture[14].
(b) A work of architecture, being a building, or a model for a building[15]: a building includes any fixed structure or a part of a building of fixed structure[16].
(c) A work of artistic craftsmanship[17]: works of artistic craftsmanship include hand-painted tiles, stained glass, wrought-iron gates, the products of high class printing, book binding, cutlery, needlework and cabinet making.

13 S4(1)(a).
14 S4(2).
15 S4(1)(b).
16 S4(2).
17 S4(1)(c).

3.7 Films and sound recordings

Although films and sound recordings may appear to be of only peripheral interest to publishers and multimedia companies, they are, in fact, of direct relevance for two reasons. First, film and sound recording rights may form part of the subsidiary rights (see paragraph 1.16) acquired by publishers. Second, works made available in multimedia formats will fall to be protected not only as literary works, but also, in some cases, as films and sound recordings (see Chapter 19).

(a) Films

In copyright parlance, a film is a recording on any medium from which a moving image may, by any means, be produced[18].

A series of moving images, shot on 35 mm film, or 16 mm film, is clearly a film. But so, too, is a recording of images recorded on video-tape, as is any series of moving images reproduced by machine code – such as a computer program with audio visual elements.

Copyright does not exist in a sound recording or a film which is a copy taken from a previous sound recording or film[19].

If the visual elements of a film are shot on 35 mm film stock, and the sound track elements are recorded separately (as is the usual practice), then, at the moment when the music, dialogue and sound effects tracks are combined and included on prints of the film there will be copies taken from a previous sound recording.

The strange effect of this curious provision is that the moving images are protected (by our 1988 copyright legislation) as a silent film and the sound track is protected as a separate series of sound recordings.

If, however, an audio visual production is shot on video-tape, only one recording is made. That recording satisfies the copyright definition of film and sound recording. It is worth noting that the 1988 Copyright, Designs and Patents Act creates a new restricted act in the form of making copies of films, sound recordings or computer programs available to the public by way of rental.

(b) Sound recordings

A sound recording is a recording of sounds from which the sounds may be reproduced[20], or a recording of the whole, or a part of, any literary, dramatic, or musical work, from which sounds reproducing the work, or part of the work, may be produced[21], regardless of the medium on which the recording is made, or the method by which the sounds are reproduced or produced.

Obviously, compact discs, 33 rpm and 78 rpm discs and audio cassettes will qualify as sound recordings. So too will audio visual cassettes, machine readable code in RAM or ROM or EPROM, as well as earlier types of technology, such as piano rolls, or wax cylinders.

18 S5(1).
19 S5(2).
20 S5(1)(a).
21 S5(1)(b).

3.8 Broadcasts and cable programmes

(a) Broadcasts

A broadcast is a transmission by wireless telegraphy of visual images, sounds or other information which is capable of being lawfully received by members of the public, or is transmitted for presentation to members of the public[22].

(b) Cable Programmes

A cable programme is any item which is included in a service which consists wholly or mainly in sending visual images, sounds or other information by means of a telecommunications system, otherwise than by wireless telegraphy, for reception at two or more places or for presentation to members of the public[23].

22 S6(1)(a) and (b).
23 S7(1).

3.9 Typographical arrangements of published editions

Besides recognising the work of authors, copyright legislation also recognises the contribution of publishers in creating published editions of works.

The typographical arrangement of a published edition of the whole, or any part, of a literary, dramatic, or musical work is protected by copyright[24]. For the purposes of copyright law, the author of the typographical arrangement of the published edition of a literary work (as distinct from the work itself) is stated to be the publisher. The copyright in the published edition is quite separate from the copyright in the work itself, and in order for an edition to qualify for copyright protection, it must be published.

Publishing a work means the issue of copies of the work to the public, in such a manner as to satisfy the public's reasonable requirements. In other words, token (or "colourable") publication will not be adequate. Although the criteria for publication of a literary, dramatic, or artistic work are met if the work is made available by means of an electronic retrieval system, in order for a typographical arrangement to be considered a published edition physical copies of the work need to be issued to the public.

It is worth noting that, in addition to the copyright which subsists in the arrangement of type, a separate copyright may exist in respect of the typeface itself. Certain provisions (see paragraph 8.36) exist to permit the use of typefaces for the purposes of making typographical arrangements, without infringing the copyright in the artistic work which consists of the design of the typeface.

24 S8.

3.10   Rental right

The owner of the copyright in a sound recording, or film, or computer program, also enjoys the right to prevent copies of the sound recording, film or computer program from being made available to the public by way of rental[25].

"Rental" is defined[26] as any arrangement under which a copy of a work is made available on terms that it will, or may, be returned for payment (in money or money's worth) or in the course of a business as part of services, or on terms that it will, or may, be returned.

Where a work is made available in multimedia format, its exploitation by way of rental will, therefore, be capable of being restricted, since the work is likely to fall into all three categories of the types of work in which a rental right subsists – as a sound recording, a film and a computer program.

Conflicts may arise if the owners of these rights are different persons, and neither legislation nor caselaw provides any definite means of resolving this conflict. It is, therefore, advisable for companies releasing multimedia titles to ensure that they are the owners (or exclusive licensees) of the copyrights in all sound recordings, films and computer programs included in the titles and that, if they are exclusive licensees, the terms of their licence grant them the exclusive right to exercise the rental right.

It is important to be aware that the rental right will not merely extend to making physical copies of a work available, but can also extend to making the work available by on-line database or by modem, or cable or other form of transmission. The right is, therefore, likely to be of increasing value to the publishing community, and it may, therefore, be appropriate for companies to negotiate for the right to participate in rental income where works are exploited in multimedia formats (see Chapter 19).

The rental right conferred by the Copyright, Designs and Patents Act 1988 is not to be confused with the rental and lending right to be conferred by the European Union Rental Directive[27] (see paragraph 17.9) or the United Kingdom public lending right provisions of the Public Lending Right Act (see paragraph 6.16). The provisions of the Rental Directive have yet to be implemented in the United Kingdom, but it is likely that they will have implications for the publishing industry in relation to the exploitation of the existing United Kingdom rental right in copyright works (see paragraphs 20.11 to 20.16).

25 S18(2).
26 S178.
27 Directive 92/100.

D.   Requirements for copyright protection in the United Kingdom

3.11   Requirements for protection and oral copyright

No formalities need to be observed in the United Kingdom in order for a work to receive copyright protection. There is no requirement, under United Kingdom laws, for a work to include a copyright notice, or for it to be registered anywhere. Copyright notices may have value to protect works in certain foreign countries (see paragraph 4.9), but they are not a pre-requisite to protection in the United Kingdom. Protection in the United Kingdom automatically applies to all works, without formality, provided that they satisfy the following requirements:

(a)   If the work is a literary, dramatic, musical, or artistic work, it must be original (see paragraphs 3.16 to 3.21)[28]. Additionally, copyright will not subsist in a literary, dramatic, musical or artistic work unless and until it is recorded in writing or otherwise. It is, therefore, possible for copyright to subsist in the spoken word if it is recorded by some means and satisfies the criterion of originality.

The criterion of originality does not need to be satisfied in relation to the other two categories of copyright works (listed in paragraphs 3.4 (b) and (c)) namely sound recordings, films, broadcasts, cable programmes and typographical arrangements of published editions.

(b)   In addition, the work will have to satisfy the requirements relating to authorship, or first publication, which are set out in the Copyright, Designs and Patents Act 1988 (referred to in paragraphs 3.12 to 3.15 inclusive). These criteria apply to all the categories of copyright works[29].

No formal action is required to be taken to obtain protection of a copyright work, but it is not uncommon for authors to wish to have some form of evidence of the date on which the material was created. This may be obtained by registering the material at Stationers Hall, Stationers Hall Court, London EC4 (071–248 2934). The registration fee is £23.50. Even though registration is not required by law, it may in certain circumstances be found useful.

An alternative method of providing evidence as to the date of the creation of a copyright work is for its author to lodge a copy of the work with a bank, or to put it into a stamped self-addressed envelope, which will then be date-franked with the date of posting. The author can then retain the envelope unopened for future reference.

28 See *Walter v Lane* [1900] AC 539, [1899] 2 Ch 749.
29 Chapter IX of the Act.

3.12   Qualifying person

A work may qualify for copyright protection either because its author was, at the time the work was made, a qualifying person, or because the work was first published in the United Kingdom, or a country to which the Copyright, Designs and Patents Act 1988 extends[30].

In the case of an individual author, a person is a qualifying person if (s)he, is a British Citizen, a British Dependent Territories Citizen, a British National (Overseas), a British Overseas Citizen, a British Subject or a British Protected Person. All of these expressions are defined in the British Nationality Act 1981[31].

An individual who is domiciled, or resident, in the United Kingdom or another country to which the Copyright, Designs and Patents Act 1988 extends, will also be a qualifying person[32].

Where the "author" of a work (see paragraphs 3.21 to 3.26) is a corporate entity, incorporated under the laws of part of the United Kingdom, or of another country to which the Copyright, Designs and Patents Act 1988 extends, that company or corporation will also be a "qualifying person"[33].

30 S154(1).
31 S154(1)(a).
32 S154(1)(b).
33 S154(1)(c).

3.13   Material time

The criteria for nationality, domicile, or residence, need to be met at the "material time". The material time for a literary, dramatic, musical or artistic work is:

– if the work is unpublished, the time when the work was made. If the making of the work extended over a period, then the "material time" will be a substantial part of that period[34].
– if the work is published, the "material time" is the time it was first published. If, however, the work is first published after an author's death, then the "material time" will be the moment immediately before the death of the author[35].

The "material time" for a typographical arrangement of a published edition is the time the edition was first published[36] (see paragraph 3.15).

In the case of films, sound recordings or broadcasts[37] (see paragraph 3.7) the "material time" is the moment when the recording, film, or broadcast was made and in the case of a cable programme the moment when the programme was included in a cable programme service.

In the case of authorship of photographs, reference should be made to paragraph 3.27.

34 S154(4)(a).
35 S154(4)(b).
36 S154(5)(d).
37 S154(5)(a), (b) and (c).

3.14   Joint authorship

Where a work is a work of joint authorship[38] (see paragraph 3.22) and the work does not qualify for protection by virtue of first publication (see paragraph 3.15), then provided one of the joint authors is a qualifying person, the work will still be protected by copyright in the United Kingdom. For some purposes, however, the law disregards the existence of the other authors which can create some peculiar situations (see paragraph 3.25 (c))[39].

38 S10(1).
39 S154(3).

3.15 First publication

If none of the authors of a work satisfies the requirements set out in paragraphs 3.11 to 3.14, the work may still qualify for copyright protection, by virtue of the fact that it is first published (see paragraph 3.9) in the United Kingdom, or another country to which United Kingdom copyright provisions extend (see paragraph 3.3), or a country to which United Kingdom copyright legislation has been applied, by virtue of an Order in Council[40].

Frequently, works may be published in one or more countries at roughly the same time. To make it slightly easier for publishers to satisfy the requirements of first publication, the law will treat previous publication of a work outside the United Kingdom, as being simultaneous with the publication in the United Kingdom (allowing the UK publication to be considered "first" publication provided that it occurs within 30 days of the non-UK publication)[41].

In the case of broadcasts and cable programmes, the provisions relating to simultaneous publication do not apply, since, if a broadcast or cable programme is ineligible for copyright protection, by virtue of its author not being a qualifying person (as to authors see paragraphs 3.23 to 3.27 and as to qualifying persons see paragraph 3.11), the broadcast or cable programme may still qualify for copyright protection, if it is sent from a place within the United Kingdom, or a country to which United Kingdom Copyright Legislation extends, or has been applied by an Order in Council[42]. The publication of a sound recording or film may not, however, amount to publication of any literary, dramatic, musical or artistic work contained in it.

Where a literary, dramatic, musical or artistic work is contained in a film or sound recording, the issue to the public of copies of that film or sound recording will not constitute publication of the literary dramatic musical or artistic works contained in it[43]. The meaning of "publication" is considered in paragraph 3.9.

40 S155(1) and (2).
41 S155(3).
42 S156(1) and (2).
43 See Laddie, Prescott and Victoria *The Modern Law of Copyright,* Chapter 3, and *Copinger and Skone James on Copyright,* Chapter 3.

E. Originality

3.16 Requirement of originality

In order for a literary, dramatic, musical or artistic work to be protected by copyright, it must be shown that the work is original[44]. In other words, the work must be the result of the application of a significant amount of skill, knowledge or creative labour.

The skill or labour must have been involved in the production of the original literary, dramatic, musical or artistic work. It is, however, permissible for the skill or labour to have been used in producing preparatory work, upon which the subsequent copyright work was based.

It is not necessary that the work itself be wholly original, and works which are wholly, or partly, based on previous works are capable of being protected by copyright. Where, however, a work is based on an existing copyright work, it will be necessary to obtain the permission in writing of the owner of the original copyright work, in order to base the subsequent work upon it. If the copyright in the original work has expired, however, no permission need be sought.

44 S1(1)(a).

3.17 Innovative nature

In order to satisfy the requirement of originality in respect of literary, dramatic, musical, or artistic works, and consequently to qualify for copyright protection, it is not necessary that a literary, dramatic, musical, or artistic work should be totally innovative. It is quite permissible, for example, for a literary work to be based upon the same real-life events as another literary work – provided that there is no direct borrowing.

Where the idea for a literary work has been suggested by the existence of another copyright literary work, care must be taken not to present (for example) historical facts in the same way as the original work, or to adopt the same manner, or approach, as the original work, if this is significant, in order to avoid claims for copyright infringement.

So long as a literary work is original, it does not matter if it is devoid of artistic merit. Works such as railway timetables, logarithms, directories, various types of forms, catalogues, and even trade figures qualify for protection as literary works, provided that they are the result of a sufficient degree of skill, originality or labour.

3.18 Ideas

Generally speaking, there is no copyright in an idea itself. Where, however, an idea is incorporated in a work in a particular manner, and a subsequent work uses the same idea, and also uses one or more of the methods of treatment of the same idea by the original work, then the subsequent work may be infringing copyright. Use of an idea may, however, represent a breach of confidence in the circumstances referred to in paragraph 1.3.

3.19 Titles, slogans, trade marks and passing off

As a general rule, the titles of works, and any associated names, are not protected by copyright. This does not mean to say that free and unrestricted use can be made of names or titles, since the user of the name (or title) may have registered the name as a trade mark or service mark in respect of a particular class of goods or services. Where a name has been so registered, its use may be a violation of trade mark or service mark rights and may be prevented (see paragraphs 3.41 to 3.45 and 13.11 to 13.17).

Furthermore, even where a name has not been registered as a trade mark or service mark, the proprietor of the name may be able to prevent its use by third parties by means of an action in passing off.

There are five essential characteristics which must be present in order to create a valid cause of action in passing off[45]. There must be:

(a)   a misrepresentation;
(b)   made by a trader in the course of trade;
(c)   to prospective customers of the trader or ultimate consumers of goods or services supplied by the trader;
(d)   as a result of which it is a reasonably foreseeable consequence that damage will be caused to the business or goodwill of another trader;
(e)   which misrepresentation causes actual damage or will probably do so.

It is, conceivably, possible that a slogan may qualify for copyright protection, if it is sufficiently original, and a sufficient degree of skill has gone into its creation. Although this possibility is somewhat remote in the context of titles of works, it is a rather more real possibility in the context of slogans. A number of advertising slogans may be eligible for copyright protection and their unauthorised use may, therefore, amount to an infringement of copyright.

45 *Erven Warnink BV v J Townend & Sons (Hull) Limited* [1980] RPC 31.

3.20   Anthologies, abridgements and compilations

Since the originality test of copyright is satisfied by the application of sufficient skill or labour, it is perfectly possible for an original copyright work to be created by means of the selection of a number of non-copyright works in an anthology which may have been compiled as a result of a sufficient amount of research and reading on the subject. In such a case the selection of works contained in the anthology would qualify for copyright protection. Compilation works may also be eligible for copyright protection in the same way as anthologies.

Where a non-copyright work is abridged by an author, the resulting abridged, or condensed, version may be the subject of a separate copyright for two reasons. First, a degree of skill or labour will have been involved in deciding what passages should be cut. Second, the bridge passages linking the selected excerpts of the text, may contain a précis of the intervening action, and these précis will, to the extent that they are original, qualify for copyright protection as literary works.

3.21   Editions

The question of typographical arrangements of published editions is dealt with elsewhere (see paragraph 3.28), but the copyright status of scholarly editions also needs to be considered.

Where a literary edition of (say) a medieval manuscript is produced, a significant amount of skill and labour may have been expended by the editor, in comparing extant manuscripts, and in researching etymological and morphological variants, in order to compile a definitive text. This definitive text will normally be glossed by footnotes and may contain a glossary, a vocabulary, a comparative analysis of metaphors and words used in the work, an introduction and other notes.

As we have seen, any elements which have been added to the text by the editor may be the subject of separate copyright protection. In addition, however, the establishment of the definitive text itself may also create a copyright work which is capable of being infringed.

F. Ownership and authorship

3.22 Who owns copyright?

The ownership of copyright is, as with the ownership of any other property, likely to change. Copyright may be transferred by way of assignment, or by way of licence[46] (see paragraphs 3.38 to 3.40).

Under United Kingdom law, however, the first owner of the copyright in a copyright work will, as a general rule, be the author. There are four exceptions to this rule including exceptions in relation to Crown copyright, Parliamentary copyright and copyright owned by certain international organisations[47]. The most important exception, however, is that where a literary, dramatic or artistic work is made by a person in the course of employment, then the employer will be the first owner of copyright in the work subject to any agreement to the contrary[48].

46 S90.
47 S11.
48 S11(2).

3.23 Authorship

The author of a work is the person who created it. In the case of sound recording or film, the author is the person by whom the arrangements necessary for the making of the recording or film were undertaken. Where a copyright work consists of the typographical arrangement of a published edition, the author is the publisher[49].

In the case of a literary, dramatic, musical or artistic work which is computer-generated, the author is the person by whom the arrangements necessary for the creation of the work were undertaken[50].

A copyright work is a work of joint authorship if it is produced by means of the collaboration of two or more authors, in which the contribution of each author is not distinct from that of the other authors[51].

49 S9.
50 S9(3).
51 S10.

3.24 Unknown authorship

Where the identity of an author of a work is unknown or, if, in the case of a work of joint authorship, the identity of none of the authors is known, the work will be a work of unknown authorship[52].

If it is not possible to ascertain the identity of an author by reasonable enquiry, that authorship will be regarded as unknown. The significance of a work being of unknown authorship is that there are circumstances in which such works may be exploited without infringing any copyright (see paragraph 8.10). Once, however, the identity of an author is known, even if the author cannot be traced, the work cannot be regarded as being work of unknown authorship.

Where there is evidence that the author of an unpublished literary, dramatic, musical or artistic work was a qualifying person (see paragraph 3.12) it shall be assumed, until the contrary is proved, that this is so, and that copyright subsists in the work.

52 S9(4).

G. Term of copyright in the United Kingdom

3.25 Literary, dramatic, musical or artistic works

The general rule is that the term of copyright in the United Kingdom in a literary, dramatic, musical, or artistic work expires 50 years from the end of the calendar year in which the author dies. This rule is, of course, subject to the copyright work satisfying the requirements of copyright protection, and is further subject to a number of exceptions set out below[53]. The European Commission has recently issued a directive which will extend this period by a further 20 years (see paragraph 17.11 and paragraphs 20.2 to 20.10).

(a) *Literary, dramatic, musical and artistic works of unknown authorship*

Where a literary, dramatic, musical or artistic work is of unknown authorship, copyright in the United Kingdom expires 50 years from the end of the calendar year in which it is first made available to the public. The general rule referred to in this paragraph will not apply, if the identity of the author becomes known more than 50 years after the end of the calendar year in which the work was made available[54].

(b) *Computer-generated literary, dramatic, musical or artistic works*

Where a work is computer-generated, copyright in the United Kingdom will expire 50 years from the end of the calendar year in which the work was made[55]. It is, of course, possible for a work to be partly computer-generated and partly human-generated. For example, the results of a computer sort programme might be rearranged by human hand, and if a sufficient degree of skill or labour has been expended (see paragraph 3.16) the work will be a work of joint authorship, and its period of protection may be based on the life of the author and may be longer than the basic 50-year period (see paragraph 3.25 (c)).

(c) Works of joint authorship

In the case of works of joint authorship, the copyright period in the United Kingdom is calculated with reference from the date of the last joint author to die. If the identity of one or more of the joint authors is not known, then, the period will run from the date of the death of the last of the authors whose identity is known. The provision relating to works of unknown authorship (see paragraph 3.23) applies only where the identity of the author (as distinct from the author's whereabouts) is not known[56].

53 S12(1).
54 S12(2).
55 S12(3).
56 S12(4).

3.26 Copyright term of photographs

Photographs are protected as artistic works (see paragraph 3.6). A photograph is any recording of light, or other radiation, on any medium, on which an image is produced, or from which an image may be produced, provided the photograph is not part of a film[57]. The Copyright, Designs and Patents Act 1988 has made significant changes in the type, and term, of copyright protection afforded to photographs in the United Kingdom, and careful enquiry may, in many cases, be necessary, both in relation to the date the photograph was taken and as to the date (if any) on which it was published, in order to calculate the relevant term of copyright protection. Three different terms may apply, being:

(a) Published photographs made between 1 July 1912 and 31 July 1989. The term of copyright in the United Kingdom will expire 50 years from the end of the calendar year in which the negative of the photograph was made[58].
(b) Photographs taken after May 1957 and unpublished as at the end of July 1989. The term of copyright protection in the United Kingdom will expire 50 years from the end of 1989 (ie 31 December 2039).
(c) Photographs taken on or after 1 August 1989. The general rule as to the term of copyright protection will apply and the term in the United Kingdom will usually be the life of the author plus 50 years[59].

The European Commission has recently issued a directive which will extend the period of United Kingdom copyright protection for photographs (see paragraph 17.11 and paragraphs 20.2 to 20.10).

57 S4(2).
58 S12(1).
59 Sch 1 paras 12.

3.27 Authorship and ownership of photographs

The identity of the author of a photograph deserves special attention. The author of a photograph taken before August 1989 is the person who at the time the photograph was taken is the owner of the material on which it is taken. This provision was originally contained in the Copyright Act 1956 (now repealed)[60].

The ownership of film stock at the time a photograph was taken has absolutely no relevance for determining the copyright ownership of photographs taken on or after 1 August 1989, since the Copyright, Designs, and Patents Act 1988 provides that the author of a post July 1989 photograph is the person who creates it[61]. This may not necessarily be the person who presses the button. Additionally, rights to privacy exist in relation to post July 1989 films and photographs (see paragraph 5.15).

60 Copyright Act 1956 S48.
61 S9(1).

3.28 Typographical arrangements

The term of copyright in the United Kingdom in the typographical arrangement of a published edition, expires 25 years from the end of the calendar year in which the edition was first published. (See also paragraph 3.9.) Publication, in the case of a published edition of the work, means the issue of copies to the public[62].

Whilst making a literary work available to the public by means of an electronic retrieval system will constitute publication in respect of the literary work, it will not constitute publication of the typographical arrangement of the work.

If only one or a few copies of a work are made available to the public, and these are not intended to satisfy the reasonable requirements of the public, this will not amount to publication.

62 S15.

3.29 Typefaces

The design of a typeface is eligible for copyright protection in the United Kingdom as an artistic work[63]. Where articles which have been specifically designed, or adapted, for producing material in a particular typeface, have been marketed by or with the licence of the copyright owner, then the term of copyright protection in respect of the use of the artwork in the typeface will expire 25 years from the end of the calendar year in which the first such articles were marketed[64].

It is not, however, an infringement of copyright to use a typeface in the ordinary course of typing, composing text, typesetting or printing[65].

Following such period, the artistic work may be copied by making articles for producing material in the typeface, or using the articles so made, without infringing copyright in the artistic work, but the term of the copyright in the artistic work is not itself ended. Where articles for the production of a typeface have been made available before 1 August 1989, the period of protection given to such articles in the United Kingdom will end on 31 December 2014, unless copyright first expires before the end of such period[66].

63 S55.
64 S52.
65 S54.
66 S52(2).

3.30 Copyright in sound recordings and films

Copyright in the United Kingdom in a sound recording or film made on or after 1 August 1989 expires at the end of the period of 50 years from the end of the calendar year in which it is made or, if it is released before the end of that period, 50 years from the end of the calendar year of release[67].

The copyright protection of films and sound recordings made before 1 August 1989 is determined by provisions contained in Schedule 1 to the Copyright Designs and Patents Act 1988. The provisions of this schedule are extremely complex and reapply some of the provisions of the Copyright Act 1956 and the Copyright Act 1911 with amendments.

Between 1912 and 1957, a film could be protected as either a dramatic work, or a series of photographs, or a sound recording – or all three. The legislation did not, however, determine with certainty who owned the copyright in a film. The 1956 Copyright Act removed the uncertainty as to ownership, stating that the copyright vested in the maker of the film, and also removed the overlapping protection of films and combined the three elements (dramatic work, photographs and sound track) into what the legislation referred to as a "cinematograph film". This legislation provided that sound recordings in the sound track of a film (other than pre-existing recordings) were treated as part of the "cinematograph film" copyright.

The 1956 Copyright Act, however, overlooked one small detail. The period of copyright protection for films was determined with reference to their date of first publication and although publication included the issue of copies of a film to the public (such as on videogram) it did not include exhibiting a film in cinemas or broadcasting it on television. The result was a technically eternal period of copyright protection for some films.

The Copyright, Designs and Patents Act 1988 removed this anomaly but another one was substituted in its place (see paragraph 20.3). The clock determining the period of copyright protection for existing unpublished films was set running on 1 August 1989, and the Act provided that for films made after this time, showing or playing them in public would constitute publication[68]. The Act also separated the copyright in the film sound track from the film itself, creating at least two separate copyrights in most films: the copyright in the silent(!) series of moving images and the copyright in the accompanying sounds. Most film sound tracks are, in fact, derived from three separate sound recordings, one containing music, one dialogue and one sound effects.

The European Commission has recently issued a directive which will extend the period of United Kingdom copyright protection for films (see paragraph 17.11 and paragraphs 20.2 to 20.20).

67 S13(1).
68 S13(2).

3.31 Publication

In the Copyright, Designs and Patents Act 1988 Part I, publication, in relation to a work, means the issue of copies to the public and includes, in the case of a literary, dramatic, musical or artistic work, making it available to the public by means of an electronic retrieval system[69], but it does not include publication which is merely colourable and not intended to satisfy the reasonable requirements of the public[70].

The following do not constitute publication:

(a) in the case of a literary, dramatic or musical work, its performance or broadcasting, or inclusion in a cable programme service (otherwise than for the purposes of an electronic retrieval system)[71];

(b) in the case of an artistic work, its exhibition, or the issue to the public of copies of a graphic work representing, or of photographs of, a work of architecture in the form of a building or a model for a building, a sculpture or a work of artistic craftsmanship, or the issue to the public of copies of a film including the work, or the broadcasting of the work or its inclusion in a cable programme service (otherwise than for the purposes of an electronic retrieval system)[72];

(c) in the case of a sound recording or film, the work being played or shown in public, or the broadcasting of the work or its inclusion in a cable programme service[73].

For the purposes of these provisions no account is to be taken of any unauthorised act[74].

69 S175(1); related expressions are construed accordingly: S175(1).
70 S175(1).
71 S175(4)(a).
72 S175(4)(b).
73 S175(4)(c).
74 S175(6).

3.32 Broadcasts and cable programmes

Where a broadcast, or cable programme, is eligible for copyright protection, its copyright will expire 50 years from the end of the calendar year in which the broadcast was made, or the cable programme was included in a cable programme service[75].

Where the broadcast, or cable programme, is a repeat of an earlier broadcast, or cable programme, the copyright in the repeat will expire at the same time as the copyright in the earlier broadcast or cable programme[76].

It should be noted that the copyright in the broadcast, or cable programme, is separate and distinct from the copyright in any other element included in it.

75 S14(1).
76 S14(2).

3.33   University copyrights

The Copyright Act 1775 conferred on the Universities of Oxford, Cambridge, St Andrew's, Glasgow, Aberdeen and Edinburgh, and each college and house of learning at the Universities of Oxford, Cambridge, Trinity College Dublin, and the Colleges of Eton, Westminster and Winchester, the exclusive right of printing of all books which had been bequeathed or given to them. This right applies to all bequests and gifts made before 1 July 1912 and was, before the 1988 Act, a perpetual right, unless the bequest specified a limited period. The 1988 Act now provides that the rights of the relevant Universities and Colleges will expire on 31 December 2039[77].

77 Sch 1 paras 13.

3.34   Unpublished literary, dramatic, musical and artistic works

Where the author of a literary, dramatic or musical work has died at the commencement date of the Act and none of the Acts restricted by the 1956 Act has been performed in respect of the work, then copyright in the work will expire on 31 December 2039[78].

In the case of a literary, dramatic, musical or artistic work which is anonymous or pseudonymous then if such work is unpublished on the commencement date copyright will expire on 31 December 2039, unless, before such time, the work is first made available to the public, in which case it will run from the date the work is made available, unless before or after the work is made available, the identity of the author becomes known, in which case the period will be the author's life plus 50 years[79].

This period will, of course, be extended by the directive recently issued by the European Commission (see paragraph 17.11 and paragraphs 20.2 to 20.20).

78 S12(1).
79 S12(2) and Sch 1 paras 12(3)(b).

3.35   Peter Pan

The Copyright, Designs and Patents Act 1988 contains special provisions which confer on trustees of the Hospital for Sick Children in Great Ormond Street, London, the right to a royalty in respect of the public performance, commercial publication, broadcast or inclusion in a cable programme of the play "Peter Pan" by Sir J M Barrie, or any adaptation of it[80]. The scope of this provision will apply only to those territories to which the United Kingdom copyright legislation extends (see paragraph 3.3).

80 S301 and Sch 6.

H. Crown and Parliamentary copyright

3.36 Crown copyright

Where a work is made by Her Majesty or by an officer or servant of the Crown in the course of their duties, copyright in such a work is stated to be Crown Copyright. The term of copyright protection for literary dramatic or musical works which are Crown Copyright is 125 years from the end of the year in which the work was made or, if the work is published commercially before the end of 75 years from which it was made, the copyright will expire 50 years from the end of the year of publication[81].

In the case of a work of joint authorship the provision will apply to the extent only of the contribution of the relevant author[82].

The copyright in every Act of Parliament and Measure of the General Synod of the Church of England belongs to Her Majesty and subsists from Royal Assent until 50 years from the end of the calendar year in which the Royal Assent was given[83].

81 S163(3)(b).
82 S163(4).
83 S164(1)(2).

3.37 Parliamentary copyright

Where a work is made by or under the direction or control of the House of Commons or the House of Lords, the House by whom or under whose direction or control the work is made is the first owner of copyright of the work[84].

If it is made by both Houses jointly, they will be joint first owners of copyright. Such works are referred to as Parliamentary copyright, and where they are literary, dramatic, musical or artistic works, the copyright period will expire 50 years from the end of the year in which the work was made[85].

Copyright in private Bills and personal Bills (after they have been carried to the House of Lords) belong to both Houses jointly[86].

84 S165(1).
85 S165.
86 S166(3).

I. Transfers of copyright

3.38 Transfer of copyright under United Kingdom law

Copyright may be transferred under the laws of the United Kingdom by way of assignment, or by way of licence, or by way of testamentary disposition, or by way of operation of law[87]. Assignments and licences are dealt with in paragraphs 3.39 and 3.40.

Where a bequest in an author's will leaves an unpublished literary, dramatic, musical or artistic work to an individual, the copyright in such work, will (so far as the person making the bequest was the owner of the copyright) pass to the person to whom the bequest is made, unless the will or any Codicil to the will indicates otherwise[88].

Where an author or owner of copyright becomes bankrupt, then any copyrights owned by such person will, by operation of the law, automatically be transferred to the individual's trustee in bankruptcy. The individual will have no right to make any assignment or licence or other dealing with the property[89].

Stamp duty is payable on the transfer of intellectual property rights (see paragraph 11.29). There is a possibility that if a document evidencing the transfer of intellectual property rights is produced to a court and stamp duty has not been paid on that document, the court might refuse to accept such document as proof of the transfer of such rights.

87 S90(1).
88 S93.
89 See *Mawman v Tegg* (1826) 2 Russ 385; *Lucas v Moncrieff* (1905) 21 TLR 683.

3.39 Assignments and licences

Under United Kingdom law, assignments and licences of copyright may be limited in two ways:

(a) they may be limited to one or more (but not all) of the things which the copyright owner has the exclusive right to do (see paragraph 3.2); and/or

(b) they may be limited to part but not the whole of the period for which copyright is to subsist[90].

Where assignments and licences extend to rights outside the United Kingdom, the provisions of English law may not be relevant, and specific regard must be paid to local laws.

In general, assignments and licences of copyright are not effective unless they are in writing, and signed by, or on behalf of, the copyright owner[91]. Where a document is signed on behalf of a person (by an agent, for example), it is important to establish that the person actually signing it has the authority to bind the person on whose behalf (s)he purports to contract. There is one exception to this provision, in that it would appear that it remains possible for non-exclusive licences to be granted verbally. It is also possible to enter into an oral contract (or verbal agreement) which imposes on a copyright owner a binding contractual obligation to execute a written assignment or licence.

Where a copyright owner grants a licence, the licence will be binding on every successor in title to the copyright owner, other than a purchaser in good faith, for valuable consideration, without notice of the licence[92].

90 S90(2).
91 S90(3).
92 S90(4).

3.40 Differences between assignments and licences

Under English law, as a general rule, an assignment of copyright will be an outright transfer, and a licence will be a transfer, subject to the performance of certain conditions. Both assignments and licences may be limited in the respects set out in paragraph 3.39. Although assignments are generally for the full period of copyright protection, including all renewal periods, they may be limited in time by the insertion of provisions requiring the assignee to reassign to the assignor the relevant rights at the end of a specified period or, if certain events have not taken place, within a given time. Alternatively, the period for which the assignment is to take effect may be framed by reference to the occurrence of an event of default, upon which the term of rights will expire automatically. The effect of such a provision on a subsequent assignee would need, however, to be considered in the light of all relevant circumstances.

The most significant difference between an assignment and licence is that a licensor may (depending on the provisions of a contract), generally speaking terminate a licence, if the licensee fails to perform any of its obligations. On termination the copyright licence will cease, leaving all rights vested in the licensor. This situation will not generally apply in the case of an assignment where all rights are assigned to the assignee outright, and the assignor does not retain any interest in them. This means that where an assignee is in breach of (for example) obligations to pay the assignor, then the assignor will be required to sue to enforce the debt, rather than simply terminate the licence, and seize any infringing materials.

Where a company enters into an agreement with a licensee of a copyright work which grants the company a sub-licence in the work, and the licensee subsequently fails to perform obligations owed towards the copyright owner and loses its licence, the company's exclusive rights will also terminate. For this reason, where significant sums are being invested in the exploitation of a copyright work which has been acquired from a licensee pursuant to a licence (as opposed to an assignment from the copyright owner), it is a prudent step to seek assurance from the relevant copyright owner, so that, in the event of termination of the licence, the sub-licensee may continue to exploit the rights in the work.

J. Trade marks and service marks

3.41 Trade marks generally

The Trade Marks Act 1938 (as amended) provides for the registration of 34 classes of trade mark and eight classes of service mark, subject to the Trade Mark and Service Marks Rules 1986. The Trade Mark Register is divided into two parts[93]. In order for a trade mark or service mark to be registrable in Part A of the Register the mark must be distinctive within the meaning of the 1988 Act[94]. In order for a mark to be registrable in Part B of the Register, it must be capable of distinguishing goods[95].

Registration of a mark in Part A carries the presumption of validity after seven years and[96], where proceedings are brought for infringement of a Part

A mark, the fact that the infringing act took place is considered to be conclusive proof of the infringement[97]. Where an action is brought in respect of infringement of a Part B mark, a defence is available by showing that the use complained of is not likely to deceive or cause confusion. It will be seen, therefore that registration in Part B of the Register is less secure than registration in Part A of the Register.[98]

93 Trademarks Act 1938 S1.
94 Ibid S9.
95 Ibid S10.
96 Ibid S13.
97 Ibid S46.
98 Ibid S5(2).

3.42   Assignment of trade marks

Registered trade marks and registered service marks are assignable or transmissible, either in connection with the goodwill of the business or not[99], but an unregistered mark cannot be transferred independently of the business to which it relates. Such marks may be assigned or transmitted in respect of all the goods or services in respect of which they are registered, or of some, but not all, of the goods or services[100]. A trade mark or service mark is not, however, assignable or transmissible where, as a result of such assignment or transmission, more than one person would have exclusive rights relating to the use of marks nearly resembling each other, or relating to identical marks used in connection with the same goods or services, or goods or services of the same description, or associated with each other if, having regard to the similarity of the goods or services, or their association or description, and the similarity of the marks, the use of the marks would be likely to deceive or cause confusion[101].

Where a trade mark or service mark is assigned otherwise than in connection with the sale of the goodwill of the business to which the trade mark or service mark relates, the assignment may not take effect until after the assignee has applied to the Registrar of Trade Marks for directions relating to the advertisement of the assignment and has advertised the assignment in such form and manner, and within such period, as the Registrar directs. The Act does not currently permit the assignment of a pending application for registration of a trade mark or service mark, except where another registered trade mark or service mark is being transferred at the same time[102].

99 Trademarks Act 1938 S22(1).
100 Ibid S22(2).
101 Ibid S22(4).
102 Ibid S22(7).

3.43   Licences of marks

Persons other than the registered proprietors of trade marks or service marks are permitted to be registered as users of marks[103]. A registered user may commence proceedings for infringement of a trade mark, or service mark, in the user's own name if the proprietor of the mark refuses or neglects to do so within two months from being called upon so to do[104]. Any application for registration as a registered user must be made by both the proprietor and the proposed registered user. Subject to the Registrar being satisfied that the use of the trade mark or service mark in respect of the proposed goods or services would not be contrary to the public interest, the Registrar may register the proposed registered user in respect of the goods or services[105].

The Registrar is, however, required to refuse any application for registration as a registered user if it appears to the Registrar that such registration would tend to facilitate trafficking in a trade mark or service mark[106]. "Trafficking" in a trade mark has been defined as dealing in the mark as a commodity in its own right and not primarily for the purpose of identifying or promoting merchandise in which the proprietor of the mark is interested. The 1984 case[107] involving the character "Holly Hobbie" and generally known by that name involved an application for registration as a registered user. Notwithstanding the fact that the proposed user agreements contained quality control provisions, the application was refused on the grounds of trafficking.

103 Trademarks Act 1938 S28(1).
104 Ibid S28(3).
105 Ibid S28(4) and (5).
106 Ibid S28(6).
107 *Re American Greetings Corporation Application* [1984] 1 All ER 426.

3.44 Proposed reforms of trade mark law

Proposed reforms in trade mark law are set out in the draft European Commission Council Regulations[108] and the White Paper entitled "Reform of Trade Marks Law"[109]. The Draft Regulations and White Paper signal the intention of the Government to depart from the legislation currently contained in the Trade Marks Act 1938 in a number of areas, including principally:

(a) The establishment of a Community Trade Mark Office to administer the new property right, the community trade mark which will have effect throughout the European Union and will be obtained by registration at the Community Trade Mark Office. The same law will apply to both trade marks and service marks, which will be collectively referred to as marks.

(b) Parts A and B of the Trade Mark Register will be combined, and there will no longer be a presumption of validity of registration after seven years.

(c) It will be possible to seek registration in several classes at once by one application.

(d) The provision restricting trafficking of marks will be repealed.

(e) The requirement to advertise assignments of marks without the goodwill of businesses will be ended.

(f) The definition of a mark will be expanded so as to include, among other matters, colours, or shades of colours, and signs denoting sound, smell or taste, if these are capable of being represented graphically, as well as the distinctive appearances of packaging, and are capable of distinguishing the goods or services.

59

The United Kingdom government introduced a Trade Marks Bill[110] into Parliament in November 1993.

108 European Commission Council Regulations 4595/91.
109 Cmnd 1203.
110 ISBN 0-10-870054-2.

3.45 What should a publisher or multimedia company do about trade marks?

Trade marks (and service marks) are an important element of the business assets of a publisher or multimedia company. They provide an effective means of projecting the image of the publisher or multimedia company, and form an important element of the "goodwill" of any business. Although something as intangible as goodwill is somewhat difficult to value in financial terms, evaluation techniques for goodwill and marks, both registered and unregistered are evolving. The Accounting Standards Board has issued proposals for reform of accounting practice in relation to goodwill,[111] and it will soon be possible for banks and other lenders to take effective security over registered trade marks.

It is therefore a matter of great importance for publishers and multimedia companies to protect their goodwill and trade and service marks, not only because these items are now beginning to be recognised as balance sheet items in their own right which form part of a publisher's or multimedia company's assets and may therefore in some circumstances be used as security to provide finance but also because failure to register a mark in a particular class of goods or in a particular country might provide a publisher's or multimedia company's competitors with an opportunity to acquire market share.

The advent of the Community Trade Mark Office and the emergence of electronic publishing represent dual threats/opportunities. Not only is the territorial scope of protection which can be achieved by a single registration being widened to European Union and European Free Trade Association (EFTA) countries but the field of publishing and multimedia activity (and consequently of the number of classes in which registration is advisable) is also broadening.

Publishers and multimedia companies should, therefore, consider taking the following action:

(a) compile a list of all names, marks and imprints (see paragraphs 9.15 and 9.16) currently or previously used by the business;

(b) establish which marks are of economic or cultural significance;

(c) identify which marks are registered, producing for each mark a list of the classes of registration, the countries of registration and renewal dates;

(d) assess whether the classes and countries of registered marks offer protection (particularly in relation to anticipated future activities by the publisher in the field of electronic publishing or by the publisher's or multimedia company's competitors in EU/EFTA countries);

(e) effect any additional registrations considered appropriate;

(f) arrange for an evaluation to be effected of the publisher's or multimedia company's "brand" mark and goodwill assets;

(g)   implement mark renewal procedure;

(h)   implement mark monitoring service to provide warning of competitors' activities.

It will be appreciated that the above matters may not only require lengthy commercial deliberation but also detailed legal advice. The potential gains and losses which might be suffered by publishers and multimedia companies through inattention to these matters fully justify such close attention.

111 Accounting Standards Board Discussion Paper "Goodwill and Intangibles".

4. International copyright protection and reversion of copyright

[IMPORTANT NOTE: Please read the section "About this book" on page v, before referring to any of the matters in this chapter]

A. Introduction

4.1 Purpose of this chapter

International trade is an important feature of the publishing and multimedia world and although some companies confine their activities to the United Kingdom, they will still benefit from understanding how the international copyright conventions work, since these determine the copyright protection not only of foreign works in the United Kingdom but also (and perhaps more importantly) the protection of British works overseas.

The first part of this chapter, therefore, identifies and explains the principal copyright conventions, and the chapter then examines aspects of copyright protection in the United States of America, the Commonwealth of Independent States and the European Union.

The symbol © is a familiar sight to all of us. We all know what it means, but few people understand its origins, or its relevance. The second part of this chapter examines the role and importance of copyright notices.

Ownership of copyright is obviously important, but there are occasions where British or American laws provide that copyrights revert. United Kingdom law provides that a total automatic reversion of certain copyrights will occur 25 years after their author's death. The provision is a time bomb which will represent a threat to publishers and multimedia companies until well into the next century, yet many people are unaware of it. The chapter identifies the problem and suggests a solution.

Finally, the chapter examines some of the difficulties in acquiring or transferring ownership of foreign copyrights, and offers some advice as to how publishers and multimedia companies might deal with this.

B. International copyright protection

4.2 Copyright conventions

Copyright legislation in the United Kingdom extends only to the United Kingdom (and, subject to certain provisos, the Isle of Man, the Channel Islands and Hong Kong) but, besides providing protection to works written or created by British nationals and to works first published in the United Kingdom, our legislation also provides protection to works written or created by foreign nationals, or works which have been first published outside the United Kingdom. How then, are United Kingdom copyright works protected overseas?

This protection is effected by means of the three principal Copyright Conventions. These Conventions are the Berne Convention, the Universal Copyright Convention (commonly referred to as the UCC) and the Rome Convention.

The Conventions are international treaties and they oblige each country which is a signatory (and most countries in the world are signatories of one, if not both) to apply certain minimum standards of copyright protection to works originating from other signatory countries.

Although the laws of each country throughout the world are obviously different, the treaty provisions provide certain minimum standards which must be observed in each country and, as a result, the type of copyright protection accorded by the various signatory countries is broadly similar. Certain formalities may, however, be required in order to obtain copyright protection in countries which are not signatories to the Berne Convention.

Both the Berne Convention and the Universal Copyright Convention state minimum provisions which must be enacted in the copyright laws of states which have signed the Treaty. There are, however, a number of ways in which the provisions of the Berne Convention and the Universal Copyright Convention differ.

4.3 Berne Convention[1]

The Berne Convention requires its signatory countries to provide for moral rights, according to their laws. Despite this treaty obligation, the United States of America, which has recently become a signatory to the Berne Convention, provides no moral rights protection for authors of literary, dramatic, or musical works, or directors of films, and provides only limited protection of artists' moral rights.

The United Kingdom itself, however, failed to comply fully with the Berne Convention's moral rights obligations until the coming into force of the 1988 Copyright, Designs and Patents Act on 1 August 1989.

Traditionally, the effect of accession to the Berne Convention has been presumed to be retroactive. Where a copyright work which originates in country A is not accorded copyright protection under the laws of country B, because country A is not a signatory to the Berne Convention, the work will not have copyright protection in country B, and is said to be "in the public domain". If, however, country B joins the Berne Convention, the normal retrospective effect of the Convention is that works which originated in country A, and which were in the public domain in country B, will fall into copyright in country B, if they are still in copyright in country A.

This effect has, however, been expressly excluded by the United States of America as a condition of becoming a signatory to the Berne Convention. The result is that a number of European and other works, which are eligible for copyright protection under the provisions of the Berne Convention, which were previously unprotected by United States copyright laws (either as a result of non-registration or non-renewal of copyright registration or failure to meet other United States criteria), will remain unprotected in the United States, even though the United States of America has joined the Berne Convention and will obtain its retrospective protection of United States works which were previously in the public domain in the Berne Convention countries.

1 See *Copinger and Skone James on Copyright,* Chapter 17.

4.4   Universal Copyright Convention and other conventions[2]

The Universal Copyright Convention recognises that it will be necessary in some cases to comply with formalities (such as the registration of copyright and the renewal of copyright etc) in order to obtain copyright protection in certain countries. It should be noted that where a country is a signatory to both the Berne Convention and the Universal Copyright Convention, since that country will have agreed to accord copyright protection to works originating in other Berne Convention States without formality, it may be possible to disregard the provisions of the Universal Copyright Convention.

Because of the enormous difficulties which publishers and authors would face if they were required to ensure compliance with the formalities required in every UCC signatory country, the UCC contains a provision which deems these formalities to have been satisfied if a copyright notice in the form referred to in paragraph 4.9 is affixed to all copies of copyright works from the time of their first publication.

Since Universal Copyright Convention protection extends only to the initial period of copyright protection, it is important that in any country (such as the United States up to 1978) where protection for a subsequent period is dependent on renewal of copyright or some other procedure, these formalities must be complied with in a timely manner.

The third major copyright convention is the International Convention for the Protection of Performers, Producers of Phonograms and Broadcasting Organisations (which is frequently referred to simply as the Rome Convention). This Convention provides certain minimum standards of protection relating to sound recordings. The minimum standards of protection are observed by United Kingdom law. The Rome Convention also contains a provision which deems formalities relating to registration of sound recordings to have been satisfied if they contain notice in the prescribed form (see paragraph 4.9).

Other relevant conventions are the Convention for the Protection of Producers of Phonograms against Unauthorised Duplication of their

Phonograms, the Convention Relating to the Distribution of Programme-Carrying Signals Transmitted by Satellite, and the European Agreement on the Protection of Television Broadcasts.

2 *Copinger and Skone James on Copyright*, Chapter 17, 17–71.

C. The United States of America and the former Union of Soviet Socialist Republics and the European Union[3]

4.5 Copyright in the United States of America and the former Union of Soviet Socialist Republics

Until 1 March 1989 (when the United States of America formally accepted the provisions of the Berne Convention other than retroactive application and certain moral rights provisions)[4] the United States of America and the Union of Soviet Socialist Republics were the two most prominent countries who had agreed to the provisions of the Universal Copyright Convention but not the Berne Convention.

Before the United States acceded to the Universal Copyright Convention in 1957, it was common practice for rights owners to acquire copyright protection both under the laws of the United Kingdom and under the laws of the United States by means of simultaneous publication. If a work was published within the same 30-day period in both countries, it was deemed to have been first published in each country, and therefore protected under the laws of each country. Since first publication in the United Kingdom gave access to Berne Convention publication, the work would additionally be protected in all Berne signatory states. The simultaneous publication requirements were relaxed by both countries during the two World Wars and, despite the absence of formal convention protection, many works published in the United Kingdom or the United States between 1939 and 1950 may, therefore, qualify for copyright protection. In the United States, copyright protection of pre-1978 works would lapse after the initial period of protection provided by United States law, unless the copyright in the works was renewed (see paragraph 4.6).

The Union of Soviet Socialist Republics did not accede to the Universal Copyright Convention until 1972. The result is that all literary, dramatic, musical, artistic works, films or sound recordings made before this time in the Union of Soviet Socialist Republics will be in the public domain in the United Kingdom unless, at the time of first publication, they satisfied the requirements then subsisting in relation to United Kingdom copyright protection. The copyright treaty position of each of the former Soviet Republics now needs to be considered in its own right, in respect of works written, or first published, in such states on or after 1 January 1992 (or their secession from the Soviet Union if earlier). Furthermore, in view of the retroactive effect of the Berne Convention (see paragraph 20.3), when former states of the Union of Soviet Socialist Republics accede to the Berne Convention, it is likely that many works will fall into copyright in the United Kingdom (see paragraph 4.3) and throughout the rest of the Berne Union.

A number of members of the Commonwealth of Independent States do not provide adequate protection for copyright works of their own citizens or citizens of other states. Although many countries are in the process of amending and revising their intellectual property legislation, and while the basic provisions of the copyright conventions (see paragraphs 4.2 to 4.4) are likely to be reflected in each Commonwealth of Independent State's future legislation, suitably qualified foreign legal advice should be obtained in relation to dealings involving the Commonwealth of Independent States.

3 *Copinger and Skone James on Copyright,* Appendix E.
4 Berne Convention Implementation Act 1988.

4.6 Copyright protection before 1978 in the United States of America

Before 1 January 1978, the relevant United States Statute controlling copyright was the Copyright Act 1909 (USA). This Act provided for an initial period of copyright protection of 28 years[5]. The initial period of protection was granted subject to the registration of the work in the United States Copyright Registry and subject to the inclusion on all published copies of the work of a notice similar in form to that specified in the Universal Copyright Convention[6] (see paragraph 4.9). The initial period was capable of extension by a further 28-year period provided that notice of renewal of copyright was filed in the United States Copyright Registry prior to the termination of the initial period[7].

The total 56-year period of copyright protection in the United States of America which was created by the 28-year initial term and the 28-year renewal term was extended by a number of interim provisions in the 1960s to a new total of 75-years (being the initial period of 28-years plus the 28-year extension period plus a further 19-year extension period).

5 Copyright Act 1909 (USA) S24.
6 Ibid SS10, 19.
7 Ibid S28.

4.7 Copyright protection after 1977 in the United States of America

The Copyright Act 1909 (USA) was repealed and replaced by the Copyright Act 1976 (USA) which came into effect on 1 January 1978. The United States Act of 1976 applies to works made or published after 1 January 1978 and provides for a term of copyright protection in general equal to the length of the author's life plus 50 years or, in respect of anonymous works and "works made for hire", a term of 75 years from the year of first publication, or 100 years from the year of creation, whichever expires first[8].

United States copyright registration or renewal may be effected in the United States Library of Congress. It is also possible to search the Registry maintained in the Library of Congress in respect of existing works. Failure to renew copyright in the United States of America before the expiry of the initial period (see paragraph 4.6) results in copyright protection for the work in the United States of America being lost. The United States of America has, however, recently clarified the position relating to works which were still the subject of copyright protection on 1 March 1989 and were in their initial period of protection. If such works originated in a Berne Convention country, no application need be made for renewal of copyright to qualify for the full United States term of protection.

Publishers should, however, always register their copyrights in the United States Library of Congress, because although United States law no longer requires registration of British copyrights as a prerequisite to commencing proceedings, or as a formality to obtain copyright protection, damages cannot be awarded for any infringement which occurs before registration[9].

8 Copyright Act 1909 (USA) S302(a), (c).
9 US Copyright Act 1976 S412.

4.8 European Union law

In 1988 the European Union published a Green Paper which contained proposals for the reform of copyright legislation, in order to achieve harmonisation and conformity of copyright laws throughout the European Union. An addendum to the Green Paper was published in 1990.

The European Union is governed according to the principles set out in the European Community Treaty (formerly known as the Treaty of Rome) which was signed in 1972 by the original member states. One of these principles is that the laws of the Union prevail over the national laws of its member states which are required to conform their laws to Union directives and regulations.

The Union is committed towards achieving a single European Market within which there is free movement of goods and services between member states. In order to ensure that the market between member states is free from anti-competitive or restrictive practices or abuses arising from dominant positions, there are a number of provisions in European Union law, and in United Kingdom statutory legislation, which control these areas (see Chapter 16).

Additionally, the European Commission has issued a number of directives and proposals for directives which will change United Kingdom legislation. The proposals and directives are summarised in Chapter 17 and their possible effect is considered in Chapter 20.

D. Copyright notice, disclaimer, warning and presumptions

4.9 Copyright notice, disclaimer and warning

There is no requirement under United Kingdom law for a form of copyright notice to appear on copyright works. Where it is desired to insert a notice, it should, if possible, accord with that specified in the Universal Copyright Convention[10].

The copyright notice should be in the following form:

Copyright [name of copyright owner] [year of publication]

Note the requirement for the name of the copyright owner to be inserted. Copyright is divisible, so the owner of publication rights in a work may be different from the owner of (say) film and television rights. The important thing to be aware of is that it is the copyright owner's name which counts, not the author's.

The above form of notice is prescribed in the Universal Copyright Convention Article III(1). Appearance of the notice on all published copies of copyright works satisfies all formalities such as deposit, registration, provision of notaries' certificates, payment of fees, manufacture or publication in countries which have acceded to the Universal Copyright Convention, to the extent such formalities are necessary to procure copyright protection for any initial period. Although the requirement is not necessary for copyright protection in the United States of America in respect of works published in the United Kingdom after 1 March 1989 (see paragraph 4.7) the requirement should be observed so as to secure copyright protection elsewhere.

In addition to the Universal Copyright Convention notice, many rights owners include a disclaimer notice to provide protection for the author and the publisher from actions for negligent misstatement (see paragraphs 9.34 and 9.35). This notice may be in the following form:

"No responsibility for loss occasioned to any person acting or refraining from acting as a result of the material contained in this publication will be accepted by the author or [name of publisher]."

Additionally, it is normal for a work to contain a copyright warning along the following lines:

"No part of this publication may be reproduced in any material form whether by photocopying or storing in any medium by electronic means whether or not transiently or incidentally to some other use for this publication without the prior written consent of the copyright owner except in accordance with the provisions of the Copyright, Designs and Patents Act 1988 or under the terms of the licence issued by the Copyright Licensing Agency Limited of 33–34 Alfred Place London WC1.

Warning: The doing of any unauthorised act in relation to this work may result in both civil and criminal liability."

The Rome Convention provides[11] that if copies of a sound recording bear a notice in the form

℗ [date of protection] [owner of copyright]

such notice shall be considered to be compliance with formalities required by laws of states which are signatories to the Rome Convention for the purpose of protecting the rights of compliance which produce sound recordings.

The inclusion of ℗ notices on multimedia carriers such as CD-ROMs, CD-Is and computer discs is, therefore, advantageous to rights owners (see paragraphs 3.7 and 3.10). It may, additionally, be advisable to include a notice indicating that rental and/or lending of the sound recording, film or computer program may not be carried out without the consent of the copyright owner (see paragraphs 3.10 and 19.26).

The inclusion of © and ℗ notices on all copies of copyright works has further additional advantages in assisting the establishment of ownership of copyright (which needs to be proved in order to commence any action for infringement) for the reasons set out in paragraph 4.10.

10 Universal Copyright Convention Article III (1).
11 Rome Convention Article 11.

4.10 Copyright presumptions[12]

A number of presumptions exist under United Kingdom law in respect of the ownership or existence of copyright.

In order to bring proceedings for infringement of copyright, it is necessary to prove that the person bringing proceedings is the owner or the owner's exclusive licence. Where the copyright is old (and remember that most copyrights survive their authors by two or more generations) the requirement of proving ownership in many cases involves the production to the court of long chains of assignments and licences.

Frequently there are gaps in the "chain of title" caused by missing or unsigned documents. Copyright infringers were aware of the difficulties which legitimate copyright owners used to face in producing clear unbroken evidence to the courts in the United Kingdom, and frequently used to challenge ownership on the basis that the owner would be unable to produce the required documentation.

Since the implementation of the Copyright, Designs and Patents Act 1988, the United Kingdom has significantly simplified the task of copyright owners by establishing a number of legal presumptions as to copyright, which are presumed correct unless proved incorrect.

Where complete chain of title documentation is available, it should be remembered that stamp duty is payable on the transfer of intellectual property rights (see paragraph 11.29). There is a possibility that if a document evidencing the transfer of intellectual property rights is produced to a court, and stamp duty has not been paid on that document, the court might refuse to accept such document as proof of the transfer of such rights.

(a) Authorship presumption[13]

Where a name purporting to be that of the author appears on copies of a published work, or on a work when it was made, it is presumed (unless it can be proved otherwise) that the person whose name appears is the author of the work and that the work was not made in the course of that person's employment. Where the work is a work of joint authorship, this provision applies in respect of each author.

(b) Ownership presumption[14]

Where no author's name appears on a published work, or on the work when it was made but:

69

– the work is eligible for copyright protection by virtue of its country of first publication (see paragraph 3.15); and
– a name purporting to be that of a publisher or copyright owner appears on copies of the work as first published or issued to the public

then it is presumed, unless it can be proved otherwise, that the named person was the owner of the copyright in the work at the time of publication or issue to the public.

(c) Other presumptions[15]

If the author of a work is dead, or if the author's identity cannot be ascertained by reasonable enquiry, then in the absence of evidence to the contrary it is presumed that the work is an original work. Additionally, in any court proceedings where details of the country and time of first publication are given, these details are also be presumed to be correct in the absence of evidence to the contrary.

12 Copyright, Designs and Patents Act 1988 Chapter VI SS104–109.
13 Ibid S104(1)(2)(3).
14 Ibid S104(4).
15 Ibid S104(5).

E.   Termination and recapture of copyright

4.11   Pre-1988 United Kingdom legislation

There are no statutory provisions in United Kingdom law which provide for the reversion or recapture of rights in copyright works by their authors, if the works were first assigned after 1 June 1957, when the provisions of the Copyright Act 1956 (repealed and replaced with effect from 1 August 1989 by the Copyright Designs and Patents Act 1988) came into force. Before June 1957 the laws relating to copyright in the United Kingdom were contained in the Copyright Act of 1911 which came into force on 1 July 1912.

One of the significant achievements of the Copyright Act 1911 was that it extended the period of copyright protection applying to copyright works in the United Kingdom and the British Dominions. Before July 1912, the period of copyright protection for a literary work under UK law was governed by the Copyright Act 1842 and the Dramatic Copyright Act 1833. This term was, in fact, the longer of two periods being either 42 years from first publication of the work, or the life of the author plus seven years.

4.12   Post-July 1912 partial reversions of copyright

The Copyright Act of 1911 extended the existing term of copyright so that it became a period equal to the life of the author plus 50 years[16]. This brought the United Kingdom belatedly into line with its obligations pursuant to the Berne Convention, to which the United Kingdom acceded in 1887.

Because the extension of the copyright period brought about by the Copyright Act 1911 effectively lengthened the time period during which an author or other rights owner could require the payment of fees or royalties for the exploitation of the copyright in a work, it was decided that the author (and not the author's assignee) should benefit from the extension of the copyright period.

For this reason, a provision was inserted in the Copyright Act 1911 which gave the author, or the author's estate, the right to recapture rights which had been assigned by the author before 1 July 1912[17].

This recapture right was exercisable by written notice which had to be given not more than one year and not less than six months before the copyright in the work would have expired under the old legislation (ie the later of 42 years from first publication or seven years from the author's death).

The recapture of copyright in a work by the author did not prevent the author's assignee from exercising, on a non-exclusive basis, the rights previously assigned to such person, provided they observed certain conditions, including the payment of royalties.

Some works which are today still protected by copyright are exploited pursuant to arrangements made subsequent to the operation of this provision.

16 Copyright Act 1911 S3.
17 Copyright Act 1911 S24 (repealed).

4.13 Pre-June 1957 automatic recapture right

The Copyright Act 1911 also provides for the automatic recapture of all rights in copyright works by authors' estates in certain circumstances irrespective of the terms and conditions in any agreement. The recapture right does not need to be exercised. It is automatic and absolute. It applies to all rights in copyright works which were first assigned by their author between 16 December 1911 and 1 June 1957.

The rights automatically revert to the author's estate 25 years from the date of the author's death. The provision was abolished by the Copyright Act 1956[18] and does not apply to works first assigned after 1 June 1957 but its abolition does not affect assignments entered into before such date since its effect is preserved by both the 1956 Copyright Act and the Copyright, Designs and Patents Act 1988.

It will be appreciated that this automatic reversion of rights can cause immense difficulties to publishers, and other rights owners, as well as being a significant asset to an author's estate. The provision is likely to be of great commercial importance for a significant period of time.

18 Copyright Act 1956 S50(2), Sch 9 (repealed).

4.14 Effect of recapture

Rights owners, authors' estates, and authors' representatives should take legal advice on the effect of contractual arrangements entered into by authors before the dates referred to in paragraphs 4.12 and 4.13. It is possible for rights owners to revive or extend the period of their rights by entering into supplemental arrangements with authors' estates (see paragraph 4.16). It is possible for authors' estates either to agree to extend the period of the rights owner's rights for a further advance, or a revised royalty, or to allow all the rights owner's rights to terminate, or to license to the rights owner on new terms some, but not all, of the rights originally granted.

In cases where a rights owner discovers that, unknown to the author, the rights owner's rights have terminated, or conversely, where the author discovers that, unknown to the rights owner, the rights owner's rights have terminated, urgent action is obviously necessary. Where substantial stocks of a publication are still being marketed, or where a work is the subject of subsidiary or ancillary exploitation (such as by way of merchandising, or motion picture, or television exploitation), the consequences for a rights owner, both in terms of loss of stock and third party claims, could be significant.

4.15 United States termination rights

In the United States of America complex termination rights exist for any work which is not a "work made for hire". A "work made for hire" is a work made by an employee in the course of his or her employment, or a work specifically ordered or commissioned for use as a contribution to a motion picture or audio visual (or other specified) work, provided that the parties assign an acknowledgement in writing stating that the work is to be considered a work made for hire[19].

Under United States Federal law, pre-1978 transfers, or licences, of rights may be terminated in certain circumstances at any time during a period of five years beginning on the later of 56 years from the date on which copyright renewal was first secured, or 1 January 1978[20].

As has been seen above (paragraph 4.6), the period of copyright protection in the United States of America for any qualifying copyright work written before 1 January 1978 was an initial term of 28 years, a renewal term of 28 years and a further extension of 19 years. The termination provisions apply only to the 19-year extension, and are effected by means of giving written notice at least two years, and not more than ten years, in advance of the date chosen for termination. This date may be at any time during the five-year period, beginning on the later of the 56th year of the term, or 1 January 1978[21].

Pursuant to the Copyright Act 1976 (USA) an author can in certain circumstances terminate a new grant of rights within five years following the earlier of 35 years from publication, or 40 years following the execution of the grant of rights, notwithstanding any agreement to the contrary[22]. The above termination provisions do not apply to any work which is a work made for hire[23].

19 See the Copyright Act 1976 (USA) S101.
20 Ibid S304(c)(3).
21 Ibid S304(c)(4).
22 Ibid S203(a)(3), (5).
23 Ibid SS203(a), 304(c).

4.16 Advice to rights owners on reversion of copyright

The matters referred to in paragraphs 4.13 to 4.15 are clearly capable of having a materially adverse impact on a rights owner's business. It is possible, however, in many cases for the effect of reversions to be anticipated and blocked.

Where a copyright work originates in the United States of America, the provisions of the United States Copyright Acts will need to be considered. There are a few United Kingdom solicitors who are familiar with the relevant legislative provisions and who may be able to offer initial guidance. Frequently, however, there may be factual matters which may need to be clarified by investigation in the United States Library of Congress in Washington, and these will usually be technical aspects on which United States legal advice is advisable, so the involvement of a United States lawyer is desirable. In many cases United States termination rights are exercisable by surviving spouses and heirs, and a short release document can be prepared, pursuant to which such persons undertake not to exercise their rights in return for payment of such sum and on such other terms as may be agreed.

Where a rights owner has acquired a copyright pursuant to a contract with an author, and the contract was entered into between 16 December 1911 and 1 June 1957, if the rights owner wishes to preserve its rights after the death of the author, the rights owner will need to enter into an additional agreement. The following action may be appropriate on the part of the rights owner:

(a) identify whether any works in the rights owners catalogue were acquired by authors' contracts entered into between 16 December 1911 and 1 June 1957;
(b) check to see whether any additional agreement (see paragraph 2.2) was entered into either with the author after the last date referred to in (a) or with anyone else;
(c) establish the date of decease of author and the reversion date;
(d) establish the identity of the current copyright owner in the work (this may be the person receiving royalties, but the terms of the author's will and any subsequent transfers of the work will need to be considered);
(e) obtain the appropriate agreement from all relevant persons.

It should be noted that United Kingdom legislation permits rights owners to enter into appropriate agreements with authors or their successors in title before the reversion date occurs. An appropriate form of document may be found in Document 9 or in Document 26, but it will be appreciated that these documents will not be suitable for use in every case. The arrangements may, on occasion, need to be presented with some diplomacy, but not in such a way that the nature of the agreement, or the reasons for it being requested, are misunderstood by the person entering into it, for the reasons set out in paragraphs 2.17 to 2.23.

4.17   Acquisition of copyright outside the United Kingdom

The legal formalities required to be performed in order to effect the valid transfer of copyright outside the United Kingdom will vary from country to country.

There are a number of members of the Commonwealth of Independent States who do not provide adequate copyright protection for works of their own citizens or citizens of other states. Specialist advice must be taken in dealing with these countries.

Detailed investigation of foreign laws is often an expensive and time-consuming process, but there is a simple means of avoiding this. Rights owners should always contract under the laws of England and Wales (or Scotland or Northern Ireland). Provided they do this, and ensure that the definition of "copyright" extends to all analogous rights in the territory (the laws of some countries do not refer to "copyright" as such), and insert in the document a covenant for further assurance, most of the anticipated difficulties can be avoided.

A covenant for further assurance obliges the person granting the rights to do any further acts and execute any further documents that may be required by the rights owner, in order to perfect or enforce any of the rights granted to the rights owner throughout the world. An example of such a provision can be found in Clause 14.2 of Document 4.

5. Moral rights and rights of privacy and personality

[IMPORTANT NOTE: Please read the section "About this book" on page v, before referring to any of the matters in this chapter.]

[In this chapter all statutory references are to the Copyright, Designs and Patents Act 1988]

A. Introduction

5.1 Purpose of this chapter

This chapter is a reference chapter. Its primary function is to describe the moral rights which are provided by the Copyright, Designs and Patents Act 1988, as well as the circumstances in which they may be exercised and the circumstances in which they do not apply.

Publishers and other rights owners will appreciate that there are circumstances in which it will be appropriate for them to obtain waivers of moral rights from authors. This chapter does not deal with the arguments which may be raised by authors when asked to waive their moral rights. These matters and the general application of moral rights legislation are considered in Chapter 7 (particularly paragraph 7.8) and elsewhere in this work.

A general analysis of how moral rights legislation is capable of affecting a publisher's or other rights owner's activities is contained in paragraph 5.22.

B. Types of moral rights

5.2 Moral rights generally

The right to be identified is the first of four types of moral rights provided in the United Kingdom under the Copyright, Designs and Patents Act 1988 (as to moral rights outside the United Kingdom see paragraphs 5.20 and 5.21). The rights are:

(a) the right to be identified as the author or director of a copyright work[1];
(b) the right to object to derogatory treatment of a copyright work[2];
(c) the right not to suffer false attribution of a copyright work[3]; and
(d) the right to privacy in respect of certain films and photographs[4].

The right not to suffer false attribution of a work was provided in the Copyright Act 1956: the remaining three rights are new.

1 Copyright, Designs and Patents Act 1988 S77(1).
2 S80(1).
3 S84(1).
4 S85(1).

C. The right to be identified

5.3 The right to be identified

The author of a copyright literary, dramatic, musical or artistic work and a director of a copyright film each have a right to be identified as the author or director of the work. The right extends only to the United Kingdom and applies only to copyright works which qualify for protection under the Copyright, Designs and Patents Act 1988[5].

The right to be identified does not extend to the creator of a sound recording. The right of an author of a literary, dramatic or musical work to be identified extends to any adaptation made from the work[6].

5 le under ss 154–156.
6 S77(2).

5.4 Artistic works, architecture and films

The author of an artistic work has the right to be identified whenever the work is published commercially or exhibited in public, or a visual image of it is broadcast or included in a cable programme service[7], or whenever a film including a visual image of the work is shown in public, or copies of a film are issued to the public[8].

The author of a copyright work, which is a work of architecture, in the form of a building or a model for a building, a sculpture, or a work of artistic craftsmanship shall have the right to be identified whenever copies of a graphic work representing it, or of a photograph of it, are issued to the public[9]. The author of a work of architecture, in the form of a building, also has the right to be identified on the building, as constructed, or, where more than one building is constructed to the design, on the first to be constructed.

The director of a film has the right to be identified whenever the film is shown in public, broadcast, or included in a cable programme service, or copies of the film are issued to the public[10].

7 S77(4)(a).
8 S77(4)(b).
9 S77(4)(c).
10 S77(6).

5.5 Manner of identification

The right of an author, or director, in the case of commercial publication, or issue to the public, of copies of a film, or sound recording, is to be identified in or on each copy or, if that is not appropriate, in some other manner likely to bring the identity of the author, or director, to the notice of the person acquiring a copy[11].

Otherwise, the right is to be identified, in a manner likely to bring the identity of the author, or director, to the attention of the person seeing, or hearing, the performance, exhibition, showing, broadcast or cable programme in question[12].

The identification must, in each case, be clear, and reasonably prominent[13]. If the author, or director, in asserting the right to be identified, specifies a pseudonym, or initials, or some other particular form of identification, that form must be used, otherwise any reasonable form of identification may be used[14].

11 S77(7)(a).
12 S77(7)(c).
13 S77(7).
14 S77(8).

5.6 Circumstances in which right arises

For the purpose of determining whether the right to be identified arises or not, the expression "commercial publication", when used in relation to a literary, dramatic, musical, or artistic work, means issuing copies of the work to the public, at a time when copies made in advance of the receipt of orders are generally available to the public, or making the work available to the public by means of an electronic retrieval system[15].

In the case of a sound recording, or film, playing or showing the work in public, or broadcasting the work, or including it in a cable programme service, does not constitute publication[16]. It will be remembered (see paragraph 3.7) that a book exploited in multimedia format might also satisfy the copyright criteria to enable it to be classified simultaneously as a book/film/sound recording/computer program.

Publication, in relation to all classes of copyright works, is defined as the issue of copies to the public, and will include, in the case of a literary, dramatic, musical, or artistic work, making the work available to the public, by means of an electronic retrieval system[17]. Any publication which is merely colourable and not intended to satisfy the reasonable requirements of the public is not considered publication by the Copyright, Designs and Patents Act 1988[18].

15 S175(2).
16 S175(4)(c).
17 S175(1).
18 S175(5).

5.7 Assertion of the right

The right to be identified is not infringed unless it has been asserted in accordance with the provisions of the Copyright, Designs and Patents Act

1988[19]. It is also necessary to check the transitional provisions of the Copyright, Designs and Patents Act 1988 (see paragraph 5.19) to determine whether the right applies.

The right to be identified may be asserted in the following ways:

(a) On an assignment of copyright in the work by including a statement that the author, or director, asserts the right to be identified. Note that this provision does not extend to licences of copyright and for the difference between an assignment and a licence (see paragraphs 1.18, 3.38 to 3.40 and paragraph 11.2)[20].

(b) By an instrument in writing signed by the author, or director. Where the right to be identified exists in respect of a work of joint authorship, the right of each joint author is the right to be identified as a joint author and must be asserted by each joint author, in relation to him or herself. If the right to be identified has not been asserted before the death of the author, and the moral rights pass to more than one person by testamentary disposition, then the right may be asserted by any of such persons[21].

(c) In the case of an artistic work, by ensuring that the author is identified on the original, or on a copy made by the author, or on a frame, or mount, or other thing to which the work is attached at the time when the author, or first owner, parts with possession of the original, or copy. An alternative method is to include in the licence by which the author, or other first owner of copyright, authorises the making of copies of the work a statement, signed by, or on behalf of, the person granting the licence, that the author asserts the author's rights to be identified, in the event of a public exhibition of a copy, made in pursuance of the licence[22].

19 S78(1).
20 S78(2)(a).
21 S78(2)(b).
22 S78(3).

5.8 Persons bound by assertion

Where assertion is made on an assignment, then the person to whom the rights are assigned and anyone claiming through such person will be bound whether or not they have notice of the assertion[23].

In the case of assertion made by an instrument in writing, which is not part of an assignment, anyone to whose notice the assertion is brought is bound by it[24].

Where the assertion is made by affixing a name to the original, or copy, then anyone into whose hands the original, or copy, comes (with or without the identification) will be bound by the assertion. Where the assertion is made in a licence of an artistic work then the licensee, and anyone into whose hands a copy of the artistic work, made in pursuance of the licence, comes, will be bound[25].

It will be appreciated from the above that if an author wishes to assert their right to be identified, the assertion should be contained in the document assigning copyright. Where copyright is reserved to the author, and the publisher is granted a licence, there may be circumstances where it may be advisable to assert the right to be identified, although the value of such an assertion is sometimes questionable for the reasons set out in paragraph 7.8.

23 S78(4)(a).
24 S78(4)(b).
25 S78(4)(d).

5.9 Exceptions to the right to be identified

The right to be identified as author or director does not apply to, or in relation to, the following:

(a) computer programs[26];
(b) typeface designs[27];
(c) computer-generated works[28];
(d) anything done by or with the copyright owner's authority, where copyright in the work originally vested in the author's employer, as being a work produced in the course of employment[29];
(e) anything done by, or with, the copyright owner's authority, where copyright in the work originally vested in a director's employer as being the person treated as author of a film[30];
(f) any work made for the purpose of reporting current events;[31]
(g) the publication in a newspaper, magazine, or other periodical, or in an encyclopedia, dictionary, year-book, or other collective work of reference, of a literary, dramatic, musical, or artistic, work made for the purpose of such publication, or made available with the author's consent, for the purposes of such publication[32];
(h) any work in which Crown or Parliamentary copyright subsists, or any work in which copyright originally vested in an international organisation, unless the author or director has previously been identified as such in or on published copies of the work[33];
(i) additionally, the right is not infringed by any act which would not infringe copyright in the work by virtue of the fair dealing provisions or permitted acts referred to in Chapter 8[34].

26 S79(2)(a).
27 S79(2)(b).
28 S79(2)(c).
29 S79(3)(a).
30 S79(3)(b).
31 S79(5).
32 S79(6).
33 S79(7).
34 S79(4).

D. Derogatory treatment

5.10 The right to object to derogatory treatment of a work

The author of a copyright literary, dramatic, musical, or artistic work, and the director of a copyright film, have the right not to have their works subjected to derogatory treatment[35]. It will be remembered (see paragraph 3.7) that a book exploited in multimedia format might also satisfy the copyright criteria to enable it to be classified simultaneously as a book/film/sound recording/computer program.

A treatment of work is any addition to, deletion from, alteration to, or adaptation of, the work other than a translation of a literary or dramatic work, or an arrangement, or transcription, of a musical work which involves no more than a change of key, or register[36]. A treatment of work is derogatory if it amounts to distortion, or mutilation, of the work, or is otherwise prejudicial to the honour or reputation of the author or director[37].

35 S80(1).
36 S80(2)(a).
37 S80(2)(b).

5.11 Derogatory treatment of works

In the case of a literary, dramatic or musical work, the right is infringed by a person who publishes commercially, performs in public, broadcasts, or includes in a cable programme service a derogatory treatment of the work, or issues to the public copies of a film, or sound recording of, or including, a derogatory treatment of the work[38].

In the case of an artistic work, the right is infringed by a person who publishes commercially, or exhibits in public a derogatory treatment of the work, or broadcasts, or includes in a cable programme service a visual image of a derogatory treatment of the work, or shows in public, a film including the visual image of a derogatory treatment of the work, or issues copies of such a film to the public[39].

In the case of a film, the right is infringed by a person who shows in public, broadcasts, or includes in a cable programme service, or issues to the public, copies of a derogatory treatment of the film, or the film's sound track[40].

The right to object to derogatory treatment is also infringed by a person who possesses in the course of business, or sells, or lets for hire, or exposes, or offers for sale or hire, or in the course of business, exhibits in public, or distributes, otherwise than in the course of business, an article which that person knows or has reason to believe is an infringing article in such manner as to affect prejudicially the honour or reputation of the author or director[41].

38 S80(3).
39 S80(4)(a)(b).
40 S80(6).
41 S83.

5.12 Exceptions to the right to object to derogatory treatment

The right to object to a derogatory treatment of a copyright work does not apply in relation to:

(a)   a computer program, or any computer-generated work[42];
(b)   any work made for the purpose of reporting current events[43];
(c)   the publication in a newspaper, magazine, or similar periodical, or an encyclopedia, dictionary, year-book, or other collective work of

reference, of a literary, dramatic, musical or artistic work, made for the purposes of such publication, or made available, with the consent of the author, for the purpose of such publication[44];

(d)   works whose copyright originally vested in the author's employer by reason of their being produced in the course of employment, or which vested in the director's employer by reason of the employer being treated as author of the film, unless the author or director is identified at the time of the relevant act, or has previously been identified in, or on, published copies of the work[45];

(e)   works in which Crown or Parliamentary Copyright subsists, or in which copyright originally vested in an international organisation, unless the author, or director, is identified at the time of the relevant act, or has previously been identified, in or on, published copies of the work[46].

42 S81(1).
43 S81(3).
44 S81(4).
45 S82(1)(a) and (2).
46 S82(1)(b) and (2).

5.13   Non-infringement of right to object to derogatory treatment

The right to object to derogatory treatment of a work is not infringed by:

(a)   any act which will not infringe copyright by virtue of the provisions relating to anonymous or pseudonymous works[47];

(b)   anything done for the purpose of avoiding the commission of an offence, or complying with the duty imposed, by or under, an enactment, or, in the case of the BBC, avoiding the inclusion of anything in a programme which offends good taste, or decency, or is likely to encourage or incite to crime, or lead to disorder, or be offensive to public feeling, provided however that where the author or director is identified or has previously been identified there is a sufficient disclaimer[48].

A sufficient disclaimer is a clear and reasonably prominent indication, which is given at the time of the act, which might otherwise have been capable of infringing an author's right to object to derogatory treatment of a work, that the work has been subjected to treatment to which the author or director has not consented. The indication must appear along with any identification given to the author or director[49].

47 S81(5).
48 S81(6).
49 S178.

E.   False attribution and privacy

5.14   The right not to suffer false attribution of a work

A person has the right not to have a literary, dramatic, musical or artistic work falsely attributed to him or her as author, or a film falsely attributed to him or her as director[50]. The attribution may be express or implied[51], and the right is infringed by any person who issues to the public copies of the work on which there is a false attribution, or exhibits in public an artistic work, or a copy of an artistic work, in or on which there is a false attribution[52].

The right is also infringed by a person who, in the case of a literary, dramatic, or musical work, performs the work in public, broadcasts it, or includes it in a cable programme service, as being the work of a particular person or, in the case of a film, shows it in public, broadcasts it or includes it in a cable programme service as being directed by a particular person, in either case knowing, or having reason to believe, that the attribution is false[53].

The right is infringed by the issue to the public, or the public display, of material containing a false attribution in connection with any of the acts mentioned above[54]. It is also infringed by a person who in the course of a business possesses, or deals[55] with, a copy of a work, in or on which there is a false attribution (or, in the case of an artistic work, possesses, or deals with the work itself, where there is a false attribution, in, or on it) knowing or having reason to believe that there is such an attribution and that it is false[56].

In the case of an artistic work the right is also infringed by a person who, in the course of a business, deals with a work which has been altered after the author parted with possession of it as being the unaltered work of the author, or deals with a copy of such a work as being a copy of the unaltered work of the author knowing, or having reason to believe, that this is not the case[57].

50 S84(1).
51 S84(1).
52 S84(2).
53 S84(3).
54 S84(4).
55 S84(7).
56 S84(5).
57 S84(6).

5.15   The right to privacy

This right, which exists under the laws of the United Kingdom, should not be confused with any foreign rights of privacy or publicity (see paragraph 5.21).

Where a person has commissioned the taking of a photograph, or the making of a film, for private and domestic purposes, and where copyright subsists in the resulting work, that person has the right not to have copies of the work issued to the public, or the work exhibited, or shown in public, or the work broadcast, or included in a cable programme service, and any person who does, or authorises the doing of, any of those acts, infringes that right[58]. The right is not infringed by acts which, by virtue of certain statutory provisions, would not infringe copyright in a work[59] (see Chapter 8).

It should be noted that the right is enjoyed by the person who commissions the taking of the photograph, or the making of the film, as opposed to the person who owns the copyright in the photograph or the film. The right does not extend to uncommissioned photographs or films.

58 S85(1).
59 S85(2).

F. Duration and transmission of moral rights

5.16 Duration of moral rights

The right to be identified as author or director, the right to object to derogatory treatment and the right to privacy subsist for as long as copyright subsists in the work (see paragraphs 3.25 to 3.37)[60]. The right not to have a work falsely attributed continues until 20 years after the death of the relevant person[61].

60 S86(1).
61 S86(2).

5.17 Transmission of moral rights

Moral rights cannot be assigned or licensed in the same way as copyright[62]. The right to prevent false attribution of a work is exercisable after a person's death by that person's personal representatives. The three remaining moral rights – the right to be identified as author or director, the right to object to derogatory treatment, and the right to privacy – may be transmitted by testamentary disposition (ie by will or codicil) in such manner as the owner of the rights specifically directs[63].

If there is no direction in a will, but the copyright of the work in question forms part of the author's or director's estate, the moral right attached to the work will pass to the person to whom the copyright passes[64]. If, or to the extent that, the moral rights do not pass in either of the above two ways, they are exercisable by the personal representatives of the author or director[65].

Where copyright passes partly to one person, and partly to another, any right which passes with the copyright is correspondingly divided. Where the right to identification of an author or director is exercisable by more than one person, it may be asserted by any of them[66]. The right to object to derogatory treatment of a work or the right to privacy of certain photographs and films may be exercised by each of the persons jointly entitled to such right, and is satisfied in relation to any of them if such person consents to the treatment of the act in question[67]. Where the moral rights are jointly owned, the waiver of any right by any one person does not affect the rights of the others[68]. Persons to whom moral rights pass, are bound by any previous consents or waivers[69].

Any infringement after a person's death of the right not to suffer false attribution is actionable by that person's personal representatives[70]. Any damages recovered by personal representatives in respect of an infringement, after a person's death, will devolve as part of that person's estate as if the right of action had subsisted, and been vested in that person, immediately before death[71].

62 S94.
63 S95(1)(a).
64 S95(1)(b).
65 S95(1)(c).
66 S95(3)(a).
67 S95(3)(b).
68 S95(3)(c).
69 S95(4).
70 S84(3).
71 S95(6).

5.18 Consent and waiver

It is not an infringement of any moral rights to do any act to which the person entitled to the right has consented[72]. Any moral right may be waived by an instrument in writing signed by the person giving up the right[73]. The waiver may relate to a specific work, to works of a specified description, or to works generally, and may relate to existing or future works[74]. The waiver may also be conditional, or unconditional, and may be expressed, to be revocable[75]. Unless a contrary intention is expressed the waiver is presumed to extend to the copyright owner's licensees and successors in title[76].

72 S87(1).
73 S87(2).
74 S87(3)(a).
75 S87(3)(b).
76 S87(3).

5.19 Transitional provisions

With the exception of the right to prevent false attribution, which was contained in the Copyright Act 1956, no act done before the commencement date of the Copyright, Designs and Patents Act 1988 (ie 1 August 1989) is actionable by virtue of any provision dealing with moral rights[77]. The right to be identified as author or director, and the right to object to derogatory treatment, do not apply in relation to a literary, dramatic, musical or artistic work the author of which died before August 1989 or in relation to a film made before that date.

The rights in relation to a literary, dramatic, musical, or artistic work existing at 1 August 1989 do not apply, in the case where copyright first vested in the author, to anything which may be done without infringing copyright; by virtue of an assignment of copyright made, or licence granted, before 1 August 1989[78]. Where copyright first vested in a person other than the author, the rights do not apply to anything done by or with the licence of the copyright owner[79]. In addition, these rights do not apply to anything done in relation to a record made pursuant to a statutory licence granted under Section 8 of the Copyright Act 1956[80]. The right to privacy does not apply to photographs taken or films made before August 1989[81].

77 S170 Sch 1 paras 22(1) and (2).
78 Sch 1 paras 23(1) and (2).
79 Sch 1 paras 23(3).
80 Sch 1 paras 23(4).
81 Sch 1 paras 24.

G. Foreign moral rights and rights of privacy and personality

5.20 Moral rights outside the United Kingdom

Moral rights exist pursuant to the laws of a number of countries. Because the Berne Convention (see paragraph 4.3) makes specific provision for countries which become signatories to it, to provide for moral rights in their legislation, many countries have now done so. One notable exception is the United States of America, which has refused to enact any moral rights provisions in US domestic law to authors of literary, dramatic or musical works or directors of films, although it has provided very limited protection for artists.

Although the United Kingdom was a signatory to the 1971 revision of the Berne Convention (which provided for moral rights) the United Kingdom itself did not provide any operative laws to protect moral rights until some 18 years later. Since the provisions of the laws of the United Kingdom were enacted in response to the requirements of the Berne Convention it is possible, as a basic rule of thumb, to work on the basis that the laws of other countries may in some circumstances follow a similar pattern. There will, however, be notable differences and local legal opinions should be obtained, in any case, where there is doubt.

In some countries – such as France – moral rights are not capable of being waived. It is submitted, however (for the reasons set out in paragraph 7.8), that the correct course of action for publishers and multimedia companies is to protect authors' moral rights in order to enhance the value of the copyright for their mutual benefit.

A number of additional moral rights may exist under the laws of foreign countries. One such right is the "droit de suite" which applies to paintings and sculptures during their copyright term, and entitles the artists, and the artists' heirs, to a share in the proceeds of each resale of their works[82]. This right enables the artists to participate in the increased value of paintings which resell at prices far higher than those which may originally have been paid to the artists. Belgium, France, Germany and Italy all have schemes which provide for the "droit de suite", and the right appears to exist, in theory, in Algeria, Brazil, Chile, Czechoslovakia, Luxembourg, Morocco, Norway, Portugal, Tunisia, Turkey and Uruguay.

82 See Stockholm Convention Article 14 ter.

5.21 Rights of privacy and personality

In the United States of America, legislation exists which protects persons' rights of privacy (not to be confused with the British right to privacy) and their rights of personality. The right of privacy is, however, counterbalanced by the American Constitution which guarantees freedom of speech. In some States of the United States of America, it is criminal misdemeanour to exploit a person's name, likeness, or biography, without their consent. It is also unlawful, in some States, to invade a person's privacy without consent. Rights of privacy and/or personality are also protected by legislation in Australia, Canada, France and Germany. It is important to be aware of these rights and take appropriate steps to ensure they are not infringed.

H.   Moral rights and publishers

5.22 How moral rights might affect publishers

Many sectors of the publishing industry in the United Kingdom have failed to come to grips with moral rights, and much of the documentation currently used in the publishing industry is, from the publisher's point of view, inadequate (see paragraph 7.22).

The impact of moral rights on multimedia applications is examined in paragraphs 19.10 to 19.12. Multimedia corporations do, however, have a direct interest in examining how the publishers with whom they have dealings treat moral rights in their contracts.

Suggestions that authors should, in certain circumstances, waive their statutory moral rights in favour of contractual provisions giving them similar protection, but permitting publishers to carry out their activities, have resulted in highly emotional responses from authors and their representatives – who in some cases do not fully understand the issues. An even-handed resolution, which accords protection to authors in a way which does not undermine publishers' economic interests, is suggested in paragraph 7.8.

The impact on publishers of the four moral rights (see paragraph 5.2) might briefly be summarised as follows:

(a) The right to be identified

Since it is common practice for publishers to accord credit to authors on copies of their works (except in the case of collective works of multiple authorship where the right to be identified is excluded – see paragraph 5.9), publishers should feel able to accommodate the author's assertion of this right (see paragraph 7.8).

(b) The right to object to derogatory treatment of a work

This right is capable of having a materially adverse impact on a publisher's activities. Because the definition of "treatment" is so wide (see paragraph 5.10), and because the test of what is, or is not, derogatory seems likely in many cases to be subjective (there is no British case law on this yet, but reported cases in Italy and France do little to assuage publishers' concerns), it would be unwise for publishers to issue contracts to authors, if the contracts do not contain provisions which ensure that the authors' moral rights cannot be used unreasonably in such a way as to interfere with the publisher's business activities.

Unless the issue is tackled in the author's contract, publishers may find that they cannot make textual corrections to conform works to their house style, or remove legally objectionable material, or even approve translations which they have commissioned, without the threat of legal action from authors in relation to the alleged derogatory treatment of their works.

(c) The right not to suffer false attribution of a copyright work

This right is unlikely to cause publishers any difficulty. It has slumbered un-noticed in British copyright law since 1956. There are no reported cases on the right, so why it should be defended so fiercely by authors is puzzling, to say the least.

There is no reason why publishers should insist on a waiver of this right. If a publisher falsely attributes a work, it is likely that the publisher may be committing an offence under the Trade Descriptions Act (see paragraph 12.40) and, in practice, there can be few situations where a publisher would wilfully wish to misattribute a work.

The author's contract could, if required, contain an express provision which states that the moral right not to suffer false attribution is reserved to the author absolutely.

(d) Right to privacy

The right to privacy exists in relation to photographs and films commissioned for private and domestic purposes on or after 1 August 1989.

This right will have some impact on publishers, in that it will require additional permissions to be obtained, and may limit the choice of available photographic material. Since it is normal to require authors to obtain all necessary releases, and permissions, relating to the inclusion of photographs and other third party material in books, the right to privacy is unlikely to interfere with publishers' rights, provided due attention is paid to obtaining and checking all necessary permissions and releases (see paragraphs 8.2 to 8.5). It is advisable, however, for publishers to pay close attention to rights clearance procedures (see paragraph 8.44).

Subject to observing clearance procedures, there is no reason why the author's contract should not contain an express provision which states that the moral right to privacy of the author is reserved to the author absolutely except in relation to those films and photographs which the author has consented to making available or being used.

6. The Copyright Tribunal, performer's rights, public lending rights and licensing bodies

[IMPORTANT NOTE: Please read the section "About this book" on page v, before referring to any of the matters in this chapter.]

[In this chapter all statutory references are to the Copyright, Designs and Patents Act 1988 unless otherwise specified]

A. Introduction

6.1 Purpose of this chapter

The chapter is a reference chapter and completes the analysis of the rights provided by United Kingdom legislation and the limitations which can be placed on their exercise. The Copyright, Designs and Patents Act 1988 applied[1], for the first time, the provisions of United Kingdom competition law to copyright licensing, and gave the newly re-named Copyright Tribunal jurisdiction over collective licensing schemes and licensing bodies. The Copyright Tribunal is capable therefore of having a direct effect on the activities of publishers and multimedia companies.

One of the innovations of the Copyright, Designs and Patents Act 1988 was to provide civil rights for performers. The performers' protection provisions are of no relevance to book publishers, but are of direct relevance to companies who are active in multimedia applications, and are examined more closely in Chapter 19.

In 1979 the United Kingdom introduced a public lending right for authors. The principal provisions of this legislation are summarised in the chapter which concludes with a short analysis of publishing industry licensing bodies. Other licensing bodies are referred to in paragraph 19.21.

1 S144.

B. The Copyright Tribunal

6.2 The Copyright Tribunal generally

The Copyright Tribunal was established (as the Performing Right Tribunal) under the Copyright Act 1956 and was renamed and extended by the

Copyright, Designs and Patents Act 1988. The Tribunal consists of a chairman, two deputy chairmen and not less than eight members. The chairman and deputy chairmen are appointed by the Lord Chancellor and the ordinary members are appointed by the Secretary of State[2].

The quorum for proceedings of the Copyright Tribunal consists of the chairman (either the chairman or one of the two deputy chairmen) and two or more ordinary members. Decisions are by majority vote if not unanimous, and where the votes are equal the chairman has a casting vote.[3]

The purpose of the Copyright Tribunal is to hear and determine proceedings under the sections of the Copyright, Designs and Patents Act which relate to licensing schemes and licensing bodies[4]. The Copyright Tribunal also has the right to hear applications for the royalties or other sums which are payable in respect of the rental of sound recordings, films or computer programs to be determined[5]. It may also hear applications for terms of copyright licences which are available as of right to be determined[6].

The Tribunal may also hear applications requesting the consent of the Tribunal for the purpose of giving performers consents[7], and for the purposes of determining any royalties or other remuneration to be paid to trustees to the Hospital for Sick Children in respect of the work "Peter Pan" (see paragraph 3.35)[8].

2 S145.
3 S148.
4 S149 and SS118, 119 or 120.
5 S142.
6 S144(4) – such a licence is available as of right in consequence of the exercise of the powers conferred by the Fair Trading Act 1973 Sch 8 Part I pursuant to the Copyright, Designs and Patents Act 1988 S144(1).
7 Ie under S190.
8 Ie under Sch 6 para 5.

6.3 Licensing schemes

A licensing scheme is a scheme which sets out the categories in which its operator is willing to grant copyright licences and the terms on which those licences will be granted[9]. Licensing schemes in relation to any typographical arrangement of published editions may be the subject of references or applications to the Copyright Tribunal.

Licensing schemes relating to copyright in literary, dramatic or artistic works which cover the terms in which the work may be copied or performed, played or shown in public, or broadcast, or included in a cable programme service may not form the basis of references or applications to the Copyright Tribunal unless they satisfy two criteria. They must be operated by licensing bodies (see paragraph 6.4) and must cover the works of more than one author[10].

Where a proposed licensing scheme will fall within the jurisdiction of the Copyright Tribunal, the terms of the scheme proposed may be referred to the Tribunal by an organisation which claims to represent persons who will require licences of a type to which the scheme would apply. The Tribunal may hear the reference or decline to do so on the grounds that it is premature. If the Tribunal hears the reference it may make an order confirming or varying the terms of the proposed scheme, in such manner as the Tribunal sees fair[11].

Where a licensing scheme which falls within the jurisdiction of the Copyright Tribunal is in operation, and a dispute occurs between the operator of a scheme and a person claiming that they require a licence of the type the scheme applies to, then a reference may be made to the Copyright Tribunal. Where a scheme has been referred to the Tribunal it shall remain in operation until the reference has been heard. The Copyright Tribunal may make such order either confirming or varying the licensing scheme, so far as it relates to cases of the same type as the one being heard. The order may be made in such manner as the Tribunal determines is reasonable in all the circumstances[12].

A person who claims that the operator of a licensing scheme has refused to grant them or procure the grant to them of a licence, or has failed to grant a licence within a reasonable time of being asked, may also apply to the Copyright Tribunal. The Copyright, Designs and Patents Act 1988 further contains provisions for an application for the review of an order made by the Copyright Tribunal and also for further reference of schemes to the Tribunal[13].

9 S116(1).
10 S117.
11 S118.
12 S119.
13 S121.

6.4 Licensing bodies

A licensing body is a society or other organisation which has as one of its main objects the negotiation or granting of copyright licences. The licences may be granted by the body, either as owner or prospective owner of copyright, or as agent for such a person. The objects of a licensing body are required to include the possibility of granting licences covering works of more than one author.

All licences which relate to typographical arrangements for published editions or computer programs may be referred to the Copyright Tribunal if their licence is granted by a licensing body otherwise than pursuant to a licensing scheme[14].

Licences which relate to copyright in literary, dramatic, musical or artistic works may be referred to the Copyright Tribunal if they cover works of more than one author and were granted by a licensing body otherwise than pursuant to a licensing scheme[15].

The terms on which a licensing body proposes to grant a licence may be referred to the Copyright Tribunal, which may either hear the reference or decide it is premature[16]. If the Tribunal decides to hear the reference it shall consider the terms of the proposed licence and may make such order either confirming or varying these terms as the Copyright Tribunal determines is reasonable in all the circumstances[17].

A licensee under a licence which is due to expire, either by effluxion of time or as a result of notice given by a licensing body, may make an application to the Copyright Tribunal on the grounds that it is unreasonable in the circumstances that the licence should cease to be in force[18]. This application may not be made until the last three months before the licence is due to expire[19]. Where reference has been made to the Copyright Tribunal, the licence will remain in operation until proceedings on a reference are concluded[20].

Where the Copyright Tribunal makes an order as a result of any reference of the type described in the two preceding paragraphs, a person who has the benefit of the order will not infringe any copyright, if such person pays to the licensing body any charges payable in accordance with the order or, where the amount cannot be ascertained, gives an undertaking to pay such charges and at the same time complies with the order[21].

14 S116(2).
15 S124.
16 S125(2).
17 S125(3).
18 S126(1).
19 S126(2).
20 S126(3).
21 S128.

6.5   Factors considered by Copyright Tribunal

In determining what is reasonable on a reference or application relating to a licensing scheme, or licence, the Copyright Tribunal is required to consider the availability of other schemes, or the granting of other licences to other persons in similar circumstances, and the terms of those schemes or licences. The Tribunal is also required to exercise its powers so as to secure that there is no unreasonable discrimination between licensees and prospective licensees of the scheme to which the reference or application relates, and licences under other schemes or licences operated to or licensed by the same person[22].

Where any application to the Copyright Tribunal relates to the licensing of reprographic copying of a published literary, dramatic, musical or artistic work or the typographical arrangement for published edition the Tribunal is required to consider the extent to which published editions of the work in question are otherwise available, the proportion of the work to be copied and the nature of the use to which the copies are likely to be put[23].

22 S129.
23 S130.

6.6   Reprographic copying

The Copyright Tribunal has jurisdiction over certain schemes for the licensing of reprographic copying of published literary, dramatic, musical or artistic works or the typographical arrangements or published editions as well as jurisdiction over licences granted by licensing bodies for reprographic copying of such nature. The jurisdiction arises where the scheme or licence does not specify the works to which it applies in enough detail to enable prospective licensees to determine whether the work is covered by the scheme or licence[24].

The Copyright, Designs and Patents Act 1988 implies into every scheme or licence to which it applies an undertaking by the person operating the scheme on granting the licence to indemnify the licensee against any liability incurred by reason of the licensee having infringed copyright by making or authorising the making of reprographic copies of a work in circumstances which were within the current scope of the licence[25].

The Secretary of State has the power to extend the licensing scheme or a licence granted by a licensing body to authorise the making by or on behalf of educational establishments, for the purpose of instruction, of reprographic works or printed literary, dramatic, musical or artistic works or of the typographical arrangement of published editions[26].

The Secretary of State also has the power to appoint an enquiry into what new provisions are required to authorise the making by or on behalf of educational establishments of reprographic copies of the works of a description which appear not to be covered by any existing licensing scheme or general licence. If the inquiry recommends the making of a new provision the Secretary of State has power to make appropriate orders[27].

24 S136(1).
25 S136(2).
26 S137.
27 S140.

C. Performances

6.7 Circumstances in which rights are conferred

The Copyright, Designs and Patents Act 1988 confers rights in respect of dramatic performances, musical performances, readings or recitations of literary works, performances of variety acts or similar presentations which are live performances given by one or more individuals, if such performances are given by a qualifying individual or take place in a qualifying country[28]. A qualifying individual is a citizen or subject of, or a resident in, a qualifying country, and a qualifying country includes the United Kingdom, any member state of the European Union or any state in whose favour an Order in Council is made having reciprocal protection under the Copyright, Designs and Patents Act, which will include countries which are parties to conventions relating to performers' rights to which the United Kingdom is also a party such as the Rome Convention[29] (see paragraph 4.4).

The Copyright, Designs and Patents Act confers rights on a performer, and also on a person who is a party to and has the benefit of such a contract to which the performance is subject, or to whom the benefit of such a contract has been assigned, provided that person is also a qualifying person[30].

28 Part II S180.
29 S206.
30 S180(1).

6.8 Infringement of performer's rights

A performer's rights are infringed:

(a) by a person who, without the performer's consent, makes otherwise than for that person's private and domestic use a recording of the whole or any substantial part of a qualifying performance, or broadcasts live or includes live in a cable programme service the whole or any substantial part of a qualifying performance[31]; or

(b) by a person who, without consent, shows or plays in public or broadcasts or includes in a cable programme service the whole or any substantial part of a qualifying performance by means of a recording which was, and which that person knows or has reason to believe was made, without the performer's consent[32]; or

(c) by a person who, without the consent of that performer, imports into the United Kingdom otherwise than for that person's private and domestic use, or in the course of a business possesses, sells or lets for hire, offers or exposes for sale or hire, or distributes a recording of a qualifying performance which is and which that person knows or has reason to believe is, an illicit recording[33].

A recording is a film or sound recording which is made directly from a live performance or from a broadcast or cable programme including the performance, or a recording which is made directly or indirectly from another recording of the performance. Any illicit recording, for the purpose of performers' rights, is a recording of the whole or any substantial part of a performance which is made otherwise than for private purposes without consent[34].

31 S182.
32 S183.
33 S184.
34 S180(2).

6.9 Infringement of recording rights

The rights of a person having recording rights are infringed by any person who without his or her consent or the consent of the performer:

(a) makes a recording of the whole or any substantial part of the performance, otherwise than for that person's private and domestic use[35];

(b) shows or plays in public, or broadcasts or includes in a cable programme service, the whole or any substantial part of the performance by means of a recording which was, and which that person knows or has reason to believe was, made without the appropriate consent[36];

(c) imports into the United Kingdom otherwise than for that person's private and domestic use, or in the course of a business possesses, sells or lets for hire, offers or exposes for sale or hire, or distributes, a recording of the performance which is, and which that person knows or has reason to believe is, an illicit recording[37].

For the purposes of recording rights, a recording is illicit if it is made, otherwise than for private purposes, without the consent of the person having recordings rights, or that of the performer[38].

35 S186(1).
36 S187.
37 S188(1).
38 S197(2) and (3).

6.10 Consent

The consent of a performer or a person having recording rights may be given in relation to a specific performance, a specified description of performances or performances generally, and may relate to past or future performances. A person having recording rights in a performance is bound by any consent given by a person through whom (s)he derives his or her rights under the exclusive recording contract, or licence, in question[39].

39 S193(1) and (2).

6.11 Remedies for infringement

Any infringement of the rights of a performer or a person having recording rights is actionable as a breach of statutory duty[40]. In addition, the court may make an order for delivery up of illicit recordings, and there is a right to seize illicit recordings[41]. Certain categories of infringement, including the making for sale or hire, importing or dealing in the course of a business with an illicit recording, are subject to criminal sanctions[42].

40 S194.
41 S195(1).
42 S198.

6.12 Duration and transmission of rights

The rights of performers, and persons having recording rights, continue to subsist in relation to a performance until the end of the period of 50 years from the end of the calendar year in which the performance takes place[43].

In general, the rights are not assignable or transmissible. However, on the death of a person entitled to performers' rights, the rights pass to such person as (s)he may by testamentary disposition specifically direct, and if or to the extent that there is no such direction, the rights are exercisable by his or her personal representatives[44].

43 S191.
44 S192(1) and (2).

6.13 Permitted acts

Certain acts may be done in relation to a performance or recording notwithstanding the existence of performers' rights or recording rights; these include fair dealing for the purposes of criticism or review, incidental inclusion and things done for instructional or education purposes. The permitted acts in relation to performances are broadly analogous to those relating to copyright which are referred to in paragraphs 8.6 to 8.38[45].

45 Sch 2.

6.14 Qualifying countries

The following countries are qualifying countries and performances which take place in these countries or involve their nationals (see paragraph 6.7) may be protected by United Kingdom legislation[46]:

Austria
Barbados
Brazil
Burkina
Chile
Colombia
Congo, People's Republic of
Costa Rica
Czechoslovakia
Denmark (including Faeroe Islands)
Dominican Republic
Ecuador
El Salvador
Fiji
Finland
France (including all overseas departments and territories)
Germany
Guatemala
Ireland, Republic of
Italy
Luxembourg
Mexico
Monaco
Niger
Norway
Panama
Paraguay
Peru
Philippines
Sweden
Uruguay

46 Sch 2.

6.15 Application to the Copyright Tribunal for performer's consents

There may be occasions where a producer wishes to incorporate in a new film, an existing film or sound recording, which contains a performance by a performer whose whereabouts are not known, or who refuses unreasonably to consent to the proposed use[47].

In such cases the producer may apply to the Copyright Tribunal to give consent on behalf of the relevant performer. The Copyright Tribunal may give consent, subject to conditions if it considers this appropriate. Where a performer withholds consent, the Tribunal may not consent unless it is satisfied that the performer's reasons for withholding consent do not include the protection of any legitimate interest of the performer.

In such cases, it is up to the performer to show what reasons exist[48]. The Tribunal will take into account whether the original recording was made with the performer's consent, and whether it is lawfully in the possession of the person proposing to make the further recording[49].

The Tribunal will also consider whether the making of the further recording is consistent with the purposes for which the original recording was made, and is consistent with the obligations of the parties under such arrangements as were made relating to the original recording[50].

The Tribunal may make such order as it thinks fit as to the payment to be made to the performer in consideration of the consent being given[51].

47 S190(1).
48 S190(4).
49 S190(5)(a).
50 S190(5)(b).
51 S190(6).

D. Public Lending Right

6.16 Public Lending Right Act 1979

The Public Lending Right Act 1979 established a public lending right for authors. The purpose of the Act was to provide a central fund out of which authors would be entitled to receive payment calculated with reference to the number of loans made of the relevant authors' books to the public by local libraries in the United Kingdom[52].

The total amount available for distribution to authors in each year is currently £3.5m, and the administration of this fund is provided by a scheme approved by the Secretary of State[53].

In order to be eligible for public lending right, a book must be registered[54]. Some books are not eligible for registration, such as books which do not have international standard book numbers, books with more than four authors, or newspapers, magazines and journals[55]. In order to register, the author (or one of the authors) must have his or her only or principal house in the United Kingdom or Germany, or have been residing there for 12 out of the preceding 24 months[56].

The rights last for the life of the author plus 50 years and the scheme contains provisions which permit the transfer of rights of deceased authors[57].

52 Public Lending Right Act 1979 S1(1).
53 S2: increase to £3.5 m by the Public Lending Right (Increase of Limit) Order 1988 (SI 1988/609).
54 Public Lending Right Act 1979 S1(7) and S4.
55 Sections 6 and 6A.
56 Sections 5 and 5A and Sch 5.
57 S1(6).

E.   Publishing industry licensing bodies

6.17   CLA, DACS and ERA

The following licensing bodies are active in the United Kingdom:

(a)   The Copyright Licensing Agency Limited
      90 Tottenham Court Road
      London W1P 9HE
      Tel 071 436 5931

The CLA issues licences to permit the copying of books, journals and periodicals by colleges, Government departments, libraries and universities. It has recently introduced a rapid clearance service (CLARCS) for issuing photocopying licences to business users. Details of this service may be obtained from its licensing administrator who may be contacted at the above address or on 071 636 3745.

(b)   The Design and Artists Copyright Society Limited
      St Mary's Clergy House
      2 Whitechurch Lane
      London E1 7QR
      Tel 071 247 1650

The DACS issues licences for the use of artistic works.

(c)   The Education Recording Agency
      32–34 Alfred Place
      London WC1E 7DP
      Tel 071 436 4883

The ERA issues licences to educational establishments to permit the off-air recording of broadcasts and cable programmes.

There are a number of circumstances in which licences may not be required in relation to certain types of use of copyright works and a licence from the above organisations may not be required. These circumstances are set out in paragraphs 8.3 to 8.39.

Othe licensing bodies are referred to in paragraph 19.21.

7. The author's contract

[IMPORTANT NOTE: Please read the section "About this book" on page v, before referring to any of the matters in this chapter]

A. Introduction

7.1 Purpose of this chapter

The purpose of this chapter is to examine one of the most valuable of publishers' assets – the author's contract. Although the chapter relates primarily to the authors' agreements, many of the comments will apply equally to other agreements which are in common use in the publishing and multimedia industries such as rights licensing agreements, rights acquisition agreements, merchandising licences, distribution agreements, translation licences and translation agreements, and many of the other documents contained in this work.

The chapter begins by examining a number of general matters relating to the commissioning of authors, including what restrictions may fairly be imposed on them, and then examines issues arising in relation to the death of authors, and also the nature of the fiduciary duties which may be assumed by a publisher or multimedia company in relation to the acquisition of subsidiary rights (see paragraph 1.16, paragraphs 2.26 to 2.30 and paragraphs 11.10 to 11.26).

The chapter then examines issues relating to copyright, publication rights, underlying rights and moral rights (see chapter 5), before considering the question of reverse assignments. There are many circumstances in which it may be appropriate to provide reverse assignments of rights from publishers to authors, where rights of copyright have been created by the publisher or its employees.

A number of specific provisions which are common to authors' contracts are then examined, in the order in which these provisions appear in the authors' agreement included as Document 4, and aspects relating to delivery of disk-based materials, and associated production and editing requirements, are also dealt with.

The chapter concludes with an analysis and summary of the principal commercial terms relating to advances and royalties which have been agreed pursuant to the minimum terms agreements currently in force between the Writers' Guild of Great Britain, the Society of Authors and a number of British publishers.

B. General matters relating to authors' agreements

7.2 Restrictions on authors

In some cases, publishers may wish to restrict authors from writing similar works. For example, in the case of a technical work, the existence of a competing publication might reduce the publisher's market considerably. In such cases a publisher clearly has a legitimate interest to protect, but the protection of this legitimate interest must be balanced by the need not to impose on the author terms which are too harsh, since there is a risk that such terms might be void.

Where any such restriction is imposed, great care needs to be taken by publishers to ensure that the restriction is reasonable. If the restriction is too far-reaching, the agreement may be unenforceable, by reason of it being in restraint of trade, or by reason of it being entered into as a result of undue influence or duress (see paragraph 2.23).

The courts draw a distinction between, on the one hand, standard form contracts which are entered into freely between parties who are bargaining on equal terms and, on the other hand, standard form contracts which have not been the subject of negotiations between the parties, and whose terms have been dictated by the party who enjoyed superior bargaining power. When dealing with contracts of the second type, the courts will consider all provisions, to see whether the bargain that has been made was fair and should be upheld by the law.

In order to determine whether a particular bargain was fair, the courts will consider whether the restrictions were:

(a)   reasonably necessary for the protection of the legitimate interests of the person requiring them; and

(b)   commensurate with the benefits given to the person who accepted them.

If an agreement imposes total commitment and restrictions on one party but imposes no obligations on the other party, there is a risk that the agreement will be held by the courts to be an unreasonable restraint of trade and therefore void.

A total prohibition on an author writing any competing work for an open-ended period is likely, therefore, to be unenforceable. If a restriction does need to be imposed, the publisher should make the restriction as specific as possible and limit the period for which it is applicable (see Document 6(a)).

The precise relationship between the publisher and an author will need close scrutiny in some circumstances, particularly when young persons who have not received any independent legal advice are involved, and where these persons rely entirely on the publisher to be given a fair deal. Although such instances are rare the publisher may be under a legally enforceable duty to observe the utmost good faith towards the author. Additionally, where a close relationship exists between an author and a publisher, and the author has been sufficiently influenced by the publisher to sign an unfair agreement, it is possible that the agreement may be set aside by the courts as having been procured by undue influence.

It is important for publishers to be aware of the consequences of dealing with bankrupts, or minors, or persons of unsound mind, and there may be occasions when specific legal advice should be taken.

7.3 Death of an author

What happens when an author dies before completing a work, which the author has contracted to write? This question needs to be dealt with in the author's contract. If the work has been substantially completed, and is a work of reference, it may be possible for it to be completed by another author. Such a step would, however, be entirely inappropriate in the case of a work of fiction, although there may be instances where writing teams or co-authors were involved, and such a provision might be acceptable.

The death of an author who has failed to complete a contracted work will normally release both publisher and author from all further obligations to each other unless specific provision is made in the agreement. Where an advance has been paid to the author, the question of whether it should be repaid will depend on the precise terms of the contract. If the advance is described as non-returnable, there may be circumstances where it is not repayable and it may be useful in some circumstances to insert a specific provision in the Author's Agreement which deals with the situation (see Document 4 Clause 12.4).

Where a substantial advance has been paid, a publisher may wish to protect its investment by providing that the publisher has the right to finish a work by using a co-author who has been approved by the author's personal representatives or executors, or who will be chosen in consultation with such persons. The cost of engaging such a person, and the method of allocation of royalties will also need to be addressed, and it may be advisable to insert arbitration provisions so that any disputes can be dealt with swiftly.

Before deciding how to proceed, some thought ought to be given as to how the work is defined and how the rights are assigned. If the assignment clause assigns all rights in the manuscript by way of future assignment of copyright, then the publisher will own whatever parts of the work exist as at the date of death of the author. The publisher may, therefore, be free to deal with the work in accordance with the terms of the original agreement (subject to being able to do so without infringing moral rights – see Chapter 5 and paragraph 7.8). If, however, the contract defines the work as the completed manuscript or the completed typescript, then, because this will not have been brought into being as at the date of death of the author, the publisher may have acquired no rights at all.

7.4 Fiduciary obligations of publishers

The duties and obligations of agents have already been considered (see paragraphs 2.24 to 2.30), and it is important for publishers to avoid putting themselves in situations where conflicts exist between their commercial priorities and the duties which they may owe to authors.

It is possible that a conflict of this type could exist where a publisher is appointed as the agent of an author for the purpose of exploiting subsidiary rights (see paragraph 2.27). There are certain advantages for publishers in being appointed as agents – principally the elimination of risk (see paragraph 2.30).

Where publishers act as agents for the exploitation of subsidiary rights, they should achieve the best obtainable arm's length terms in licences which they negotiate or grant. They must also keep the authors they represent fully apprised of all relevant information, and must avoid putting themselves in conflict with the authors' commercial interests. This means that a publisher should not, in its capacity as agent, grant rights to one of its subsidiaries, when it might have obtained better terms from a third party.

There is no restriction, however, on a publisher's activities when it is not acting as agent, and publishers may generally freely dispose of any rights which are assigned or licensed to them (as opposed to rights for which they are appointed agent) on any terms they like. Where a publisher wishes to grant paperback rights or subsidiary rights to a company which is in the same group as the publisher, or is connected with the publisher, it may be preferable from the publisher's point of view for these rights to be licensed by the author to the publisher as part of the publication rights rather than being retained by the author and being exploited as subsidiary rights under an agency arrangement.

C. Copyright and moral rights

7.5 Publication rights

The question of whether the publisher should obtain an assignment of publication rights or a licence has already been considered (see paragraphs 1.18 to 1.20 and paragraphs 3.38 to 3.40). From a publisher's point of view, under United Kingdom law, there is little practical difference between an assignment and an exclusive licence, other than the fact that the licence may usually be terminated for breach. Provided that the definitions of the work and the publication rights are carefully worded, the publisher would, under an exclusive licence, normally obtain all rights which it would be likely to need in the ordinary course of business, leaving the author with the ownership of the copyright.

There are, however, some circumstances in which an exclusive licence is inappropriate and the publisher should obtain an assignment of copyright. Such instances include multiple contributions to works written by a number of authors, and works which have been developed specifically by an author or authors at the express request of the publisher which are destined to fulfil a gap in the market. Other examples where assignments of copyright may be appropriate are circumstances where rights are granted by an author to a packager, who is obliged pursuant to its agreement with a publisher to obtain and assign to the publisher the entire copyright in the work. Similarly, assignments will normally be required in arrangements in relation to works which are to be exploited in multimedia or electronic format (see Chapter 19).

Assignments and licences may be limited by reference either to territory or to term, or to both territory and term. A publisher, therefore, has the choice of a number of different alternative possibilities, some of which are listed in Documents 5(a) to 5(e).

The choice of the appropriate alternative is a matter for the publisher but, as a general indication, it is in the interests of the publisher to obtain the longest duration of rights and the widest possible territory which can be achieved without increasing the amount of any advance or royalty. An assignment of the entire copyright throughout the world for the full copyright period is, therefore, from a publisher's point of view, preferable to a licence for a territory for a limited period.

7.6   Reverse assignments

One of the areas of change introduced by the Copyright, Designs and Patents Act 1988 was the possibility of creating copyright in oral contributions to works. This has meant that it is, in some cases, arguable that a commissioning editor, or copy editor, may have made a contribution of sufficiently skilful and/or original character to permit that person to be considered as one of the "authors" of the work. In such circumstances, it may be appropriate for the author's contract to contain a provision confirming that neither the publisher, nor any of its staff, nor any of the persons engaged by it for the purpose of commissioning or editing the work, has any claim in relation to its copyright.

An example of such a provision can be found in Clause 8.2 of Document 4. Although this provision is not currently standard practice in the publishing industry, it is submitted that the inclusion of such a clause constitutes good practice, and provides reassurance to authors without, in any way, undermining the interests of publishers.

7.7   Underlying rights material

The author's contract normally requires the author to identify any literary or artistic material (such as quotations and illustrations) which has been written by third parties and has been used by the author. Depending on the nature and type of the work, it is normally the responsibility of the author to acquire the right to use such underlying or third party material. In practice, however, all publishers should check that their authors have properly carried out all underlying rights clearances.

This is advisable for three reasons. First, the publisher will be liable at civil and criminal law if any published material infringes third party rights, and the publisher knew or had reason to believe that this was the case (see paragraphs 13.2 to 13.8). Second, it is unlikely that any individual author will have the same level of expertise as a publisher in making the necessary contractual arrangements to effect underlying rights clearances. An author might obtain merely a simple licence permitting the use of material. This would generally not be adequate to a publisher, since it might be revoked at any time. Third, the parties giving consent to use excerpts may, in some cases, require some form of acknowledgement from the publisher, which the author will normally not be in a position to confirm.

Persons making suggestions which are included in a work, may have the right to be identified in certain circumstances, and the author may wish to acknowledge their contributions. The author's contract should recognise the author's commitment to such persons, and encourage the author to inform the publisher of their identity, so as to avoid problems later (see Document 4 Clause 1.7).

7.8 Moral rights

Moral rights have been considered at some length in this work (see Chapter 5). Of the four types of moral rights, one right can generally be ignored by publishers. This is the right not to have a work falsely attributed to oneself. The making of any false attribution might make a publisher liable in relation to the Trade Descriptions Act (see paragraph 12.40) and it is unlikely that publishers would wilfully wish to infringe this right. There is certainly no record of proceedings having been brought for its infringement since it was introduced in the Copyright Act 1956.

A second category of moral rights (the right to privacy in relation to photographs and films) is likely to be relevant only in relation to biographies and reporting current events. Where photographs are used, a form of release or "permission" (see paragraphs 8.2 to 8.5) will usually be obtained, and the terms of this permission will normally include the necessary confirmation in relation to moral rights (see Documents 16 to 30). Where photographs are obtained from persons other than the moral rights owners, it is advisable for publishers to obtain consents from the moral rights owners.

The remaining two types of moral rights (the right to be identified and the right to object to derogatory treatment) are rights which cause authors concern. In many cases, authors do not fully understand the extent or significance of their rights, and the contractual provisions which deal with them may need to be explained tactfully.

It is common for publishing agreements to require publishers to print authors' names on all published copies of works. In addition to this contractual obligation, the publisher also has a statutory obligation to identify the author, if the author's right to be identified is asserted. The statutory obligation and any contractual obligation exist independently of each other, and provide overlapping protection on terms which might possibly conflict.

It is clearly in the interests of both authors and publishers that any confusion, in an area of such emotional significance for authors, should be eliminated. For this reason, it is submitted that a sensible course of conduct might be as follows.

(a) The right to be identified

This right should be asserted by authors in a form agreed upon by the parties, in accordance with normal publishing practice (see Clause 2.4 in Document 4). Casual or inadvertent failure to comply with obligations of this nature is normally excluded in certain types of agreements, and the contract should therefore contain the standard exclusion wording (see Clause 2.4 in Document 4). Without this wording, inadvertent failure by the publisher or its licensee to comply exactly with the credit provision might permit the author to obtain an injunction and prevent publication of the work by the publisher. Clearly this is not an acceptable commercial risk.

(b) The right not to suffer derogatory treatment

Most publishers have great respect for the work of their authors, and wish to protect it from derogatory treatment.

The protection afforded to authors by the Copyright, Designs and Patents Act 1988 is, however, of such a wide nature, that it is capable of being used in such a way as to prevent publishers from making any alterations to text, such as correction, copy editing, conforming to house style, complying with legal advice or authorising translations.

Clearly, publishers must be able to carry out such activities, and the author's agreement should contain a provision allowing them to do so (see Clause 2.5 in Document 4), whilst at the same time respecting the author's moral right.

The practice has developed in recent years for certain publishers to include in the preliminary pages of their publications a statement to the effect that the author has asserted his or her right to be identified. The effect of this statement is considered below.

If an author's right to be identified is asserted by specific reference in an assignment of copyright, the publisher and all persons acquiring rights through the publisher will be bound by the assertion whether or not they have notice (see paragraph 5.8). Where the right to be identified is not inserted in any assignment, but the author's contract contains a provision obliging the publisher to name the author on all copies of the work, the author will have similar rights to those the author would have had if the rights had been asserted. If the publisher breaches the contractual obligation, the author will be able to sue the publisher, and may even be able to obtain an injunction restraining publication of the work, since the loss of an opportunity to enhance one's reputation is not adequately compensated by damages (see paragraphs 13.11 to 13.13).

A similar position applies where rights are licensed to a publisher. Breach by the publisher of its contractual obligation to identify an author is actionable, and the author may be able to obtain damages and an injunction. Where an author's contract requires a publisher to ensure that sub-licensees identify the author in a particular form (see for example Document 4 clause 2.7), any failure of the sub-licensees may be an actionable breach of the obligations of the publisher. This may entitle the author to obtain damages from the publisher, though possibly not an injunction. Additionally, the author may be able to obtain damages from the publisher's licensee for interference with contractual rights (see paragraph 13.10) and also, possibly, for infringement of moral rights (although this would depend on whether moral rights were observed under the laws of the country of the licensee, and also upon remedies available under those laws).

If any third party copies an author's work without the consent of the copyright owner and fails to identify the author, such copying will amount to an infringement of copyright – unless it falls within the scope of the permitted acts, (see paragraphs 8.6 to 8.44). Even where third party action falls within the scope of the permitted acts, there are a number of circumstances where a third party would be required to give "sufficient acknowledgement" to the author (see paragraphs 8.6 and 8.7 for example). This sufficient acknowledgement will require the identification of the author, thus preserving the author's right to be identified, even though it has not been asserted.

For the above reasons, it is submitted that statements on books to the effect that the author has asserted his or her right to be identified are of doubtful value. Surely the fact of this assertion is implicit from the appearance of the name of the author on the spine, cover and frontispiece of a book? In circumstances where a publisher has undertaken a contractual obligation to accord credit in the customary form, it is submitted that the inclusion in publications of a written statement of the assertion adds nothing to the author's rights.

Some publications contain statements to the effect that "the author's moral rights have been asserted". Out of the four moral rights (see paragraph 5.2) only one – the right to be identified – needs to be asserted. Statements that the author's moral rights have been asserted are, therefore, incorrect, and are to be avoided.

D. Specific provisions in authors' agreements

7.9 Commissioning the work

The fundamental purpose of an author's agreement is to commission the work. Whether a publisher is commissioning a work pursuant to an author's agreement, or acquiring rights in a work under a third party licence, it is essential for the contract to contain an adequate description of the work. The contract should specify the number of pages of text and illustrations, and also should contain a brief description of the work (ie whether it is a work of fiction or a biography or analysis of events) and should state whether the work is to be based on material previously submitted by the author to the publisher.

The author's agreement also normally contains a date by which the author is required to deliver the manuscript or typescript to the publisher, and in some cases a provision giving the publisher the right to require revisions to be made to the work, and requiring the author to deliver the revised version within a set number of days.

The contract will also need to contain provisions dealing with the creation of an index, and to the obtaining by the author of releases or permissions (see paragraphs 8.2 to 8.5). The cost of paying for permissions, and the cost of obtaining the right to use illustrations also needs to be covered in the contract.

7.10 Editing corrections and credit

The author's agreement will frequently contain a provision under which the publisher agrees to consult with the author in relation to copy editing, illustrations, jacket design, introduction, cover notes, and the like. The contract will also normally state in whose name the copyright notice on the preliminary pages of the work will appear. If the copyright is reserved by the author, the copyright notice should contain the author's name. If, however, the copyright is assigned to the publisher, the notice should be in the name of the publisher.

Additionally, a contract will normally state the form of credit to be given to the author, and provision will also usually be made permitting the publisher to make alterations to the text for the purpose of complying with house style, and complying with the advice of legal advisers, and removing any material which might be actionable at law, or which might damage the publisher's reputation or business interests. These aspects have been touched upon earlier in this chapter (see paragraph 7.8).

The contract will also contain a provision dealing with proofing and correction of the work. It is normal for an author to have 21 days to read and correct proofs, and it is also normal for the cost of corrections above a certain level to be borne by the author.

Where a work contains material which might, in the opinion of the publisher, expose the publisher to liability to third parties (see Chapters 9, 10 and 12) or damage the publisher's reputation or business interests, the agreement will normally give the publisher the right either to reject the work, or to make changes to the work, or to require the author to make changes to the work.

7.11 Publication

Many authors wish their contracts to contain details of the anticipated print run and retail price of their work, and there may be no objection to such information being included in the contract, provided that it does not take the form of an absolute obligation imposed on the publisher.

Publishers are sometimes willing to undertake to publish works to their customary standard, but an absolute undertaking to publish the work is generally avoided for two reasons. First, the work, as delivered, might be defamatory or create other legal liability on the part of the publisher (see Chapters 9, 10 and 12). Second, the publisher might require alterations to be made to the work, or the work, as delivered, might fail to achieve the desired standard.

It is normal also for contracts to make provision for a number of free copies of the first published edition to be supplied to the author, and some contracts give the author the right to require the publisher to return any typescript or manuscript to the author.

In some cases, the publisher will wish the author to provide assistance in relation to the production of publicity and advertising material, and the publisher may wish the author to provide a list of suitable recipients for review copies of the work. If any special promotional activities are required to be carried out by the author, the contract should state what these are, and state whether the author is entitled to receive any remuneration for them. Frequently promotional activities are carried out free of charge (save for the reimbursement of pre-approved expenses and/or the payment of a small per diem fee), but such obligations are generally made subject to the author's pre-existing contractual arrangements with third parties.

7.12 Corrections and proofs

Part of an author's duties involves the correction of galley proofs, and occasionally page proofs. This is a most important part of the publishing process, which is designed to ensure that the work will, in its final published form, be correct and accurate. Publishing contracts generally give an author a specified period (normally 21 days) to return corrected proofs to the publisher. They also make the author responsible for repaying to the publisher the cost of printers' corrections, to the extent that these exceed a percentage (normally 10%) of the typesetting cost. In practice, the amount of any excess cost may be recovered by the publisher from royalties, in the same way as the advance.

Although such correction clauses are standard, there are many occasions when they should be amended. For example, where a work is of a topical nature and last-minute changes are expected, the correction allowance may need to be extended. Another instance is the engagement of a general editor, who should not be made liable for corrections which need to be made to material which has been written by third parties.

Where a work is to be delivered on disk, or by other electronic means, the method of calculating the excess costs may need to be changed since, if the work is typeset automatically, the cost may be lower, and the point at which the author becomes liable for corrections may be reached sooner.

7.13 Electronic delivery material

Where a publisher intends to accept delivery of a work on disk, the author's contract will need to contain a number of additional provisions. Wording that may be suitable for incorporation in an author's contract is contained in Document 6(c).

The materials which a publisher will need to obtain from an author are of three types. The first type will be disks, containing the work in machine readable format. The size of the disks, the word processing program system, and any relevant database format, will need to be specified. Each disk or tape should be clearly labelled and numbered. The second category of material is an index which should contain details of all information stored on the disks. The information should include all file and directory names, together with any other information needed to produce a print-out of the work using the disks. The third element of the delivery material is a print-out of the work, which should be clearly typed and securely bound. It is important that the print-out should have been made from the disks which have been delivered, or identical duplicate copies. The print-out should conform in all respects to the contents of the disks.

As soon as delivery materials have been received by the publisher, they should be converted to whatever system or process the publisher's typesetter uses, and tested to ensure that they are error free, and capable of producing a print-out which conforms to the print-out delivered by the author. It may be advisable to carry out a trial run so that any difficulties or areas of incompatibility between the author's hardware and software, and those of the typesetter can be identified at an early stage. Once materials have been delivered, the author and the publisher will need to agree which party is to be responsible for editing the text.

A publisher may be asked to give an absolute undertaking to use the delivery material to typeset the work automatically. From an author's point of view, there are certain advantages, since the standard of proof-reading required where the material has been typeset automatically, using the author's disks, is lower than that required where the work has been typeset ab initio. The publisher will not normally accept an absolute obligation to have the work typeset automatically, since problems may arise in the typesetting stages for one of three reasons.

First, it is possible that the disks may contain errors. Second, the conversion process may distort the information on disk. Third, the typesetter's hardware or software may be unable to deal with the material in the desired manner. The problems in the first category can be dealt with by giving the author an agreed time period in which to provide error-free materials. Problems of the second and third categories can only be resolved by the typesetter or the publisher.

Where electronic delivery materials are not used for automatic typesetting of the work, the time specified in the agreement by which proof-reading is to be completed may need to be extended. Where electronic delivery materials are used for automatic typesetting of the work, the standard author's corrections clause may need to be amended since the amount above which the author becomes liable for corrections (generally 10% of typesetting costs – see Clause 2.2 in Document 4) will be reduced.

A number of different possibilities exist for remunerating an author who provides disk-based delivery materials. Either the author can receive a fixed sum per disk, or perhaps a fee which may be calculated by reference to the publisher's estimated savings. Alternatively it may be appropriate to pay the author an agreed sum per printed page. It should be noted, however, that the savings are generally not significant.

The author may additionally seek to impose upon the publisher a number of conditions relating to the disks. The publisher should ensure that any such conditions do not prohibit the grant of a licence to the publisher, permitting the disk material to be used in the automatic typesetting process. An author may require an acknowledgement that property and ownership of the disks belong to the author, together with an acknowledgement that the author will not be liable to the publisher, if the author is unable to deliver acceptable disk-based delivery materials as a result of any occurrence beyond the control of the author – otherwise the author may incur liability for the additional costs incurred by a publisher in having the work typeset ab initio.

7.14 Remuneration and rights

The precise amount of the remuneration payable to the author, and the precise description of the rights to be acquired by the publisher, are the two most important elements of any author's agreement.

An author is normally entitled to receive an advance against future sums payable by way of royalty. An analysis of the commercial practice prevailing among those publishers who have entered into minimum terms agreements with the Society of Authors and the Writers' Guild of Great Britain is contained in paragraph 7.21.

The question of defining precisely what publication rights should be acquired by the publisher has been considered elsewhere in this work (see paragraph 1.14), as has the description and method of exploiting subsidiary rights (see paragraphs 2.26 to 2.30 and paragraphs 11.9 to 11.29).

Where an author is represented by an agent, the author's contract may contain a payment direction, requiring the publisher to pay all royalties to the author's agent, to enable the agent to recover his or her commission. Royalties are normally payable 90 days after 30 June and 31 December in each year, and it is usual for agreements to give publishers the right to deduct and retain reserves from royalties, to cover the publisher from any liability in relation to claims made by third parties, or liability in relation to returned books, or liability imposed on the publisher by reason of exchange control restrictions or withholding taxes in any part of the world.

Although the sale of books is currently Value Added Tax exempt, the provision by an author of services to a publisher is taxable, and an author will be liable to account to Customs and Excise for Value Added Tax in relation to the author's earnings if they exceed the Value Added Tax threshold. Where an agreement does not make express provision for Value Added Tax to be paid, the remuneration is deemed to be inclusive of Value Added Tax, and the omission of appropriate Value Added Tax provision in an author's agreement may result in a substantial diminution of the author's net income. An appropriate provision is contained in Document 4 in Clause 11.6.

There is one aspect of remuneration which is frequently overlooked in documents, and this is the recovery of damages from infringement by third parties. It is advisable to make specific provision in publishing contracts for the commencement of infringement actions, in order to state who will bear the cost of proceedings, and how the proceeds of successful proceedings will be shared. Although a publisher will have the right, as exclusive licensee, to sue to restrain infringement in the United Kingdom, there may be some jurisdictions in which the publisher will need the author to become a party to proceedings. An appropriate provision covering these points may be found in Document 4 in Clauses 14.1 and 14.2.

7.15 Warranties and indemnities

Publishing contracts contain a number of standard warranties, and in many cases an indemnity provision. It is important for publishers to understand the meanings which the law attaches to these expressions.

Breach of a warranty in an agreement will entitle the innocent party to claim damages for that party's loss. Additionally, the agreement may contain a provision which permits the innocent party to terminate the agreement, but the innocent party remains primarily liable to bear the damages it incurs. It will be able to recover damages from the party in breach when it has been established that this party is responsible, and when evidence acceptable to a court substantiating the innocent party's loss, has been produced.

An indemnity provision amounts to a directly enforceable undertaking to ensure that no loss is occasioned by the innocent party, and entitles the innocent party to demand payment of any expenses it incurs as a result of a breach of warranty, without having first established the basis of the claim, and proved the amount of its loss. An indemnity provision, therefore, confers quite extensive protection – although its value will depend on the financial position of the person giving the indemnity.

Whether or not it is appropriate to impose an indemnity obligation on an author is a matter which publishers should consider carefully. An indemnity obligation is potentially without limit, and the person giving the indemnity frequently has no control over the matters in which publishers may incur costs, or over the amount of such costs.

Indemnity provisions are capable of imposing severe financial hardship on authors, who (apart from a comparatively small band of superstars) are generally not highly remunerated. Unlike publishers, who are able to take advantage of the shield of limited liability, authors are personally liable, and the amount of their personal liability is without limit. Unlike insolvent publishers, who may find escape from liability in liquidation, death does not permit the author to avoid financial accountability, since the author's debts must be borne by his or her estate.

The imposition of harsh indemnity provisions on authors may, therefore, be considered morally unconscionable, and, although there are strong arguments which may be advanced against indemnity provisions on the part of authors, there appear to be few justifications for publishers to insist on having indemnity protection from every author, as a standard requirement, although there may be circumstances where an indemnity might be a reasonable requirement. If an author is prepared to give full unqualified normal warranties, a publisher will be able to recover its losses from the author (and the author's estate) in respect of any breach of the warranties, provided that the publisher attempts to mitigate its loss. If a publisher has effected insurance cover, it will in many cases have the benefit of indemnity cover from insurers. The insistence on an indemnity from an author in circumstances where insurance cover exists, means that the author is being asked to reinsure the insurers, but without charging a premium. Many persons would regard such insistence as being unreasonable.

A further factor counting against the unilateral imposition of indemnity clauses is that there are a number of reasons why a court might refuse to enforce such provisions against an author, on the grounds of undue influence, duress, restraint of trade or breach of fiduciary duty. There may, however, be circumstances where it is fair and reasonable, and necessary, for indemnity provisions to be included, particularly where a publisher is placing reliance on the veracity or accuracy of facts which can be known solely to the author. In such cases publishers should ensure that the nature and consequences of the provision are understood by authors, and, it is submitted, should permit the author's legal advisers to participate in the defence of any claim, and should agree not to settle any proceedings otherwise than on the advice of counsel.

Authors' agreements normally require authors to give warranties on a number of different matters, including the following:

(a) the author is the sole author and owner of the work;
(b) the author has not entered into any conflicting agreement;
(c) the work is original and does not infringe any right of copyright or moral right or right of privacy or right of publicity or any other right and does not constitute a contempt of court or violation of secrecy laws;
(d) the work is not obscene, or blasphemous, or offensive to religion, or defamatory, and does not contain any other unlawful material;
(e) all statements purporting to be facts in the work are true and correct, and no recipe, advice or formula or instruction in the work is capable of causing loss or damage if used or followed;
(f) there is no present or prospective claim in relation to the work;
(g) copyright in the work is valid and subsisting throughout the world;
(h) the author will keep all information relating to the agreement and the publisher confidential.

7.16 New editions

Where an author's agreement is for a work of reference, or a technical work, it will be appropriate for the agreement to contain provisions relating to future editions which will be produced, when needed, in order to ensure that the work remains up to date and accurate. Normally the production of new editions will be in the interests of both the author and the publisher. The length of notice required to be given to the author in order to authorise the publisher to engage new personnel should be specified in the agreement.

An author will normally be particularly concerned to ensure that the publisher is obliged to commission the author to produce the updated or finished work. Where the author dies or becomes incapacitated, or is unable, or simply unwilling, to update or produce a new edition of the book, then agreement will need to be reached on a number of matters. Will the person engaged by the publisher be entitled to a credit? Will the copyright in the material produced by the new editor vest in the original author (or the publisher)? To what extent may the royalty payable to the original author be reduced?

An appropriate provision for new editions, giving the publisher control over all relevant aspects may be found in Document 6(a). This provision will only work effectively, however, if it is included in an agreement which contains an assignment (as opposed to a licence) of copyright in the work.

7.17 Subsequent works

An author's contract will frequently give the publisher an option over the author's next work. Sometimes the option is limited to works of the same type as the work for which the contract was issued. The option normally requires the publisher to exercise it within a designated time after delivery of the manuscript or typescript. Where an author has entered into contracts with several publishers, great care should be taken by the author to ensure that the option rights which have been given to the various publishers do not conflict with each other or overlap.

The type of option provision which is currently included in many publishing contracts is legally unenforceable, since in most cases it constitutes merely an agreement to agree. Although the courts will enforce a contract to enter into a contract, an agreement to agree has no contractual effect whatever (see paragraphs 2.2 to 2.8). This means that a publisher cannot sue to enforce an option of this type, and it is suggested that there is therefore no point in including it.

A contractually enforceable option clause is included in Document 6(b), and this clause is capable of being inserted in an author's contract.

7.18 Termination and reversion of rights

Some publishing contracts provide that the rights granted to a publisher will revert to the author in certain circumstances. The technical means of effecting the reversion depend on whether the rights were granted in an assignment or a licence. If the rights were assigned, they must be reassigned but, if they were licensed, the licence can normally be terminated by notice in certain circumstances. The circumstances in which termination rights arise can usually be divided into three separate categories, being:

(a) where the publisher is in breach of some material obligation, and has not remedied the breach within a certain specified time after having received notice from the author;
(b) where the publisher has gone into or been put into liquidation;
(c) where the publisher has not published the work within a specified period of time, or has allowed the work to go out of print for a designated period.

It is not always appropriate for reversion of rights provisions to be inserted into an author's agreement. Where a high advance is being paid by a publisher, the publisher may feel that the amount paid will be adequate compensation to the author, irrespective of whether the work is published or not. This argument may be further supported by the fact that many high advances which are now being paid by publishers are not recouped from the author's royalties. The work might equally well, however, be of a type where a reversion of rights is not permissible. Such works would include a part work or an encyclopedia, which may be the work of many authors.

Whenever rights revert, the position of the publisher's sub-licensees needs to be considered. The termination of a publisher's licence will automatically end any sub-licences granted to third parties, unless specific provision to the contrary is made in the author's contract. An author's contract may, therefore, provide that any such licences will remain effective, and that the publisher shall remain entitled to receive income payable from licensees, and to deduct the percentage of rights income to which the publisher is entitled. An example of a contractual provision of this type may be found in Document 4 in Clause 16.3.

The termination of an agreement, or the operation of a reversion of rights provision, will have an effect on other provisions in an author's agreement. An author may feel that it would not be right for the publisher to continue to have an option over the author's next work (paragraph 7.17), or for the author to continue to be bound by a provision restricting the author from writing any competing work (see paragraph 7.16), and may wish such rights to cease on termination.

Where a work has gone out of print, or is the subject of remainder sales, an author may wish to have the right to buy up the publisher's stock. An appropriate provision covering this is contained in Document 4 in Clause 13.

7.19 Alternative dispute resolution

Many publishing agreements contain provisions requiring disputes to be submitted to arbitration. Arbitration of disputes is a far from an ideal solution, since it is both time-consuming and costly.

A far more effective solution to arbitration is to insert in the author's contract a provision which requires both parties to submit to an alternative dispute resolution procedure. An effective procedure has been established by the Centre for Alternative Dispute Resolution and a model provision may be found in Document 4 in Clause 15.

E.   Minimum terms agreement

7.20   Minimum terms agreements generally

The Writers' Guild of Great Britain and the Society of Authors have established a set of what they consider to be minimum terms for the engagement of authors, the text of which is contained in their standard Minimum Terms Agreement. Since 1978, the Writers' Guild of Great Britain and the Society of Authors have been involved in negotiations with a number of publishers who have signed negotiated variants of the Minimum Terms Agreement. Although each of the signed agreements is derived from a common ancestor, there are numerous differences, both in relation to agreed commercial terms and in relation to contractual provisions.

The publishers who have entered into minimum terms agreements with the Writers' Guild of Great Britain and the Society of Authors are Journeyman Press, Hamish Hamilton Limited, BBC Publications, Faber & Faber publishers Limited, Headline Book Publishing plc, Century Hutchinson Limited, Bloomsbury Publishing Limited, Hodder & Stoughton Limited, OPG Services Limited (Methuen), Sinclair-Stephenson Limited, Chapmans publishers, WH Allen & Co Limited, the Penguin Group, Harper Collins and Random House.

7.21   Prevailing commercial practice

A brief analysis of the principal financial terms of the minimum terms agreement, which have been signed by the publishers referred to in paragraph

7.20, reveals a number of common features which, it is submitted, might be considered prevailing commercial practice in the publishing industry in the United Kingdom. The provisions are:

(a) Advance

The advance normally equals 65% of the estimated author's receipts, or 55% of estimated author's receipts if the agreement is for both hardback and paperback rights.

In order to calculate the estimated author's receipts, the total estimated sales or print-run of the work should be multiplied by the royalty percentage, royalty rate and retail price.

(b) Instalments of advance

The advance payments are, in the case of non-commissioned works, one half on signature and one half on the earlier of one year from signature or publication of the work. In the case of commissioned works instalment payments are one third on signature, one third on delivery and one third on the earlier of one year from delivery or publication of the work.

(c) Home hardback royalties

Home hardback royalties are 10% of the published price for the first 2,500 copies, 12½% of the published price for the next 2,500 copies and 15% of the published price after that.

Some agreements provide for a variation on sales at discounts of less than 45% or 50%.

(d) Overseas hardback royalties

Overseas hardback royalties are 10% of the price received on the first 2,500 copies, 12½% of the price received on the next 2,500 copies and 15% on the price received after that.

Some agreements provide for royalties calculated as percentages of the British published price at discounts of less than 50%.

(e) Royalties on hardback licences

There are two approaches to dealing with royalties on hardback licences. Either the publisher's receipts are shared in the proportions 60% to the author and 40% to the publisher (as with BBC Publications) or the author is paid a royalty of 10% on the first 1,500 to 2,000 copies, 12½% on the next 2,000 copies and 15% after that.

(f) Royalties on paperback licences

Royalties on paperback licences are expressed as a percentage of the publisher's receipts. The applicable percentage is 60% to the author and 40% to the publisher up to a point to be negotiated, or the first 35,000 copies, or the first £5,000, and after this point has been reached 70% to the author and 30% to the publisher.

(g) Book clubs

Three different bases and percentages exist, namely 7½% of the book club list price on the first 10,000 copies and 10% after that, or 10% of publisher's receipts on bound copies or sheets sold to the book club, or 60% of the publisher's receipts on copies of the book manufactured by the book club.

(h) Subsidiary Rights

The following percentages of publisher's receipts are paid to authors by way of royalty in relation to subsidiary rights:

Anthology and Quotation Rights	60%
Digest Rights	75%
First Serial Rights	90%
Merchandising Rights	80%
Motion Picture and Television Rights	90%
Paperback Rights	60% rising to 70% at points to be negotiated
Reading Rights	75%
Second and Subsequent Serial Rights	75%
Single Issue Rights	75%
Translation Rights	80%
US Rights	80%

7.22 Publishers and minimum terms agreements

Whilst the minimum terms agreements represent an undeniable improvement on the terms and conditions offered to authors, the form of the agreements was pioneered as long ago as 1978. In view of subsequent changes and developments in United Kingdom copyright legislation (principally the Copyright, Designs and Patents Act 1988), the current effect of the minimum terms agreements, from a publisher's point of view, is not entirely acceptable.

All negotiated agreements are capable of improvement, and the various minimum terms agreements are no exception in this regard. The principal respect in which the minimum terms agreements pose a threat to publishers, is that none of them deals adequately with the potential liability which might be encountered by publishers, as a result of the enactment of moral rights provisions in United Kingdom law.

For the reasons set out in paragraph 5.21 and paragraph 7.8, it is submitted that no publisher should sign any author's contract which omits to make specific provision protecting the publisher against capricious exercise by the author of that author's moral rights.

The minimum terms agreements require publishers who have signed them to enter into authors' contracts solely in the form permitted by the minimum terms agreement (ie without providing any protection to publishers in relation to moral rights). Whilst the minimum terms agreements remain in force, any change made by signatory publishers to their authors' contracts may constitute a breach of the minimum terms agreement.

It is submitted that all affected publishers should – as a matter of urgency – review their relevant arrangements and seek legal advice on the various alternatives which may be open to them, in order to limit or eliminate their potential liability in this area.

8. Permissions, fair dealing, rights, clearances, permitted acts and Crown and Parliamentary copyright

[IMPORTANT NOTE: Please read the section "About this book" on page v, before referring to any of the matters in this chapter.]

[*In this chapter all statutory references are to the Copyright, Designs and Patents Act 1988*]

A. Introduction

8.1 Purpose of this chapter

It is important for publishers and multimedia companies to be able to identify when their copyrights are being infringed, and when they need to seek consent or authorisation to avoid infringing other people's rights. This chapter provides a quick guide to what can, and what cannot, be done in the areas of conventional book publishing, multimedia and electronic exploitation.

Obtaining permission to use extracts from works is a laborious and time-consuming task, but it is a very necessary part of the business activity of a publisher or a multimedia company. This chapter begins by examining precisely what a permission is, and why it is necessary.

A number of acts may, however, be carried out in relation to copyright works by means of fair dealing. The concept of fair dealing is explained, as well as the recommendations of the Copyright Licensing Agency in relation to it.

Further exemptions from infringement of copyright are provided by legislation, for the reporting of current events, and other matters. The chapter examines each of the acts which are permitted by legislation to be done without infringing copyright, by educational establishments and libraries and archives, as well as the more generally applicable permitted acts. The chapter also contains a summary of the guidelines which have been established for the use of Crown and Parliamentary Copyright material.

Finally, the chapter examines the types of rights clearance procedures which publishers and multimedia companies should follow. Specific advice in relation to multimedia exploitation may be found in paragraphs 19.4 to 19.30.

B. Permissions and fair dealing

8.2 What are permissions?

Although a publisher or multimedia company acquires the exclusive rights of copyright in the original material contained in a work which has been written by an author, it is likely that certain limited, non-exclusive rights of copyright in the underlying material contained in the work will be owned or controlled by third parties. Permissions and consents (or rights clearances) will need to be obtained from these parties, since the publication of a work containing another person's copyright material without their consent would be an infringement of copyright which would expose the publisher or multimedia company to both civil and criminal liability (see paragraphs 13.2 to 13.17). Various forms of permission are contained in Documents 16 to 29.

The author's contract will normally assign the copyright, or grant an exclusive licence, in relation to all material written by the author. The contract may also impose obligations on the author to obtain non-exclusive licences or consents for the use of the underlying material (see paragraph 1.17). Before issuing an author's contract, a publisher or multimedia company should consider what types of underlying rights clearances may be necessary and should then ensure that all licences, consents and permissions which may be required to enable the publisher to publish any underlying material have been obtained. Failure to do this may expose the publisher or multimedia company to both civil and criminal liability.

A check-list of rights clearance procedures is contained in Document 30. The list offers a guide to the types of steps which it may be appropriate to follow, but additional steps may well be necessary, depending on the facts of each case.

8.3 Fair dealing generally

The Copyright, Designs and Patents Act 1988 provides that a number of acts are permitted to be done without infringing copyright or performers' rights.

Fair dealing with a work for the purpose of criticism or review will not infringe any copyright, provided that it is accompanied by a sufficient acknowledgement[1]. A sufficient acknowledgement is an acknowledgement which identifies the work in question by its title and also identifies the author, unless the work has been published anonymously, or the work is an unpublished work, where it is not possible to identify the author by reasonable enquiry[2].

Fair dealing with a literary work for the purposes of research or private study will not infringe any copyright work, or, in the case of a published edition, the typographical arrangement[3]. Copying by a person other than the researcher is not fair dealing, if the person doing the copying knows, or has reason to believe, that it will result in copies of substantially the same material being provided to more than one person, at substantially the same time, for substantially the same purpose[4].

If the use of the work cannot be authorised by the fair dealing provisions, and does not fall within the other categories of permitted acts (see paragraphs 8.6 to 8.43), then a specific permission will need to be obtained.

As far as concerns rights in performances, the fair dealing with the performance or recording for the purpose of criticism or review or for the purpose of reporting current events will not infringe any rights in respect of the performances.

1 Copyright, Designs and Patents Act 1988 S30(1).
2 S178.
3 S29(1).
4 S29(3)(b).

8.4 What is fair dealing?

If a publisher intends to rely on fair dealing as a substitute for obtaining a rights clearance, it is extremely important to ensure that the proposed use is, in fact, fair dealing. So, what is fair dealing? The expression "fair dealing" is frequently used in publishing circles, but does not have a precise legal definition. The Government White Paper of 1986 entitled *Intellectual Property and Innovations* concluded that to give the expression "fair dealing" a definition in the Copyright, Designs and Patents Act 1988 would be disadvantageous because, whether an action was fair, or not, depended on a wide number of variable circumstances. It was felt that it would be imprudent of the legislature to try to anticipate and encapsulate these in a statutory provision.

Some guidelines as to what constitutes fair dealing are, however, available. The following factors will be relevant, namely:

(a) the amount and importance of the part of the work which has been taken;
(b) the purpose for which any fair dealing is carried out; [the reason for this is that it might be permissible to take a substantial part of the work for the purposes of private study (which is permitted as fair dealing), but if the same amount were reproduced for commercial purposes (such as research) that might not be permissible.]
(c) whether the alleged fair dealing is in fact competing, or rivalling, the copyright which is being used;
(d) any intention on the part of the person making the fair dealing to obtain unfair commercial advantage over the copyright owner of the work used.

8.5 Copyright Licensing Agency Limited's views on fair dealing

The Publishers' Association reviews at regular intervals the levels of fees which are appropriate for using copyright material. Publishers' Association Document 102/90 contains recommendations for the permission fees which are applicable for prose and poetry. These recommendations have been submitted to and approved by the Office of Fair Trading.

Publishers' Association Document 14/91 contains rates for use of published material by means of radio and television broadcast. These rates are subject to periodic review.

Quotations may be made from any work for the purpose of criticism or review, provided the use is accompanied by a sufficient acknowledgement (see paragraph 8.6), or (except in the case of a photograph) for the purpose of reporting current events (see paragraph 8.6).

The fair dealing provision does not authorise the use of quotations from existing works where they are not used for the purpose of criticism or review without specific consent. The use of quotations for illustrative purposes or for reference purposes technically requires authorisation.

Although it is common practice in the publishing world for authors to quote small quantities from other works, without requesting permission, and without making payment of any fees by giving an acknowledgement of the work, technically the consent of the copyright owner (either the publisher or the author) may be required.

The Copyright Licensing Agency and the British Copyright Council interpret copyright legislation as permitting a reader of a work to "copy out extracts for his or her own retention" and state that this "copying may reasonably be done to a fair extent by photocopying for the reader's strictly personal use". In other words it is not permissible, in the view of the Copyright Licensing Agency and the British Copyright Council, for an individual to photocopy the whole of a work for the purposes of research or private study. It is submitted that this interpretation is incorrect and is unlikely to be acceptable to the courts; the question of whether such use does or does not constitute fair dealing will be more complex and will depend on a number of factors including those set out in paragraph 8.4.

On a practical level, the interpretation would not permit a person carrying out research into a literary work to copy it by typing it into a word-processor (or by scanning it) for the purpose of effecting (say) an electronic analysis of the text. It is submitted that such an act would constitute fair dealing, and the British Copyright Council/Copyright Licensing Agency interpretation would not be accepted by the courts, because it would not be in the public interest for persons to be prevented from making fair use of technological advances for the purpose of research or private study.

The European Commission and the United Kingdom has authorised the reverse engineering of computer programs (which are literary works – see paragraph 3.6) in certain circumstances (see paragraph 17.7) and this must implicitly permit the electro-copying of the whole of a literary work for certain purposes. Although the legal position is not entirely clear, it would be curious indeed if the copying and electronic analysis and decompilation of a computer program were to be permitted, but the same type of analysis of a great novel, a play or musical work were not permitted.

It is to be hoped that the British Copyright Council/Copyright Licensing Agency will review their interpretation of the meaning of "fair dealing".

C. Reporting events, incidental inclusion, use of notes, public reading

8.6 Research and private study

Fair dealing with a literary, dramatic, musical or artistic work for the purposes of research or private study does not infringe any copyright in the work itself or any separate copyright in its typographical arrangement, if the work is contained in a published edition[5] (see paragraphs 3.4 and 3.9).

If a person other than the researcher or student makes copies of a work, that copying will not be considered fair dealing if it would not be permitted under the regulations applying to libraries and archives (see paragraphs 8.16 to 8.21) or if the person doing the copying knows, or has reason to believe, that it will result in copies of substantially the same material being provided to more than one person, at substantially the same time, for substantially the same purpose[6].

During the passage of the Copyright, Designs and Patents Act through Parliament, it was proposed that fair dealing for research purposes should be limited to private research. The final wording of the Act is not, however, limited to private research use, and use of a copyright work research for commercial purposes would appear to be permitted provided, however, that the use constitutes fair dealing (see paragraphs 8.2 to 8.5).

5 S29(1).
6 S29(3).

8.7 Criticism and review

Fair dealing with a work for the purposes of criticism or review (of that work or of another work, or of a performance of any work) does not infringe copyright in the work, provided it is accompanied by a sufficient acknowledgement[7].

Sufficient acknowledgement means an acknowledgement identifying the work in question by its title or other description and identifying the author, unless the work is a published work which has been published anonymously, or unless the work is an unpublished work and it is not possible to identify the identity of the author by reasonable inquiry[8].

Before the passing of the 1988 Copyright, Designs and Patents Act, the fair dealing provisions for criticism and review extended only to literary, dramatic, musical and artistic works. The provisions now extend to dealing with films, sound recordings, broadcasts, cable programmes and typographical arrangements of published editions.

It is submitted that the use of films and sound recordings in multimedia works will not constitute fair dealing if such use is by way of background or illustrative use only, unless the use is made by way of criticism or review.

7 S30(1).
8 S30(2) and S178.

8.8 Reporting current events

Fair dealing with a work (other than a photograph) for the purpose of reporting current events does not infringe any copyright in the work which is used, provided that it is accompanied by a sufficient acknowledgement[9].

Sufficient acknowledgement means an acknowledgement identifying the work in question, by its title or other description, and identifying the author, unless the work is a published work which has been published anonymously, or unless the work is an unpublished work, and it is not possible to ascertain the identity of the author by reasonable inquiry[10].

No acknowledgement is required in connection with the reporting of current events by means of a sound recording, film, broadcast or cable programme[11].

9 S30(2).
10 S178.
11 S30(3).

8.9 Incidental inclusion

Copyright in a work is not infringed by its incidental inclusion in an artistic work (see paragraph 3.6), sound recording or film (see paragraph 3.7), or broadcast or cable programme (see paragraph 3.8). Nor is it infringed if the work in which it is included is played, showed, broadcast, or included in a cable programme, or copies of it are issued to the public[12].

A musical work, or words which are spoken or sung with music, or any part of a sound recording or broadcast or cable programme which includes a musical work, or words spoken or sung with music, shall not be regarded as being incidentally included in another work if it is deliberately included[13]. Unfortunately neither legislation nor case law has elucidated this rather delphic statement.

12 S31(1) and (2).
13 S31(3).

8.10 Unknown authorship

Copyright in a literary, dramatic, musical or artistic work in not infringed by an act done at any time when it is not possible, by reasonable enquiry, to ascertain the identity of the author, and it is reasonable to assume that copyright has expired, or that the author died, 50 years or more before the beginning of the calendar year in which the act is done[14]. This provision does not apply to any work in which Crown copyright subsists, or where a work is of joint authorship (see paragraphs 3.14 and 3.23). The provision will only apply if it is impossible to ascertain the identity of any of the authors.

14 S57(1).

8.11 Use of notes or recordings of spoken words

Where a record of spoken words is made in writing, or otherwise, for the purpose of reporting current events, or for the purpose of broadcasting or including in a cable programme service, the whole or any part of the words, it is not an infringement of any copyright in the words to use the record, or material taken from it, for that purpose, provided the following conditions are met[15]:

(a) the record is a direct record of the spoken words and is not taken from any previous record, or film, or broadcast or cable programme;
(b) the making of the record was not prohibited by the speaker, and, where copyright already subsisted in the work, it did not infringe the copyright;

(c) the use made of the record, or material taken from it, is not of a type of use prohibited by or on behalf of the speaker or the copyright owner before the record was made; and

(d) the use is made by, or with the authority of, a person who is lawfully in possession of the record[16].

15 S58(1).
16 S58(2).

8.12 Public reading or recitation

The reading, or public recital, by one person of a reasonable abstract from a published issue of a dramatic work does not infringe any copyright if it is accompanied by a sufficient acknowledgement[17]. Copyright is not infringed by the making of a sound recording, or the broadcast or inclusion in a cable programme service, of a reading, or recitation, which does not infringe copyright in a work, provided that the recording, broadcast or cable programme, consists mainly of material in relation to which it is not necessary to rely on this exemption[18].

17 S59(1).
18 S59(2).

D. Permitted acts by educational establishments

8.13 Things done for the purposes of instruction or examination

Copyright in a literary, dramatic, musical or artistic work is not infringed by its being copied in the course of instruction, or preparation for instruction, provided the copying is done by a person giving or receiving instruction, and is not by means of a reprographic process[19].

Copyright is not infringed by anything done for the purposes of an examination, by way of setting the questions, communicating the questions to the candidates or answering the questions[20]. This provision does not extend to the making of a reprographic copy of a musical work for use by an examination candidate performing the work[21].

Where a copy does not infringe copyright by virtue of the above provisions, if that copy is subsequently dealt with otherwise than for the purpose permitted by the relevant section of the Copyright Designs and Patents Act, it shall be treated as an infringing copy[22] (see Chapter 13).

19 S32(1).
20 S32(3).
21 S32(4).
22 S32(5).

8.14 Anthologies for educational use

The inclusion of a short passage, of a published literary, or dramatic work, in a collection, which is intended for use in educational establishments, and which consists mainly of material in which no copyright subsists, will not infringe copyright in the work included, subject to a number of conditions.

The conditions are that the collection must not only be intended for use in educational establishments, but must also be described as such in its title, and in any advertisements to be issued by or on behalf of the publisher. Additionally, the work from which a short passage is taken must not be a work which is intended to be used in educational establishments. Finally, the short passage included must be accompanied by a sufficient acknowledgement[23] (see paragraph 8.6).

This provision does not, however, authorise the inclusion of more than two excerpts from copyright works by the same author in collections published by the same publisher over any period of five years[24]. Where a copyright work is written by a number of authors in collaboration, any passage excerpted from work will count as a work by any of the authors[25]. In other words, only two excerpts written by any of the collective authors may be used by the same publisher in a five-year period.

23 S33(1).
24 S33(2).
25 S33(3).

8.15   Reprographic copying, public performance and recording by educational establishments

Reprographic copies of passages from published literary, dramatic, or musical works may, in certain circumstances, be made by or on behalf of an educational establishment, for the purposes of instruction, without infringing any copyright in the work, or in the typographical arrangement[26].

Not more than 1% of any work may be copied by, or on behalf of, an establishment, by virtue of the section, in any quarterly period, calculated over the fixed calendar year of 1 January to 31 December. Additionally, the exemption cannot be relied on if licences could be available, authorising the copying in question, and the person making the copies knew, or ought to have been aware of, such fact[27].

The section provides that if any licence to an educational establishment authorising reprographic copying for the purposes of instruction, purports to limit the amount of work which may be copied, to less than 1% of the work in any quarterly period, then such limitation will be of no effect[28].

Copies of works made pursuant to the above provisions, will not infringe copyright, but, where such copies are subsequently dealt with outside the scope of the above provisions, they will be deemed to be infringing copies[29].

The performance of a literary, dramatic or musical work, before an audience consisting of teachers and pupils of, and other persons directly connected with, an educational establishment, by a teacher, or pupil, or other person at the establishment, for the purposes of instruction, will not infringe copyright in the work, nor will showing or playing a sound recording, film, broadcast, or cable programme, before such an audience, for the purposes of instruction. A person is not directly connected with the activities of the educational establishment, simply because that person is the parent of a pupil at the establishment[30].

A recording of a broadcast, or cable programme, or a copy of such recording, may be made by or on behalf of an educational establishment for educational purposes of that establishment, without infringing the copyright in the work. This exemption does not apply if there is a licensing scheme in effect (see paragraphs 6.3 and 6.17) which would apply in relation to the work[31].

The expression "educational establishment" includes schools and other establishments specified by order of the Secretary of State[32].

26 S36(1).
27 S36(2) and (3).
28 S36(4).
29 S36(5).
30 S34.
31 S35(1) and (2).
32 S174.

E. Libraries and archives

8.16 Articles and periodicals

The librarian of a prescribed library may make, and supply, a copy of an article in a periodical, without infringing any copyright in any text or illustrations, if certain conditions are complied with[33]. These conditions are:

(a) copies are supplied only to persons who satisfy the librarian that they require copies for the purpose of research, or private study, and they will not use them for any other purpose[34];

(b) no person is provided with more than one copy of the same article, or with copies of more than one article from the same issue of a periodical[35];

(c) persons to whom copies are supplied, are required to pay a sum not less than the cost attributable to their production, including a contribution to the general expenses of the library[36].

33 S38(1).
34 S38(2)(a).
35 S38(2)(b).
36 S38(2)(c).

8.17 Parts of published works

The librarian of a prescribed library may, if the conditions are complied with, make and supply from a published edition a copy of part of a literary, dramatic, or musical work, other than an article in a periodical without infringing any copyright in the work, or any illustrations, accompanying the work, or in a typographical arrangement of the work[37].

The conditions are:

(a) copies are supplied only to persons who satisfy the librarian that they require the copies for the purposes of research or private study, and will not use them for any other purpose[38];

(b) no person is provided with more than one copy of the same material or with a copy of more than a reasonable part of any work[39];

(c) persons to whom copies are supplied are required to pay a sum not less than the cost attributable to their production including a contribution to the general expenses of the library[40].

125

This means that prescribed libraries and archives are required by law to procure the observance of the conditions by users of the library or archive.

37 S39(1).
38 S39(2)(a).
39 S39(2)(b).
40 S39(2)(c).

8.18 Restriction of multiple copies

It should be noted that the conditions referred to in paragraphs 8.15 and 8.16, relating to the copying of articles and parts of published works, are conditions which are included in the regulations made by the Secretary of State in respect of prescribed libraries and archives[41].

This means that prescribed libraries and archives are required, by law, to procure that their users observe the conditions referred to in paragraph 8.17.

41 S40.

8.19 Supply of copies to other libraries and replacement copies of works

A librarian in a prescribed library may make, and supply to another prescribed library, a copy of an article, or periodical, or the whole or part of a published edition of a literary, dramatic or musical work, without infringing any copyright in the text of the article or, as the case may be, in any illustration accompanying it, or any type of typographical arrangement.

It should be noted that the exemption will not permit the copying of photographs (which are artistic works) although if a photograph appears as an illustration in the text of a work, the copying would appear to be permissible.

The exemption will not, however, apply if, at the time the copy was made, the librarian who made it, knew, or could by reasonable enquiry ascertain, the name and address of the person entitled to authorise the making of the copy[42].

A librarian or archivist of a prescribed library or archive may, if the prescribed conditions are complied with, make a copy of any item in the permanent collection of the library or archive without infringing copyright in any literary, dramatic or musical work, or any illustrations accompanying such a work, or in the typographical arrangement of such a work.

The prescribed conditions include provisions restricting the making of copies to circumstances where it is not reasonably practicable to purchase a copy of the item in question. Additionally, the copy must be made in order to preserve or replace the item, by placing a copy in the permanent collection of the prescribed library or archive, in addition to or in place of the original item, or in order to replace in the permanent collection of another prescribed library or archive an item which has been lost destroyed or damaged[43].

42 S41.
43 S42.

8.20 Copying unpublished works

The librarian or archivist of a prescribed library or archive may, if certain conditions are complied with, make and supply a copy of, the whole or part of a literary, dramatic or musical work from a document in the library or archive, without infringing any copyright in a work, or any illustrations accompanying it[44].

This exemption will not apply if the work in question has been published before the document was deposited in the library or archive, or if the copyright owner had prohibited copying of the work, or at the time the copy was made the librarian or archivist who made it was aware, or ought to have been aware, of such fact[45].

The conditions include the following:

(a) copies are supplied only to persons satisfying the librarian, or archivist, that they are required for the purposes of research, or private study, and will not be used for any other purpose[46];
(b) no person is provided with more than one copy of the material[47]; and
(c) persons to whom copies are supplied are required to pay a sum not less than the cost attributable to their production, including any contribution to the general expense of the library or archive[48];
(d) any additional provisions contained in any regulations made by the Secretary of State.

44 S43(1).
45 S43(2)(a) and (b).
46 S43(3)(a).
47 S43(3)(b).
48 S43(3)(c).

8.21 Condition of export

If an article of cultural, or historical, importance, or interest, cannot be exported from the United Kingdom unless a copy of it is made and deposited in the appropriate library or archive, it is not an infringement of copyright to make that copy[49].

49 S44.

8.22 Recordings of folksongs

A recording of a performance of a song may be made by certain designated bodies, for the purpose of including it in an archive, without infringing any copyright in the words, as a literary work, or the accompanying musical work, provided that the words are unpublished, and of unknown authorship, at the time the recording is made, the making of the recording does not infringe any other copyright, and its making is not prohibited by any performer[50].

Copies of a sound recording made by a designated body may be supplied by the archivist without infringing copyright in the recording or the works included in it if:

(a) copies are only supplied to persons satisfying the archivist that they require them for the purpose of research, or private study, and will not use them for any other purpose[51]; and

(b) no person is furnished with more than one copy of the same recording[52].

50 S61(1) and (2).
51 S61(4)(a).
52 S61(4)(b).

F. Other permitted acts

8.23 Transfer of works in electronic form

The Copyright, Designs and Patents Act 1988 contains specific provisions which apply to copies of works in electronic form, which have been purchased on terms which, expressly, or impliedly, or by virtue of any law, allow the purchaser to copy the work, or adapt it, or make copies of an adaptation in connection with the purchaser's use of it[53].

If there are no express provisions prohibiting transfer by the purchaser, or imposing any obligations which continue after transfer, or prohibiting assignment or transfer, or providing for the terms on which a transferee may do what the purchaser was permitted to do, then anything which the purchaser was permitted to do may also be done by the transferee without infringement of copyright[54].

The provisions apply even where the original purchased copy is not available, and a further copy, which is used in its place, is transferred[55]. The provisions also apply to transfer to subsequent transferees[56], but where a copy, or adaptation, made by the purchaser is not transferred, then that copy is treated as an infringing copy after the date of the transfer[57].

The effect of the statutory provisions will, therefore, prevent the copying of electronic works as a substitute for purchasing them, and the provisions will not apply if they are excluded by the provisions of any relevant software licence.

53 S56(1).
54 S56(2).
55 S56(3).
56 S56(4).
57 S56(2).

8.24 Computer programs

A number of new permitted acts have been created as a result of the amendment of the Copyright, Designs and Patents Act 1988 by regulations implementing Directive 91/250 (see paragraph 17.7).[58]

It is not an infringement of copyright for a lawful user of a copy of a computer program to make any back-up copy for the purposes of the user's lawful use.[59] It is not an infringement of copyright for a lawful user of a copy of a computer program expressed in a low level language to convert it into a version expressed in a higher level language, or incidentally in the course of so converting the program, to copy it[60] provided certain conditions are met. The conditions are that it is necessary to decompile the program to achieve interoperability and that any information obtained is not used for any purpose other than the permitted objective.[61]

A lawful user of a computer program may also copy or adapt it, provided the copying is necessary for the user's lawful use and is not prohibited under any term or conditions of an agreement regulating the use of the program[62].

Any term of an agreement which prohibits or restricts the making of back-up copies of a program, or its decompilation is void[63], as is any term which prohibits or restricts the use of any device or means to observe study or test the functioning of the program in order to understand the ideas and principles which underlie it.[64]

58 The Copyright (Computer Programs) Regulations 1992, SI 1992 No 3233.
59 S 50 A.
60 S 50B(1).
61 S 50B(2).
62 S 50(1).
63 S 296 A(1)(a) and (b).
64 S 296 A(1)(c).

8.25 Artistic works, adaptations and abstracts

It is not an infringement of copyright in an artistic work to copy it, or to issue copies of it for the purpose of advertising the sale of the work[65].

Where the author of an artistic work is not the copyright owner, the author will not infringe the copyright by copying the work, and making another artistic work, provided that the author does not repeat or imitate the main design of the earlier work[66].

Where an act is permitted in respect of the copyright in a literary, dramatic or musical work, if that work is an adaptation of a previous work then the permitted act will not infringe the copyright in the work from which the adaptation was made[67].

Where an article on a scientific or technical subject is published in a periodical accompanied by an abstract indicating the contents of the article, it is not an infringement of copyright in the abstract, or in the article, to copy the abstract or issue copies of it to the public[68].

65 S63(1).
66 S64.
67 S76.
68 S60(1).

8.26 Playing of sound recordings for purposes of a club

It is not an infringement of the copyright in a sound recording to play it as part of the activities of a club, society or other organisation for the benefit of any such body if[69]:

(a) the body is not established or conducted for profit, and its main objects are charitable or are concerned with the advancement of religion, education or social welfare[70]; and

(b) the proceeds of any charge for admission to the place where the recording is to be heard are applied solely for the purposes of the organisation[71].

69 S67(1).
70 S67(2)(a).
71 S67(2)(b).

8.27 Rental of sound recordings, films and computer programs

The Secretary of State may provide by order that the rental to the public of sound recordings, films or computer programs shall be treated as licensed by the copyright owner subject only to the payment of such royalties as may be agreed or in default of agreement may be determined by the Copyright Tribunal[72].

72 S66(1).

8.28 Incidental recordings for purposes of broadcast or cable programme

Where a person is authorised to broadcast or include in a cable programme service a literary, dramatic or musical work or any adaptation of such a work, or an artistic work, or a sound recording or film, that person shall be treated as being licensed by the owner of the copyright of the work to have the following rights for the purposes of the broadcast or cable programme[73]:

(a) in the case of a literary or dramatic or musical work, or an adaptation, the right to make a sound recording, or film of the work, or adaptation[74];
(b) in the case of an artistic work, the right to take a photograph, or make a film of the work[75];
(c) in the case of a sound recording or film, the right to make a copy of it[76].

The licence is subject to the condition that the recording, film, photograph or copy in question shall not be used for any other purpose and shall be destroyed within 28 days of first being used for broadcasting the work, or including it in a cable programme service[77].

73 S68(1).
74 S68(2)(a).
75 S68(2)(b).
76 S68(2)(c).
77 S68(3).

8.29 Recording for supervision of broadcast

Copyright is not infringed by the making or use by the British Broadcasting Corporation of recordings of programmes, for the purpose of maintaining supervision and control over programmes. A similar provision exists in respect of the Independent Television Commission[78].

78 S69.

8.30 Recording for the purposes of time-shifting

The making, for private and domestic use, of a recording of a broadcast, or cable programme, solely for the purpose of enabling it to be viewed or listened to at a more convenient time does not infringe any copyright in the broadcast or cable programme, or any work included in it[79].

79 S70.

8.31 Photographs of television broadcasts or cable programmes

The making, for private and domestic use, of a photograph of the whole or any part of an image forming part of a television broadcast, or cable programme, or a copy of such a photograph, does not infringe any copyright in the broadcast or cable programme, or any film included in it[80].

80 S71.

8.32 Free public showing or playing

The showing or playing in public of a broadcast, or cable programme, to an audience who have not paid for admission to the place where the broadcast or programme is to be seen, or heard, does not infringe any copyright in the broadcast or cable programme, or any sound recording or film included in it[81].

The audience can be treated as having paid for admission to a place, if they have paid for admission to a place, of which it forms part, or of goods or services supplied to that place, at prices which are substantially attributable to the facilities afforded for seeing or hearing the broadcast programme, or at prices exceeding those usually charged there, and which are partly attributable to those facilities[82].

Persons who are admitted as residents or inmates of the place, or are admitted as members of a club or society, where the payment is only for membership of the club or society, and the provision of facilities for seeing or hearing broadcasts of programmes is only incidental to the main purposes of the club or society, shall not be regarded as having paid for admission[83].

81 S72(1).
82 S72(2).
83 S72(3).

8.33 Reception and re-transmission of broadcasts

Where a broadcast is made from a place in the United Kingdom and is, by reception and immediate retransmission, included in a cable programme service, the copyright of the programme is not infringed if the inclusion is pursuant to a requirement imposed under the Cable and Broadcasting Act 1984 S13(1), or Broadcasting Act 1990 Sch 12, if the broadcast is made for reception in the area in which the cable programme service is provided, and is not a satellite transmission, or an encrypted transmission[84].

84 S73.

8.34 Provision of sub-titled copies

Certain designated bodies may, for the purpose of assisting people who are deaf or hard of hearing, or physically or mentally handicapped in other ways, provide them with copies of television broadcasts or cable programmes which are sub-titled, or otherwise modified for their special needs, and make copies and issue copies to the public without infringing any copyright in the broadcasts, or cable programmes, or works included in them[85].

85 S74.

8.35 Recording for archival purposes

A recording of a broadcast or cable programme may be made for the purpose of being placed in an archive maintained by a designated body, without infringing any copyright in the broadcast, or cable programme, or in any work included in it[86].

86 S75.

8.36 Typefaces

It is not an infringement of copyright in an artistic work which consists of a design, or a typeface, to use a typeface in the ordinary course of typing, composing text, typesetting, or printing, or to possess an article for the purpose of such use, or to do anything in relation to material produced by such use[87].

87 S54.

8.37 Designs

It is not an infringement of copyright in any design document, or model, which records or embodies a design (other than one for an artistic work or a typeface) to make an article to the relevant design, or copy any such article[88].

The Copyright, Designs and Patents Act creates a new design right, which applies to articles made by industrial process, and such articles are no longer protected by copyright, but by the new design right which subsists for 15 years from the end of the year in which the design document or model was created[89] or, if articles made from the design are made available for sale or hire within five years from the end of that calendar year, ten years from the end of the calendar year in which they were so made available[90].

Where an artistic work has been exploited with the consent of its copyright owner by making articles, through an industrial process, and these articles have been marketed, it will not be an infringement of copyright in the work to make articles of any description after 25 years from the end of the calendar year in which the first articles were marketed[91].

88 S51(1).
89 S216(1)(a).
90 S216(1)(b).
91 S52(2).

132

8.38   Public administration

Copyright is not infringed by anything done for the purposes of parliamentary or judicial proceedings[92], or for the purpose of reporting such proceedings[93], or those of a Royal Commission or statutory inquiry[94].

Where material is open to public inspection, or is on a statutory register, any copyright in the material is not infringed by copying, or issuing copies, of certain factual material[95].

Additional exemptions exist in relation to certain acts of the Crown[96], public records[97] and acts authorised by Acts of Parliament[98].

92 S45(1).
93 S45(2).
94 S46(1).
95 S47.
96 S48.
97 S49.
98 S50.

8.39   Performances and moral rights

Although certain acts are permitted in relation to copyright works, it is important to remember that acts which may be done without infringing copyright (by virtue of the provisions referred to in paragraphs 8.6 to 8.38) may still infringe performers' rights or violate moral rights.

The Copyright, Designs and Patents Act 1988 contains provisions which provide in relation to performers' rights the same types of exemptions as those referred to in paragraphs 8.12 to 8.38, but where a publisher is making material available in electronic or multimedia format (see Chapter 19) it is possible that this material may contain performances, the reproduction of which is prohibited unless certain acts are complied with (see paragraphs 6.7 to 6.15).

It is equally important for publishers to be aware that the use of a copyright work by virtue of the "fair dealing" provisions (see paragraphs 8.3 to 8.5) will not immunise a publisher from liability to an author for the derogatory treatment of the author's work (see paragraphs 5.10 to 5.13).

G.   Use of Crown and Parliamentary copyright

8.40   Her Majesty's Stationery Office ("HMSO")

The 1956 Copyright Act provided that copyright in all works commissioned by a Government department was claimed for the Crown. Under the 1988 Copyright, Designs and Patents Act, Crown copyright now covers only those works "made by her Majesty or by an officer or servant of the Crown in the course of [their] duties"[99]. The authority to administer Crown Copyright is granted by her Majesty to the controller of HMSO by means of Royal Letters Patent and all rights in relation to Crown Copyrights and other copyrights belonging to the Crown are administered by HMSO.

The Copyright, Designs and Patents Act 1988 created a new category of

Parliamentary copyright[100]. The authority for Parliamentary copyright lies with the Clerk of the Parliaments for House of Lords material and with the Speaker of the House of Commons for Commons material. Those Parliamentary items which HMSO publishes are administered by the Controller of HMSO on the conditions similar to those pursuant to which Crown copyright is administered[101].

For copyright purposes, Crown and Parliamentary copyright material is divided into the following general categories:

(a) statutory material including Bills and Acts of Parliament, Statutory Rules and Orders and Statutory Instruments;
(b) reports of House of Lords and House of Commons debates (Hansard), Lords Minutes, the Vote Bundle, the Commons Order-Books and Commons Statutory Instruments List;
(c) other Parliamentary papers published by HMSO, including reports of select committees of both Houses;
(d) other Parliamentary material not published by HMSO;
(e) non-Parliamentary material, comprising all papers of Government departments and Crown bodies – both published and unpublished – not contained in other classes;
(f) charts and navigational material published by the Ministry of Defence (Hydrographic Department), and maps and other items in all media published by Ordnance Survey.

99 S163.
100 S165.
101 See general notice dated 25 June 1990.

8.41 Reproduction of Crown and Parliamentary copyright material

Considerable freedom is permitted in relation to the reproduction of material listed in paragraph 8.40(a) to (c). All Crown rights in relation to this material are, however, reserved, and will be asserted in cases where the material is reproduced in an undesirable context, or where the reproduction of the material falls outside conditions specified in HMSO's guidelines for reproduction, or where reproduction could result in a significant loss of sale of official publications.

The guidelines issued by HMSO in relation to the material listed in paragraph 8.40 are as follows.

(a) Statutory material

There is no objection to the reproduction of extracts (defined as being up to 30% of the original publication) provided that the source is acknowledged as being Crown or Parliamentary Copyright, as appropriate. Permission is, however, required if the HMSO official publication is to be used as camera-ready copy. Copies of Acts of Parliament, Statutory Rules and Orders, and Statutory Instruments, other than those reproduced by the order of HMSO, do not have the legal standing of officially published versions produced by HMSO.

The reproduction of excerpts of more than 30% of the original publication or the complete text is not normally allowed during the following embargo periods:

– for Bills and Acts of Parliament, six months from the date of publication; and
– for Statutory Instruments, Orders and Rules, three months from the date of publication.

The above embargo periods will be waived if the texts are reproduced as part of a book or journal, which contains substantial annotations to the text, or commentary on them, in which case no permission is required, unless the official publication is to be used as camera-ready copy. Again, the source must be acknowledged as being either Crown or Parliamentary Copyright, whichever is appropriate.

Outside the above embargo periods, there is no objection to the reproduction of material in this category.

(b)   Official reports and House business papers

Reproduction of this material is not allowed in relation to advertising, but these publications may otherwise be reproduced freely, provided the source is acknowledged as Parliamentary copyright, and provided that extracts are produced verbatim.

If it is intended to use an official publication as camera-ready copy, or if extracts form a substantial part of the reproduction, then permission will be required.

Where it is intended to publish unofficial reports of proceedings in Parliament, HMSO warns relevant persons that even though the material may comprise verbatim reports of speeches as reported in the official report, anyone publishing it will not have the same rights of privilege in proceedings for defamation (see paragraph 9.27) as those enjoyed by the official report.

(c)   Other Parliamentary papers

There is no objection to the reproduction of brief extracts of up to 5% of the whole publication, and it is not necessary to seek permission from HMSO before doing so, and no fees are levied. The source must, however, be acknowledged as either Crown or Parliamentary Copyright.

Extracts of longer than 5% must not be reproduced without the formal permission of HMSO, which will not normally permit reproduction until six months after the date of publication by HMSO.

(d)   Other Parliamentary material published by HMSO

All applications for reproduction of this material must be referred to the officials of the relevant House.

(e) Non-Parliamentary material

This category covers a very wide range of material published by HMSO, Government departments and bodies. It also covers unpublished material.

While it is desirable that information of this nature should be widely known, official publication is the usual channel for the purpose, and the exercise of the Crown's copyright is necessary to prevent official material from misuse by unfair or misleading selection, undignified association, or undesirable use for advertising purposes.

The rights of the Crown will, therefore, normally be enforced in relation to material in this category, and acknowledgement of the sources and of the permission of the Controller of HMSO or the department and bodies which have delegated authority to HMSO to grant such permission will be required, as well as payment of suitable fees payable to authorise reproduction.

The Controller of HMSO has discretion to waive or reduce fees in respect of applications for use of material for professional, technical or scientific purposes, where profit is not a primary purpose of reproduction. Consideration for reducing or waiving fees will also be given in the case of reproduction in works of scholarship, journals of learned societies and similar non-profit-making bodies, reproduction for educational purposes and for other purposes where the need for the fullest assimilation of official information is paramount, and the commercial or other aspects are relatively unimportant.

(f) Charts and navigational material

The administration of Crown copyrights relating to this category of material is subject to arrangements for delegation between the Controller of HMSO and the Ministry of Defence (Hydrographic Department) and Ordnance Survey and applications for permission to reproduce the material should be made to such parties.

8.42 Limitations on HMSO consent

Consent will normally authorise printed reproduction and publication in the United Kingdom only. Where consent is sought in relation to computer software (which is treated in copyright terms as a literary work – see paragraph 3.5) it is the policy of the Crown to acquire use of the software rather than to buy the copyright of the software. The Central Computer and Telecommunications Agency will, if requested, provide guidance on how Crown requirements are met in such situations. The right to reproduce Crown or Parliamentary copyright material outside the UK or in other than printed form will need advance clearance from HMSO and, in some cases, permissions from third parties.

8.43 Royal Arms

It is not permitted to reproduce the Royal Arms or other official printing and publishing imprints, nor is it permitted for reproduction to purport to have been published by authority of Her Majesty.

H. Rights clearances

8.44 Clearance procedures for publishers

The process of obtaining permissions and other necessary releases, licences and consents is an important process for publishers. Although an author's contract will frequently require authors to obtain all necessary permissions (see Document 4 Clause 1.7), it would be neither safe, nor advisable, for a publisher to rely totally on the author having taken all necessary actions.

It is therefore advisable for publishers to devise standard procedures, or rules, which they will apply to all their publications, in order to ensure that the publications:

(a) do not infringe any rights of copyright (see Chapters 3 and 4);
(b) do not infringe any moral rights (see Chapter 5);
(c) do not infringe any performers' rights (see paragraphs 6.7 to 6.15);
(d) do not give rise to liability in defamation, negligent misstatement, or other matters (see Chapter 10);
(e) do not give rise to any liability in respect of contempt of court, breach of official secrets legislation, or privacy legislation (see Chapter 10);
(f) do not give rise to any other liability (see, for example, paragraphs 2.17, 2.18, 13.9, 13.10).

A basic checklist, outlining some of the points which may need to be considered in relation to permissions, can be found in Document 30. The list will not necessarily be comprehensive and will need to be reviewed in the light of all the circumstances, as will the various permissions, releases and waivers which may be found in Documents 16 to 29.

Additional factors may need to be considered in relation to multimedia use (see Chapter 19) and, depending on the manner of implementation of European legislation relating to rental rights and harmonisation of the term of copyright, there may be a number of areas of complexity which will require close examination (see paragraphs 20.2 to 20.16).

9. Liability for content

[IMPORTANT NOTE: Please read the section "About this book" on page v, before referring to any of the matters in this chapter]

A. Introduction

9.1 Purpose of this chapter

This chapter examines some of the large number of areas in which publishers might incur potentially vast financial liability in relation to the content of their works. It is not to be read by persons with a nervous disposition. The number of areas in which publishers and multimedia companies may incur liability, and the wide scope of these areas attests to the degree of skill, knowledge, and expertise required by them, if they are simply to stay in business.

The principal areas in which liability may be incurred are organised in alphabetical order in this chapter, starting with advertising standards and ending with statutory deposit obligations.

The chapter does not cover liability in relation to matters relating to the press, such as contempt of court, reporting restrictions, secrecy and national security, the Press Complaints Commission, or proposed reforms of legislation relating to privacy and the press – these matters are considered in Chapter 10. Nor does this chapter cover liability in relation to the sale of goods, or consumer protection matters, or liability under the Trade Descriptions Act – these matters are considered in the context of distribution of product under Chapter 12. Copyright infringement and trade mark infringement are also outside the scope of this chapter, and are dealt with in Chapter 13.

The financial liabilities which companies may face under proceedings brought in connection with the matters referred to in this chapter are potentially enormous. The importance of taking proper legal advice cannot be over-emphasised. This chapter should be used only to enable the reader to identify whether or not a potential liability exists. If a particular risk or problem is not referred to here, it should not be assumed that it is safe to proceed.

Any reader using this chapter as a substitute for taking proper legal advice does so at their peril.

B. Advertising standards

9.2 Misleading advertising

The Advertising Standards Authority administers the British Code of Advertising Practice and the British Code of Sales Promotion Practice in conjunction with the Code of Advertising Practice Committee. The Authority also administers the rules for database management which are set out in paragraphs 18.12 to 18.17.

This self-regulatory system has been established pursuant to the Control of Misleading Advertising Regulations 1988 which gives effect to a European Union Directive on misleading advertising.

The regulations give the Director General of Fair Trading power to obtain an injunction to ban the publication of misleading advertisements in the press, in direct mail, in magazines and in posters. The Director General is empowered to act only when a complaint has been received, and is not permitted to clear advertisements in advance of publication although (s)he can start proceedings to prevent the publication of an advertisement which will be misleading[1].

1 Control of Misleading Advertisements Regulations 1988, SI 1988/915 Reg 5.

9.3 Circumstances where the Director General of Fair Trading cannot act

The Director General may not act in relation to any advertisement if the relevant complaint is about taste or decency, or is frivolous or vexatious[2].

The Director General is also unable to act if the complaint is about:

(a) activities, products or services which are alleged to be objectionable or unsatisfactory in their quality or performance as opposed to complaints about the advertisements themselves;

(b) advertisements which are not likely to affect the economic behaviour of the persons to whom they are aimed, or injure a competitor of the advertiser;

(c) advertisements published by private individuals not acting in a business capacity, such as advertisements for selling personal possessions through the classified columns of local newspapers.

There are other situations where the Director General may not act. It is outside the power of the Director General to seek compensation, or other forms of redress for the person making the complaint, since the Director General is concerned with preventing publication of misleading material.

2 Control of Misleading Advertisements Regulations 1988 Reg 4(1).

9.4 Circumstances where the Director General can act

The Director General is empowered to act on receipt of any complaint in relation to a misleading advertisement.

An advertisement is "any form of representation which is made in connection with a trade, business, craft or profession in order to promote the supply or transfer of goods or services, immovable property, rights or obligations". The definition has a wide scope which will also cover editorial mentions of products, competitions or sponsored events[3].

An advertisement is misleading if it in any way deceives, or is likely to deceive, persons to whom it is addressed and by reason of its deceptive nature is likely to affect those persons' economic behaviour, or to injure or be likely to injure a competitor of the person whose interest the advertisement seeks to promote[4].

An advertisement will be likely to affect the economic behaviour of consumers if it induces, or is likely to induce, them to part with money for what is being advertised. There are a number of ways in which an advertisement can be misleading, such as containing a false statement of fact – which it is possible to prove or disprove by evidence – or concealing or leaving out important facts. Where the Director General considers that the gravity of the misleading is such as to warrant court action, and no immediate undertaking is given to amend or discontinue the advertisement, the Director General may seek a High Court injunction, or in Scotland an interdict, which will prevent publication of the offending advertisement, until the case can be fully argued in court.

The court can order any person who is concerned with the publication of the advertisement, to provide evidence to show that the factual claims made of the advertisement are accurate, and if such person fails to provide adequate evidence to substantiate the claims, the court may refuse to regard the claims, as being accurate[5].

3 Control of Misleading Advertisements Regulations 1988 Reg 2(1).
4 Ibid Reg 2(2).
5 Ibid Reg 6(3).

9.5 British Code of Advertising Practice

The rules of the British Code of Advertising Practice apply to:

(a) advertisements and newspapers, magazines and other printed publications;
(b) indoor and outdoor posters and advertisements;
(c) cinema and videocassette commercials;
(d) advertisements on viewdata services;
(e) advertising material such as brochures and leaflets which are mailed or

delivered directly or reach their public as inserts in newspapers or other publications[6].

The Code's rules do not apply to:

(a)   broadcast commercials;
(b)   advertisements in media principally intended for circulation outside the United Kingdom;
(c)   advertisements addressed either directly or in professional journals to members of the medical or allied professions in their professional capacities[7].

6 See British Code of Advertising Practice Part A 1.1.
7 Ibid Part A 1.2.

9.6   The principal points of the Code

(a)   All advertisements should be legal, decent, honest and truthful[8].
(b)   All advertisements should be prepared with a sense of responsibility to the consumer and society[9].
(c)   Advertisements should conform to the principles of fair competition generally accepted in business[10].

8 Ibid Part B 2.
9 Ibid Part B 15.
10 Ibid Part B 21.

9.7   Legal, decent, honest and truthful

(a)   The advertisements should contain nothing which is in breach of the law or is likely to bring the law into disrepute, or omit anything which the law requires[11].
(b)   No advertisement should contain any matter which is likely to contain grave or widespread offence or give expression to attitudes or opinions about which society is divided[12].
(c)   No advertiser should seek to take improper advantage of any character-istics or circumstance which may make consumers vulnerable, and the design and presentation of advertisements should be such as to permit each part of the advertiser's case to be easily grasped and clearly understood[13].
(d)   No advertisement, whether by inaccuracy, ambiguity, exaggeration, ommission, or otherwise, should mislead consumers of any matter likely to influence their attitude to the advertised product[14].
(e)   Advertisements which contain political claims should be readily recog-nisable as advertisements, and cause no confusion as to the identity or state of the advertiser[15].
(f)   Where a product is advertised as being "free", any incidental costs which will need to be incurred in acquiring it must be clearly indicated. Advertisers may not seek to recover costs of a "free" product by imposing additional charges which they would not normally make, or

by inflating any incidental expenses, or by altering composition or quality, or by increasing the price of any other product which they require to be bought as a precondition of obtaining the "free" product[16].

It should be noted that incidental minor inaccuracies, unorthodox spelling and the like will not infringe the Code's rules on truthful presentation, nor will obvious untruths and exaggerations which are evidently intended to attract attention and cause amusement, if there is no likelihood of consumers misunderstanding.

The rules of the Code as to truthful presentation do not place any constraint upon free expression of opinions, including subjective assessments of the quality or desirability of a product, provided that it is clear what is being expressed in the opinion, and there is no likelihood that the opinion, or the way it is expressed, is misleading customers.

11 British Code of Advertising Practice Part B 2.1.
12 Ibid Part B 3.1.
13 Ibid Part B 4.1.
14 Ibid Part B 5.1.
15 Ibid Part B 6.3.
16 Ibid Part B 8.1.

9.8 Responsibility to society

(a) No advertisement should play on fear, or excite distress, without good reason[17].

(b) Advertisements should neither condone, nor incite, violence, or anti-social behaviour[18].

(c) Advertisements should not portray or refer to any living persons, unless their express prior permission has been obtained, although the reference or portrayal may be acceptable without prior permission where the advertisement contains nothing which is inconsistent with the position of the person to whom reference is made, and does not abrogate that person's right to enjoy a reasonable degree of privacy. A reference or portrayal may also be acceptable where the purpose of the advertisement is to promote a book or a film, where the person concerned is the subject of that book or film[19].

(d) Advertisements should not show, or advocate, dangerous behaviour or unsafe practices, except in the context of promotion of safety[20].

17 British Code of Advertising Practice Part B 15.1.
18 Ibid Part B 16.1.
19 Ibid Part B 17.1 and 17.2.
20 Ibid Part B 19.1.

9.9 Fair competition

(a) Advertisers should not seek to discredit the product of their competitors by any unfair means[21].

(b) No advertisement should so closely resemble another advertisement as to be likely to mislead or confuse[22].

21 British Code of Advertising Practice Part B 22.1.
22 Ibid Part B 24.

C. Blasphemy

9.10 Blasphemy generally

Blasphemy is a criminal offence and may be punished by fine or imprisonment, at the discretion of the court. The offence is committed by anyone who publishes contemptuous, reviling, scurrilous, or ludicrous matter, relating to God, Jesus Christ, the Bible or the formularies of the Church of England.

It is not blasphemy to attack any religion except christianity. The person committing the offence must intend to publish, but need not intend that the words amount to blasphemy. It is irrelevant whether the words are spoken or written, but if they are written they may constitute blasphemous libel.

D. Financial Services Act

9.11 Financial Services Act generally

The Financial Services Act 1986 provides that a person may carry on the business of giving investment advice only if that person is an authorised person or an exempt person[23]. Authorisation is from the Securities and Investments Board or may be obtained by virtue of being a member of a self-regulating organisation, or being certified by a recognised professional body[24].

In order for authorisation to be needed by a publisher or journalist the following factors have to exist:

(a) investment advice must be being given;
(b) the advice must be being given during the course of a business giving investment advice; and
(c) the advice must fall outside certain freedom of the press exemptions.

23 Financial Services Act 1986 S3.
24 Ibid Chapter III SS7–34.

9.12 Giving investment advice

Investment advice is given when a person gives advice on the merits of buying, selling, subscribing or underwriting an investment to another person in their capacity as investor[25]. Offering or agreeing to offer advice is also counted by the Financial Services Act as giving investment advice, and potential investors are also counted as investors. The Financial Services Act extends to any advice in connection with exercising any right conferred by an investment to buy, sell, underwrite or convert an investment[26].

A number of matters do not count as investments for the purpose of the Financial Services Act. These include bank accounts, building society accounts, national savings accounts, houses, land, insurance policies which do not have any savings element, works of art, coins and stamps.

Investments include stocks and shares, unit trusts, pension plans which consist of life assurance or unit trusts, futures and options, and life assurance policies which have savings[27].

Advice on investment business or general generic advice on investments does not count as investment advice; nor does neutral information. But advice on merits of specific investments is counted as investment advice.

25 Financial Services Act 1986 Sch 1 Part II Para 12.
26 Ibid Sch 1 Part II Para 15.
27 Ibid Sch 1 Part I.

9.13 The business of giving investment advice

Where advice is given by a person to their friends or relations they will not need to be authorised by the Financial Services Act. They will, however, need to be authorised if the advice is given in the course of a business which they are carrying on.

Even where a newspaper or publication gives free advice, for example to readers' letters, the business of giving advice is being carried on.

When a newspaper or periodical runs a feature on an investment, in connection with suspected fraud for the purpose of warning investors and potential investors, the Securities and Investment Board does not currently consider that such a feature would be caught by the provisions of the Financial Services Act, although this would be a question for the courts to decide.

Where any fee is given for advice in connection with an investment the activity will clearly come within the scope of the Financial Services Act.

9.14 Freedom of the press

The business of giving investment advice does not extend to advice given in a newspaper, journal or magazine or other periodical publication if the principal purpose of the publication is not to lead persons to invest in any particular investment[28].

The Securities and Investment Board has the power to issue a certificate to the proprietor of any such newspaper, magazine or periodical. Investment advice given in any publication which has a certificate, or is eligible for one, will not be counted as investment advice[29]. The exemption does not cover advice given outside the pages of a certified, or certifiable, publication, and it applies only in respect of periodical publications.

28 Financial Services Act 1986 Sch 1 Part II Para 25(1).
29 Ibid Sch 1 Part II Para 25(2).

E. Imprints

9.15 Name and address of printer

The Newspapers, Printers and Reading Rooms Repeal Act 1869 (as amended by the Criminal Justice Act 1982 S 46) requires the name and address of the printer to appear on the first or last page of each book which is intended to be published or distributed. The printer is required to print in legible characters his or her name and usual place of abode or business, as is every person "who shall publish or disperse or assist in publishing or dispersing" any printed paper or book. Failure to comply with the obligation will give rise to a fine of not more than level 1 on the standard scale[30].

The requirements of the Newspapers, Printers and Reading Rooms Repeal Act 1869 have been relaxed by the Printers Imprint Act 1961 which states that a printer shall not be required to print the statement of the printer's name and usual place of abode or business (referred to in the Act as the "Printers' Imprint") on any paper or book unless it comprises either[31]:

"(a) Words grouped together in a manner calculated to convey a message other than words calculated to convey only a greeting invitation or other message in a conventional form[32] or

(b) a drawing illustration or other picture other than a design representing only a geometrical floral or other design or a registered trade mark or any combination thereof.[33]"

30 See the Newspapers, Printers and Reading Rooms Repeal Act 1869 Sch 2 S2.
31 See the Printers Imprint Act 1961 S1(1).
32 Ibid S1(1)(a).
33 Ibid S1(1)(b).

9.16 Preservation of copies

The Second Schedule of the Newspapers, Printers and Reading Rooms Repeal Act 1869 (as amended by the Criminal Justice Act 1982 S 46) requires printers "to keep a copy of every paper they print and write thereon and name and abode of their employer". The printer is also required to keep the copy and the information for six months after printing and to produce and show it to any Justice of the Peace within such times requires to see it. The maximum fine for omission, neglect or refusal is level 2 on the standard scale[34].

The Printers Imprint Act 1961 S 1 further relaxes the 1869 Act by providing that printers shall not be required to preserve, keep or prohibit any person from publishing or dispersing or assisting in publishing or dispersing a copy of any paper or book which is not required by either Act to bear the Printers' Imprint.

34 See the Newspapers, Printers and Reading Rooms Repeal Act 1869 Sch 2 S29.

F. Libel and slander

9.17 What is defamation?

Defamation is the making of a defamatory statement. A defamatory statement can be written or spoken, and can be made directly, or by innuendo. A defamatory statement has been defined variously in a number of ways. It may be a statement which is calculated to injure the reputation of another person, by exposing that person to hatred, contempt or ridicule[35]. Or it may be a statement which conveys an imputation on a person which is disparaging or injurious to that person in their office, profession, calling, trade or business.

Or it may be words which would tend to lower a person in the estimation of right-thinking members of society generally.

35 Per Parke B, in *Parmiter v Coupland* (1840) 6 M&W P108.

9.18 Libel and slander

If a defamatory statement is made in writing or some other permanent form it will be libel. If the statement is oral it will constitute a slander. Slander and libel are actionable at civil law, although if a libel was intended to provoke a person to commit a breach of the peace or against the public interest criminal proceedings might be brought against the person making the defamatory statement. Dead people cannot be defamed, nor can a class of persons be defamed, although an action might lie from an individual if the individual could establish that they were the person referred to and defamed.

(a) Libel

A libel action may be brought in respect of defamatory statements made or conveyed by written or printed words, or in other permanent form, concerning an individual, which is published to a person other than that individual.

(b) Slander

An action for slander may be brought in respect of any defamatory statement made, or conveyed, by spoken words, sounds, looks, signs, gestures or some other non-permanent form about an individual, which is published to a person other than the individual.

In the case of an action for slander, however, the individual is required to show that they have suffered actual damage which must be proved, although some types of slander are actionable without providing this proof (see paragraph 9.20). Slander is not actionable as a criminal offence.

9.19 What is defamatory?

A number of stages must be gone through to determine whether a statement is defamatory or not. First, it must be established that the words in question would, under the circumstances in which they were published, have been understood by a reasonable man in a defamatory sense.

Second, the meaning of the words must be decided on. This meaning may go beyond the literal meaning of the words, and be an inference to be drawn from the context in which the words were published. The combination of this literal meaning, and any inference from the context is referred to as the natural and ordinary meaning. The secondary or extended meaning which a phrase may have will depend upon knowledge of external facts, and this secondary extended meaning is referred to as innuendo. The question of determining the natural and ordinary meaning of an expression is not governed by the legal rules for construction, but, rather, the meaning which the words would convey to ordinary people. Statements which allege fraud, dishonesty or dishonourable conduct on a person are actionable as are allegations of anti-social behaviour, mental incapacity, financial difficulty and all statements disparaging property or goods (see paragraph 9.24).

9.20 When is a slander actionable?

The following types of slander are actionable without proof of special damage (see paragraph 9.18(b)).

(a) Allegations that a person has committed a crime which is punishable by a prison sentence

Words which impart merely the suspicion that such an offence has been committed will not support a slander action unless special damage can be proved. The intention of the speaker is irrelevant[36].

To allege that a person is a villain or a swindler is not actionable without proof of special damage, unless the commission of an offence which is punishable by imprisonment is imputed to the person, or the allegation is calculated to disparage a person in the way of their trade.

(b) Words calculated to disparage a person in any office, trade, profession, calling or business held or carried on by them at the time of the publication of the words[37]

It is not necessary that the words are spoken of the person in connection with the office, trade, profession, calling or business. A statement will be disparaging if it imputes to any person a lack of some general essential quality for the office, trade, profession or calling such as honesty, fidelity, capacity, competence, experience, qualification, knowledge, skill, judgment or efficiency[38].

(c) Allegations of immoral conduct and allegations relating to contagious diseases

Generally any allegation of immoral conduct is defamatory but allegations of sexual immorality may not in some circumstances be defamatory. It is, however, defamatory to allege unchastity (which includes lesbianism) to a woman or girl[39]. A statement that a person is suffering from venereal disease is defamatory and it may be defamatory to state that a person suffers from an infectious disease, although it may not be defamatory to say that a person has suffered in the past from such a disease.

147

36 *Persen v Rainbow* [1922] 1 WWR 592; *Lewis v Daily Telegraph* [1964] AC 234.
37 Defamation Act 1952 S2.
38 *Robinson v Ward* (1958), *Times* 16 June.
39 Slander of Women Act 1891.

9.21 Publication of libel

A libel action can only be brought if there has been publication of the libel. If a person wishes to bring an action they have to show that the person against whom they are bringing it (the defendant) published a libel or caused it to be published to a third party[40]. Publication may occur by post, telegraph post and telegram or telex.

The requirement to have the defamatory statement published to a third party is satisfied if there is publication to the defamed person's wife or husband or employees, or the employees of the defendant. The requirement is not satisfied by publication to the person bringing the action, or publication to the defendant's spouse. A person who originally publishes a libel is not responsible for its subsequent re-publication. However, the spouse of the defendant may be the defendant's agent in publishing a libel to a third party, so as to make the defendant a publisher.

It should be noted that although publication to a third party is necessary for civil libel, in the case of criminal proceedings (see paragraph 9.25) publication to the person defamed will be enough.

Publication of a libel occurs when a defamatory statement which has been reduced in some permanent form is made known. Simply writing down the defamatory words does not amount to publication of a libel. Each time a libel is communicated, it amounts to a separate publication for which proceedings may be brought.

Unintentional publication may be actionable, as will negligently permitting another person to read a defamatory document. Incidental publication of defamatory statements may also amount to libel.

Incidental publication occurs where, for example, a person dictates a defamatory letter to their secretary. Publication of the slander will occur at the time of dictation and publication of the libel at the time it is typed, or read, by the secretary. Even where allegations are addressed to the person who is being defamed, if they are not marked "strictly private and confidential" they may be opened by that person's secretary, or another person, and the libel will then be published. If a letter containing a libel which is intended for, and addressed to the person libelled, is wrongly opened by somebody else, in error, then there may be no publication.

40 *Pullman v Hill* [1891] 1 QB.

9.22 Liability for publication

Every person or company which publishes or participates in the publication of libellous matter will be liable as a publisher.

The owner of a newspaper is answerable at law for the actions of its employees, and will be liable unless the owner can prove, by way of defence, that the publication in question was made without the owner's authority, consent, or knowledge, and that the incident of publication did not occur as a result of lack of due care or caution on the owner's part.

A printer who distributes a libellous statement will be liable as a publisher of such a statement, and may also be liable if a defamatory illustration is contained in a work, even though the illustration may not have been printed by the printer, if the text printed by the printer contains a reference to the illustration.

A printer may also be liable if a defamatory statement printed by the printer is made known to the printer's compositors, or other employees, even though it may never be printed.

A company who employs a person is liable for any publication of a libel carried out in the course of that person's employment, within the scope of their authority or employment. If the employee in the course of their employment writes and publishes defamatory statements which are known to be untrue, the employer will be liable.

In some cases the original publisher of a libel will be liable for its republication, if the person making the subsequent publication was simply following instructions from the original publisher who provided the text of the defamatory matter, which the subsequent publisher used unchanged.

It is not, however, a defence for a person to say that they published a libel at the request of the author and disclosed the author's name at the time of publication. This will not be a defence, even where the subsequent publisher believed the statement to be true, but any damages award may be mitigated.

The innocent publication of a libel will not be actionable. For example, postmen delivering libellous letters are not liable for their contents nor will booksellers, or librarians, be liable for circulating defamatory books, provided at the time of circulation they did not know that the books were defamatory. Newspaper sellers are in a similar position.

Where a person wishes to establish innocence, the person must prove that they did not know the document concerned was libellous, and that their ignorance was not due to any negligence on their part and that it was unreasonable for the person to suppose that the document was libellous[41].

41 Contempt of Court Act 1981 S3.

9.23 Publication of slander

A slander is published when words which are defamatory of the person defamed are spoken in the presence of a third party, who hears them and understands them, in a defamatory sense. Dictating what is to become a libellous letter will amount to publication of a slander (see paragraph 9.18 (b)). It may be that, where a slanderous statement has been reduced into printed form, the (silent) reading of that printed statement will be the publication of a libel.

Even if a person repeats what they already heard, the act of repetition may constitute a slander. The original speaker is responsible for the original act of publication of a slander but, where the words are repeated, the original speaker will not, generally, be liable for the repetition. The repetition of the slander will, of course, give rise to a separate course of action against the person repeating it. Where the original slanderer is liable for the repetition, that person may also be liable for subsequent damages.

The original speaker will be responsible for the repetition, where that person intended the slander to be repeated to a subsequent person, and authorised it to be repeated.

9.24 Slander of title, goods and malicious falsehood

(a) Slander of title

In order to bring a successful claim for slander of title of goods, the person bringing the action must prove that the relevant words were false, that they were published maliciously, and that they caused special damage[42].

Slander of title occurs when a person falsely and maliciously disparages the right of ownership of a person's land or personal property and causes special damage. There are certain exceptions, which do not require special damage to be proved[43]. Disparagement consists in alleging that the owner's rights of ownership are defective, or the owner has a limited right to deal with the property, and the disparagement may be oral or in writing.

In an action for slander of title the person bringing the action is required to prove a bad motive (or malice) on the part of the person who committed the slander. There will be no malice if the words spoken were honestly or wrongly believed[44], or they were spoken in the honest execution of a supposed duty. In determining whether or not the person being sued (the defendant) had a bad motive, or not, a court will consider whether, in all the circumstances, a defendant acted in good faith, paying regard to the character, situation, prejudices and passions of the defendant, and not whether the defendant's belief was founded on such grounds as would be held of a man of sound sense and business knowledge.

(b) Slander of goods

Slander of goods occurs where a person falsely and maliciously publishes words relating to goods, and causes special damage, although the need to prove special damages is not necessary in some cases[45]. A mere puff, such as where a person states in an advertisement that their goods are superior to their rivals, will not be actionable, but where the words spoken or written go beyond this, and contain untrue statements of fact about a rival's goods, it will be actionable[46].

(c) Malicious falsehood

Where falsehoods are published maliciously either orally, or in writing, and are calculated, in the ordinary course of things, to produce actual damage, and do produce actual damage, then the person who suffers the damage may bring an action for malicious or injurious falsehood.

(d) Malice and damage

In actions for slander of goods and malicious falsehood, malice is an important element which needs to be proved. For this purpose it is necessary to show a dominant motive which is dishonest. There would be no malice if the defendant spoke or wrote honestly, even if wrongly, or carelessly, believing the words to be true, or merely for the purpose of advancing the sale of the defendant's own goods, or in pursuit of the defendant's duty.

In an action for slander of title, slander of goods or malicious falsehood, it is not necessary to allege, or prove, special damage if:

– the words on which the action was founded were calculated to cause pecuniary damage to the person bringing the action, and were published in written or other permanent form[47]; or
– the words were calculated to cause pecuniary damage to the person bringing the action in respect of any office, profession, calling, trade or business, held, or carried on by, that person at the time of publication[48].

42 *Ratcliffe v Evans* [1892] 2 QB, CA.
43 Defamation Act 1952 S3(1).
44 *Balden v Shorter* [1933] 1 Ch 427.
45 Defamation Act 1952 S3(1).
46 *Harman v Delany* [1731] 2 Str.
47 Defamation Act 1952 S3(1)(a).
48 Ibid S3(1)(b).

9.25 Defamatory libel

Any person who maliciously publishes any defamatory libel may face criminal proceedings where the publication is likely to disturb the peace, or seriously affect the defamed person's reputation. No proceedings for criminal libel will be brought where the defamatory words were spoken, although the defendant may be bound over to good behaviour depending on the circumstances. A libel on a foreign ambassador is an offence at common law, and punishable by reason of its ability to interrupt peaceful relations between this country and the ambassador's country. Where a person threatens to publish libel on a living or dead person, the criminal offence of blackmail may also be committed.

Criminal prosecutions cannot, without the order of a judge, be brought against any proprietor, publisher, editor or other person responsible for the publication in a newspaper of any libel. Where such proceedings are brought, they may be dismissed summarily, if a court receives evidence to show that publication was for the public benefit, or that matters charged were true, or that the report was fair and accurate and published without malice.

Where a newspaper is so charged it may plead that the matters were true[49] and that their publication was for the public benefit. A further defence is that the publication was in fair comment[50]. Additionally, where the matter relates to a newspaper report of judicial proceedings, the newspaper will have a defence of privilege in respect of any report published contemporaneously with those proceedings, provided it does not contain any blasphemous or indecent matter. Fair and accurate reports of proceedings of a public meeting which are published in a newspaper are also privileged[51].

49 Libel Act 1843 S6.
50 *Goldsmith v Pressdram* [1977] QB 83.
51 Law of Libel Amendment Act 1888 S4.

G. Defences to defamation

9.26 Justification

The defence of justification is available where the statement complained about was true in substance and in fact. Because the law presumes that every man is of good repute until the contrary is proved, the defendant is required to prove that the defamatory words are true, or substantially true. Where justification is used as a defence, the defendant must show that the statements of fact are true, or substantially true, and any inferences are also true. It is possible to use truth, not only as a defence to all defamatory statements, but also as a defence to just part of them.

Where justification is pleaded in respect of a comment, both the facts on which the comment is based, and any inference, is required to be shown to be justified. Where a defendant has written a letter of apology in respect of certain statements made by the defendant, the apology will not prevent the defendant from using justification as a defence in respect of subsequent statements.

Where a person makes a statement which purports to be the reported speech of an identified third party, the reported statement will still be actionable.

Where a person is a rehabilitated offender, whose convictions no longer have to be disclosed, a defendant may use the fact of the spent conviction to support a plea of justification, but if publication of the spent conviction has been made with malice, the plea of justification will not succeed.

Where an allegation is not justified at the time it is made but facts occur which subsequently justify or support the allegation, then these facts may be used in any defence.

9.27 Absolute privilege

It is in the public interest for persons in certain positions, such as members of the judiciary, to be permitted to express themselves with complete freedom. In order to secure the independence of judges, witnesses and lawyers, their words and actions in court proceedings are the subject of absolute privilege. In other words, no legal proceedings may be taken against them for words spoken in the ordinary course of any judicial proceedings.

The proceedings which are the subject of absolute privilege include the full gamut of legal proceedings in the House of Lords, the Appeal Court, the High Court, County Courts, Coroner's Courts, Magistrates' Courts and proceedings before Tribunals and enquiries. Communications passing between solicitors and their clients are also the subject of absolute privilege and are free from actions of the type referred to in paragraphs 9.17 to 9.25.

Words spoken in Parliament by a Member of Parliament are absolutely privileged[52]. The privilege does not, however, extend to words spoken by an

MP outside Parliament[53]. Authorised reports and copies of Parliamentary proceedings in certain circumstances enjoy absolute privilege.

Fair and accurate reports in any newspaper or broadcast are similarly privileged provided they do not include any blasphemous or indecent matter, and provided such reports are published contemporaneously with the relevant proceedings[54].

52 *Ex parte Wason* [1869] LR 4 QB 573.
53 *R v Lord Abingdon* (1794) 1 Esp 226.
54 Defamation Act 1952 S7.

9.28 Qualified privilege

Qualified privilege is a defence to proceedings in defamation, which exists for any person acting in good faith, without any improper motive, who makes a statement about another, which is untrue and defamatory. The number of circumstances for which qualified privilege may exist is very large. Generally speaking they all share one common feature, which is that there is a duty or interest on the part of the person making the communication towards the person who receives the communication.

In order to rely on the defence of qualified privilege, the person making the statement has to show that a duty to disclose information exists[55]. To defeat the defence, the person bringing the action may show that the words complained of were actuated by express malice. If the words were not the subject of privilege, the defence would not arise, and the person uttering them would be liable if they were defamatory. Even where a defendant is not acting out of malice, and believes the occasion to have been privileged, the defendant may still be liable.

Occasions when communications are privileged are occasions where the person who makes the communication has a legal, social or moral duty, or interest, to make the communication to the person who receives it, and the person who receives it has a corresponding duty or interest to receive the communication. Privileged statements are statements which are made in pursuance of any social, legal or moral duty, to a person with a corresponding duty, or interest, to receive them. Additionally, statements which are made in protection of a common interest, and statements which are made in answer to enquiries, are also the subject of qualified privilege.

Statements made by employers as to employees' characters are protected by qualified privilege, even if they are untrue. This privilege may in certain circumstances extend not only to communications made to persons who are thinking of engaging the employee, or who have already taken the employee on, but also to communications made to previous employers. Obviously, however, great care should be taken in relation to statements made about current or former employees.

Other examples of communications which are the subject of privilege include statements made in reasonable protection of a person's interests, publication of information from statutory registers and statements made in investigating crime. Where a communication is privileged, the privilege is extended to acts of publication which are incidental to the communication of the privileged information. For example, where privileged communication occurs in a letter, the act of dictating, or typing, or opening the letter will not amount to publication.

55 *Pullman v Hill* [1891] 1 QB 524.

9.29 Fair comment

Fair comment is a separate defence from the defence of privilege. It must be based on facts which are proved to be true and, if used to justify statements which are expressions of opinion, rather than statements of fact, both the facts and any inferences drawn from the facts and any comments on the facts need to be shown to be true.

In order to use the defence of fair comment, the following must be shown:

(a) the comment must have been on a matter of public interest[56];
(b) the comment must have been based on one or more facts which were stated accurately;
(c) the comment must have amounted to a fair comment on the facts.

Where a comment is published maliciously the defence of fair comment will be defeated.

56 *London Artists Limited v Littler* [1969] 2 QB 375.

9.30 Apology and amends

The defence of apology is available in respect of libels which are published in newspapers or periodicals. In order to use this defence, it must be shown that the libel was inserted without malice and without gross negligence, and that before actions were commenced, or at the earliest opportunity after they were, the person who published the libel inserted a full apology for it. Where newspapers or periodicals are published at intervals of more than one week, the defence may also be used where an apology has not been published, but the defendant has offered to publish an apology in any newspaper or periodical selected by the person complaining[57].

This defence may only be pleaded if the defendant at the same time makes a payment of money into court by way of amends[58].

Where a person has published a defamatory statement about another person, and claims that the words are published innocently, the person who has published the statement may make an offer of amends. This means an offer to publish a rebuttal, or correction, or apology, together with the taking of such steps as are reasonably practicable, to notify parties who have received copies of the words which are alleged to be defamatory.

57 Libel Act 1843 S2 (as amer ded by the Libel Act 1845 S2).
58 Ibid S2(d).

H. Defamation insurance

9.31 Cover provided

Libel insurance policies may provide a company with cover for any claim of libel, injurious falsehood, slander of title of goods, passing off, infringement of trade mark, copyright, patent or registered design contained in publications. Additionally, cover may be provided against slander committed by the company in the course of its business.

The cover is normally up to a maximum limit, and there will generally be an excess, or deduction, or contribution required to be borne by the company before the insurer becomes liable. Frequently this amount is 10% of any claim.

The policy will cover the company's legal liability for damages, costs and expenses in respect of any claim together with the expenses of withdrawal of any affected publication, or the cost of making alterations to the publication, together with any additional costs incurred by the company with the approval of the insurer.

The policy will not normally cover any damages or expenses incurred as a result of ill-will or spite of the company, nor will it generally cover criminal libel, infringement of copyright or patent connected with computer software, or any claim made outside the United Kingdom. Additionally, if the company accepts liability the terms of the cover may be prejudiced (see paragraph 9.32).

9.32 Conditions of cover

The conditions of cover will generally require the company to submit any matter which is likely to lead to a claim in the insured publication to a lawyer with relevant experience, and to follow all recommendations which are made by the lawyer in order to remove the likelihood of any successful claim. If the company does not follow the recommendations of the lawyer, then the company will normally be required to provide the insurer with details of the recommendations, and the relevant matter, before publication, accompanied with a relevant written opinion from the lawyer if requested by the insurer. The insurer will then determine whether to accept the risk of the publication, or not, and may notify the company either that the risk is accepted or that it is rejected, or that the insurer will accept the risk if the company makes certain alterations to the publication.

The policy normally requires the company to notify the insured as soon as the company receives any claim from third parties, together with full appropriate details.

9.33 Insurance contracts generally

Insurance contracts are contracts where a relationship of the utmost good faith (uberrimae fidei) exists between the insured and the company. This means that the insured is required to display the utmost good faith towards the company. This means that in any application for insurance the insured must disclose all facts which might be relevant to the contract of insurance. Failure to disclose any facts which might be material may give the insurance the company the right to avoid the policy.

When insurance cover is effected, the insurer is subrogated to the company's rights of action. In other words, the insurer has the right to exercise the company's right of defence against any claim. This is a logical state of affairs, since the insurer is liable to pay for the company's losses arising from any insured claims. It does, however, mean that the company must not make any acknowledgement of liability, or settle any claim or do anything which would compromise the defence by the insurer of any insured claim and, if the company does this, it may lose the benefit of the policy of insurance.

The company will normally be required by the policy to do any acts reasonably required by the insurer in order to enable the insurer to defend an insured claim. These acts may include making apologies and offering amends if Counsel so advises (see paragraph 9.30). The insurer may also exercise the company's rights of action against the author of a work which contains a defamatory statement, and require the author to pay to the company the sum insured pursuant to an indemnity provision in the author's contract (see paragraph 7.15). Receipt of this sum may constitute settlement of the insurer's obligations under the policy.

I. Negligent misstatement

9.34 Negligent misstatement generally

Each person has a duty to avoid making careless or negligent statements which could result in harm to others. The harm may be caused to a person, or to property, and may be economic loss.

Where information is given to a person with whom the provider of the information has a close relationship, or in circumstances where the recipient of the information could reasonably be expected to rely on the skill or care of the person providing the information, then a duty of care will exist and the information-provider may be liable. It would appear, however, to be necessary for the person giving the advice or information to be fully aware of the nature of the transaction which the person intending to rely on the advice had in mind, to know that the advice should be communicated to that person, and to know that it was likely that the person would rely on the advice or information in deciding whether or not to engage in the transaction contemplated. If a statement was in more or less general circulation, and might foreseeably have been relied on by strangers to the person making the statement, for any one of a variety of different purposes which the person making the statement had no specific reason to anticipate, there might not be any liability.

A publisher might, however, incur liability in the case of a specialist publication with a controlled or limited circulation where readers might legitimately expect a certain degree of expertise by the publisher in relation to the subject matter of the publication, and therefore might rely on the publication for advice. A further area where a publisher may incur liability is in the case of a specific "reader advice" or "information" section in relation to, for example, money matters. Any service where individual readers' queries are answered increases the probability of a special relationship based on the publisher's knowledge of the reader's reliance on the advice.

9.35 Exclusion of liability for negligent misstatement

A publisher may not totally exclude liability for negligent misstatement. The Unfair Contract Terms Act 1977 (see paragraphs 2.14 to 2.16) permits the exclusion of liability for negligence only so far as such exclusion satisfies the requirement of reasonableness[59]. In other words, the courts must be of the view that it is fair and reasonable to allow a publisher to rely on the exclusion clause, having regard to all relevant circumstances.

A number of factors may be relevant in considering whether an exclusion clause was fair or reasonable, including, in the case of advice, whether it would have been reasonably practicable to have obtained the advice from an alternative source, the difficulty of the nature of the task for which liability was excluded, and whether it would have been possible for the party disclaiming liability to effect insurance cover against negligence as an alternative to excluding liability.

59 Unfair Contract Terms Act 1977 S11.

J. Obscenity

9.36 Definition of obscenity

Pursuant to the Obscene Publications Act 1959 it is an offence to publish an obscene article whether for gain or not, or to have an obscene article for publication[60].

An article is obscene if its effect, or the effect of any of its items, is, when taken as a whole, such as to deprave and corrupt persons who are likely, having regard to all relevant circumstances, to read, or see, or hear whatever is contained in the article. Any kind of article which contains or embodies matters to be read or looked at falls within the scope of the Obscene Publications Act[61].

A person publishes an article if that person distributes it, sells it, lets it on hire, gives it, lends it or offers it for sale or for letting on hire. A person is deemed to have an article for publication for gain if that person has the article in their ownership, possession, or control with a view to publication[62].

Although European Union legislation provides for the free movement of goods between member states, the European Community Treaty makes express provision permitting member states to prohibit the import of goods on grounds of obscenity and other matters (see paragraph 16.9).

60 Obscene Publications Act 1959 S2.
61 Ibid S1(1).
62 Ibid S1(3).

9.37 Defences

A person may not be convicted of publishing an obscene article, or suffer a forfeiture order being made, if it can be proved that the publication of the article in question is justified as being for the public good. In order to justify an article, it must be shown that its publication is in the interests of science, literature, art, learning or some other object of general concern[63].

The opinion of experts as to the literary, artistic, scientific or other merits of an article may be admitted in any proceedings to establish the ground that publication is for the public good[64].

A person may not be convicted of publishing an obscene article, or of having one for publication for gain, if it can be proved that the person had not examined the article, and had no reasonable cause to suspect it was of such a nature as would make him or her liable to be convicted of the offence[65].

63 Obscene Publications Act 1959 S4(1).
64 Ibid S4(2).
65 Ibid S2(5).

9.38 Taking and distributing indecent photographs of children

It is an offence for a person to take, or permit to be taken, any indecent photograph of a child. It is also an offence to distribute or show indecent photographs, or have them in your possession, with a view to them being distributed by yourself or another. Equally, it is an offence to publish or cause to be published any advertisement which is likely to be understood as conveying information that the advertiser distributes, or shows, indecent photographs, or intends to do so[66].

Where a person is charged for possession, or distribution of photographs, it is a defence for that person to prove:

(a)   that there was a legitimate reason for distributing or showing the photographs, or having them in the person's possession[67]; or
(b)   that the person had not seen the photographs, and did not know or have any cause to suspect them to be indecent[68].

66 Protection of Children Act 1978 S1(1).
67 Ibid S1(4)(a).
68 Ibid S1(4)(b).

9.39 Possession of indecent photographs of children

It is an offence for a person to have any indecent photographs of children in their possession[69]. Where a person is charged with such an offence, it is a defence to prove:

(a)   that the person had a legitimate reason for having the photographs[70]; or

(b)   the person had not seen the photographs and did not know or have any reason to suspect them to be indecent[71]; or

(c)   that the photographs were sent to the person without any prior request and were not kept for an unreasonable time[72].

Various powers of search, seizure and forfeiture exist in respect of indecent photographs of children.

69 Criminal Justice Act 1988 S160(1).
70 Ibid S160(1)(a).
71 Ibid S160(1)(b).
72 Ibid S160(1)(c).

9.40 Sending of obscene or indecent matter by post

It is a criminal offence for a person to send, or attempt to send, or procure to be sent, a postal packet which encloses any indecent or obscene print, painting, photograph, lithograph, engraving, cinematograph film, book, card or written communication, or any other indecent or obscene article whether or not similar to the above[73]. It is also an offence for a person to send, attempt to send, or procure to be sent a postal packet which has on it, or on its cover, any words, marks or designs which are grossly offensive or of an indecent or obscene character[74].

A person who sends, or causes to be sent, to another person, any book, magazine, or leaflet, or advertising material, or any of these, which the person knows, or ought reasonably to know, is unsolicited, and which describes or illustrates human sexual techniques, is guilty of a criminal offence.

73 Post Office Act 1953 S11(1)(b).
74 Ibid S11(1)(c).

9.41 Offensive communications

It is a criminal offence to send a message, or other matter, that is grossly offensive, or of an indecent, obscene or menacing character, by means of a public telecommunication system. It is also an offence to send, by means of such a system, for the purpose of causing annoyance, inconvenience or needless anxiety, any message which is known to be false, or persistently to make use of any system for such purpose[75].

It is a criminal offence to send to another person, a letter, or other article, which conveys a message, that is indecent, or grossly offensive, or conveys a threat, or conveys information, which is false, and known, or believed to be false, by the sender. It is also a criminal offence to send any other article which is in whole, or in part, of an indecent or grossly offensive nature.

A person is not guilty of an offence in respect of the making of a threat, if a person can show the threat was used to reinforce a demand which the person believed they had reasonable grounds for making, and believed that the use of the threat was a proper means of reinforcing the demand.

75 Telecommunications Act 1984 S43.

9.42 Interception of communications

It is an offence for a person to intercept a communication in the course of its transmission by post, or by means of a telecommunication system[76].

The offence is not committed if the person intercepting the communication has reasonable grounds for believing the person to whom, or by whom the communication is sent, consented to the interception. No offence is committed if the communication is intercepted in obedience to a warrant issued by the Secretary of State or for purposes connected with the provision of postal or public telecommunication services, or the enforcement of Acts of Parliament relating to use of those services or for purposes connected with the Wireless Telegraphy Act 1949[77].

Proceedings in relation to offences may not be instituted without the consent of the Director of Public Prosecutions[78].

The Act provides the machinery permitting the Secretary of State to issue a warrant requiring the interception of communications by post or public telecommunications, if the Secretary of State considers such interception is necessary in the interests of national security, or for the purpose of preventing or detecting serious crime, or for the purpose of safeguarding the economic well-being of the United Kingdom[79].

76 Interception of Communications Act 1985 S1(1).
77 Ibid S1(2)(3).
78 Ibid S1(4).
79 Ibid S2.

9.43 The Interception of Communications Tribunal and Commissioner

The Interception of Communications Act 1985 provides for the establishment of a tribunal for the purpose of investigating complaints from persons who believe that communications sent to them have been intercepted. On application, the Interception of Communications Tribunal will investigate whether a relevant warrant or certificate has been issued by the Secretary of State and conclude whether or not there has been a contravention of the provisions relating to the issue of warrants or certificates by the Secretary of State. The Tribunal will give notice to the person applying stating their conclusion, and make a report of their findings to the Prime Minister and, if they think fit, they may make an order quashing the relevant warrant or certificate, directing the destruction of copies of all intercepted material, and direct the Secretary of State to pay compensation to the applicant[80].

The Tribunal's details are:

Interception of Communications Tribunal
PO Box 44
London SE1 OTX
Tel 071 273 4093

The Act also provides for the appointment by the Prime Minister of a person who holds or has held high judicial office to act as Commissioner to keep under review the implementation by the Secretary of State of the powers conferred on him by the Act in relation to issuing warrants or certificates authorising the interception of material and also to give all such assistance as the Tribunal may require for the purpose of enabling it to carry out its functions under the Act.

The Commissioner has the power to obtain from Crown servants or persons engaged in the business of the Post Office, or running a telecommunication system, documents and information for the purpose of enabling the Commissioner to carry out his or her functions. The Commissioner is also required to make a report to the Prime Minister, if it appears to the Commissioner that there has been any contravention of the provisions authorising the interception of communications[81]. The current Commissioner is Sir Thomas Bingham, The Master of the Rolls.

A number of safeguards are contained in the Act in relation to the use of material obtained pursuant to a warrant, or certificate for interception, limiting to the minimum that is necessary, the extent to which the material is disclosed, the number of persons to whom any material is disclosed, the extent to which the material is copied, and the number of copies made of the material. The Act also requires each copy made of any material to be destroyed, as soon as its retention is no longer necessary[82].

80 Interception of Communications Act 1985 S7.
81 Ibid S8.
82 Ibid S6(2) and (3).

K. Racial hatred

9.44 Inciting racial hatred

The Public Order Act 1986 creates offences in respect of certain acts which may stir up racial hatred.

Racial hatred, is hatred of any group of persons in Great Britain, whether such persons are defined by reference to their colour, their race, their nationality, their citizenship or their ethnic or national origins[83]. Ethnic origins of a group include cultural traditions, language or literature, common ancestry, common religion and long history. The Public Order Act does not contain a definition for hatred but this will include intense dislike, animosity or enmity.

If a person uses threatening, abusive or insulting words or behaviour or displays written material which is threatening, abusive or insulting, then an offence will be committed if[84]:

(a) the person intends to stir up racial hatred[85]; or
(b) having regard to the circumstances racial hatred is likely to be stirred up[86].

Where words or behaviour are used inside a dwelling, or written material is displayed inside a dwelling, and the words and material are not heard or seen except by other persons in that or another dwelling, no offence is committed[87].

A person who publishes, or distributes, written material which is abusive, threatening or insulting to the public, or a section of the public, will be guilty of an offence if that person intends to stir up racial hatred or, having regard to the circumstances, racial hatred is likely to be stirred up[88].

It is a defence for a person who is not shown to have intended to stir up racial hatred to prove that the person was not aware of the content of material published or distributed, and did not suspect, and had no reason to suspect, that this material was threatening, abusive or insulting[89].

A person who has in their possession written material which is threatening, abusive or insulting, with a view to it being displayed, published or distributed is guilty of an offence, if that person intends racial hatred to be stirred up or, having regard to the circumstances, racial hatred is likely to be stirred up[90].

It is a defence for a person who is not shown to have intended to stir up racial hatred to prove that the person was not aware of the content of the written material, or recording, and did not suspect, and had no reason to suspect, that it was threatening, abusive, or insulting[91].

83 Public Order Act 1986 S17.
84 Ibid S18(1).
85 Ibid S18(1)(a).
86 Ibid S18(1)(b).
87 Ibid S18(2).
88 Ibid S19(1)(a) and (b).
89 Ibid S19(2).
90 Ibid S23(1).
91 Ibid S23(3).

L.   Sex discrimination

9.45   Sex discrimination generally

It is unlawful to discriminate against men, or against women, in a number of areas including employment and education. It is also unlawful for any person to discriminate against a man, or a woman, in connection with the provision of goods, facilities, or services, by refusing, or omitting, to provide them, or providing them on different terms than those on which they are available to the opposite sex[92].

It is not permitted to discriminate against a person of either sex by treating them less favourably than a single person of the same sex[93].

92 Sex Discrimination Act 1975 Parts I, II and Part III.
93 Ibid S3.

9.46   Advertisements

It is also unlawful to publish any advertisement which indicates or might reasonably be understood to indicate an intention to discriminate in a way contrary to the Sex Discrimination Act[94]. The effect of this is not only that advertisers are responsible for the contents of their advertisements but so are the persons who publish them.

Where a person publishes an unlawful advertisement, however, a defence is provided by the Sex Discrimination Act if the publisher can prove that the advertisement was published in reliance of a statement made by the advertiser, to the effect that the content of the advertisement would not offend the Sex Discrimination Act, and that it was reasonable for the publisher to rely on this statement.

Where an advertiser knowingly makes a statement which is untrue, or makes a statement recklessly, and the statement is false or misleading, then the advertiser may be liable on summary conviction to pay a fine[95].

The Sex Discrimination Act provides that if a job description, or an advertisement for a job, contains a sexual description (such as waiter, salesgirl, postman or stewardess), the mere use of such word would be presumed to indicate an intention to discriminate, unless a contrary indication is contained in the advertisement.

Either the job title should be advertised in the masculine and feminine forms or, if there is no distinct form for each gender, the wording of the advertisement should make it clear that the position is open to applicants from both sexes.

An advertisement for a job must not contain any statement or requirement which would amount to indirect discrimination (advertise for applicants at 6ft tall or people who wear skirts). Where illustrations are given, care should be taken to ensure that pictures of women appear as well as men (and vice versa).

94 Sex Discrimination Act 1975 S38(1).
95 Ibid S42.

9.47 Genuine occupational qualifications

Discrimination on grounds of sex is permitted where:

(a) Being a man is a genuine occupational qualification for the job. This is the case only where the essential nature of the job calls for a man for reasons of physiology (excluding physical strength) or stamina or in dramatic purposes or other entertainment, for reasons of authenticity, so that the essential nature of the job would be materially different if turned out by a woman[96].

(b) The job needs to be held by a man to preserve decency or privacy[97].

(c) The job is likely to involve the holder of the job doing work, or living in a private home, and the job needs to be held by a woman, because objection might reasonably be taken to allowing a man to perform such a job[98].

(d) The nature or location of the establishment makes it impracticable for the holder of the job to live elsewhere, other than in the premises provided by the employer, and such premises are lived in, or normally lived in, by men, and are not equipped with separate sleeping accommodation, and sanitary facilities, for women, or facilities which could be used by women in privacy from men, and it is not reasonable to expect the employer to equip the premises with such accommodation or facilities[99].

(e) The nature of the establishment, or part of it, requires a job to be held by a man because it is a hospital, prison, or other establishment for persons requiring special care, supervision, or attention, and those persons are all men, and it is reasonable that the holder of the job should not be a woman[100].

(f)   The holder of the job provides individuals with personal services, promoting their welfare, or education, and those services can most effectively be provided by a man[101].

(g)   The job needs to be held by a man because it is likely to involve duties outside the United Kingdom in a country whose laws or customs are such that the duties could not effectively be performed by a woman[102].

(h)   The job is one of two to be held by a married couple[103].

96 Sex Discrimination Act 1975 S7(2)(a).
97 Ibid S7(2)(b).
98 Ibid S7(2).
99 Ibid S7(2)(c).
100 Ibid S7(2)(d).
101 Ibid S7(2)(e).
102 Ibid S7(2)(f).
103 Ibid S7(2)(f).

9.48   Positive discrimination

Positive discrimination is also permitted in certain circumstances including where an employer has no employees of one sex, or only a comparatively small number of persons of one sex, doing a particular job during the proceeding 12 months. In such cases, it is permissible for an employer to put forward employees of the sex in question for access to facilities, or training, which would enable them to carry out such work, and to encourage women to take opportunities for doing such work.

It would not, however, be lawful for an employer to encourage women to apply for every vacancy advertised, since in some positions the number of women engaged may be greater than the number of men. Equally, it would not be lawful for an employer to establish a quota system for employees of both sexes, since the Sex Discrimination Act still requires that people should be engaged on grounds of merit and not on grounds of their sex.

M.   Statutory deposit

9.49   Statutory deposit generally

A statutory deposit scheme for books currently exists in the United Kingdom. The system is provided by the Copyright Act 1991 S 15 (the sole section of this Act which remains unrepealed) and imposes on the publisher of every book which is published in the United Kingdom two obligations.

First, the publisher is obliged to deliver, at the publisher's expense, a copy of the relevant book to the British Library Board within one month of publication. The copy to be delivered has to be one of the "best copies of the book" published "and on the best paper on which the book is printed".

Second, the publisher has to deliver a further copy of the book to each of the remaining five deposit libraries if they demand a copy. The relevant deposit libraries are the Bodleian Library, Oxford, University Library, Cambridge, the National Library of Scotland, the Library of Trinity College, Dublin and the National College of Wales. Demand may be made by these libraries either before publication or at any time up to 12 months after publication and the publisher is required to deposit a copy within one month from demand made after publication or, if demand is made before publication, upon publication.

The obligation extends to all books published in the United Kingdom, irrespective of whether the books are entitled to copyright protection, and irrespective of whether they were first published in the United Kingdom.

Any publisher failing to perform its deposit obligations is liable to a fine not exceeding £50 plus the value of the book. This fine must be paid either to the British Library Board or to the authority to whom the book should have been delivered.

The Theatres Act 1968 provides that where the public performance of a new play which is based on a written script is given in Great Britain, the person who presented the performance is required to deposit a copy of the script on which the play is based with the British Library Board within one month from the date of performance[104].

104 Theatres Act 1968 S11(i).

10.   Periodicals and the press

[IMPORTANT NOTE: Please read the section "About this book" on page v, before referring to any of the matters in this chapter.]

A.   Introduction

10.1   Purpose of this chapter

The purpose of this chapter is to address issues which are frequently encountered by publishers of periodicals and by the press.

These issues are, in some cases, relevant to the activities of book publishers and multimedia companies who should not, therefore, completely overlook this part of the book.

The first section of this chapter examines the potential liability faced by publishers and multimedia companies in relation to contempt of court. Restrictions exist in relation to what can and cannot be reported in newspapers and magazines.

The law relating to secrecy and national security has received a great deal of attention in recent years but has recently been reformed. Relevant provisions of the new Official Secrets Act are examined as are provisions of the Prevention of Terrorism Act.

The chapter then examines the establishment of the Press Complaints Commission and its code of practice and concludes with a brief summary of the law reforms recommended by the Calcutt Review of Press Self-Regulation.

The financial liabilities which companies may face under proceedings brought in connection with the matters referred to in this chapter are potentially enormous. The importance of taking proper legal advice cannot be over-emphasised. This chapter should be used only to enable the reader to identify whether or not a potential liability exists. If a particular risk or problem is not referred to, here, it should not be assumed that it is safe to proceed.

Any reader using this chapter as a substitute for taking proper legal advice does so at their peril.

B. Contempt

10.2 Types of contempt

Contempt of court can be divided up into a number of separate categories:

(a) Interference with the outcome of judicial proceedings

This would include disclosure of an accused person's previous convictions. Normally such matters are kept secret from the jury, so as not to prejudice a fair trial. This category would also include intimidating witnesses, bribing or intimidating jurors or judges, perverting or obstructing the course of justice, or bringing improper pressure on a party to settle legal proceedings.

(b) Disobedience or breach of undertaking

This includes any failure to comply with a court order or any breach of an undertaking given to the court.

(c) Interfering with the administration of justice

Conduct which threatens to interfere with the administration of justice, even though it does not place in jeopardy any particular proceedings, may be contempt. The naming of blackmail victims, whose identity has not been revealed by the court, would be a contempt.

(d) Contempt in the face of the court

This category includes disturbance or unacceptable behaviour in court.

(e) Scandalising the court

This category includes the publication of any abusive or highly critical statement about the court or judges, if the statement is perceived as a scurrilous abuse of the court or of judges or if it attacks the integrity of the administration of justice.

10.3 The strict liability rule

The strict liability rule states that conduct may be treated as interference with the course of justice (a contempt of court of the type referred to in paragraph 10.2 above) irrespective of intent[1].

In other words, the person who has engaged in such conduct will be liable, whether that person intended to engage in such conduct or intended such conduct to have the effect that it did. This rule is known as the strict liability rule.

The proceedings to which the rule applies will include proceedings in Magistrates' Courts, County Courts, Courts Martial, Coroners' Courts, Consistory Courts, Tribunals of Enquiry set up by Parliament and also probably apply to Industrial Tribunals and various tribunals.

1 Contempt of Court Act 1981 S1.

10.4 Application of the rule

There must be a publication which creates a substantial risk that the course of justice in the proceedings in question will be seriously impeded or prejudiced.

The following conditions therefore have to be satisfied:

(a) there must be a publication which will include any speech, writing, broadcast or other communication in whatever form which is addressed to the public at large or to any section of the public[2];

(b) there must be a *substantial* risk that the course of justice will be *seriously* impeded or prejudiced[3];

(c) the proceedings in question must be active at the time of the publication[4].

2 Contempt of Court Act 1981 S2(1).
3 Ibid S2(2).
4 Ibid S2(3).

10.5 When are proceedings active?

The Contempt of Court Act 1981 Sch 1 contains detailed provisions which specify when proceedings are active. A general simplification is as follows:

(a) Criminal proceedings are active from any of the following initial steps:
  – arrest without warrant issue or in Scotland grant of a warrant for arrest;
  – issue of a summons to appear (in Scotland grant of a warrant to cite);
  – service of an indictment or other document specifying the charge;
  – oral charge (but not in Scotland)[5].
  Criminal proceedings will remain active until they are concluded by:
  – acquittal or sentence;
  – any other verdict, finding, order or decision which ends proceedings;
  – discontinuance of proceedings or operation of law[6].

(b) Non-criminal proceedings are active from a time when arrangements for the hearing are made or when the case is set down for trial in the High Court or when a date for the hearing is fixed or if no such arrangement is previously made from the time the hearing begins until the proceedings are disposed, of discontinued or withdrawn[7].

(c) Appeal proceedings are active from the time they are started by:
  – application for leave to appeal or to apply for review;
  – notice of application for such leave;
  – notice of appeal or application for review;
  – other appeal-originating process[8].

The proceedings remain active until they are disposed of, abandoned, discontinued or withdrawn.

5 Contempt of Court Act 1981 Sch 1 Para 4.
6 Ibid Sch 1 Para 5.
7 Ibid Sch 1 Para 12.
8 Ibid Sch 1 Para 15.

10.6 Defences

A publisher of any matter to which the strict liability rule applies will not be guilty of contempt under the rule if at the time of the publication the publisher does not know, and has no reason to suspect, that relevant proceedings are active, and has taken all reasonable care. A distributor of a publication which publishes matter to which the strict liability rule applies, will not be liable for contempt if, at the time of distribution, having taken all reasonable care, such distributor does not know and has no reason to believe that the publication actually contains, or is likely to contain, any matter to which the strict liability rule may apply. It is up to the publisher or distributor to prove the elements of their defence[9].

A person will not be guilty of contempt under the strict liability rule in respect of any fair and accurate report of legal proceedings held in public which is published contemporaneously with such proceedings and in good faith[10].

A court is, however, free to order that publication of any report of its proceedings (or any part of them) should be postponed for whatever period the court considers necessary if the court considers such an order is necessary to avoid a substantial risk of prejudice to the administration of justice on those proceedings[11].

A publication which is made as a discussion in good faith (or a part of such discussion) of public affairs or other matters of general public interest will not be treated as contempt of court under the strict liability rule if the risk of impediment or prejudice to particular legal proceedings is merely incidental to the discussion[12].

9 Contempt of Court Act 1981 S3.
10 Ibid S4(1).
11 Ibid S4(2).
12 Ibid S5.

10.7 Disclosure of information

No court can require a person to disclose the source of information contained in a publication for which that person is responsible, unless it can be established to the satisfaction of the court that disclosure is necessary in the interests of justice or national security or for the prevention of disorder or crime. No person will be guilty of contempt for refusing to disclose the source of information unless this is established[13].

A court will, however, order disclosure if it is in the interests of justice that a person should be able to bring civil proceedings against a source to recover documents, or otherwise protect that party's rights.

Where a court allows the name, or other details, relating to a person in proceedings to be withheld from the public, the court may also give directions prohibiting the publication of that name, or any other matter which appears necessary to the court to be withheld, and the name or material may not be the subject of publication in connection with the proceedings.

13 Ibid S10.

C. Reporting restrictions

10.8 Committal proceedings

It is unlawful to publish in Great Britain, any written report of committal proceedings in England and Wales which contains matter other than permitted facts[14].

The permitted facts which may be published in a report without an order from the court are:

(a) identity of the court, and names of the examining justices[15];

(b) names, addresses and occupations of the parties and witnesses, and the ages of the accused and witnesses[16];

(c) the offence or offences (or a summary of them) with which the accused is or are charged[17];

(d) names of counsel and solicitors engaged in the proceedings[18];

(e) any decision of the court to commit the accused, or any of the accused, for trial, and any decision of the court on the disposal of the case against any accused not committed[19];

(f) where a court commits the accused, or any of the accused, for trial, the charge, or charges, or a summary of them, on which they are committed, and the court to which they are committed[20];

(g) where the committal proceedings are adjourned, the date and place to which they are adjourned[21];

(h) any arrangements as to bail, on committal or adjournment[22];

(i) whether legal aid is granted to the accused or any of them[23].

Where an application is made with reference to any committal proceedings by the accused, or any of them, the Magistrates' Court may order that the restriction contained in this Section will not apply to reports of the proceedings[24].

Where a Magistrates' Court determines not to commit the accused for trial, it is not unlawful to publish a report of the committal proceedings containing facts other than those committed after the date the court has so determined[25].

Where a court commits the accused for trial, it is not unlawful to publish a report of committal proceedings containing facts other than those committed after the date of the accused's trial or, as the case may be, the trial of the last of the accused to be tried[26].

14 Magistrates' Courts Act 1980 S8(1).
15 Ibid S8(4)(a).
16 Ibid S8(4)(b).
17 Ibid S8(4)(c).
18 Ibid S8(4)(d).
19 Ibid S8(4)(e).
20 Ibid S8(4)(f).

21 Ibid S8(4)(g).
22 Ibid S8(4)(h).
23 Ibid S8(4)(i).
24 Ibid S8(2).
25 Ibid S8(3)(a).
26 Ibid S8(3)(b).

10.9   Rape reporting

After an allegation has been made that a woman has been the victim of a rape offence, neither the woman's name, nor her address, nor a still or moving picture or likeness of her shall during her lifetime be published in England and Wales, in a written publication available to the public, if it is likely to lead members of the public to identify her as an alleged victim of such an offence, unless such publication is authorised by a direction given pursuant to the Sexual Offences (Amendment) Act 1976 S4[27].

After a person is accused of a rape offence, no matter which is likely to lead members of the public to identify the woman as the complainant in relation to that application shall, during the woman's lifetime, be published in England and Wales, in any written publication which is made available to the public, except as authorised by direction given pursuant to the Sexual Offences (Amendment) Act 1986 S4[28].

The above provisions do not prohibit the publication of matter consisting only of a report of criminal proceedings, other than proceedings at, or intended to lead to, or on an appeal arising out of, the trial at which the accused is charged with the offence[29].

Where a person is charged with an offence in respect of the publication of any matter of the type described above, it shall be a defence to prove that the publication in which the matter appeared, was one in respect of which the woman had given written consent to the appearance of matter of that description. Written consent will not be a defence, if it is proved that any person interfered unreasonably with the woman's peace or comfort, with intent to obtain the consent[30].

27 Sexual Offences (Amendment) Act 1976 S4(1)(a).
28 Ibid S4(1)(b).
29 Ibid S4(1)(b).
30 Ibid Ss5A and 5B.

10.10   Fraud trials

In the case of serious frauds, the Criminal Justice Act 1987 contains a procedure for bypassing committal proceedings in a Magistrates' Court and provides that a notice of transfer may be served transferring the case direct to the Crown Court[31]. The Criminal Justice Act 1987 also contains restrictions on reporting applications for dismissal, and preparatory hearings of transferred charges, if the report contains any matter other than permitted matter[32].

The matters permitted by the Criminal Justice Act are:

(a)   the identity of the court, and the name of the judge[33];
(b)   the names, ages, home addresses, and occupations of the accused and witnesses[34];

(c)   any relevant business information[35];

(d)   the offence, or offences, or a summary of them with which the accused is charged[36];

(e)   the names of counsel and solicitors engaged in the proceedings[37];

(f)   where the proceedings are adjourned, the date and place to which they are adjourned[38];

(g)   any arrangements as to bail[39];

(h)   whether legal aid was granted to the accused[40].

31 Criminal Justice Act 1987 S4.
32 Ibid S11(1), (1A) and (2).
33 Ibid S11(8)(a).
34 Ibid S11(a)(b).
35 Ibid S11(8)(c).
36 Ibid S11(8)(d).
37 Ibid S11(8)(e).
38 Ibid S11(8)(f).
39 Ibid S11(8)(g).
40 Ibid S11(8)(h).

10.11   Relevant business information

Relevant business information within the meaning of the Criminal Justice Act is defined as:

(a)   any address used by the accused, for the carrying on of a business on the accused's own account[41];

(b)   the name of any business which the accused is carrying on, for the accused's own account at any relevant time[42];

(c)   the name of any firm in which the accused was a partner at any relevant time, or by whom the accused was engaged at such time[43];

(d)   the address of any such firm[44];

(e)   the address of any company of which the accused was a director at any relevant or time, or by whom the accused was engaged at any such time[45];

(f)   the address of the registered, or principal, office of any such company[46];

(g)   any working address of the accused, in the accused's capacity as a person engaged by any such company[47].

The Act provides machinery for the courts to lift reporting restrictions relating to accused persons.

41 Ibid S11(9)(a).
42 Ibid S11(9)(b).
43 Ibid S11(9)(c).
44 Ibid S11(9)(d).
45 Ibid S11(9)(e).
46 Ibid S11(9)(f).
47 Ibid S11(9)(g).

10.12   Matrimonial proceedings

The Judicial Proceedings (Regulation of Reports) Act 1926, provides that it is not lawful to print, or publish, or cause to, or procure to, be printed or published in relation to any judicial proceedings for dissolution of marriage, for nullity of marriage, or for judicial separation, or for restitution of conjugal rights other than the following particulars[48]:

(a) the names, addresses and occupations of the parties and witnesses[49];

(b) a concise statement of the charges, offences and counter-charges in support of which evidence has been given[50];

(c) submissions on any point of law arising in the course of the proceedings, and the decision of the court on them, or the summing up of the judge and finding of the jury (if any) and the judgment of the court, and observations made by the judge in giving judgment[51]. No person other than a proprietor, editor, master printer, or publisher is liable to be convicted under the Act[52].

48 Judicial Proceedings (Regulation of Reports) Act 1926 S1(1)(b).
49 Ibid S1(1)(b)(i).
50 Ibid S1(1)(b)(ii).
51 Ibid S1(1)(b)(iii) and (iv).
52 Ibid S1(2).

10.13 Domestic proceedings

In the case of domestic proceedings in the Magistrates' Court (other than proceedings taken under the Adoption Act 1976) the Magistrates' Courts Act 1980 provides that it is unlawful for the proprietor, editor or publisher of a newspaper or periodical to print or publish, or cause or procure to be printed or published, any particulars in the proceedings, other than the following:

(a) names, addresses and occupations of the parties and witnesses[53];

(b) grounds of the application and a precise statement of the charges, defences, and counter-charges in support of which evidence has been given[54];

(c) submissions on any point of law arising in the course of the proceedings, and the decisions of the court on the submissions[55];

(d) the decision of the court and any observations made by the court in giving it[56].

In the case of domestic proceedings in the Magistrates' Court under the Adoption Act 1976, information in sub-categories (a) and (b) may not be printed or published. Additionally, for the purpose of determining whether an offence has been committed, the expression "particulars of the proceedings" will include the name, address and school of the child, any picture which is or includes a picture of a child, and any other particulars which are calculated to lead to the identification of the child. None of these may be printed or published[57].

53 Magistrates' Courts Act 1980 S71(1A)(a).
54 Ibid S71(1A)(b).
55 Ibid S71(1A)(c).
56 Ibid S71(1A)(d).
57 Ibid S71(1B)(2).

10.14 Children

The Children and Young Persons Act 1933 (as amended), provides that in relation to any proceedings in any court, the court may direct that, except so far as may be permitted by the direction of the court, no newspaper report of the proceedings shall reveal the name and address of the school or include any particulars calculated to lead to the identification of any child, or young person, concerned in the proceedings, either as being the person by or against or in respect of whom proceedings are taken, or as being the witness. Additionally, no picture may be published in a newspaper as being, or including a picture, of any child or young person concerned in such proceedings[58].

The Administration of Justice Act 1960 further provides that the publication of information relating to proceedings which relate to the wardship, or adoption of an infant, or wholly or mainly to the guardianship, custody, maintenance or upbringing of an infant, or rights of access to an infant shall in itself amount to contempt of court (see paragraph 10.2).

58 Children and Young Persons Act 1933 S39(1).

D. Secrecy

10.15 Security and intelligence services

The Official Secrets Act 1989 has now replaced the Official Secrets Act 1911 under which many recent prosecutions including Sarah Tisdall, Clive Ponting and Anthony Blunt have been brought. A person who is or has been a member of the security and intelligence services or a person who is notified that he or she falls within the scope of the Act will be guilty of an offence if, without lawful authority, that person discloses any information, documents or other article relating to security or intelligence which is or has been in that person's possession[59].

Notification that a person is affected by the Official Secrets Act is by notice in writing served by a Minister of the Crown and is given pursuant to S1 of the Act, where the work of the person in question is connected with the security and intelligence services, and it is in the interests of national security to do so[60].

The notice is in force for a period of five years beginning with the day on which it is served, and may be renewed by further notices for periods of five years at a time. The notice may be revoked at any time, and the Minister is required to do so as soon as the work undertaken by the relevant person stops being connected with the security and intelligence service, and being a type where the interests of national security require the person to be restricted. Expiry of the notice will not release the individual from obligations in relation to information or documents acquired by the person before the date of expiry[61].

59 Official Secrets Act 1989 S1.
60 Ibid S1(6).
61 Ibid S1(7) and (8).

174

10.16 Offences under the Official Secrets Act

(a) Security and Intelligence Offence

It is an offence under the Official Secrets Act to make any statement which purports to be a disclosure of information of the type referred to or is intended to be taken as being such a disclosure. Any person who is or has been a Crown servant or Government contractor is guilty of an offence if, without lawful authority, that person makes a disclosure of any information, document or other article relating to security or intelligence which is, or has been, in that person's possession by virtue of their position, where the circumstances in paragraph 10.17 do not apply (Section 1). A disclosure is damaging if it causes damage to the work of the security or intelligence services or any part of them or is a disclosure of information or a document or other article which would be likely to cause such damage or which falls within a class of information which would be likely to have that effect (Section 1)[62].

(b) Defence-related offence

A person who is or has been a Crown servant or Government contractor is guilty of an offence if that person without lawful authority makes a damaging disclosure of any information, document or other article relating to defence which is or has been in their possession by virtue of their position (Section 2). A disclosure is damaging if it damages the capability of any part of the Armed Forces or leads to loss of life or injury to members of the forces or damage to their equipment or installations. It may also be damaging if it endangers the interests of the United Kingdom abroad or seriously obstructs the promotion or protection by the United Kingdom of those interests or endangers the safety of British citizens abroad. A disclosure will also be damaging if it consists of information or a document or an article which is of such a type that its unauthorised disclosure would be likely to have any of the effects referred to above[63] (Section 2).

62 Official Secrets Act 1989 S1(3) and (4).
63 Ibid S2(1) and (2).

10.17 Defences

It is a defence to a charge brought under Section 1 of the Official Secrets Act 1989 (see paragraph 10.15) if the person charged can prove that at the time of the alleged offence that person did not know, and had no reasonable cause to believe, that the information, document or article in question related to security or intelligence or (so far as the previous paragraph is concerned) that the disclosure would be damaging within the meaning of the Official Secrets Act[64].

It is a defence for a person charged with an offence under Section 2 of the Official Secrets Act 1989 to prove that at the time of the alleged offence the person did not know and had no reasonable cause to believe that the information, document or article in question related to defence or that its disclosure would be damaging within the meaning of the Official Secrets Act[65].

Defence has a wide meaning in the act and includes:

(a)   the size, shape, organisation, logistics, order of battle, deployment, operations, state of readiness and training of the armed forces of the Crown[66];

(b)   the weapons, stores or other equipment of the armed forces and the invention, development, production and operation of such equipment and research relating to it[67];

(c)   defence policy and strategy, military planning and intelligence[68];

(d)   plans and measures for the maintenance of essential supplies and services that are and would be needed in time of war[69].

64   Official Secrets Act 1989 S1(5) .
65   Ibid S2(3).
66   Ibid S2(4)(a).
67   Ibid S2(4)(b).
68   Ibid S2(4)(c).
69   Ibid S2(4)(d).

10.18   International relations and Section 3 of the Official Secrets Act

A person who is, or has been, a Crown servant or Government contractor is guilty of an offence if, without lawful authority, that person makes a damaging disclosure of any information, document, or other article, relating to international relations, or any confidential information, document, or other article, which is obtained from a state other than the United Kingdom, or an international organisation in that person's possession, by virtue of their position[70].

A disclosure is damaging if it endangers the interests of the United Kingdom abroad, seriously obstructs the promotion or protection by the United Kingdom of those interests or endangers the safety of British citizens. It will also be damaging if information, or a document, or article which is of such a type that its unauthorised disclosure would be likely to have any of the effects above, and in this case the fact that the information, document or article is confidential, or its nature or contents may be sufficient to establish that disclosure would be likely to have such effect[71].

It is a defence for a person charged with an offence under Section 3 of the Official Secrets Act 1989 to prove that at the time of the alleged offence the person did not know, and had no reasonable cause to believe, that the information, document, or article in question was of the type mentioned above, or that its disclosure would be damaging within the meaning of the Official Secrets Act[72].

Where information is communicated in confidence to another state, or international organisation, and comes into a person's possession as a result of having been disclosed without the authority of such state, or organisation, any further disclosure, without lawful authority, would be an offence under Section 6 of the Official Secrets Act.

70   Official Secrets Act 1989 S3(1).
71   Ibid S3(2) and (3).
72   Ibid S3(4).

10.19 Unauthorised disclosure

When any information, document or other article which is protected against disclosure by the provisions of the Official Secrets Act 1989 comes into the possession of a person as a result of it having been disclosed without lawful authority, then the disclosure by the recipient of the information is an offence under S5 of the Official Secrets Act. It is also an offence if a person who receives information on terms which are required to be held in confidence discloses the information without lawful authority, knowing, or having reasonable cause to believe, that it is protected against disclosure. In cases of information relating to security and intelligence, or defence, or international relations, a person will not commit an offence unless the disclosure is damaging, and it is made by the person knowing, or having reasonable cause to believe, that it would be damaging[73].

So far as information in respect of defence is concerned, a person does not commit an offence if information has come into that person's possession as a result of it having been disclosed by a Government contractor without lawful authority, or on terms of confidence, unless the disclosure was made by a British citizen or took place in the United Kingdom or in any of the Channel Islands or in the Isle of Man or a colony[74].

A person is guilty of an offence if, without lawful authority, that person discloses any information, document or other article which came into that person's possession as a result of a contravention of S1 of the Official Secrets Act 1911[75].

73 Official Secrets Act 1989 S5.
74 Ibid S5(4).
75 Ibid S5(6).

10.20 The safeguarding of information

Where a Crown servant, or Government contractor, possesses or has under their control, a document or article of which the Official Secrets Act 1989 prohibits the disclosure, without lawful authority, the Official Secrets Act imposes on that person certain obligations to keep the information or article secure.

A Crown servant will be guilty of an offence if that person retains a document or article contrary to their official duty. This offence is also committed by any person who has notice served on them pursuant to S1 of the Official Secrets Act[76] (see paragraph 10.15 above).

A Government contractor commits an offence if that person fails to comply with any official direction for the return or disposal of a document or article. Additionally, an offence would be committed if a Government contractor fails to take such care as might be reasonably expected in order to prevent the unauthorised disclosure of any document or article[77].

The offence also extends to cover certain information received from unauthorised disclosures, information entrusted in confidence, and information originally communicated in confidence to other states or international organisations.

An additional offence is committed under S8 if a person discloses any official information, document or other article which can be used for the purpose of obtaining access to any information, document or other article which is protected by the Official Secrets Act. The offence is committed if the circumstances in which the information, or document, or article is disclosed are such that it would be reasonable to expect that the item disclosed might be used for the purpose of obtaining access to any protected item without proper authority[78].

76 Official Secrets Act 1989 S8(1)(a).
77 Ibid S8(1)(b).
78 S8(6).

10.21 Lawful authority

A number of principles are established in Section 7 of the Official Secrets Act to determine whether a disclosure is lawful or not:

(a) in the case of a Crown servant, or a person who is not a Crown servant but who has been notified for the purposes of Section 1(1) (see paragraph 10.15) the disclosure is made with lawful authority only if it is made in accordance with that person's official duty[79];

(b) in the case of a disclosure by a Government contractor, that disclosure will be made with lawful authority only if it was made in accordance with an official authorisation, or it was made for the purposes of the functions for which the person is a Government contractor without contravening any official restriction[80];

(c) in the case of a person who is not a Crown servant or a Government contractor, a disclosure is made with lawful authority only if it is made to a Crown servant for the purposes of that person's functions, or in accordance with the appropriate official authorisation, given or imposed, by a Crown servant, or Government contractor[81];

(d) it is, in some circumstances, a defence for a person who is charged with an offence under the Official Secrets Act to prove that at the time of the alleged offence the person believed that they had lawful authority to make the disclosure in question, and did not have reasonable cause to believe otherwise[82].

79 S7(1).
80 S7(2).
81 S7(3).
82 S7(4).

E. Prevention of Terrorism

10.22 The Prevention of Terrorism (Temporary Provisions) Act

The Prevention of Terrorism (Temporary Provisions) Act 1982 contains extensive provisions in relation to the prevention of the use of violence for political ends including the use of violence for the purpose of putting the public or any section of the public in fear. This is the statutory definition of "terrorism"[83].

The Act contains provisions permitting a warrant or order to be issued by a Justice of the Peace or a Circuit Judge, in relation to material which is likely to be of substantial value, whether by itself or together with other material, to the investigation of terrorism[84].

Where any warrant or order has been issued, a person is guilty of an offence if, knowing or having reasonable cause, to suspect that the investigation has taken place, the person makes any disclosure which is likely to prejudice the investigation or falsifies, conceals or destroys, or otherwise disposes of, or causes; or permits, the falsification, concealment, destruction or disposal of material which is or is likely to be relevant to the investigation[85].

Refusal of a request to identify the source of information on the grounds of protection of confidentiality will be an offence under the Act.

The Act further creates a positive duty to provide the Police or a member of Her Majesty's Forces in Northern Ireland with any information which might be of material assistance in preventing an act of terrorism, or apprehending, prosecuting or convicting a person suspected of terrorism in connection with the affairs of Northern Ireland. This obligation would extend to advance knowledge of the likely whereabouts of terrorists which might be obtained, for example, with the making of arrangements for interviews, as well as to films or sound recordings identifying terrorists and other information including names[86].

83 Prevention of Terrorism (Temporary Provisions) Act 1982 S20.
84 Ibid Sch 7 Part I Para 2.
85 Ibid S17(2).
86 Ibid S18.

F. The Press Complaints Commission

10.23 The Press Complaints Commission generally

The Press Complaints Commission is an independent body which was founded following the recommendation of the Calcutt Committee Report which was published in June 1990. It is an independent body whose objective is to oversee self-regulation of the press and comprises 16 members drawn from the lay public and the press including 7 editors of national regional and local newspapers and magazines.

The Commission deals with complaints of the public in relation to the contents and the conduct of British newspapers and magazines. It also advises editors on journalistic ethics.

The Press Complaints Commission is responsible for enforcing a Code of Practice which was framed by the newspaper and periodical industry. The main role of the Commission is to deal with complaints from people in organisations about the failure of newspapers or magazines to follow the letter or spirit of the Code of Practice.

The primary objective of the Press Complaints Commission is to help the parties as speedily and fairly as possible to resolve any complaints that the

Code has been broken, and to this objective the procedures of the Press Complaints Commission are uncomplicated. If resolution of the complaint fails, the Commission adjudicates whether or not there has been a breach of the Code.

A monthly report is published by the Press Complaints Commission which includes reports of adjudications and details of all complaints which have been resolved directly with editors as well as a précis of complaints which raise no breach of the Code.

10.24 Code of Practice

All members of the press have a duty to maintain the highest professional and ethical standards. In doing so, they should have regard to the provisions of this Code of Practice and to safeguarding the public's right to know.

Editors are responsible for the actions of journalists employed by their publications. They should also satisfy themselves as far as possible that material accepted from non-staff members was obtained in accordance with this Code.

While recognising that this involves a substantial element of self-restraint by editors and journalists, it is designed to be acceptable in the context of a system of self-regulation. The Code applies in the spirit as well as in the letter.

Any publication which is criticised by the PCC under one of the following clauses is duty bound to print the adjudication which follows in full and with due prominence.

(a) Accuracy

Newspapers and periodicals should take care not to publish inaccurate, misleading or distorted material.

Whenever it is recognised that a significant inaccuracy, misleading statement, or distorted report has been published, it should be corrected promptly and with due prominence.

An apology should be published whenever appropriate.

A newspaper or periodical should always report fairly and accurately the outcome of an action for defamation to which it has been a party.

(b) Opportunity to reply

A fair opportunity for reply to inaccuracies should be given to individuals or organisations when reasonably called for.

(c) Comment, conjecture and fact

Newspapers, while free to be partisan, should distinguish clearly between comment, conjecture and fact.

(d) Privacy

Intrusions and enquiries into an individual's private life, without his or her consent including the use of long-lens photography to take pictures of people on private property without their consent are not generally acceptable, and publication can only be justified when in the public interest. Note: Private property is defined as any private residence, together with its garden and outbuildings, but excluding any adjacent fields or parkland; in addition, hotel bedrooms (but not other areas in a hotel) and those parts of a hospital or nursing home where patients are treated or accommodated.

(e) Listening devices

Unless justified by public interest, journalists should not obtain or publish material obtained by using clandestine listening devices, or by intercepting private telephone conversations.

(f) Hospitals

Journalists or photographers making enquiries at hospitals, or similar institutions, should identify themselves to a responsible official, and obtain permission before entering non-public areas.

The restrictions on intruding into privacy are particularly relevant to enquiries about individuals in hospitals or similar institutions.

(g) Misrepresentation

Journalists should not generally obtain or seek to obtain information or pictures through misrepresentation or subterfuge.

Unless in the public interest, documents or photographs should be removed only with the express consent of the owner.

Subterfuge can be justified only in the public interest and only when material cannot be obtained by any other means.

(h) Harassment

Journalists should neither obtain nor seek to obtain information or pictures through intimidation or harassment.

Unless their enquiries are in the public interest, journalists should not photograph individuals on private property without their consent; should not persist in telephoning or questioning individuals after having been asked to desist; should not remain on their property after having been asked to leave and should not follow them.

It is the responsibility of editors to ensure that these requirements are carried out.

(i) Payments for articles

Payments or offers of payment for stories, pictures or information should not be made to witnesses or potential witnesses in current criminal proceedings, or to people engaged in crime, or to their associates—which includes family, friends, neighbours and colleagues—except where the material concerned ought to be published in the public interest, and the payment is necessary for this to be done.

(j) Intrusion into grief or shock

In cases involving personal grief or shock, enquiries should be carried out and approaches made with sympathy and discretion.

(k) Innocent relatives and friends

Unless it is contrary to the public's right to know, the press should generally avoid identifying relatives, or friends of persons convicted, or accused, of crime.

(l) Interviewing or photographing children

Journalists should not normally interview or photograph children under the age of 16 on subjects involving the personal welfare of the child, in the absence of, or without the consent of, the parent or other adult who is responsible for the children.

Children should not be approached or photographed while at school, without the permission of the school authorities.

(m) Children in sex cases

The press should not, even where the law does not prohibit it, identify children under the age of 16 who are involved in cases concerning sexual offences, whether as victims, or as witnesses or defendants. In any press report of a case involving a sexual offence against a child—the adult should be identified; the term "incest", where applicable, should not be used; the offence should be described as "serious offences against young children" or similar appropriate wording; the child should not be identified; care should be taken that nothing in the report implies the relationship between the accused and the child.

(n) Victims of crime

The press should not identify victims of sexual assault, or publish material likely to contribute to such identification, unless, by law, they are free to do so.

(o) Discrimination

The press should avoid prejudicial or pejorative reference to a person's race, colour, religion, sex or sexual orientation, or to any physical or mental illness or handicap.

It should avoid publishing details of a person's race, colour, religion, sex or sexual orientation, unless these are directly relevant to the story.

(p) Financial journalism

Even where the law does not prohibit it, journalists should not use for their own profit, financial information they receive in advance of its general publication, nor should they pass such information to others.

They should not write about shares or securities in whose performance they know that they or their close families have a significant financial interest, without disclosing the interest to the editor or financial editor.

They should not buy or sell, either directly or through nominees or agents, shares or securities about which they have written recently or about which they intend to write in the near future.

(q) Confidential sources

Journalists have a moral obligation to protect confidential sources of information.

(r) Public Interest

There are a number of clauses of the Code which refer to the public interest.
   In all these clauses the public interest includes:

- detecting or exposing crime or serious misdemeanour;
- protecting public health and safety;
- preventing the public from being misled by some statement or action of an individual or organisation.

10.25 Freedom and Responsibility of the Press Bill

A Private Members' Bill entitled "Freedom and Responsibility of the Press" was introduced into the House of Commons by Mr Clive Soley MP in June 1992. It is the seventh such bill on privacy since 1961. (The others were introduced by Lord Mancroft in 1961, Mr Alex Lyon in 1967, Mr Brian Walden in 1969, Mr William Cash in 1987, Mr John Browne in 1988, and Lord Stoddart in 1989).

Mr Soley's Bill would introduce an independent press authority with responsibility for promoting the highest standards of journalism in newspapers, producing and promoting codes and professional and ethical standards and investigating and monitoring these. The Bill would, if enacted, also provide the right to correction of factual inaccuracies under which aggrieved parties would have the right to procure the printing of a correction, free of charge, in the next possible edition of the same newspaper, the correction to be given the prominence equivalent to that of the material complained of, and of whatever length necessary to correct the material, having regard to its original context. If an editor or newspaper failed or refused to publish a correction a complainant would have the right under the Bill to apply to the independent press authority for the enforcement of the right to correction.

Mr Soley's Bill was considered during the Calcutt review which concluded that a statutory press complaint's tribunal would need to encompass not only the areas which Mr Soley's Bill sought to cover, but other matters as well, and that a somewhat different statutory body with wider functions and powers would be needed.

10.26 The Calcutt Review

On 9 July 1992 Sir David Calcutt QC was invited to conduct a review of press self-regulation, from the date of the report of the Committee on Privacy and Related Matters (the "Privacy Committee Report") which led to the establishment of the Press Complaints Commission.

The purpose of the Review was to assess whether the current arrangements for self-regulation of the press by the Press Complaints Commission have been effective. The Review concluded that the Press Complaint's Commission was not an effective regulator of the press, that it had not been set up in a way and was not operating a code of practice which enabled it to command press or public confidence. The review also concluded that the Press Complaints Commission did not hold the balance fairly between the press and the individual, and was not the truly independent body that it should be since, as constituted, it was in essence a body set up and financed and dominated by the industry which was operating a code of practice devised by the industry which was over-favourable to the industry.

The Review concluded that it was unlikely that the press would be willing to make or would in fact make the changes which would be needed to establish an independent body which would command the confidence of the public and therefore recommended that the Government should establish a new statutory body in the form of a Press Complaints Tribunal.

10.27 The Press Complaints Tribunal

One of the matters considered by the Calcutt Review was the Code of Practice of the Press Complaints Commission. The Privacy Committee which reported in 1990 proposed a code of practice for the press, but this was not the code which was adopted by the Press Complaints Committee. It was the view of the Calcutt Review that "the protection for individuals which the Privacy Committee's proposed code would have provided has been significantly reduced by the [Press Complaints Committee] code; and that code does not hold the balance fairly".

One of the primary functions of the Statutory Press Complaints Tribunal which the Calcutt Review recommended should be established would be to draw up and keep under review a code of practice. In addition, the Press Complaints Tribunal would have the following functions and powers:

(a)   to restrain publication of material in breach of the code of practice;
(b)   to receive complaints of alleged breaches of the code of practice;
(c)   to inquire into those complaints;
(d)   to initiate its own investigations about a complaint;
(e)   to acquire a response to its inquiries;
(f)   to attempt conciliation;
(g)   to hold hearings;
(h)   to rule on alleged breaches of the code of practice;
(i)   to give guidance;
(j)   to warn;
(k)   to require the printing of apologies, corrections and replies;
(l)   to enforce publication of its adjudications;
(m)   to award compensation;
(n)   to impose fines;
(o)   to award costs;
(p)   to review its own procedures;
(q)   to publish reports;
(r)   to require the press to carry at reasonable intervals an advertisement to be specified by the Tribunal, indicating to its readers how complaints to the Tribunal can be made.

10.28 Physical intrusion and infringement of privacy

The Review recommends the establishment of the following criminal offences in England and Wales:

(a)   entering or remaining on private property without the consent of the lawful occupant, with intent to obtain personal information with a view to its publication; or
(b)   placing a surveillance device on private property without the consent of the lawful occupant, with intent to obtain personal information with a view to its publication; or

(c)   using a surveillance device (whether on private property or elsewhere) in relation to an individual who is on private property, without the consent of the individual to such use, with intent to obtain personal information about that individual with a view to its publication; or

(d)   taking a photograph, or recording a voice of an individual, who is on private property without his or her consent with a view to its publication, and with intent that the individual should be identifiable.

The Review proposes a number of defences to the proposed offences where the act was done:

– for the purpose of preventing, detecting or exposing the commission of a crime or other seriously anti-social conduct; or
– for the purpose of preventing the public from being misled by some public statement or action of the individual concerned; or
– for the purpose of informing the public about matters directly affecting the discharge of any public function of the individual concerned; or
– for the protection of public heath and safety; or
– under any lawful authority.

The Review also proposes a civil remedy giving individuals concerned a right to obtain injunctions, restraining publication of information obtained by means of any act which constitutes an offence, as well as the right of action against any person publishing any such information in relation to any loss suffered by the individual, and the right to call for an account of profits accruing to the person publishing it. It is proposed that this civil remedy would also be available if the act in question took place outside England and Wales, if done with a view to publication in England and Wales.

As an alternative to establishing a new criminal offence the Calcutt Review recommended the incorporation of the substance of the proposed criminal offences into the statutory code which the statutory Press Complaints Tribunal would administer if established.

10.29 Data protection and telecommunications

The Data Protection Act (see paragraphs 18.2 to 18.5) regulates the use of automatically processed information relating to individuals[87]. It applies to personal data which comprise information relating to a living individual who can be identified from that information including an expression of opinion about that individual. It also defines "processing" in relation to that data as meaning amending, augmenting, deleting or rearranging the data or extracting the information constituting the data, but not the performance of any operation carried out solely for the purpose of preparing the text of documents[88].

Most newspapers and magazines today use electronic technology, and while it could be argued that this technology is used solely for the purpose of preparing the text of documents, there is equally an argument that the technology is capable of greater processing than simply preparing text, and that accordingly personal information held electronically by newspaper publishers is personal data for the purposes of the 1984 Act.

Were the counter argument to be accepted, then an individual who is the subject of personal data held by a newspaper who suffered damage by reason of the inaccuracy of that data, would be entitled to compensation from the data user for that damage and for any distress which the individual had suffered by reason of the inaccuracy. The Review recommended that further consideration should be given to the extent to which the Data Protection Act might contain provisions which are relevant for the purposes of misrepresentation or intrusion into personal privacy by the press.

The Review also identifies gaps in the legislation designed to protect private telephone conversations, and recommended that the Government should give consideration to further legislation.

While the Interception of Communications Act 1985 makes it an offence intentionally to intercept communication in the course of its transmission by means of a public telecommunication system, no further offences are committed under the Act if the communication is recorded, nor does the Act provide offences relating to the publication of intercepted material[89]. Additionally, there may be difficulty in producing evidence to establish whether or not a call has been intercepted and even where a tape which purports to be a recording of a telephone call exists, it may require the parties to the call to confirm its authenticity before a prosecution could be brought. The offence applies only in relation to public telecommunication systems, yet there are a number of private telecommunications systems in the United Kingdom. Whether a system is private or public, if it is a fixed system it will end at the network termination point, which is in domestic premises the master socket on the wall. Signals passing between a customer's handset and the radio base station, are not systems on a public network. The interception of communications, once signals have left the public network, or before the signals have reached the public network, is not caught by the Interception of Communications Act.

87 Data Protection Act 1984 S2.
88 Ibid Sch 1 Part II.
89 Interception of Communications Act 1985 S1.

10.30   Infringement of privacy

Because of the conclusion reached in the Review that the Press Complaints Commission was not operating as an effective regulator of the press the Review recommended that consideration should be given to the establishment of a new tort of infringement of privacy. Before any such tort could be introduced, it would be necessary for the subject area to receive detailed consideration in order to balance the protection of privacy with freedom of information and expression.

A White Paper on privacy rights is expected to be issued by the Department of National Heritage shortly.

11.   Buying and selling rights

[IMPORTANT NOTE: Please read the section "About this book" on page v, before referring to any of the matters in this chapter]

A.   Introduction

11.1   Purpose of this chapter

The earlier chapters of this book have examined copyright, moral rights and the law of contract, which are areas of specific importance to a publisher's or multimedia company's business. They have also considered the documentation which a publisher or multimedia company needs to obtain in order to exploit copyrights (Chapter 7 'the author's contract' and Chapter 8 'Permissions, etc') and the liability of publishers and multimedia companies in relation to the printed word (Chapters 9 and 10).

This chapter examines how a publisher or multimedia company can go about exploiting rights in works which the publisher or multimedia company has acquired, and also examines the terms on which works can be acquired.

Because rights acquired by publishers and multimedia companies are capable of extending across a very wide spectrum, this chapter examines not only buying and selling publication rights, but also dealing with subsidiary rights, merchandising rights, motion picture rights and other rights.

In practice, most licences are expressed to be "exclusive" or "sole and exclusive", but it is most important that this fact should be expressly stated in the agreement. All licences of intellectual property rights are likely to be affected by European Union and United Kingdom competition laws which are examined in Chapter 16, which should be read in conjunction with this Chapter.

This chapter concludes with a section examining the taxation consequences of buying and selling rights.

B. Buying and selling publication rights

11.2 Buying publication rights

Where a publisher or multimedia company (the "buyer") acquires rights from a seller, the buyer will generally prefer to have the rights assigned (rather than licensed) to it, since assignments are generally not capable of determination for breach (but see paragraph 11.3). A precise definition of the publication rights to be acquired by a buyer is of great importance. The extent of the rights acquired will depend upon commercial negotiation.

Publication rights may be limited to volume rights only, and may exclude sheet form rights. Volume rights may be further divided into hardback rights and paperback rights. Where hardback rights alone are acquired, a buyer may wish to prevent the seller of the rights from granting licences of the paperback rights in the work to other persons in the territory, until sufficient time has elapsed to enable the buyer to exploit the full sales potential of the work in hardback form.

The buyer may even wish to prevent any other person acquiring rights from advertising that the paperback rights will soon be available in the territory. This might, of course, damage sales of the hardback version since potential purchasers might simply decide to delay purchasing the book for a few more months until the paperback version is issued.

The entry of a book in competitions for literary prizes is a further matter which might need to be considered. By convention, the hardback publisher is generally responsible for making arrangements to enter works into competitions, but there is no reason, however, why a buyer acquiring paperback rights in a territory should not also acquire the right to enter the book for designated competitions or prizes in the country. In such circumstances, it would be normal for a buyer to require a warranty from the seller of the rights that any hardback licence or other relevant agreement entered into by the seller contained a provision prohibiting the licensee from entering the work for any competition or prize. This type of warranty would provide the paperback purchaser with some basic protection.

Various forms of newspaper and magazine exploitation rights may be considered to be subsidiary rights (see paragraph 1.16). If a buyer acquires these rights, the buyer will also enjoy the benefit of the income derived from their exercise, and the amount of income payable to the seller of the rights may be applied towards recoupment of any advance paid to the seller by the buyer. Where rights are reserved by the seller, a buyer may wish to pay a lower advance, and, additionally, may seek to prevent the exercise of any reserved rights, before or after specific periods, to prevent them from conflicting with the buyer's rights.

When a buyer acquires rights, the question of whether the buyer should also acquire the right to publish a work electronically, such as by way of its inclusion in an electronic database (see Chapter 19) or on CD-ROM should also be considered, and appropriate amendments can be made, if necessary to the subsidiary rights clauses, or the grant of publishing rights.

A buyer should also specify whether the rights acquired by the buyer are limited to one particular language, or include the right to make translations. Where the right to make translations is included, the seller of the rights may require the buyer to assign to the seller the copyright in any translation of the work commissioned by the buyer. This will enable the seller to exploit (say) a Spanish language translation created by the publisher's Spanish licensee in South America at no additional cost.

Documents 31 and 38 might be suitable for the acquisition of publication rights.

11.3 Selling publication rights

Where a publisher or multimedia company (the "seller") sells rights, the seller will generally wish the sale to be effected by way of licence. This means that, in the event of any default by the buyer, the seller will be free to terminate the licence, and enter into new arrangements with third parties in respect of the rights. Where a grant of rights is effected by way of an assignment, and the buyer commits a serious breach of the agreement permitting the seller to terminate the agreement, the seller will have to obtain a court order providing for the reassignment of the rights before being able to contract with third parties. It is, however, possible to assign rights for a period of time after which they revert, and there is no reason why the expiry of the period should not be defined as being the occurrence of a particular event, such as the giving of notice of non-payment. Although this form of provision has not previously been used in the publishing industry a sample clause is included in Document 5(e).

The ability to assign rights to a buyer depends on the rights having been assigned (as opposed to having been licensed) to the seller in the first place. Where the seller disposes of rights by way of a licence the seller should seek to exclude the ability of the buyer to grant further sub-licences (see paragraph 11.2). Sale agreements frequently contain provisions stating that the arrangements are personal to the licensee, and the licensee may not sub-license any of the rights.

Since sellers generally want to receive royalties from all sales of works in the territory (whether the sales are by the original buyer or any subsequent sub-licensee), publishing agreements frequently contain wording making it clear that the actions of any associated companies, sub-licensees or assignees of the buyer will be considered as actions of the buyer, and that the buyer will be liable to pay royalties on sales of the work by such persons. This is not an oppressive provision and is designed to protect sellers from situations where licensees enter into sub-licences with connected companies which do not pay the licensees who, therefore, do not pay their seller licensors (see also paragraph 11.22).

A seller may wish to limit the scope of the rights granted to a buyer. Limitations may be made in respect of both exclusivity and territory. Where a book is licensed by the seller for translation in a territory, and the territory granted to the buyer is not the only territory in the world where the particular language is spoken, the seller may wish to acquire ownership of the translation, in order to be able to make the translation available to the seller's other licensees in other countries where the language is spoken.

In such cases the seller may insert a provision which assigns to the seller the copyright in any translation made by the licensee, and confirms that the seller has the right to make the translation available to third parties. This provision will also be supported by an obligation on the licensee to make available to the seller a copy of the translation in typescript or disk form and the licensee should also be required to give certain warranties to the seller in respect of the translation.

Documents which might be suitable for the licensing of rights on a commercial basis can be found in Documents 32 and 33 and on a non-commercial basis in Documents 40 to 42.

11.4 Territory

Once a precise definition has been agreed for the rights which are to be granted, the next stage is for the territory to be defined. Although, under European Union law, it is possible for a licence to be limited to one or more particular countries in the European Union, it is not possible for a seller to agree that its licensee in (say) France will be protected against the seller's Belgian licensee exporting copies of the work from Belgium and selling them in France. Such copies are known as "parallel imports". (See paragraph 16.15.) Publishers acquiring exclusive English language rights for the United Kingdom face the possibility that English language rights could be sold to a licensee for a small European territory (such as Luxembourg). The United Kingdom publisher would not be able to prevent the parallel import of competing books from Luxembourg (or elsewhere in the European Union).

Linked to the choice of territory is the choice of language rights. A seller may, for example, grant English language rights for the entire European Union to one buyer. If a buyer retains English language rights in a work for the whole European Union (and European Economic Area – see paragraph 16.28) this will effectively protect the buyer from parallel imports. Where the grant of rights is for a language other than English (say French or Spanish), and for a territory which includes the European Union, the question of ownership of any foreign language material commissioned by the buyer will also be relevant, since the work may have sales potential in countries outside the territory (such as South America). The existence of foreign language material may assist sales in those countries.

Where the territory is defined by reference to the European Union, a seller should also consider whether the agreement is to extend to the European Union as it exists at the date of the agreement, or whether it is to include all member states of the European Union (or European Economic Area – paragraph 16.28) from time to time during the term.

11.5 Term

The term (or period of duration) of the agreement is a relatively straightforward provision to decide upon. Either the term will be for the full period of copyright in respect of the work or film (see paragraph 3.30) or it will be for a lesser period, normally a term of years. Where the term is calculated by reference to the copyright period in a work, it should be remembered that this period may be extended by making new editions or versions of the work, each of which may be the subject of a separate copyright (see paragraph 3.21). There will be circumstances when it will be appropriate to limit the grant of rights to the period of copyright of the original edition, as distinct from any revised edition or new edition of the work.

Where rights of different categories or media are acquired by a buyer, the agreement may provide for different terms in respect of the various different categories of rights or media. Alternatively, the periods in which certain rights are acquired may be limited and may be specified in the agreement.

Sellers will in many cases wish to avoid selling rights for the full period of copyright protection. The argument used to support the request for a limited term is that the majority of the income to be earned in respect of the book will be generated during the first few years of the term. This will not, however, be the case if the work becomes a classic – and there is probably no way of knowing whether or not this will be the case.

The factors which determine the length of the term of rights will depend not only on the identity of the author, but also upon the type of work concerned. For example, books of a technical nature soon go out of date, and can be expected to have limited periods of exploitation.

A further line of argument which a seller might use in order to justify a limited term of years, is that one of the main commercial factors considered by the seller in entering into the agreement was the buyer's ability to exploit the work to the full. While the seller may have every reason to believe that the buyer will continue to be an effective market force in the foreseeable future, there can be no guarantee that the buyer will still be in existence at the end of the term of copyright in the work and, for this reason, a specified term of years is preferable.

11.6 Remuneration

Agreements for the sale of rights normally require the seller to pay the seller an advance or a minimum guarantee plus a royalty or a percentage of profits or both. The advance or minimum guarantee will normally be recoupable by the seller from royalties or net profits payable by the seller to the seller.

For a more detailed examination of remuneration provisions see paragraphs 11.22 to 11.29.

11.7 Due diligence

An important aspect of any sale of rights is the procedure for verifying whether the seller actually owns the rights being sold. This is frequently referred to as carrying out due diligence, and is normally carried out by a lawyer with specialist knowledge. The matters which a purchaser will wish to be reassured about are, first, that the work is actually protected by copyright in the territory and, second, that the rights of the seller have been validly acquired by the seller.

In order to demonstrate ownership of works it is normal to request the seller to produce what is known as a chain of title of the work. The chain of title begins with the author of the work and tracks each disposition of rights in the work until the point where the seller acquires the work. In order for the purchaser to show that the purchaser has acquired good title to (ie owns) the work, the purchaser will need to produce a copy of each instrument transferring rights at each point in the chain, back to the original author.

If the purchaser is unable to produce this documentation, the purchaser may be unable to sue third parties to prevent infringement of copyright, since the purchaser will be unable to prove ownership to the satisfaction of the court. In the United Kingdom, however, certain presumptions exist in relation to notices printed on works (see paragraph 4.10) and if the copyright notice on the work correctly identified the seller, this will be of assistance.

There is no register of ownership of copyrights in the United Kingdom (although Stationer's Hall maintains a voluntary system – see paragraph 3.11). A register of ownership is maintained at the United States Copyright Office in the Library of Congress, and there may be occasions when a search of the United States Copyright Registry may reveal useful information.

11.8 Obligations and warranties

Agreements for the sale of rights normally contain a number of standard obligations and warranties on the part of the company selling the rights ("seller") for the benefit of the company acquiring rights ("buyer"). Examples of the types of warranties and undertakings which may be requested by a buyer from a seller are:

- the seller has the right to enter into the agreement and grant the rights;
- the seller will, throughout the term of the agreement, control the rights;
- nothing contained in the work is obscene, or blasphemous, or libellous, or defamatory;
- the work does not infringe any right of copyright, right of privacy, publicity, or moral right;
- the buyer will not incur any liability in relation to the exploitation of the rights;
- the work complies with all contractual, credit and other obligations owed by the seller;
- all importation and other requirements and costs, fees and charges will be observed, performed and paid for by the seller;
- the seller will indemnify the buyer, and keep the buyer indemnified, in respect of all costs, claims, awards and damages.

Agreements for the purchase of rights normally contain a number of standard obligations and warranties on the part of the buyer. Examples of the types of warranties and undertakings which may be requested from a buyer are:

- the buyer will not impair, or prejudice copyright, in the work and acknowledges that all rights of copyright other than those specifically licensed, or assigned, are reserved to the seller;
- the buyer will return to the seller the delivery material on the expiry of the term;
- the buyer will pay all sums punctually;
- the buyer will not license, assign, charge or sub-license any of the buyer's rights under the agreement;
- the buyer will pay all customs charges, import and export duties;
- the buyer will prevent any unauthorised exploitation of the work in the territory;

193

- the buyer will exploit the rights licensed/assigned to the best of its skill and ability;
- the buyer will indemnify the seller, and keep the seller fully and effectively indemnified, in respect of all costs, claims, proceedings etc.

11.9 Commercial terms relating to sale of subsidiary rights

The principal commercial terms contained in any sale of subsidiary rights will generally be similar to those outlined in paragraphs 11.2 to 11.8. The method in which a seller will exploit subsidiary rights will depend on the manner in which the seller has acquired them. For an analysis of the types of subsidiary rights see paragraph 1.16.

If the subsidiary rights have been assigned to the seller, the seller will generally be free to deal with them. If rights have been licensed to the seller with the power to grant further licences, then the seller will be free to license them on to third parties. In each of these situations, the seller will be contracting in its own right and will be liable to any licensee if there is any defect in the work or if the work is defamatory or if the work infringes the copyright of a third party. This may expose the seller to substantial liability towards third parties in some circumstances.

If, however, the seller has acquired the subsidiary rights as agent (see paragraphs 2.26 to 2.30) the seller will be able to contract for the exploitation of the subsidiary rights as the disclosed agent of the author, or other person from whom the rights were acquired.

In such circumstances, the seller will not incur any liability, and cannot be sued in its own right. This is a general rule, and there are obviously circumstances where the publisher may incur liability in its own right, as, for example, where it makes representations which are untrue (see paragraph 2.17).

C. Book packaging and book clubs

11.10 Book packaging

The book packaging industry is a comparatively recent development in the publishing industry worldwide. A book packager is a specialist company which will perform all the actions normally performed by a publisher in-house. The advantages to publishers in entering into arrangements with book packagers is that publishers may acquire high quality books, in bound, printed copies, immediately ready for distribution without having to apply their own time and resources directly on the production of the books.

The advantages to a publisher of using a book packager are that the publisher may be able to operate at a significantly lower overhead level, since the packager will assume and perform all the obligations and tasks normally required to be performed by a publisher, such as identifying and commissioning potential authors and other contributors, issuing contracts, organising and supervising editing, design, layout and production, entering into arrangements with printers and procuring delivery of the work.

Additionally, the packager may be able to negotiate the printing and binding of copies of the work on more advantageous terms than the publisher can.

Some packaging arrangements are fixed-price agreements, where a packager will produce and deliver a set number of books to a publisher for a set price. There are a number of commercial factors in which variations may be agreed between the parties, and these factors may be identified by contrasting the two types of packaging agreements contained in Documents 36 and 37, one of which (Document 36) is drafted from the point of view of a publisher, the other of which (Document 37 – being the Book Packagers' Associations recommended guidelines) is drafted from the point of view of a book packager. The factors which are capable of variation and which might be considered include the question of ownership of copyright, territory, term, extent of rights acquired, remuneration, commercial terms relating to the sale of subsidiary rights and the obligations and warranties and other matters referred to in paragraphs 11.2 to 11.9.

11.11 Book clubs

Arrangements with book clubs are an important part of a publisher's activities. Book clubs are capable of creating a significant increase in the numbers of books sold, and an increase in the returns to publishers, without having a markedly adverse detrimental effect on the revenues derived by publishers from the normal trade market.

There are three common forms of agreement with book clubs, being:

(a) licensing agreements pursuant to which publishers license to a book club the right to print and publish books; or

(b) sheet sale agreements pursuant to which publishers will print sheets or bound copies of books and deliver these to a book club; and

(c) combined license/sheet sale agreements pursuant to which a publisher will agree to license to the book club specified rights for a specified territory and deliver a specified amount of stock.

The commercial factors to be considered by a publisher in relation to licence agreements are examined in paragraphs 11.2 to 11.9 and 11.22 to 11.29. The commercial terms which apply to sheet sales will include the same matters as those which need to be considered in relation to licensing agreements and, additionally, matters which are analogous to those which should be considered in relation to distribution agreements (see Chapter 12).

Copies of a book club licence and a book club sale and licensing agreement are contained in Documents 34 and 35 and the provisions contained in these agreements might usefully be examined and compared with those contained in distribution agreements (Documents 47 and 48) and other acquisition and licensing agreements.

The Publishers' Association has devised a set of regulations for the conduct of book clubs and recommends that publishers of books should license books only to those book clubs which appear on the Publishers' Association register, as having signed and agreed to abide by the regulations currently in force. It is therefore recommended that all publishers contracting with book clubs should check their status with the Publishers' Association and should also obtain copies of the current Publisher's Association rules for the conduct of book clubs, and the concordat relating to fair competition between book clubs.

D. Merchandising rights

11.12 The essentials of a merchandising licence

Although the exercise of merchandising rights may have little relevance to the activities of publishers of academic books, there are numerous areas of publishing (particularly children's books and popular books) and multimedia where a literary, or artistic, property will have substantial revenue-generating potential. A form of merchandising licence is contained in Document 50.

Merchandising rights are included in the vast range of rights which may be acquired by companies from authors under the heading "subsidiary rights" and, although there are occasions when an author, or the author's agent, will exclude merchandising rights from the scope of the rights granted, there will equally be instances where these rights are acquired by companies. In these circumstances, an understanding of how they may be exploited will be necessary.

Where a company controls merchandising rights in a book, the company may wish to enter into merchandising licences with third parties in order to exploit the rights. A merchandising licence is a licence to exploit the goodwill of a literary or artistic property and any associated trade mark by means of incorporating it in an item of manufactured product.

Merchandising licences need to contain definitions of three essential components, being first, the *property* which is to be licensed (such as, for example, Roger Hargreaves' *Mr Men* books) and, second, the *generic type of product* on which it is to be applied (such as, for example, yoghurt). Once the property has been applied to the product, a third concept emerges, being the *licensed product*. The licensed product is any product of the generic type which incorporates some part of the property or on which the property has been applied (such as *yoghurt pots which contain illustrations of Mr Men*).

11.13 Rights granted in a merchandising licence

The rights granted pursuant to a merchandising licence will generally include the non-exclusive right to manufacture the licensed product, in the designated territory, during a specified term of years, together with the sole and exclusive right to package, market, sell and distribute the licensed product in the territory during the term.

It is advisable to make the manufacturing rights non-exclusive, because it is possible that the territory for which the merchandising rights are granted may have within it the largest, or best, or most competitive, manufacturing facility for the type of goods in question, and this facility might be used by licensees in neighbouring territories. There would clearly be advantages (particularly in the case of Hong Kong, Singapore and Taiwan) for these manufacturing facilities to be available to suppliers for other territories.

If, however, a rights owner grants exclusive manufacturing rights in (say) Hong Kong to a company in Hong Kong, this company may be able to prevent licensees for European territories using Hong Kong manufacturers. Even if this is not the case, there may be advantages to granting only a non-exclusive manufacturing licence. For example, where the property has not yet been widely licensed in surrounding territories, future licensees for other countries may be able to reduce their manufacturing costs, by using the manufacturer who has been chosen by the licensee for the first licensed territory.

Normally a merchandising licence will make provision for the delivery of whatever materials a licensee needs in order to be able to manufacture the licensed product. In some cases, the only materials needed will be 35mm transparencies, but frequently materials of other descriptions may be required. The licensee will usually accept an obligation to return materials delivered to the rights owner as soon as they have been used, and in any event on the expiry of the term.

On the expiry of the term, any rights granted to the licensee will, of course, expire. Normally this will mean that the licensee does not have the right to manufacture any further product. The question of what is to be done with product which has been manufactured but has not been sold needs also to be settled. Frequently this position is covered by the inclusion in the licence of a "sell-off" period at the end of the term, during which the licensee has the right to sell off any licensed product manufactured by the licensee during the term. At the end of the "sell-off" period, the licensee is usually required either to destroy the licensed product, or to deliver it up to the licensor, or to sell it to the licensor.

"Sell-off" periods are frequently thought to be concessions in favour of licensees, to permit them to sell off their stock lawfully but, in fact, the opposite is the case. In many territories, it is not possible to restrict the sale of manufactured goods once they have been put into circulation (even on a sale or return basis). For this reason, from the point of view of the licensor, it is prudent to ensure that all licences contain a provision which permits the licensor to obtain possession of existing stocks made by the licensee at the end of the term (or licence period). Many "sell-off" clauses limit the numbers of copies of works which licensees may manufacture during the latter periods of their rights (see paragraph 12.4). This is to prevent them from stockpiling copies and then "schlocking" them (dumping them at low prices in order to spoil the subsequent market).

11.14 Relevance of trade marks to merchandising licences

The value of certain types of literary and artistic properties may be more easily protected and enhanced if trade mark protection is obtained. Trade marks may be registered in relation to any element of a property which is distinctive, or capable of distinguishing, one item of product from another.

The principal advantage of trade mark protection is that it offers owners of intellectual property rights an effective way of preventing unauthorised exploitation of their properties. Although trade mark protection is not available to certain names – those with geographical associations, for example, or those which are simply not distinctive – it is possible to register as a trade mark, a distinctive logo, which may incorporate a non-registrable word.

Where a trade mark is registered, it is important that the merchandising licence should contain provisions which oblige the licensee to observe certain standards, which relate to quality and design of the licensed product. A number of quality control provisions are frequently found in agreements of this nature. These will include provisions where the licensee will agree that:

- the licensed product will be of high standard, and of such style, appearance, and quality, as to be adequate and suited to exploitation to the best advantage of the property, and to protect and enhance the value of the property, and the goodwill associated to it;
- the licensed product will be manufactured, sold, and distributed in accordance with all applicable laws in the territory;
- the policy of sales and distribution shall be consistent with earning the highest possible royalties, and marketing the licensed product to the best possible standards;
- the licensee will, before manufacturing any licensed product, make samples available for inspection, in reasonable numbers and quantities;
- the packaging and advertising material will comply with any requirements, and will not depart from any agreed standard;
- the method of design or construction of the licensed product will follow certain pre-specified requirements.

Failure to include such provisions may lead to the registration of the mark being challenged and disputed, on the basis that there is no trade connection between the proprietor of the mark and the goods which are manufactured, and that the proprietor has treated the mark as a commodity in own right, instead of an indication as to the quality and source of the manufactured goods.

This area has been of concern to the merchandising industry for some time, and various anomalies are likely to be resolved following the proposed reform of trade mark laws (see paragraph 3.44). The reforms in the law will also lead to the establishment of a community trade mark office which will accept registration of marks throughout the European Union.

11.15 Labelling of product

A merchandising licence will normally contain provisions which require the licensee to incorporate in the licensed product, or to annex or attach to it, notices which will be designed to protect the intellectual property rights which are being licensed. The notices will generally comprise:

(a) a copyright notice in accordance with the Universal Copyright Convention:
"[specify name of copyright owner] [specify year of manufacture] All Rights Reserved".

(b) a trade mark notice:
"[Name of trade mark] is a trade mark used under licence from [name of licensor]":

(c) notice in respect of any patent comprised in the licensed product:
"[specify name of patent owner] [specify patent number]

Additionally, a merchandising licence will normally require a licensee to make sure that the licensed product, and all packaging, bears the trade mark, and any appropriate notice required by all applicable laws in the territory. The merchandising licence will normally prevent the licensee from using any trade mark or name which is similar to the licensed trade mark or the property. The licensee will usually agree to co-operate fully in preserving and enforcing, and securing, any intellectual property rights in the property in the territory.

11.16 Enhancements

Enhancements are relevant to persons licensing intellectual property, because it is not unknown for licensees to develop or invent ways of enhancing the property licensed, in one way or another.

The question of enhancements may appear to have little relevance to publishers or multimedia companies, in view of the fact that merchandising users can extend across a very wide range of produce (Edwardian Lady Country Diary, Ninja Turtles, Thomas the Tank Engine etc). Improved or enhanced ways of making soap, or toy engines, or pizza have little relevance to the activities of a publisher or multimedia company, but there are instances where enhancements or improvements may have significance, such as where the licensee is granted the rights to manufacture (say) a three-dimensional toy based on a two-dimensional cartoon character.

The development of samples featuring a character for manufacture may literally add new dimensions to the original character. Enhancements or improvements may not be limited merely to physical attributes of the character itself, but may include accessories of the character and special powers. The rights owner will, quite naturally, want to have the right to incorporate any enhancements or improvements or new dimensions of its character in the original on screen or other version.

Enhancements are particularly important where themes or characters are likely to be exploited in a CD-I or multimedia or computer game or motion picture context.

11.17 Remuneration

Generally, the remuneration payable pursuant to a merchandising licence is an advance, or minimum guarantee, plus a royalty or percentage of net profits. The royalty will be based on either the retail price of the licensed product, or its recommended retail price or wholesale price.

The definition of net profits will be subject to negotiation. There is no such thing as a "standard" definition of "net profits" (see paragraph 11.24).

As an alternative to an advance, a licensee may provide the rights owner with an annual guarantee in respect of income. The guarantee will be payable in arrears, rather than in advance. Obviously an advance is preferable to a minimum guarantee.

Remuneration provisions are considered generally in paragraphs 11.22 to 11.27.

11.18 Licensees' undertakings and warranties

The undertakings and warranties normally expected of a licensee in a merchandising licence are broadly analogous to those expected of the licensee in a rights licence (see paragraph 11.8). A merchandising licence will additionally contain certain obligations on the part of the licensee to effect product liability insurance and, depending on the territory concerned, there will be further provisions relating to consumer protection (see paragraphs 12.30 to 12.43).

E. Motion picture and television rights

11.19 Motion picture and television rights generally

In former years, motion picture and television rights invariably formed part of the subsidiary rights (see paragraph 1.16) granted to publishers, but nowadays this is not always the case. Where a publisher does obtain these rights, the publisher will generally remit to the author 80%, or 90%, of the income received by the publisher from the exploitation of the motion picture and television rights. Whether the publisher will enter into film and television rights agreements in the publisher's own name, or as agent for the author, may need to be considered (see paragraphs 2.26 to 2.30).

Where a publisher enters into film or television rights agreements in its own name it will, generally, be liable if there is any breach of warranty, or other claim under the agreement. In many cases a publisher will have no control over the events which may give rise to a breach of warranty or claim, since only the author will know if (s)he has plagiarised another work, or defamed an innocent person. Because the financial liabilities which may be incurred by a publisher entering into agreements of this type in the publisher's own name are significant, it is not generally advisable for publishers to assume such risks.

11.20 Option agreements

From the point of view of the rights owner, it is bad business practice to sell film or television rights in a work to a production company on an outright basis. If the production company goes into liquidation, loses interest in the project, or is unable to raise the production finance for it, the rights owner will not receive the benefits which would otherwise be received from a finished film. This benefit would normally take the form of increased sales of the work, and a participation in any profits made from the film.

Because of the risks involved in giving production companies rights on an outright basis, rights owners will normally only be prepared to grant them an option to acquire motion picture or television rights during a specified option period for an agreed purchase price.

If the production company exercises the option and pays the agreed purchase price during the option period, then the production company will own the rights. If the production company does not exercise the option and fails to pay the purchase price during the option period then, at the end of the option period, the production company's rights will lapse and the rights owner will be free to enter into arrangements with other interested parties. The production company will, once it has paid the option price, have no liability to pay the purchase price, unless it exercises its option.

The option period is generally an initial period of at least 12 months, which may be extended by one or more further periods of 12 months. The production company will normally pay the rights owner an option price on signature of the option agreement and will also usually pay a further sum if the option period is extended.

The price payable on the signature of the option agreement (the option price) is normally 10% of the price payable on the exercise of the option (the purchase price). It is usual to treat the option price (and sometimes any fees payable for extending the option period) as payment on account of the purchase price. The purchase price is usually reduced by the amount of any prepayments. The purchase price may be a specified amount, ie US$[amount] or £[amount], or, in some cases will be a specified amount plus a percentage of the budget of the film. Additionally, the rights owner will, in some cases, wish to receive participations in profits derived from the film or television series. Whether or not this is appropriate will depend on the relative strengths of bargaining power of the parties.

11.21   Remake and sequel rights, live stage and radio rights

Where film rights are granted to a production company, the remuneration payable to the rights owner in respect of a remake is generally 50% of the remuneration payable for the first film and, in the case of a sequel, $33^1\!/_3$%. For television exploitation the rights owner may receive a fee calculated by reference to the duration of each episode of any television series, or by reference to its exploitation in various countries throughout the world.

A precise definition of the rights acquired by the production company will always depend on the project, the nature of the work and the rights available. In addition to motion picture, television, film and series rights, a production company will always require certain subsidiary and ancillary rights, such as the right to exploit recording and merchandising elements in the work and the right to publish limited synopses of the work. The production company will also need the right to make adaptations of the work, and the right to use the work with other literary material so that the production company can make adaptations of the work, and base the screenplays on it.

Normally a rights owner will reserve publication rights, and it is also usual to reserve live stage and radio rights. A production company will generally seek to impose a restriction preventing the exercise of live stage and radio rights during a certain period, and will normally obtain the right to make and exploit a synopsis of the work of between 7,500 and 10,000 words for publicity purposes.

In practice, synopsis rights are generally obtained from a publisher through a publisher's release, or quitclaim. Despite its American-sounding origin, "quitclaim" is a medieval French word which means a formal discharge or release. A quitclaim is normally required by a production company from all known publishers of a work in order to confirm that the publisher's agreement with the author does not entitle the publisher to any of the motion picture or television rights. A form of quitclaim may be found in Document 29.

F.   Remuneration provisions in rights agreements

11.22   Advances and minimum guarantees

There are many circumstances in which a purchaser will acquire rights in return for the payment of a single fee. This fee may be referred to as a fee, as an advance or even a minimum guarantee.

In agreements where a flat fee is payable, the only matter which may require negotiation is when the fee is payable. There are generally three alternative time points: signature of the agreement, delivery of the work, and publication of the work. Frequently the fee is divided into instalments, payable on those dates.

Where a purchaser agrees to pay an advance, it is usual also for the advance to be paid in instalments in certain stages. An advance is normally only paid where a purchaser has agreed to make additional payments, either by way of royalty, or by way of profits, and is literally an advance payment on account of royalties. This will mean that the purchaser will be entitled to recover an amount equal to the advance out of the sums payable by way of royalties. In other words, the advance is recoupable. Many contracts, however, do not specifically provide that advances are recoupable.

Although it may be possible to draw the inference from surrounding circumstances that the parties intended that the advance would be recoupable, it is advisable to state this fact clearly. If an advance is non-recoupable, the purchaser will not be entitled to recover an equivalent amount from the royalties and will have to pay these from first exploitation of the work.

A further aspect relating to advances which may need to be clarified, is whether the advance is to be returnable or non-returnable. Even if the contract does not make specific provision for the advance to be repaid, a purchaser may be able to sue for the recovery of damages up to the amount of the advance and also any other losses incurred by the purchaser (see paragraph 13.13) if the other party to the contract is in breach of its material obligations under the contract.

Where, however, the performance of a contract is frustrated (see paragraphs 2.19 and 2.20) by some event beyond the control of the parties, the purchaser may be entitled to seek repayment of any advances which have been paid. This entitlement may, however, be jeopardised if the contract pursuant to which the advance was paid states that the advance is non-returnable, and purchasers should for this reason avoid agreeing to pay non-returnable advances, if possible.

Contracts which state that advances are returnable, normally meet with objections from the person entitled to be paid the advance. Since, from a purchaser's point of view, the main priority is to avoid describing advances as non-returnable, it is perfectly acceptable to a purchaser if a contract simply refers to "an advance of £[*amount*] recoupable from the royalties payable pursuant to Clause [*number*]".

Where a purchaser is entitled to be paid an advance by a sub-licensee, there may be occasions when it is advisable for the purchaser to negotiate the highest possible advance figure, rather than negotiate for a high royalty and a small advance.

There are two reasons for this. First, there is no guarantee that the sales of the work will ever actually reach the amount of the advance, which could therefore be regarded as a guarantee that the purchaser will receive a minimum amount.

The second reason is that interest is not generally charged on advances and is not recouped from royalties (although there is no reason why a person paying an advance should not be permitted to recover interest on it), and the recipient of the advance might be regarded as having the interest-free use of the advance until it is recouped.

Some contracts contain remuneration provisions which refer to minimum guarantees. Many people use the term "minimum guarantee" in a sense that is synonymous with "advance". In the strict sense of the word, however, an advance is usually payable in advance while a minimum guarantee is a guarantee that the person entitled to receive payment will receive a minimum sum (see paragraph 11.17). Minimum guarantees may be payable at the end of an accounting period, or at the end of the term of an agreement, or at the end of a specified year, rather than in advance.

11.23 Royalties

Where a purchaser has licensed rights to a third party, and is entitled to receive royalty payments, the purchaser will normally wish to ensure that the royalty is payable on all sales of the work by the third party and any sub-licensees of the third party.

While the percentage amount of any royalty is of obvious importance, the basis on which the percentage is calculated is equally important, and should be examined closely by any person who is entitled to receive royalties.

The price on which the royalty is based (or royalty base price) is normally the recommended retail price, although it is not unknown for the royalty base price to be the sub-licensee's wholesale price or the actual selling price of the work net of all deductions and discounts. The royalty is normally calculated on all copies of the relevant work which have been sold and paid for and have not been returned. Many agreements contain provisions which permit the distribution of copies of works as surplus or review copies or for publicity purposes without the payment of royalties.

Where a company is entitled to receive a percentage of the receipts of a third party, these payments are not royalty payments in the strict sense of the word, but might better be described as participations in receipts, or participations in profits.

G. Participations in receipts and profits

11.24 Receipts – gross, net, source, or remitted?

The expressions "gross receipts" "net receipts" and "net profits" have no absolute fixed meaning: they are variables whose precise sense will depend on how they are defined in the contract in which they are used (see paragraph 11.17). Definitions of the terms should always be provided and should be examined carefully.

When dealing with participations it is important to be able to distinguish between source receipts and remitted receipts. Source receipts are sums which arise "at source" or at the point of sale or exploitation of a work. Remitted receipts are the sums remitted to, and actually received by, the third party who is contractually liable to pay the participation to the company. (It is similarly important to be conscious of the distinction between received and receivable income for the reasons referred to in paragraph 12.8.)

A participation which is based on remitted receipts will be much less than a participation based on source receipts. For example, where a company licenses rights in a work to a third party in return for 15% of that third party's receipts, the company will be entitled to receive 15% of sums remitted to that third party, not 15% of sums generated by the work. If the third party sub-licenses the work to a sub-licensee in return for a 15% royalty, the company will be entitled to receive only 2.25% of the third party's receipts (15% of 15%) leaving the third party with 12.75%.

If, however, the company negotiates a participation which is calculated on the receipts of the third party and its (and their) sub-licensees, then the company will be entitled to participate in source receipts and, if the figures in the preceding paragraph were to apply, the company would be entitled to all sums received by the third party (namely 15% of the sums received by the third party's sub-licensee).

If a company is to permit third parties to whom it grants rights to sub-license them, it is most important for the question of sub-licensing to be tackled directly. The company must protect itself from the third party selling those rights onward to an entity which it is connected with it for a nominal sum, say £1, and accounting to the company on the nominal sum only, leaving the connected company with the majority of the income derived from the work. This abuse is, of course, prevented if the company is entitled to participate in the receipts of the third party, its sub-licensees and all other persons authorised by or through them.

Where a company is entitled to participate in a third party's net receipts, the third party will usually be entitled to deduct certain items of expenditure from its receipts. Many agreements fail to specify precisely what items may be deducted – and this must be done clearly. It is also prudent to limit the deduction entitlement to reasonable amounts of expenditure, wholly and exclusively incurred and expended by the third party, directly in connection with the book. Agreements which provide for the payment of royalties do not usually permit expenses to be deducted from them, since the amount of expenses and costs could easily exceed the amount of the royalty. There may, however, be circumstances where this might be appropriate.

11.25 Onerous provisions

In transactions where a company is entitled to receive a participation in receipts (gross or net, source or remitted) there are ways in which a third party can reduce the amount receivable by the company.

One way is the insertion of a provision which states that sums received by the third party, by way of advance or minimum guarantee, do not constitute receipts unless and until they are fully earned. This will mean that any such sums payable to the third party by its sub-licensees or sub-distributors will not be counted as income for the purpose of the third party's arrangements with the company, until the sub-licensees have recouped their advances or minimum guarantees and started paying royalties to the third party.

The effect of such a provision is that, even where an advance may be non-returnable (see paragraph 11.22), and is therefore the property of the third party, it will not be brought into account unless it is fully earned. In some situations advances are never recouped, and this provision would be detrimental to a company's interests since it permits their licensees to accumulate cash on which they are not liable to make payments.

A further means of reducing a company's entitlement is for the third party to deduct from receipts sums which either did not form part of them, or have already been deducted, such as sums payable by way of value added tax (which is payable on services) and sub-distributors and sub-licensees' commissions and expenses. Where a third party obtains the right to deduct the above items from remitted receipts (see paragraph 11.24) there will be a double deduction, since these sums will already have been deducted from receipts before they were remitted to the third party. The amount deducted by the third party will therefore constitute an additional profit centre, unless the provision is amended.

11.26 Accounting provisions

Most rights licences in the publishing industry provide for accounting to be effected on a half-yearly basis up to 31 December and 30 June in each year. A statement of account is normally remitted to the author, or proprietor, within a set number of days after the expiry of the accounting period. This number is frequently 90 days, although shorter periods may, in some cases, be negotiated. Indeed, there is no reason why, in appropriate cases, the accounting periods should not be quarterly, although this will affect the cashflow of companies. In the audio-visual industries, accounting periods are normally quarterly, ending on 31 March, 30 June, 30 September and 31 December in each year, with payment due 30 or 45 days after the end of the accounting period.

Each statement of account is normally accompanied by payment of all sums which are indicated to be owing to the rights owner, subject of course to any provision which provides for the recoupment of advances, or minimum guarantees, and retention of reserves. Where sums are received in currencies other than pounds sterling, currency conversion provisions may be inserted. In some cases, it may be appropriate to impose on a distributor or licensee an obligation to convert sums which have been received in a foreign currency into the currency in which accounts are to be rendered, in the event of any materially adverse currency fluctuation.

A rights owner will normally require its licensees to keep full and proper books of account, relating to the books being distributed, and will require a right of access to the accounts and records, as well as rights of inspection and audit together with the right of inspection of the premises on reasonable prior notice during the term of the agreement.

It is also common for agreements to provide that where an accounting error has been discovered in excess of 5% or 10% of sums due to the rights owner in any accounting period, then the third party shall pay the rights owner the costs of its audit or inspection together with the sums due.

H. Taxation

11.27 Direct taxation

The double taxation and withholding tax implications of any payments made from one jurisdiction to a recipient located in a different jurisdiction should be considered at an early stage. Normally, a rights owner third party distributor or licensee will require the right to make any deductions or withholdings which are required by law in respect of remittances of money to the rights owner. The exercise of this right should be made conditional on the third party providing receipts, certificates and other documents or information required in order to enable the publisher to obtain any tax credit in respect of the deduction or withholding.

The right to make reserves against returns or other liabilities will, of course, be subject to commercial negotiations and will normally be resisted by the rights owner. Alternatively it may be possible (under the terms of a relevant double tax agreement) to make payments gross provided that permission to do so is obtained in advance from the fiscal authorities of the payer's jurisdiction. Specific professional advice should be taken as appropriate.

11.28 Value Added Tax

If an agreement makes no provision for Value Added Tax to be paid in addition to any contractual payment and Value Added Tax is chargeable on the supply in question, any amounts payable will be deemed to be inclusive of Value Added Tax and netted down by the Value Added Tax fraction (currently 7/47). This will have an adverse impact on the rights owner's receipts. Accordingly, all amounts payable should be stated as being exclusive of Value Added Tax and the documentation should incorporate a contractual right for the supplier to claim Value Added Tax from the recipient should Her Majesty's Customs and Excise (or any other Value Added Tax authority) require it to be accounted for subsequently.

Value Added Tax is chargeable on royalties in the United Kingdom and should be considered at the time of agreeing the royalty fee and drafting the related documentation. If a royalty payment is received in the United Kingdom from a non-United Kingdom source, a Value Added Tax reverse charge may arise. Reverse charges are considered in more detail in paragraph 12.28. Whether this will have any real financial consequences for the recipient will depend on its own Value Added Tax position.

The assignment of copyright will be a supply of services if made to a person in the United Kingdom and will also be standard rated for Value Added Tax purposes. If a transaction involves payments to and receipts from more than one jurisdiction then the Value Added Tax implications should be examined carefully in advance. The precise position will depend on whether the supply is to a recipient within or outside the European Union and if within the European Union whether the Value Added Tax supply is received in a business capacity as well as whether the supplier and recipient are registered, in the same or different member states. Similarly, the Value Added Tax consequences of any assignment of a copyright from outside the UK to a person in the United Kingdom should be taken into account. Reverse charges are considered in more detail in paragraph 12.28.

The Value Added Tax consequences of the sale of books and distribution agreements are considered in paragraphs 12.22 to 12.29. Although the sale of printed books generally is assumed to be a zero-rated supply in the United Kingdom (which is not the case throughout the European Union), an increasing number of books is being treated as standard rated for Value Added Tax purposes, and Her Majesty's Customs and Excise will seek to apply the standard rate if the book in question does not satisfy the tests they apply. Furthermore, the sale of an actual manuscript of a book, or a shorthand transcript, will be standard rated for Value Added Tax purposes.

11.29 Stamp duty

The stamp duty consequences of any transaction for the sale of rights and the implementing documentation should also be considered at an early stage. An assignment of copyright, for example, will be liable to ad valorem stamp duty at the rate of 1% as will, in certain circumstances, the grant of an exclusive licence (which is regarded as the conveyance of property) but usually no duty is charged on the grant of a revocable licence or upon arrangements which are not exclusive.

One particular stamp duty problem which often arises in transactions for the sale of rights (where the right to exploit copyright in a book may have little value without the right to the physical chattel) is the question of apportionment of consideration between the tangible property (which is deliverable and therefore not liable to stamp duty) and the copyright. If the apportionment of the consideration by the parties is bona fide, then even if the allocation is not necessarily indicative of their respective values it should be possible to avoid a reallocation of the consideration by the United Kingdom Stamp Office. The parties should not overlook other tax consequences of the proposed apportionment, however, which could prove more costly than stamp duty.

It is sometimes possible to reduce the charge to stamp duty on the assignment of copyright or grant of an exclusive licence if non-United Kingdom rights and United Kingdom rights are dealt with in separate documents provided that the assignment, transfer or grant of non-United Kingdom rights is not executed in the United Kingdom and the related documentation is retained offshore. It would be important to confirm that no similar transfer duty would be charged in the jurisdiction where the non-United Kingdom grant or assignment is actually executed and retained.

A transaction will qualify as a small transaction where the consideration for the property being assigned does not exceed £60,000 (currently) provided that it does not form part of a larger transaction or series of transactions for which the aggregate amount of consideration would be in excess of £60,000. A certificate in appropriate form should be included in the relevant document or may be endorsed on it subsequently, as long as it is signed by all relevant parties.

If the consideration for an assignment is uncertain at the time of execution (for example, in the case of royalties, which will depend on profits) then unless it is possible to calculate the amount which will be received (which could be subject to a maximum or a minimum) documents executed on or after 8 December 1993 will be charged with ad valorem stamp duty on the open market value of the property transferred. This supersedes the previous rule that where sums which cannot be quantified at the date of execution, and which are not subject to a minimum or maximum, the assignment will only bear fixed duty of 50 pence. This means that, in such cases, valuations must be agreed with the Stamp Office of the Inland Revenue which could be an expensive and time-consuming process. In such cases, advance consideration of the likely value of the assets transferred (backed up by documentation) is recommended. If a minimum or maximum is expressed, ad valorem stamp duty of 1% will be charged on that amount irrespective of whether that amount is finally received. Great care should be taken in how unascertained consideration is expressed in any related documentation.

If a document evidencing the transfer of ownership of intellectual property rights is produced to a court, and if stamp duty has not been paid on that document, it is possible that a court might refuse to accept such document as proof of the transfer of such rights.

12. Distribution agreements – the commercial terms

[IMPORTANT NOTE: Please read the section "About this book" on page v, before referring to any of the matters in this chapter]

A. Introduction

12.1 Purpose of this chapter

Acquiring rights from authors, or other rights owners, and licensing rights to third parties is only a small part of the activity of a publishing or multimedia company. The overriding commercial imperative of a publisher or multimedia company is to get their works printed or duplicated and on shelves in shops. The numerous practical matters which are required to take a book or other multimedia work through production form an essential part of the skills of a publisher or multimedia professional, but are outside the scope of this book.

Contractual arrangements for the supply of plant and machinery could have been dealt with in this book, but have been excluded, partly on grounds of space, but primarily because contractual arrangements for the supply of machinery are variable and are normally determined by transaction-specific details, and are frequently for substantial sums of money, and are therefore matters on which companies ought to take specific legal advice.

Contractual arrangements with printers, manufacturers, and duplicators, have also been excluded from this book, again partly on grounds of space, but primarily because the relationships are frequently close, and invariably extremely complex.

This chapter therefore focusses solely on matters relating to the distribution of printed books, discs and other items of manufactured product. The contractual arrangements relating to the distribution of finished product are of fundamental importance to the continued existence of a publisher or multimedia company. If proper attention is not given to distribution arrangements, a company may face not only loss of the items of manufactured product themselves, but also the loss of all proceeds from their sale. In fact, a number of companies have suffered substantial losses in recent years through failing to deal with such matters in their distribution arrangements.

This chapter, therefore, looks at the principal terms of distribution agreements and their financial provisions. It also examines the legal rules which determine when property and risk in goods pass, the effect of sale or return transactions, and certain standard obligations normally assumed by companies and their distributors.

The chapter also examines commission arrangements in distribution agreements and contains a detailed analysis of the impact of Value Added Tax on distribution arrangements. The chapter concludes with an analysis of those areas in which a company might incur legal liability in relation to the distribution of printed or manufactured product. The chapter does not examine European Union and United Kingdom Competition laws. These have a definite bearing on distribution agreements and are examined in Chapter 16 which, it is suggested, should be read in conjunction with this chapter.

To place the chapter in a practical perspective it may be useful to refer to a distribution agreement. Two forms of distribution agreement are included in Documents 47 and 48.

B. Principal terms

12.2 Rights

The rights which a company grants to a distributor under a distribution agreement will be for a defined term and will extend throughout a designated territory. Frequently the distributor will wish to distribute all works owned or controlled by the company. It may be preferable for the company to limit the scope of the agreement to designated imprints, which will leave the company with some flexibility if the company wishes to expand or widen its activities in the future.

Where a company's catalogue, or any work that has been the subject of a prior distribution arrangement with a third party whose rights have ended, the distributor may be required to accept a limited right of competition from the third party during any so-called "sell-off" period (see paragraph 12.4) enjoyed by the third party.

12.3 Exclusivity

The rights acquired by a distributor will usually include the exclusive rights to sell and distribute all works owned or controlled by the company in the territory during the term. Frequently, the distributor may acquire the right to use publicity material which is provided by the company for the purpose of advertising and promotion, but this will depend on the precise arrangements between the parties relating to advertising.

The rights granted to a distributor may be a mixture of exclusive rights and non-exclusive rights. A distributor may, for example, have exclusive rights in one country and non-exclusive rights in another country.

The degree of exclusivity enjoyed by a distributor will depend on the laws in force in the territory concerned. The provisions of the European Community Treaty (see paragraphs 16.9 to 16.15) affect exclusivity in the European

Union and the European Economic Area. Other countries also have laws affecting the exclusivity of distributors (Australia has recently enacted legislation in this area) and suitably qualified foreign legal advice should be sought, where appropriate.

12.4 Term

When agreeing upon the term of a distribution agreement, no less than four separate elements need to be considered, namely the period (or term) the agreement will last, the period of distribution rights to be enjoyed by the distributor, the length of any sell-off period and the extent of any collection period.

The first two elements may appear to be identical (and in many agreements the difference is not of particular relevance) but where a distribution agreement relates to a company's entire catalogue (or certain imprints) and is for a term of (say) two years, the period of distribution rights in relation to a work first distributed in month 21 would only be three months. This would clearly be too short a period for most distributors, and in many circumstances it will be in the interests of both company and distributor for the distributor's rights to continue for a longer period – in order to avoid confusion in the market-place and loss of incentive. In such circumstances, the agreement can provide for the distributor to enjoy distribution rights in works for a minimum distribution period – regardless of when the works are delivered.

The question of a "sell-off" period may not always be relevant and will depend on the precise nature of the arrangements between company and distributor. The sell-off period is the period during which the distributor is permitted to sell off stocks of works in the distributor's possession. It is in the publisher's interest (see paragraph 11.13) for the "sell-off" period to be as short as possible so as not to interfere with the activities of the new distributor. Technically there is no reason for the distributor to have any sell-off period at all and the distribution agreement could provide for the distributor to deliver up to the company the entire stock of unsold works held by the distributor at the end of the term.

The collection period is the period during which the distributor is entitled to collect outstanding debts. Since most distribution agreements will entitle the distributor to receive a commission on sales, it would be unfair to deprive the distributor of commission on sales made during the term, merely because payment was not received until after the term had expired. It would equally not be in the company's interest if the company were obliged to pay commission to a distributor on debts collected by the company after the end of the distribution agreement if these debts had been regarded as bad or doubtful debts and provision had been made for them by the distributor.

An effective commercial compromise is for the company to allow the distributor to have the benefit of a collection period. The distributor will receive commission on payments for sales made by the distributor during the term, if the payments are made during the collection period. If the payments are not made during the collection period, the distributor will not be entitled to any commission.

211

12.5 Basis of calculation of distribution commission

The starting point for the calculation of a distributor's commission will usually be the amount of gross receipts generated, since the distributor will normally be entitled to receive a commission which is a percentage of this amount. If the distribution agreement is drafted from the point of view of the distributor, then the definition of gross receipts may be linked to receipts "at source" (see paragraph 11.24) which would lead to the company paying more by way of commission.

If the agreement is drafted from the point of view of the company, then the definition of gross receipts may be linked to receipts calculated on a so-called "remittance" basis (see paragraph 11.24) which will lead to the company paying less by way of commission. The cost to the company is further reduced where the commission is calculated on a net receipts basis. In this instance these are first deducted from the gross receipts (preferably from the company's point of view calculated on a remitted basis rather than a source basis) the distributor's expenses, and the commission is based on the net amount of receipts remaining after the deduction of these expenses.

In calculating commission bases it is important to be clearly aware of the distinction between received and receivable income (see paragraph 12.8).

12.6 Commission basis favourable to the company

Where a company appoints a distributor, the method of calculating commission which is most favourable to the company will be as follows:

(a) gross receipts will be calculated on a "remittance" (see paragraph 11.24) basis;

(b) the distributor will be permitted to deduct from the gross receipts the distributor's pre-approved expenses which will be limited to a maximum sum or percentage of income in any period;

(c) the balance of gross receipts remaining after the deduction of expenses will constitute net receipts;

(d) the commission payable to the distributor will be calculated as a percentage of the net receipts;

(e) if the net receipts suffer deduction of tax at "source" (see paragraph 11.24) the distributor will gross up the net amounts so that the company receives the amount it would have received had there been no such deduction.

12.7 Commission basis favourable to the distributor

Where a company is acting as the distributor of another company, the method of calculating which is most favourable to the distributor will be as follows:

(a) gross receipts will be calculated on a "source" basis (see paragraph 11.24);

(b) from the gross receipts, the commission of the distributor will be deducted;

(c)   the balance of gross receipts remaining after deduction of the commission or distribution fee will be applied towards payment of the distributor's expenses;

(d)   the net sums remaining after the deduction of commission and expenses is remitted to the publisher subject to (e) and (f) below;

(e)   the distributor will require the right to make reserves out of sums to be remitted to the supplier in order to cover the distributor in respect of future liability for distribution expenses which may include bad debts, and also to cover the distributor's potential liability in respect of future manufacturing expenses, and future returned stock;

(f)   additionally, where a distributor provides additional services (such as the printing or manufacture or packing of a product), the distributor may require an undertaking from the company to pay the distributor any short-fall between the amount of gross receipts actually received, and the amount of the commission owed to the distributor plus the amount of costs and expenses incurred by the company in relation to the additional services.

12.8   Received and receivable income

It is of crucial importance, when negotiating commission arrangements, to be conscious of the difference between received income and receivable income. A distributor will normally wish its commission to be calculated with reference to receivable income. Where this is accepted, the company will be paying a commission on income which may never be received – since at least some part of receivable income will constitute bad debts.

Where receipts are calculated on a "source" basis, a distributor will normally protect itself from having to pay the company the amount of any bad debts by providing that bad debts are permitted deductions from receipts.

Where a commission is calculated by reference to actual receipts, a distributor will only be entitled to receive commission in respect of sales for which payment has been made. It is not necessary to deduct the amount of bad debts from actual receipts, since the amounts comprising the bad debts will not have been counted as receipts in the first place. Where provision is included it may operate as a double deduction and constitute a hidden profit centre in favour of the distributor.

12.9   The reduction of financial risk

The accounting provisions which should be included in distribution agreements are of a different type to those contained in author's agreements (see Chapter 7), or agreements for the sale or purchase of rights (see paragraphs 11.2 to 11.8).

The appointment of an exclusive distributor by a company involves the assumption, by the company, of risks of the highest commercial significance, since the distributor acquires effective control of the company's entire turnover. For this reason, it is essential that the arrangements offer the company the highest degree of security permissible.

Many distribution arrangements do not, however, offer companies any protection from the high-risk factors and, in some cases, companies are asked to place all their faith in the existence of a good personal relationship with a director of the distributor, who will normally have no personal liability.

The primary concern of the company which is entering into a distribution agreement must be to prevent its turnover and profits being made available to fund the distributor's business, or to satisfy the claims of the distributor's secured creditors. The consequences of either of these possibilities may lead to the company's own insolvency, because although it might be deprived of all its income, the company will nonetheless have incurred liabilities which it has to meet.

The greatest level of financial protection which a company can achieve is to persuade the distributor to agree to pay all distribution revenue into an account managed by and in the name of the company. In practice, very few distributors are prepared to do this, although there may be occasions where the strength of bargaining power of the company may be such that this is acceptable. In some circumstances, a distributor may agree to maintaining an account in the joint names of the company and the distributor. The terms on which the account may be operated will need to be stipulated.

Alternatively, the distributor may be appointed as the agent of the company which will impose certain fiduciary obligations (see paragraph 12.16) or the distributor may agree to hold the distribution receipts on trust, which may have the same effect. In order for these protections to be effective the distribution income will need to be clearly identifiable and will need to be kept separate from, and not commingled with, other income. In practice, this is extremely difficult to achieve, and failure to ensure complete separation will undermine the legal efficacy of the solution (see paragraph 12.17).

A further alternative, at least in theory, is for the company to take a legal charge over the distributor's bank account, but in practice this is likely to be unacceptable, not only to the distributor, but also to the distributor's bank.

Whatever the legal or contractual position, in practical terms there is a great deal which a company can do to avoid calamity.

- First, the period when the distributor holds money should be as short as possible, and linked to the regular payment dates of the distributor's main customers, where known.
- Second, it is possible to operate a two-speed system of accounting, where substantial sums over a pre-specified amount must be paid over by the distributor in five or seven days, and other sums paid over monthly.
- Third, the company should monitor the distributor's business as closely as is reasonable, in order not only to raise efficiency, but also to receive advance notice of any warning signs.
- Fourth, before entering into distribution arrangements, a careful check should be made on the distributor's creditworthiness, the level of indebtedness to banks and the extent and type of security which they may have over the distributor's business. If, for example, a company's investigation reveals that the distributor's bank has advanced a large loan which remains outstanding, and that the bank has a charge over the distributor's bank account, it would probably be inadvisable for the company to permit its distribution income to be held in the distributor's bank account.

There may be circumstances in which it would be prudent for the company to carry out periodic checks on its distributor's financial stability. Since financial instability is often associated with poor or unreliable accounting, audit rights should be exercised on a reasonable basis, in order to encourage efficiency as well as to check on accuracy. Where the terms of the arrangements permit, the company should consider obtaining access to books, records and accounting statements of the distributor's customers. The distributor should be required, where relevant, to pursue any queries raised, and to follow them up by way of audit.

C. Delivery and risk

12.10 Delivery obligations

Distribution agreements generally contain provisions dealing with the method of delivery of product, and the period in which books or other items of product are required to be delivered. The method of delivery may be delivery to the premises of the distributor, or delivery ex-works, FOR-FOT, FOB-airport, FAS, FOB, C&F, CIF, ex-ship, ex-quay and frontier duty paid. All the above expressions have an international standard meaning and are defined in the Inco-terms of the International Chamber of Commerce.

Where a distribution agreement is drafted from the point of view of the distributor, it is normal to expect delivery of books or other items of product to a distributor's place of business. The agreement may also provide that the company will bear all costs in relation to delivery, but this will not, of course, always be acceptable to the company.

A distributor will generally wish to secure a specific time limit within which delivery must be made by the company. For the purpose of delivery obligations, time may be made of the essence of the contract (see paragraph 2.10). In other words, any dates, or time limits, contained in the contract must be strictly complied with, or the company will be in breach. With books and multimedia product time of delivery is of particular importance, not merely to eliminate any disruption to business, but also to exploit their topicality.

Frequently, a company may wish to avoid altogether, or else mitigate, its liability for failure to deliver within a specified time period, and in some cases a company's will include wide-ranging force majeure clauses, which exclude the company from delay outside the company's control (see paragraph 2.20).

12.11 Risk of loss or damage

It is important for a company to specify exactly when the risk in books and other items of multimedia product delivered under distribution agreements passes to the distributor. The reason for this is that, once risk has passed to the distributor, then the distributor will be liable for any loss or damage occasioned to the product. In distribution agreements which have been drafted from the point of view of the distributor, the risk in product (see paragraph 12.13) may pass to a distributor only when the distributor appropriates the product to a particular order placed by the distributor's customers. These provisions may be linked to provisions in the distributor's standard terms and conditions of sale, which may provide that risk passes to the distributor's customers when the distributor appropriates product to serve that customer's order.

In such circumstances the distributor will never have any liability if the product is lost or damaged, and this is not a state of affairs that is likely to be acceptable to most companies, who will generally seek to provide that if books or other items of product are destroyed or damaged while they are in the possession of the distributor, then the distributor will be liable. The provision is frequently backed up by an obligation on the distributor to effect insurance cover in relation to such liability. Whether or not the cost of such cover is recovered by the distributor as a distribution expense, is a matter for negotiation.

If loss or damage occurs after appropriation of books or other items of product, by the distributor pursuant to a third party contract then, although the distributor may remain liable to the company (depending on the terms of the relevant agreement), the third party customer will be liable to pay the purchase price to the distributor as a contract debt (subject to the terms of sale of the distributor, and any special contract terms). It is important for a company to examine its distributor's terms and conditions of sale of books or other items of product to ensure that they are adequate and do not conflict with the terms of the company's own arrangements or undermine its security arrangements.

12.12 Credit risk

Where a distributor accepts orders from customers for books or other items of product and fulfils the orders, then, depending on the financial provisions in the distribution agreement, the distributor may become liable to pay the company the sale price of the company for supplying the books or other items of product of the distributor. Alternatively, the distributor may become liable to pay to the company the distributor's resale price, less a fee and expenses. The precise terms will depend upon the arrangements.

The liability owed by the distributor to the company will probably be absolute and the distributor may therefore protect its position, and ability, to make the payment by reserving title in the books or other items of product which the distributor sells to its customer.

The question of who is to accept the credit risk relating to the distributor's customers is a further aspect which needs to be considered. If the distributor sells to a customer which does not pay, who is to be responsible for the bad debt?

From the company's point of view, the most preferable alternative is to oblige the distributor – which will mean that the distributor is liable to pay the company whether or not it receives payment from its customer.

Conversely the distributor may wish to assume liability to pay the company only when the distributor's customer has paid. This is not entirely satisfactory from the company's point of view, since the distributor may supply customers who do not, in the company's opinion, represent a good credit risk. If such customers do not pay, and the stock is not recovered, the company will suffer loss.

It is normal for the parties to a distribution agreement to agree upon a policy relating to a bad debt. There will be certain customers who the company will not want the distributor to supply, unless the distributor assumes the credit risk. Conversely there may be customers whom the company wishes the distributor to supply, but the distributor refuses to supply unless the company assumes the credit risk. Hopefully there will be a larger numbers of customers which both company and distributor wish to supply.

Where a company agrees to assume liability for bad debts, it would be normal for the company to wish to have the benefit of any right which the distributor might have to commence proceedings for the recovery of the debts, as well as the right to receive payment of any sums recovered by such action. In view of the lack of an enforceable contract directly between the company and the distributor's customer (unless the distributor was acting as the publisher's agent) the distribution agreement may need to contain a provision requiring the distributor to bring proceedings necessary to recover the debts, usually at the cost of the company.

12.13 Ownership

Property (or ownership) of books or other items of product will normally remain with the company until the books or other items of product have been appropriated by the distributor, in order to fulfil a customer's order. This will, of course, mean that the stock risk, or the risk of being able to sell the books or other items of product, will remain with the company. This is normal and is a risk which is considered by companies when calculating how large the print or manufacturing run of each book or other product should be. At some point, property (or ownership) of the product must, however, pass both to the distributor and to the distributor's customer, in order to ensure that the distributor is capable of fulfilling the order and selling the product to its customers.

The distributor will not, however, wish ownership of the product to pass to its customer until the customer has paid in full. Normally a distributor's standard terms of sale will contain a retention of title provision (see paragraph 12.14), which reserves ownership of the product until payment in full has been made to the distributor.

In the same way as a distributor will normally reserve title (or ownership) of books or other items of product until its customer has paid, a distribution agreement will normally provide that the title and property in the product will pass to the distributor only on receipt of payment by the company. Technically, this means that the distributor cannot legally convey ownership of the product until the company receives payment. This provision might be combined with a minimum annual, quarterly, or monthly order level of product, which is required to be met by the distributor.

Where a minimum order level is provided in an agreement, normally the risk in relation to items of product ordered, or required to be ordered, will be for the account of the distributor. In other words, if the items of product are lost, or unsold, the distributor will have to absorb the loss.

D. Retention of title

12.14 Retention of title generally

Retention of title clauses are used by companies, and their distributors, to retain ownership (or title) in items of product even after they have been delivered to distributors or customers, until certain conditions contained in the contract of sale have been fulfilled. Parties to a contract are entitled to decide when title in goods should pass, and their intention is construed in accordance with the contract, which may provide the express right to retain title in goods after delivery.

The usual aim of retention of title clauses in distribution agreements is to ensure that goods are paid for and, more importantly, that in the event of a distributor's insolvency the company's goods do not form part of the distributor's assets and are not used to satisfy the distributor's creditors. In a distributor's insolvency, the company may be merely an unsecured creditor and will be unlikely to receive any payment, even though the proceeds of the company's goods may be used to satisfy higher ranking creditors. A successful retention of title clause will allow a company to reclaim what it has supplied, before the assets of the insolvent distributor are calculated, and before they are applied towards the distributor's liabilities.

12.15 Retention of title clauses

There are two types of clauses, being:

– *All money clauses:* These clauses only permit title in product to pass to the distributor when it has paid all debts owed to the company[1].
– *Particular debt clauses:* These clauses only permit title to pass in product when the invoices relating to it have been paid off. This creates two particular problems. First, in order to repossess books, the company must be able to identify those items of product which directly relate to unpaid invoices, and not merely those which the company delivers. Second, particular indebtedness clauses may prevent a company from tracing proceeds of sale[2] (see paragraph 12.16).

In order to succeed in a retention of title claim, a company must establish:

(a)   that the retention of title clause has been properly incorporated into the contract with the distributor[3];
(b)   that the company can identify the books which are subject to the claim[4];
(c)   that the clause in question is not, in some way, defective.

1 *Aluminium Industrie Vaassen BV v Romalpa Aluminium Limited* [1976] 2 All ER.
2 *Re Peachdart Limited* [1984] Ch 131, *Clough Mills Limited v Martin* [1985] 1 WLR 111.
3 *Aluminium Industrie Vaassen BV v Romalpa Aluminium Limited*, above.
4 *Re Peachdart Limited*, above.

12.16   Tracing and fiduciary relationships

If a company cannot recover enough of the product it has supplied to eliminate the debt owed by the distributor, then the company may be able to claim that the company's interest in the product has been transferred to the proceeds of sale of the product.

In order to claim the proceeds of sale of the product the company must be able to show a fiduciary relationship (ie a relationship of good faith) between itself and the distributor, imputing a duty on the distributor to account to the company for the proceeds of sale. Clauses which attempt to establish such a relationship may provide that the distributor holds unsold items of product on behalf of the company, and has a licence to sell the items of product as the agent of the company, and when they are sold will be a trustee of the proceeds of sale, which the distributor will hold for the benefit of the company[5].

In order for a fiduciary relationship to exist the following need to be demonstrated:

(a)   the company retains legal and beneficial title to the items of product which are held by the distributor on the publisher's behalf (technically "as bailee")[6];

(b)   the distributor will have a right to resell items of product as the agent of the company in a fiduciary capacity and will keep proceeds of resale in a separate account[7];

(c)   a true fiduciary relationship exists between the parties and not (for example) a charge (see paragraph 12.17).

5 *Aluminium Industrie Vaassen BV v Romalpa Aluminium Limited* [1976] 2 All ER.
6 Ibid.
7 *Re Bond Worth Limited* [1980] Ch 228.

12.17   Charges

A charge is a form of security interest, which does not pass ownership to the person entitled to it, but prevents the person granting it from disposing of the charged asset, in order to provide security over the proceeds of sale.

Under United Kingdom law, where a company grants a security interest by way of charge to a third party, in order for that security interest to be enforceable against a liquidator of that company, or anyone who buys the property which is subject to the charge, particulars of the charge must be registered against the company[8].

However, even where a charge is registered by a company against a distributor, a customer of the distributor who has no notice of the company's security interest, and who has bought items of product in good faith, will acquire good title to (or ownership of) the items of product.

The end result of the legal provisions referred to in this paragraph, and the preceding one, is that there is currently no cast-iron, guaranteed effective way of securing interests over proceeds of sale under United Kingdom law – but this is an area of law in which reforms are being considered.

8 Companies Act 1985 S395(1).

E. Sale or return

12.18 Sale or return arrangements generally

Sale or return transactions are of significant importance in distribution agreements, since they may have a distorting effect on the amount of revenue to be remitted to the publisher. If the distribution agreement permits a distributor to deal with returned items of product by deducting their invoice value as distribution expenses, the distributor will receive commission on items of product, where no sales revenue has been generated.

For this reason, the company may require the value of all returned items of product to be debited from the amount of receipts in the relevant period, and for the amount of any commission taken by the distributor on the returned items of product to be paid back or credited against future liability.

12.19 Returned stock and sale or return stock

A distributor will normally wish to cover the possibility that items of product may be returned by the distributor's customers. A distributor will normally wish to cover its liability in respect of items of product returned by the distributors and customers because they are damaged. The distribution agreement may require the distributor to insure goods in transit, in which case the distributor should assume liability for the sale price and any administration costs. Where items of product are returned because they have been supplied in error by the distributor, the distributor should similarly bear any administration costs.

Further provision may need to be made to cover consignments by a distributor on a "stock balancing" basis (ie where returns of one particular company's items of product are permitted in exchange for the supply of another company's items of product). Returns of the stock balancing type should be permitted by a company only in respect of that company's own items of product, since the ability by the book distributor to accept returns of one company's items of product against resale of another company's items of product may be capable of manipulation by the distributor to the disadvantage of either company, by artificially increasing the number of commission-bearing supplies.

Where a distributor is permitted to supply items of product on a sale or return basis, the company may wish to impose an upper limit on the number or percentage of items of product which can be returned. The distributor, for its part, will want to establish a reserve to be deducted from sums payable to the company, in order to provide cover for the distributor where items of product are, in fact, subsequently returned.

The question of items of product being returned to a distributor, following the end of the distribution agreement, is another instance where the distributor may wish to make a reserve. This may be dealt with by providing that, on the final accounting date, the distributor will retain a percentage of the sums payable to the company, in order to indemnify the distributor for any liability to its customers in respect of returned items of product. The company will expect all reserves made by the distributor (less any amounts paid out by way of claims) to be liquidated and paid to the company within a specified number of days, or months, following the date when the reserve was made.

F. Undertakings and obligations

12.20 Companies' warranties and obligations

A distributor will normally require the publisher or multimedia company whose books or other items of product it distributes to give a number of warranties and undertakings in a distribution agreement. These may include warranties on the following points:

(a) the company has the right to enter into the agreement and grant to the distributor the exclusive rights granted in it;

(b) the company controls, and will throughout the term control, all rights necessary to grant to the distributor the rights granted;

(c) the books or other items of product will not infringe any copyright, trade mark, patent, or other right of any person and will not contain anything which is obscene, blasphemous, offensive to religion, defamatory, or likely to cause a breach of public order;

(d) the books or other items of product will be in a first-class condition when delivered;

(e) the distributor will not incur any liability in relation to any name, logo, or trade mark incorporated on the books or other items of product;

(f) the books or other items of product will not contain any false attribution of authorship;

(g) nothing contained in the books or other items of product, or any associated advertising or publicity material, will contain any misleading indication as to price;

(h) if the distribution arrangement is exclusive, the company will not supply books or other items of product falling within the scope of the agreement to any third party in the territory;

(i) if the distribution agreement is exclusive, the company will refer to the distributor all orders and enquiries for books or other items of product received by the supplier from persons in the territory;

(j) the company will conform with all customs and excise requirements relating to the import of the books or other items of product and also with any requirements of any professional association within the territory;

(k) the company will indemnify the distributor in respect of all actions and claims arising as a result of any breach, or non-performance, by the supplier of the company's obligations under the agreement.

12.21 Distributors' warranties and obligations

A publisher or multimedia company may wish to impose a number of obligations on its distributor. A distribution agreement may contain the following types of warranties and obligations given by the distributor to the publisher or multimedia company:

(a) the distributor shall distribute the books or other items of product to the best of the distributor's skill and ability, throughout the territory during the term;

(b) the distributor shall spend a specified amount in each year of the term by way of advertising or promotion for the books or other items of product;

(c) the distributor will supply monthly statements of shipments and sales;

(d) the distributor will give the company full particulars of any threatened or actual claim in respect of the books or other items of product;

(e) the distributor will take out and keep in effect, during the term, certain insurances in respect of the books or other items of product;

(f) the distributor will market the books in accordance with the provisions of the agreement;

(g) the distributor will pay all costs, fees, import, export, re-importation duties, customers' freight, packaging, transportation, collection of sales taxes and other taxes;

(h) the distributor will comply with all local industry, trade union and guild collective bargaining and other agreements relating to books or other items of product;

(i) the distributor will return to the company or sell to the company, at the end of any sell-off period, any unsold stocks of books or other items of product in the possession of the distributor;

(j) the distributor will indemnify the company in respect of all actions, proceedings and claims arising directly or indirectly as a result of any breach by the distributor of its obligation.

G. Value Added Tax

12.22 Value Added Tax on payments

Unless it is stated specifically that payments pursuant to a distribution agreement in respect of which Value Added Tax is due are exclusive of Value Added Tax then such payments will be deemed to be Value Added Tax inclusive and will be netted down by the Value Added Tax fraction (currently 7/47), which will reduce the net proceeds of the recipient. All amounts should therefore be stated as being exclusive of any Value Added Tax and a contractual obligation should be included in the agreement requiring the payer to account for Value Added Tax in addition to any payment, as appropriate.

12.23 Commission

Commission charged by a distributor to a company should in particular be expressed as being Value Added Tax exclusive. A United Kingdom distributor will be required to charge Value Added Tax at the standard rate (currently 17½%) on its commission. Where the company is located in a different jurisdiction, the Value Added Tax position will require further consideration depending on the location of the parties involved.

12.24 Value Added Tax on book sales

The sale of books (including literary works, reference books, directories and looseleaf manuals) is zero rated in the United Kingdom although the sale of school work books, educational texts in specified formats and certain other specified types of publication are standard rated.

The supply of books is not, however, zero rated throughout the European Union and may come under threat in the United Kingdom so it is preferable for distribution agreements to state that consideration is exclusive of Value Added Tax which will be payable in addition at the appropriate rate for the jurisdiction or jurisdictions where the supply is made.

12.25 Sale or return

Distribution agreements may provide for books to be supplied to distributors on a sale or return basis. In the United Kingdom, the tax point for such supply is the time when it is certain that a supply has taken place or (if sooner) 12 months from the removal of the books, unless the supplier first issues a tax invoice when the tax point will be the date of issue of that invoice. Different rules may apply outside the United Kingdom. If a distribution agreement provides for sale and return arrangements and the distributor wants to keep cash flow costs to a minimum by triggering any tax point as late as possible, it is advisable to include specific provisions in the agreement to address this.

12.26 Self-billing

If either party wishes to operate a self-billing system (by providing a document to itself for the supply of goods and/or services to it by the other party) then, in the United Kingdom, that document can only be treated as a Value Added Tax invoice with Customs and Excise's approval. The party must submit a written request explaining why self-billing is necessary and showing that the supplier has agreed to self-bill and will not itself issue tax invoices for the relevant transactions.

Self-billing invoices should also be appropriately endorsed. If self-billing is to be operated, the distribution agreement should contain appropriate provisions obliging the relevant party to obtain Customs and Excise approval. Other European Union member states may specify different requirements before similar procedures can be adopted.

12.27 Value Added Tax and the Single Market

The arrival of the Single Market on 1 January 1993 has resulted in significant changes in the treatment of movement of goods within Europe. The old system of imports and exports remains in place for supplies of goods between the United Kingdom (or any other member state) and non-European Union countries but there is a new system, based on acquisitions and despatches, for movements between member states.

There are also complicated new administrative requirements relating to such movements. While there are no specific provisions which should be included in distribution agreements as a standard matter, if goods will cross borders pursuant to the arrangements, the Value Added Tax consequences and ancillary administrative requirements should be considered at an early stage.

12.28 Reverse charges

Where a United Kingdom Value Added Tax registered recipient receives a supply of services in the United Kingdom from a person belonging outside the United Kingdom who is not registered for Value Added Tax here, that recipient must account for Value Added Tax in the United Kingdom on the payment made to the foreign supplier, under the reverse charge procedure.

This is to eliminate any distortion which would otherwise arise, if overseas suppliers could make supplies free of United Kingdom Value Added Tax. The services to which the reverse charge applies include transfers and assignments of copyrights, patents, licences and trade marks, advertising services, the services of consultants, and the supply of staff.

The reverse charge means that a recipient must account for output tax on the deemed supply, and can recover input taxes of an equivalent amount, subject to normal rules. Where a United Kingdom business receives these kinds of supplies from an overseas supplier, the Value Added Tax status of that supplier should be ascertained, so that proper account can be made for the reverse charge. This is particularly important if the United Kingdom is partially exempt, because it may suffer a real (as distinct from a cash-flow) Value Added Tax cost on imported services.

It should be noted that the supply of such services outside the United Kingdom, whilst outside the scope of United Kingdom Value Added Tax, may, if supplied in another member state, become liable to that country's Value Added Tax. These rules are complex, and specific advice should always be obtained regarding the Value Added Tax liability of international services.

12.29 Distance selling

Distance sales are sales by a supplier in one European Union state to non-registered persons in a different member state where the goods are delivered by the supplier. Non-registered customers include private individuals, public bodies, charities and small businesses making supplies beneath the registration threshold as well as exempt businesses. If a supplier in one member state sells goods in excess of the threshold limit in any other member state then the supplier must either register there or appoint a tax representative there (if it has no place of business) and then account for Value Added Tax at the appropriate local rate in that state on future sales.

Distance selling can give rise to significant administrative complexities as the supplier will need to monitor sales in each state to see if the threshold has been reached which will mean recording all sales to non-registered suppliers on a country by country basis.

While there are no specific provisions which ought to be included in a standard distribution agreement, parties to such agreements should be aware of the distance selling rules and whether they are likely to apply especially as there are a number of ways in which their effects can be mitigated or avoided if appropriate steps are taken at an early stage.

12.30   Triangulation

Triangulation is the situation where goods and invoice trails differ because there are more than two parties to an arrangement and the goods are delivered by the first party in the chain directly to the last. Such situations often arise where manufacturing sources are located in one member state while customers are located in another member state and the original supplier is located in yet another member state.

The new rules applying to triangular (and indeed, chain) transactions are complex and, if it is contemplated under the terms of a distribution agreement that goods and invoices trails will differ, then appropriate expert advice should be obtained at an early stage.

H.   Distribution and sale of goods

12.31   Product liability under the Consumer Protection Act

The Consumer Protection Act 1987 contains provisions that cover product liability. The Act provides that, where a defective product is supplied, a number of different categories of persons will be liable. These persons are:

(a) the producer of the product[9]; and
(b) any person who holds themselves out as the producer of the product by putting their name or trade mark on it[10]; and
(c) any person who has imported the product into a member state of the European Union in the course of a business for the purpose of supplying it to another[11].

A product is defective if its safety is not such as persons are generally entitled to expect. The safety requirement extends not only to the product, but items comprised in the product, and covers risk of damage to property as well as risk of death or physical injury. For the purpose of determining what level of safety persons are generally entitled to expect, all the circumstances relating to the product, and its supply, are taken into account. These circumstances include the manner in which the product is marketed, the method with which it is marketed, any instructions or warnings with respect to the product or its use, the time of supply of the product, and the actions which might reasonably be expected to be done with or in relation to the product[12].

The Act also imposes liability on any supplier of a defective product, if the person who suffered damage requests the supplier to identify any of the persons in the categories referred to above, and the request is made within a reasonable period after the damage occurred and it is not practicable for the person who has suffered the damage to identify all the relevant persons who might fall within the categories. If a supplier fails within a reasonable period to comply with a request to identify the person who supplied the product to the person, then the supplier will be liable under the Act[13].

It should be noted that the importer is the first importer into the European Union and not the importer into the country of supply. Additionally, a supplier who supplies goods which are incorporated into a third parties' goods will still be liable.

9 Consumer Protection Act 1987 S2(2)(a).
10 Ibid S2(2)(b).
11 Ibid S2(2)(c).
12 Ibid S3.
13 Ibid S2(3).

12.32 Defences

There are a number of defences which are available in respect of proceedings brought against a person pursuant to the Consumer Protection Act. These defences are:

(a) the defect was attributable to compliance with a statutory requirement or any regulation made pursuant to any statutory requirement or to any community obligation[14];

(b) the person proceeded against did not supply the product to the person making the claim[15];

(c) the supply of the product was not made in the course of business, and the person proceeded against falls within the scope of the Act only by virtue of the things done by that person, which were not done with a view to profit[16];

(d) the defects did not exist in the product at the relevant time of supply[17];

(e) the state of scientific and technical knowledge at the time of supply was not such that the producer might be expected to have discovered the defect, if it had existed in the product, while it was under the producer's control[18];

(f) the defect constituted a defect in a subsequent product, in which the product in question had been comprised, and was wholly attributable to the design of the subsequent product, or the compliance of the person in question with the instructions given by the producer of the subsequent product[19].

14 Consumer Protection Act 1987 S4(1)(a).
15 Ibid S4(1)(b).
16 Ibid S4(1)(c).
17 Ibid S4(1)(d).
18 Ibid S4(1)(e).
19 Ibid S4(1)(f).

12.33 Misleading indications as to price

Part 3 of the Consumer Protection Act makes it an offence to give a misleading price indication in respect of goods, facilities, services or accommodation, or failing to take proper steps to correct the misleading indication[20].

An offence will be committed if either:

(a) a person gives a misleading indication as to price to consumers in the course of that person's business[21]; or
(b) alternatively, a person gives an indication as to price in the same circumstances, and this indication becomes misleading[22], and
  (i) some or all of the consumers might reasonably be expected to rely on the indication after it has become misleading[23];
  (ii) the person who first gave the indication failed to take all such steps as are reasonable to prevent those consumers from relying on the indication[24].

It is irrelevant whether the person who gave the indication was acting on their own behalf or on behalf of another. The person who makes the indication does not have to be the person from whom the goods, services, accommodation or facilities are available. An offence would be committed if the indication becomes misleading only to part of the consumers to whom it was given[25].

The Consumer Protection Act extends to all services and facilities including banking insurance services and the provision of credit. The Consumer Protection Act does not apply to statements relating to accommodation or facilities which are to be provided by the creation or sale of certain property[26].

20 Consumer Protection Act 1987 S20(1).
21 Ibid S20(1).
22 Ibid S20(2)(a).
23 Ibid S20(2)(b).
24 Ibid S20(2)(c).
25 Ibid S20(3).
26 Ibid SS22 and 23.

12.34 Meaning of misleading

Information may be misleading as to price both by what it says and by what consumers might reasonably be expected to infer from the information. A number of different types of indication would be caught by the Act such as:

(a) an indication that the price is less than it is[27];
(b) an indication that the price does not depend on other circumstances when, in fact, it does[28];
(c) an indication that the price is inclusive, when additional charges are made[29];
(d) an indication that a person expects the price to be increased or reduced or maintained when, in fact, that person has no such expectation[30];
(e) an indication that the facts by which consumers might be expected to make a comparison are not what they seem[31].

A misleading price indication may also be given as to the method of calculating a price, if the indication says, or consumers might be expected to understand that it contains, a statement which conveys any one of a number of matters broadly analogous to those set out above[32].

27 Consumer Protection Act 1987 S21(1)(a).
28 Ibid S21(1)(b).
29 Ibid S21(1)(c).
30 Ibid S21(1)(d).
31 Ibid S21(1)(e).
32 Ibid S21(2).

12.35 Defences to offence of misleading information

Where an indication is contained in an advertisement, it is a defence for a company charged to show that:

- the company carries on the business of publishing, or arranging for the publication of advertisements[33];
- the advertisement was received in the ordinary course of business[34]; and
- at the time of publication, the company did not know, and had no grounds for suspecting, that publication would constitute an offence[35].

It is a defence for a person who has given a misleading indication of price to any consumer if the person can show that:

(a) the indication did not relate to the availability from the person making the statement of any goods, services, accommodation or facilities[36];

(b) a price had been recommended to every person from whom the goods etc were indicated as being available[37];

(c) the indication related to the recommended price, and was misleading only because of the failure of a third party to follow the recommendation[38]; and

(d) it was reasonable for the person giving the indication to assume that their recommendation was, for the most part, being followed[39].

Where proceedings are brought in respect of an indication published in a book, newspaper or magazine it is a defence for the publisher of the book, newspaper or magazine to show that the indication was not contained in an advertisement[40].

33 Consumer Protection Act 1987 S24(3)(a).
34 Ibid S24(3)(b).
35 Ibid S24(3)(c).
36 Ibid S24(4)(a).
37 Ibid S24(4)(b).
38 Ibid S24(4)(c).
39 Ibid S24(4)(d).
40 Ibid S24(2).

12.36 Sale of goods

The Sale of Goods Act 1979 is the principal Act of Parliament which relates to the sale of goods, both to businesses and to consumers. The Sale of Goods Act implies certain warranties in contracts for the sale of goods.

First, there is a warranty that the seller has the right to sell the goods. Second, there is a warranty that the goods are free and will remain free from any charge or encumbrance not disclosed or known to the buyer before the contract is made. Third, there is a warranty that the buyer's possession of the goods will not be disturbed by any third party[41].

41 Sale of Goods Act 1979 S12.

12.37 Quality of goods and fitness for purpose

The Sale of Goods Act additionally implies terms relating to quality and fitness in relation to goods which are sold by a seller in the course of its business.

These terms are that the goods supplied are of merchantable quality, but the terms will not apply in respect of defects which are specifically drawn to the attention of the buyer before the contract is entered into, nor will they apply if the buyer has examined the goods before the contract is made, to the extent that this examination should have revealed the defects concerned[42].

Where the buyer expressly, or by implication, makes known to the seller any particular purpose for which the goods are being bought, there is an implied condition that the goods are reasonably fit for that purpose[43].

42 Sale of Goods Act 1979 S14(2).
43 Ibid S14(3).

12.38 Right of ownership of goods

The right of ownership (or property) in goods, passes when the parties intend. A number of specific rules exist for determining the intention of the parties as follows:

(a)   In an unconditional contract for goods which can be delivered, the right of ownership (or property) in the goods passes to the buyer when the contract is made. It is irrelevant whether payment or delivery occurs later[44].

(b)   Where there is a contract for the sale of specific goods, and the seller has to do something to the goods to put them into a deliverable state, property (or ownership) will not pass to the buyer until the thing is done and the buyer has notice that it has been done[45].

(c)   Where there is a contract for the sale of specific goods which are in a deliverable state, but need to be tested, measured or weighed by the seller, or to have some other thing done to them, in order to calculate the price, then the property will not pass until the relevant thing is done and the buyer has notice[46].

(d)   Where goods are delivered to the buyer on approval, or on a sale and return basis, the property (ie ownership) in the goods passes to the buyer when the buyer signifies approval or acceptance, or does any act adopting the transaction. If the buyer does not signify approval, or acceptance, but keeps the goods without rejecting them beyond the time which has been fixed for the return of the goods (or if no time has been fixed beyond a reasonable time), then property will pass[47].

(e)   Where there is a contract for the sale of unascertained goods, and goods of that description in a deliverable state are unconditionally appropriated, either by the seller with the assent of the buyer or by the buyer with the assent of the seller, then property (or ownership) in the goods will pass to the buyer. Assent may be express or implied, and may be given before or after appropriation[48].

(f) Where the seller delivers goods to the buyer, or to a carrier, or other bailee, for the purpose of transmission to the buyer without reserving the right of disposal, the seller is taken to have unconditionally appropriated the goods to the contract[49].

44 Sale of Goods Act 1979 S18 Rule 1.
45 Ibid S18 Rule 2.
46 Ibid S18 Rule 3.
47 Ibid S18 Rule 4.
48 Ibid S18 Rule 5(1).
49 Ibid S18 Rule 5(2).

12.39 Liability for the destruction of goods and delivery of goods

The risk (or liability) for the destruction of goods remains with the seller until the property in the goods is transferred to the buyer, unless the parties agree otherwise. When property is transferred to the buyer, the goods are at the buyer's risk irrespective of whether delivery has been made or not[50].

Where delivery has been delayed through the fault of either the buyer, or the seller, the goods will be at the risk of whichever party is in default, so far as concerns any loss which would not have occurred but for such default[51].

Unless it is agreed otherwise, the duty of the seller to deliver and the duty of the buyer to pay will be concurrent[52]. Whether the contract requires the buyer to take possession, or the seller to deliver, is a question of fact in each case. If no express agreement is reached as regards the place of delivery, this is to be the seller's place of business, or the location of the contracted goods if they are somewhere else. Where no time is fixed for the despatch of goods, it is implied that they will be despatched within a reasonable time[53].

Where a seller is authorised, or required, to send the goods to the buyer, delivery of goods to a carrier will be deemed to be delivery to the buyer unless otherwise agreed. Where a seller contracts with a carrier, the contract must be reasonable, having regard to the nature of the goods. If the seller does not make a reasonable contract, the buyer may hold the seller responsible in damages, or may decline to accept that delivery to the carrier constitutes delivery to the buyer[54].

Where the seller agrees to deliver goods, at the seller's own risk, to a place other than that where they were sold, the buyer must accept any risk of deterioration of goods in transit unless otherwise agreed[55].

Where a buyer has not previously examined goods which are delivered, the buyer will have a reasonable opportunity to examine goods, to determine whether they conform with the agreement[56]. The buyer is deemed to have accepted the goods when the buyer intimates acceptance to the seller, or does any act consistent with such acceptance, or if (s)he does not intimate rejection of the goods, after the lapse of a reasonable time[57].

Where goods are delivered to a buyer and the buyer refuses to accept them, and has the right to do so, the buyer is not bound to return the goods to the seller, but may simply intimate that the buyer refuses to accept them[58].

50 Sale of Goods Act 1979 S20(1).
51 Ibid S20(2).
52 Ibid S28.
53 Ibid S29.
54 Ibid S32.
55 Ibid S33.
56 Ibid S34.
57 Ibid S35.
58 Ibid S36.

12.40 Trade descriptions

The Trade Descriptions Act 1968 provides that any person who, in the course of a trade or business, applies a false trade description to any goods or supplies, or offers to supply, any goods to which a false description is applied is (subject to certain exceptions) guilty of an offence[59].

A trade description is any direct or indirect indication, made by whatever means, in respect of certain specified matters with regard to goods, or any parts of goods[60].

The specified matters are:

(a) quantity, size or gauge[61];
(b) method of manufacture, production, processing or reconditioning[62];
(c) composition[63];
(d) fitness for purpose, strength, performance, behaviour or accuracy[64];
(e) any characteristics not included in the proceeding four categories[65];
(f) testing by any person and results of testing[66];
(g) approval by any person or conformity with an approved type[67];
(h) place or date of manufacture, production, processing or reconditioning[68];
(i) identity of person manufacturing, producing, processing or reconditioning[69];
(j) other history including previous ownership or use[70].

The expression "quantity" includes length, width, height, area, volume, capacity, weight and/or number[71].

A false trade description is any trade description which is false to a material degree and will include any trade description which, although it is not false, is misleading. "Misleading" means likely to be taken for an indication of any of the matters which may constitute a trade description, if such indication is false to a material degree.

Anything which is not a trade description, but is likely to be taken for an indication of any of the matters referred to above, is also considered to be a false trade description, if it would be false to a material degree if taken to be such an indication. A false indication that goods comply with a specified, or recognised, standard is also considered to be a false trade description, if there is no such recognised or specified standard[72].

59 Trade Descriptions Act 1968 S1.
60 Ibid S2(1).
61 Ibid S2(1)(a).
62 Ibid S2(1)(b).
63 Ibid S2(1)(c).
64 Ibid S2(1)(d).
65 Ibid S2(1)(e).

66 Ibid S2(1)(f).
67 Ibid S2(1)(g).
68 Ibid S2(1)(h).
69 Ibid S2(1)(i).
70 Ibid S2(1)(j).
71 Ibid S2(3).
72 Ibid S3.

12.41   Application to goods in a trade or business

A person applies a trade description to goods if they affix or annex the description to, or on, the goods, or anything in which they are contained, or mark it on, or incorporate it within the goods, or their container.

Alternatively, the description may be applied where goods are placed in, on or with anything upon which the description has been marked, or incorporated in, or where the trade description is used by a person in any manner likely to be taken as referring to the goods[73].

A verbal statement may amount to the use of a trade description. The business in which the description is made need not be a retail business and need not be full-time[74].

Where a trade description is made in an advertisement, a number of provisions apply. The trade description is taken to refer to all goods of the relevant class, whether or not they are in existence at the time the advertisement is published, for the purpose of determining whether a false trade description has been applied to any goods, and for the purpose of determining whether the supply, or offer to supply, has been made in respect of any goods to which a false description is applied.

In determining whether goods are of a class to which a trade description has been applied in an advertisement, regard must be paid not only to the form or content of the advertisement, but also to the time, place, manner and frequency of its publication, and all other matters making it likely or unlikely that the person to whom the goods are supplied would think of the goods as belonging to the class in relation to which the trade description was used in the advertisement[75].

73 Trade Descriptions Act 1968 S4(1).
74 Ibid S4(2).
75 Ibid S5.

12.42   False indications

It is an offence to make or give any false indication, either directly or indirectly, that any goods or services are of a kind supplied to or approved by Her Majesty or any member of the Royal Family[76].

It is also an offence to use without the authority of Her Majesty any device or emblems signifying the Queen's Award to Industry or anything resembling such a device, or any device or emblem signifying a Royal warrant[77].

It is an offence to make, directly or indirectly, any false indication in the course of any trade or business that any goods or services supplied are of a kind supplied to any other person. Additionally, it is an offence for any person in the course of a trade or business, to make a statement which they know to be false, or recklessly to make a statement which is false, in connection with the provision of any services or facilities in the course of a trade, or their nature, or the time at which or manner in which or persons by whom they are provided, or the examination or approval or evaluation by any person of such services or facilities[78].

It is an offence to import into the United Kingdom any goods bearing a false trade description relating to the manufacture, production, processing or reconditioning of any goods[79].

76 Trade Descriptions Act 1968 S12(1).
77 Ibid S12(2).
78 Ibid SS13 and 14.
79 Ibid S16.

12.43 Defences

A number of defences exist in respect of proceedings brought under the Trade Descriptions Act. It is, in some circumstances, a defence to prove that the commission of the offence was due to a mistake, or due to reliance on information supplied by or due to the act or default of another person, or an accident or some other cause beyond the control of the alleged defender. It is also a defence to show that the offender took all reasonable precautions, and exercised all due diligence, to avoid the commission of an offence, both by the offender and any person under the offender's control[80].

Where a defence is based on the act, or default, of another person or reliance on information supplied by another person, the defence may not be relied upon, unless the alleged defender has served on the prosecutor, not less than seven clear days before the hearing, notice in writing giving such information in relation to the identification, or assisting the identification of the person whose alleged act, or default, is being used in defence, to the extent that such information is in the possession of the alleged defender[81].

Where proceedings relate to an offence of supplying, or offering to supply, goods to which a false trade description is applied, it is also a defence of the person charged to prove that they did not know the goods did not conform to the description, or that the description had been applied to the goods, and that they could not with reasonable diligence have ascertained such facts[82].

Where proceedings are brought for an offence committed by the publication of an advertisement, it is a defence for the person charged to prove that they are a person whose business it is to publish, or arrange for the publication of advertisements, and that they received the advertisement for publication in the ordinary course of business, and did not know, and had no reason to suspect, that publication would amount to an offence under the Trade Descriptions Act[83].

80 Trade Descriptions Act 1968 S24(1).
81 Ibid S24(2).
82 Ibid S24(3).
83 Ibid S25.

12.44 Unsolicited goods and services

Where a person receives unsolicited goods, the recipient of those goods is, subject to complying with certain provisions, entitled to use, deal with, or dispose of the goods, as if they were an unconditional gift, and the sender's rights to the goods are extinguished. The provisions apply only if the recipient does not have cause to believe the goods were sent with a view to their being acquired for the purpose of a trade or business, and do not apply if the recipient has agreed to acquire the goods, or agreed to return them, and the provisions require notice to be sent by the recipient to the sender, in a particular form, within six months from receipt of the goods[84].

It is a criminal offence for a person to make a demand for payment, or assert a right to receive payment, for what that person knows are unsolicited goods which have been sent to another person,[85] unless the person making the demand has reasonable cause to believe that there is a right of payment in the course of any trade or business. It is also a criminal offence for a person who does not have reasonable cause to believe there is a right to payment for unsolicited goods to threaten to bring legal proceedings, or place or threaten to place the name of any person on a list of defaulters or debtors, or invoke any collection procedure, or threaten to do so[86].

It is a criminal offence for a person to recover payment, by way of charge, for including or for arranging for the inclusion of a directory entry relating to a person, or their trade or business, unless an order form has been signed by the person[87]. The order form is required to comply with a number of provisions and must state the amount of the charge being made for inclusion, must identify the directory, give details of the proposed date of publication, the price and minimum number of copies which are to be available for sale, the minimum number of copies which are to be distributed free of charge and must also contain reasonable particulars of the entry proposed[88].

It is a criminal offence for a person to send, or cause to be sent to any other person, any book, magazine, leaflet or advertising material, which the sender knows, or ought reasonably to know, is unsolicited, and which describes or illustrates human sexual techniques[89].

84 Unsolicited Goods and Services Act 1971 S1.
85 Ibid S2.
86 Ibid S2(2).
87 Ibid S3(1).
88 Ibid S3(3).
89 Ibid S4(1).

13. Infringement and enforcement

[IMPORTANT NOTE: Please read the section "About this book" on page v, before referring to any of the matters in this chapter.]

[*In this chapter all statutory references are to the Copyright, Designs and Patents Act 1988 unless otherwise specified*]

A. Introduction

13.1 Purpose of this chapter

The purpose of this chapter is to identify the various classes of action which are capable of infringing copyright. It is important for publishers and multimedia professionals to be aware of the categories of infringing acts, not only in order to prevent others from infringing their rights but also to eliminate the possibility of inadvertently infringing other persons' rights. Infringement of copyright may also involve infringement of trade marks.

The chapter also examines the position of the innocent infringer as well as the law relating to criminal liability for infringement, and the circumstances in which individual officers of companies may be held personally liable for copyright infringement.

There are other related areas in which publishers and multimedia professionals may incur liability, and the chapter contains brief summaries of the law relating to trespass to goods, and interference with third party contractual rights. These summaries may assist publishers and multimedia professionals in identifying or avoiding problems of this nature.

Finally, the chapter sets out some of the possible legal remedies which may be obtained to prevent, or provide compensation for, copyright or trade mark infringement.

B. Infringement

13.2 Infringement of copyrights and trade marks

Copyright is infringed when a person does any of the acts restricted by copyright legislation, without the consent of the copyright owner or other authorised person[1]. The acts restricted by copyright under English law are listed in paragraph 3.2. Infringement of copyright is capable of being both a civil and a criminal offence (see paragraphs 13.3 to 13.8). Where an act of criminal infringement is committed by a company, in certain circumstances individuals associated with or employed by the company may also be personally liable to criminal proceedings[2] (see paragraph 13.7).

All infringements of copyright give rise to civil liability. In certain additional cases, criminal liability may exist. The types of act which give rise to copyright infringements may be divided into primary infringement and secondary infringement. In order to be able to commence proceedings for copyright infringement in the United Kingdom, the plaintiff must be either the copyright owner or the exclusive licensee of the copyright owner in respect of the medium infringed (see paragraph 13.11).

In some cases, infringement of copyright may also involve infringement of trade marks (see paragraphs 3.41 to 3.45 and paragraph 17.6). The remedies in relation to the infringement of trade marks are examined in paragraphs 13.11 to 13.17.

1 Copyright, Designs and Patents Act 1988 S16.
2 S110.

13.3 Primary infringement

There are five different types of act which constitute primary infringement of copyright under United Kingdom law. These acts are referred to in copyright parlance as "acts restricted by copyright".

Only the copyright owner (or the owner's licensee or assignee) has the right to do or authorise the doing of the acts which are restricted by copyright. The copyright owner (or licensee or assignee) therefore has the exclusive right to:

(a)   copy a copyright work[3];
(b)   issue copies of a copyright work to the public[4];
(c)   perform, show or play a copyright work in public[5];
(d)   broadcast the copyright work or include it in a cable programme service[6];
(e)   make an adaptation of a copyright work or do any of the acts in (a) to (d) in respect of an adaptation[7].

For an infringement of copyright to occur, it is not necessary that a complete work is copied or issued to the public, or performed or broadcast or adapted. It will be enough if any of the acts restricted by copyright is performed in relation to a substantial part of a work by an unauthorised person. The infringement may be either direct or indirect and, in the case of an indirect infringement, it is irrelevant whether any of the acts performed prior to infringement were themselves infringements, or whether they were authorised acts[8].

In some cases it is permissible for acts restricted by copyright to be carried out without the authorisation of the copyright owner pursuant to the fair dealing provisions, permitted act provisions and copyright licensing provisions of the Act (see paragraphs 6.3 to 6.6 and 8.1 to 8.39).

3 S16(1)(a).
4 S16(1)(b).

5 S16(1)(c).
6 S16(1)(d).
7 S16(1)(e).
8 S16(2) and (3).

13.4 Copies

Copying a work means reproducing it in any material form and includes storing the work in any medium by any electronic means[9].

A copy will include any object which is transient or incidental to some other use of a work, and in the case of artistic works the copy may be in three dimensions or two dimensions[10].

For an infringement of copyright to occur, it is not necessary that a complete work is copied or issued to the public, or performed or broadcast or adapted. It will be enough if any of the acts restricted by copyright is performed in relation to a substantial part of a work by an unauthorised person.

The infringement may be either direct or indirect and, in the case of an indirect infringement, it is irrelevant whether any of the acts performed prior to infringement were themselves infringements, or whether they were authorised acts[11].

In some cases it is permissible for acts restricted by copyright to be carried out without the authorisation of the copyright owner pursuant to the fair dealing provisions, the permitted act provisions and the copyright licensing provisions of the Act (see paragraphs 6.3 to 6.6 and 8.1 to 8.39).

9 S17(2).
10 S17(3).
11 S16(3).

13.5 Adaptations

It should be remembered that an adaptation of a copyright work may itself be capable of qualifying for copyright protection. The consequence is that in the case of adaptations two, or more, infringements may occur – infringement of the original work, if it is still in copyright, and infringement of the adaptation[12].

In the case of a literary or dramatic work, an adaptation includes a translation (which when used in the context of a computer program would include computer languages or codes). It also includes the conversion of a dramatic work into a non-dramatic work and vice versa. It will also include adapting a literary or dramatic work into a version in which the story is conveyed wholly or mainly by means of pictures in a form suitable for reproduction in a book, newspaper, magazine or similar periodical[13].

12 S76.
13 S21.

13.6 Secondary infringement of copyright

There are six types of secondary infringement of copyright under United Kingdom legislation.

(a) Importing without the licence of the copyright owner, otherwise than for private and domestic use an article which the importer knows, or has reason to believe, is a copy of a copyright work[15].

(b) Possessing or dealing with an infringing copy of a copyright work. The requirements for secondary infringement of this type are, first an infringer must, without the licence of the copyright owner of a copyright work, possess an article which is an infringing copy of the work and which the infringer knows or has reason to believe is an infringing copy. (In other words, first, an infringing copy has to be in existence, second, it has to be in the possession of the secondary infringer and, third, the secondary infringer must either know that the article (s)he possesses is an infringing copy, or have reason to believe it is an infringing copy.) The offence is committed if:
  – the secondary infringer possesses the article in the course of a business[16]; or
  – sells or lets for hire or exposes for sale or hire the article[17]; or
  – in the course of a business exhibits the article in public or distributes it[18]; or
  – distributes the article otherwise than in the course of a business to such an extent as to affect prejudicially the owner of the copyright[19].

(c) Providing the means for making infringing copies. This type of secondary infringement occurs where the secondary infringer, again without the licence of the copyright owner, makes an article specifically designed or adapted for making copies of a particular copyright work, or imports such an article into the United Kingdom, or possesses such an article in the course of a business, or sells or lets for hire, or exposes for sale or hire such an article. The secondary infringer must know or have reason to believe, however, that the article is to be used to make infringing copies[20].

(d) A further type of secondary infringement occurs where a person, without the licence of a copyright owner, transmits a copyright work by means of a telecommunications system. The secondary infringer must know or have reason to believe that infringing copies of the work will be made by means of reception of the transmission in the United Kingdom or outside the United Kingdom. A telecommunications system is a system for conveying visual images, sounds or other information by electronic means. Electronic means includes any electric, magnetic, electromagnetic, electrochemical or electromechanical means[21].

(e) Permitting the use of premises for an infringing performance. Where the copyright in a literary, dramatic or musical work is infringed by a performance at a place of public entertainment, any person who gave permission for that place to be used for the performance is also liable for the infringement unless that person believed on reasonable grounds, when giving permission, that the performance would not infringe copyright[22].

(f) A person who supplies apparatus which is used for the public performance of a copyright work or to show, play or receive it in public will be liable for the infringement if the person, at the time of supply of the apparatus, knew, or had reason to believe, that it was likely to be used to infringe copyright. Where the normal use of the apparatus involves public performance or the showing or playing of copyright works in public, the person supplying it will be liable unless that person believed on reasonable grounds that the apparatus would not be used so as to infringe copyright[23].

An occupier of premises who gave permission for the apparatus to be brought into the premises is liable if, when giving permission, the occupier knew, or had reason to believe, that the apparatus was likely to be used to infringe copyright[24].

A person who supplied a copy of a sound recording or film used to infringe copyright is liable for the infringement if, when supplying it, the person knew or had reason to believe that what was supplied or any copy made directly or immediately from it was likely to be used so as to infringe copyright[25].

14 SS25 and 26.
15 S22.
16 S23(a).
17 S23(b).
18 S23(c).
19 S23(d).
20 S24(1).
21 S24(2).
22 S25(1).
23 S26(1) and (2).
24 S26(3).
25 S26(5).

13.7   Criminal and personal liability

It is a criminal offence if any person without the licence of the copyright owner:

(a)   makes for sale or use; or
(b)   imports into the United Kingdom otherwise than for private and domestic use; or
(c)   possesses in the course of business with a view to committing any act infringing copyright; or
(d)   in the course of a business
  – sells or lets for hire;
  – offers or exposes for sale or hire;
  – exhibits in public;
  – distributes; or
(e)   distributes otherwise than in the course of a business to such an extent as to affect prejudicially the owner of the copyright an article which that person knows, or has reason to believe, is an infringing copy of a copyright work[26].

A separate offence exists where a person makes or has in their possession an article which is specifically designed or adapted for making copies of a particular copyright work, knowing, or having reason to believe, that it is to be used to make infringing copies for sale, or hire, or use in the course of a business[27].

Where copyright is infringed (otherwise than by reception of a broadcast or cable programme), by the public performance of a literary, dramatic or musical work, or by the playing or showing in public of a sound recording or film, any person who caused the work to be performed, played, or shown, is guilty of an offence if that person knew or had reason to believe that copyright would be infringed[28].

Where it can be proved that an offence involving criminal copyright liability has been committed by a body corporate, with the consent or connivance of a director, manager, company secretary, or other similar officer, or a person purporting to act in any such capacity, then, that person will be guilty of the criminal offence, as well as the body corporate, and will be liable to be proceeded against and punished accordingly[29].

26 S107(1).
27 S107(2).
28 S107(3).
29 S110(1).

13.8 Innocent infringement

No knowledge is required for primary infringement[30]. Where the primary infringement is innocent a court will not, generally, make an order for an account of profits.

Before the coming into force of the Copyright, Designs and Patents Act 1988, knowledge was required for secondary infringement. It now appears that knowledge may be inferred by the court, if the infringer knew or had reason to believe that an infringement would occur. Where it is shown that, at the time of the infringement, the infringer did not know, and had no reason to believe, that copyright subsisted in the work in question, no damages will be awarded against the infringer, without prejudice to any other remedy[31] (see paragraph 13.11).

In the case of criminal liability, it is again sufficient for the court to find that the infringer had "reason to believe" that the article possessed by the infringer was an infringing copy[32]. The test is likely to be the same as the test for civil liability, but in view of the serious consequences of criminal proceedings, it is possible that the test may be applied in a more stringent manner.

For an individual officer of a company to be liable for proceedings, two requirements must be satisfied. First, the body corporate must have committed criminal copyright infringement and, second, that infringement must be proved to have been committed with the consent or connivance of the director, manager, company secretary or other similar officer[33].

30 *Mansell v Valley Printing Company* [1908] 2 Ch 441; *Byrne v Statist Company* [1914] 1 KB 622.
31 Copyright, Designs and Patents Act 1988 SS22, 23 and 24.
32 SS107(3) and 108(1)(b).
33 S110(1).

C. Trespass and interference

13.9 Trespass to goods

In addition to facing potential liability for infringement of copyright, and infringement of trade mark, there are circumstances where publishers and multimedia companies may also face potential liability in relation to the tort (ie unlawful act giving rise to civil but not criminal liability) of trespass to goods.

Trespass to goods is the wrongful physical interference with them, such as their unlawful removal from the place where they are kept (which, if coupled with an intent to deprive the owner permanently, might also constitute the criminal offence of theft) or destroying goods or causing physical damage to them or using them in an unauthorised manner.

There are occasions where an action in trespass to goods may succeed, in circumstances where an action for infringement of copyright will not. What is the position if a publisher or multimedia company has received a collection of old photographs or illustrations from an individual, suggesting that a selection of the photographs or illustrations could be made available for publication? Would the publisher or multimedia company be free to make copies of the works, return them to the sender, subsequently select items for publication and then publish or otherwise exploit them without entering into any agreement with the sender?

Generally a company will not be free to behave in such a manner, since, although the company's actions may not amount to infringement of copyright in either the photographs/illustrations or in any selection or compilation made of them by the sender (see paragraph 3.20), the actions of the company may, however, amount to a breach of the terms and conditions on which the material was originally sent (see paragraph 1.3). Additionally, the company's actions may amount to trespass to goods, since the company would have used the material submitted to the company in order to make additional copies without the consent of the sender.

13.10   Interference with contractual relations

A further area where rights may be infringed is where a company pursues a course of action which constitutes the unlawful interference with another party's contractual rights. Such action might be unlawful (at civil law not at criminal law) and the enforcement of civil contractual rights may, on occasions, be used in order to prevent actions which would not constitute infringement of copyright or infringement of trade mark rights.

If an author enters into a contractual arrangement with Company A pursuant to which Company A has an option to acquire all rights in the author's next work, and Company B, in the knowledge of Company A's option, enters into a contract with the author to acquire all rights in the next work, then Company A may be able to bring proceedings against Company B, and claim damages (see paragraph 13.13) and apply for an injunction, restraining Company B and the author (see paragraph 13.12), as well as applying for an order requiring specific performance by the author of the author's obligations (see paragraph 13.14 – but note that the circumstances in which an order for specific performance may be obtained are limited).

A further illustration of unlawful interference with contractual rights would be where an author contracted with Company A not to write a competing work on the same subject within a designated period and was subsequently contracted by Company B to do so. In this situation, however, the question of whether the restriction on the author was enforceable (see paragraph 7.2) would need to be considered.

The practical advice for companies who are faced with a situation where they are able to buy rights from an author (or another company) who has entered into a contract to sell them elsewhere, is: "Don't do it."

D. Remedies

13.11 Principal remedies for copyright and trade mark infringement

An infringement of copyright is actionable by the copyright owner (which includes any person to whom copyright in a work is assigned)[34]. An exclusive licensee has, except as against the copyright owner, the same rights and remedies in relation to matters occurring after the licence as if the licence had been an assignment. The licensee's rights are, however, concurrent with those of the copyright owner[35].

Where concurrent rights of action exist, neither the copyright owner nor the exclusive licensee of the right in question may proceed with any court action (other than interlocutory relief), unless the other party is added as a defendant. Any party which is added as a defendant for the purpose of commencing proceedings is not liable for any costs in the matter, unless such person takes part in the proceedings[36].

Where concurrent rights of action exist, the court may apportion the damages between the copyright owner and the exclusive licensee of the right in question[37].

An infringement of trade mark rights is generally actionable by the trade mark proprietor, although there are circumstances where a licensee may have the right to commence proceedings (see paragraph 3.43).

The remedies which exist under English law for an infringement of copyright, or trade mark, or breach of contract, are briefly summarised in paragraphs 13.12 to 13.17.

34 S96(1).
35 S101.
36 S102(1) and (2).
37 S102(4)(c).

13.12 Injunctions

Where an obligation is negative in nature, a breach of it may be restrained by an injunction. A restrictive injunction is an order of the court, which will require the person against whom it is made, to refrain from doing a particular act. In order to obtain an injunction, a plaintiff must show that:

(a) the payment of financial compensation (ie damages) would not be an appropriate remedy for the person's losses[38]; and

(b) the person did not acquiesce whilst the act complained of took place, or threatened to take place; and

(c)   the person did not delay unreasonably after the infringement of their rights had taken place, so that it would be unjust for the court to grant the injunction.

Injunctions are a most powerful remedy, but the decision whether or not to award one is always at the discretion of the court, which has the right to consider the conduct of the plaintiff, if appropriate.

An injunction may be granted without a full trial, on very short notice, and without the prior knowledge of the person against whom it is granted. The remedy is frequently used in connection with service contracts, to restrain ex-employees from competing with their previous employers, or to restrain them from disclosing confidential information of a specific nature.

38   *American Cyanamid Company v Ethicon Limited* [1975] AC 396.

13.13   Damages

Damages are awarded in court actions to successful plaintiffs. Where damages are awarded as a result of breach of contract, the intention is to place the plaintiff in the same position that (s)he would have been in, had the contract not been breached. An innocent party to a contract is, in principle, entitled to recover any anticipated net profits, and incidental expenditure of a type contemplated by the parties, at the time the contract was entered into. Generally the courts will not award gross profits.

(a)   General damages

These are awarded in respect of damage which results from the infringement of a legal duty or right.

(b)   Special damages

These are damages which can be calculated precisely.

(c)   Liquidated damages

These are damages which have been agreed and fixed by the parties, or else fixed by statute.

(d)   Unliquidated damages

These are damages which are not immediately quantifiable at the time the damages are claimed (ie when proceedings are commenced), and are left by the plaintiff, to be assessed by the jury or judge.

(e)   Exemplary damages

These are punitive damages, which are awarded against the defendant. In any action for infringement of copyright, a court may also award additional damages, having regard to all the circumstances, and in particular to the flagrancy of the infringement and any benefit accruing to the defendant by reason of the infringement. Where, however, the defendant did not know and had no reason to believe that copyright subsisted in the work in question, no damages will be awarded, without prejudice to any other remedy.

A plaintiff may not recover a portion of the damages in one action, and the remainder in a subsequent action. The plaintiff must claim damages for all prospective loss stemming from the same cause of action at the same time.

A plaintiff may not be allowed a claim for damages if the damage occasioned to the plaintiff is too remote. The modern interpretation of the rule on remoteness of damages has been stated as follows: "A type or kind of loss is not too remote a consequence of a breach of contract if, at the time of contracting (and on the assumption that the parties actually foresaw the breach in question), it was within their reasonable contemplation as a not unlikely result of that breach."

Damages for breach of a contract usually will be assessed at the date the cause of action arose, in other words, the date of the breach, unless this would lead to an injustice.

A plaintiff's damages for breach of contract may be reduced where the damage suffered was partly caused by the plaintiff's own negligence, but only in cases where the breach also gave rise to an independent action in tort[39].

A plaintiff is under a duty at law to attempt to mitigate the loss suffered, and will not be able to recover damages for any loss arising from the breach that the plaintiff could have avoided by taking reasonable steps.

39 Law Reform (Contributory Negligence) Act 1945 S1.

13.14 Specific performance

Specific performance is a discretionary remedy, and usually is granted only where damages are not an adequate remedy. The remedy compels performance by the defendant of its contractual obligations. The court will refuse to grant a decree of specific performance, if doing so would cause severe hardship to the defendant, or if the plaintiff's conduct was such that to do so would not be just, would make it impossible for the defendant to perform its obligations.

13.15 Restitution

The principle behind restitution is to provide a remedy for unjustifiable enrichment. The remedy obliges the defendant to restore, or pay for, a benefit received from the plaintiff. An example of restitution is where one party has performed its part of the contract and has not received any part whatever of the benefit of the agreed counter-performance. Such a party may be entitled to restitution in respect of its own performance. If performance consists of payment of money, the plaintiff may seek the return of the money by commencing a court action for what is known as "money had and received".

Where an innocent party has carried out work under a void contract, the fact that it is void will not automatically disentitle that party from recovering payment on a "quantum meruit" basis (what the job is worth), if the other party accepted the benefit of those services knowing that they were not intended to be gratuitous.

Similarly, in a contract for work to be done, or a contract for sale of goods, if no scale of remuneration, or price for the goods, has been fixed, the law imposes an obligation to pay what the job is worth.

The law may impose such an obligation where the plaintiff has commenced work pursuant to a letter of intent, and the defendant failed either to put a financial ceiling on the value of any preliminary work, or failed to specify the applicable rates and prices. In either event, the law may impose an obligation to pay a reasonable sum, considerably in excess of the financial ceiling or "contract" rate or price.

13.16 Limitation periods

It is a well-known fact that a prospective plaintiff in search of proceedings should not delay unreasonably in instituting them, and, thus there are certain periods of limitation laid down by law. After the expiration of the appropriate period, the law does not permit any action to be brought. A court action founded on a simple contract must be brought within six years from the date the cause of action arose (ie a breach[40]). In cases of fraud, deliberate or concealed breach, and mistake, the limitation period may be extended[41]. With regard to personal injury and death, the limitation period is three years from the date the cause of action arose or the date of the plaintiff's knowledge, if later.

40 Limitation Act 1980 S5.
41 Ibid S32.

13.17 Additional remedies for copyright infringement

While an injunction may be the first remedy a court is asked for, and damages may be the last, there are a number of other orders which a court may make in proceedings including:

(a) An order for accounts to be rendered.
(b) An Anton Piller order. This is an order which permits a plaintiff in an action to enter into premises of a defendant and seize property or documents subject to stringent conditions which the plaintiff must meet.
(c) A Mareva Injunction. This is used to prevent assets of a defendant being taken out of the jurisdiction.
(d) A garnishee order. This is an order where a sum of money is frozen and then attached by a court in order to satisfy a judgment debt.
(e) An order for delivery up. This order may be made against a person who possesses infringing copies of copyright works in the course of business[42].
(f) An order for disposal. This order may be made in respect of any infringing copy delivered up or seized. The order may be for the copy to be destroyed or made available to the copyright owner.

245

(g) The right to seize. This is an additional right for which no court order is necessary. The right may be exercised in circumstances where a copyright owner finds infringing copies of a work exposed, or immediately available, for sale or hire, in circumstances which would ordinarily entitle the copyright owner to apply for an order for delivery up of these goods[43].

Once seized, the goods are subject to the order of the court relating to their disposal. Before goods may be seized, notice of the time and place of the proposed seizure must be given in a prescribed form to a local police station.

A person exercising the right may not, however, seize any possession in the custody or control of a person at a permanent or regular place of business, and may not use force. The person may, however, enter premises to which the public have access. If any goods are seized in the exercise of this right, the person seizing the goods is required to leave notice in a prescribed form, giving details of the identity of the person on whose authority the goods were seized and on what grounds they were seized[44].

42 Copyright, Designs and Patents Act 1988 S99.
43 S100(1).
44 S100(3) and (4).

14. Termination of contracts and recapture of rights

[IMPORTANT NOTE: Please read the section "About this book" on page v, before referring to any of the matters in this chapter]

A. Introduction

14.1 Purpose of this chapter

The purpose of this chapter is to set out the circumstances in which a publisher or multimedia company may be able to terminate or rescind a contract, and to establish what the consequences of such action might be.

The chapter explains the difference between accepting repudiation of a contract, and terminating a contract, and explains the commercial advantage of the former course of action.

Any person consulting this section with a view to resolving contractual difficulties (by acceptance of repudiation or termination) should resist any temptation to act without taking legal advice. If notice of termination of a contract (or notice of acceptance of repudiation) is served without cause, the service of the notice may itself constitute repudiation and place the innocent party in breach. There will generally also be other legal aspects which will need to be considered before action is taken, and, in such circumstances, suitably qualified legal advice must always be taken.

After examining repudiation and breach, the chapter concludes with an examination of the circumstances in which rights may be recaptured, the events which normally permit agreements to be terminated, and the effect of determination.

B. Termination, rescission and repudiation of contracts[1]

14.2 Termination of contracts by performance

Where the parties to a contract perform their obligations in accordance with the requirements of the contract, they will be discharged from their

247

obligations. Where a contract is entered into for an allotted term which has expired, the contract will have terminated through effluxion of time.

Contracts may also be terminated (or discharged) by agreement (see paragraph 4.3). Rights in works which are the subject of a contract may also be terminated or recaptured in certain circumstances (see paragraphs 4.11 to 4.17).

Additionally, it is normal for contracts to contain specific provisions permitting the parties to terminate the contract on the happening of certain events by giving written notice of termination. Examples of typical events may be found in Clause 6 of Document 32. Once notice of termination has been given, the contract will usually be at an end, but it is common for contracts to contain specific provisions which provide what will happen on termination.

The inclusion of termination provisions in a contract will not always be advantageous to a party. Termination of a contract on grounds of breach will not permit the party terminating to recover damages for consequential loss, and it will generally be preferable for that party to accept the other's repudiation of the contract.

1 For a more detailed analysis on the discharge of agreements see *Chitty on Contracts* (Sweet & Maxwell, 26th edn.), Vol 1, 'General Principles', Chapter 22 or *Cheshire Fifoot and Furmston's Law of Contract* (Butterworths, 12th edn) Chapters 18 and 19.

14.3   Termination of contracts by agreement

Apart from performance of a contract, or its expiry by effluxion of time, there are a number of ways in which contractual obligations may be discharged by agreement between the parties:

(a)   the parties may terminate a contract by agreeing to rescind it[2]; or

(b)   the parties may terminate or alter a contract by an agreement to vary the terms[3]; or

(c)   one party may waive certain rights under a contract[4]; or

(d)   one party may be bound by estoppel (ie prevented from enforcing its rights) where that party has represented that it will not insist on its strict rights under a contract, and the other has relied on the representation or promise to its detriment[5];

(e)   the parties may novate a contract (enter into a new one) discharging one party from obligations under the original contract, either in respect of future obligations only, or in respect of past and future obligations) and creating a new contract with new terms[6]; or

(f)   the parties may agree upon an accord and satisfaction between the parties. In effect, this is the purchase of a release from the original contractual obligations for valuable consideration (see paragraph 2.10) other than the actual performance of the contractual obligations themselves[7].

A contract may also be terminated by the exercise of a contractual termination right (see paragraph 14.2) or by act of rescission (see paragraph 14.4) or acceptance of repudiation (see paragraph 14.5).

Rights in works which are the subject of a contract may also be terminated or recaptured in certain circumstances (see paragraphs 4.11 to 4.16).

2 *Chitty* Chapter 22, paras 1592–1598; *Cheshire Fifoot and Furmston* Chapter 9.
3 *Robinson v Page* (1826) 3 Russ 114.
4 *Hickman v Haynes* (1875) LR 10 CP 598.
5 *Hughes v Metropolitan Railway* (1877) 2 AC 439.
6 *Scarf v Jardine* (1882) 7 AC 345.
7 *British Russian Gazette and Trade Outlook Ltd v Associated Newspapers Ltd* [1933] 2 KB 616.

14.4 Rescission for breach of contract[8]

Where a contracting party has committed a serious breach, by defective performance, or by repudiating its obligations under a contract, the other party may rescind the contract. In other words, the other party may treat itself as discharged from further performance of its obligations, and may sue for damages for any loss suffered that was caused by the breach.

There is no specific test for deciding whether breaches lead to a right to rescind or not but, in general, where a party renders a defective performance, the defect must attain a certain degree of seriousness, before the innocent party can rescind. If breach by one party of its obligations under a contract results in a situation radically different from anything the parties contemplated when the contract was agreed, there will be a fundamental or serious breach that may entitle the innocent party to rescind. The courts will look to the construction of the contract in deciding what is, or is not, a fundamental or serious breach.

In deciding whether the performance of a contract was so defective that the innocent party can treat the contract as discharged, it is necessary to examine the terms of the contract to establish whether there are conditions or warranties. In general, any breach of a condition will allow the innocent party to rescind the contract and claim damages for loss suffered whereas (subject always to any contractual term providing otherwise) the innocent party may only be able to claim damages for a breach of warranty. Many contracts, however, permit innocent parties to terminate for breach of warranty, as well as breach of condition.

If a breach deprives the innocent party of substantially the whole benefit of the contract, in other words, the breach goes to the root of the contract, the innocent party may have a remedy in damages and also may rescind the contract.

8 See *Chitty* Chapters 22 and 24; *Cheshire Fifoot and Furmston* Chapter 9.

14.5 Repudiation[9]

Where a party places itself in breach of the contract by showing an intention to repudiate its obligations under that contract, this may amount to repudiation even though the time to perform the obligations has not come. The repudiation may be either express or implied and will give the innocent party the right to rescind the contract and claim damages. If the repudiation occurs before the time fixed for the performance of the contract, it will constitute what is known as an "anticipatory breach".

For a repudiation to exist, one party must have refused to do something that goes to the root of the contract. Whether or not the refusal goes to the root will depend on the construction of the contract, and the circumstances surrounding the refusal. The question of whether the breach constitutes a repudiation sufficient to give rise to the right to rescind, or simply constitutes a breach which will give rise to a claim for damages only, will be decided by various factors.

Repudiation may be implied from failure of one party to perform its contractual obligations or, in cases of anticipatory breach, by the party placing itself in a position which makes it unlikely that the party will be able to perform its obligations at the time that is fixed for their performance. In order to rely on repudiation implied by conduct, the innocent party must be able to show that the other party conducted itself in such a manner as to lead a reasonable person to believe that it would not perform, or would be unable to perform, its obligations under the contract.

Where a party accepts repudiation of a contract by another party, the accepting party will generally be able to recover damages for consequential loss. This type of loss will not be recoverable if the innocent party were to have chosen to terminate the contract as opposed to accepting its repudiation.

Clearly it will normally be preferable for a publisher to accept repudiation of a contract rather than terminate it, since the acceptance of repudiation will generally permit the publisher to recover consequential losses[10].

9 See *Chitty* Chapter 24; *Cheshire Fifoot and Furmston* Chapter 9.
10 See *Chitty* Chapter 26, para 1827; *Cheshire Fifoot and Furmston* Chapter 9.

C.   Consequences of breach and determination

14.6   Rights of the parties

A serious breach of contract, such as a breach constituting a failure of a condition precedent, failure of consideration, breach of condition, breach going to the root of the contract, fundamental breach, or repudiation will give the innocent party the right to choose whether to treat the contract as still subsisting, or at an end.

If the innocent party chooses to treat the contract as still subsisting, the contract will remain in existence, but this will not affect the innocent party's right to claim damages for breach of contract. If the innocent party chooses to treat the contract as at an end, it may sue for damages for any loss suffered (including the future non-performance of the contract) and will not be liable to perform any further obligations under the contract. However, the basic principle is that termination for breach does not have any retrospective effect (ie does not take away vested rights). The innocent party generally may not choose to affirm any one part of the contract, and at the same time treat the remainder at an end, but must choose either to affirm the entire contract, or rescind it.

Whether or not the innocent party has elected to affirm or rescind a contract is a question of fact. The exercise of a valid right to rescind must be made without undue delay and will result in the innocent party being freed from its obligations under the contract as a consequence of the breach, but the innocent party will lose its right to rescind for breach if it chooses to affirm the contract. The party in breach will still be able to claim damages for any breach by the innocent party which occurred before the termination of the contract.

Breach of contract normally will involve only civil liability and the innocent party will be able to obtain only remedies available in civil proceedings – damages, restitution, a decree of specific performance or, in certain cases, for example breach of confidentiality undertaking, an injunction to restrain a continuing or further breach of the contract.

14.7 Damages and injunction[11]

When a contract has been breached, an action for damages is available as of right. Claims for specific performance and injunctions are subject to the discretion of the court and are available only in certain circumstances.

The legal principle governing the award of damages is that, so far as possible, they should place the plaintiff in the same position as the plaintiff would have been in, if the contract had been performed. Damages for breach of contract compensate the plaintiff for damage, loss, or injury suffered as a result of the breach. If the plaintiff is unable to establish actual loss, the plaintiff will be entitled only to nominal damages, which may be awarded for the purpose of establishing and recording the infringement of the plaintiff's legal rights.

In principle, the innocent party is entitled to recover, by way of damages, its anticipated net profit, and any incidental expenditure of a type contemplated by the parties at the time the contract was entered into. Generally, the anticipated gross profit (full contract price and disbursements) will not be awarded. Alternatively, "reliance" damages may be awarded to compensate for expenditure wasted as a consequence of the breach, subject to proof that the net profit would not have covered such expenditure.

The types of damages which may be recoverable and other remedies are examined in paragraphs 14.9 to 14.15.

11 See *Chitty* Chapter 26, Damages; *Cheshire Fifoot and Furmston* Chapter 21.

D. Termination and recapture of rights

14.8 Recapture of rights generally

There are a number of circumstances in which rights may be recaptured by an author, or by a company which has licensed publication rights. Depending on the nature of the arrangements, the recapture may be effected through the termination or expiry of a contract, or through the happening of an event which entitles an author or company to require a reassignment of rights or through some statutory provision.

Recapture pursuant to statutory provisions under United Kingdom law and United States law is dealt with in paragraphs 4.11 to 4.16. Reference should also be made to the provisions of US law which provide for rights of copyright to cease to exist if certain renewal formalities are not observed (see paragraph 4.9) and, where other foreign laws are involved, to any local copyright registration requirements.

The degree of relevance of local legal requirements to an extent depend on whether the country in question is a signatory to the Berne Convention or the Universal Copyright Convention (see paragraphs 4.3 and 4.4).

14.9 Events leading to termination or recapture

It is normal in copyright agreements to provide for a number of events which will give rise to termination of a licence, or permit the exercise of the right to require a reassignment of rights. These may include the following:

(a) The work is not exploited by the company within a certain time, or goes out of print and ceases to appear in the company's catalogue.

(b) The company does not pay to the author or proprietor any sums due under the agreement. In practice a cure period is normally given to a company, who may have a certain time after receiving notice from the proprietor or author in which to comply with the accounting obligations. Additionally, these obligations may be expressed to be subject to the compliance and observance by the author with certain obligations and warranties on the part of the author in an agreement. If these obligations and warranties are not observed or performed, the company may have a counterclaim against the author or proprietor or be entitled to withhold payment of royalties.

(c) The company is in breach of obligations under the agreement other than those referred to in (a) and (b) above. Again a period is normally provided for any breach to be remedied.

(d) The company transfers or disposes of part of its assets, which in the opinion of the proprietor would materially inhibit the performance by the company of its obligations. This provision would protect a proprietor where its sub-publisher sold off a large part of its operations. A provision such as this is especially relevant in the case of a distribution agreement, but in many other agreements, its inclusion may be successfully resisted by the company.

(e) Any indebtedness of the company is not paid at the due time.

(f) The company is declared or becomes insolvent.

(g) The company convenes a meeting with its creditors or a petition is presented or other steps are taken for the winding up of the company or a trustee, receiver, liquidator or administrative receiver is appointed in respect of any of the company's assets.

(h) Control of the company changes.

(i) The company abandons or announces that it intends to abandon the business of publishing or distributing books or multimedia product.

14.10   Effect of determination

On the happening of any event entitling a proprietor or author to terminate a licence, or to recapture rights which have been assigned, the consequences will depend both on the type of agreement concerned, and on the provisions contained in the agreement. The following generalisations may, however, be relevant.

Where rights are granted by way of licence, the licence will normally be terminated automatically and the licensee will no longer be permitted to do what was originally authorised. Where rights are assigned to a company, the author or proprietor will need to secure their reassignment in order to stop them being exploited by the company. In some cases, an agreement may specifically provide that if the company refuses to reassign the rights, then the author or proprietor will have the power to do this as the attorney of the company.

Where a rights owner has licensed rights to a company and the company has sub-licensed the rights to another company, the termination of the owner/company licence will normally automatically terminate the sub-licence, and the other company's rights will expire immediately.

15. Insolvency and directors' liabilities

[IMPORTANT NOTE: Please read the section "About this book" on page v, before referring to any of the matters in this chapter]

A. Introduction

15.1 Purpose of this chapter

The purpose of this chapter is to set out a brief summary of the consequences of insolvency for individuals and for companies.

The field of insolvency law is one of immense complexity, but is of increasing relevance, particularly in the context of terminating contractual arrangements. One of the economically significant aspects of insolvency laws is the fact that legal proceedings, generally speaking, cannot be commenced against companies in liquidation, administration or administrative receivership. The potentially dire consequences of this fact are examined in paragraph 15.4.

Where a company becomes insolvent, there are circumstances in which the directors of the company may become personally liable, or may become the subject of court proceedings. It is clearly important to be aware of these provisions, however remote their applicability to one's present position may seem. A short summary of the provisions is contained in paragraphs 15.5 to 15.8.

B. Insolvency

15.2 Insolvency of an individual

The insolvency of an individual is referred to as bankruptcy. When a person is declared bankrupt, that person's property vests in their trustee in bankruptcy. This means that the trustee will be entitled to receive all income derived from the exploitation of any property owned by the individual and the individual will not be permitted to enter into any agreement for the disposition of any of the individual's property after the date of the bankruptcy order – since from that date the property belongs to the trustee in bankruptcy[1].

The duty of the trustee in bankruptcy is to administer the property of the bankrupt, so as to make payment of the bankrupt's debts to all creditors so far as possible[2]. A specific order for the distribution of the assets of the bankrupt is provided for. First, the income is applied towards the expenses of the bankruptcy. Next it is applied towards certain preferential creditors, including debts due to the Inland Revenue, to HM Customs and Excise, Social Security contributions, contributions to occupational pension schemes and remuneration of employees. Next the income is applied towards payment of the debts of ordinary creditors, and after that towards payment of interest arising on the debts of both preferential and ordinary creditors since the bankruptcy. After this any debts which are due to the bankrupt's spouse are paid, together with interest on such debts and any balance remaining is returned to the bankrupt[3].

A trustee in bankruptcy may apply to the court to avoid any transaction at an undervalue, or any attempt by a bankrupt to give preference to a creditor or guarantor, for any of the bankrupt's debts. The court may, in such an instance, make such order as it thinks fit in order to restore the position to what it would have been if the transaction had not been entered into[4].

1 Insolvency Act 1986, the second group of parts, Parts VIII to XI.
2 Ibid S305(2).
3 Ibid SS328 and 386.
4 Ibid S339.

15.3 Insolvency of a company

The winding-up of a company may be voluntary or compulsory. The members of a company may at any time decide to wind it up, to pay off all its liabilities and distribute its assets amongst its shareholders. Once a company is wound up, it is removed from the Register of Companies maintained at Companies House.

A compulsory winding-up order will be made by the court in various circumstances[5]. Liquidation of the company may be either solvent or insolvent. Where assets exceed liabilities, a company is solvent. Where, on the other hand, the liabilities exceed the company's assets, the company is insolvent.

A company may be wound up by the court if it is unable to pay its debts. A company is presumed unable to pay its debts if:

(a)   there is non-compliance with a "statutory demand" (ie where a written demand for at least £750 in the prescribed form is left at the registered office and is not answered after three weeks);[6] or
(b)   the company fails to satisfy a judgment debt;[7] or
(c)   it is proved to the satisfaction of the court that the company is unable to pay its debts as they fall due;[8] or
(d)   it is proved to the satisfaction of the court that the value of the company's assets is less than its liabilities. (Liabilities include contingent and prospective liabilities[9].)

The effect of the presentation of a petition to wind up a company or the making of a voluntary winding-up order may place the company in breach of obligations pursuant to its financing or trading agreements. Where a company is insolvent, either the court or the company's creditors may appoint a receiver or administrative receiver to manage the company's affairs. An administrative receiver will normally attempt to continue trading, but if this is impossible the company may be forced to enter into liquidation and the liquidator will be appointed to dispose of all the company's assets, which are then applied towards payment of the company's debts in a prescribed order, similar to the order of application of a bankrupt's assets.

As with a trustee in bankruptcy, a receiver, administrative receiver, or liquidator has the power to make application to the court for orders avoiding transactions that are at an undervalue, or transactions which attempt to give preference to creditors[10].

5 Insolvency Act 1986 S122.
6 Ibid S123(1)(a).
7 Ibid S123(1)(b).
8 Ibid S123(1)(e).
9 Ibid S123(2).
10 Ibid S138.

15.4 Proceedings against insolvent companies

Where an administrator, or administrative receiver, or liquidator, is appointed in relation to a company, the effect of such an appointment is that all legal proceedings against the company (including petitions presented to wind the company up) are automatically dismissed, and no proceedings may be brought against the company and no judgments may be enforced against it without the consent of the court[11].

Where rights have been assigned to a company which becomes insolvent and fails to pay, the operation of the above provision will mean that a publisher or multimedia company cannot sue to recover royalties. The intention of the insolvency provisions is to relieve pressure on companies in order to assist them to recover – but this recovery is frequently at the expense of their creditors.

Fortunately the law does not prevent a publisher or multimedia company who has entered into a contract licensing rights to a company which subsequently enters into insolvent liquidation, from exercising any right which the contract gives the publisher to terminate the licence. In circumstances where a publisher or multimedia company has assigned rights, however, the assignment will not lapse and the rights will not revert unless the contract contains specific provision for this.

How best can companies protect themselves from being trapped by insolvency laws? There is no guaranteed failsafe protection, but it is submitted that it would be good business practice for companies to review all existing important contractual relationships to determine what the company's position would be if the other party became insolvent. Existing contractual arrangements can frequently be varied by negotiation, and future contracts should ideally contain licences rather than assignments of rights, and should contain provisions which can be activated to eliminate the insolvency risk.

Where any company has licensed rights to a company in the United States, there are provisions in the United States Bankruptcy Act (which applies to corporations) which permit the exercise of contractual termination rights against companies entering so-called Chapter 7 and Chapter 11 arrangements (the rough equivalent of an administrative receivership and liquidation provisions). Any company which has entered into large-scale licensing arrangements in the United States would be well advised to review their existing arrangements from an insolvency viewpoint to ensure their rights are adequately protected.

11 Eg Insolvency Act 1986 S10.

C. Directors' liabilities

15.5 Disqualification

A disqualification order must be made by a court against any person who has been a director of a company which has become insolvent during or after the time the person was a director, where the court is satisfied that the person's conduct as a director was such that they are unfit to be concerned in the management of a company[12].

The power to make a disqualification order is contained in the Insolvency Act 1986 and extends not just to persons who are directors of a company but also to shadow directors[13]. A shadow director is a person in accordance with whose directions or instructions the directors of a company are accustomed to act. A person giving advice to a company in its professional capacity will not, however, be deemed to be a shadow director.

A disqualification order prevents a person from being a director, administrator, liquidator, or receiver, or manager of any company's property. It also prevents that person from being directly or indirectly concerned with or taking part in the promotion, formation or management of a company. The order, therefore, prevents persons from acting as management consultants or company directors, where they have been disqualified[14].

The period of a disqualification order may be anything from two years to fifteen years, although the disqualified person may apply for an exemption at any time during the period, or also may apply for the order to be lifted[15].

12 Company Directors Disqualification Act 1986 S6(1).
13 Ibid S6(3).
14 Ibid S1(1).
15 Ibid S6(4).

15.6 Restriction on use of company names

Where a person is a director or shadow director of a company which has gone into insolvent liquidation or has been a director or shadow director of such a company at any time in the period of 12 months before the company went into liquidation, that person is prohibited from doing certain acts for a period of five years from the date of commencement of the liquidation[16].

The person may not be a director of any company which is known by a prohibited name, or in any way directly or indirectly be concerned with or take part in the promotion, formation or management of such a company, or the carrying on of a business under the prohibited name[17].

A prohibited name is the name of the company at the time it went into insolvent liquidation, or any other name by which it was known 12 months before commencement of liquidation, or a name so similar as to any of the above as to suggest an association. The name therefore extends not only to the company name itself but also its trading name[18].

16 Insolvency Act 1986 S216.
17 Ibid S216(3).
18 Ibid S216(2).

15.7 Wrongful trading

Directors of companies are liable, in certain circumstances, for the liabilities and debts of the companies of which they are directors.

Wrongful trading provisions apply only where a company is wound up and involve an application being made to the court by a liquidator[19]. A court may find a director (or shadow director) liable for wrongful trading if:

(a) the relevant company has gone into insolvent liquidation[20]; and
(b) at some time before the liquidation, the director, or shadow director, knew, or ought to have known, that there was no reasonable prospect of avoiding insolvent liquidation of the company[21]; and
(c) the director was a director or shadow director at the time they had the knowledge (or should have had the knowledge) referred to in (b)[22].

If, however, a director or shadow director took every step that a reasonably diligent person would have taken in order to minimise the potential loss to the company's creditors, a court will not make a finding of wrongful trading against such a person[23].

Where a court finds that a person is liable in respect of wrongful trading, then the court may make a declaration that the director or shadow director is liable to make a contribution to the company's assets and the amount of the contribution will be such amount as the court considers proper[24].

19 Insolvency Act 1986 S214(1).
20 Ibid S214(2)(a).
21 Ibid S214(2)(b).
22 Ibid S214(2)(c).
23 Ibid S214(3).
24 Ibid S214(1).

15.8 Fraudulent trading

In addition to the provisions relating to wrongful trading, the Insolvency Act 1986 contains provisions which deal with fraudulent trading. The Act provides that if any business of the company is carried on with the intention of defrauding creditors of the company, or creditors of any other person, or for any fraudulent purpose, then every person who is knowingly a party to the carrying on of the business in this manner will be liable to imprisonment, or to a fine or to both. The provision applies whether or not the company has been wound up or is in the course of being wound up[25].

The above provision is a criminal provision, but additionally a civil law remedy is contained in the Insolvency Act, which provides that a court may on the application of a liquidator declare that any person who was knowingly a party to the fraudulent trading will be liable to make such contribution to the company's assets as the Court considers proper[26].

The courts have considered the precise meaning of the words "intention to defraud" and have concluded that if a company continues to carry on business, and incur debt, at the time when there is to the knowledge of the directors no reasonable prospect of creditors ever receiving payment, it will generally be proper to draw the inference that the company is carrying on business with intent to defraud[27].

25 Insolvency Act 1986 S207.
26 Ibid S213.
27 Ibid S214(2)(b).

259

16. Competition law

[IMPORTANT NOTE: Please read the section "About this book" on page v, before referring to any of the matters in this chapter]

A. Introduction

16.1 Purpose of this chapter

The purpose of this chapter is to provide a brief explanation of the principles of United Kingdom and European Union competition law, and to explain their relevance to the publishing and multimedia world.

A basic familiarity with the subject would be advantageous to publishers and multimedia professionals – particularly those whose business involves trade with other European Union member states, since failure to comply with relevant United Kingdom or European Union law may result in contracts being unenforceable or in rights of exclusivity being lost.

The chapter deals first with aspects of United Kingdom competition law (such as the Restrictive Trade Practices Act 1976, Resale Prices Act 1976 and the Competition Act 1980) and then explains, in general terms, the principles underlying Articles 85 and 86 and Articles 30 to 36 of the European Community Treaty, and the reasons behind the European Union so-called "block exemptions".

The chapter then explains what provisions of European Union and United Kingdom law are relevant to the four principal types of contractual arrangement most commonly entered into by publishers and multimedia professionals, examining in turn distribution agreements, purchasing agreements, licensing agreements, and agency agreements, before concluding with a short explanation of the European Free Trade Association (EFTA).

B. United Kingdom competition law

16.2 Restrictive Trade Practices Act 1976

The Act controls the type and extent of restrictions which can be agreed to in arrangements between entities which carry on business in the United Kingdom[1].

The Act provides that agreements of a certain type must be submitted to the Office of Fair Trading before the restrictions come into effect. If particulars of the agreement are not provided to the Office of Fair Trading in due time, the restrictions will be void and unenforceable[2]. If the Restrictive Practices Court holds that any of the restrictions would have a significant effect on competition, the restrictions will be void and unenforceable[3].

It is, of course, quite possible that parties may innocently enter into anti-competitive agreements, or may fail to register them. In such circumstances the Office of Fair Trading has no power to fine the relevant parties, but it may refer the matters to the Restrictive Practices Court which has the power to order the parties not to give effect to any registrable agreement which has not been registered or any agreement which will have a significant effect on competition[4].

The Act does not simply apply to written agreements, but extends to verbal agreements, and agreements which are not legally enforceable, as well as agreements and recommendations made by trade associations.

Agreements between two or more parties which carry on business in the United Kingdom under which at least two parties agree not to supply certain goods or services, or to supply them only subject to certain restrictions, are registrable[5]. Parties to an agreement are not required to be in the same line of business, or to accept the same restrictions. The type of restrictions covered by the Act include[6]:

(a) Agreements to supply goods or services at fixed charges. This implies a restriction not to supply at different charges.

(b) Agreements to give priority in the supply of goods or services to particular customers. This implies a restriction on supplying other customers in a way which would conflict with third parties.

(c) Agreements giving privileges or benefits to a person only if that person complies with conditions, or imposing obligations if the party fails to comply with conditions, or containing remuneration provisions which are calculated to penalise supply, production, or acquisition of goods, or the supply or obtaining of services.

1 Restrictive Trade Practices Act 1976 SS6, 7, 11 and 12.
2 Ibid S35.
3 Ibid S2(1).
4 Ibid S2.
5 Ibid SS6 and 11.
6 Ibid S6(2)(b).

16.3 Resale Prices Act 1976

The Act prohibits a supplier from imposing minimum resale prices on a dealer, or wholesaler, in relation to the resale of goods in the United Kingdom. If a provision in an agreement purports to impose minimum resale prices, the provision will be void[7].

It is also unlawful to take indirect measures, such as withholding supplies, in order to enforce resale price maintenance. Although it is lawful to recommend minimum prices, it is unlawful to make recommendations where the recommended minimum price is intended to be the very minimum price[8].

The Act also takes steps to prevent collective resale price maintenance, such as supplier cartels, under which suppliers agree to withhold supplies from dealers who do not observe the minimum prices, or dealer cartels, pursuant to which dealers agree to refuse to deal with suppliers who do not enforce resale price maintenance[9].

The Act does, however, permit contracts for the sale of goods with not more than two parties, to contain resale price provisions which link the price of goods sold under the contract to the price of other goods of the same description under an exclusive dealing arrangement[10].

7 Resale Prices Act 1976 S9(1).
8 Ibid S1(1).
9 Ibid S2(1).
10 Ibid S5.

16.4 Net Book Agreement

By virtue of the acceptance by the Office of Fair Trading of the Net Book Agreement, it is permissible for a publisher to specify a minimum retail price for books. The publishing industry and the pharmaceutical industry are the only industries which are permitted to specify minimum resale prices. The Net Book Agreement is currently under review by the Office of Fair Trading.

If the Net Book Agreement is abolished, protection of the amount payable by way of royalty may be achieved by requiring a publisher to pay not less than a certain sum by way of royalty for each book sold. Such a requirement does not prohibit the book from being sold at a price which is less than that on which the royalty is calculated.

16.5 Fair Trading Act 1973

The Act gives the competition authorities in the United Kingdom power to investigate monopoly situations, where one person, company, or group of companies supplies, or purchases, at least 25% of particular goods in the United Kingdom, or where two or more unconnected persons do so, and conduct their affairs in such a way as to prevent, restrict, or distort competition. Where such situations are found, the Act may be used to prohibit anti-competitive practices by the monopoly parties[11].

11 Fair Trading Act 1973 S6.

16.6 Competition Act 1980

The Act gives power to the United Kingdom competition authorities to investigate anti-competitive practices of individual companies or firms. An anti-competitive practice is defined as a course of conduct pursued by a party in the course of business which:

> "of itself or when taken together with a course of conduct pursued by persons associated with [the party] has, or is intended or is likely to have, the effect of restricting, distorting, or preventing competition in connection with the production supply, or acquisition of goods in the United Kingdom, or any part of it, or the supply, or securing, of services in the United Kingdom, or any part of it[12]."

If the existence of an anti-competitive practice is established, the competition authorities may seek undertakings from the parties concerned to end the practice, or if the practice operates against the public interest, orders may be made prohibiting the practice[13].

The Act will not, however, apply to any person or company which has (together with any connected corporations) less than a 25% share of the relevant market and an annual turnover (with that of any connected corporation) in the United Kingdom of less than £5 million.

12 Competition Act 1980 S2(1).
13 Ibid SS9 and 10.

16.7 Restraint of trade

Under English common law, any restriction on a person's freedom to carry on business is unenforceable, unless it can be shown to be both reasonable as between the parties and in the public interest.

In the context of distribution, licensing, and agency agreements this is probably most relevant to terms which restrict the freedom of the parties after termination of the agreement.

While the doctrine should not be overlooked, most of the restrictions which it might provide in the field of competition law are now covered by the Acts referred to in paragraphs 16.2 to 16.6.

16.8 Proposed new legislation

In July 1989 the British government issued a White Paper containing proposals for new legislation to replace the Restrictive Trade Practices Act 1976 and the Resale Prices Act 1976. This was followed in November 1992 by a Green Paper which stated the case for a new system to replace the two Acts, which would be modelled on Articles 85 and 86.

In January 1994 the United Kingdom Government introduced the Deregulation and Contracting Out Bill. This proposes a number of refinements to the Restrictive Trade Practices Act which, it appears, is to remain on the statute book, after all, amended by the introduction of the concept of "non-notifiable agreements" and other matters.

C. European Union competition law

16.9 European Union law – the general principles

European Union law is made primarily by treaties between the member states, and by directives and regulations made pursuant to the powers created by the treaties. The European Court then develops the law by construing the provisions in the treaties, directives and regulations in much the same way as United Kingdom courts interpret statutes and statutory instruments.

The main treaty, the Treaty of Rome (originally made in 1957 but subsequently amended), provides that the contracting states are obliged to enact the provisions of European Union law as part of their national law. The Treaty of Rome in its latest form is now referred to simply as the European Community Treaty. The United Kingdom has done this by means of the European Communities Act 1972 Section 2(1) which provides that all obligations arising under the European Community Treaty are to be given legal effect and recognised and available in law in the United Kingdom.

The principal European Union competition law provisions are Articles 85 and 86 of the European Community Treaty whose purpose is to encourage fair competition by outlawing certain restrictive practices and abuses which may affect trade between member states. Additionally, there are complementary provisions in Articles 30 to 36, and Articles 59 to 66, of the European Community Treaty which are designed to achieve the free movement of goods within the Union, and the freedom to provide services in any member state.

Article 36 of the European Community Treaty, however, recognises that there are occasions when member states may impose prohibitions or restrictions on imports, exports or goods in transit. The grounds on which member states are permitted to act include grounds of public morality; public policy or public security; the protection of health and life of humans, animals or plants; the protection of national treasures possessing artistic, historic or archaeological value; or the protection of industrial and commercial property.

16.10   Prevention, restriction or distortion of competition

Article 85 of the European Community Treaty prohibits all agreements between undertakings, decisions by associations of undertakings, and concerted practices, which may affect trade between member states, and which have as their object or effect the prevention, restriction or distortion of competition, and in particular those which:

(a)   directly or indirectly fix purchase or selling prices or any other trading conditions;
(b)   limit or control production, markets, technical development or investment;
(c)   share markets or sources of supply;
(d)   apply dissimilar conditions to equivalent transactions with other trading parties, thereby placing them at a competitive disadvantage;
(e)   make the conclusion of contracts subject to acceptance by other parties of supplementary obligations which, by their nature or according to commercial usage, have no connection with the subject of such contracts.

This list is merely illustrative and not exhaustive. By Article 85(2), any such agreements or decisions are automatically void. However, the European Court has interpreted Article 85(2) as meaning that restrictions in any Agreement which are contrary to Article 85(1) are void. By Article 85(3), the provisions of Article 85(1) may be declared inapplicable in certain circumstances.

Article 86 prohibits the abuse by an undertaking, or undertakings, of a dominant position within the European Union or a substantial part of it in so far as it may affect trade between member states. The ownership and exercise of industrial property rights (which by their very nature give to their owner a degree of monopoly) do not of themselves give rise to a dominant position within the meaning of the Article. However, this does not mean that such an owner may not in fact have a dominant position which the owner may use their industrial property right to maintain or extend, and this use may be caught by Article 86. Authors' rights societies and collecting societies (such as those referred to in paragraphs 6.17 and 19.21) are often the subject of proceedings under Article 86.

Where an agreement contains provisions which are contrary to Article 85(1) the provisions will be void. There are, however, circumstances in which the provisions of Article 85(1) (which prohibit the restrictions referred to above) may be declared inapplicable, pursuant to Article 85(3). Such circumstances might be where, for example, a restriction imposed in a trading agreement might bring about a countervailing benefit to consumers (eg increased sources of supply, lower cost etc).

Additionally the European Commission has issued certain regulations (known as block exemptions) which automatically exempt agreements "en bloc" from the scope of the Article 85(1) restrictions, provided the agreements fall within the scope of the block exemptions.

To summarise all this: it is permissible to impose obligations which might prevent, restrict or distort competition in trade between member states if the agreements fall within the scope of the block exemptions (see paragraph 16.11) or constitute a so-called "open" licence (see paragraph 16.12).

16.11 Block exemptions

The European Commission has issued block exemptions which apply to distribution agreements (see paragraph 16.16), purchasing agreements (see paragraph 16.22) as well as franchising, patent licensing and know-how licensing.

A distribution agreement normally involves a supplier agreeing to appoint only one distributor in a specific territory, or a distributor agreeing not to handle competing goods. This type of arrangement is, therefore, capable of limiting the sources of supply of goods, and will fall within the scope of European Union competition rules (see paragraph 16.10).

Both the European Commission and the Office of Fair Trading in the United Kingdom recognise that such agreements may confer economic benefits which outweigh the potential detriment caused by the restriction on competition. For example, exclusive distribution agreements may increase the likelihood of goods or services being distributed more widely to consumers.

The European Commission has, therefore, issued a block exemption (Regulation 1983/83)[14] for certain categories of exclusive distribution agreement. The provisions of this block exemption are examined in paragraph 16.16.

An exclusive purchasing agreement normally requires the purchaser to buy all its requirements of particular goods from one supplier. If these types of arrangement continue for any length of time, their effect may be to restrict competition, since the purchaser will be unable to obtain goods from sources other than the supplier, and other suppliers will therefore be prevented from supplying the purchaser with the particular type of goods. This type of arrangement will, therefore, fall within the scope of European Union competition rules (see paragraph 16.10).

The European Commission is of the opinion that certain exclusive purchasing agreements may have beneficial effects. They permit both parties to enjoy some certainty as to future supplies, and may make it possible for production and distribution costs to be reduced, and market penetration facilitated.

The European Commission has, therefore, issued a block exemption (Regulation 1984/83)[15] which applies to certain categories of exclusive purchasing agreement. The provisions of this block exemption are examined in paragraph 16.22.

14 Official Journal 1983 L173/1.
15 Ibid L173/5.

16.12 Open licences

The provisions of Article 85(1) of the European Community Treaty will, however, apply. The European Court of Justice has stated that a certain kind of licence (an "open" licence) would not be caught by Article 85(1). An open licence is a licence which contains an agreement on the part of the licensor not to compete with the licensee for the licensee's territory, and not to grant any additional licences for that territory, provided the licence does not contain any undertaking giving the licensee any absolute territorial protection from competition through parallel imports.

It is not clear how far the European Court of Justice or the European Commission is willing to extend the principle of open licences, and it may therefore be advisable to bring intellectual property licence agreements into line with the provisions contained in the European Community Regulations (the so-called "block exemptions") for patent licences and know-how licences.

The block exemptions do not permit the imposition of restrictions barring exports, or parallel imports, nor do they permit the imposition of tie-ins which oblige licensees to buy goods and/or services from a licensor, nor do they permit the imposition of restrictions on the licensee's pricing policies, or other unnecessary anti-competitive restrictions. It is therefore advisable to ensure that licence agreements meet these requirements.

16.13 Abuse of dominant position

Article 86 of the European Community Treaty prohibits the abuse by an undertaking, or undertakings, of a dominant position within the European Union, or a substantial part of it, in so far as it may affect trade between member states.

Copyright and other intellectual property rights confer on their owners a degree of monopoly (since the owners are in a position to prevent unauthorised exploitation of their works), but the ownership of exclusive intellectual property rights (in, say, one book, or one song) will not, of itself, result in the owner being in a monopoly position.

Collective ownership, or administration, of intellectual property rights may well, however, result in a dominant position, and therefore the provisions of Article 86 may need to be considered by large multinational companies, and also by collecting societies, such as the Performing Right Society Limited and the Authors' Licensing and Collecting Society – each of which may be in a dominant position.

In fact, the current requirement by the Writers' Guild of Great Britain and the Society of Authors that all their members should also be members of the Authors' Licensing and Collecting Society appears to contravene the provisions of the Competition Act 1980 (see paragraph 16.6) and Article 85 of the European Union Treaty (see paragraph 16.10) although the activities of the Authors' Licensing and Collecting Society would appear to be entirely permissible.

16.14 Free movement of goods and services

One of the objectives of the European Union is to establish an internal market in which the free movement of goods and services is ensured. The intention is that national boundaries are not to be obstacles to the free movement of goods in the European Union, or the provision of services in any member state. This is the basic effect of Articles 30 to 36 (which apply to goods), and Articles 59 to 66 (which apply to services), of the European Union Treaty.

Rights of copyright, and other intellectual property rights, are frequently exploited, by licensing their use on a territory-by-territory basis. The national laws of most member states permit the owners of copyright, in any country, to prevent the import of articles derived from such copyright (books, records, films etc) if they have been manufactured outside the territory without the owner's consent. Thus the United Kingdom copyright owner of a book can prevent the import, into the United Kingdom, of copies of that book, which have been printed in the United States of America, if such copies are intended for resale.

Clearly, if such a situation were permitted within the European Union, it would impede the free movement of goods (and services). The European Union has resolved the potential conflict between the exercise of intellectual property rights, controlled by an owner or licensee, and the free movement of goods manufactured by the owner or licensee in a neighbouring territory. The means by which the conflict has been resolved is the application of the principle of "exhaustion" to what the European Union refers to as "parallel imports".

16.15 Exhaustion and parallel imports

A parallel import is an article incorporating intellectual property rights, which has been lawfully manufactured in one member state (the first state) with the consent of the owners of the rights in that state, and is imported into another member state (the second state) where it is sold in parallel to articles incorporating the same intellectual property rights, which have been made in the second state.

European law has resolved the conflict in such a way as to permit parallel imports, and at the same time protect the rights of intellectual property rights owners. It is obviously in the public interest for companies which expend considerable sums on research or development of (say) pharmaceutical products, or in producing films, to be able to protect their product in the market place, so as to recover and make a reasonable return on their investment. Normally the result of this investment will be a material product or article which will be sold on the open market. Once the product has been sold, the owner of the intellectual property rights from which it has been derived will normally be unable to control its subsequent use and resale. In other words the act of first sale (either by the owner or someone acting with the owner's authority such as under licence) will have "exhausted" the owner's intellectual property rights.

Once the intellectual property rights in an article have been "exhausted" in any part of the European Union, they cannot be used to stop the article being resold anywhere else in the community. It is, however, possible for a rights owner to impose certain restrictions on its licensee in (say) France, but it will not be able to protect its French licensee from parallel imports being made into France from (for example) Belgium (see paragraph 16.17). The principle of exhaustion presents particularly interesting questions which must be resolved if the European Union copyright harmonisation programme is to be achieved (see paragraphs 17.11 and 20.7).

United Kingdom law provides that one of the acts which a copyright owner is able to restrict is the rental of copies of films, sound recordings and computer programs to the public. The laws of certain other member states of the European Union contain similar provisions. Where a video cassette of a film is marketed in one member state, European Union law does not permit any restriction on the export of the video cassette to another member state by the copyright owner of the film, whose rights to control the use or resale of the video cassette are "exhausted" by the first sale.

Where, however, the member state into which the video cassette is exported provides for a rental right for films, the copyright owner's right to control the rental of the imported video cassettes in the territory to which they have been exported will not have been "exhausted" by the first sale of cassettes, and the copyright owner will be able to prevent the cassettes being made available by way of rental in the country to which they have been exported. The copyright owners of sound recordings and computer programs (see paragraphs 3.10 and 19.26) have similar rights.

D.   Distribution agreements

16.16   **Distribution agreements generally**

For the reasons referred to in paragraph 16.11, the European Commission has issued a block exemption for certain categories of exclusive distribution agreements (Regulation 1983/83)[16]. Agreements which fall within these categories are exempted from the scope of both Article 85(1) and the Restrictive Trade Practices Act 1976, provided that they contain only those restrictions permitted by block exemption, and comply with certain other specified requirements.

This Regulation applies to distribution agreements which impose exclusive supply obligations on a supplier. The agreements which impose exclusive purchasing obligations are dealt with elsewhere (see paragraph 16.22).

The block exemption is aimed at any agreements between not more than two undertakings where one party to the agreement agrees to supply to the other, on an exclusive basis, goods for resale within the whole or a defined area of the European Union.

For the purpose of determining the number of undertakings, connected bodies are counted as one undertaking.

Agreements which fall within the scope of the block exemption are excluded from the effect of Article 85(1), and would not be unenforceable by virtue of any provision contained in Article 85(1).

16 Official Journal 1983 L173/1.

16.17   Circumstances outside regulation 1983/83[17]

Block exemption 1983/83 will not apply:

(a)   where manufacturers of identical or competing goods enter into reciprocal exclusive distribution agreements or non-reciprocal exclusive distribution agreements in respect of their goods unless (in the latter case) at least one of them has an annual turnover in all goods and services (together with the turnover of connected bodies) of no more than 100 million European Currency Units;

(b)   where users can obtain the relevant goods in the relevant territory only from the distributor, and have no alternative source of supply outside the territory;

(c)   where one or both parties makes it difficult for intermediaries or users to obtain contract goods from other dealers outside the European Union or (so far as an alternative source of supply is available) from outside the European Union.

17 Official Journal 1983 L173/1.

16.18   Restrictions which may be imposed on a supplier

Where the supplier of goods agrees to supply a distributor on an exclusive basis, the distributor cannot take any action to prevent the supplier from supplying goods to a foreign distributor who resells in the first distributor's exclusive territory.

It is, however, permissible for the distribution agreement to contain a provision which prohibits the supplier from supplying the contract goods to end-users in the exclusive territory.

Provisions which permit the supplier to supply certain customers in the exclusive territory, with or without payment of compensation to the exclusive distributor, are permitted, provided that the customers in question are not themselves resellers.

16.19 Restrictions which may be imposed on a distributor

Obligations may be imposed on a distributor not to manufacture or distribute competing goods, as may the obligation to obtain goods only from the supplier. It is also permissible for a distributor to be prohibited from seeking customers for the goods outside the exclusive territory, or to be prevented from establishing any branch or distribution depot outside the exclusive territory.

A distributor may be required to buy complete ranges of goods, or minimum quantities, or to sell goods under trade marks, or to pack and present goods in a manner specified by the supplier. It is also permissible to require a distributor to advertise goods, to maintain a sales network, or a stock of goods, and to provide customer and guarantee services, as well as employing specialised staff.

Any further restrictions included in a distribution agreement will take the agreement outside the block exemption, and will require individual exemption from the European Commission.

The Regulation does not permit any provision under which the parties undertake to refrain from cross-border trade or to prevent it. Such provisions will fall outside the block exemption, as will agreements pursuant to which the parties are not able to determine their prices, or conditions of business, independently.

16.20 Selective distribution

The block exemption does not apply to distribution agreements which impede the distributor in its free choice of customers. An agreement which permits a distributor to supply only certain categories of customers (such as retailers), and prohibits the distributor from supplying other categories (such as department stores), which are supplied by other local distributors, falls outside the block exemption.

It is, however, permissible for a distributor to be prevented from supplying goods to unsuitable dealers, provided that admission to the distribution network is based on objective criteria of a qualitative nature which relate to the professional qualifications of the owners of the distribution/retail business or its staff, or the suitability of their business premises, and provided that the criteria are the same for all potential dealers, and are applied in a non-discriminatory manner.

Any selective distribution system which does not fill these conditions will fall outside the scope of the block exemption, but may, however, obtain individual exemption.

16.21 United Kingdom law relating to distribution agreements

Agreements between a foreign company and a United Kingdom distributor will not fall within the scope of the Restrictive Trade Practices Act 1976 provided that the foreign company does not also have a place of business within the United Kingdom. This applies only to agreements between two or more persons carrying on business in the United Kingdom.

For the Act to apply to a distribution agreement, it is necessary for at least two parties to except relevant restrictions under the agreement. If the distribution agreement imposes relevant restrictions only on the distributor, the Act will not apply.

Any terms which relate, exclusively, to the goods supplied pursuant to the distribution agreement, are disregarded for the purpose of determining whether an agreement falls within the scope of the Act. For example, a provision which requires a distributor to sell goods in particular packaging could be disregarded.

The Resale Prices Act 1976 also applies to distribution agreements, and a supplier cannot require a distributor to resell goods at, or above, a minimum price set by the supplier.

Distribution agreements which fall outside the scope of the Restrictive Trade Practices Act, may still be investigated under the Fair Trading Act 1973, where a monopoly situation prevails (see paragraph 16.5), or under the Competition Act 1980 (see paragraph 16.6).

In the case of the Competition Act 1980, it is necessary to establish a course of conduct which is anti-competitive, and it is therefore unlikely that a single distribution agreement (as opposed to a network of such agreements) would be investigated.

E. Purchasing agreements

16.22 Purchasing agreements generally

For the reasons referred to in paragraph 16.11, the European Commission has issued a block exemption (Regulation 1984/83)[18] for certain types of exclusive purchasing agreements. The block exemption applies to bilateral arrangements, where the purchaser agrees with the supplier to purchase certain specified goods for resale, solely from the supplier, or from a party connected to the supplier, or from third parties designated by the supplier.

An obligation may be imposed on the supplier not to distribute the relevant goods, or any competing goods, in the purchaser's principal area of business and at the purchaser's level of distribution, but any further restrictions on the supplier's activities will prevent the block exemption from applying.

It is also permissible to impose obligations on a purchaser not to manufacture or distribute competing goods, to purchase a complete range of goods, to purchase minimum quantities of the contracted goods, to sell the contracted goods under trade marks, to sell the goods in a particular package, to advertise the goods, to maintain a sales network or pre-specified stock level of the goods, to provide customer and guarantee services, or to employ specialised staff.

18 Official Journal 1983 L173/5.

16.23   Circumstances outside regulation 1984/83[19]

The block exemption provided by Regulation 1984/83 does not apply where:

(a)   manufacturers of identical or competing goods enter into reciprocal or exclusive purchasing agreements, or non-reciprocal agreements in relation to such goods, unless (in the latter case) one of them has a total annual turnover in all goods and services (together with turnover of connected bodies) of no more than 100 million European Currency Units;

(b)   the exclusive purchasing obligation is in relation to more than one type of goods, and these are not connected by either their nature or commercial custom;

(c)   the agreement is for an indefinite term or for a period longer than five years.

19 Official Journal 1983 L173/5.

F.   Licensing agreements

16.24   European Union laws relating to licensing agreements

A licensing agreement may broadly be described, as an agreement, under which an owner of intellectual property rights, grants a licence to another person (the licensee) to manufacture and sell items of product. Under a licence agreement, it is the licensee who manufactures goods, prints books, duplicates video cassettes etc.

A licence agreement is, therefore, fundamentally different from a distribution agreement, which involves the sale of finished items of manufactured product (books, records, video cassettes etc).

Although certain distribution agreements are expressly exempted from the scope of European Union law by virtue of a block exemption (see paragraph 16.11), no block exemption exists in relation to licensing agreements.

It is thought, however (see paragraph 16.12), that "open" licences may not fall foul of European Union competition legislation. It is advisable to ensure that the provisions of licence agreements conform with the provisions of the block exemptions. These do not permit the imposition of restrictions banning exports or parallel imports, or the imposition of "tie-ins" which oblige licensees to buy goods and/or services, or the imposition of restrictions on pricing policies and other matters. It is advisable not to include such provisions in licensing agreements.

16.25   United Kingdom laws relating to licensing agreements

The criteria which apply to licensing agreements are broadly analogous to those referred to in paragraph 16.21.

G. Agency agreements

16.26 European Union laws relating to agency agreements

Directive 86/653 has been issued by the European Commission in relation to agency agreements and was implemented in the United Kingdom on 1 January 1994. The effect of the regulations in the United Kingdom is considered in paragraph 16.27. European Commission Directives and their implementation are examined in paragraphs 17.2 and 17.3.

The European Commission has stated that it considers that a true agency agreement, as opposed to an agreement between a supplier and an independent trader, is not covered by the prohibition contained in Article 85(1).

In order, however, for Article 85(1) not to apply to agency arrangements, it is essential that the party acting as agent should neither undertake, nor engage in any activities, which might be proper to an independent trader in the course of commercial operations.

The decisive criterion which distinguishes a commercial agent from an independent trader, is that the agent must not either expressly or impliedly assume any financial risk which results from the transaction.

Factors which indicate that a party is not an agent, but is an independent trader, include provisions in agreements which require a party to keep a considerable stock of goods, or provisions, or which require a party to organise or maintain a substantial service to customers free of charge. Where a party is able to determine the prices or the terms of a business, or does do so, such ability is also consistent with the function of an independent trader rather than a commercial agent.

Where a so-called agent is determined to be an independent trader, Article 85(1) will, of course, apply to the agreement, irrespective of what it is called, since the European Commission would examine the substance of the transaction in order to determine its true character.

In 1990 the European Commission issued a draft notice setting out an updated view on the agency relationships to which Article 85(1) would not apply. As yet the draft notice has not been formally published.

16.27 United Kingdom laws relating to agency agreements

The Restrictive Trade Practices Act 1976, the Fair Trading Act 1973 and the Competition Act 1980 do not differentiate between agency agreements and distribution agreements. The criteria for establishing whether they apply to any particular agency agreement are the same as those for determining whether they apply to distribution agreements. (See paragraph 16.21.) Where an agent is merely soliciting orders for goods, and the person represented by the agent sells the goods, the Resale Prices Act 1973 will not be relevant to the agency agreement.

Regulations implementing European Union Directive 86/653 on Agency Agreements were laid before Parliament in December 1993 and these Regulations[20] came into effect on 1 January 1994. The regulations apply to persons who negotiate the sale or purchase of goods, but they do not apply to persons negotiating the sale or purchase of services. The precise scope of the definition of "goods" is unclear. In some legislation "goods" includes rights of copyright. It is possible, therefore, that the regulations may apply to authors' agents and to the sale of rights of copyright. The Department of Trade and Industry which drafted the regulations had intended to issue guidance notes covering these and other issues but, at the date of publication, these notes were unavailable.

All authors' and publishers' agency agreements should be reviewed in order to determine the precise extent of any new obligations created by the regulations.

The regulations specify a number of basic rights and obligations which apply to the activities of agents, and the persons they represent. The regulations state that, where any agreement contains terms or conditions which conflict with the regulations, those terms and conditions will be void. Because the regulations contain certain minimum provisions relating to remuneration, there is a possibility that remuneration clauses in contracts which do not comply with the regulations might, in some circumstances, be void. This might mean that there might be no valid consideration (see paragraph 2.7) and the contract itself would be void (see paragraphs 2.21 to 2.23).

The regulations, besides specifying minimum terms of commission, also specify minimum dates by which commission payments are to be made, and provide that agents are in some cases entitled to receive commission after the termination of their appointment (which represents a departure from the current legal position – see paragraphs 2.28 to 2.30). The regulations also provide minimum levels of compensation for agents on termination, and they limit the restrictions which can be placed on an agent's activities after termination of the agency arrangement. Restraint of trade clauses may not exceed two years after termination, must be in writing, must relate to the agent's geographical area and the specific goods (but may also relate to customers), and must be reasonable from the point of view of the agent, the person whom the agent represents, and their common customers.

20 The Commercial Agents (Council Directive) Regulations 1993, SI 1993 No 3053.

H. European Free Trade Association

16.28 European Free Trade Association (EFTA) generally

Agreement was reached by the European Union and the European Free Trade Association on 21 October 1991 to form a European Economic Area. The aim of the European Economic Area is to extend the European Union single market principles to EFTA countries at the same time as the European Union single market is achieved.

The original EFTA countries were:

Austria
Finland
Iceland
Liechtenstein
Norway

Sweden
Switzerland

Switzerland has since withdrawn from EFTA.

The EFTAns are required to adopt some 12,000 pages of existing European Union legislation – known as the *acquis communautaire* – and are required to adopt new European Union legislation on which they will be consulted.

The Agreement covers the free movement of goods, services, capital and people as well as enhanced co-operation on side issues such as the environment, research and development and social policy.

Manufactured goods in EFTA countries will enjoy free circulation in the European Economic Area, subject to satisfying European Union technical and safety standards. The European Economic Area is not a customs union, so border controls and origination procedures will still apply to goods arriving from EFTA countries, although controls will be simplified.

Present trading arrangements with EFTA countries do not cover services, and the new arrangements are a positive move away from highly protective markets towards liberalisation. EFTA countries will set up their own institutions to enforce competition law and compliance with European Economic Area rules. Public procurement will be opened up for the first time in all 19 countries.

Credit institutions which are licensed in the European Union will be able to set up operations in EFTA countries on the basis of the "single passport approach". Non-trading policies include matters affecting the environment, social policy, safety at work, equal opportunities for men and women, employment for disabled people, consumer protection and tourism.

17. The European Commission and the Council of Europe

[IMPORTANT NOTE: Please read the section "About this book" on page v, before referring to any of the matters in this chapter]

A. Introduction

17.1 Purpose of this chapter

The purpose of this chapter is to summarise the principal areas of legislation which are likely to change as a result of directives adopted by the European Commission.

The chapter begins by examining precisely what a directive is, and then summarises the key points of directives relating to trade marks, computer programs, television without frontiers, rental rights, satellite broadcasting and cable retransmission, and the harmonisation of the term of copyright.

Next, the chapter examines proposals for a directive relating to the processing of personal data. The European Community directive relating to commercial agents and its implementation in United Kingdom law have been considered in the context of competition legislation in paragraphs 16.26 and 16.27. The proposals for a directive relating to the processing of data are considered in paragraphs 18.7 to 18.11.

The chapter concludes with a brief explanation of the activities of the Council of Europe, which is situated in Strasbourg. This organisation is often confused with the European Commission, based in Brussels and the European Parliament, which is based in Strasbourg.

B. European Union directives

17.2 European Union directives generally

A directive is a formal act or instruction issued by the Council of Ministers (the legislative body of the European Union) and the European Commission, requiring member states to implement what is set out in the directive.

Article 189(3) of the Treaty of Rome (which set up the European Union and is now referred to as the European Community Treaty) provides:

> "A directive shall be binding, as to the result to be achieved, upon each member state to which it is directed, but shall leave to the national authorities the choice of form and methods."

Directives must be addressed to member states, and cannot be addressed to individuals. As such, they do not immediately have effect in the United Kingdom in such a way as would entitle a United Kingdom citizen to rely directly on the terms of the directive.

However, in certain circumstances (as to which see below) the directive may be deemed to have such effect, for limited purposes.

Such an effect would arise where:

(a)   a directive is drafted in such detail that it leaves little or no discretion to the member state, so that transformation into the domestic format is a formality; and

(b)   the time limit for implementation of a directive by the member state has passed; and

(c)   the European Union citizen claiming rights under the directive has a "direct and individual concern" under the directive.

It is thought that the directive would then give the individual a defence to prosecution under national laws which are at variance with the directive, and possibly also rights in other limited circumstances. In addition, the offending state may be made the subject of enforcement proceedings before the European Court of Justice.

17.3   Implementation of directives

The formulation and publication of a directive is subject to the scrutiny of the European Court of Justice. Generally directives will not become binding in member states without implementing legislation.

The European Court of Justice has jurisdiction in an action brought by a member state, or the Council of Ministers, or the European Commission to pronounce an act "void" on the grounds of "lack of competence, infringement of an essential procedure requirement, infringement of the Treaty or of any rule of law relating to its application, or misuse of powers" (European Community Treaty Article 173(1)). This is rare, however.

There is no right of appeal for a European Union citizen against the terms of a directive. A directive which is not reviewed by the European Court of Justice may only be amended or repealed by a supplementary directive, but a directive may be appealed against in limited circumstances by a member state, the Council of Ministers, or the European Commission.

However, as a matter of practice, once a directive has been adopted it is likely that any procedural error (eg a directive passed under the wrong Article) will be ratified by the European Court of Justice (on application by a member state) or by the Council of Ministers, by means of a supplementary directive with the original directive not being withdrawn.

The consultation and investigation procedures pursued prior to adoption of a draft directive are of such a nature that it is unlikely that a directive would be adopted where one or more member states regarded it as having such defects which were not also procedural defects.

Any person having an interest in a proposed directive should express his or her viewpoint during the consultation process prior to the adoption of the directive. Such representations will fall on deaf ears after the date of adoption of the directive.

It is possible that trade organisations, government departments, or the European Commission itself will inform parties which are likely to have an interest in any proposed directive that European "legislation" is pending. Otherwise a party may lobby members of the European Parliament on such a matter, prior to a vote being taken on the directive, or may declare an interest in a particular area to the relevant directorate of the European Commission, and seek consultation.

C. European Union directives and proposals for legislation relevant to the media

17.4 Relevant media directives and the European Commission's views on books

This section contains a short summary of certain relevant European Union directives and proposals. It is not a comprehensive list, nor are the summaries of the documents exhaustive. While the European Union directives themselves are in final form, implementing legislation in member states may vary. Proposals for directives are subject to change, primarily through the European Parliament.

The following directives are among those which are relevant to the publishing and multimedia industries:

- 89/104 on trade marks;
- 89/552 on television without frontiers;
- 91/250 on computer programs;
- 91/263 on telecommunications terminal equipment;
- 92/100 on rental rights;
- 93/83 on satellite broadcasting and cable transmission;
- 93/98 on the harmonisation of the term of copyright.

The European Commission has made its views on the publishing industry public in the Commission communication *Books and Reading: Cultural Challenge for Europe*[1]. The Commission regards publishing as one of the major vehicles for promoting and disseminating culture, as well as being of considerable economic importance in terms of employment, total added value, investment and external trade. The Commission outlines a number of specific areas in which the Commission proposes action.

(a) Creation of books

The Commission wishes to improve the social status of writers and translators by means of progressive harmonisation of legislation governing tax and social security arrangements. It also wishes to harmonise items of copyright protection and associated rights and encourage collective agreements guaranteeing writers and translators a minimum level of protection and fair remuneration, and stimulate the adoption by all member states of public lending right legislation, and examine the effects of reprography on the market.

(b) Publication of books

The Commission wishes to implement a programme for the publication of cultural statistics in liaison with the Council of Europe and UNESCO, and examine the application of the European Union Treaty rules on competition in the light of technological and economic developments, and concentration and internationalisation of publishing.

(c) Translation of books

The Commission wishes to launch a number of schemes to stimulate and encourage translation, and training, and professional status, of translators.

(d) Dissemination of books

The Commission also proposes the examination of distribution systems, with particular reference to training and computerisation, the adoption of an action plan for inter-library co-operation and data processing, co-operation between libraries in the areas of conservation and preservation, the formulation of European standards for "permanence" of paper and board, the launch of a campaign to promote the use of "permanent" paper, an examination of prevailing retail price maintenance, a search for alternative measures to promote book publishing and distribution, the consideration of the problem of Value Added Tax rates on books, and communications and postal policy.

(e) Promoting books and reading

The Commission contemplated the organisation of a campaign to raise public awareness of reading, the definition of guidelines for action to promote literature on radio and television, and a series of studies on cultural habits in the European Union, including particularly reading habits.

1 COM (89) 258 Final Brussels 1989.

17.5 Proposals for directives and green papers

The following proposals for directives are relevant to the publishing and multimedia industries:

- proposals for a directive on the legal protection of databases;
- pluralism and media concentration in the European Union (Green Paper)[2].

A summary of the proposals for a directive on the legal protection of databases is contained in paragraph 17.12.

In September 1993 the Economic and Social Committee of the European Union produced an opinion[3] on the Commission's Green Paper on pluralism and media concentration. In the opinion of the Committee, the safeguarding of pluralism and freedom of opinion depends on rules designed to prevent media concentration processes which could lead to a monopoly-type mergers. The Committee feels that the Commission should take action to safeguard pluralism in the supply of television programmes, and consequently safeguard the freedom and variety of opinions. The action to be taken should, in the view of the Committee, define the limits to media concentration, so as to protect pluralism in the European Union against media companies which dominate entire sectors of opinion-forming activity in certain regions. The Committee considers that rules on national and trans-national media companies are considered to be necessary, and any proposed directive should not concentrate exclusively on the removal of barriers to market access, but should also set precise limits to media-specific concentration.

The Economic and Social Committee has urged the European Commission to take steps to ensure that ownership conditions in the press and electronic media sector are made completely public, and to require transparency in financial transactions, and full disclosure of worldwide company holdings, cross-holdings and concealed third-party holdings. It is the view of the Committee that such transparency is a pre-condition of legal protection for freedom of opinion and information.

The Economic and Social Committee proposes rapid European Union action with the aim of:

- defining standard European Union-wide concentration rules for the print and electronic media;
- setting a minimum democratic standard to ensure "internal" broadcasting and press freedom in the interests of safeguarding the variety of opinion and freedom of information;
- guaranteeing the right to report on cultural and sporting events (even of a commercial nature) and precluding unjustified interference by commercial interests;
- making public the advertising revenue of all broadcasters.

The Economic and Social Committee additionally makes a number of specific proposals for a media directive:

- In view of the existence of international multimedia corporations, it is the opinion of the Committee that ownership restrictions must be introduced in respect of the press.
- In the opinion of the Committee, neither media nor non-media enterprises must be allowed to dominate the market in several media sectors

(television, radio, press) in one or more national markets; similarly, no enterprise that already controls a national media sector must be allowed to extend its market dominance.

- In the view of the Committee, media or non-media companies which already dominate the market in one national media sector should not be allowed to acquire a majority holding in media holdings elsewhere in the Union.
- In the view of the Committee, before a media company which is already active in one media sector is allowed to operate in another media sector, all its holdings and cross-ownership arrangements must be disclosed in full.

Finally, the Economic and Social Committee proposes the foundation of a media code which, in addition to dealing with the control of media company power, will provide for the analysis of consumer requirements, bearing in mind the maintenance and safeguarding of the freedom of information and opinions, the protection of minors against violent and pornographic programmes, the protection of human (particularly female) dignity and the prohibition of the glorification of violence and armed conflict.

2 COM (92) 480 Final Brussels 1992.
3 CES 891/93 Economic and Social Committee 1993.

D. Specific directives

17.6 Directive 89/104 on trade marks[4]

European Union trade mark law contains certain disparities between the legislation in member states, which may impede the free movement of goods, the freedom to provide services, and is also capable of distorting competition. It is the objective of this Directive to provide that the conditions which apply to obtaining and holding registered trade marks in member states are identical, and that trade marks enjoy the same protection under the legal systems of all member states. The Directive requires all member states to pass legislation harmonising Union trade mark law prior to 31 December 1992. Currently the majority of member states, including the United Kingdom, has not passed such legislation.

One of the secondary objectives of the Directive is to reduce the total number of trade marks registered in the Union. To this end the establishment of a Community Trade Mark Office is proposed. Draft rules relating to the registration of trade marks in the Community Trade Mark Office have been published and the United Kingdom has published a White Paper on the reform of trade mark law, which contemplates numerous reforms including the abolition of the restriction on "trafficking" trade marks which has a direct impact on the character merchandising industry in the United Kingdom (see paragraphs 3.41 to 3.44). A Trade Mark Bill was introduced into the United Kingdom Parliament in November 1993.

4 Council Directive to Approximate the Laws of the Member States Relating to Trade Marks (89/104/EEC) 21 December 1988.

17.7 Directive 91/250 on computer programs[5]

The legislation of some member states does not clearly provide protection for computer programs, and legislation in other member states provides varying levels of protection. Differences in the legal protection afforded to computer programs have direct and negative effects on the function of the Common Market. The Directive aims to eliminate these differences and inconsistencies, by providing that all member states should accord protection to computer programs under copyright law as literary works. The Directive also aims to establish precisely which restricted acts, copyright owners should be able to authorise or prohibit. The Directive extends not only to software computer programs but also programs which are "burnt into" hardware, as well as preparatory design work.

Part of the function of a computer program is to communicate, and work with, other components of a computer system. In addition to common elements of physical interconnection, a common standard relating to software, and hardware, is required, in order to enable different elements of software and hardware to work together. This functional interconnection and interaction is generally known as "interoperability" (ie the ability to exchange information and then mutually use information which has been exchanged). The Directive aims to make it possible to connect all components of a computer system, including those of different manufacturers so that they can work together.

Some computer programs incorporate ideas and principles, such as logic algorithms and programming languages, which are commonly used in other applications. The Directive clarifies the fact that only the computer program itself is protected, not the ideas and principles which underlie any element of the program. This permits the free use of these ideas and principles in other applications[6]. The Directive also clarifies the fact that the rental of computer programs should be an act which the copyright owner is capable of authorising or prohibiting[7].

Certain types of activity which would normally amount to the infringement of copyright are required to be performed by the purchaser of an item of computer software or hardware who, in most circumstances, will not have acquired the copyright in the item purchased. Such acts include loading and running programs, making back-up copies of programs, the correction of errors, and also the decompilation of programs in order to obtain the information necessary to achieve interoperability with other programs. The Directive recognises and provides that member states should legitimise this type of activity. The Directive also permits the observation, study and testing of functions of programs provided such acts do not infringe copyright in programs[8]. This Directive has now been implemented in the United Kingdom by the Copyright (Computer Programs) Regulations 1992[9].

5 Council Directive on the Legal Protection of Computer Programs (91/250/EEC).
6 Ibid Article 1(2).
7 Ibid Article 4(C).
8 Ibid Article 5.
9 SI 1992 No 3233.

17.8   Directive 89/552 on television without frontiers[10]

The objective of the Directive is to eliminate the barriers which divide Europe, with a view to permitting and assuring the transition from national programme markets to a common programme production and distribution market. The Directive also aims to establish conditions of fair competition without prejudice to the public interest role which falls to be discharged by television broadcasting services in the European Union.

The European Community Treaty provides for the free movement of all services normally provided for payment, without exclusion on grounds of cultural or other content, and without restriction on nationals of member states.[11] This is a specific example of a more general principle of European Union law, namely the principle of freedom of expression as is found in Article 10(1) of the Convention for the Protection of Human Rights and Fundamental Freedoms, which convention has been ratified by all member states.

The laws of all member states relating to television broadcasting and cable operations contain disparities which may impede the free movement of broadcasts within the European Union and may distort competition. All such restrictions are, however, required to be abolished.

All broadcasts emanating from, and intended for reception within, the European Union are required to respect the law of the state in which such broadcasts originate. The originating member state is required to verify that such broadcasts comply with its national law, in order to ensure the free movement of broadcasts within the European Union without secondary control[12].

It is the aim of the European Union to promote the establishment of a market of sufficient size for television production in the member states to recover its necessary investments, not only by reference to individual national markets, but also by reference to pan-European markets.

Member states are free to specify detailed criteria relating to language etc. Additionally, member states are permitted to lay down different conditions relating to the insertion of advertising in programmes within the limits set out in the Directive[13].

All television advertisements relating to cigarettes and tobacco products are to be prohibited as is television advertising for medicinal products and treatment. Strict criteria are laid down relating to television advertising of alcoholic products. Additionally, the Directive provides for rules to be laid down in relation to the sponsorship of the financing of television programmes[14].

Member states are required to provide where practicable that broadcasters reserve a proportion of their transmission time (excluding time apportioned to news, sports events, games, advertising and teletext services) to European works or alternatively at least 10% of their programming budget (excluding news, sports events, games, advertising, teletex services) to European works created by independent producers[15].

Member states shall ensure that television broadcasters do not broadcast any cinematographic work (unless otherwise agreed between the rights holder and the broadcaster) until two years from the time the work was first shown in cinemas in one of the member states of the Union. The period in the case of cinematographic works co-produced by broadcasters is reduced to one year[16].

The amount of advertising is not to exceed 15% of daily transmission time and the amount of spot advertising within a given one-hour period shall not exceed 20%[17].

Member states are required to take appropriate measures to ensure television broadcasts do not include programmes which might impair the physical, mental or moral development of minors[18]. The Directive also requires member states to give the right of reply to any person whose legitimate interests, in particular their reputation and good name, have been damaged by the insertion of incorrect facts in a television programme[19].

The provisions of the Directive have been enacted pursuant to the Broadcasting Act 1990.

10 Council Directive of 3 October 1989 (89/552/EEC).
11 Ibid Article 2(2).
12 Ibid Article 2(1).
13 Ibid Chapter IV Articles 10–16.
14 Ibid Articles 13, 14 and 15.
15 Ibid Article 5.
16 Ibid Article 7.
17 Ibid Article 11.
18 Ibid Article 22.
19 Ibid Article 23.

17.9 Directive 92/100 on rental rights

Member states are required to make provision in their legislation for a right to authorise or prevent the rental and lending of originals and copies of copyright works. "Rental" means making available for use for a limited period of time, for direct or indirect advantage[20].

The rental right belongs to:

(a) the author in respect of the original and copies of the author's work;
(b) the performer in respect of fixations of the performance;
(c) the phonogram producer in respect of the phonograms; and
(d) the producer of the first fixation of the film (which designates an audio or audiovisual work whether or not accompanied by sound)[21].

The director of a film is considered as its author or one of its authors. The rental rights may be transferred or assigned, or subject to the granting of contractual licences. In the case of performers, the rental right is deemed to be transferred automatically to the film producer, subject to agreement to the contrary, and subject to the performer's right to receive equitable remuneration. The legislation of member states may provide a similar provision relating to the rights of authors[22].

Authors or performers have, pursuant to the Directive, an unwaiveable right to receive equitable remuneration. The administration of this right to obtain equitable remuneration may be entrusted by authors or performers to a collecting society. The member states may regulate whether and to what extent collecting societies may administer the right[23].

The rental right is without prejudice to any public lending rights provided for in any legislation[24].

Member states are required to provide a right for performers in relation to the fixation of their performances, a right for phonogram and film producers in relation to their phonograms and first fixations of their films, and a right for broadcasters in relation to the fixation of broadcasts and their broadcast and cable transmissions[25].

In addition to the so-called "fixation" right referred to above, the Directive requires member states to provide for a "reproduction right" giving performers, phonogram producers, film producers and broadcasting organisations the right to authorise or prohibit the direct or indirect reproduction of their copyright works[26].

So far as concerns broadcasting and communication to the public, member states are required to provide a right on the part of performers and other rights owners to receive equitable remuneration[27].

The Directive also requires member states to provide for performers, film producers, phonogram producers and broadcasting organisations to have exclusive rights to make available their work by sale or otherwise – known as the "distribution right". Member States need not apply the rental right to audio visual works created before 1 July 1994 and are free to determine a date no later than 1 July 1997 from which it shall apply.

20 Council Directive on Rental Rights (92/100/EEC), Article 1.
21 Ibid Article 2.
22 Ibid Article 2.
23 Ibid Article 4.
24 Ibid Article 5.
25 Ibid Article 6.
26 Ibid Article 7.
27 Ibid Article 8.
28 Ibid Article 13.

17.10   Directive 93/83 on satellite transmission and cable retransmission[29]

Differences between national rules of copyright, and some uncertainty as to law in some member states, mean that owners of copyright in works which are the subject of cross-border satellite broadcasting and cable transmission may not currently be entitled to remuneration. The Directive provides a definition which specifies when the act of communication of a programme takes place, and avoids the cumulative application of several national laws to one single act of broadcasting.

Communication to the public by satellite occurs, for the purpose of the Directive, only when, and in, the member state where the programme-carrying signals are introduced under the control or responsibility of the broadcasting organisation into an uninterrupted chain of communication leading to the satellite and down towards the earth. Normal technical procedures relating to programme-carrying signals are not considered as interruptions to the chain of broadcasting. The Directive also examines protection for authors, performers, producers of phonograms and broadcasting organisations.

The Directive requires member states to provide that the author of a copyright work will have the exclusive right to authorise or prohibit communication to the public by satellite. The member states are also required to provide that rights of performers, phonogram producers and broadcasting organisations are protected in accordance with the provisions of Directive 92/100. Certain transitional arrangements are intended to apply in relation to works exploited pursuant to agreements in force on 1 January 1995.

The Directive requires member states to ensure that copyright owners may grant or refuse authorisation to a cable operator for cable retransmission of a broadcast only through a collecting society. The cable retransmission right exists, however, solely in relation to the programme, not in relation to the broadcast – the copyright of which will remain controlled by the broadcaster.

29 Official Journal, 6 October 1993, No L248/15.

17.11   Directive 93/98 on harmonising the term of protection of copyright and certain related rights

The term of protection originally laid down by the Berne Convention was intended to provide copyright protection to an author and the first two generations of the author's descendants. The average life-span in the European Union has grown longer, to the point where the original duration is no longer sufficient to provide protection for two generations. Additionally, certain member states have provided extensions to the term of copyright protection in order to offset the effect of the World Wars.

The Commission has stressed the need to harmonise the protection of copyright and neighbouring rights throughout the European Union in the 1988 Green Paper, and in the follow-up to the Green Paper of 1991. The Commission regards these rights as fundamental to intellectual creation, and to the maintenance and development of creativity, in the interests of authors, cultural interests, consumers and society as a whole. The due regard for the established rights of persons is one of the general principles of law which is protected by the Union's legal order. Any harmonisation of the term of protection of copyright cannot, therefore, have the effect of reducing the protection currently enjoyed by rights holders in the European Union.

The Directive provides that the term of copyright should be harmonised throughout the Union at 70 years after the death of the author irrespective of the date the work is lawfully made available to the public[30]. The term for related rights is 50 years from the event which starts the term, namely first publication, communication to the public, transmission or fixation.[31]

The principal director of a cinematographic or audio visual work is considered as its author or one of its co-authors[32]. Member states are free to designate other co-authors. The term of protection expires 70 years after the death of the last of the following persons to survive, whether or not they are designated as co-authors: the principal director, the author of the screenplay, the author of the dialogue, the composer of any specially commissioned music[33].

Where a rights holder who is not a Union national qualifies for protection under International Convention (either Berne or Universal Copyright Convention) the term of protection of related rights should be the same as that laid down in the Directive, except that it should not exceed the term fixed in the country of origin of the work[34].

Anonymous or pseudonymous works are protected for 70 years from the date the work is made available to the public. If the pseudonym adopted by the author leaves no doubt as to his or her identity, or if the author discloses his or her identity before the expiry of 70 years from first publication, the period shall be calculated from the date of death of the author[35]. In the case of works published in volumes, parts, instalments, issues or episodes, the period is calculated for each item separately.

The Directive also provides that rights of performers shall run for 50 years from the date of the performance or, if later, from the point at which the fixation of the performance is lawfully made available to the public for the first time, or if this has not occurred, from the first assimilation of the performance.

The rights of producers of phonograms will run 50 years from the first publication of the phonogram, but shall expire 50 years after the fixation was made if the phonogram has not been published during that time. A similar provision applies to the rights of the producers of the first fixations of cinematographic works, and of sequences of moving images, whether or not accompanied by sound. The rights of broadcasting organisations run for 50 years from the first transmission of the broadcast[36].

The Directive provides that the person who makes available to the public a previously unpublished work which is in the public domain, shall have the same rights of exploitation in relation to the work as would have fallen to the author. The term of protection is 25 years from the time when the work was first made available to the public[37].

The Directive will apply to all works which are protected by at least one member state from 1 July 1995, as a result of the application of national provisions of copyright and related rights[38]. This is also the date by which the Directive must be implemented. The provisions relating to the authorship of cinematograph films need not be applied to works created before 1 July 1994[39]. All periods specified in the Directive are calculated from the first day of January of the year following the event which gives rise to them[40].

30 Directive 93/98 Article 1.
31 Ibid Article 3.
32 Ibid Article 2(1).
33 Ibid Article 2(2).
34 Ibid Article 7(2).
35 Ibid Article 1(3).
36 Ibid Article 3(2), (3) and (4).
37 Ibid Article 4.
38 Ibid Articles 10, 10(1) and 13(1).
39 Ibid Article 10(2).
40 Ibid Article 8.

E. Proposals for directives

17.12 Proposals for a directive on the legal protection of databases[41]

A number of divergencies and anomalies exist in relation to the legislation of member states on the question of legal protection of databases. Current database services are provided by on-line information services and CD-ROM databases.

Databases are currently protected by member states in various forms, either through statutory legislation or case law, but the level of protection varies from state to state.

The proposals for a directive recognise that, while the development of a database requires investment of considerable human technical and financial resources, information from databases can be extracted and copied at a fraction of the cost needed to develop it. The proposals for a directive conclude that unauthorised access to a database and removing its contents can have the gravest economic and technical consequences.

The draft directive suggests that the basis on which collections of data should be eligible for copyright protection should be the action taken by the author in effecting the arrangement of the contents of the database. No criteria other than originality should be applied and, in particular, no aesthetic or qualitative criteria should be applied to databases.

The proposals for a directive apply only to database material which is made by electronic means that and the expression "database" does not apply to any computer program used in the construction or operation of a database. The rights of author's works incorporated in a database are not affected by any provisions of the proposals, nor are any moral rights.

In addition to protecting the copyright of the original selection or arrangement of the contents of the database, the proposals seek to safeguard the position of databases by a special right to prevent the unauthorised right of extraction or re-use of the contents of databases for commercial purposes.

The proposals for a directive recognise that licences to use databases should be fair and non-discriminatory, and that a body should be provided to monitor licensing. Additionally, the proposals for a directive recognise the need to protect individuals in relation to the processing of personal data, particularly in relation to the right of privacy, which is recognised in Article 8 of the European Convention for the Protection of Human Rights and Fundamental Freedom.

The proposals for a directive further recognise the right to prevent unlawful extraction should not be capable of being exercised in such a way as to prevent a lawful user from quoting from, or otherwise using, a work for commercial purposes.

The right to prevent unlawful extraction of any information from databases, is proposed to expire ten years from the end of the date on which the database was first lawfully made available to the public.

41 Proposal for a Council Directive on the Legal Protection of Databases COM(92)24 Final – SYM393.

F.   The Council of Europe

17.13   Origins and membership

The Council of Europe was established in 1949. It is an inter-Governmental political organisation which groups 27 European democracies. It is quite separate and distinct from the 12-nation European Union. The headquarters of the Council of Europe are in the Palais de L'Europe in Strasbourg.

Member states of the Council are Austria, Belgium, Bulgaria, Cyprus, Czechoslovakia, Denmark, Finland, France, Germany, Greece, Hungary, Iceland, Ireland, Italy, Liechtenstein, Luxembourg, Malta, Netherlands, Norway, Poland, Portugal, San Marino, Spain, Sweden, Switzerland, Turkey and the United Kingdom. A number of other countries have applied for membership of the Council of Europe including Albania, Estonia, Lithuania, Latvia, Romania, Russia and Slovenia.

The aims of the Council are to work for European unity by protecting and strengthening pluralist democracy and human rights, seeking solutions to the problems facing European society and promoting awareness of a European cultural identity.

The Council of Europe operates through the Committee of Ministers and the Parliamentary Assembly. The Committee of Ministers is composed of the Ministers for Foreign Affairs of the 27 member states and the Parliamentary Assembly is composed of 210 members from the 27 national parliaments. The official languages of the Council are French and English, although German, Italian, Spanish, Portuguese, Dutch and Turkish are also used as working languages by the Parliamentary Assembly. The Council of Europe's budget for 1992 was 135,000,000 ECUS or approximately £97,000,000.

17.14 Achievements of the Council of Europe

The Council has pioneered over 145 legally binding European treaties or conventions, most of which are open to non-member states. In addition, the Council of Europe has been responsible for researching and issuing policy guidelines on matters which are of major concern to Governments and the establishment of Europe-wide public awareness campaigns.

In the area of human rights, the Council of Europe established the 1950 European Convention on Human Rights which provides a sophisticated monitoring and protection system through the European Commission and Court of Human Rights, and permits any individual to complain about alleged breaches of their rights for which redress is unavailable in the national courts and the 1981 Convention for the Protection of Individuals.

To date over 19,000 cases have been dealt with by the Council of Europe. The Council has also established a convention to eradicate torture, and in the area of social rights, established the 1961 European Social Charter and its additional 1988 protocol and the European Code for Social Security. The Council's activities in the sphere of security include a convention to prevent spectator violence at sports, which was drawn up following the May 1985 Heysel Stadium tragedy, and the 1977 European Convention on the Suppression of Terrorism.

In the field of health, the Council has been active in relation to pharmaceuticals, blood transfusions, drug abuse and anti-doping in sport, the subject of a 1989 Convention. The Council is also active in the fields of environment and responsible for the 1979 Bern (sic) Convention on the Conservation of European Wildlife in Natural Habitats as well as being active in the area of finance where it has produced a 1989 Convention to help in the detection of insider trading on Stock Exchanges, and a Convention on the Laundering, Search, Seizure and Confiscation of the Proceeds of Crime to prevent money laundering. It is also responsible for a Convention on International Aspects of Bankruptcy enabling liquidators of bankruptcy to exercise their powers abroad and allowing for the opening of secondary bankruptcies.

In the area of education and culture, the Council was responsible for the 1954 European Cultural Convention, the 1985 Convention for the Protection of Architectural Heritage of Europe, the 1992 Convention on the Protection of Architectural Heritage and the 1985 European Charter of Local Self-Government.

In the area of media the Council pioneered the 1989 Convention on Transfrontier Television which is designed to foster co-production and distribution of European cinematographic and audio visual works. The Council was also responsible for the establishment of the 1992 Convention on European Cinematographic Co-Productions and is pioneering a Convention to guarantee the preservation of the European audio visual heritage.

18. Data protection

[IMPORTANT NOTE: Please read the section "About this book" on page v, before referring to any of the matters in this chapter.]

A. Introduction

18.1 Purpose of this chapter

This chapter is primarily a reference chapter, whose function is to provide publishers and multimedia professionals with a guide to data protection legislation in the United Kingdom, its implications for publishers and multimedia professionals, as well as current proposals for its reform.

This area of law is of significance to publishers and multimedia professionals for two reasons. First, many companies carry out activities which require them to register with the Registrar of Data Protection and a number of people are unaware of the legal requirement to register.

Second, the provision by publishers and multimedia professionals of information in CD-ROM or multimedia format or by electronic means can have data protection implications and, in some circumstances, is capable of violating the data protection principles.

The protection of individual rights which may be infringed by processing personal data is the subject of a European Convention, whose aims are summarised. The European Commission has also proposed a directive for the protection of personal data, whose provisions are briefly described.

In addition to international conventions and directives, there are a number of practical recommendations which exist in relation to the use of personal data contained in databases. These are contained in the British Code of Advertising Practice for Database Management, which is set out in full at the end of the chapter.

B. Data protection

18.2 Scope of Data Protection Act

The Data Protection Act 1984 applies to automatically processed information, normally information which has been processed by a computer, but does not apply to manually held information, which is contained in files or other paper records. Not all information falls under the scope of the Act but only information which relates to living individuals. The Act does not, therefore, cover information which relates solely to a company or to a dead individual[1].

The Act gives individuals the right to find out about what information is recorded on computer relating to them[2]. They also have the right to challenge the information and, if appropriate, claim compensation in some circumstances[3]. Persons who record and use personal data (who are referred to as data users in the Act) must register with the Registrar of Data Protection, and must also follow certain practices, which are known as the data protection principles[4].

The Act defines data as information recorded in a form in which it can be processed by equipment which operates automatically, in response to instructions given for that purpose. Data therefore includes information processed by a computer, or information processed by mechanical means[5].

Personal data is defined by the Act as data which consists of information which relates to a living individual, who can be identified from that information alone or in conjunction with other information held by the data user. It includes the expression of opinions about the individual, but not indications of the data used as intentions towards the individual[6].

1 Data Protection Act 1984 S1.
2 Ibid S21(1).
3 Ibid S22.
4 Ibid S2 and Sch 1.
5 Ibid S1(2).
6 Ibid S1(3).

18.3   Exempt data

Some kinds of data are exempt from the Act, do not need to be registered, and the individual concerned does not have any right of access to the information. Exempt data includes:

(a) personal data held for domestic or recreational purposes[7];
(b) information that the law requires to be made public[8];
(c) information maintained to safeguard national security[9];
(d) information held for payroll, pensions, and accounts purposes, subject to certain conditions being satisfied[10];
(e) information relating to unincorporated members clubs[11];
(f) mailing lists, subject to certain conditions[12].

Every data user who holds personal data must register under the Act, unless all the data held by such a user is exempt from registration. Computer bureaux, which process personal data for other persons, are also required to register under the Act[13].

7 Ibid S33(1).
8 Ibid S34.
9 Ibid S27.
10 Ibid S32.
11 Ibid S33(2)(a).
12 Ibid S33(2)(b).
13 Ibid S5.

18.4 Data protection principles

The data protection principles are required to be observed by all data users, and are as follows:

(a) the information to be contained in personal data must be obtained fairly and lawfully, and the data must be processed fairly and lawfully[14];

(b) personal data must be held only for one or more specified and lawful purposes[15];

(c) personal data held for any purpose shall not be used or disclosed in a manner which is incompatible with the purpose[16];

(d) personal data held for any purpose must be adequate, relevant and not excessive in relation to the purpose[17];

(e) personal data must be accurate and, where necessary, kept up to date[18];

(f) personal data held for any purpose must not be kept for longer than is necessary for that purpose[19];

(g) an individual must be entitled at reasonable intervals, and without undue delay or expense, to be informed by any data user whether that user holds personal data relating to the individual. The individual is also entitled to have access to any such data and, where appropriate, to have the data corrected or erased[20].

If a company keeps a mailing list of its customers, simply naming the company, then the information will be exempt. If the company names the individual employees and their job descriptions, the information will be personal data and will need to be registered. If the data user's processing is aimed simply at communicating with a customer, then the personal data will not need to be registered. If the intention is to communicate with the individual then the personal data will need to be registered.

14 Ibid Sch 1, para 1.
15 Ibid Sch 1, para 2.
16 Ibid Sch 1, para 3.
17 Ibid Sch 1, para 4.
18 Ibid Sch 1, para 5.
19 Ibid Sch 1, para 6.
20 Ibid Sch 1, para 7.

18.5 Implications of Data Protection Act for publishers and multimedia companies

There are two main implications which the Data Protection Act has for publishers and multimedia professionals, namely:

(a) Where a publisher or multimedia company maintains a computerised list of authors, titles of books or works and the numbers of books or works sold, such a list will amount to personal data relating to the authors who are still alive. If the publisher or multimedia company removes the names of the authors from the descriptions of the books or works, they will still amount to personal data since the authors can be identified from information on the computer, together with other information in the possession of the publisher or multimedia company. If the information is held merely for the purpose of checking how many of the stock items have been sold, the publisher or multimedia company need not register, but if the information is held in order to provide information about a particular author, for example to identify the number of books or works which (s)he has written or discover how popular his or her works are, then the publisher or multimedia company will be required to register.

(b) The second implication of the Act is that the supply by publishers and multimedia companies of certain types of material on CD-ROM or in other electronic format may in some circumstances require the purchaser of the material to be registered with the Data Protection Registrar. It may therefore be appropriate for CD-ROM material or material supplied in electronic format to contain a suitable warning notice, so that the publisher and multimedia company can be seen to have brought the requirements of the law to the attention of their customers. It should be emphasised, however, that this particular aspect of the Data Protection Act is unclear, and is likely to be the subject of review. Further advice should be taken depending on the relevant circumstances.

C. Data protection and the media

18.6 Freedom of expression

There is an inherent conflict between the individual's right to be protected in relation to the automatic processing of personal data, and the freedom of expression which is necessary to guarantee an independent free press.

The individual's right to protection in relation to the processing of personal data is contained in the European Convention for the Protection of Individuals with Regard to the Processing of Personal Data. This provides that everyone has a right to freedom of expression including freedom to hold opinions and receive and impart information and ideas without interference by public authority and regardless of frontiers.

The European Court of Human Rights expressed the view that freedom of expression "constitutes one of the essential foundations of a democratic society and one of the basic conditions for its progress and for each individual's self fulfilment...[21]." It is applicable not only to "information" or "ideas" that are favourably received or regarded as inoffensive, or as a matter of indifference, but also to those that offend, shock or disturb. Such are the demands of pluralism, tolerance and broadmindedness, without which there is no democratic society. These principles are of particular importance, so far as the press is concerned.

The Parliamentary Assembly of the Council of Europe recognised the conflict between press freedom and privacy and stated that "the exercise of the former right [freedom of expression] must not be allowed to destroy the existence of the latter [the right to privacy][22]."

The question of unlawful data collection by technical devices has been considered by the European Court of Human Rights[23]. The Court expressed the opinion that national law should provide a right of action enforceable at law against persons responsible for such infringements of the right to privacy. The Court of Human Rights was of the view that the limits of acceptable criticism as regards a politician are wider than a private individual, on the grounds that politicians inevitably and knowingly lay themselves open to close scrutiny of their every word and deed both by journalists and the public at large. They must therefore display a greater degree of tolerance[24].

The Committee of Ministers has proposed certain guidelines in relation to the right to reply to the press, radio and television. These guidelines were as follows:

(a)   a right to reply should exist in relation to individuals and corporate bodies, with regard to whom facts have been made accessible to the public which the natural legal person feels are inaccurate;

(b)   at the request of the person concerned, the medium in question should be obliged to make public the reply which the person concerned sent in;

(c)   publication of the reply should be without undue delay, and should be given as far as possible the same prominence as was given to the information contained in the facts claimed to be inaccurate;

(d)   any dispute in relation to the application of the rules should be brought before a Tribunal, which should have power to order immediate publication of the reply.

A right of reply in relation to television programmes which have been broadcast is contained in Article 8 of the European Convention on Transfrontier Television.

21   The *Lingens Case* (Series A, No.103).
22   Resolution 428, 1970.
23   *Klass and Others v The Federal Republic of Germany* (Series A, No.28); *Malone v The United Kingdom* (Series A, No.82).
24   *Lingens v Austria* (Series A, No.103).

D.   Proposals for a directive protecting personal data[25]

18.7   Objectives

One of the objectives of the European Union is to encourage the constant improvement of the living conditions of its peoples and preserve and strengthen peace and liberty and promote democracy on the basis of the recognition of the fundamental rights specified in the European Convention for the Protection of Human Rights and Fundamental Freedoms. The proposals for the above directive is subject to the principles contained in the Council of Europe Convention of 28 January 1981 for the Protection of Individuals (see paragraph 17.14).

The proposals recognise that, while data processing systems are designed to serve society, such systems must be required to respect the fundamental freedoms and rights of individuals, in particular their right to privacy. Because a parallel objective of the European Union is to ensure the free movement of goods, persons and services, the attainment of this objective will require the free flow of personal data which is increasingly used in various spheres of economic and social activity. Because of the differences in the level of protection and freedom of individuals accorded by the laws of member states, notably in relation to the right of privacy, the variations of the laws in member states of the European Union might constitute an obstacle to the free flow of personal data. The proposals for the directive aim to remove the divergencies between the various laws and to protect the right to privacy of individuals enshrined in Article 8 of the European Convention for the Protection of Human Rights and Fundamental Freedoms[26].

25 Proposal for a Council Directive on the protection of individuals with regard to the processing of personal data and on the free movement of such data, COM(92)422 Final – SYM 287.
26 Ibid Article 1.

18.8 Personal data

The proposals define personal data as meaning any information relating to an identified or identifiable natural person who is referred to by the proposals as a "data subject". The proposals would apply to any processing of personal data by automatic means or processing by non-automatic means of any data which forms part of a personal data file. A personal data file is any structured set of personal data which is accessible according to specific criteria and whose object or effect is to facilitate the use or alignment of data relating to data subjects[27].

The proposals will require member states to provide that the processing of personal data is only lawful if carried out in compliance with the directive. Member states must provide that personal data must be processed fairly and lawfully, collected for specified explicit and legitimate purposes, must be adequate, and relevant in relation to the purposes for which the data are processed, and must be accurate and where necessary kept up to date. It must be kept in a form which permits identification of data subjects for no longer than is necessary.[28]

The proposals will require member states to provide that personal data may be processed only if the data subject has consented, and the processing is necessary for the performance of a contract with the data subject, to comply with an obligation imposed by law, to protect the vital interests of the data subject, for the performance of a task in the public interest, and certain other specified circumstances.

27 Ibid Article 2.
28 Ibid Article 7.

18.9 Prohibited data processing

The proposals will require member states to prohibit the processing of data revealing racial or ethnic origin, political opinions, religious beliefs, philosophical or ethical persuasion or trade union membership and of data concerning health or sexual life but such data may be processed where the data subject has given his or her written consent, or the processing is carried out by a foundation or non-profit-making association of a political, philosophical, religious or trade union character, or is performed in circumstances where there is manifestly no infringement of privacy or personal freedom.

The proposals would permit member states to lay down exemptions on the grounds of public interest relating to all data, including data relating to criminal convictions, and the proposals would permit member states to determine the conditions under which a national identification number might be used. The proposals would also permit member states to prescribe exemptions for processing of personal data solely for journalistic purposes by the press, the audio visual media and by journalists[29].

29 Ibid Article 8.

18.10 Right of access

If the proposals were adopted member states would be required to ensure that any person was entitled on request to know the existence of any data processing operation, as well as its purposes, and the categories of data concerned and certain other information, subject to certain exemptions which may be provided in relation to national security, defence, criminal proceedings, public safety, public interest, monitoring or inspection by public authority and equivalent rights and freedoms of others[30]. Where data is provided to third parties, member states will be required to provide that the data subject was informed of this provision and given certain information, which would permit the data subject to have a right of access to obtain details of personal data relating to such subject, an indication of their source and general information on their use, and would permit the data subject to rectify inaccurate or incomplete data, or erase such data, if they have been processed in breach of the proposals. Exemptions to such access may be provided[31] where restriction is necessary to safeguard:

(a) national security;
(b) defence;
(c) criminal proceedings;
(d) public safety;
(e) a duly established paramount economic and financial interest of a member state or of the European Union;
(f) a monitoring or inspection function performed by a public authority;
(g) an equivalent right of another person and the rights and freedoms of others.

30 Ibid Article 10.
31 Ibid Article 14.

18.11 Right to object

If the proposals were adopted member states would be required to give data subjects the right to object to the processing of data relating to the data subject on certain grounds, and require any person effecting data processing to take appropriate technical and organisational measures, to protect personal data against accidental or unlawful destruction or loss or unauthorised alteration or disclosure, and to provide and maintain a suitable level of security. The proposals will also require member states to provide a register of notified processing operations, to provide every person with the right to judicial remedy for breach of their rights under the proposals, as well as a right to receive compensation where they suffered damage as a result of any unlawful processing operation, or any act incompatible with the proposals for a directive. The proposals, however, envisage that member states may provide exemptions in relation to liability, where it can be proved that the controller of data has taken suitable steps to satisfy the requirements of the proposals. The proposals also contain provisions relating to the transfer of data to third countries, the establishment of codes of conduct of trade associations, the supervision of the protection of personal data by an independent public authority and the establishment of a working party for the protection of individuals in relation to the processing of personal data.[32]

32 Ibid Article 11.

E.   British Code of Advertising Practice rules for database management

18.12   Database management rules

The Council of the Advertising Standards Authority has extended the scope of the British Code of Advertising Practice to regulate the use of personal data for direct marketing purposes and also to cover the use and maintenance of lists and databases used to market consumer products and services.

Information is required to be fairly obtained, and personal data is required to be fairly processed, and held, in accordance with the data protection principles set out in the Data Protection Act 1984 (see paragraphs 18.2 to 18.5).

Compliance with the Data Protection Act is required, in addition to observance of the Code.

18.13   General rules

All reasonable steps should be taken to ensure that lists are accurate and up to date, that they should avoid duplication of mailings to the same name and address, and that prompt action is taken, upon request, to correct personal information. This is primarily the responsibility of the list owner[33].

All list owners should be able to identify those individuals who have objected to them, regarding the use of their data. List owners who make their lists available to third parties should be able to identify individuals who have objected to their personal information being used in such a way, or who have not been given an opportunity to object[34].

All who supply lists are required to satisfy themselves that the use to which the list is put, and any literature used in the promotion, conforms both to the spirit and to the letter of the Code[35].

All list owners, brokers, managers and advertisers holding databases and/or using rented-in lists should respond promptly to requests from individuals for suppression of any of their personal information, and should refrain from mailing such individuals for a minimum of five years from the date of the request[36].

Requests made by individuals to receive no further promotional mailings from a particular company will be taken to concern that company's mailings only. If an individual wishes to reduce significantly consumer mailings from all sources, the recipient should promptly refer the individual to the Mailing Preference Service (MPS)[37].

List users should maintain records which permit requests for the source of mailing lists to be identified, in order that such information can be supplied promptly upon request[38].

Personal information should at all times be held securely and safeguarded against unauthorised use, disclosure, alteration or destruction[39].

33 See The British Code of Advertising Practice, Rules for Direct Marketing including List and Database Management, CV1(B) 2.1.
34 Ibid 2.2.
35 Ibid 2.3.
36 Ibid 2.4.
37 Ibid 2.5.
38 Ibid 2.6.
39 Ibid 2.7.

18.14 Obtaining personal data

The advertiser or the data user (if they are different) should ensure that the general purpose for which personal information, including an individual's name and address, is being supplied should be transparently clear at the time that such a request is made. The notification should also identify the data user, any significantly different use for which the personal information might be used, and any intended disclosure to other companies including those associated with or forming part of the same group, where such a relationship is either not obvious or not generally known[40].

The extent to which an individual can be expected to recognise associations which exist, for example, between companies within the same group, should be considered carefully before personal information is used by the group as a whole[41].

When extensive personal information is sought, for example in "lifestyle" questionnaires, an explanation regarding the purpose of its collection should be given[42].

The extent and detail of any personal information held for any purposes should be adequate, relevant and not excessive for those purposes[43].

The data user obtaining personal information through direct response advertisements may use such information to make follow-up offers, except where specifically excluded by a subsequent suppression request[44].

When it is proposed to use personal information for a purpose significantly different from that for which it was originally collected, the individual should be informed and given an opportunity to object. A period of not less than 30 days should be allowed for such objections before personal information is used or disclosed for a purpose significantly different from that originally intended[45].

Both users and suppliers of lists are responsible for ensuring that the lists they use or make available do not include individuals who have objected to the use of their names[46].

Advertisers should take particular care in using sensitive personal data (including race, political opinions, religious and other beliefs, physical and mental health, specific salaries and investments, sexual orientation and criminal convictions – attention is drawn to the requirements of the Rehabilitation of Offenders Act 1974[47]) so as to avoid causing offence or harm to individuals. They should also, where appropriate, seek the prior permission of individuals to the use of sensitive personal data.

Published personal information which falls within the public domain can be used without informing the individual concerned in advance provided that such information is not used if the individual is listed on the MPS Suppression File[48].

40 Ibid 3.1.
41 Ibid 3.2.
42 Ibid 3.3.
43 Ibid 3.4.
44 Ibid 3.5.
45 Ibid 3.6.
46 Ibid 3.7.
47 Ibid 3.8.
48 Ibid 3.9 (and see paragraph 18.13).

18.15   List maintenance

Notification of the death of an individual held on a consumer list should be acted upon as soon as possible to stop all future mailings. The list user should also, in appropriate cases, promptly refer the notifier of the death to the MPS[49].

49 Ibid 4.1 (and see paragraph 18.13).

18.16   Mailing lists rented in

Users of rented lists should use their best endeavours to ensure that the category of individual is not inappropriate to the product or service on offer, particularly where there are specific criteria (eg age or income) which must be satisfied[50].

In order to ensure that rented lists contain the latest corrections and suppressions, the interval between the date of supply of the list and the date of mailing should preferably be no longer than three months, but should not exceed six months unless suppressions and/or corrections have been incorporated[51].

If individuals included on a list request the list user to refrain from further mailings, their names should be suppressed from that and any subsequent lists rented in[52].

If individuals included on a rented list request corrections to inaccuracies in their personal data, the list user should inform the list owner within 60 days[53].

50 Ibid 4.2.
51 Ibid 4.3.
52 Ibid 4.4.
53 Ibid 4.5.

18.17   Mailing lists rented out

List owners should ensure that prospective list users:

(a)   give an assurance to observe the requirements of the Code both in its general and specific rules;

(b)   satisfy them that the form and content of the intended mailing conforms with the general requirements of the Code;

(c)   either return the list to the supplier or incorporate suppressions and/or corrections, if the distribution of the mailing is delayed by more than six months;

(d)   pass back to them all requests for corrections to an individual's data within sixty days[54].

List owners and brokers should ensure that any consumer list offered for rental will not be used unless it is run against the MPS Suppression File[55]. List owners should hold records to demonstrate compliance with the requirements of the Code with regard to list rental and make these available, upon request, to the Advertising Standards Authority and the Committee of Advertising Practice[56].

54 Ibid 4.6.
55 Ibid 4.7 (and see paragraph 18.13).
56 Ibid 4.8.

19. Multimedia

[IMPORTANT NOTE: Please read the section "About this book" on page v, before referring to any of the matters in this chapter.]

A. Introduction

19.1 Purpose of this chapter

The purpose of this chapter is to deal with specific issues facing the multimedia industries, which are not covered elsewhere in this book. Although this is the only chapter in this book to deal specifically with multimedia issues, the multimedia professional will find that many of the topics covered in earlier chapters will also be of direct relevance to the world of multimedia.

Earlier parts of this book have been specifically written with multimedia users in mind. Chapter 3, for example, contains a detailed summary of copyright laws relating to films and sound recordings. This may be of limited interest to some publishers, but will be essential reading for the multimedia professional. Moral rights (which are covered in Chapter 5) and permissions (Chapter 8) are also of particular relevance to the multimedia world. If the multimedia industry becomes reliant on collective administration of rights, then the Copyright Tribunal (covered in Chapter 6) will assume an important role.

The essentials of contract law (covered in Chapter 2), the commercial aspects of buying and selling rights (Chapter 11), and commercial terms of distribution agreements (Chapter 12) are of direct relevance to the multimedia professional, as are matters relating to copyright infringement, termination of rights and insolvency (Chapters 13 to 15 respectively).

Defamation, obscenity and other matters covered in Chapter 9 may be relevant to the multimedia professional, as may matters relating to the public reporting of certain events (Chapter 10). Aspects of competition law (Chapter 16) are likely to be especially relevant to the multimedia industry if the telecommunications sector becomes an active player, and data protection legislation (Chapter 18) is clearly relevant.

It can be seen, therefore, that many of the concerns of the publishing and multimedia professional are shared. There are, however, a number of areas which are of specific concern to persons who are active in multimedia or electronic publishing, and these aspects are covered in this chapter.

The chapter starts with an attempt to define multimedia, both in terms of the marketplace as it currently exists, and in terms of current copyright legislation.

The chapter next examines the particular consents and permissions which are required for the development and exploitation of multimedia works. The relevance of performers' rights, moral rights and personality rights, in the specific context of the multimedia sector, is examined.

The chapter then examines the incorporation of music in multimedia product, and other aspects relating to copyright ownership, rental rights and subsidiary rights, in multimedia product.

A number of practical aspects relating to developing and producing multimedia product are then examined and a detailed analysis of the main component parts of multimedia development and production agreements is provided.

The next topic covered is the licensing and distribution of multimedia product, in which context a number of basic principles which may be useful to multimedia professionals are set out. Then the various possibilities open to companies wishing to co-publish, co-produce, or enter into multimedia joint venture agreements, are examined.

A short summary of certain aspects of telecommunications law, which may be relevant to multimedia professionals is then set out. This is followed by a summary of the law relating to computer misuse, and other aspects of legislation which may be relevant to companies active in software and video publishing and distribution.

B. What is multimedia?

19.2 Multimedia defined in market terms

The word "multimedia" is of relatively recent coinage and is used to describe a technological advance which is still at a very early stage of development. The arrival of digital recording has meant that it is possible to store text, sound recordings and moving images in binary electronic form on computers. Multimedia involves the storage and use of text, sounds, graphics and moving images in digital format. A computer equipped with a video card and sound card (which may be purchased for a few hundred pounds each) is capable of producing digital stereo sound and full motion video from digital information which is input into the computer by disk, by CD-ROM, by CD-I or by modem.

The same computer will also permit a photograph which has been digitally scanned to be stored on disk, and to be altered or manipulated in a number of ways. It is similarly possible to alter, and manipulate, digitally recorded music, or to create one's own music, and reproduce this, together with self-produced or altered images. Reproduction may either be by means of playback, through a computer-monitor and stereo sound system, or by means of copying the digital information on to disk or CD-ROM, or CD-I or by means of transmission by modem to another computer.

The multimedia market is still in its infancy, and although rapid growth of the market is predicted, it is unclear in what direction it will develop. It is currently possible to categorise the multimedia industry in a number of different ways. Although it is not the intention to provide an exhaustive current definition, it is possible to identify the following applications which exist:

(a) CD-ROM

CD-ROM disks can, when used on a personal computer which is fitted with a sound card and a video card, provide full motion video and digital stereo sound. Personal computers which are fitted with CD-ROM drives are additionally capable of reading and manipulating vast amounts of data which may be stored on CD-ROM disks.

(b) CD-I

CD-I disks are the same size as CD-ROM disks but they are designed to be used not on personal computers but on specific CD-I players. CD-I players also offer full motion video and digital stereo sound. The principal difference between a CD-I player and a CD-ROM player is that a CD-I player is connected to a television and is more "user-friendly".

(c) Electronic books

The electronic book is a new application. Sony has recently launched its data disk-man electronic book player (which is a multimedia walkman). It is capable of playing 8mm CDs which reproduce speech and music, as well as reproducing text and graphics. It can be linked up with either a television or a personal computer.

(d) On-line applications

The above three applications are all carrier-based (ie the information is carried on a disk). Since digital information may be accessed by modem, it is possible to obtain digitally recorded sound, graphics and text by means of on-line access to a computer.

(e) Interactive television and video on demand

Interactive television offers a wide range of possibilities. At the lowest level of interaction it is possible for viewer-response to be measured (to quiz shows and current affairs programmes etc). Interactivity may also be used to permit certain home-services such as home shopping and banking. It also makes possible the provision of Video on Demand services, by means of which consumers may order audio visual product for home viewing, and have the same controls (pause, rewind, fast-forward etc) as they would on a domestic video cassette recorder.

(f) Location-based applications

Location-based applications include not only virtual reality product which may be experienced at games centres, but also arcade-style machines which may offer a higher level of sophistication than that attainable by home personal computers.

It will be appreciated that the above breakdown is not intended to be exhaustive, and it will be remembered that, in addition to the applications and sectors listed above, there are a wide range of service providers and technologies concerned with the design and manufacture of technologies, the creation of new means of data compression and new operating systems and technologies which do not fall into any single one of the above categories.

19.3 Multimedia defined in intellectual property terms

Because its component parts are of such a wide and varied nature, a multimedia work is simultaneously protected by United Kingdom (and international) copyright legislation in a number of different ways.

(a) Literary elements

Any original literary elements of a multimedia work are protected as literary works.

(b) Dramatic elements

Any original dramatic elements of a multimedia work are protected as dramatic works.

(c) Musical elements

Music contained in a multimedia work will be protected as a musical work. Words accompanying a musical work are protected as literary works.

(d) Artistic works

Any graphic work, or photograph, or drawing or model contained in a multimedia work is protected as an artistic work.

(e) Moving images

Any series of moving images contained in a multimedia work will be protected in the same way as a film.

(f) Sound recordings

Any sound recordings contained in multimedia product are protected in the same way as other sound recordings.

(g) Typographical arrangements

Where a multimedia work contains the typographical arrangement of a published edition of a literary, dramatic or musical work, this typographical arrangement is also protected by copyright.

(h) Computer programs

Where a multimedia work contains a computer program, this program is also protected by copyright as a literary work.

(i) Choreographic routines

Where a multimedia work contains a choreographic routine, this routine is protected by copyright as a literary work.

In addition to the specific types of copyright protection set out above, the owner of copyright in a multimedia work will also have the right to restrict the rental of the multimedia work to the public. In addition to the specific rights which are protected by copyright, multimedia product may also be protected by the law of patent (see paragraph 19.29), by trade mark law (see paragraphs 3.41 to 3.45) or by passing off (see paragraph 3.19).

C. Consents and permissions required for multimedia works

19.4 Copyright licences generally

The consent or licence of all owners of copyright works which are to be included in a multimedia product needs to be obtained before such works can be copied or otherwise used. The multimedia producer should ensure that the licence extends to the entire territory which it requires for a term of years sufficient to justify the investment, and for the media which are required. The licence should also contain warranties as to certain facts. Examples of matters on which warranties may be required can be found in paragraph 7.15 and Document 31 clauses 7.1 to 7.9.

The licence needs to be obtained in relation to each of the elements of copyright works referred to in paragraph 19.3. The precise nature of the licence will depend on all the circumstances, but the licence should extend to at least three of the five acts which are restricted by copyright (see paragraph 13.3). The multimedia company should obtain:

(a)   the right to copy the work;
(b)   the right to issue copies of the work to the public;
(c)   the right to adapt the work: and also possibly
(d)   the right to perform, show or play the work in public; and
(e)   the right to broadcast the work or include it in a cable programme service.

One of the areas in which multimedia differs from other parts of the copyright industry, is that purchasers of multimedia works will themselves be using, adapting and manipulating these works. The purchaser of a record or a video cassette will not normally make copies of the record or cassette. Generally, purchased records and cassettes may only be used by being played back in the purchaser's own home. As the British Phonographic Industry repeatedly reminds us, the home taping of records is illegal.

There are three aspects to note where a computer program is involved:

– The making of backup copies of the program and decompilation of the program is permitted, as is copying, adaptation, and error correction unless such copying, adaptation and error correction is prohibited by a term of a licence (see paragraph 8.24).
– It is not fair dealing in relation to a computer program to convert it from low-level to high-level language (see paragraph 8.24).
– Any term of a licence in relation to a computer program which prevents the making of backup copies or decompilation or using any device or process to observe, study or test the functioning of the program to understand the underlying ideas and principles is void (see paragraph 8.24).

19.5   What rights should multimedia companies acquire?

Multimedia works are expressly designed and intended to be copied and adapted by their purchasers. Copying for the purposes of United Kingdom copyright legislation, includes storing a work in any medium by electronic means. It also includes the making of copies which are transient or are incidental to some other use of the work.

CD-ROM based multimedia works will frequently contain elements which need to be copied onto a personal computer's hard disk. Even where this is not the case, when the CD-ROMs are used, it is likely that their use will result in a transient copy of part of the work contained on the CD-ROM being made either in Random Access Memory, or in the personal computer's disk cache.

Any licence obtained by a multimedia company will therefore need to permit not only the multimedia company to copy the relevant work but also permit purchasers of the multimedia application to copy it. The copying of works is permitted for the purposes of research or study (paragraph 8.6) and certain other acts involving copying are classed as "permitted acts" (paragraphs 8.7 to 8.39). Any use of a work for the purpose of research or private study is permitted (see paragraph 8.6). Purchasers of CD-ROMs will therefore have the right to use them and copy and adapt them. It will be remembered that copying of computer programs can be prohibited in certain circumstances (see paragraph 19.4). Even if a licence in relation to a computer program expressly prohibits the copying of a computer program (which United Kingdom legislation does not define), purchasers of the program will, it appears, be able to copy or adapt any literary, dramatic, musical or artistic works, or films, or sound recordings contained in it, although they will not, of course, be able to issue copies of such works to the public, or perform them in public. There will be many circumstances where the purchaser of multimedia product will not be able to use copyright works without the benefit of a licence from the owner of such works which expressly extends to the purchaser.

The making of adaptations of any copyright work is also an act restricted by copyright. Any licence obtained by a multimedia company will need not only to permit it to adapt the copyright work but will also need to extend to purchasers of its product. The adaptation of works has certain moral rights implications. These are considered in paragraphs 19.10 to 19.12.

In those cases where a multimedia company is producing a product which is designed to be shown or played in public (such as a program permitting the making of slide presentations), the multimedia company may need to ensure that any licence obtained from third parties permits their material to be shown or played in public by purchasers of the product. In the circumstances, where it is unclear whether such rights are licensed to purchasers, the purchasers should check they are authorised to use the works in public.

There will also be occasions where a multimedia company intends its product to be made available in an "on-line" situation (see paragraph 19.45). Such use may fall within the United Kingdom statutory definition of "cable programme service" (see paragraphs 3.8 and 3.32) and the company or any purchaser who intends to use elements of the product in such a way should ensure that the copyright owner has licensed the appropriate rights.

In addition to rights acquired from third party companies, multimedia companies will need to acquire rights of copyright (and other rights) from individuals whom they engage. Such persons may be engaged either as employees, or as independent contractors. Some of the relevant factors which need to be considered are examined in paragraphs 19.9 and 19.32.

19.6 Performers' consents generally

Where a multimedia product incorporates recordings of performances, certain consents will need to be obtained from various categories of performers. Performers' rights exist in relation to musical performances, dramatic performances, readings or recitations of literary works, and performances of variety acts. The rights will exist if the performance is given by a qualifying individual, or the performance took place in a qualifying country (see paragraphs 6.1 to 6.15).

Performers' rights exist not only in relation to sound recordings and films which are included in multimedia product, but also in speech and, in some cases, in programmed music. Many countries (including the United States of America) do not recognise rights in performances. Any performance made by a United Kingdom national in the United States within the last 50 years may not be reproduced in the United Kingdom (or any other countries recognising performers' rights) without the consent of the relevant performer.

United Kingdom legislation does not require consent to be given in writing. Whether the consent has been given, or not, is, therefore, a question of fact. The extent of any consent is also questionable. A consent which authorises the manufacture of a record, or the showing of a film in cinemas, does not necessarily extend to exploiting the record or film in CD or video format. It is certainly questionable whether a consent given in relation to a long-playing sound recording in the 1940s or 1950s would extend to multimedia exploitation. It should not be assumed that it would. It is necessary either to examine underlying documentation in every case, or to obtain a specific warranty from the person supplying the recording, to ensure that all relevant performers' consents have been obtained.

Many companies and corporations are happy to supply films and sound recordings on terms which require their users to obtain all necessary consents. Because of the low level of copyright protection given by United States laws until recently (see paragraphs 4.5 to 4.8), many copyright works which are in the public domain in the United States are protected by copyright under the laws of the United Kingdom, and the rest of the European Union. Many United States corporations are therefore able to sell rights which may have expired in the United States, but which may not have expired elsewhere. These companies are quite prepared to make material available to third parties on terms which require the third parties to obtain clearances in relation to all necessary rights.

19.7 Performers' consents and the Copyright Tribunal

The clearance of performing rights is frequently difficult, especially when the recordings have been made some time ago. There are a number of problems. First, the identity of the performers may not be readily ascertainable. Even though lead or featured musicians are identifiable, the performances of backing musicians and singers will also need consents, as will the performance of chorus girls and crowd extras, if these persons are qualifying individuals or their performances were qualifying performances (see paragraph 6.14).

Even where the relevant performers are identified, they might be difficult to locate. They could even be dead. Under United Kingdom law, the right to give consent on behalf of a performer is transmissible on their decease, but in view of the recency of United Kingdom legislation (and also in view of the fact that a performers' consent may be exercisable by more than one person), the tracing of all heirs of deceased performers is not only extremely labour-intensive and tiresome – it is also generally unproductive.

Fortunately, United Kingdom legislation has provided a means to deal with these two difficulties. Since August 1989 (when most of the Copyright, Designs and Patents Act 1988 came into effect) the jurisdiction of the old Performers' Right Tribunal was extended, and its name was changed to the Copyright Tribunal. The legislation specifically empowers the Copyright Tribunal to hear applications where the identity or whereabouts of performers is not capable by reasonable enquiry of being ascertained.

The Copyright Tribunal has power to give performers' consents on behalf of individuals whose identity or whereabouts may not be reasonably ascertained, or who unreasonably withhold their consent. The consents may be given upon such terms as the Copyright Tribunal considers appropriate (see paragraph 6.15). The effect of any consent given by the Copyright Tribunal is that the reproduction of performances given by the relevant performers in the United Kingdom does not infringe any performers' rights legislation, provided that the conditions of the Copyright Tribunal order are adhered to. The availability of the Copyright Tribunal will not, however, remove the need to obtain performers' consents in relation to acts which are to be performed outside the United Kingdom.

19.8 Practical advice on performers' clearances

There are a number of practical precautions which might be taken by multimedia producers. As a general guideline, material should not be incorporated in any multimedia product unless:

(a) the person making available the material is prepared to warrant (see paragraph 7.15) that it does not infringe any performers' rights (in addition to the other normal copyright warranties referred to in paragraph 19.4);

(b) the person supplying the material is prepared to indemnify the multimedia producer (see paragraph 7.15); and

(c) the multimedia producer is satisfied that the person giving the indemnity is of sufficient substance to perform their indemnity obligations; and

(d) the consent extends (where appropriate) to the use of multimedia products in the circumstances referred to in paragraphs 19.5(d) and (e).

It is worth noting that performers' rights cannot be infringed by a person who copies a recording for their private and domestic use[1]. The making of such a recording will, of course, infringe copyright in the recording (the copyright is likely to be owned by someone other than the performer) unless the consent of the copyright owner has been given, or the use falls within the fair-dealing provisions or other permitted acts (see paragraphs 8.1 to 8.44).

1 Copyright, Designs and Patents Act 1988 S182(1)(a).

19.9 Performers' rights of employees and independent contractors

Where a multimedia producer employs or engages persons to develop or produce multimedia material, it is important for the producer to obtain such persons' consent to their performances being used in any and all media by any means. When a company obtains rights of copyright from persons who have been engaged or employed, the status of such persons (whether they are an employee or an independent contractor) is a relevant factor. Where a person is an employee, all rights of copyright in literary, dramatic, musical or artistic works produced in the course of their employment belong to the employer. If the person is an independent contractor, they will, however, retain ownership of all rights of copyright in such works.

This state of affairs does not, however, prevail in relation to performers' rights. Even where the performer is an employee, the employer will have no right to give consent to authorise the making of recordings of the employee's performances, unless the employee has entered into an exclusive recording contract[2] entitling the employer, to the exclusion of all other persons, to make recordings of the employee's performances with a view to commercial exploitation.

Multimedia production companies should, therefore, ensure that if there are circumstances where employees may give performances which are digitally recorded (by reading literary or dramatic works or by playing music, for example), an appropriate performers' consent is contained in the employment contract. Sample wording may be found in Document 51 Clause 15.4.

Even where an employment contract gives an employer the exclusive right to make recordings of performances, the employer does not have sole control of these rights – and they are therefore not really "exclusive". The problem is that while the employer's so-called "exclusive" recording rights are exclusive in relation to the first fixation of the recording, the performer can authorise additional reproductions of the performance – even if the employer refuses to do so.

In many cases this will not present problems, since, although the employer may not be able to use performers' legislation to prevent copies of a performance being made, the employer may still use copyright legislation. If the employer made the sound recording, then the employer will own the copyright in the recording. Since any reproduction of the performance will also be a reproduction of the sound recording, it will constitute an infringement of the copyright in the sound recording unless its use falls within the fair-dealing provisions or other permitted acts (see paragraphs 8.1 to 8.44) and can be stopped by the employer.

Where an independent contractor is engaged by a multimedia company, and the independent contractor renders services which result in performances being given, it is important for multimedia producers to ensure that not only do the terms of that engagement assign to the producer all rights of copyright, but they additionally transfer all necessary performers' consents to the producer. Since both performers' rights and multimedia applications are recent developments, this point is easily (and frequently) overlooked. Multimedia companies should take care to apply appropriate procedures.

2 Ibid s 185(1).

19.10 Moral rights generally

Moral rights are of importance to multimedia producers both in relation to the rights which they acquire and in relation to the rights which they assign or license to third parties.

Where a literary, dramatic, musical or artistic work is made in the course of the person's employment, that person has no moral rights. In the case of a sound recording the arrangements for whose making were undertaken by an employee, no moral rights exist, but the director of a series of moving images will be entitled to moral rights unless the copyright in the moving images first vested in the director's employer.

Copyrights in films and sound recordings belong to the person(s) who undertook the arrangements which resulted in the film being made. It is therefore a prudent step for multimedia companies to make sure that their contracts of employment make it completely clear that arrangements for the making of films and sound recordings which are undertaken by any individual are done so expressly on the understanding that they are made on behalf of the company.

The possibility also exists that individual employees may make arrangements or create literary, dramatic, musical or artistic works outside their strict working hours. The terms and conditions of employment of such persons should (where it is appropriate) clarify that works made in such circumstances belong to the employer. Appropriate provisions may be found in Clause 15 of Document 51 and Clause 2 of Document 52.

19.11 Moral rights, computer-generated works and computer programs

Moral rights do not exist at all in relation to certain types of copyright works, such as designs of typefaces, computer programs and computer-generated works. These last two items are of special interest to multimedia companies.

A computer-generated work is any work which is generated entirely by computer, in circumstances where there is no human author. Most multimedia products are, as we have seen (see paragraph 19.3), a combination of a variety of different rights of copyright. Even if one element of a multimedia work is completely computer-generated, it is likely that there will be other elements which have human authors. The significance of identifying computer-generated works is that their period of copyright protection is significantly less than that of works by human authors (see paragraph 3.25(b)).

An example of a computer-generated work would be a selection of data extracted from a database, which has been organised and made entirely through the operation of a computer program. If computer-generated data are subsequently taken by a human author who makes a further selection of data from a variety of different computer-generated works, then the result may be protected by copyright as a compilation (see paragraph 3.20).

The absence of moral rights (and specifically the right to be identified and the right to object to derogatory treatment) in relation to computer programs also bears closer examination. It will be remembered that copyright in a computer program is protected as a literary work (see paragraph 3.5). Where a computer program is operated in such a way as to produce a series of moving images, these images may also qualify for copyright protection as films (see paragraph 3.7). Where the program can reproduce sound, it may also qualify for copyright protection as a sound recording (see paragraph 3.7).

Therefore, even though no moral rights exist in relation to cold computer code, moral rights may very well exist in relation to other aspects of a computer program. Furthermore, depending on the manner on which the sound elements have been "captured", performers' rights may also subsist in

312

relation to the program. If sounds have been programmed on a keyboard using a MIDI interface to store data, which is subsequently used as part of a computer program, a performers' consent may be necessary (see paragraphs 19.6 to 19.9).

19.12 Moral rights and users of multimedia product

When a multimedia producer engages persons to perform services which may result in the creation of copyright works, the producer will in some circumstances need to obtain a waiver from such persons in relation to their moral rights. Waivers may be conditional and may be revoked, and it is generally advisable for the waivers to be expressed to be unconditional and irrevocable.

The question of whether moral rights owners can exercise or enforce their moral rights against purchasers of multimedia works also needs to be considered. If a purchaser of a multimedia work uses it in private, such use will not infringe the right to be identified, the right to object to derogatory treatment, the right not to have a work falsely attributed, or the right to privacy. These moral rights exist only where a copyright work is published or performed in public in some manner (see paragraphs 5.1 to 5.22). Use of a multimedia work in an "on-line" situation, or in public, is capable of being an infringement of moral rights, as well as of copyright, and purchasers of multimedia works who intend such use should ensure that it will not constitute an infringement of moral rights.

Where a multimedia producer is not able to obtain waivers of moral rights, it is still possible for the producer to make use of the relevant copyright works (subject to obtaining all necessary copyright and performers' consents) within limited circumstances, if the producer takes certain precautions.

First the producer should ensure that all relevant persons are identified in the appropriate manner (see paragraph 5.5) in relation to every copyright work which is used. Second, the producer will need to take care that the treatment of the work in question is not derogatory (see paragraphs 5.10 to 5.13). Whether the use of a work constitutes derogatory treatment or not, may not always be capable of being clearly established from the circumstances, so great care should be taken. It should be remembered, too, that these steps may not provide effective protection against claims for infringement of moral rights brought under foreign laws.

19.13 Personality rights

Although United Kingdom legislation does not provide for personality rights, the right of a person to prevent their name, likeness or biography from being used without their consent exists in a number of jurisdictions including the United States of America (see paragraph 5.21). Consequently, any United Kingdom multimedia producer of product intended for the world market should obtain the right to use names, likenesses and biographies of individuals whose names appear on credits or packaging of multimedia products.

Where an individual is featured in multimedia product, either in an animated version or in full motion video, multimedia companies will also need to obtain the specific right to use the likeness of the person in the product, as well as on associated packaging and advertising. The exploitation of the likeness of a person in multimedia format (in CD-I or CD-ROM) may increase the income-earning potential of that person in other product endorsement purposes not connected with the product.

While it would not be appropriate for a multimedia producer to request a percentage of an individual's income derived from unconnected product endorsement, or personal public appearances, or other means of exploiting their personality rights, there will undoubtedly be situations where merchandising opportunities associated with multimedia product will be created. (For a brief analysis of merchandising rights see paragraphs 11.12 to 11.18.) These opportunities may result in further exploitation of the likeness of individuals, either on figurines, or on packaging and associated advertising, or by means of other applications.

The multimedia producer should, therefore, ensure that all contractual arrangements with relevant individuals permit merchandising exploitation. The commercial terms which relate to merchandising applications are obviously subject to individual negotiation. Where a multimedia producer is committing a substantial sum to develop and produce a product, it is not unreasonable for the multimedia producer to wish to apply all their merchandising revenue towards recovering the cost of production of the product. Once the cost of production has been recouped, the multimedia producer could agree, where appropriate, to pay the individual a percentage of the net receipts. Unless, however, the individual has previous and substantial celebrity status, it would probably be inappropriate for the producer to pay the individual a fixed sum of merchandising revenue.

D. Music in multimedia

19.14 Synchronisation rights

The use of music (and lyrics) in synchronisation with, or in timed relation to, moving images, requires the consent of the copyright owner, as we have seen (paragraph 19.4). This consent is frequently given in a form of document which is referred to as a synchronisation licence. Where music (or lyrics) have been written by a composer who has entered into contractual arrangements with a music publisher, the music synchronisation rights are likely to be controlled by the music publisher.

Before the arrival of videograms in the early 1980s, it was the existing practice in the motion picture industry for synchronisation licences to be obtained on a "buy out" basis. In other words, film and television producers would pay music publishers, or other rights owners, a fixed fee which would authorise worldwide all media exploitation of their music by any manner or means. Since the 1980s, the payment of mechanical royalties has been a common requirement in synchronisation licences. The mechanical royalty system is examined in paragraphs 19.16 and 19.17.

19.15 Synchronisation licences

Music has international appeal, and songs written by British composers enjoy success all over the world, in the same way that the British public responds to songs from a wide variety of different cultures. Because of the international aspect of the music industry, the practice has developed for music publishers to appoint foreign music sub-publishers to administer their catalogues in other territories, and to stimulate the local exploitation of their songs. While, in many cases, the right to grant synchronisation licences is retained by the main publisher, this does not always happen. In some cases, sub-publishers may have the right to authorise synchronisation use of music.

Multimedia companies acquiring synchronisation rights in works will in many cases need to acquire these from the main publisher (sometimes re-ferred to as the head publisher). In circumstances where a multimedia com-pany is acquiring synchronisation rights from a sub-publisher, appropriate verification should be obtained that the sub-publisher does have the right to grant licences of synchronisation rights. Where a previous course of dealings exists between the multimedia company and the sub-publisher, it may be appropriate for the multimedia company to rely on an indemnity from the sub-publisher (see paragraph 7.15).

There will be some circumstances where the right to grant a synchronisa-tion licence remains with the head publisher, but the right to authorise mechanical reproduction (see paragraph 19.16) belongs to the sub-publisher. In such circumstances a multimedia producer will need to acquire a syn-chronisation licence from the head publisher, and a mechanical licence from the relevant sub-publisher in the territory in which the product is to be manufactured or exported.

19.16 Mechanical rights

In the United Kingdom, for most of the twentieth century, a statutory licensing scheme gave companies the right to manufacture records incor-porating musical works, subject to payment of a royalty which was fixed by statute (a statutory royalty). The scheme was established by the Copyright Act 1911, and continued until the implementation of the Copyrights Designs and Patents Act on 1 August 1989, when it was ended. The statutory licence scheme authorised persons to manufacture contrivances which permitted music and lyrics to be reproduced by mechanical means. The royalty payable to the copyright owner was fixed by statute at 6¼% of the retail price.

What became known as a "mechanical use licence" would be issued by the copyright owner of the musical work (in many cases a music publisher). In practice many music publishers granted mechanical licences through the Mechanical Copyright Protection Society Limited (a company which is owned by the Music Publishers Association). The MCPS would grant "mech-anical licences" conditional on the payment of royalties. The royalties were frequently referred to as "mechanical royalties" or "mechanicals" and were fixed at the rate provided by the Copyright Act 1911 and the Copyright Act 1956. The statutory rate was 6¼%.

The music and lyrics of the songs recorded on each record manufactured under the statutory licence scheme would remain the property of the music publisher (or other copyright owner), subject to the mechanical licence granted to the record company to manufacture the recordings. The copyright in the recordings themselves (as distinct from the songs performed on them) would belong to the record company. The record company would pay the music publisher (or copyright owner) mechanical royalties for the right to use the songs. The record company would also have to pay fees (and in appropriate cases royalties) to artists engaged by the record company to perform the songs incorporated in the recordings.

19.17   "Mechanicals" and multimedia companies

The definition of "record" in United Kingdom copyright law at the time the video industry began in the early 1980s, was contained in the Copyright Act 1956. This definition was wide enough to include videograms and other audio visual recordings. Some owners of copyright in films found that while they might have obtained valid synchronisation licences (authorising the incorporation of music in the film, and the subsequent manufacture of prints and their public exhibition and broadcast), in many cases these licences did not permit the manufacture of video cassettes, video discs, or records. In such situations mechanical fees would be payable.

A multimedia company wishing to use existing music in multimedia discs is likely to find itself in a similar situation. The terms which authorise the use of existing music in multimedia product are likely to require payment not only of a synchronisation fee, but also of a mechanical use fee.

19.18   Commissioned music in multimedia

Where a multimedia company commissions a composer to write music specifically for the multimedia product, it is possible for the multimedia producer to acquire all rights of copyright in this material, subject to rights which are vested in the Performing Right Society Limited ("PRS") (see paragraph 19.21). Where the composer of music which has been originally commissioned for use in a multimedia product is an employee of the multimedia company, the company will already own all rights in the product of the employee's services, and will therefore control the music copyright.

In those circumstances, however, where the composer is a member of the PRS, the terms and conditions of the composer's membership assign to the PRS the right to authorise the public performance and broadcast of all music written by their members. The terms and conditions of employment of any PRS member should therefore be amended to reflect any commitment they have undertaken by virtue of their membership of the PRS (see Document 51 Clause 15 and corresponding annotation).

Where a multimedia company owns the copyright in any music or lyrics incorporated in its product, not only will the company be able to exploit these rights itself, without the payment of mechanical fees, but the company will also be able to license rights to third parties on terms which require them to pay mechanical fees to local mechanical collecting societies. These fees will then be passed back to the multimedia company (or its associated publisher) by way of royalties, and are normally shared in an agreed percentage with the composer.

19.19 Non-commissioned music in multimedia

Where multimedia companies wish to make new recordings of existing music, and incorporate these in multimedia product, they should ensure that the licence permits purchasers of the multimedia product mechanically to reproduce the music and to copy it and make adaptations of it. These rights are required for the reasons explained in paragraph 19.5.

Even where a multimedia company does not own the entire copyright in music, it is possible for it to receive a participation in the mechanical fee income payable on the manufacture of CD-Is or CD-ROMs. The multimedia company will suggest to any relevant music publisher, that if the publisher wishes the multimedia company to use composers who are signed to that publisher under exclusive composers' agreements, or if the publisher wishes the multimedia company to use the publisher's catalogue in multimedia format, then the multimedia company will wish to receive a percentage of the mechanical and other music publishing income generated.

The possibility of spin-off or subsidiary exploitation of music which is used for the first time in multimedia product should not be ignored. The inclusion of catchy music in a successful game could lead to other commercial opportunities. These might permit the generation of income, not merely through mechanical licences payable on the manufacture of records and disks, but also income from the PRS derived from broadcasting and public performance. The making of recordings themselves (in which separate copyright exists) could be a further source of income, as could the various other recognised means of merchandising exploitation.

19.20 Use of existing sound recordings in multimedia

Where a multimedia company wishes to use not just a particular song, but an existing recording of a song, by a designated performer or performers, a synchronisation licence (frequently referred to as a master use licence) has to be obtained in relation to the sound recording. The provisions of a master use licence will, in many respects, be similar to those provisions which apply to licences of the music and lyrics (see paragraphs 19.15 to 19.19).

E. Collective licensing schemes

19.21 Collecting societies generally

A number of collective licensing organisations exist in the United Kingdom including:

(a) *Authors Licensing and Collecting Society:* This society licenses the exploitation of literary and dramatic works created by its members (see paragraph 16.13).

(b)   *Design and Artists Copyright Society Limited:* This society licences to exploitation of artistic works created by its members (see paragraph 6.17).

(c)   *Mechanical Copyright Protection Society Limited:* This company licenses the exploitation of rights in musical works (see paragraph 19.16).

(d)   *Performing Right Society Limited:* This society controls the public performance and broadcasting, including satellite and cable broadcasting, of musical works written by its members (see paragraph 19.18).

(e)   *Phonographic Performance Limited:* This company licenses the public performance and broadcasting of sound recordings owned by its members.

(f)   *Videogram Performance Limited:* This company authorises the public performance and broadcasting of videograms controlled by its members.

Collecting societies may in future play an important role in the licensing of rights for various multimedia uses. For the present, however, their role is likely to be limited. This is partly because many of these societies are of recent origin. A more important limiting factor, however, is the existence of a vast number of copyright works which are not controlled by collecting societies, but which are still owned and controlled by authors, their representatives, heirs or successors. These rights cannot, therefore, be licensed for multimedia use by collecting societies.

19.22   Collecting societies and multimedia

If collecting societies are to play a fuller role in future, they will need to respond to the needs of their customers. The customers of collecting societies are persons who wish to be granted the right to use copyright material controlled by the society – copyright "users". There are a number of fundamental requirements of users which will need to be reflected in any licensing scheme that is intended to have multimedia application.

(a)   Warranties

Any grant of rights in copyright material to a "user" should contain warranties as to certain facts. The facts in relation to which warranties are obtained are: the person granting the rights actually owns them; they do not infringe any other rights etc. Examples of other matters on which warranties may be required can be found in paragraph 7.15 and Document 31 Clauses 7.1 to 7.8.

(b)   Indemnity

It is also normal in many cases for rights licences to contain indemnity provisions in order to protect users. An explanation of the term "indemnity" may be found in paragraph 7.15 and a sample indemnity clause may be found in Document 31 Clause 7.9. In the case of licences for the reprographic reproduction of works an express statutory obligation is imposed on the licensing body (see paragraph 6.6). This obligation requires the licensing body to indemnify any licensee against any liability incurred by reason of the licensee infringing copyright in a work within the apparent scope of the licence granted. There is, therefore, legislative precedent for licensing schemes to give indemnity protection to copyright users, and this is a strong argument for indemnity protection being included in any licensing scheme applying to multimedia works.

(c) No limitation on liability

Because the damages awarded in relation to copyright infringement are capable of being substantial, it is submitted that any provision in a copyright licence which limits the liability of the company, or society, granting the rights to the total licence fee paid by the user is unreasonable. A user acquiring rights from a company or society which does not own them, could face legal claims for sums many times greater than the licence fee actually paid. Additionally, the user could have expended considerable sums in developing or manufacturing a product incorporating the rights. If the licence is defective, the user will not be able to exploit the rights, and the user will lose this investment, as well as being left with the liability to pay damages, which might be substantial.

(d) Territoriality

A problem which may arise in dealing with national societies, is the territorial limit of the rights which they control. National collecting societies may not always have the right to license the free and unrestricted exploitation and export of works which they control, outside their own territory. If a multimedia company manufactures product for the world market, it will need to acquire rights for the world – not just the United Kingdom or the European Union.

(e) Non-exclusivity

One matter which falls completely outside the current system of collective licensing schemes is the grant of exclusive licences. Most collecting societies encourage the widest possible exploitation of the works they control, by as many people as possible, in every conceivable medium, by every imaginable means. This system of multiple concurrent non-exclusive licensing is incompatible with the requirements of the exclusive licensee (see paragraph 1.19) who wishes to be the *only* person who can exploit the rights for a substantial period of time.

19.23 Collecting societies and agency

A further factor which may from time to time cause difficulty is the operation of agency principles. Where a collecting society grants a licence on behalf of one of its members as their agent, and discloses this fact, the collecting society generally incurs no liability (see paragraphs 2.26 to 2.30). A company which relies on the warranty and indemnity of a collecting society in relation to copyright infringement, will normally be influenced by the substance and standing of the society.

If the society is merely acting as the agent of a £100 limited liability company with no assets and a defective chain of title, any user could find itself exposed to huge claims for damages, without being able to claim compensation from the collecting society (see paragraph 2.30).

It will be remembered that, in the case of copyright infringement, innocence is no defence (see paragraph 13.8), and even if the company has no reason to believe it is infringing any copyright, it will still be liable in damages if it is wrong.

19.24 Collecting societies and the Copyright Tribunal

United Kingdom law recognises the special position of collecting societies, and has given the Copyright Tribunal (see paragraphs 6.2 to 6.6) jurisdiction in relation to licensing schemes and licensing bodies. Where a licensing body in the United Kingdom incorporates in its licensing conditions any term (such as, for example, limitation on its liability if it makes an error in granting the licence), and this term is unfair in the opinion of any licensee, or prospective licensee under the scheme, application may be made to the Copyright Tribunal. The Copyright Tribunal has power to alter or amend the provisions of licensing schemes and has jurisdiction over licensing bodies (see paragraphs 6.2 to 6.6).

In addition to challenge through the Copyright Tribunal, any onerous provision contained in a licensing scheme may also be subject to challenge on the grounds that it is unenforceable, in view of the provisions of the Unfair Contract Terms Act (see paragraph 2.13). Its enforceability would depend on all the relevant circumstances.

F. Copyright ownership, rental rights, subsidiary rights and patents

19.25 Copyright ownership

Where a third party licensee creates a new copyright work based on the original work, the licensee may retain copyright ownership of what (s)he produces. At the end of the period of the licence of the original copyright work, the new elements created by the licensee are effectively sterilised. The reason for this is that, if the new elements are based on the original work, then they will constitute copies or adaptations of the original work. The original copyright owner can therefore prevent such copies or adaptations being exploited (see paragraph 19.4). Equally, there are circumstances where the copyright owner will wish to own whatever the licensee produces (see paragraph 11.3). In such circumstances the owner of a copyright work will be prepared to license the copyright to a third party for use, but will also wish to acquire ownership of elements created by the third party.

From the point of view of a multimedia company which develops existing product, it is clearly possible for it to create original material which is not directly or indirectly based on the rights licensed. Material of this type could substantially enhance the value of the licensed rights. In such circumstances, the multimedia company may wish to become a joint copyright owner of both the new and old material. This situation is not so commercially naive as it might at first appear.

If material is successfully converted from one medium to another, it may be difficult to assess the extent of the contribution which is made by the material created for the new medium in increasing the popularity of the original material. Where licensing adapted original material for merchandising purposes, it is very difficult to assess the relative weighting of importance. Is it the new adaptation which makes the merchandising application attractive, or is it the original material? Sometimes it is the combination of new and old, and in these circumstances joint ownership may offer an equitable solution.

19.26 Rental of multimedia product

The right to rent films, sound recordings and computer programs to the public is one of the acts restricted by copyright (see paragraph 13.3). Multimedia productions are likely to be included in at least one, if not all of the above categories. The rental of multimedia product to the public can, therefore, generally be restricted.

The significance of this for multimedia producers is that copies of multimedia product can be sold on terms which expressly prohibit them from being rented. These terms can be displayed on labels, and in container packaging, as well as in statements contained in the multimedia works.

A number of outlets in the United Kingdom have recently started making multimedia product available to customers on rental terms, in the same way as videograms are rented. There is nothing wrong or illegal about this. The possibility exists, however, for copyright owners of multimedia product to specify the terms on which copies of their product may be rented to the public.

Because the United Kingdom copyright definition of "copy" is so wide, it is possible that rental use may extend not just to the hiring out of physical copies of films, sound recordings and computer programs, but also to video on demand use. Aspects relating to rental use are clearly matters which would benefit from receiving closer commercial consideration by multimedia companies.

19.27 Directive 92/100 on rental rights

The European Union Directive 92/100 will give producers of audio visual works, and certain other persons, the right to receive remuneration. It will also require certain creative personnel to be paid equitable remuneration for their services (see paragraph 17.9).

A great many questions remain to be answered in relation to the implementation of the Directive, and the effect it may have on various persons (see chapter 20). One factor which may be relevant to multimedia companies is that the rental right vests in the producer of the product. What is the situation, however, where a multimedia company commissions and pays for a multimedia work, which is to be produced by a production company?

Each of the entities might regard itself as being the "producer" within the meaning of whatever legislation implements the rental directive in the United Kingdom. Until this legislation is framed, there is no reason why the commissioning company should not require the production company to agree that the commissioning company is deemed to be the producer for the purpose of any legislation implementing Directive 92/100. This would give the commissioning company the right to control the administration of rental rights in the multimedia product.

Such a provision will obviously need to be reviewed in the light of subsequent legal and commercial developments.

19.28   Subsidiary rights

The transferability of rights in multimedia product from the multimedia arena into other media is another aspect which needs to be monitored closely. Current indications are that films will not necessarily transfer successfully into multimedia format. Although their implementation may be successful, they may not receive the same consumer response as they did on the big screen. The converse may also be true. Certain computer games have earned significantly more revenue from the consumer game market than the films which have been derived from them. Whether these facts are a reflection of the lack of maturity of the multimedia market or an indication of general trends remains to be seen.

There are some aspects of multimedia which appear unlikely to compete with other established sectors. While the multimedia possibilities for creating reference media for works of art are exciting, and while the colour and intensity and resolution of fine art works in multimedia is stunning, can these applications compete with the sumptuous reproduction and immediacy of access of coffee-table-type books? It is thought not.

Where a multimedia product has achieved success in the marketplace, it is likely that subsidiary rights will exist in such product which are of an analogous nature to those which exist in relation to books (see paragraph 1.16). These subsidiary rights will lead to opportunities in relation to film, television, the live stage, music, publishing, records, merchandising and product placement – as well as book and other publication rights!

As with any new market or product, it is likely that substantial profits will be made by persons or companies who are able to anticipate demand in areas before it has materialised. The development of the multimedia market is therefore of great interest.

19.29   Patents, trade marks and branding

Patentability of computer software is an issue which has been much discussed on both sides of the Atlantic. There is still currently some uncertainty as to whether it is possible to patent elements of computer software, although the patentability of certain applications which may be described in algorithmic format does seem possible.

The patentability of a process is a useful way of creating a semi-monopoly – although for a shorter period of time than that of copyright – and locking-in suppliers, or even competitors, to using one's product or process. Patented products increase brand awareness, and in any new market brand loyalty and awareness are factors which have substantial value.

The corporate profile, image, trade and service mark protection and patent portfolio of multimedia corporations will be of increasing significance to the value or market capitalisation of these businesses. New techniques are evolving for the valuation of intangible assets, and the Accounting Standards Board has issued a discussion paper on the valuation of goodwill and intangibles. It will be necessary, therefore, for multimedia companies to take active steps to protect the value of these assets.

19.30 Digital information super-highway

The term "digital information super-highway" is not crisp enough to be a buzz word, but it has been much mentioned in recent times.

The exploitation of digital multimedia product and applications may occur either by "on-line" or "off-line" means. The manufacture and sale of physical carriers (CD-Is, CD-ROMs, CDs, computer disks) involves and enables the transfer of information by off-line means. It is the off-line means which are examined most closely in this publication. Although on-line use of digital information does currently occur in a number of different formats, an established pattern of commercial trading has not yet emerged.

It is undeniable that the on-line use of digital multimedia applications and products has exciting (and terrifying) implications for our future. At the date of publication, the process of commercial and legislative change which will be brought about by these applications is only just beginning, and they have, therefore, been omitted from the scope of this book.

G.   Development and production of multimedia works

19.31   Developing multimedia works generally

Companies which are engaged in the business of producing or commissioning the production of multimedia works will frequently wish to assess the viability of any given project before committing substantial production finance to it. In such circumstances, it may be appropriate for a company wishing to commission multimedia product to enter into a development agreement with an established multimedia producer. The end result of the development agreement will be to permit the company to assess the viability of a project, to gain an idea of its "look and feel", to assess whether necessary clearances and permissions are available, and if so at what cost, as well as to carry out market tests or research on the product. There will be occasions when the release of a competing title from a competitor may eliminate a fully developed project before it goes into production. Equally there will be occasions where a company may wish to develop a "me-too" project to compete with an existing title on the market.

The essential terms of the development agreement are normally that the company pays a fixed fee, in return for which the producer produces development material and assigns to the company all rights in it.

The terms of the development agreement normally require the producer to bear the entire cost of producing the development material. The company engaging the producer may wish the producer to keep books and records of expenditure. Normally the producer will be required to expend the development money in the most cost-effective manner, and will be required to use reasonable endeavours to keep expenditure to a minimum without compromising the standard of the development material. (See Clauses 1.1 to 1.6 of Document 43.)

The precise nature of the various items which are required to form part of the delivery material needs to be specified. The agreement will also need to identify whatever consultation rights are required, and it may be necessary to establish an approvals procedure.

19.32   Clearance procedures in developing multimedia works

Every multimedia project will require a number of releases, permissions, consents and licences (see paragraphs 8.1 to 8.41). It is important that the development agreement obliges the producer to obtain all necessary releases and permissions, and to follow the company's rights clearance procedures. If third parties are engaged by the producer to produce the development material, then the company will need to check that the producer has acquired rights of copyright and other rights in the services of these persons. Such rights may be acquired, either by means of a simple assignment of copyright (as in Document 8) or under a freelance form of engagement (as in that contained in Document 52). In appropriate cases (see paragraphs 19.6 to 19.19) the producer will also need to obtain performers' consents.

Where services are carried out by employees of the producer, it may be appropriate to check the terms of the employees' contracts of employment. As a general rule, the copyright in a work is owned by its author. Where, however, a literary, dramatic, musical or artistic work is made by a person in the course of their employment, then their employer will be the first owner of copyright in the work subject to any agreements to the contrary (see paragraph 3.22).

Because multimedia works contain audio and audio-visual recordings, and because the rights in these do not pass automatically to a person's employer, all employment contracts entered into by producers of multimedia product should contain express provisions transferring all rights in audio and audio visual and other material from the employee to the employer. An appropriate provision may be found in Clause 15.2 of Document 51.

A development agreement will normally require the producer to give a number of warranties, both in relation to the producer's own activities, and in relation to the development material, and will also generally require the producer to give an indemnity. (The precise legal meaning of warranties and indemnities is examined in paragraph 7.15.) Paragraphs 4.1 to 4.12 of the Schedule of Development Standard Conditions annexed to Document 43 contain a number of warranties which may be suitable for inclusion in development agreements.

19.33 Producing multimedia works generally

The documentation required to give adequate protection to a company financing the production of a multimedia product is of a fundamentally different nature from the contractual documents normally required by a publisher. A publisher's interests can normally be adequately protected by means of an Author's Agreement (such as Document 4) or alternatively by means of a Packaging Agreement (such as Document 36) or a Distribution Agreement (such as Document 48).

None of these documents, however, affords adequate protection to a company which is financing the production of a multimedia project. Because of the nature of the medium, the documentation required is closer in nature to that required to produce a film or television programme than any documentation so far traditionally associated with the publishing world. The medium on which a multimedia product is distributed (currently principally CD-I or CD-ROM) also impacts on the commercial structure of the transactions, in that multimedia production companies are remunerated in some transactions on a royalty basis. For this reason the production documentation may need to contain royalty provisions which will more closely resemble those normally contained in an agreement with a recording artist than those usually found in an agreement for the commissioning of a book.

The drafting of standard form documentation for multimedia production therefore requires not only a wide range of legal experience (in film and television production, in the music and record business as well as in publishing) but also a certain creative approach, to create the right synthesis.

The multimedia production agreement contained in Document 44 is a relatively short, but comprehensive, document which affords a high level of protection to the company financing the production. There are of course many alternative shapes which the document could have taken, and the requirements of every commercial situation cannot be satisfied by just one agreement.

Because of the complexity of the issues involved in multimedia production, it is strongly advised that any company or person engaged in this activity should obtain suitably qualified legal advice as to the terms and conditions of their documentation. This precaution is particularly important in any new sector of commercial activity.

19.34 Production and delivery

The production agreement must clearly define precisely what is to be produced and precisely what obligations a producer is to undertake.

Normally, a producer is required to agree to produce a multimedia product for an amount not exceeding an agreed budget in accordance with a production schedule. The producer will have to deliver certain designated items of delivery material to the company by a specified date.

The contract should identify a number of essential elements which must be included in the multimedia product, and should also specify each item of delivery material which the company needs. A producer should also be required to observe and maintain certain technical specifications. These technical specifications may be those agreed by Philips and Sony (commonly known as the Green Book), or they may be specifications specific to the company commissioning the project.

19.35 Copyright and other rights

The production agreement should require the producer to assign to the commissioning company all rights of copyright in the finished multimedia product. The company should ensure that persons engaged by the producer have assigned all their rights to the producer. It will be noted that while United Kingdom law provides that rights in literary, dramatic, musical and artistic works made in the course of their employment pass automatically to the employer, specific provision is required to be made in relation to audio and audio visual work (see paragraphs 3.22 and 19.34).

Additionally, consent must be obtained from all persons who give performances which are contained in the multimedia material (see paragraphs 19.6 to 19.9). Where names, likenesses and biographies are used, consents will need to be obtained from various individuals. Additionally, the agreement will require the producer to obtain all necessary releases, permissions, licences etc and to follow the company's rights clearance procedures from time to time, and disclose to the company all relevant information. These provisions are absolutely essential if the company is to ensure that it has the necessary right to exploit the multimedia product.

All companies engaged in multimedia production or distribution should ensure that they operate, on a rigorous basis, detailed rights clearance procedures (see paragraph 8.44). It is not necessary for these procedures to be carried out by legally qualified staff, but whatever system is implemented should contain some provision for documentation to be checked by legal advisers. It should be remembered that the objective of rights clearance procedures is to identify and resolve potential problems before they arise. If rights clearance procedures are not followed, there is a possibility that third parties may be able to prevent exploitation of the product causing, at worst, substantial loss or, at best, delay, inconvenience and frustration.

19.36 Production contracts

Normally, the producer will be obliged to engage the services of a wide range of people to produce a single item of multimedia product. Such persons will include actors, musicians, animators and computer programmers. The production agreement will normally require the producer to engage these persons on a "buy-out" basis. There will, however, be occasions where persons are required to be engaged under guild or union standard terms and conditions (which apply to actors, musicians etc), and on these occasions the company may require the producer to pay scale remuneration only.

At the date of publication, the Rental Rights Directive 92/100 has not been implemented. The provisions of this Directive have been summarised in paragraph 17.9 and its potential effect on the copyright industries is examined in paragraphs 20.11 to 20.16.

The remuneration provisions will need to be reviewed in the light of United Kingdom legislation implementing the Directive.

19.37 Warranties

A production agreement will normally require the producer to give a number of warranties and an indemnity. (The legal significance of these expressions is examined in paragraph 7.15). A number of warranties which are suitable for inclusion in production agreements may be found in Clauses 4.1 to 4.26 of Document 44.

The warranties are designed to ensure that the multimedia product is produced on schedule and for the budget. They are also designed to ensure that the producer follows rights clearance procedures, that the producer owns the rights in the multimedia material and that nothing contained in it is obscene, blasphemous or defamatory, or infringes any right of copyright or any other rights of third parties or constitutes a contempt of court.

19.38 Other production matters

The production agreement will normally provide that the company has the right to appoint a designated individual as production representative. The producer will be obliged to provide the production representative with whatever information (s)he requests, and to permit the production representative to be present at all rough cuts and edits.

It is also normal to provide for full insurance cover to be taken out in relation to the production. The company should have its interest noted on any insurance policy.

Additionally, the agreement will contain provisions relating to screen credits and there may be occasions where classification by the British Board of Film Classification is necessary (see paragraph 19.55).

Other important provisions include banking arrangements. Depending upon the amount of expenditure involved, it may be sensible to require the producer to open a designated production account and to provide that this account may only be operated with the joint signature of a representative of the producer and the production representative nominated by the company. The company will normally wish to know precisely how much has been expended on the production and, for this reason, the production agreement will normally contain a provision requiring the producer to deliver a statement of cost of production, and requiring the producer to keep the usual books of account.

19.39 Under-spend and over-spend

A clause commonly found in production agreements is one which entitles the producer to the benefit of any savings in the budget. Normally, the company

327

will agree to make sums up to the amount of the budget available to the producer. The budget, however, is, at best, only an estimate, and there are frequently occasions when savings can be made.

The savings will not always, however, represent true savings, since certain items specified in the budget may not have been used, or the numbers of personnel used may be less than originally estimated, or the producer may have given over-estimates in relation to taxation or National Insurance, or the production schedule may have been reduced, or there may have been alterations, substitutions or amendments to essential elements.

In any of the above circumstances, it may not be appropriate for a producer to share in savings. It would certainly not be appropriate for the producer to share in money which had been allocated by the company in order to meet contingencies which had not arisen.

The flip side of the under-spend coin is, of course, over-spend. It is normal for the production agreement to make the producer liable for any over-spend (or excess costs) incurred in production of the product. The transaction, from the company's point of view, represents a fixed price contract. The producer is insulated, to a certain extent, by the inclusion of a contingency element in the budget, and also has the further benefit that the company is providing the finance on a cashflow basis. An alternative means of the company acquiring the same protection as that offered by a specific over-spend provision, would be for the company to agree to pay the cost of production specified in the budget, such sum to be payable on delivery of all material specified in the agreement. This would not only guarantee the company a fixed price contract, but also make the producer liable for financing the production of the product from commencement, until completion and delivery of the delivery material.

19.40 Default and takeover

The production agreement will normally specify a number of acts of default which will permit the company to terminate or accept the repudiation by the producer of its obligations under the agreement (the concepts of termination and repudiation are examined in paragraphs 14.2 to 14.5).

Additionally, the company will require the right to take over production of the project if it falls materially behind schedule, or if it goes over budget, or on the happening of certain events. Examples of takeover and default provisions which may be appropriate may be found in Clauses 13 to 15 of Document 44.

19.41 Remuneration

The nature and amount of remuneration to be paid pursuant to a production agreement will depend on the various circumstances.

Currently, the most significant part of multimedia distribution is effected by CD-based carrier (either CD-I or CD-ROM). In those circumstances where the company is prepared to permit the producer to participate in the success of the project, a disc-based royalty structure may be appropriate.

While most publishers will assume that they are familiar with royalty-based remuneration systems, there is one fundamental difference between royalty agreements in the publishing industry, and royalty agreements outside it. That difference is the Net Book Agreement, which permits publishers to stipulate a minimum retail price. The effect of the Net Book Agreement and the Resale Prices Act 1976 are examined in paragraphs 16.3 and 16.4. In practical terms, royalty provisions for the sale of CD-Is, CD-ROMs and other carriers will usually link the royalty either to the achieved wholesale price or the company's recommended selling price. The reason for this is that discs and tapes may freely be sold for less than whatever price is recommended by the distributor. Royalties linked to the *actual retail* price would, therefore, be impossible to calculate. Whichever price is chosen will depend on the transaction. Normally, however, if the wholesale price is chosen, the figure which the royalty is based on, will be net of rebates and discounts.

The price which the royalty is calculated on, is frequently referred to as the "royalty base price". In the record industry, it is common practice for record companies to deduct what are known as "packaging deductions" from the retail or wholesale price. In such circumstances, the royalty base price is the retail or wholesale price after the deduction of packaging deductions (which normally range from 15% to 25% of the price). The royalty rate itself is normally payable on net sales of discs – in other words, all those discs which have been sold for which the company has received payment, after the deduction of any returns (faulty goods or stock sent in error) and credits (which may be given against sale or return consignments or other matters).

There are a number of circumstances in which both the royalty base price and the royalty rate are adjusted, to take into account certain practices in the marketplace. In the record industry, it is normal to find adjustments in relation to sales to club operations, sales to libraries or educational institutions, sales which are promoted by television advertising, sales to multiple stores or chains at a discount, sales of product incorporating product derived from other sources, distribution of samples, sales of "cut-outs", discontinued goods or deletions and sales through licensees who apply different royalty terms. Provisions dealing with reserves against returns, the recoupment of the cost of production and the payment by the producer of creative royalties to persons engaged by the producer are also commonplace.

H. Licensing distribution and joint ventures

19.42   Licensing and distributing multimedia product

The principles which apply to the buying and selling of publication rights and the distribution of books (which have been examined in Chapters 11 and 12) apply equally to licensing and distribution agreements in relation to multimedia product.

A distinction, however, needs to be made between licensing multimedia product itself, and licensing to a third party the right to adapt and exploit the literary, dramatic or artistic property by means of developing and distributing multimedia product. A form of licence for an existing multimedia product may be found in Document 45. A licence of the right to make a multimedia product incorporating an existing property may be found in Document 46.

The provisions of a licence for existing multimedia product (as contained in Document 45) are very similar to those contained in a licence for an existing publication, where the publisher is supplying production materials (as in Document 32).

The possibility exists, however, that, in certain foreign territories, legislation may exist relating to classification of multimedia material, and data protection and other legislation. Specific provision should be made to counter these eventualities. Additionally, a licence of an existing multimedia product may need to contain restrictions relating to rental, public performance, broadcasts and transmission by cable, and it may also be necessary to consider the position of local collecting societies.

19.43 Licensing multimedia rights to third parties

A form of licence agreement pursuant to which rights in a property are licensed to a third party for multimedia exploitation is included in Document 46. The following general principles might be of assistance to publishers considering the licensing of their works to third parties for multimedia:

(a) grant the licence for a short term;

(b) do not grant an extensive territory;

(c) do not license on-line use or ensure that such on-line use does not take place outside the United Kingdom. Most European states do not give the same level of copyright protection to databases as the United Kingdom (see paragraph 17.12);

(d) grant the rights on a non-exclusive basis;

(e) identify the proposed use to which the work is to be put by the licensee and ensure that any accompanying material is of satisfactory quality;

(f) ensure that all moral rights in the licensed work have been waived by the author and obtain an indemnity from the licensee (see paragraph 7.15) in relation to non-violation of moral rights. The purpose of this provision is to avoid the publisher being exposed to any claim by an author for derogatory treatment of the author's work (see paragraph 5.11);

(g) where appropriate, obtain pre-approval rights of sample material and an appropriate number of complimentary copies;

(h) ensure that the licence contains "sell-off" provisions (see paragraph 12.4) and the right to inspect premises following expiry or sooner termination;

(i) ensure that the licence is terminable for breach, insolvency etc (see paragraphs 14.2 to 14.10 and paragraphs 15.2 to 15.4);

(j) adjust the remuneration provisions to fit the circumstances, either a flat fee or royalty basis, or percentage of gross, or net, receipts, as appropriate.

19.44 Multimedia co-publishing, co-production and joint venture agreements

There are a number of different collaborative ventures which publishers and multimedia production companies are capable of entering into which fall within the general description of co-publishing, or co-production, or joint venture arrangements. The range of variables is, however, so wide, and the documentation required to give legal effect to these arrangements depends so much on the circumstances of each particular venture, that no precedent document has been provided.

For these types of arrangements, it is generally better to start with a blank sheet of paper, and work out the commercial priorities, rather than to attempt to shoe-horn any set of given facts into a rigid precedent document structure. It is, however, possible to distinguish between three broad types of co-publishing or co-production arrangements, namely:

– co-financing arrangements;
– co-production arrangements;
– joint venture arrangements.

A co-financing arrangement is where one person does all the work, another provides all (or most) of the finance and one of the parties (or a third party) distributes the finished product, and the profits, or royalties, are dealt with in an agreed manner.

A true co-production arrangement involves both parties (if there are two) equally sharing in all co-production arrangements.

A joint venture arrangement would include a situation where one party provided the rights, the other party provided the finance or carried out all the production work.

Whatever the form the arrangement is to take, there are a number of basic facts which may need to be established before the documentation can be produced:

– Who is to provide the finance for the project?
– Is one party to provide it all, or is it to be contributed in agreed proportions?
– Will one party be providing finance by deferring their fees, or providing services, or goods, or facilities?
– Who is to carry out the production work?
– Who is to obtain the underlying rights which are required to complete the product?
– What value is to be attributed to these rights?
– Is a price to be paid for the rights during production, or will the value form part of one partner's contribution?
– How are the rights in the finished product to be shared?
– If the agreement is with companies situate in different countries, will each company take the rights for their own country?
– How will the remaining territories be dealt with?
– Are they to be licensed by both companies jointly, or will one company distribute them for the rest of the world?
– How is the copyright in the finished product to be owned?
– Will it be owned by both parties jointly, as tenants in common?
– Will it be held in equal shares, or in another percentage?
– Who is to have control over the physical aspects of production?

- What happens if there is a dispute?
- Are there designated approvals procedures which need to be followed?
- Who has the final say in relation to the product?
- If more than one language version is being produced, does each partner have the right of final say for the version for their territory?
- What is the scope of the arrangements to be?
- Is it to be a single product arrangement or a multi-product arrangement?
- Will it run for a term of years? Will it be exclusive to each party's catalogue?
- What rights do the partners have to opt out of the arrangement?
- Are the opt-out rights exercisable on a single-project basis, or exercisable only in relation to the agreement as a whole?
- Is the ownership of the underlying rights material to be affected by termination of the arrangement?
- What effect will the licensing of multimedia product have upon the licensing of merchandising rights in the underlying rights material?
- Is the multimedia producer to share in the benefits derived from enhanced merchandising possibilities by the owners of underlying rights?
- What restrictions are to be imposed on each of the parties?
- Are there to be post-termination restrictive covenants?
- Will staff be protected by no-poaching arrangements?
- What procedure is envisaged for notifying the arrangements to appropriate competition authorities?
- What is the respective market share of the parties?

Once all these questions have been identified, it will be possible to determine an appropriate structure for the transaction.

As with all new industries, it is likely that the custom and practice of the multimedia industry will take a while to become sufficiently established and for a definite pattern to emerge. This custom and practice is likely to be influenced more by commercial factors, including those referred to above, than it will be influenced by purely legal matters.

I. Databases and telecommunications

19.45 Databases generally

Broadly speaking, there are two types of databases, being on-line databases and off-line databases. An on-line database is a database which is supplied by means of a telephone or other communication system. An off-line database is a database which is self-contained and may be used by a user without resorting to a public telecommunications system. For example, information contained in a CD-ROM and accessed on a home computer is an off-line database.

Where information is being supplied by an on-line database, the publisher or other supplier will need to obtain what is referred to as a VADS (or Value Added and Data Services) licence. A VADS licence is a telecommunications class licence for the running of systems which provide value added or data services. The Telecommunications Act 1984 empowers a Secretary of State to issue class licences which cover private telecommunications systems[3]. One of these class licences is the VADS licence.

The licence is available automatically to all persons who run relevant systems, provided they are not persons to whom the licence has been revoked and provided they are not companies which are connected with public telecommunications operators (frequently referred to as PTOs or PTTs).

No action is required by the licensee under a VADS licence, but if the licensee's turnover from value added and data services exceeds £1,000,000 or if the group turnover of the licensee's group is in excess of £50,000,000 per year, then the licensee will need to register its company name and address with the Director-General of Telecommunications. Additionally, where a company provides switching services between a public network and another unconnected company, by means of a line leased from a PTO, then the company will need to register with the Director-General of Tele-communications.

The licence is given to run a telecommunications system, and running the system is not limited simply to day-to-day operations but includes control over how the system is made up and used. It is not necessary to own a system in order to run it. Apart from mobile radio apparatus, any type of telecom-munication system may be run including those which send and receive speech, or other sounds, data signals, visual signals, telemetry, and tele-control signals whether these are analogue or digital so long as the system is located within the United Kingdom of Great Britain and Northern Ireland.

3 Telecommunications Act 1984 S7.

19.46 Activities permitted by VADS licence

The VADS licence permits the licensee to run a telecommunication system only in a single set of premises, but if the system is situated in more than one set of premises, provided the premises are occupied solely by the same company or members of the same group of companies and are in the same building, they will be counted as a single set of premises. Additionally, where the separate premises are within 200 metres of all other premises, a group may be served by a single system, without any obligation to use circuits leased from a public telecommunications operator.

It can be seen therefore, that apart from the above two exceptions, only public telecommunications operators may run links between different locations. The VADS licence further requires the VADS licensee to use approved apparatus, and restricts the systems to which the licensed system may be connected, as well as restricting the type of telecommunications service which may be provided.

19.47 Connection rights of VADS licensee

A VADS licensee may connect the system either directly or via a public telecommunications system to any of the following, namely:

(a) another system run under the VADS licence, or under a general licence;
(b) systems run under the branch systems general licence;
(c) certain named public telecommunications systems;
(d) systems run by associates of public telecommunications operators for providing value added services and data services;
(e) systems run by the Crown;
(f) any system which is already licensed and which is specified by the Secretary of State;
(g) any other system authorised by future licences to connect to the licensee's system.

19.48 VADS services

The services which may not be provided under a VADS licence are as follows:

(a) cable programme services;
(b) land mobile radio services;
(c) basic voice telephony or basic telex except to persons outside the licensee's group. This restriction does not prevent a licensee from providing a value added service where the provision of basic voice telephony or basic telex plays a part, provided that the value of the added part of the service is a substantial element of the overall service that is offered.

J. Computer misuse

19.49 Computer misuse generally

The Computer Misuse Act 1990 creates three criminal offences in relation to computers, being:

(a) unauthorised access to computer material[4];
(b) unauthorised access with intent to commit or facilitate commission of further offences[5];
(c) unauthorised modification of computer material[6].

4 Computer Misuse Act 1990 S1.
5 Ibid S2.
6 Ibid S3.

19.50 Unauthorised access to computer material

The Computer Misuse Act 1990 provides that a person is guilty of an offence if:

(a) that person causes a computer to perform any function with intent to secure access to any program or data held in any computer[7];
(b) the access which the person intends to secure is unauthorised[8], and

(c)   the person who causes the computer to perform the function knows at the time that this is the case[9].

For an offence to be committed it is not necessary for a person's actions to be directed towards any particular program, or data, or computer[10].

7 Ibid S1(1)(a).
8 Ibid S1(1)(b).
9 Ibid S1(1)(c).
10 Ibid S1(2).

19.51   Unauthorised access with intent to commit or facilitate commission of further offences

This offence is committed if a person obtains unauthorised access with the intention of committing any further offence for which the sentence is fixed by law, or for which a person of 21 years of age or over, not previously convicted, might be sentenced to imprisonment, for a term of five years[11].

A person will be guilty even where the commission of a further offence is impossible, and it is immaterial whether any further offence is to be committed on the same occasion as the unauthorised access offence, or on any future occasion[12].

11 Ibid S2(1) and (2).
12 Ibid S2(3) and (4).

19.52   Unauthorised modification of computer material

This offence is committed if a person does any act which causes an unauthorised modification of the contents of any computer, and at the time when the act is committed the person has the requisite intent and requisite knowledge[13].

The requisite intent is the intention to cause a modification of the contents of any computer, and by so doing to impair the operation of any computer, to prevent or hinder access to any program or data held in any computer, or to impair the operation of any such program, or the reliability of any such data[14].

The intent need not be directed at any particular computer or program, or data, or any particular modification, and the requisite knowledge is knowledge that any modification intended by the person is unauthorised. It is immaterial whether the unauthorised modification is, or is intended to be, permanent, or merely temporary, and if the modification of the contents of the computer does impair or damage its physical condition, then a further offence will be committed under the Criminal Damage Act 1971[15].

The Act covers computer misuse which either originates from, or is directed against, computers located in this country, regardless of where the offence was committed[16]. Under the law of England and Wales, it is a criminal offence to conspire to commit a criminal offence, even if the conspiracy is not resolved in the commission of any act which is actually illegal. Incitement to commit a criminal offence is also punishable at law, as will be the commission of an offence or an attempt to commit an offence[17]. In the case of conspiracy or incitement in England and Wales to commit a computer misuse offence which will occur abroad, such conspiracy or incitement will not be capable of prosecution in England and Wales, unless the act contemplated would if done be punishable under the law of the country in which the act were to take place. Where offences are committed abroad, the courts have the power to make an order for extradition of the offender[18].

13 Ibid S3(1).
14 Ibid S3(2).
15 Ibid S3(3), (4), (5) and (6).
16 Ibid S4.
17 Ibid S6.
18 Ibid S8.

K.   Software publishing and video publishing

19.53   Software publishing

Many of the legal aspects relating to the sale of a work on computer disk, or tape, will be the same as those considered in relation to the sale of the work in volume or sheet form, in particular those relating to the law of contract, law of copyright, confidentiality and those setting out the publishers liability for the content of the work. (See Chapter 1, and Chapters 9 and 10.)

When computer disks are sold to consumers, the provisions of the Consumer Protection Act 1987 will apply (see paragraphs 12.31 to 12.35) and the warranties implied by the Sale of Goods Act 1979 in respect of all goods sold will equally apply (see paragraphs 12.36 to 12.38). Where the computer software being sold is, itself, the product of a computer (in other words what the law refers to as a "computer generated work" which category includes compiler programs created by computer), the term of copyright protection is different from that of a work created by a human author (see paragraph 3.25(b)).

The transfer and copying (for back-up purposes) of electronic works is permitted in certain circumstances. These circumstances are explained in paragraphs 8.14 and 8.24.

Any publisher who develops computer software, using the services of third parties, should ensure that they acquire all necessary rights of copyright and performers' rights from the individual or company concerned. This basic point is frequently overlooked. A form of engagement for freelance staff may be found in Document 52, a form of contract of employment in Document 51, and a form of copyright assignment in Document 8. These may be suitable for use in certain circumstances.

Because a computer program is treated as a literary work, provided it is created in the course of a person's employment, and no agreement exists to the contrary, then the copyright in that work will initially vest in the employer. No moral rights (see Chapter 5) subsist in works created during the course of employment[19].

Where a book or other literary or dramatic work is contained in computer software in machine form only, and where the work has not previously been published in printed form, it would appear that a publisher is not capable of claiming the copyright in the typographical arrangement of the work[20]. As has been examined above (see paragraph 3.28), for the purposes of determining who is the owner of a typographical arrangement of a published edition the publisher is, for copyright purposes, considered the author (!). The term of copyright in a typographical arrangement ends 25 years from the end of the calendar year in which the edition was first published.

Literary, dramatic, musical or artistic works may be published by being made available to the public through an electronic retrieval system, but in the case of other copyright works, publication means the issue of copies to the public. A typographical arrangement of a published edition would, therefore, appear to have been published, if made available to the public on disk in sufficient numbers to meet demands, but would appear not to have been published, if made available by means of an electronic retrieval system.

19 Copyright Designs and Patents Act 1988 S11(2).
20 Ibid S79(2)(b).

19.54 Video publishing

Pursuant to the Video Recording Act 1984, it is an offence to supply or offer to supply, or possess for the purpose of supplying, a video recording containing a work to which the Act applies, unless the work has been classified by the British Board of Film Classification, and has been labelled in accordance with the statutory labelling regulations[21].

Certain video recordings are exempt, if they are designed to inform, educate or instruct, or if they are concerned with sport, religion or music, or if they are video games. However, this exemption is lost if the video recording, to any significant extent, depicts human sexual activity, or acts of force or restraint, associated with such activity, or mutilation or torture of, or other acts of gross violence towards humans or animals, or human genital organs, or human urinary or excretory functions, or if such video recordings are designed to stimulate or encourage activity of such nature[22].

Certain forms of supply of video recordings are exempted supplies, such as the giving of private gifts, records of private occasions as supplied to participants, video recordings as supplied to the cinema, or to the British Broadcasting Corporation or the Independent Television Commission, or the British Board of Film Classification, and video recordings supplied for export only[23].

Certain types of computer games are currently not required to be submitted to the British Board of Film Classification for classification, in the same way as video recordings. Some computer programs do, however, fall within the criteria specified by the Act and are required to be submitted for classification. In view of the blurring of boundaries between the video industry and the computer game industry, many persons feel that all computer games should be submitted for classification and the situation is likely to be the subject of review.

21 Video Recordings Act 1984 S9.
22 Ibid S2.
23 Ibid S3.

19.55 Classification

Pursuant to the Act, it is an offence for a recording to be sold, or offered for sale or hire, if it contains a work which has not received a British Board of Film Classification classification certificate, or it is supplied or offered in breach of the terms of the classification[24]. There are five classification categories currently available for supply at ordinary unlicensed shops, being "U" "UC" "PG" '15" and "18". The "UC" category is not currently in use in cinemas and is an optional category indicating recordings intended particularly for young children. There is one further additional category, restricted 18, and video recordings with this classification may be sold only in sex shops licensed by a local authority[25].

The Video Recordings (Labelling) Regulations 1985 require all video works which have received a British Board of Film Classification classification certificate, and the packaging of such works, to be labelled in such a manner as to display the classification certificate symbol. It is an offence to sell, or offer for sale or hire, a video recording to which labels have been affixed, if the recording contains a video work which has not received a classification certification. Where a video recording contains more than one work, the most restricted classification is required to be displayed. Thus where an "18" classified trailer for a "18" classified film is contained in a cassette which also contains a "PG" classified work, the packaging will need to display the more restrictive "18" classification indication. If, however, only the most restricted classification is displayed, the indication may amount to a trade description within the meaning of the Trade Descriptions Act 1968 (see paragraph 12.40), and if it is false or misleading to a material degree it will contravene the provisions of the Trade Descriptions Act. It would therefore seem prudent to display all classifications.

A self-regulatory scheme controlling packaging has been established by the British Board of Film Classification, and is administered by the Video Packaging Review Committee which considers all artwork and proofs for video packaging before the issue by the British Board of Film Classification of a classification certificate. Where artwork and transparencies have been submitted to the Video Packaging Review Committee for approval, no British Board of Film Classification classification certificate will be issued in respect of the relevant recording, unless the Video Packaging Review Committee is satisfied as to the matters displayed on the packaging.

24 Ibid SS9 and 11.
25 Ibid S7.

20. Publishing and multimedia – the future

[IMPORTANT NOTE: Please read the section "About this book" on page v, before referring to any of the matters in this chapter.]

A. Introduction

20.1 Purpose of this chapter

The purpose of this chapter is to identify and examine some of the issues which may determine the shape of the publishing and multimedia industries in the future.

The final years of this century will see the implementation of some of the greatest changes in United Kingdom copyright legislation since 1911, as a result of the implementation of the European Union harmonisation programme, and these changes will have enormous commercial and economic consequences for publishers and multimedia companies.

At the date of publication of this work, the manner of implementation of these changes has yet to be decided, and a number of important issues remain to be determined in relation to copyright works whose period of protection is renewed or extended.

These issues are considered in this chapter, together with the question of copyright protection in the United Kingdom of works which are in the public domain in the United States of America, or elsewhere. The chapter then examines some of the issues which fall to be considered in relation to the implementation in United Kingdom law of Directive 92/100 (summarised in paragraph 17.9) and Directive 93/98 (summarised in paragraph 17.11).

One of the crucial areas in which commercial and legislative consensus is required, is the redefinition of our contemporary system of classifying copyright works (as literary, dramatic, musical or artistic works, or as films or as sound recordings or published editions). This current system of classification is stretched when dealing with a work that is in multimedia format. The chapter examines this issue, and also considers how collective administration of copyright works might in future be effected.

Finally, the anticipated development of technology raises a number of moral and cultural issues which are considered in this chapter. These issues include personal freedom, GATT, cultural protection, cultural integrity, moral rights for information users, avoidance of economic responsibility, the so-called "information tap", and pricing issues.

B. Harmonisation of the term of copyright

20.2 Existing Berne Convention term of copyright

The term of protection provided by the Berne Convention for literary, dramatic, musical and artistic works expires 50 years *post mortem auctoris* (pma). The Berne term is, however, a minimum period, and a number of countries have chosen to provide for longer periods of protection in relation to literary, dramatic, musical and artistic works, notably Germany where the period is 70 years pma, Spain where the period is 60 years pma, and France, where the period is 60 years pma, or 70 years pma for musical compositions.

In addition to the differences of the term of rights pma, further discrepancies in protection accorded by different member states arise out of wartime extensions, and former legislation. Belgium has provided a wartime extension of 10 years, Italy an extension of 12 years, and France extensions of 6 and 8 years respectively in relation to the First and Second World Wars. In France a further period of 30 years is provided in the case of copyright works whose authors were killed in action.

In Spain the former legislation provided for a period of 80 years pma, which continued to apply to copyrights protected under the Spanish law of 1879, until its reform in November 1987.

20.3 Retroactive effect of the Berne Convention

The retroactive effect of the Berne Convention is generally well known. Unlike the Universal Copyright Convention, the Berne Convention provides that when countries join the Berne Union, copyright works originating from those countries which are not protected in countries of the Berne Union will, subject to certain conditions, fall *into* copyright.

The Berne Convention will protect works which have not fallen into the public domain in their country of origin by virtue of the expiry of the term of protection, at the date of that country's accession to Berne[1]. This provision will not, however, operate to give retroactive copyright protection to works which have fallen into the public domain in their country of origin as a result of failure to comply with formalities such as registration or renewal.

Additionally, if a work has fallen into the public domain in the country in which protection is claimed, by virtue of the expiry of that country's term of protection, the work will not be protected anew[2].

The Berne Convention leaves countries free to grant a term of protection in excess of that minimum term provided by the Berne Convention[3].

Current United Kingdom law[4] does not specifically apply the principle set out in the Berne Convention, which prevents the retroactive granting of Berne protection for works which have fallen into the public domain in their country of origin. Current United Kingdom legislation[5] appears to provide retroactive protection to works of United States citizens or subjects even though these works may be in the public domain in the United States of America, and even where these works were in the public domain in the United Kingdom before the United States of America acceded to the Berne Convention (see paragraph 20.4).

1 Berne Convention Article 18(1).
2 Ibid Article 18(2).
3 Ibid Article 7(6).
4 Copyright (International Conventions) Order 1979 as amended by SI 1989 No 157.
5 Ibid para 3(6).

20.4 Reciprocal United States protection for United Kingdom works

The retroactive effect of the Berne Convention, and its implementation under United Kingdom law in relation to the United States have been considered at paragraph 20.3.

When the United States of America acceded to the Berne Convention with effect from 1 March 1989, United States law[6] not only failed to provide for protection of moral rights (although limited moral rights protection for certain visual artists was subsequently introduced), but also expressly excluded the retroactive effect of the Berne Convention.

The result is that a very large number of European works which are protected throughout the Berne Union are denied copyright protection in the United States of America, while works which are in the public domain in the United States of America are the subject of copyright protection in the United Kingdom and possibly other European Union states.

The question of whether non-European Union states should benefit from the renewal term or extension term is dealt with in Directive 93/98 which provides[7]:

> "where the country of origin of a work within the meaning of the Berne Convention is a third country and the author of a work is not a Community national the term of protection granted by the Member States shall expire on the date of expiry of the protection granted in the country of origin of the work but may not exceed the term laid down in Article 1".

It seems likely that the enactment of this provision in United Kingdom law will remove the existing anomaly where works which are in the public domain in the United States appear to be accorded copyright protection pursuant to United Kingdom law[8].

6 Berne Convention (Implementation) Act 1988 (US).
7 Directive 93/98 Article 7(1).
8 Copyright (International Conventions) Order 1979 (as amended in 1989).

20.5 Effect of harmonisation on United Kingdom public domain works

How are the interests of persons who have exploited copyright works which were in the public domain likely to be affected, if the copyright in such works is renewed?

It is likely that United Kingdom legislation would determine the position of such persons in accordance with the provisions of the legislation referred to in paragraphs 20.3 and 20.4[9]. These provisions state:

> "Where any person has before the commencement of this Order incurred any expenditure or liability in connection with the reproduction or performance of any work or other subject-matter in a manner which at the time was lawful, or for the purpose of or with a view to the reproduction or performance of a work at a time when such reproduction or performance would, but for the making of this Order, have been lawful, nothing in this Part of this Order shall diminish or prejudice any right or interest arising from or in connection with such action which is subsisting and valuable immediately before the commencement of this Order unless the person who by virtue of this Part of this Order becomes entitled to restrain such reproduction or performance agrees to pay such compensation as, failing agreement, may be determined by arbitration."

The wording is (drafting amendments excepted) an almost verbatim reproduction of the provisions of the Copyright Act 1911. The provision applied to any actions taken before 26 July 1910, but the commencement date of the Copyright Act 1911 was 1 July 1912. Any expenditure in the two-year period between 26 July 1910 and 1 July 1912 did not entitle the person making such expenditure to compensation.

9 Copyright (International Conventions) Order 1979.

20.6   Future application of current United Kingdom legislation

It falls to be considered whether current United Kingdom legislative provisions, which originated in the Copyright Act 1911, offer adequate protection to owners of rights against exploitation possibilities afforded by new technology, or against commercial abuses which are these days normally restricted by contract.

One specific issue which needs to be dealt with is the sale of previously manufactured copies of works which were in the public domain when they were made, and have had their copyright subsequently renewed. An analogy may be found by considering what acts are permitted to be performed in relation to goods manufactured under a copyright licence after the expiry of the licence. In the absence of an express provision restricting the sale of copies after a sell-off period (usually six months) the owner of copyright is unable to prevent the sale of previously manufactured copies of works if such copies have previously been put into circulation in the United Kingdom.

The application of a provision along the lines of the 1911 Copyright Act provision (referred to in paragraph 20.5) would be likely to cause damage to the economic interests of publishers and others, since the provision would not prevent stockpiling of works and their subsequent issue to the public. The exemption could, however, be limited so as to prevent further actions occurring after renewal of copyright in any work, such as the issue of copies of the work to the public, other than copies which have been previously put into circulation in the United Kingdom or elsewhere. This would fit in with more recent legislation[10].

Stockpiling of works could be prevented by providing that copies of a work would not be considered to have been put into circulation, to the extent that the numbers of copies so circulated exceeded the reasonably anticipated requirements of the public.

It would also be inappropriate to apply the 1979 Order provisions to previously public domain works which have been incorporated in other new copyright works – such as films, sound recordings or books. It is submitted that where previously public domain material is incorporated in good faith in another copyright work, the owner of copyright in such other copyright work should be free to do, or authorise the doing of, any act which such person was entitled to do before the commencement of the harmonisation provisions.

The question of whether a work is incorporated in good faith or not would easily be capable of determination by the application of the same criteria which are used to determine whether any given act constitutes "fair dealing" (see paragraphs 8.3 and 8.4).

10 Copyright, Designs and Patents Act 1988 s 18(2).

20.7 Exhaustion

A further matter which will require clarification is the application of the exhaustion principle (see paragraph 16.15). The *Patricia* case[11] involved the import of records into Germany where an exclusive right still existed from Denmark where the protection period had expired. Although the "exhaustion" principle (see paragraph 16.15) permits goods made in a European Union state with the consent of the copyright owner to be lawfully marketed in any other European Union state, it does not apply where the country in which the goods are made does not recognise rights which are recognised in the country to which the goods are exported.

Because of the different provisions relating to wartime protection and previous legislation in France, Italy and Spain, the free circulation of copyright works may not be possible between the European Union and these countries, and barriers may exist to the free movement of goods and services unless further amendment is made to the proposals.

It is submitted that the proposals for harmonisation of the term of copyright should be amended, so as to provide that copies of any works which are made after the expiry of the period of protection provided by the harmonisation directive may be legitimately exported or imported into, or made available for rental or lending in, any other member state without contravening any laws of such state.

11 *EMI Electrola GmbH v Patricia Im-umd Export and Others* [1989] ECR 79.

20.8 Will the renewal period accrue to the benefit of the rights owner?

The answer to this question could depend on two factors, the enabling legislation and contractual terms. These are now considered.

Legislative precedent exists in the United Kingdom for the extension of the period of protection of copyright works. During the passage through Parliament of what became the Copyright Act 1911, the effect which the extension of copyright protection would have on the economic interests of authors and publishers was considered in detail. The 1911 Copyright Act extended the term of protection for certain copyright works from a period of 42 years from publication or 7 years post mortem auctoris, to 50 years post mortem auctoris.

It was not thought right that the entire extension period should pass to the benefit of publishers and other interested parties, depriving the surviving dependants of authors from the additional benefit which might have accrued to them, had the advance and other remuneration terms pursuant to which rights in the work were granted to the publisher (or other interested party) reflected the extended period of copyright, as opposed to the original period.

The legislature succeeded in striking a delicate balance, protecting the economic interests of authors' dependants whilst at the same time preserving the rights of publishers. The means by which this was achieved were to provide that the copyright in any work would at the end of the original period of protection revert to the author (or the author's estate), but the person who was the owner of the right immediately before the date at which the right would have expired was entitled either:

(a) on giving notice to the author not less than 6 and not more than 12 months before the date of expiry of the right, to acquire the assignment or grant of a similar interest in the work for the remainder of the term, for such consideration as, failing agreement, was determined by arbitration; or

(b) without any assignment or grant, to continue to exercise the same rights subject to payment of such royalties as, failing agreement, were determined by arbitration, if demand for payment was made by the author within three years following expiry.

Where the second option was chosen, the publisher, or other authorised party, was permitted to continue to exploit the rights granted as an exclusive licensee of the original owner, but such exclusive licence extended only to what the 1911 Copyright Act referred to as His Majesty's Dominions. This is a logical provision, since it would clearly be impossible for British law to extend to countries other than those which are governed by British law.

20.9 Conflict of laws

The Copyright, Designs and Patents Act 1988 extends to England and Wales, Scotland and Northern Ireland, and may by Order in Council be extended to any of the Channel Islands, the Isle of Man or Hong Kong. Any provision which determines the identity of the person entitled to the benefit of any extension period will, therefore, apply only to those territories whose laws are controlled by those of the United Kingdom.

Since each European Union state is responsible for implementing the Directive it is theoretically possible for each state to legislate in different terms on the renewal of copyright in works, and the nature of acts in relation to works whose copyright had been renewed which require the consent of authors' estates.

20.10   Contractual rights

If future United Kingdom legislation provides that the ownership of any extension or renewal term should be determined not by the legislation itself but by the contractual arrangements which exist between the parties, then it will be necessary to consider the precise terms of each contractual arrangement. A model form of copyright assignment is set out below:

> "The Author assigns to the Publisher the entire copyright and all other rights of whatever nature in and to the Work including all vested future and contingent rights to which the Author is now or may in the future be entitled under the laws in force in any part of the world TO HOLD the same unto the Publisher its successors assignees and licensees absolutely for the full period of copyright protection throughout the world including all reversions renewals and extensions and after that so far as permissible in perpetuity."

This assignment expressly includes all future and contingent rights to which the author is at the date of the assignment or may in future be entitled under the laws in force in any part of the world. The assignment also expressly includes all renewals and extensions to the copyright period and also includes all reversions.

The effect of a copyright assignment provision along the lines of that outlined above might therefore (depending on future United Kingdom legislation) be sufficient to transfer to the publisher or other rights owner the benefit, not only of any extended, or renewed, period of copyright, but also of any rights which the author had if the copyright of the work ever reverted to him or her.

The existence of the United Kingdom copyright reversion is well known to publishers. It has become widespread practice since the introduction of the Copyright Act 1956 for publishers and other interested parties to obtain additional confirmation from authors or their estates, transferring the benefit of any reversionary right created by the 1911 Act. The terms of any such confirmation obtained will need to be considered, where appropriate, in order to determine the ownership of any renewal term or extension term.

C.   Rental rights and publishers

20.11   Definition of "rental"

A number of issues arise in relation to the rental right which is to be introduced following Directive 92/100 (see paragraph 17.9).

"Rental" means making available for use for a limited period of time and for direct or indirect economic or commercial advantage. The definition of "rental" is not restricted merely to the hiring out of physical copies of videograms or records, but could extend to the making available of material on a "pay per view" or subscription basis. Making material available through an on-line basis could also constitute "rental".

The precise formulation of the definition could have a far-reaching effect on publishers.

20.12 Apportionment of income

A number of different interested parties may have rights in relation to the rental right. The categories include authors of copyright works, publishers, performers of the work, producers of sound recordings, producers of films, directors of films and other persons who might be considered to be authors of films. Such other persons might, for example, include composers of music used in films.

The question arises as to how this income will be apportioned between the relative contributors. Is it to be apportioned on a percentage basis between each separate category of work? Or is it to be apportioned on a numerical basis between each contributor of copyright works?

Is each contributor to be accorded equal importance in relation to his or her contribution to the work? If not, how is the relative weighting to be determined? Will the nature or duration of the contribution be considered? Or will the respective weightings of the contributions of individuals be determined by a third party such as a producer of a film or a producer of a phonogram?

20.13 Equitable remuneration

The right to equitable remuneration given to authors, performers, phonogram producers and film producers includes a right to equitable remuneration. It is clear[12] that this equitable remuneration may be paid on the basis of one, or several payments, at any time on or after conclusion of the relevant contract.

Different commercial terms exist for the engagement of each of the respective categories of rights owners. Is it to be anticipated that the determination of what constitutes equitable remuneration will be adjudicated by applying different criteria for each creative category?

12 Directive 92/100 Article 13(9).

20.14 Is the rental right capable of assertion by an author or by the author's publisher?

The Directive provides[13] that the rights to equitable remuneration will apply in contracts entered into before 1 July 1994 only where authors or performers or those representing them have submitted a request that it should apply before 1 January 1997.

It is important to determine who has the right to submit the request, and who has the right to receive the income.

Will an assignment of copyright from an author to a publisher operate to transfer to the publisher the right to assert, on behalf of the author, the author's unwaivable right to equitable remuneration?

The answer to this question will depend not only on the form of assignment contained in the relevant contract, but also on the form of future legislation in the United Kingdom.

13 Directive 92/100 Article 4.

20.15 Can the right to administer an author's rental right be transferred under a copyright assignment?

The answer to this question depends equally on not only the form of the copyright assignment, but also the provisions of future legislation to be implemented in the United Kingdom.

As a matter of copyright and contract law, it would appear that (subject to statute and case law developments) the form of assignment contained in paragraph 20.10 may operate to transfer to the publisher the rental right in works, although the provision ought clearly to be reviewed in the light of subsequent legislation and developments.

20.16 Collection of rental income

The Directive states[14] that the administration of the right to obtain equitable remuneration may be entrusted to collecting societies representing authors or performers. How is the equitable remuneration to be calculated? How is the equitable remuneration to be divided between eligible persons?

The Directive provides[15] that member states may regulate whether and to what extent administration by collecting societies of the right to obtain equitable remuneration may be imposed. Member states may also decide on whom the equitable remuneration may be collected from.

The role of collecting societies in the multimedia industries has been considered elsewhere (see paragraphs 19.21 to 19.24). To what extent should United Kingdom legislation enhance their position in the marketplace, in view of the dominant position which they might subsequently attain (see paragraph 16.10)?

14 Directive 92/100 Article 4(4).
15 Ibid Article 4.

D. Economic, moral and cultural issues

20.17 Economic issues

One of the major economic issues facing the publishing and multimedia industries is the convergence of areas which have, up to now, been regarded as separate and distinct. In previous years the distinction between the various conventional media was clear, and easy to understand. Technology now presents us with multimedia product which is capable of being classified by copyright legislation in multiple overlapping categories, as a literary work, a dramatic work, a musical work, an artistic work, a computer program, a published edition, a film, a sound recording and even as a database. The difficulties in assimilating multimedia product into our classification system for copyright works are further compounded by the possibilities offered by digital broadcasting, which now permits the broadcast transfer of digital information. Until comparatively recently, this type of transfer could only be made by means of a cable or other similar link. Digital broadcasting technically permits the broadcasting of computer games and other data applications. Data compression technology can already deliver full motion video on CD-I, and public telecommunications operators and film rights owners are examining the possibility of offering access to films over telecommunications networks on a pay-per-view or video on demand basis. Asynchronous transfer mode technology now offers even further enhancements to the data transfer process.

The technological developments which are currently known about, or anticipated, offer interesting possibilities to authors and rights owners, in permitting them to control, or share in, the proceeds of distribution and exploitation of their works. Legislative reforms currently required by European Union legislation (in particular the implementation of Directives 92/100 and 93/83 on rental right and satellite transmission and cable re-transmission – see paragraphs 17.9 and 17.10) contemplate, or require, the establishment and co-operation of collecting societies for the new rights to be administered.

Contemporaneously, the basis of the remuneration arrangements for performers of films and television programmes in the United Kingdom is changing from one in which performers are entitled to receive so-called "residual" payments (payments calculated as a percentage of the fees originally paid to them on the exploitation of certain rights) to a basis on which performers will be entitled to receive a royalty percentage of the receipts of the relevant production company. The fact that the average term of existence of film and television production companies is an extremely short period when compared to the duration of copyright protection (see paragraph 17.11) of the films and television programmes created by such companies, or the duration of rights in relation to the performances contained in the films and television programmes that they produce (see paragraph 6.12), raises obvious implications for the performers concerned, and may lead to the establishment of a collecting society to collect and administer payment obligations on behalf of performers and producers.

The above factors all point to an increase in the activities of collecting societies in the European Union. While competition between collecting societies would have obvious cost advantages for authors, publishers and other rights owners, it is unlikely that a proliferation of collecting societies would be advantageous to any party (other than the societies themselves). In the United Kingdom, a number of collecting societies are currently active, including the Performing Right Society Limited, the Mechanical Copyright Protection Society Limited, Phonographic Performance Limited and Videogram Performance Limited. To these might be added the Copyright Licensing Agency Limited, the Design and Artists Copyright Society Limited, the Education Recording Agency, the Authors' Licensing and Collecting Society Limited and the Directors' and Producers' Rights Society Limited.

It is in the interests of publishers, producers, authors and other rights owners, that the terms on which the various parties and collecting societies become involved in the field of multimedia are agreed, in order to minimise conflict.

Additionally, the finalisation of a convention relating to the protection of the European audio-visual cultural heritage is likely to introduce a scheme for the statutory deposit of films, and associated sound recordings, and other material, in member states which adhere to the Council of Europe (see paragraph 17.14). Such a convention will lead to a standard international standard film number along the lines of the ISBN for books and the ISRN currently being introduced for sound recordings. All these developments will require significant investment in information technology and data processing. While the terms on which such information may be exploited and made available to others is controlled by European Union and United Kingdom legislation (see paragraphs 6.2 to 6.6 and paragraphs 16.2 to 16.15), there are obvious licensing and competition law implications.

20.18 Moral and cultural issues

The changes brought about by technological and commercial developments can be expected to raise a number of moral and cultural issues, some of which have already been identified.

Reference has already been made in this book to the views of the Copyright Licensing Agency Limited on "fair dealing" (paragraph 8.5), and while it is believed that these views will not achieve widespread acceptance, a number of arguments (which appear to be seriously flawed) have recently been advanced to justify the imposition by rights owners of fees on persons wishing to read books, or view works, on screen in their homes, and to subject all acts done in private to an exclusive right of the rights owner to control the fate of these works[16]. These suggestions have fundamental civil rights implications, and, it is submitted, must be resisted, since their acceptance cannot be in the public interest.

Aspects relating to data protection, freedom of expression, and protection of individual rights of privacy, have been dealt with elsewhere in this work (see Chapter 18), but in view of the extremely rapid development of technology, many issues remain. Current information technology enables the assembly and compilation of information from a wide variety of sources relating to individuals, and identifiable groups of individuals. It is currently possible to collate a wide range of information (financial, medical, criminal, social, psychological) on families. Parental identities may be accessed through a number of different possible sources and the establishment of computerised medico-socio-economic genealogies on individuals is more than just a possibility. The availability of such information would have profoundly serious implications for all of us.

Another issue is that of moral rights for users. It has been suggested that, although the Berne Convention protects moral rights of authors, persons using the works of authors should also be protected from deliberate disinformation and from the prejudicial withdrawal of the works in question[17]. The ability of companies producing and selling computer software to exclude all liability for consequential loss or damage (other than death or personal injury caused through negligence) caused by their software to business users also needs to be re-examined. Companies and individuals who buy expensive software can suffer serious economic loss or damage, through defects in the software and have no legal redress in such circumstances.

A further moral right, for information users, is the guarantee of integrity of the information. The distortion of information does not have merely economic consequences, but potentially serious cultural and ideological consequences. If we are to enter an era where the primary means, and medium, for making literary works available to readers is provided by digital technology, and this technology enables each individual copy of a work to be altered, in a way which is tailored to its ultimate recipient, without that person's knowledge, society must provide a guaranteed means of preventing the global deletion or replacement of its sociological and political structure.

The protection of European national culture from destruction is already the subject of heated debate. The United States of America sought to use the recent Uruguay round negotiations on the General Agreement for Tariffs and Trade (GATT) and Trade-Related Intellectual Property issueS (TRIPS) to enforce on the European Union, and on developing countries, obligations which require them to protect American economic interests in relation to intellectual property. The United States of America were, until accession to the Universal Copyright Convention in 1957 (see paragraph 4.4), beyond any doubt the world's biggest copyright pirate. Although the European audio-visual industry was, at the last minute, excluded from the scope of the GATT Agreement, its future remains in the balance, and is dependant, largely, on the level of enlightenment of decisions which are to be taken by the Monopolies and Mergers Commission in its investigation into the supply of films in the United Kingdom, and the European Commission in relation to the continuation (or hopefully non-continuation) of the exemption granted by the European Commission in 1985 to United International Pictures in relation to Article 85 of the European Community Treaty.

The United States of America still fail to accord copyright protection to vast numbers of copyright works protected by every other country in the world (see paragraph 20.4). The United States of America also (despite having assumed treaty obligations to do so pursuant to the Berne Convention) have failed to make adequate protection for moral rights. It is submitted that it is morally reprehensible for the United States of America to attempt to impose on developing countries obligations which the United States of America did not accept while they considered themselves to be a "developing country" – which they appear to have done until as recently as 1957 when they joined the Universal Copyright Convention.

A further issue which has been identified[18] is that developing countries are concerned that the "information tap" will be "shut off" as a result of changes in the global strategies of technology leaders. These countries have already experienced loss of access to information in the fields of computers, nuclear technology and space technology. The right to share in the knowledge of others, and the obligation to make advances of learning freely available, should be fundamental tenets of international law.

Another major issue which needs to be considered is that of pricing. The pricing of digital technologies and delivery systems is geared to the living standards of people in the developed countries and

"it is very difficult to justify the import and use of such technologies in the developing countries unless the pricing is designed to make the cost benefit ratios attractive for local market conditions. It is, therefore, necessary to develop pricing structures which bring the technology within the economic reach of users in different countries. The prices should bear a relationship to the productivity benefits achieved by the use of the technology in economies having different standards of living. As a case in point, the pricing model of books, which have different editions and affordable prices for different geographic regions of the world, seems to have worked well"[19].

The developed countries have a clear moral obligation to share technology and information with developing countries, in order to alleviate suffering, hardship and famine. The publishing industry has traditionally accepted this obligation, and, it is to be hoped that the multimedia and information technology industries will, for their part, continue this tradition of supporting developing countries[20].

16 Paper prepared by Mr Thomas Dreier, Head of Department, Max-Planck Institute for Foreign and International Patent, Copyright and Competition Law, Munich entitled "Copyright Digitized: Philosophical Impacts and Practical Implications for Information Exchange in Digital Networks" presented at the WIPO World Symposium on The Impact of Digital Technology on Copyright and Neighbouring Rights at Harvard University between 31 March and 2 April 1993.
17 Paper prepared by Mr Ashok Bhojwani, Advanced Information Technologies, Managing Director of TSG Consultants, New Delhi entitled "Digital Recording Technologies and Intellectual Property: Promises and Pitfalls for Development" presented at the WIPO World Symposium on The Impact of Digital Technology on Copyright and Neighbouring Rights at Harvard University between 31 March and 2 April 1993 – paragraph 2.13.
18 Ibid para 3.2.
19 Ibid para 3.5.
20 All royalties from this book will be applied by Actionaid towards the relief of famine and poverty in the developing countries.

The Documents

About the Documents

Annotations

Where the annotations refer to *paragraphs*, the references relate to paragraphs of the text in Chapters 1–20.

Where the annotations refer to *clauses*, the references relate to clauses in Documents 1–52.

Style

The documents in this section contain:
- no gender words
- no archaic language
- no punctuation

List of documents

A. Preliminary

B. Commissioning

C. Permissions, releases, reversionary assignments and waivers

A. Preliminary

DOCUMENT 1

Confidentiality agreement

[IMPORTANT NOTE: Please read the section "About this book" on page v, before copying or using this Document]

Purpose of this Document

This Document is intended for use in circumstances where a publisher or multimedia company needs to disclose to a third party information which is of a confidential nature but which is not protected by the laws of copyright or trade mark. The Document creates a contract between the publisher or multimedia company and the person to whom the information is submitted, and imposes confidentiality obligations on the recipient of the information.

Relevant text

The text of this Work covers a number of topics which are relevant to documents of this nature including:

- ideas and confidentiality (paragraphs 1.2 to 1.4)
- confidentiality and publishers (paragraphs 1.5 to 1.12)
- the law of contract and agency (Chapter 2)

Document 1 *Confidentiality agreement*

From   :   [*name of publisher*] of [*address*] ("Publisher")

To   :   [*name of company*] of [*address*] ("Company")

Dated   :   [*date*]

Dear [*insert name*]

[*Name of Project*] ("Project")
Certain discussions have taken place between the Publisher and the Company in relation to the possibility of entering into an agreement to [*state purpose*] in relation to the Project. In order to carry out a full evaluation of the Project the Company requires the Publisher to disclose certain information.

This letter is to confirm the terms and conditions pursuant to which the Publisher is prepared to disclose details of the Project to the Company. In order to induce the Publisher to disclose such details and in consideration of the sum of £1 paid by the Publisher to the Company receipt of which the Company acknowledges the Company warrants undertakes and agrees with the Publisher as follows:

1. This undertaking is binding upon the Company and all its associated companies and associates (as defined in the Income and Corporation Taxes Act 1988 Sections 416 and 417) and all officers employees servants agents or professional advisers of such persons (together "Relevant Persons").

2. This undertaking extends to all information of whatever nature in whatever form relating to the Project obtained from any source including without limitation information received from the Publisher and information obtained as a result of being allowed access to any premises where the Publisher may carry on business ("Confidential Information") but does not extend to information which at the time it is obtained is in the public domain.

3. The Company shall treat all Confidential Information as being strictly private and confidential and shall take all steps necessary to prevent it

Unnumbered paragraph 1 The nature of the agreement proposed between the Publisher and the Company, and a general description of the project to which it relates need to be specified. The use of the defined term "Publisher" may be replaced by a company name or abbreviation if the company in question is not in the business of publishing.

Unnumbered paragraph 2 The sum of £1 is paid by the Publisher to the Company in order to provide consideration to enable a binding contractual commitment to be created. The concept of "consideration" is examined in paragraph 2.7 and the elements required in order to create binding contractual obligations are examined in paragraphs 2.2 to 2.8.

Clause 1 This provision makes the company liable for the actions and omissions of group companies, associated companies, employees, servants and agents.

Clause 2 This paragraph defines what constitutes Confidential Information, which is not limited specifically to information disclosed by the Publisher, but extends to all information relating to the project obtained by the Company from whatever source.

from being disclosed or made public to any third party by any Relevant Person or coming by any means into the possession of any third party.

4. The Company shall use the Confidential Information solely for the purpose of evaluating whether or not to enter into an agreement with the Publisher relating to the Project or to perform any obligations which the Company may undertake or have undertaken with the Publisher relating to the Project and the Company shall not use any part of the Confidential Information for any other purpose whatever.

5. The Company shall not use or disclose or permit the disclosure by any person of the Confidential Information for the benefit of any third party or in such a way as to procure that the Company may at any time obtain commercial advantage over the Publisher.

6. Neither the Company nor any of the Relevant Persons shall by any means copy or part with possession of the whole or any part of the Confidential Information without the prior consent of the Publisher.

7. The Confidential Information and its circulation shall be restricted to circulation and disclosure to individuals whose identity shall have been approved by the Publisher prior to disclosure in writing.

8. The Company shall keep all materials containing Confidential Information in a safe and secure place and return them to the Publisher immediately on determination of discussions in relation to the Project or on the Publisher's prior request.

9. The Company undertakes to indemnify and keep the Publisher at all times fully indemnified from and against any loss or disclosure of Confidential Information and from all actions proceedings claims demands costs (including without prejudice to the generality of this provision the legal costs of the Publisher on a solicitor and own client basis) awards and damages however arising directly or indirectly as a result of any breach or non-performance by the Company of any of the Company's warranties undertakings or obligations under this agreement.

10. This Agreement shall be governed and construed in accordance with the

---

Clause 3   The Company is required not only not to disclose the Confidential Information but to prevent it being disclosed by any of the persons referred to in clause 1.

Clause 4   This paragraph specifically prevents the Company from using any part of the information for the purposes of its business.

Clause 6   The contractual restriction imposed by this paragraph will override any "fair dealing right" which the Company may have in relation to the Confidential Information (see paragraphs 8.3 to 8.39).

Clause 8   This provision imposes specific liability on the Company for loss of the materials. There are circumstances in which the Company might have no liability in relation to scripts or other materials (see paragraph 1.11).

Clause 9   This provision creates an indemnity obligation on the Company. For an explanation of the difference between warranties and indemnities reference should be made to paragraph 7.15.

laws of England and Wales whose courts shall be courts of competent jurisdiction.

Yours faithfully

for and on behalf of
[*name of Publisher*]

We agree and confirm the above and agree to be bound by it.

SIGNED BY
[   ]
for and on behalf of
[*name of Company*]

Clause 10   Where a contract is made between two entities in England and Wales, it will generally not be necessary to insert a provision of this nature, but where a contract is to be created with a foreign company (or a company situate in Scotland or Northern Ireland) this provision should always be included.

DOCUMENT 2

Submission agreement

[IMPORTANT NOTE: Please read the section "About this book" on page v, before copying or using this Document]

Purpose of this Document

The purpose of this Document is to provide a publisher or multimedia company with protection against claims from persons who have submitted unsolicited material. There are occasions when ideas which have been developed by a publisher or multimedia company may match or bear a close resemblance to ideas which are submitted to a publisher or multimedia company. Even where there is no direct link between the two projects a publisher will not be able to prevent claims being made by third parties. The use of this letter may prevent claims being made for breach of confidentiality but a publisher or multimedia company may still incur liability through indirect or subconscious infringement of copyright and appropriate clearance procedures will still need to be followed (see paragraph 8.44 and Document 30).

Relevant text

The text of this Work covers a number of topics which are relevant to documents of this nature:

- ideas and confidentiality (paragraphs 1.2 to 1.4)
- confidentiality (paragraphs 1.5 to 1.12)
- infringement of copyright (paragraphs 13.2 to 13.8)
- the law of contract and agency (Chapter 2)

Document 2 *Submission agreement*

From   :   [*Author*]
              of [*Address*]

To   :   [*Publisher*]
              of [*Address*]

Dated   :   [*Date*]

Dear [*insert name*]

I am now submitting to you for your consideration the material ("Material") enclosed under cover of this letter [which is based on the material owned or controlled by third parties ("Third Party Material") details of which are specified below]:

[*Insert details of Material and any Third Party Material*]

I understand that it is not your practice to accept unsolicited material for examination and in order to induce you to accept the Material for examination and in consideration of your so doing I warrant represent and agree with you as follows:

1.   I am the [sole author and] sole legal and beneficial owner of the Material which is original [to me] [except to the extent that it is based upon the Third Party Material], and does not infringe any rights of copyright patent trade mark rights of privacy rights of publicity moral rights or any other rights whatever of any person.

2.   Except as disclosed in the Schedule the Material is not the subject of any assignment or licence or other arrangement pursuant to which any third party has any rights whatever.

3.   The Material has been submitted to you on the understanding that you shall not produce any publication based on the Material or use the Material unless you have entered into an agreement with me for such use but I acknowledge that this submission is not being made in confidence and you do not owe me any duty to keep the Material or any part of it confidential and that the submission of the Material shall not prevent you from originating or publishing publications which contain similar or identical features or elements to those contained in the Material or from originating or participating in or publishing publications which are

Unnumbered paragraph 1   A Publisher will wish to know whether submitted material is based upon or incorporates other third party material, the rights in which are controlled by third parties, since appropriate copyright licences, releases and permissions will need to be obtained. Some of these matters are referred to in paragraph 8.44 and Document 30. The use of the defined term "Publisher" may be replaced by a company name or abbreviation, if the company in question is not in the business of publishing.

Clause 1   The text of this paragraph will need to be amended to suit appropriate circumstances.

Clause 2   Even where the person submitting material is the owner of the rights in the material, it is still possible for third parties to have been licensed rights in the material or to have been granted options over it. The purpose of this paragraph is to identify any third party right which might in future conflict with the rights intended to be acquired by the Publisher.

based on any part of the Material which is not new or novel or which is in the public domain or which is not otherwise legally protected by copyright or which was obtained by you from other sources.

4. If you determine you have the independent legal right to use material containing elements or features similar to those contained in the Material without reaching any agreement with me and I disagree with your assumption then any dispute between us shall be submitted to an arbitrator acting as an expert experienced in the publishing industry and chosen by us jointly or in the absence of agreement to such person who may be nominated by the Publishers Association and the findings of any person to whom the dispute is submitted shall be binding on us.

5. I agree that the Material is submitted to you on an unsolicited basis and you shall have no liability to me in the event that such material is mislaid lost or destroyed.

6. I acknowledge that it is in my interest that you should have the right to copy the Material make adaptations of the Material and the right to submit the Material to third parties and I agree that you shall not be responsible for the actions of such third parties or any actions of any of your employees which have not been ratified by you or undertaken pursuant to your specific instructions.

7. If any provision of this Agreement shall be prohibited or adjudged by a court to be unlawful void or unenforceable such provision shall to the extent required be severed from this Agreement and rendered ineffective as far as possible without modifying the remaining provisions of this Agreement and such provision shall not in any way affect any other circumstances the validity or enforcement of this Agreement.

Clause 3 This provision expressly excludes confidentiality obligations (see paragraph 1.6) and may prevent any claim being brought by the Author if a Publisher suddenly develops similar material. The possibilities of subconscious infringement may, on occasions, present difficulties. For this reason Publishers should ensure that their clearance procedures are designed to prevent, as far as possible, indirect copying or unconscious use of elements which have been submitted and are protected by copyright.

Clause 4 The provisions of this paragraph are designed to ensure that any dispute is referred to arbitration, rather than being dealt with through the courts.

Clause 5 Publishers may in some circumstances (see paragraph 1.11) be liable in relation to unsolicited material.

Clause 6 This provision licenses the Publisher the right to copy and make adaptations of the material. These rights are restricted by copyright (see paragraphs 3.2 to 3.4) and the carrying out of such acts is unlawful without the consent of the owner of the copyright (see paragraphs 13.2 to 13.8). Where the Material incorporates third party material, a Publisher will additionally need to seek the consent of the owners of third party material. The person submitting the material should already have obtained all necessary consents for inserting third party material in the material submitted. The identity of relevant owners of copyright and other rights should be disclosed in the schedule pursuant to the provisions of paragraph 2.

Clause 7 The concept of severance is discussed in paragraph 2.22. This provision gives significant protection to publishers, but it will not assist them if the person signing the submission agreement is mad, since such persons lack the capacity to enter into binding contracts (see paragraph 2.23). The insertion of a warranty in the letter that the person signing it has mental capacity (which is, on occasion, seen in American documentation) is no use either, since if the contract is void, any warranty contained in it will also be void!

8. The benefit of this Agreement shall enure to your successors assignees and licensees.

9. This Agreement shall be governed and construed in accordance with the laws of England and Wales whose courts shall be courts of competent jurisdiction.

The Schedule

Disclosed Arrangements

(Paragraph 2)

Date   *Description of Document*   *Parties*

Yours faithfully

[*Name of Author*]
[*Address*]

Clause 8   The purpose of this paragraph is to establish that any licence given pursuant to this agreement is not simply personal and that all such rights may be transferred by the Publisher.

Clause 9   Where a contract is made between two entities in England and Wales, it will generally not be necessary to insert a provision of this nature, but where a contract is to be created with a foreign company (or a company situate in Scotland or Northern Ireland) this provision should always be included.

DOCUMENT 3

Pre-contract checklist

[IMPORTANT NOTE: Please read the section "About this book" on page v, before copying or using this Document]

Purpose of this Document

The purpose of this Document is to provide guidelines as to what information may need to be established before an author's contract can be issued. The information contained in these guidelines is intended primarily for use by publishers internally, not for disclosure to authors. The form which the offer to an author should take is discussed in paragraph 1.23.

Relevant text

The text of this Work covers a number of topics which are relevant to documents of this nature including:

- terms of an offer (paragraphs 1.22 and 1.23)
- acquiring rights generally (paragraphs 1.13 to 1.16)
- factors to be considered in relation to acquiring rights (paragraphs 1.17 to 1.21)
- the author's contract (Chapter 7)

Document 3 *Pre-contract checklist*

The following basic terms need to be established before an Author's Agreement can be prepared. References to clause numbers are to clauses of Document 4 unless otherwise indicated. It will not necessarily be appropriate for details of all the matters specified in this list to be communicated to the Author until the contract is sent.

1. THE WORK

(a) Title and length of the Work (Clause 1.1).
(b) Description of the Work (Clause 1.2).
(c) Description and source of illustrations (Clause 1.3).
(d) Delivery date (Clause 1.4).
(e) Requirement for index (Clause 1.6).
(f) Amount of fees payable in relation to illustrations (Clause 1.8).

2. RIGHTS

(a) Identify precise scope of Publication Rights to be acquired by the Publisher (see the definition of this term in Clause 18.1).
(b) Identify whether the Publication Rights are to be licensed or assigned to the Publisher (see Document 5 (a) to (e)).
(c) Identify whether the Publication Rights assigned or licensed are granted for the period of copyright or for its shorter term (see Document 5(a) to (e)).
(d) Identify whether the Publication Rights assigned or licensed are granted for the entire world or a designated territory (see Document 5(a) to (e)).
(e) Specify whether any Subsidiary Rights (see the Schedule to Document 4) are to be acquired by the Publisher and ensure there is no overlap between the definitions of Subsidiary Rights and Publication Rights.
(f) Specify period during which Publisher will have the right to sell the Subsidiary Rights.

3. PUBLICATION

(a) Set the likely number of first print run (Clause 3.2).
(b) Will first publication be in hardback or paperback format (Clause 3.2).
(c) Set the anticipated retail price of the Work (Clause 3.2).

4. REMUNERATION

(a) Identify amount of advance payable to the Author (Clause 5).
(b) Identify instalments of advance and dates of payment (Clause 5).
(c) Specify amount of royalties payable to Author and royalty base – published price or Publisher's receipts as appropriate (Clause 6).

5. ACCOUNTS

(a) Specify details of Author's agent for payment direction (Clause 11.1).
(b) Specify amount of reserves against returns (Clause 11.3) – unless the Publisher has a fixed policy on returns.

6. ADDITIONAL CLAUSES

(a) Identify whether specific provision is needed in relation to new editions of the Work or competing Works (see Document 6(a)).
(b) Identify whether an option provision is needed in relation to subsequent Works (see Document 6(b)).

7. PERMISSIONS AND CLEARANCES

(a) Where the Work involves extensive third party rights and releases or permissions are likely to be required from third parties, reference should be made, where appropriate, to the Publisher's guidelines (if any) for the use of such material.
(b) Where the Work contains material of a sensitive nature which may lead to legal liability (in defamation security or otherwise) reference should be made, where appropriate, to the Publisher's guidelines (if any) for the use of such material.

B. Commissioning

DOCUMENT 4

Author's agreement

[IMPORTANT NOTE: Please read the section "About this book" on page v, before copying or using this Document]

Purpose of this Document

The purpose of this Document is to acquire publication rights and subsidiary rights in works from their authors. The Document has been drafted from the point of view of the publisher and is intended to provide a comprehensive form of author's agreement.

Alternative rights clauses are provided for in Document 5, and Document 6 contains a number of additional clauses which may be suitable for inclusion, depending on the circumstances. A number of the provisions in the contract conform with the provisions of minimum terms agreements (see paragraphs 7.20 to 7.22).

A shorter and less comprehensive form of author's agreement is contained in Document 7, and other forms of agreement which may be useful to publishers in the commissioning process are contained in Documents 8 to 15.

Many of the clauses in the author's agreement are modelled on the principles established by the Writer's Guild of Great Britain and the Society of Authors in their negotiated minimum terms agreements (see paragraphs 7.20 to 7.22).

Relevant text

The text of this Work covers a number of topics which are relevant to documents of this nature including:

- general matters relating to authors' agreements (paragraphs 7.2 to 7.4)
- copyright and moral rights (paragraphs 7.5 to 7.8)
- specific provisions in authors' agreements (paragraphs 7.9 to 7.19)
- minimum terms agreements (paragraphs 7.20 to 7.22)
- acquiring rights generally (paragraphs 1.13 to 1.16)
- factors to be considered in relation to acquiring rights (paragraphs 1.17 to 1.21)
- commercial terms of publishers' offers (paragraphs 1.22 and 1.23)
- the law of contract and agency (paragraphs 2.1 to 2.30)
- creation, existence and transfer of copyrights (paragraphs 3.1 to 3.45)
- international copyright protection (paragraphs 4.1 to 4.17)
- moral rights (paragraphs 5.1 to 5.22)
- permissions, fair dealings and rights clearances (paragraphs 8.1 to 8.44)
- liability for content (paragraphs 9.1 to 9.49)
- buying and selling rights (paragraphs 11.1 to 11.29)
- infringement enforcement (paragraphs 13.1 to 13.17)
- termination and recapture (paragraphs 14.1 to 14.10)
- competition law (paragraphs 16.1 to 16.28)
- multimedia (Chapter 19)

THIS AGREEMENT is made the   day of   199

BETWEEN

(1) *[name]* LIMITED of *[address]* ("Publisher"); and

(2) *[name]* of *[address]* ("Author")

IT IS AGREED as follows:

1. THE WORK

1.1 The Publisher engages the Author to write the original literary [dramatic] Work entitled "*[title]*" of not less than *[number]* pages of text and *[number]* pages of illustrations ("Work") and the Author undertakes to write the Work and deliver it to the Publisher in accordance with the provisions of this Agreement.

1.2 The Work shall be *[state description of the Work ie original Work of fiction or biography or historical analysis of certain events etc]* and shall be based on the original outline of the Work written by the Author [dated *[date]* or submitted to the Publisher on *[date]*] and shall *[state additional requirements]*.

1.3 The illustrations of the Work shall be [original to the Author] [selected by the Author in consultation with the Publisher from *[specify sources]*].

1.4 The Author shall complete and deliver to the Publisher two copies of a clearly typed legible typescript of the Work by no later than *[date]*. It shall be the responsibility of the Author to keep duplicate copies of all material

---

Statement of parties Where there is more than one Author, it will be necessary to alter the statement of parties so that the defined term "Author" extends to all relevant persons. A suitable statement of parties might look as follows:

(1) [*name*] LIMITED of [*address*] ("Publisher"); and
(2) [*name*] of [*address*]; and
(3) [*name*] of [*address*]
(the second and third parties jointly and severally referred to as the "Author")

It will also be necessary to change the defined term "Author" to the plural form, although, in view of the provision of clause 18.4 (which provides that singular forms include plural) this change is of cosmetic/grammatical import rather than being legally significant.

The inclusion of the words "joint and several" means that each Author is liable for his or her own acts and omissions as well as the acts and omissions of all other Authors. In other words, if one Author is in breach of his or her obligations under the contract, the Publisher can sue that Author and every other Author in relation to the breach.

The words "joint and several" are legal jargon, and although their replacement with "individually and collectively" may achieve the same effect, it is possible that argument to the contrary might be advanced.

Clause 1.1 This clause constitutes the engagement of the Author by the Publisher to write the Work. The text needs to be varied to suit the circumstances. The engagement does not make the Author the Publisher's employee. This possibility is expressly excluded by clause 19.1.

Clause 1.2 This clause is of fundamental importance since it provides a full description of the Work. The clause should be adjusted to suit appropriate circumstances.

Clause 1.3 If illustrations are to be obtained from third parties, the agreement will usually contain provisions relating to the cost of the illustrations (clause 1.8) and it will also be necessary for the Publisher to ensure that various rights clearance procedures are followed (see paragraph 8.44).

submitted to the Publisher and whilst the Publisher undertakes to take all reasonable steps to safeguard copies of the Work in the Publisher's possession the Publisher shall have no liability for loss or destruction of any material submitted to it.

1.5   Within [*number*] days from delivery to the Publisher of the typescript of the Work the Publisher shall have the right to notify the Author of changes which the Publisher requires to have made in the Work and the Author shall within [*number*] days from the date of notification effect such changes as are requested by the Publisher and deliver to the Publisher two copies of clearly typed legible typescript of the Work containing the changes and/or revisions which shall be clearly indicated.

1.6   If in the opinion of the Publisher an index is required for the Work and the Author does not wish to undertake the preparation of an index the Publisher shall have the right to engage an indexer and the costs of such engagement shall be borne equally by the Author and the Publisher the amount of the Author's share being deducted from sums payable to the Author under this Agreement.

1.7   The Author shall obtain releases or permissions in a form satisfactory to the Publisher signed by all relevant persons in relation to all quotations illustrations photographs and other third party material used in the Work and shall deliver original or certified copies to the Publisher on the date referred to in Clause 1.4. The Author irrevocably confirms that the benefit of all consents releases and permissions obtained by the Author shall extend to the Publisher throughout the territory and term for which the Publication Rights are granted to the Publisher pursuant to this Agreement. The Author shall advise the Publisher in writing on the date referred to in Clause 1.4 of the identity of all persons who have made suggestions for the Work or contributions to the Work and the identity of all persons whose assistance the Author wishes to acknowledge.

1.8   The Publisher shall pay fees for illustrations agreed between the Publisher and the Author up to £[*amount*] and any additional sums payable in relation to illustrations shall be the responsibility of the Author and shall

---

Clause 1.4   The delivery date needs to be inserted. Although the document does not provide that time is of the essence of the contract (see paragraph 2.10) it would be possible for the Publisher to make time of the essence if the Author failed to deliver by the specified date. The Publisher would need to give the Author a reasonable period of notice requiring the Author to perform his or her obligations by the end of such period. Clause 12.3 permits the Publisher, however, to give notice terminating its obligations under the agreement if the Author fails to deliver by the due date.

Clause 1.5   This clause permits the Publisher to require the Author to make alterations to the text of the Work. The right is in addition to the Publisher's right to make corrections to the Work, to conform it to the Publisher's house style or remove material which might give rise to liability. These matters are covered in clause 2.5.

Clause 1.6   This provision is a standard indexing requirement. Where a detailed index is required, the costs of preparation are frequently borne by the Publisher. In addition to indexes, other reference material may be required (such as, for example, tables of cases and statutes in many legal publications) which the Publisher may prepare.

Clause 1.7   Releases and permissions are of fundamental importance, and should always be double-checked by Publishers. There are circumstances when permissions and releases may not be required (see paragraphs 8.2 to 8.39). Publishers should ensure that appropriate clearance procedures are followed (see paragraph 8.44 and Document 30).

either be paid by the Author or at the discretion of the Publisher shall be advanced by the Publisher and deducted from sums payable to the Author under this Agreement.

2.   EDITING CORRECTIONS AND AUTHOR'S CREDIT

2.1   The Publisher shall consult with the Author in relation to the copy editing of the Work the numbers and types of illustrations the jacket design and the introduction and cover notes and shall give good faith consideration to the Author's views.

2.2   The Author shall read check correct and approve all proofs of the Work submitted to the Author by the Publisher and shall return to the Publisher clearly marked corrected proofs within 21 days from receipt [time being of the essence of this Clause]. The Author shall bear the cost of all corrections and alterations to proofs other than printer's errors in excess of 10% of the cost of composition or typesetting of the Work and/or origination of artwork and the Publisher shall have the right to deduct such costs from any sums which may be payable to the Author pursuant to this Agreement without prejudice to the Publisher's rights. If the amount of such extra costs exceeds the amount of Advances payable to the Author pursuant to this Agreement the Author shall within 30 days from demand by the Publisher pay to the Publisher the amount by which such extra costs exceed the Advances.

2.3   All copies of the Work published by the Publisher shall contain the following copyright notice:

[conform to reflect copyright position determined by Clause 8]

2.4   The Author asserts the Author's right to be identified in relation to the Work on the title page and cover in the following form:

[state form of identification required]

and the Publisher undertakes to comply with such request and to require all sub-publishers and other licensees to honour this right. The Author acknowl-

---

Clause 1.8   Where illustrations are commissioned by an Author from third parties, Publishers should ensure that appropriate agreements are entered into by the persons providing the illustrations.

Clause 2.1   The obligation on the Publisher to consult does not require the Publisher to reach agreement with the Author, or to follow the Author's directions. The obligation merely requires the Publisher to seek the Author's views on the matters.

Clause 2.2   Time is made of the essence of this clause (see paragraph 2.10) because time is frequently critical during production schedules. The level beyond which the cost of corrections is borne by the Author is fixed at the conventional level of 10% although it may be appropriate to change this where electronic delivery material is provided by the Author (see paragraphs 7.12 and 7.13).

Clause 2.3   The copyright notice should state the identity of the copyright owner. If copyright is assigned to the Publisher, the copyright owner will be the Publisher. If copyright is reserved to the Author and the Author grants an exclusive licence to the Publisher, the copyright owner will be the Author. It is possible for the copyright owner in one country to be different from the copyright owner in another country (see paragraph 1.20).

There are a number of other notices which traditionally appear on publications (see paragraph 4.9) and there are legal advantages to ensuring that the copyright information on publications is correct (see paragraphs 4.9 and 4.10). In some countries – notably the United States – there are strong advantages to registering copyright works in the relevant foreign copyright registry (see paragraph 4.7).

edges that no casual or inadvertent failure by the Publisher or by any third party to comply with this provision shall constitute a breach by the Publisher of this Agreement or the Author's rights and in the event of any breach of this Clause the Author shall not have the right to seek injunctive relief and the sole remedy of the Author shall be a claim for damages.

2.5   The Author acknowledges that it is necessary for the purposes of publication for the Publisher to have the right to make alterations to the text of the Work in order to make corrections and conform the text to the Publisher's house style and also for the purpose of authorising translations of the Work or removing any material which might in the opinion of the Publisher be actionable at law or which might damage the Publisher's reputation or business interests and for the purpose of complying with the advice of the Publisher's legal advisers and for other general copy-editing purposes and the Author consents to the exercise by the Publisher of such rights and agrees that the product of such exercise shall not be capable of being considered a distortion mutilation or derogatory treatment of the Work.

2.6   The Publisher undertakes not to change the title of the Work (except for the purpose of exploiting the Work in the United States of America or authorising or exploiting translations of the Work) without the consent of the Author which shall not be unreasonably withheld.

2.7   The Publisher shall at the request of the Author disclose to the Author the size of all print runs of the Work produced by the Publisher.

2.8   If it is necessary in the opinion of the Publisher for the Work to be read by a legal adviser the costs relating to such reading and subsequent advice shall be borne equally between the Publisher and the Author the amount of the Author's share being deducted from sums payable to the Author under this Agreement.

Clause 2.4   This clause contains an assertion of the Author's right to be identified (see paragraphs 5.3 to 5.9). The assertion is included for the reasons referred to in paragraph 7.8. There are circumstances in which a person who, for example, loses the opportunity to enhance their reputation can apply for injunctive relief (see paragraph 13.12) and restrain the publication or distribution of works which do not contain appropriate credit wording. The final sentence of the clause is intended to eliminate this risk.

Clause 2.5   This clause contains a confirmation from the Author that certain acts will not violate the Author's right to object to derogatory treatment of the Author's work (see paragraphs 5.10 to 5.13). The clause has been inserted for the reasons referred to in paragraph 7.8, and is a more acceptable alternative (from an Author's point of view) to a complete waiver of moral rights. Although provisions of this nature are not generally found in minimum terms agreements (see paragraph 7.20), there are strong commercial arguments to support their inclusion (see paragraph 7.22). They may not be effective in certain foreign territories.

Clause 2.6   A similar provision is contained in the minimum terms agreements (see paragraph 7.20). This provision is not onerous from a Publisher's point of view, since the consent of the Author may not be unreasonably withheld.

Clause 2.7   A provision of this nature is included in the minimum terms agreements (see paragraph 7.20) and it is submitted that in most circumstances Publishers will not consider this provision to be unreasonable.

Clause 2.8   There are some works which would be of a sensitive nature and which are intended to contain information which may be scandalous or may have security implications. This clause is particularly aimed at these works.

3.   PUBLICATION

3.1   Subject to the Acceptance by the Publisher of the Work and subject to the remaining provisions of this Agreement the Publisher undertakes to publish the Work to the customary standard of the Publisher at the cost and expense of the Publisher on or around such date as may be indicated by the Publisher pursuant to Clause 3.4.

3.2   It is the intention of the Publisher to print [*number*] copies of the Work in [hard][paper] back format with an anticipated retail price of [*price*] but nothing contained in this Clause 3.2 shall constitute an obligation on the part of the Publisher in relation to the print run or pricing of the first or any subsequent edition of the Work and the Author acknowledges that the Publisher shall have sole control of all matters in relation to the production and publication of the Work including without limitation print runs numbers of reprints and editions marketing price advertising editorial production distribution and terms of sale.

3.3   If the Publisher has in the Publisher's possession the original typescript of the Work (or any revised version) and the Author gives the Publisher notice in writing within 30 days of first publication of the Work in the United Kingdom requiring the Publisher to return such original typescript or revised version to the Author the Publisher shall at its election either make such material available for collection by the Author or the Author's representative from the office of the Publisher or despatch it to the Author by prepaid post.

3.4   The Publisher shall consult with the Author in relation to the publication date of the Work and shall use all reasonable endeavours to give the Author advance notice of such date.

3.5   The Publisher shall provide the Author with 12 free copies of the Work on first publication in hardback format [and in the case of any paperback edition up to 20 free copies] and the Author shall have the right to purchase additional further copies at a discount of [*percentage*]% of the Publisher's list price for the personal use of the Author but not for resale purposes.

Clause 3.1   The Publisher's obligation to publish the Work is subject to acceptance by the Publisher of the Work (see clause 12). Publication costs are generally borne by Publishers, although in the area which is referred to as "vanity publishing" it is usual for Authors to pay to have the privilege of seeing their works in print.

Clause 3.2   This clause requires the Publisher to state the intended print run and publication price. The statements will not bind the Publisher for the future and the clause makes it clear that the Publisher retains sole control over production matters. A similar provision is contained in the minimum terms agreements.

Clause 3.3   This provision requires the Publisher to return original typescript material which is in the Publisher's possession if requested by the Author. The obligation of the Publisher is limited to making such material available for collection, or to despatching it by pre-paid post. The Publisher does not guarantee that the Author will actually receive the returned material. A similar provision is contained in the minimum terms agreements.

Clause 3.4   The consultation obligation does not oblige the Publisher to follow the Author's requirements. A similar provision is contained in the minimum terms agreements.

Clause 3.5   The number of free copies of the Work and the provisions relating to purchase of additional copies are matters on which the practice varies from publisher to publisher. A similar provision is contained in the minimum terms agreements.

4. PROMOTION

4.1   The Author shall supply the Publisher with details of suitable persons and other information relating to publicity and advertising of the Work and shall provide the Publisher with a list of suggested individuals and periodicals who might be suitable recipients for review copies of the Work.

4.2   The Publisher shall not place any advertising inserts in copies of the Work without the consent of the Author.

4.3   The Publisher shall have the right to use the name likeness and biography of the Author in advertising and publicity material relating to the Work but not for the purposes of product endorsement.

5. ADVANCE

Subject to and conditional upon the full performance and observation by the Author of all the undertakings and warranties on the part of the Author contained in this Agreement the Publisher undertakes to pay to the Author the recoupable advance ("Advance") of £[*amount*] on account of royalties which shall be payable:

5.1   as to £[*amount*] on the date of this Agreement receipt of which the Author acknowledges; and

5.2   as to £[*amount*] on Acceptance of the Work; and

5.3   as to £[*amount*] on first publication of the Work.

6. ROYALTIES

Subject to and conditional upon the full performance and observation by the Author of all the undertakings and warranties on the part of the Author

---

Clause 4.1   This provision may not always be suitable for inclusion. It does not, however, impose an obligation on the Publisher to send all notified individuals copies of the Work.

Clause 4.2   A similar restriction is contained in some minimum terms agreements (see paragraph 7.20).

Clause 4.3   The unauthorised use of a person's name or likeness constitutes a criminal misdemeanour in some states of the United States of America. This provision permits the Publisher to use the Author's name, likeness and biography without infringing any rights of privacy or publicity or personality (see paragraph 5.21) but prevents the Publisher from abusing this right by licensing photographic material for product endorsement purposes.

Clause 5   The advance is expressed to be recoupable. In other words it is paid on account of royalties and recouped from future royalties paid to the Author. The Author will not receive any royalties until the total accrued royalty obligations amount to more than the amount paid by way of advance.

It will be noted that the advance is not described as "non-returnable" since the agreement specifically provides (see clause 12.4) that there are circumstances in which the advance is repayable.

The Author's entitlement to receive the advance is subject to and conditional on full performance and observance by the Author of the Author's warranties and obligations under the agreement.

contained in this Agreement the Publisher undertakes to pay to the Author the following sums ("Royalties"):

6.1   on sales of hardback copies of the Work in the United Kingdom and the Irish Republic and on overseas sales of hardback copies of the Work at discounts of less than 15%:

(a)   [*percentage*]% of the Published Price on the first [*number*] copies of the Work which have been sold and paid for and are not returned; and

(b)   [*percentage*]% of the Published Price on all subsequent copies of the Work which have been sold and paid for and are not returned (subject to the provisions of Clause 7.2).

6.2   on sales of hardback copies of the Work overseas at discounts:

(a)   [*percentage*]% of Publisher's Receipts in relation to the first [*number*] copies of the Work which have been sold and paid for and not returned; and

(b)   [*percentage*]% of Publisher's Receipts in relation to all additional copies of the Work which have been sold and paid for and not returned (subject to the provisions of Clause 7.2)

6.3   in relation to any hardback edition of the Work published at not less than two thirds of the original published price or any special hardback edition of the Work bearing the Publisher's imprint [*percentage*]% of [the Published Price on all copies of the Work in such editions which have been sold and paid for and are not returned or [*percentage*]% of the Publisher's Receipts in relation to such editions].

6.4   on sales of copies of the Work in paperback in the United Kingdom and the Irish Republic:

(a)   [*percentage*]% of the Published Price on the first [*number*] copies of the Work which have been sold and paid for and not returned; and

(b)   [*percentage*]% of the Published Price on all subsequent copies of the

---

Clause 6   The Author's entitlement to receive the royalties is subject to and conditional upon the full performance and observance by the Author of all the Author's obligations in the agreement.

Clause 6.1   For the prevailing commercial practice in relation to royalty rates see paragraph 7.21. The provisions of clause 6.1 are intended to provide that after sales of a certain number of copies (specified in clause 6.1 (a)) the royalty will increase to the rate specified in clause 6.1 (b) which will be higher than that specified in clause 6.1 (a). In the case of reprints below a certain level, the increased royalty provision is normally excluded (see clause 7.2).

Clause 6.2   For the prevailing commercial practice in relation to royalty rates see paragraph 7.21. The provisions of clause 6.2 are intended to provide that after sales of a certain number of copies (specified in clause 6.2 (a)) the royalty will increase to the rate specified in clause 6.2 (b) which will be higher than that specified in clause 6.2 (a). In the case of reprints below a certain level, the increased royalty provision is normally excluded (see clause 7.2).

Clause 6.3   For the prevailing commercial practice in relation to royalty rates see paragraph 7.21.

Work which have been sold and paid for and not returned (subject to the provisions of Clause 7.2)

6.5 on overseas sales of copies of the Work in paperback format a royalty of [*percentage*]% of [the Published Price or the Publisher's Receipts].

6.6 in relation to Book Club Sales:

) (a) [*percentage*]% of the Publisher's Receipts in relation to bound copies or sheets of the Work sold by the Publisher to book clubs;

(b) [*percentage*]% of the Publisher's Receipts in relation to copies of the Work printed by book clubs.

6.7 in relation to sales of copies of the Work in CD-ROM format:

[*specify royalty percentage base price and deductions if appropriate*]

7. SPECIFIC ROYALTY PROVISIONS

7.1 Where the Publisher has granted paperback rights in the Work in the United States of America the following provisions shall apply:

(a) if the Publisher sub-licenses the paperback rights in the Work to a United States Publisher the Publisher shall be entitled to a commission of [*percentage*]% of all sums paid by the United States Publisher in relation to the Work and shall remit the balance of such sums to the Author after the recovery of all sums to which the Publisher is entitled pursuant to this Agreement; and/or

(b) if the Publisher sells sheets or bound copies of the Work to a Publisher or sub-Publisher in the United States of America the Author shall be entitled to receive a royalty of [*percentage*]% of the Publisher's Receipts from such sale except in relation to sales discounted by more than [*percentage*] where the applicable percentage shall be [*percentage*]%.

Clause 6.4 For the prevailing commercial practice in relation to royalty rates see paragraph 7.21. The provisions of clause 6.4 are intended to provide that after sales of a certain number of copies (specified in clause 6.4 (a)) the royalty will increase to the rate specified in clause 6.4 (b) which will be higher than that specified in clause 6.4 (a). In the case of reprints below a certain level the increased royalty provision is normally excluded (see clause 7.2).

Clause 6.5 The effect of paying a percentage of the published price or the Publisher's receipts may be determined by referring to paragraphs 11.22 to 11.26 and paragraph 12.8.

Clause 6.6 It will be necessary to adjust the provisions of this clause to fit the appropriate circumstances.

Clause 6.7 It will be necessary to adjust the provisions of this clause to fit the appropriate commercial circumstances. In particular the provision may not be appropriate to include at all and should be deleted. Alternatively, it might be appropriate for royalty percentage provisions, royalty base price provisions, packaging and other deductions to be included in CD-ROM remuneration provisions on lines similar to those prevailing in the record industry (see Document 44 clauses 11 and 12). This will be particularly relevant if CD-ROM distribution is to be effected through record and videogram distributors, who in many cases service newsagents and other outlets for printed publications.

Clause 7.1 Some agreements contain specific royalty provisions relating to sales of works in the United States of America. It may not always be appropriate for these provisions to be included.

7.2   On reprints of less than [1500] copies of the Work the royalty percentages payable pursuant to Clauses 6.1 (b) 6.2 (b) and 6.4 (b) shall be the same as those percentages specified in Clauses 6.1 (a) 6.2 (a) and 6.4 (a).

7.3   No royalties shall be payable on copies of the Work sold or given to the Author or distributed for the purposes of publicity or advertising or distributed as review copies or on copies of the Work which are lost or destroyed or for which the Publisher does not receive payment.

8.   <u>RIGHTS</u>

8.1   The Author grants the Publisher the sole and exclusive licence to exploit the Publication Rights in the Work throughout the [world or territory of *specify*] for the full period of copyright from time to time existing under the laws in force in any part of the world including all reversions renewals and extensions [or for the period commencing on the date of this Agreement and terminating [*number*] years from the delivery date specified in Clause 1.4].

8.2   The Publisher confirms to the Author that all copy editing in relation to the Work shall be undertaken by employees of the Publisher or persons who are contracted to the Publisher on terms which assign to the Publisher the entire copyright in relation to the product of the services of such persons ("Editors") and the Publisher now confirms the assignment to the Author of all rights of copyright in any revisions alterations and amendments to the Work made by the Editors or made by the Author at the suggestion of the Editors.

8.3   The Publisher confirms that the following rights are reserved to the Author:

(a)   all reprographic rights in relation to the Work (other than reprographic rights subsisting in relation to the typographical arrangement of the published edition of the Work)

Clause 7.2 This clause excludes the application of any royalty escalator in relation to reprints of the Work of less than a designated number.

Clause 7.3 It is normal for agreements to provide that royalties are not paid on copies of the Work which are given to the Author or used for publicity or advertising or are lost or destroyed.

Clause 8.1 This clause is of crucial importance to a Publisher. The clause gives the Publisher the exclusive licence of the publication rights in the work throughout the designated territory for the full period of copyright. It is important for the precise extent of Publication Rights to be defined (see paragraphs 1.13 to 1.16 and paragraphs 2.26 to 2.30 and clause 18.1). If the grant of the licence (which should be expressed to be sole and exclusive) is not for the full period of copyright then the period will need to be specified. There are certain limitations on exclusivity implied by European Union legislation (see particularly paragraph 16.15) whose provisions have important implications for publishers. It is necessary to define the territorial extent of the rights (see paragraph 11.4). The provisions of this clause will not be suitable for all acquisitions, and alternative clauses are contained in Document 5. It will be noted that the licence extends to any renewal or extension of copyright. It is submitted that all licences should be so framed in view of the European Commission Directive to extend the term of copyright (see paragraph 17.11 and paragraphs 20.2 to 20.10).

Clause 8.2 This provision contains a reverse copyright assignment. Although this is not common practice in the publishing industry, it is submitted, for the reasons set out in paragraph 7.6, that such provisions are good practice. The Publisher should ensure that it does actually acquire the relevant rights from the editors.

(b)   all rights of the Author in relation to the Work pursuant to the Public Lending Right Act 1979 and any analogous legislation in any part of the world.

All rights reserved by the Author shall be subject to the provisions of Clause 8.4 and Clause 9.

8.4   The Author warrants to the Publisher that the Author is a member in good standing of the Author's Licensing and Collecting Society Limited and warrants that the Author's Licensing and Collecting Society Limited and its overseas affiliated bodies (together with such other bodies as may be approved by both the Author and Publisher in writing) shall have the exclusive right to authorise the reprographic exploitation of the Work.

9.   SUBSIDIARY RIGHTS

9.1   The Author appoints the Publisher as the sole and exclusive agent of the Author during the [period referred to in Clause 8.1] [period of [*specify*] years from the date of this Agreement] to sell and exploit and enter into contracts and collect all income arising in relation to the exercise by third parties of the Subsidiary Rights listed in the Schedule. In consideration of such appointment the Publisher undertakes to pay to the Author the applicable percentages of Publisher's Receipts listed in Clause 9.2 arising in relation to each such Subsidiary Right.

9.2   The applicable percentages of Publisher's Receipts referred to in Clause 9.1 are as follows:

(a)   Anthology and Quotation Rights: [*percentage*]% Publisher's Receipts

---

Clause 8.3   Reprographic rights in relation to Works may be the subject of licences granted by the Copyright Licensing Agency (see paragraph 6.17). Clause 8.3 reserves reprographic rights of the Work to the Author (in other words they are excluded from the rights granted under clause 8.1) but in view of the confirmation contained in clause 8.4 (that the Author is a member of the ALCS) and in view of the fact that all ALCS-controlled works are licensed by the Copyright Licensing Agency, the end result is that although the reprographic rights are reserved to the Author initially, they are subsequently transmitted to the Copyright Licensing Agency. If the Publisher is a member of the Copyright Licensing Agency, all reprographic rights in Works controlled by the Publisher will be capable of administration by the CLA which will account for money collected in such a way that the Publisher and the ALCS receive 50% each. The Author will be entitled to collect his or her share from the ALCS after the deduction of their administration expenses.

The rights of the Author in relation to the Public Lending Right Act 1979 are set out in paragraph 6.16, and the reservation of these rights does not conflict with any of the Publisher's interests.

Clause 8.4   The effect of this clause is that although the Author reserves reprographic rights, they are transmitted to the Copyright Licensing Agency which will account between Author and Publisher on a 50/50 basis in relation to income collected (see the note to clause 8.3 of this Document).

Clause 9.1   This clause deals with subsidiary rights (see paragraph 1.16). The clause appoints the Publisher as the Author's agent for the purpose of licensing the subsidiary rights. The appointment is effected for the reasons set out in paragraph 2.30. The clause needs to be modified to contain a specific reference to the period of the Publisher's rights. This clause has been drafted on the basis that the Publisher is appointed as agent for all subsidiary rights. It should be noted that the Advance (see the definition in clause 18.1) is recoupable from all other sums payable under the Agreement. If subsidiary rights income is generated and the Advance is unrecouped, the Author's share of the subsidiary rights income will be retained by the Publisher until recoupment. However, if some subsidiary rights are being retained by the Author, then the Publisher should consider whether it is appropriate for the Publisher to obtain the agreement of the Author not to exercise such retained rights for an initial period, to avoid them being exploited in competition with the Publisher's rights. An example would be where CD-ROM rights were retained by the Author, and did not form part of the subsidiary rights. The sale of the Work in CD-ROM format might impact on other exploitation of the Work.

(b) Book Club Rights: [*percentage*]% Publisher's Receipts

(c) Braille Rights: [*percentage*]% Publisher's Receipts

(d) Computer Game Rights: [*percentage*]% Publisher's Receipts

(e) Digest Rights: [*percentage*]% Publisher's Receipts

(f) Educational Rights: [*percentage*]% Publisher's Receipts

(g) First Serial Rights: [*percentage*]% Publisher's Receipts

(h) Information Storage and
Retrieval Rights: [*percentage*]% Publisher's Receipts

(i) Merchandising Rights: [*percentage*]% Publisher's Receipts

(j) Motion Picture and
Television Rights: [*percentage*]% Publisher's Receipts

(k) Other Rights: [*percentage*]% Publisher's Receipts

(l) Paperback Rights: [*percentage*]% Publisher's Receipts

(m) Radio Rights: [*percentage*]% Publisher's Receipts

(n) Reading Rights: [*percentage*]% Publisher's Receipts

(o) Reprint Rights: [*percentage*]% Publisher's Receipts

(p) Second and Subsequent
Serial Rights: [*percentage*]% Publisher's Receipts

(q) Single Issue Rights: [*percentage*]% Publisher's Receipts

(r) Sound Recording Rights: [*percentage*]% Publisher's Receipts

(s) Translation Rights: [*percentage*]% Publisher's Receipts

(t) US Rights: [*percentage*]% Publisher's Receipts

9.3 In authorising the exploitation of the Subsidiary Rights the Publisher shall have the right to grant licences for periods up to and including the full

---

Clause 9.2 Prevailing commercial practice in relation to percentage payments of subsidiary rights is considered in paragraph 7.21. The provisions of the clause will need to be adjusted so that they conform with the definition of Publication Rights contained in clause 18.1. Publication Rights may well include book club rights, paperback rights, reprint rights, and US rights. The provisions of this clause will require careful adjustment to fit the circumstances. It should be noted that the definition of Information Storage and Retrieval Rights (in the Schedule to Document 4) covers most forms of multimedia and electronic publishing. It may, however, be appropriate to refer to these in a separate category of subsidiary rights. Alternatively if the Publisher itself wishes to exploit these rights it may be appropriate to include them within the definition of Publication Rights, and provide a separate royalty in clause 6.7.

period of copyright in the Work and the Publisher's sole and exclusive rights and obligation to administer such licences and right to collect all income arising thereunder shall subsist for the full period of such licences irrespective of the expiry or termination of the licence contained in Clause 8.1 or the expiry or termination of the Publisher's appointment as agent.

10.   AUTHOR'S WARRANTIES

The Author represents warrants undertakes and agrees with the Publisher as follows:

10.1   the Author is the sole author of the Work and the sole unincumbered absolute legal and beneficial owner of all rights of copyright and all other rights whatever in the Work throughout the world and is and shall remain at all material times during the writing of the Work a "qualifying person" within the meaning of the Copyright, Designs and Patents Act 1988 Section 154;

10.2   the Author has not assigned or incumbered or licensed or transferred or otherwise disposed of any rights of copyright or any other rights in or to the Work except pursuant to this Agreement and has not entered into any agreement or arrangement which might conflict with the Publisher's rights

Clause 9.3   This clause will be necessary where the period of the Publisher's appointment as agent under clause 9.1 is for a period of less than the full duration of copyright (see paragraphs 3.25 to 3.35 and paragraph 17.11 and paragraphs 20.2 to 20.10). The effect of this provision is to permit a Publisher who is appointed as agent for a term of (say) seven years, to grant licences to third parties during the seven year term but to provide that the period of the licences granted can be for the full period of copyright (generally the life of the Author plus 50/70 years). At the end of the Publisher's seven year appointment the licences will continue to remain in force and the Publisher will remain entitled to receive all income from the licences.

Clause 10   The legal meaning of the expression "warranty" is examined in paragraph 7.15.

Clause 10.1   This provision is necessary to confirm that the Author is the sole author of the Work and that no other persons own it (see paragraphs 3.14, 3.23 and 3.24) and that the Work qualifies for copyright protection.

Clause 10.1 is designed to ensure that the Publisher acquires a Work in which copyright subsists. There are two alternative means of obtaining copyright protection under United Kingdom law, either through first publication, or through the Author being a qualifying person. If, however, a Publisher relies on a work being eligible for copyright protection through first publication of the Work, then, until the Work is first published in the United Kingdom or in another country to which United Kingdom legislation extends, there is a possibility that a Work for which a substantial advance has been paid may lose copyright protection. Although this possibility is remote, it is not beyond the realms of contemplation.

If a Publisher wishes to contract a resident of the Commonwealth of Independent States to write a Work, and that Work is first published in the CIS, the Work may not be protected under United Kingdom law or under the laws of other adherent countries to the Berne Convention. The position will depend on whether the state has adhered to the Berne Union. Although many CIS states are negotiating to join Berne, at the date of publication most have not acceded.

It is not, therefore, safe for Publishers to rely on first publication as a means of acquiring copyright protection in the United Kingdom. An alternative means of achieving copyright protection is to satisfy the criteria relating to authorship. Persons who are British citizens, British subjects, British protected persons and a number of other categories provided by the Nationality Act 1981 are persons whose copyright works are automatically protected by United Kingdom legislation. More importantly, so are individuals who are domiciled or resident in the United Kingdom, or another country to which the relevant provisions of the Act extend.

It follows therefore that if a CIS citizen takes up residence or domicile in the United Kingdom before writing a book, and remains resident or domiciled in the United Kingdom throughout the time that (s)he writes the book up until the date of first publication of the book in the United Kingdom, then the book will be eligible for United Kingdom (and Berne Convention) copyright protection.

under this Agreement or might interfere with the performance by the Author of the Author's obligations under this Agreement;

10.3   the Work is original to the Author and does not and shall not infringe any right of copyright moral right or right of privacy or right of publicity or personality or any other right whatever of any person;

10.4   the Work is not under the laws of any jurisdiction obscene or blasphemous or offensive to religion or defamatory of any person and does not contain any material which has been obtained in violation of the Interception of Communications Act 1985 the Official Secrets Act 1989 or any analogous foreign legislation and nothing contained in the Work would if published constitute a contempt of court;

10.5   all statements purporting to be facts in the Work are true and correct and no advice recipe formula or instruction in the Work will if followed or implemented by any person cause loss damage or injury to them or any other person;

10.6   there is no present or prospective claim proceeding or litigation in respect of the Work or the title to the Work or the working title or final title of the Work or the ownership of the copyright in the Work which may in any way impair limit inhibit diminish or infringe upon any or all of the rights granted to the Publisher in this Agreement;

10.7   copyright in the Work is and shall throughout the full period of

---

Clause 10.2   Although clause 10.1 protects the Publisher by ensuring that copyright subsists in the Work, it is also necessary to ensure that the rights of copyright are owned by the Author, which is what clause 10.2 provides. The warranty assures the Publisher that the Author has not incumbered the Work (by mortgaging it or charging it) or licensed rights in the Work to third parties.

The provision also assures the Publisher that the Author has not entered into any other agreement or arrangement which might interfere with the Publisher's rights under the agreement. An option granted by the Author to another Publisher would interfere with the Publisher's rights, for example, if it is enforceable – and many in the publishing world are not (see paragraph 7.17). There may be circumstances where it will be appropriate for publishers to remind authors of the extent of matters covered by this warranty, and other warranties in this agreement.

Clause 10.3   Infringement of copyright, moral rights, rights of privacy or rights of publicity or personality could lead to legal liability on the part of the Publisher, which this provision seeks to exclude. There may be occasions when it will be useful for Publishers to give guidance to authors on matters relating to infringement. It is certainly good practice for Publishers themselves to double-check material and ensure non-infringement and non-violation, since the legal costs of prevention are generally less than those incurred in trying to remedy a situation.

Clause 10.4   This warranty is designed to eliminate any liability on the Publisher's part for the matters examined in Chapters 9 and 10.

Clause 10.5   There are occasions where a Publisher and an Author will be liable for negligent misstatement (see paragraphs 9.34 and 9.35). An example of a matter which could give rise to liability for negligent misstatement would be the printing of an incorrect chemical formula in a school chemistry textbook (which could cause an explosion).

Clause 10.6   If the Author is aware of any dispute in relation to the Work, the Author will be in breach of this warranty. It is, however, possible to exclude from the scope of warranties matters which have been expressly disclosed. If an Author discloses the existence of a dispute to a Publisher, the question of interference with contractual relations may need to be considered (see paragraph 13.10).

copyright protection be valid and subsisting pursuant to the laws of the United Kingdom and the United States of America and the provisions of the Berne Convention and Universal Copyright Convention;

10.8   the Author shall not disclose reveal or make public except to the professional advisers of the Author any information whatever concerning the Work or the business of the Publisher or this Agreement all of which shall be strictly confidential nor shall the Author make any public statement or press statement in connection with the foregoing or commit any act which might prejudice or damage the reputation of the Publisher or the successful exploitation of the Work;

10.9   the Author undertakes to indemnify the Publisher and keep the Publisher at all times fully indemnified from and against all actions proceedings claims demands costs (including without prejudice to the generality of this provision the legal costs of the Publisher on a solicitor and own client basis) awards damages however arising directly or indirectly as a result of any breach or non-performance by the Author of any of the Author's undertakings warranties or obligations under this Agreement.

11.   ACCOUNTS

11.1   All sums payable pursuant to this Agreement [(other than sums payable pursuant to Clause 5.1 to 5.3 which shall be payable to the Author)] shall as the Author irrevocably directs be payable to [*name*] of [*address*] whose receipt shall be full and sufficient discharge to the Publisher of the Publisher's liability to make such payments.

11.2   The Publisher shall keep full books and records relating to the payment of sums due to the Author pursuant to this Agreement and shall prepare and submit to the Author within 90 days from 30 September and 31 December of each year a statement of account in relation to all sums payable to the Author during the preceding six-month period. Each such statement of account [shall be in the form recommended by the Society of Authors and] shall be accompanied by a cheque in favour of [the Author] [*or name*] in the amount shown to be due.

11.3   The Publisher shall have the right to deduct and retain from payments due to the Author up to [*percentage*]% of sums payable to the Author in

---

Clause 10.7   This warranty, to an extent, reinforces the warranty contained in clause 10.1. There may be circumstances where it may be appropriate for a Publisher to reduce the scope of the warranty by limiting it to the Berne Convention and to the Universal Copyright Convention only so far as concerns any initial period of copyright protection in the Universal Copyright Convention countries.

Clause 10.8   This provision imposes confidentiality obligations on the Author (see paragraphs 1.5 to 1.12).

Clause 10.9   The extent to which it is appropriate for a Publisher to impose indemnity obligations on Authors is a matter which should be given very careful thought for the reasons set out in paragraph 7.15.

Clause 11.1   This clause permits an Author to issue an irrevocable direction to the Publisher, requiring the Publisher to pay the Author's agent. In order to avoid any claim by an Author that money paid to the Author's agent should have been paid to the Author, the latter part of the clause provides for a release in favour of the Publisher. The name of the Author's agent should be inserted.

Clause 11.2   An option is provided for the statement of account to be in the form recommended by the Society of Authors. The name of the Author's agent should be inserted.

relation to the exploitation of Publishing Rights in paperback form as a reserve against returns in any accounting period. Each such reserve shall be liquidated (to the extent not applied against returns) in the [three/four] accounting periods following which the reserve is made and at the end of such period the balance remaining in such reserve shall be paid to the Author in full.

11.4   The Publisher shall have the right to deduct and retain from payments to the Author all sums required to be deducted or retained by way of withholding or other tax pursuant to the laws of any country. In the event that the remittance of royalties to the Author is prohibited by reason of exchange control restrictions in any part of the world the Publisher shall if requested by the Author deposit the amount of any sums due to the Author in an account in the name of the Author situate in the country in question subject to the payment or reimbursement by the Author to the Publisher of the administrative costs incurred in so doing.

11.5   If any bona fide claim shall be made in relation to the Work or any of the matters relating to the Author's warranties pursuant to this Agreement the Publisher shall be entitled without prejudice to any of its rights under this Agreement to suspend payment of the Advance and/or the Royalties or to retain such sums by way of reserve as the Publisher reasonably considers appropriate until the withdrawal or settlement to the satisfaction of the Publisher and its insurers of such claim.

11.6   Value Added Tax shall to the extent applicable be payable in addition to the sums payable to the Author under this Agreement subject to the production and delivery by the Author to the Publisher of a full accurate and correct Value Added Tax invoice bearing the Author's Value Added Tax registration number and country prefix accompanied by sufficient proof of the veracity of such details as the Publisher may request.

12.   ACCEPTANCE AND REJECTION

12.1   Following receipt of the typescript of the Work and any revisions requested the Publisher agrees within a reasonable time after delivery of the typescript and revisions (such period to be determined by the Publisher in the

---

Clause 11.3   This provision permits the Publisher to make reserves from sums payable to the Author. The percentage permitted to be retained and the number of accounting periods over which it is required to be liquidated are matters which need to be specified. It may be appropriate to apply the reserve provision to hardback sales and other exploitation, in certain circumstances.

Clause 11.4   A number of countries require withholding taxes to be deducted from royalties and this provision enables the Publisher to deduct such sums from royalty payments to the Author. The second part of the clause provides a mechanism for effecting payment to an Author from any country which imposes exchange control restrictions, by permitting the appropriate sum to be deposited in a bank account in the Author's name in the territory.

Clause 11.5   This provision permits the Publisher to suspend payment obligations on the occurrence of any adverse claim in relation to the Work. It should be noted that the provision is not as onerous as an indemnity provision, since it applies only to sums payable by the Publisher to the Author, instead of requiring indemnity payments from the Author to the Publisher.

Clause 11.6   There are circumstances where provision should be made for Value Added Tax (see paragraph 11.28) and where it may be appropriate for self billing arrangements to be made (see paragraph 12.26).

light of its publication schedule and the other commitments of the Publisher
and the Author) to examine or procure the examination of the Work and to
give the Author notice of acceptance or rejection of the Work or advise the
Author of the changes or revisions which the Publisher requires to be made.

12.2   If the Work contains any material which in the opinion of the Publisher might be actionable at law or damage the Publisher's reputation or
business interests the Publisher shall have the right to

(a)   give the Author notice of rejection of the Work (notwithstanding
any previous Acceptance pursuant to the provisions of Clause 12.1);
or

(b)   request the Author to make such changes to the Work as may be
necessary or advisable to avoid any potential action or damage; and/or

(c)   make such changes to the Work as the Publisher considers
appropriate.

12.3   If the Author fails to deliver the typescript of the Work together with
all other materials provided in this Agreement in accordance with the provisions of this Agreement or if following the Publisher's request pursuant to
Clause 12.2 (b) the Author refuses or is unable to make such changes to the
Work as are satisfactory to the Publisher or if the Publisher shall have given
notice of rejection of the Work or if an event beyond the control of the
Publisher shall prevent or in the opinion of the Publisher render difficult or
impossible the publication of the Work the Publisher shall have the right to
give notice in writing to the Author specifying such fact and the receipt of
such notice by the Author shall release the Publisher from all further obligations under this Agreement.

12.4   Where the Publisher has given notice to the Author pursuant to
Clause 12.3 on the grounds of failure or inability of the Author to deliver the
Work in accordance with the provisions of this Agreement or failure or
inability of the Author to make changes or rejection of the Work by the
Publisher [the Author shall within [*number*] weeks repay to the Publisher all

---

Clause 12.1   The obligation on the Publisher to publish the Work in clause 3.1 is subject to the Work
being accepted by the Publisher. This clause requires the Publisher to examine the typescript and any
revisions delivered by the Author and advise the Author whether such material is suitable for publication
or not. No fixed time-scale is required for the Publisher to give such notice, although it is submitted that
the Publisher should behave reasonably in implementing this provision.

Clause 12.2   This clause sets out the Publisher's options if it is discovered that the Work contains
material which might be actionable, or which might damage the Publisher's reputation or business
interests. A Publisher might become aware of such fact after it has previously accepted the Work, and the
provision acknowledges this fact.

Clause 12.3   This clause permits the Publisher to give notice to the Author if the Author fails to deliver
the Work in accordance with the agreement, or refuses or is unable to make changes, or events beyond
the control of the Publisher make it difficult or impossible for publication of the Work. The effect of giving
notice is to remove the Publisher from any further liability to the Author under the agreement.

sums previously paid to the Author under this Agreement] [or the Author shall be free to re-submit the Work to third party publishers and the Publisher shall reassign to the Author or any third party publisher the rights acquired by the Publisher pursuant to this Agreement upon the repayment to the Publisher of all sums previously paid to the Author under this Agreement].

13. REMAINDER SALES AND NOTICE TO RECAPTURE

13.1   If the Publisher wishes to sell off any of its stock of copies of the Work as remainder copies the Publisher shall wherever the Publisher considers it reasonably practicable so to do give notice to the Author specifying the number of copies in stock and the proposed disposal price (inclusive of Value Added Tax if relevant) and the Author shall have the option to purchase all copies of the Work held by the Publisher. The Author shall exercise this option within [14] days from receipt of the notice from the Publisher by payment to the Publisher of the total proposed disposal price specified in the notice.

13.2   If the Publisher wishes to destroy surplus copies of the Work the Publisher shall where it considers it practicable give notice to the Author of the proposed date of destruction and shall permit the Author subject to making prior arrangements to obtain up to [20] free copies of the Work for the Author's own personal use which copies shall not be resold.

13.3   If all editions of the Work published by the Publisher or any of its licensees are out of print or if over a two-year period the average annual sales of the Work by the Publisher and its licensees are less than [100] copies in hardback format or trade paperback format or [1500] copies in mass market paperback then the Author shall be entitled to give the Publisher notice in writing requiring the Publisher to indicate whether the Publisher intends to reprint and/or reissue the Work.

13.4   If the Publisher does not within [three months] from receipt of notice under Clause 13.3 give notice that it intends to reprint the Work all Publication Rights granted to the Publisher pursuant to Clause 8 shall revert to the Author on the sooner of the expiry of six months from the date of receipt of notice or the sale of all stocks of the Work.

13.5   If the Publisher gives notice in writing to the Author that the Publisher

---

Clause 12.4   Where a Publisher has given notice to the Author, as a result of failure or inability of the Author to deliver the Work, or make changes to it, or where a Publisher has rejected the Work this clause offers two alternatives. Either the Author is required to repay all sums previously paid within a stated period of weeks, or the Author is free to submit the Work to a third party publisher, and the Publisher will release the rights to the third party publisher on repayment of sums previously paid to the Author. It will be noted that the giving of notice under clause 12.3 or clause 12.1 merely releases the Publisher from liability to the Author, and does not terminate the licence granted under clause 8.1.

Clause 13.1   This provision gives the Author the right to buy-off copies of the Work being remaindered by the Publisher. The Author is required to exercise the Author's option within a set number of days. The option may only be exercised by offering payment, and the Author is required to purchase all of the Publisher's stock of the Work, not just some of it. There may be circumstances where it is appropriate to adjust these provisions.

Clause 13.2   This provision gives the Author the right to receive additional free copies of the Work if the Publisher intends to destroy surplus copies. It is modelled on a provision contained in minimum terms agreements (see paragraph 7.20).

intends to reprint or reissue the Work or produce a new edition of the Work then the provisions of Clause 13.4 shall not apply and the Publisher shall use all reasonable endeavours to reprint or reissue the Work or produce a new edition of it within [18] months of the date it gives notice.

13.6   The Work shall be considered to be out of print if fewer than [50] copies of any hardback or trade paperback edition of the Work or [150] copies of any mass market paperback edition of the Work remain in stock with the Publisher or under the Publisher's control.

14.   ACTIONS FOR INFRINGEMENT

14.1   If at any time during the period the Publication Rights in the Work are vested in the Publisher the copyright in the Work is infringed by any person or any person is in breach of any contract in relation to the Subsidiary Rights the Author shall have the option of joining in with the Publisher in any action taken by the Publisher to prevent such infringement and of sharing costs and damages relating to such action in such proportion as may be agreed. Where any proceedings are instituted by the Publisher and no agreement exists between the Publisher and the Author in relation to the costs of such proceedings then the Publisher shall have the right to take such action as the Publisher considers appropriate and the damages in relation to such action shall be applied by the Publisher first by way of repayment of any costs incurred by the Publisher (including a reasonable allowance for overhead costs of the Publisher) second towards recoupment of the Advance to the extent outstanding and the balance remaining shall be applied [as to [*percentage*]% to the Author the remainder being retained and applied by the Publisher for its own benefit or in accordance with the provisions of Clauses 6 and 9].

14.2   The Author undertakes to do any and all acts and execute any and all documents in such manner and at such locations as may be required by the Publisher in its sole discretion in order to protect perfect or enforce any of the Subsidiary Rights or any of the other rights granted to the Publisher pursuant to this Agreement. As security for the performance by the Author of the Author's obligations under this Agreement if the Author shall have failed following 14 days notice from the Publisher to execute any document or perform any act required pursuant to this Agreement the Publisher shall have the right to do so in the place and stead of the Author as the lawful appointed attorney of the Author and the Author undertakes and warrants that the Author shall confirm and ratify and be bound by any and all of the actions of the Publisher pursuant to this Clause and such Authority and appointment

---

Clause 13.3 to 13.6   This is an important provision for Publishers. Where rights are licensed to Publishers, they may be terminated in certain circumstances. One of the circumstances in which termination rights are exercisable are if the Work goes out of print. A number of the minimum terms agreements (see paragraph 7.20) contain termination provisions of this nature. The provisions vary greatly. Some tend to favour authors more, others less. The provisions of clauses 13.3 to 13.6 are, in spirit, not far removed from the tone of the minimum terms agreement provisions which have been signed recently.

Clause 14.1   The royalty provisions do not make any specific allowance for sums recovered by the Publisher through court actions against third parties who infringe copyright in the Work. This provision permits Publisher and Author to agree upon how such sums are applied.

shall take effect as an irrevocable appointment pursuant to Section 4 of the Powers of Attorney Act 1971.

15. ALTERNATIVE DISPUTE RESOLUTION

15.1 If either party is of the opinion that the other party to this Agreement is in breach of any material condition or obligation pursuant to this Agreement including without prejudice any obligation to pay money (but excluding any matter referred to in Clause 15.4) such dispute shall be dealt with in accordance with the alternative dispute resolution procedure set out in this Clause.

15.2 The Publisher and the Author undertake that they shall endeavour in good faith to resolve any dispute or claim arising in relation to the Work or this Agreement by means of good faith negotiations which shall take place between the Author and a senior executive of the Publisher who shall have Authority to settle the dispute. If the dispute is not resolved within [14] days from commencement of good faith negotiations the Publisher and the Author shall endeavour in good faith to resolve the dispute through an alternative dispute resolution procedure carried out in accordance with the recommendations of the Centre for Dispute Resolution.

15.3 All negotiations in relation to the matters in dispute shall be strictly confidential and shall be without prejudice to the rights of the Author and the Publisher in any future proceedings. If the parties fail to reach an agreement which finally resolves all matters in dispute within 60 days of having commenced negotiations pursuant to the alternative dispute resolution procedure or if such negotiations fail to take place within 30 days from the date specified in Clause 15.2 then either party shall be entitled:

(a) to refer the matter to a single arbiter agreed upon by the Publisher and the Author whose decision shall be final and binding on the parties; or

(b) to seek such legal remedies as may be appropriate.

15.4 The provisions of Clause 15.1 to 15.3 shall not apply in relation to the exercise by the Publisher of any of its rights pursuant to Clause 12 or 14 [or any matter relating to such rights or to any dispute or claim which involves a third party].

16. TERMINATION

16.1 If pursuant to the provisions of Clause 15 the Publisher is found to be in breach of any material obligation on its part pursuant to this Agreement

---

Clause 14.2 In the United Kingdom an exclusive licensee may commence court proceedings to prevent infringement without the consent of the copyright owner. In some overseas territories the consent of the copyright owner may be required. This provision permits the Publisher to act as the lawfully appointed attorney of the Author in such circumstances. Many documents contain references to powers of attorney being coupled with an interest and therefore being irrevocable. Such powers are not irrevocable unless they are given by way of security, as in the case of this clause.

Clause 15 Many publishing agreements provide for resolution of disputes by arbitration. Arbitration is slow, ineffective and costly. Recently some publishing agreements have provided for resolution by arbitration through the Publishers' Association. There may be circumstances where Authors or Publishers do not wish the Publishers' Association to become involved in (or even know about) certain disputes. Clauses 15.1 to 15.4 of this Document provide for a quick, effective, cheap and private means of resolution of disputes.

and the Publisher shall not have remedied such breach to the extent possible within 30 days of the date of such finding or if the Publisher shall have been put into liquidation other than for the purposes of solvent reconstruction the Author shall have the right to give notice to the Publisher in writing terminating (subject to the provisions of Clause 16.3) the rights granted to the Publisher pursuant to Clause 8.

16.2   On receipt of notice of termination from the Author all rights granted to the Publisher pursuant to Clause 8 shall (subject to the provisions of Clause 16.3) revert to the Author and the appointment by the Publisher as the Author's agent pursuant to Clause 9 shall also terminate.

16.3   Termination of the grant of rights pursuant to Clauses 16.1 and 16.2 shall be without prejudice to the obligations of the parties contained in Clauses [*specify added clauses*] and [*specify added clauses*] which shall continue to bind the parties and shall be without prejudice to:

(a)   the continuation of any licence or sub-licence granted by the Publisher and the right of the Publisher to collect and account to the Author in relation to all income due to the Author under this Agreement arising pursuant to agreements entered into in relation to any Subsidiary Rights;

(b)   the right of the Author to receive remuneration from the Publisher;

(c)   any claims by the Author against the Publisher as at the date of termination.

17.   <u>NOTICES</u>

17.1   Any notice or other document required to be given under this Agreement or any communication between the parties with respect to any of the provisions of this Agreement shall be in writing in English and be deemed duly given if signed by or on behalf of a duly authorised officer of the party giving the notice and if left at or sent by pre-paid registered or recorded delivery post or by telex telegram cable facsimile transmission or other means of telecommunication in permanent written form to the address of the party receiving such notice as set out at the head of the Agreement or as notified between the parties for the purpose of this Clause

17.2   Any such notice or other communication shall be deemed to be given to and received by the addressee:

Clause 16.1 This clause provides the Author with a termination right, if alternative dispute resolution has not been successful, and if the Publisher has still failed to remedy any breach of the agreement after a 30-day remedy period. The clause applies only in relation to Publication Rights.

Clause 16.2 This clause provides that the appointment of the Publisher as the Author's agent for the purpose of exploiting the Subsidiary Rights will terminate on the exercise of the Author's termination right under clause 16.1.

Clause 16.3 This clause provides that the exercise of termination rights will not affect the rights of the Publisher under additional clauses (such as those of the type contained in Documents 6(a) and 6(b)) or in relation to the exploitation of subsidiary rights pursuant to licences previously granted.

Clause 17 A number of clauses in the Document provide for a means of exercising rights and a notice provision is therefore necessary.

(a) at the time the same is left at the address of or handed to a representative of the party to be served

(b) by post on the day not being a Sunday or Public Holiday two days following the date of posting

(c) in the case of a telex telegram cable facsimile transmission or other means of telecommunication on the next following day.

17.3 In proving the giving of a notice it should be sufficient to prove that the notice was left or that the envelope containing the notice was properly addressed and posted or that the applicable means of telecommunication was addressed and despatched and despatch of the transmission was confirmed and/or acknowledged as the case may be.

17.4 Communications addressed to the Publisher shall be marked for the attention of [*name*] with a copy to [*name*] of [*address*].

18. DEFINITIONS AND INTERPRETATION

18.1 The following definitions apply in this Agreement:

"Acceptance"
Acceptance of the Work pursuant to Clause 12

"Advance"
The sum specified in Clause 5 which shall be recoupable from all other sums payable to the Author under this Agreement

"Book Club Sales"
The sale of copies or sheets of the Work or the licensing of the Work to any book club

"Out of Print"
Not listed as available in any catalogue of the Publisher or any licensee

"Publication Rights"
The sole and exclusive right to print and/or publish the Work in volume or sheet form in paperback or hardback form [in CD-ROM and other electronic format] and the right to authorise others to do so

"Published Price"
The price recommended by the Publisher in any country for sale of copies of the Work exclusive of any amount of sales or value added or other taxes (if applicable)

"Publisher's Receipts"
100% of all sums directly and identifiably received by the Publisher in sterling in the United Kingdom (excluding any sums paid for the use of the

typographical arrangement of the Work or paid for the supply of discs plates or other pre-print materials) in relation to the categories of Publication Rights and Subsidiary Rights referred to in Clauses 6 and 9 the Publisher's Receipts in each such category being computed on a separate basis.

18.2   The following terms are defined in this Agreement in the place indicated:

"Advance": Clauses 5 and 18.1
["Arm's Length Offer": Clause [*specify*]]
["Offer": Clause [*specify*]]
"Editors": Clause 8.2
"Royalties": Clause 6
["Subsequent Work": Clause [*specify*]]
["Subsequent Work Rights": Clause [*specify*]]
"Subsidiary Rights": The Schedule
"Work": Clauses 1.1 and 18.6

18.3   Any reference in this Agreement to any statute or statutory provision shall be construed as including a reference to that statute or statutory provision as from time to time amended modified extended or re-enacted whether before or after the date of this Agreement and to all statutory instruments orders and regulations for the time being made pursuant to it or deriving validity from it.

18.4   Unless the context otherwise requires words denoting the singular shall include the plural and vice versa and words denoting any one gender shall include all genders and words denoting persons shall include bodies corporate unincorporated associations and partnerships but successors and assignees shall not be deemed to include licensees.

18.5   All warranties and obligations on the part of the Author pursuant to this Agreement shall survive the expiry of any term of years specified in this Agreement whether by determination or by effluxion of time.

18.6   The word "Work" shall include all literary dramatic musical and

---

Clause 18.1   The definitions contained in clause 18.1 will need review in order to fit the appropriate circumstances. In particular careful attention should be paid to those clauses dealing with rights (see notes to clause 9.2) and money.

Clause 18.2   The references in this clause need to be adjusted to fit the appropriate circumstances. In particular, it may be appropriate to insert additional clauses (such as those contained in Documents 6 (a) and 6 (b)) which will necessitate consequential renumbering.

Clause 18.5   This provision ensures that any obligation on the Author which was intended to remain in force after the term of rights expired (such as, for example, an option on the Author's next Work) will remain in force.

artistic material (including notes and other preparatory material drafts revisions revised rejected surplus and derivative material) written by the Author or selected by the Author pursuant to this Agreement.

18.7   The word "copyright" means the entire copyright and design right subsisting under the laws of the United Kingdom and any and all analogous rights subsisting under the laws of each and every jurisdiction throughout the world.

19.   MISCELLANEOUS

19.1   Nothing contained in this Agreement shall constitute or shall be construed as constituting a partnership or contract of employment between the parties.

19.2   Neither party shall have any obligation to the other in the event of any act or omission on the part of such party where such act or omission results from the occurrence of any event which is outside the reasonable control of such party.

19.3   Nothing contained in this Agreement shall constitute an undertaking on the part of the Publisher to publish the Work unless and until notice of Acceptance is given by the Publisher pursuant to Clause 12 and such notice is not withdrawn pursuant to the provisions of this Agreement. If the Publisher elects not to publish the Work in no event shall the Author be entitled to any compensation or remedy in respect of loss of opportunity to enhance the Author's reputation or loss of publicity or for any other reason whatever.

19.4   This Agreement and all representations obligations undertakings and warranties contained in it shall enure for the benefit of and shall be binding on the personal representatives heirs and beneficiaries of the Author and their successors and assignees and shall be binding upon the successors licensees and assignees of the Publisher.

19.5   This Agreement contains the full and complete understanding between the parties and supersedes all prior arrangements and understandings

---

Clause 18.6   The effect of this provision (when construed together with the provisions of clause 8.1) is to transfer to the Publisher the Publication Rights in all material written by the Author in relation to the Work after the date of the agreement. This may not always be appropriate but it may be relevant in circumstances where the Author dies between the time of signing the contract and delivering the Work (see paragraph 7.3).

Clause 19.1   Under English law if two parties carry on business in common with a view to profit and share profit, the arrangement is capable of being considered a partnership. This provision ensures that no partnership is created inadvertently and also expressly excludes the possibility of an employment contract being created.

Clause 19.2   This is a short form of what is frequently referred to as a "force majeure" clause. It may not always be appropriate for this clause to be included, since it may permit an Author to argue against a Publisher that the Author is not liable in certain circumstances which are beyond the Author's reasonable control.

Clause 19.3   This clause expressly excludes the possibility of any claim by the Author for compensation for loss of opportunity to enhance the Author's reputation or any other reason (see paragraph 1.23).

Clause 19.4   This provision gives the Publisher's successors, licensees and assignees the benefit of rights obtained by the Publisher and confirms the liability of the Author's estate in relation to the warranties and obligations of the Author.

whether written or oral appertaining to the subject matter of this Agreement and may not be varied except by an instrument in writing signed by all the parties to this Agreement. The Author acknowledges that no representations or promises not expressly contained in this Agreement have been made to the Author by the Publisher or any of its servants agents employees members or representatives.

19.6   This Agreement shall be governed and construed in accordance with the laws of England and Wales whose courts shall be courts of competent jurisdiction.

[certificate of value]

IN WITNESS this Author's Agreement has been duly executed as a Deed and is intended to be delivered and is delivered on the day month and year first above written

THE SCHEDULE
Subsidiary Rights
(Clause 9.1)

The expression "Subsidiary Rights" means in relation to the Work the following sole and exclusive rights throughout the world:

(1)   "Anthology and Quotation Rights" namely the sole and exclusive right to authorise the reproduction of extracts and quotations from the Work (including illustrations diagrams and maps contained in the Work) in other publications.

(2)   "Book Club Rights" namely the sole and exclusive right to license the Work to book clubs and similar organisations [*these rights may form part of the Publication Rights*].

(3)   "Braille Rights" namely the sole and exclusive right to authorise the use of the Work in braille form or in "talking-book" form.

Clause 19.5   There are occasions where oral agreements or other understandings may be created in relation to a Work, which may contain either additional obligations, or obligations which conflict with those set out in subsequent written agreement. This provision makes it clear that all previous arrangements and understandings are at an end and the contract is the only document relevant to the obligations and rights of the parties in relation to its subject matter. The final part of the clause expressly excludes the possibility of any liability of the Publisher for misrepresentation on the part of any of its servants, agents, employees or representatives (see paragraph 2.17).

Clause 19.6   Where a contract is made between two entities in England and Wales, it will generally not be necessary to insert a provision of this nature, but where a contract is to be created with a foreign company (or a company situate in Scotland or Northern Ireland) this provision should always be included.

The Schedule   The various types of subsidiary rights will require adjustment to reflect those which are retained by the Author (with the Publisher acting as agent) and those which form part of the Publication Rights. Reference should be made to the annotations against clauses 8.1, 9.1 and 9.2. Particular attention should be paid to the treatment of Book Club Rights, Computer Game Rights, Information Storage and Retrieval Rights, Paperback Rights, US Rights, Multimedia and other Electronic Exploitation Rights.

(4) "Computer Game Rights" namely the sole and exclusive right to authorise the making and exploitation of any computer game based on the Work.

(5) "Digest Rights" namely the sole and exclusive right to authorise the publication of abridgements or condensations of the Work either in volume form or in magazines journals periodicals newspapers or other works.

(6) "Educational Rights" namely the sole and exclusive right to authorise the publication of special editions of the Work which may contain additional material or limited vocabulary and which are suitable for educational use.

(7) "First Serial Rights" namely the sole and exclusive right to authorise the publication of extracts of the Work in one issue on more than one successive or non-successive issue of newspapers magazines or periodicals.

(8) "Information Storage and Retrieval Rights" namely the sole and exclusive right to authorise the use of the Work in electronic database by means of storage and retrieval systems and/or by any "on-line" or "off-line" and by any other means in any format whatever including without limitation microfilm magnetic tape reprography magnetic and/or optical disk and any other digital and/or mechanical and/or electronic means whether now known or in future invented.

(9) "Merchandising Rights" namely the sole and exclusive right to authorise the use of characters or illustrations from the Work in or upon artifacts and/or articles other than books.

(10) "Motion Picture and Television Rights" namely the sole and exclusive right to authorise the making of any film or television production or videogram based upon the Work.

(11) "Other Rights" namely any rights of exploitation in the Work other than those referred to in this Schedule.

(12) "Paperback Rights" namely the sole and exclusive right to authorise the publication of the Work in paperback format [*these rights may form part of the Publication Rights*].

(13) "Radio Rights" The sole and exclusive right to authorise the making of any radio adaptation or dramatisation of the Work.

(14) "Reading Rights" namely the sole and exclusive right to authorise the non-dramatic reading of the Work on radio or television or upon the live stage including the making of videograms or records of such non-dramatic or "straight" reading.

(15) "Reprint Rights" namely the sole and exclusive right to authorise the use by foreign publishers of materials which have been produced by the Publisher so as to enable the foreign publishers to produce their own editions of the Work.

393

(16) "Second and Subsequent Serial Rights" namely the sole and exclusive right to authorise the issue or publication of the Work in newspapers or periodicals appearing subsequent to those publications first granted licences in relation to the First Serial Rights.

(17) "Single Issue Rights" namely the sole and exclusive right to authorise the single issue or "one-shot" publication of the complete Work or a condensed version of it in a single issue of a periodical or newspaper.

(18) "Sound Recording Rights" namely the sole and exclusive right to authorise the reproduction distribution and other exploitation of the Work by means of sound recordings.

(19) "Translation Rights" namely the sole and exclusive right to authorise the making and exploitation of the Work in foreign languages.

(20) "US Rights" namely the sole and exclusive right to authorise the exploitation of the Work in hardback or paperback form in the United States of America [*these rights may form part of the Publication Rights*].

EXECUTED AND DELIVERED
AS A DEED BY
[Publisher]
acting by [a director and
its secretary] [two directors])

Director

Secretary/Director

SIGNED AND DELIVERED
AS A DEED BY
[Author]
in the presence of:)

Witness Signature
Witness Name
Witness Address
Occupation

Attestation clause This form of wording is appropriate for documents which are executed as deeds. The purpose of executing this document as a deed is to ensure that the appointment by the Publisher as the attorney of the Author permits the Publisher to execute documents by way of deed. This may be necessary to pursue actions for infringement overseas (see clauses 14.1 and 14.2 and annotations).

Certificate of Value Although it had been intended to abolish stamp duty on assignments of intellectual property at the same time as the introduction of paperless share transfer, the failure of the Stock Exchange system TAURUS has delayed the abolition of stamp duty which is still payable in relation to assignments of copyright.

The publishing industry has, traditionally, never made provision for the payment of stamp duty in assignments of copyright and for this reason no provision is included in this document – although there are now many circumstances where it is advisable. A suitable form of wording may, however, be found in Document 6 (d) and a summary of the current legislation relating to stamp duty may be found in paragraph 11.29.

DOCUMENT 5

Alternative rights clauses

[IMPORTANT NOTE: Please read the section "About this book" on page v, before copying or using this Document]

Purpose of this Document

This Document provides a number of alternative rights clauses which may be suitable for incorporation in Document 4. In each case where an alternative rights clause is inserted, a number of consequential amendments will be required to be made to Document 4. As with all documents contained in this book, care, and suitably qualified legal support, is recommended to persons wishing to make changes.

Relevant text

The text of this Work contains a number of topics which are relevant to documents of this nature:

- assignments and licences of copyright (paragraphs 1.18 to 1.21)
- creation, existence and transfer of copyright (paragraphs 3.1 to 3.40)
- international copyright protection (paragraphs 4.1 to 4.17)
- buying and selling rights (paragraphs 11.2 to 11.9)

Warning The use of any of the following sample clauses will require a number of consequential amendments to be made to Document 4, or any other appropriate document. Failure to make the appropriate adjustments could have serious consequences, and appropriate legal advice should therefore be taken.

396

5 (a) Licence for a designated territory for a specified term of years

The Author grants the Publisher the sole and exclusive licence to exploit the Publication Rights in the Work and to authorise others so to do throughout the territory of [*specify names of countries*] for the period commencing on the date of this Agreement and terminating [*number*] years from the delivery date specified in Clause 1.4

5 (b) Assignment of Publication Rights worldwide for the full period of copyright

The Author assigns to the Publisher the Publication Rights in the Work and all rights of action and all other rights of whatever nature in relation to the Publication Rights whether now or in future created to which the Author is now or may at any time after the date of this Agreement be entitled by virtue of or pursuant to any of the laws in force in any part of the world TO HOLD the same to the Publisher its successors assignees and licensees absolutely for the whole period of such rights for the time being capable of being assigned by the Author together with any and all renewals reversions and extensions throughout the world.

5 (c) Assignment of Publication Rights for a designated territory for a specified period

The Author assigns to the Publisher the Publication Rights in the Work and all rights of action and other rights of whatever nature in relation to the Publication Rights in the Work throughout the territory of [*specify*] ("Territory") and all rights of action and all other rights of whatever nature in relation to the Publication Rights in the Work whether now known or in future created to which the Author is now or may at any time after the date of this Agreement be entitled by virtue of or pursuant to any of the laws in force in the Territory TO HOLD the same to the Publisher its successors assignees and licensees absolutely for the period of [*specify period*].

5 (d) Assignment of entire copyright for the full period of copyright

The Author assigns to the Publisher the entire copyright whether vested contingent or future in the Work and all rights of action and all other rights of whatever nature in the Work whether now known or in the future created to which the Author is now or may at any time after the date of this Agreement be entitled by virtue of or pursuant to any of the laws in force in any part of the world TO HOLD the same to the Publisher its successors assignees and licensees absolutely for the whole period of such rights for the time being capable of being assigned by the Author together with any and all renewals reversions and extensions throughout the world.

5 (e) Assignment of entire copyright for a designated territory for a specified term

The Author assigns to the Publisher the entire copyright whether vested contingent or future in the Work throughout the territory of [*specify*] ("Territory") and all rights of action and all other rights of whatever nature in and to the Work now known or in the future created to which the Author is now or may at any time after the date of this Agreement be entitled by virtue of or pursuant to any of the laws in force in any part of the Territory <u>TO HOLD</u> the same to the Publisher its successors assignees and licensees absolutely for the Term.

DOCUMENT 6

Additional clauses

[IMPORTANT NOTE: Please read the section "About this book" on page v, before copying or using this Document]

Purpose of this Document

This Document comprises a number of additional clauses which may be suitable for incorporation in Document 4, depending on the commercial circumstances. Each of the clauses will necessitate consequential amendments to Document 4. As with all documents contained in this book, care, and suitably qualified legal support, is recommended to persons wishing to make changes.

Relevant text

The text of this Work covers a number of topics which are relevant to documents of this nature:

- restrictions on authors (paragraph 7.2)
- new editions (paragraph 7.16)
- subsequent works (paragraph 7.17)
- electronic delivery material (paragraph 7.13)
- stamp duty (paragraph 11.29)

Warning The use of any of the following sample clauses will require a number of consequential amendments to be made to Document 4, or any other appropriate document. Failure to make the appropriate adjustments could have serious consequences, and appropriate legal advice should therefore be taken.

Document 6 *Additional clauses*

6 (a) New editions and competing works

[.1] Before publishing a new edition of the Work the Publisher shall be entitled but not obliged to request the Author by giving the Author not less than [three] months notice in writing to update the Work. On receipt of such notice the Author undertakes to carry out such research as may be required in order to enable the Author to update the Work comprehensively. The Author undertakes to provide the Publisher by the specified date with a legible typescript indicating all additions and alterations required to bring the Work fully and comprehensively up to date. The typescript shall clearly indicate the places where such additions and alterations are required to be inserted.

[.2] If following receipt of notice from the Publisher pursuant to Clause [.1] the Author in the discretion of the Author decides that the Author does not wish to carry out the additional work referred to in Clause [.1] or the Author for any reason fails or neglects to do so the Publisher shall be entitled to make such arrangements as the Publisher considers appropriate including the engagement of other suitable persons on terms as may be acceptable to the Publisher in order to bring the Work up to date. In such event [the Publisher shall be under no obligation to pay to the Author royalties in relation to any new edition of the Work] [the amount of all expenditure incurred by the Publisher in so doing shall be recovered from sums payable by the Publisher to the Author under this Agreement] and the provisions of Clauses [2.3] and [2.4] shall be amended so as to provide that the Author shall be entitled to receive such credit and copyright notice as the Publisher considers appropriate. The assertion by the Author of the Author's right to be identified in Clause [2.4] shall be construed accordingly.

[.3] The Author shall not during the period commencing on the date of this Agreement and ending 5 years from first publication of any Work or any subsequent reissue or new edition of the Work write any English language work which [deals with the same subject as the Work] [covers substantially the same subject matter as the Work] which might reasonably be regarded by the Publisher as competing with the Work or being likely to affect sales of the Work. The Author acknowledges that the Publisher shall have the right to seek injunctive and other relief in order to prevent any breach by the Author of this provision notwithstanding the provisions of Clause [15].

Document 6 (a) This provision entitles the Publisher to request the Author to update the Work and create a new edition, but does not oblige the Publisher to do so. It does not provide for the Author to receive any advance for the additional work needed to produce a new edition. If the Author refuses or fails or neglects to carry out additional work, the Publisher is entitled to engage other suitable personnel and either recover the amount of expenditure from sums payable to the Author, or suspend payment to the Author of royalties in relation to any new editions of the work.

These are provisions which obviously need to be negotiated and consequential amendments may need to be made to credit provisions and copyright notices provided in the agreement (see clauses 2.3 and 2.4 of Document 4). In general terms it is preferable for Publishers who are acquiring rights in works which they anticipate will be the subject of new editions to acquire their rights by way of assignment of copyright so that they have acquired clear ownership of the original underlying work and are free to use it to create updated versions.

The final part of the clause contains an undertaking from the Author not to write any other book which competes with the Work, in which regard the provisions of paragraph 7.2 will be relevant. The Publisher's right to seek an injunction (see paragraph 13.12) is expressly excluded from the alternative dispute resolution provisions contained in clause 15.

6 (b)   Subsequent works

[.1]   The provisions of this Clause apply to any literary [or dramatic] work ("Subsequent Work") written by the Author alone or in collaboration with others [after the date of this Agreement and prior to the expiry of [*number*] years from the date of this Agreement] [which covers the same field or subject matter as the Work] [which contains any of the principal characters portrayed or appearing in the Work or any derivative revised or rejected or surplus material written by the Author in connection with the Work and which contains a story that is different from that contained in the Work or any literary or dramatic work which is a sequel to the Work (whether such work or sequel is temporally prior to or concurrent with or subsequent to the events portrayed or occurring in the Work)].

[.2]   The Author undertakes to deliver to the Publisher the completed manuscript or typescript of any Subsequent Work following its completion and as further consideration for the undertakings of the Publisher under this Agreement the Author agrees that the Publisher shall have the sole and exclusive right to negotiate and obtain from the Author the same rights in relation to any Subsequent Work ("Subsequent Work Rights") as those obtained by the Publisher from the Author pursuant to this Agreement upon the same terms and conditions (other than the amount of any Advance) as specified in this Agreement. The Publisher's right shall commence on the date of this Agreement and shall terminate in relation to each such Subsequent Work [three calendar months] after the manuscript or typescript of such Subsequent Work shall have been delivered to the Publisher. As soon as the financial terms relating to the acquisition of the Subsequent Work Rights in relation to any Subsequent Work have been agreed the Author undertakes to enter into a written agreement with the Publisher in the form of this Agreement or such other form as the Publisher may reasonably require.

[.3]   If following the expiry of the period referred to in Clause [.2] the parties shall not have agreed terms in relation to any Subsequent Work the Author shall be free to negotiate with third parties in respect of the Subsequent Work Rights in such Subsequent Work provided however that the Author shall give immediate written notice to the Publisher of any offer ("Offer") received by the Author in respect of the Subsequent Work Rights or any part of them. The Publisher shall have the right to acquire from the

---

Document 6 (b)   These clauses are designed to apply to subsequent works. Many Authors' Agreements contain option clauses which do not constitute enforceable contractual obligations. The provisions of Document 6(b) first define what constitutes a subsequent work – different definitions are required for fictional works or technical works etc and the clause will need to be amended as appropriate.

The clause requires the Author to deliver the typescript of any subsequent work to the Publisher, and gives the Publisher a specified period of time during which the Publisher can renegotiate the financial terms (principally the advance and royalty claims) payable in relation to the subsequent work. If, at the end of this period, the parties have agreed terms then the Author will enter into an agreement with the Publisher in the form of the Author's contract (Document 4) or such other form as may be required by the Publisher.

If, however, at the end of the designated period, agreement has not been reached, the Author is free to negotiate with third parties in relation to the acquisition of rights in the subsequent work, provided that before concluding an agreement with the third party the Author notifies the Publisher of the proposed terms, and gives the Publisher the right to match the proposed terms.

Author the Subsequent Work Rights or any part of them in such Subsequent Work upon the same financial terms as the Offer pursuant to an agreement with the Author in the form of this Agreement or such other form as the Publisher may reasonably require. If any Offer is not a bona fide arm's length offer made by a third party not directly or indirectly connected with the Author ("Arm's Length Offer") the Publisher shall have the right to acquire such rights on the same terms as would in the opinion of the Publisher constitute an Arm's Length Offer.

[.4]   The rights of the Publisher pursuant to Clause [.3] shall be exercisable by notice in writing given to the Author within [28] days following receipt by the Publisher of notice of the Offer and the Author undertakes that the Author shall immediately on the exercise by the Publisher of its rights under this Clause [.4] enter into a written agreement in relation to the Subsequent Work Rights with the Publisher or its nominee in the form of this Agreement or such other form as the Publisher may require.

[.5]   The Author undertakes not to dispose or transfer or in any way whatever incumber or agree to dispose of or transfer or in any way whatever incumber any of the Subsequent Work Rights in contravention with the terms of this Clause [.].

6 (c)   Electronic delivery material

[.1]   The Author shall complete and deliver to the Publisher a clearly typed legible typescript of the Work by no later than [*date*]. The typescript shall be accompanied by a [*size*] computer disk containing the Work in [*specify*] wordprocessing software and the typescript shall have been printed from the disk and shall in all respects conform with it. The Author shall retain a duplicate copy of the disk and typescript submitted to the Publisher and whilst the Publisher undertakes to take all reasonable steps to safeguard materials in the Publisher's possession the Publisher shall have no liability for loss or destruction of any material.

[.2]   Within [*number*] days from delivery to the Publisher of the materials referred to in Clause [.1] the Publisher shall have the right to notify the Author of changes which the Publisher requires to have made to the Work and the Author shall within [*number*] days from the date of notification effect such changes as are requested by the Publisher and deliver to the Publisher a computer disk in the size and format referred to in Clause [.1] accompanied

---

Document 6 (c) This Document contains a number of provisions which may be appropriate for inclusion in contracts where an Author has agreed to deliver materials to the Publisher on disk. The provisions specify what materials are to be delivered, the format which they are to take, states how changes are to be made to the materials and confirms that the Publisher has the right to use the materials for typesetting and other production purposes. The Publisher is also permitted to use the materials for the purpose of exploiting the Publication Rights and any other rights granted to the Publisher in the Agreement.

by a printout of the Work which shall have been produced from the disk and which shall contain all changes and/or revisions which shall be clearly indicated.

[.3]   The Publisher shall have the right to use all disks delivered to it for the purpose of typesetting editing and printing and otherwise for the purpose of exploiting the Publication Rights and other rights granted to the Publisher pursuant to this Agreement.

6 (d)   Certificate of value

The parties to this Agreement certify that the fee payable under this Agreement attributable to any assignment of copyright effected by this Agreement is £[amount] and further certify that the transaction so effected does not form part of a larger transaction or of a series of transactions in respect of which the amount or value or the aggregate amount or value of the consideration exceeds £60,000.

Document 6 (d)   This clause is a standard form for a certificate of value which is currently required in order to pay stamp duty on assignments of intellectual property. If a certificate of value is not included, the amount of the remuneration payable in relation to the transfer of the intellectual property will be adjudicated.

If a document evidencing ownership of copyright is produced to a court and stamp duty has not been paid, it is possible that a court may refuse to accept the document as evidence of the ownership of the copyright or other intellectual property rights.

For further information on stamp duty, reference should be made to paragraph 11.29.

DOCUMENT 7

Short form author's agreement

[IMPORTANT NOTE: Please read the section "About this book" on page v, before copying or using this Document]

Purpose of this Document

The purpose of this Document is to provide a shorter alternative form to Document 4. The level of protection offered in this Document to publishers is not as great as the level of protection offered by Document 4. The Document contains an assignment of the copyright in the Work (as opposed to a licence in the publication rights and an agency appointment in relation to subsidiary rights).

The provisions relating to advance payments and royalties will need to be adjusted to conform with the publisher's standard practice. Publishers may also wish to insert a provision providing remuneration in relation to the sale of Subsidiary Rights (see paragraph 1.16 and see paragraph 7.21). A number of the provisions in the contract conform with the provisions of the minimum terms agreements (see paragraphs 7.20 to 7.22).

It may be advantageous for the rights provisions to be adjusted so that the Publication Rights alone are assigned to the Publisher and the Publisher is appointed the Author's agent for the purpose of authorising the exploitation of the Subsidiary Rights (see paragraph 2.30). In this case a definition for Publication Rights will need to be inserted similar to that contained in Document 4. Document 5 and Document 6 contain additional clauses which may be suitable for inclusion.

Relevant text

The text of this Work covers a number of topics which are relevant to documents of this nature including:

- general matters relating to authors' agreements (paragraphs 7.2 to 7.4)
- copyright and moral rights (paragraphs 7.5 to 7.8)
- specific provisions in authors' agreements (paragraphs 7.9 to 7.19)
- minimum terms agreements (paragraphs 7.20 to 7.22)
- acquiring rights generally (paragraphs 1.13 to 1.16)
- factors to be considered in relation to acquiring rights (paragraphs 1.17 to 1.21)
- commercial terms of offers (paragraphs 1.22 and 1.23)
- the law of contract and agency (paragraphs 2.1 to 2.30)
- creation, existence and transfer of copyrights and trademarks (paragraphs 3.1 to 3.45)
- international copyright protection (paragraphs 4.1 to 4.17)
- moral rights (paragraphs 5.1 to 5.22)

- permissions, fair dealings and rights clearances (paragraphs 8.1 to 8.44)
- liability for content (paragraphs 9.1 to 9.49)
- buying and selling rights (paragraphs 11.1 to 11.29)
- infringement and enforcement (paragraphs 13.1 to 13.17)
- termination and recapture (paragraphs 14.1 to 14.10)
- competition law (paragraphs 16.1 to 16.28)
- multimedia (Chapter 19)

Document 7 *Short form author's agreement*

THIS AGREEMENT is made the ——— day of ——— 199 —

BETWEEN

(1) [*name*] LIMITED of [*address*]
     ("Publisher"); and

(2) [*name*] of [*address*]
     ("Author")

IT IS AGREED as follows:

1. THE WORK

1.1 The Publisher engages the Author to write the original literary [dramatic] work entitled "[*title*]" of not less than [*number*] pages of text and [*number*] pages of illustrations ("Work") and the Author undertakes to write the Work and deliver it to the Publisher in accordance with the provisions of this Agreement.

1.2 The Work shall be [*state description of the Work ie original work of fiction or biography or historical analysis of certain events etc*] and shall be based on the original outline of the Work written by the Author [dated [*date*] or submitted to the Publisher on [*date*]] and shall [*state additional requirements*].

1.3 The illustrations of the Work shall be [original to the Author] [selected by the Author in consultation with the Publisher from [*specify sources*]].

1.4 The Author shall complete and deliver to the Publisher two copies of a clearly typed legible typescript of the Work by no later than [*date*]. It shall be the responsibility of the Author to keep duplicate copies of all material submitted to the Publisher and whilst the Publisher undertakes to take all reasonable steps to safeguard copies of the Work in the Publisher's possession the Publisher shall have no liability for loss or destruction of any material submitted to it.

Clause 1.1 This clause constitutes the engagement of the Author by the Publisher to write the Work. The text needs to be varied to suit the circumstances. The engagement does not make the Author the Publisher's employee. This possibility is expressly excluded by clause 11.1.

Clause 1.2 This clause is of fundamental importance since it provides a full description of the Work. The clause should be adjusted to suit appropriate circumstances.

Clause 1.3 If illustrations are to be obtained from third parties, the agreement will usually contain provisions relating to the cost of the illustrations (clause 1.8) and it will also be necessary for a Publisher to ensure that various rights clearance procedures are followed (see paragraph 8.44).

Clause 1.4 The delivery date needs to be inserted. Although the document does not provide that time is of the essence of the contract (see paragraph 2.10) it would be possible for the Publisher to make time of the essence if the Author failed to deliver by the specified date. The Publisher would need to give the Author a reasonable period of notice requiring the Author to perform his or her obligations by the end of such period. Clause 7.3 permits the Publisher, however, to give notice terminating its obligations under the agreement if the Author fails to deliver by the due date.

1.5   Within [*number*] days of delivery to the Publisher of the typescript of the Work the Publisher shall have the right to notify the Author of changes which the Publisher requires to have made in the Work and the Author shall within [*number*] days from the date of notification effect such changes as are requested by the Publisher and deliver to the Publisher two copies of clearly typed legible typescript of the Work containing the changes and/or revisions which shall be clearly indicated.

1.6   If in the opinion of the Publisher an index is required for the Work and the Author does not wish to undertake the preparation of an index the Publisher shall have the right to engage an indexer and the costs of such engagement shall be borne equally by the Author and the Publisher the amount of the Author's share being deducted from sums payable to the Author under this Agreement.

1.7   The Author shall obtain releases or permissions in a form satisfactory to the Publisher signed by all relevant persons in relation to all quotations and other third party material used in the Work and shall deliver copies to the Publisher on the date referred to in Clause 1.4.

1.8   The Publisher shall pay fees for illustrations agreed between the Publisher and the Author up to £[*amount*] and any additional sums payable in relation to illustrations shall be the responsibility of the Author and shall either be paid by the Author or at the discretion of the Publisher shall be advanced by the Publisher and deducted from sums payable to the Author under this Agreement.

2.   EDITING CORRECTIONS AND AUTHOR'S CREDIT

2.1   The Author shall read, check, correct and approve all proofs of the Work submitted to the Author by the Publisher and shall return to the Publisher clearly marked corrected proofs within 21 days from receipt [time being of the essence of this Clause]. The Author shall bear the cost of all corrections and alterations to proofs other than printer's errors in excess of 10% of the cost of composition or typesetting of the Work and/or origination of artwork and the Publisher shall have the right to deduct such costs from any sums which may be payable to the Author pursuant to this Agreement without prejudice to the Publisher's rights. If the amount of such extra costs exceeds the amount of Advances payable to the Author pursuant to this

Clause 1.5   This clause permits the Publisher to require the Author to make alterations to the text of the Work. The right is in addition to the Publisher's right to make corrections to the Work, to conform it to the Publisher's house style or remove material which might give rise to liability. These matters are covered in clause 2.4.

Clause 1.6   This provision is a standard indexing requirement. Where a detailed index is required, the costs of preparation are frequently borne by the Publisher. In addition to indexes, other reference material may be required (such as, for example, tables of cases and statutes in many legal publications) which the Publisher may prepare.

Clause 1.7   Releases and permissions are of fundamental importance, and should always be double-checked by Publishers. There are circumstances when permissions and releases may not be required (see paragraphs 8.2 to 8.39). Publishers should ensure that appropriate clearance procedures are followed (see paragraph 8.44 and Document 30).

Clause 1.8   Where illustrations are commissioned by an Author from third parties, Publishers should ensure that appropriate agreements are entered into by the persons providing the illustrations.

Agreement the Author shall within 30 days from demand by the Publisher pay to the Publisher the amount by which such extra costs exceed the Advances.

2.2   All copies of the Work published by the Publisher shall contain the following copyright notice:

[conform to reflect copyright position determined by Clause 3]

2.3   The Author asserts the Author's right to be identified in relation to the Work on the title page and cover in the following form:

[state form of identification required]

and the Publisher undertakes to comply with such request and to require all sub-publishers and other licensees to comply honour this right. The Author acknowledges that no casual or inadvertent failure by the Publisher or by any third party to comply with this provision shall constitute a breach by the Publisher of this Agreement and in the event of any breach of this Clause the Author shall not have the right to seek injunctive relief and the sole remedy of the Author shall be a claim for damages.

2.4   The Author acknowledges that it is necessary for the purposes of publication for the Publisher to have the right to make alterations to the text of the Work in order to make corrections and conform the text to the Publisher's house style and also for the purpose of authorising translations of the Work or removing any material which might in the opinion of the Publisher be actionable at law or which might damage the Publisher's reputation or business interests and for the purpose of complying with the advice of the Publisher's legal advisers and for other general copy-editing purposes and the Author consents to the exercise by the Publisher of such rights and agrees that the product of such exercise shall not be capable of being considered a distortion mutilation or derogatory treatment of the Work.

Clause 2.1   Time is made of the essence of this clause (see paragraph 2.10) because time is frequently critical during production schedules. The level beyond which the cost of corrections is to be borne by the Author is fixed at the conventional level of 10% although it may be appropriate to change this where electronic delivery material is provided by the Author (see paragraphs 7.12 and 7.13).

Clause 2.2   The copyright notice should state the identity of the copyright owner. If copyright is assigned to the Publisher, the copyright owner will be the Publisher. If copyright is reserved to the Author and the Author grants an exclusive licence to the Publisher, the copyright owner will be the Author. It is possible for the copyright owner in one country to be different from the copyright owner in another country (see paragraph 1.20).

There are a number of other notices which traditionally appear on publications (see paragraph 4.9) and there are legal advantages to ensuring that the copyright information on publications is correct (see paragraphs 4.9 and 4.10). In some countries – notably the United States – there are strong advantages to registering copyright works in the relevant foreign copyright registry (see paragraph 4.7).

Clause 2.3   This clause contains an assertion of the Author's right to be identified (see paragraphs 5.3 to 5.9). The assertion is included for the reasons referred to in paragraph 7.8. There are circumstances in which a person who, for example, loses the opportunity to enhance their reputation can apply for injunctive relief (see paragraph 13.12) and restrain the publication or distribution of works which do not contain appropriate credit wording. The final sentence of the clause is intended to eliminate this risk.

Clause 2.4   This clause contains a confirmation from the Author that certain acts will not violate the Author's right to object to derogatory treatment of the Author's work (see paragraphs 5.10 to 5.13). The clause has been inserted for the reasons referred to in paragraph 7.8, and is a more acceptable alternative (from an Author's point of view) to a complete waiver of moral rights. Although provisions of this nature are not generally found in minimum terms agreements (see clause 7.20), there are strong commercial arguments to support their inclusion (see paragraph 7.22). They may not be effective in certain foreign territories.

2.5   If it is necessary in the opinion of the Publisher for the Work to be read by a legal adviser the costs relating to such reading and subsequent advice shall be borne equally between the Publisher and the Author the amount of the Author's share being deducted from sums payable to the Author under this Agreement.

3.   RIGHTS

3.1   The Author assigns to the Publisher the entire copyright whether vested contingent or future in the Work (other than the rights referred to in Clause 3.2) and all rights of action and all other rights of whatever nature in the Work whether now known or in the future created to which the Author is now or may at any time after the date of this Agreement be entitled by virtue of or pursuant to any of the laws in force in any part of the world TO HOLD the same to the Publisher its successors and assigns absolutely for the whole period of such rights for the time being capable of being assigned by the Author together with any and all renewals reversions and extensions throughout the world.

3.2   The Publisher confirms that the following rights are reserved to the Author:

(a)   all reprographic rights in relation to the Work (other than reprographic rights subsisting in relation to the typographical arrangement of the published edition of the Work)

(b)   all rights of the Author in relation to the Work pursuant to the Public Lending Right Act 1979 and any analogous legislation in any part of the world.

3.3   The Author warrants to the Publisher that the Author is a member in good standing of the Author's Licensing and Collecting Society Limited and warrants that the Author's Licensing and Collecting Society Limited and its overseas affiliated bodies (together with such other bodies as may be

---

Clause 2.5   There are some works which would be of a sensitive nature and which are intended to contain information which may be scandalous or may have security implications. This clause is particularly aimed at these works.

Clause 3.1   This clause provides for an assignment from the Author to the Publisher of all rights of copyright in the Work. There will be some cases where it may be preferable for the Publisher to amend this provision to an assignment of publication rights for the reasons set out above in the note under "Purpose of this Document". An assignment of publication rights may be found in Document 5 (b).

Clause 3.2   Reprographic rights in relation to works may be the subject of licences granted by the Copyright Licensing Agency (see paragraph 6.17). Clause 3.2 reserves reprographic rights of the Work to the Author (in other words they are excluded from the rights granted under clause 3.1) but in view of the confirmation contained in clause 3.3 (that the Author is a member of the ALCS) and in view of the fact that all ALCS-controlled works are licensed by the Copyright Licensing Agency, the end result is that although the reprographic rights are reserved to the Author initially they are subsequently transmitted to the Copyright Licensing Agency. If the Publisher is a member of the Copyright Licensing Agency, all reprographic rights in Works controlled by the Publisher will be capable of administration by the CLA which will account for money collected in such a way that the Publisher and the ALCS receive 50% each. The Author will be entitled to collect his or her share from the ALCS after the deduction of their administration expenses.

   The rights of the Author in relation to the Public Lending Right Act 1979 are set out in paragraph 6.16 and the reservation of these rights does not conflict with any of the Publisher's interests.

approved by both the Author and Publisher in writing) shall have the exclusive right to authorise the reprographic exploitation of the Work.

4. REMUNERATION

The Publisher undertakes to pay to the Author:

4.1 an advance of £[*amount*] which shall be recoupable from royalties payable to the Author under this Agreement;

4.2 a royalty of [*percentage*]% all sums received by the Publisher from copies of the Work sold by the Publisher or where the Work is exploited by the Publisher's licensees [*percentage*]% of sums received by the Publisher from them.

5. PUBLICATION

5.1 Subject to the Acceptance by the Publisher of the Work and subject to the remaining provisions of this Agreement the Publisher undertakes to publish the Work to the customary standard of the Publisher at the cost and expense of the Publisher and undertakes to use all reasonable endeavours to give the Author advance notice of the publication date.

5.2 It is the intention of the Publisher to print [*number*] copies of the Work in [hard][paper] back format with an anticipated retail price of [*price*] but nothing contained in this Clause 5.2 shall constitute an obligation on the part of the Publisher in relation to the print run or pricing of the first or any subsequent edition of the Work and the Author acknowledges that the Publisher shall have sole control of all matters in relation to the production and publication of the Work including without limitation print runs numbers of reprints and editions.

Clause 3.3   The effect of this clause is that, although the Author reserves reprographic rights, they are transmitted to the Copyright Licensing Agency which will account between Author and Publisher on a 50/50 basis in relation to income collected (see note to clause 3.2 of this Document).

Clause 4.1   The remuneration provisions may need to be adjusted to reflect the circumstances for the reasons set out in the note under "Purpose of this Document" above. As to the amounts of advances payable and the percentages on which they are paid see paragraph 7.21 and clause 5 in Document 4 and accompanying notes.

Clause 4.2   For guidance as to prevailing commercial practice of royalty rates reference should be made to paragraph 7.21 and to the provisions of clauses 6 and 7 of Document 4 and accompanying annotations. This clause may require further adjustment depending on the circumstances in order to provide for remuneration to the Author in relation to Subsidiary Rights.
   Paragraph 7.21 sets out current prevailing commercial practice in relation to Subsidiary Rights and reference should be made to the schedule to Document 4 and to clauses 9.1 to 9.3 of Document 4 and accompanying annotations.

Clause 5.1   The Publisher's obligation to publish the Work is subject to acceptance by the Publisher of the Work (see clause 7). Publication costs are generally borne by publishers, although in the area which is referred to as "vanity publishing" it is usual for authors to pay to have the privilege of seeing their works in print. The consultation obligation does not oblige the Publisher to follow the Author's requirements.

Clause 5.2   This clause requires the Publisher to state the intended print run and publication price. The statements will not bind the Publisher for the future, and the clause makes it clear that the Publisher retains sole control over production matters. A similar clause is contained in the minimum terms agreements (see paragraphs 7.20 to 7.22).

5.3   The Publisher shall provide the Author with 12 free copies of the Work on first publication in hardback format [and in the case of any paperback edition up to 20 free copies] and the Author shall have the right to purchase additional further copies at a discount of [*percentage*]% of the Publisher's list price for the personal use of the Author but not for resale purposes.

6.   AUTHOR'S WARRANTIES

The Author represents warrants undertakes and agrees with the Publisher as follows:

6.1   the Author is the sole author of the Work and the sole unincumbered absolute legal and beneficial owner of all rights of copyright and all other rights whatever in the Work throughout the world and is and shall remain at all material times during the writing of the Work a "qualifying person" within the meaning of the Copyright, Designs and Patents Act 1988 Section 154;

6.2   the Author has not assigned or incumbered or licensed or transferred or otherwise disposed of any rights of copyright or any other rights in or to the Work except pursuant to this Agreement and has not entered into any agreement or arrangement which might conflict with the Publisher's rights under this Agreement or might interfere with the performance by the Author of the Author's obligations under this Agreement;

6.3   the Work is original to the Author and does not and shall not infringe any right of copyright moral right or right of privacy or right of publicity or personality or any other right whatever of any person;

6.4   the Work is not under the laws of any jurisdiction obscene or blasphemous or offensive to religion or defamatory of any person and does not contain any material which has been obtained in violation of the Interception of Communications Act 1985 the Official Secrets Act 1989 or any analogous

---

Clause 5.3   The number of free copies of any Work and the provisions relating to purchase of additional copies are matters on which the practice varies from publisher to publisher.

Clause 6   The legal meaning of the expression "warranty" is examined in paragraph 7.15.

Clause 6.1   This provision is necessary to confirm that the Author is the sole author of the Work and that no other persons own it (see paragraphs 3.14, 3.23 and 3.24) and that the Work qualifies for copyright protection.
   For further explanation of the purpose of this clause reference should be made to the notes to clause 10.1 of Document 4.

Clause 6.2   Although clause 6.1 protects the Publisher by ensuring that copyright subsists in the Work, it is also necessary to ensure that the rights of copyright are owned by the Author, which is what clause 6.2 provides. The warranty assures the Publisher that the Author has not encumbered the Work (by mortgaging it or charging it) or licensed rights in the Work to third parties.
   The provision also assures the Publisher that the Author has not entered into any other agreement or arrangement which might interfere with the Publisher's rights under the agreement. An option granted by the Author to another publisher would interfere with the Publisher's rights, for example. There may be circumstances where it will be appropriate for publishers to remind authors of the extent of matters covered by this warranty, and other warranties in this agreement.

Clause 6.3   Infringement of copyright, moral rights, rights of privacy or rights of publicity or personality could lead to legal liability on the part of the Publisher, which this provision seeks to exclude. There may be occasions when it will be useful for Publishers to give guidance to Authors on matters relating to infringement. It is certainly good practice for Publishers themselves to double-check material and ensure non-infringement and non-violation, since the legal costs of prevention are generally less than those incurred in trying to remedy a situation.

foreign legislation and nothing contained in the Work would if published constitute a contempt of court;

6.5   all statements purporting to be facts in the Work are true and correct and no advice recipe formula or instruction in the Work will if followed or implemented by any person cause loss damage or injury to them or any other person;

6.6   there is no present or prospective claim proceeding or litigation in respect of the Work or the title to the Work or the working title or final title of the Work or the ownership of the copyright in the Work which may in any way impair limit inhibit diminish or infringe upon any or all of the rights granted to the Publisher in this Agreement;

6.7   copyright in the Work is and shall throughout the full period of copyright protection be valid and subsisting pursuant to the laws of the United Kingdom and the United States of America and the provisions of the Berne Convention and Universal Copyright Convention;

6.8   the Author shall not disclose reveal or make public except to the professional advisers of the Author any information whatever concerning the Work or the business of the Publisher or this Agreement all of which shall be strictly confidential nor shall the Author make any public statement or press statement in connection with the foregoing or commit any act which might prejudice or damage the reputation of the Publisher or the successful exploitation of the Work;

6.9   the Author undertakes to indemnify the Publisher and keep the Publisher at all times fully indemnified from and against all actions proceedings claims demands costs (including without prejudice to the generality of this provision the legal costs of the Publisher on a solicitor and own client basis) awards damages however arising directly or indirectly as a result of any breach or non-performance by the Author of any of the Author's undertakings warranties or obligations under this Agreement.

Clause 6.4   This warranty is designed to eliminate any liability on the Publisher's part for the matters examined in Chapters 9 and 10.

Clause 6.5   There are occasions where a Publisher and an Author will be liable for negligent misstatement (see paragraphs 9.34 and 9.35). An example of a matter which could give rise to liability for negligent misstatement would be the printing of an incorrect chemical formula in a school chemistry textbook (which could cause an explosion).

Clause 6.6   If the Author is aware of any dispute in relation to the Work, the Author will be in breach of this warranty. It is, however, possible to exclude from the scope of warranties matters which have been expressly disclosed. If an Author discloses the existence of a dispute to a Publisher, the question of interference with contractual relations may need to be considered (see paragraph 13.10).

Clause 6.7   This warranty, to an extent, reinforces the warranty contained in clause 6.1. There may be circumstances where it may be appropriate for a Publisher to reduce the scope of the warranty by limiting it to the Berne Convention and to the Universal Copyright Convention only so far as concerns any initial period of copyright protection in the Universal Copyright Convention countries.

Clause 6.8   This provision imposes confidentiality obligations on the Author (see paragraphs 1.5 to 1.12).

Clause 6.9   The extent to which it is appropriate for a Publisher to impose indemnity obligations on Authors is a matter which should be given very careful thought for the reasons set out in paragraph 7.15.

7. ACCEPTANCE AND REJECTION

7.1 Following receipt of the typescript of the Work and any revisions requested the Publisher agrees within a reasonable time after delivery of the typescript and revisions (such period to be determined by the Publisher in the light of its publication schedule and the other commitments of the Publisher and the Author) to examine or procure the examination of the Work and to give the Author notice of acceptance ("Acceptance") or rejection of the Work or advise the Author of the changes or revisions which the Publisher requires to be made.

7.2 If the Work contains any material which in the opinion of the Publisher might be actionable at law or damage the Publisher's reputation or business interests the Publisher shall have the right to

(a) give the Author notice of rejection of the Work (notwithstanding any previous Acceptance pursuant to the provisions of Clause 7.1); or

(b) request the Author to make such changes to the Work as may be necessary or advisable to avoid any potential action or damage; and/or

(c) make such changes to the Work as the Publisher considers appropriate.

7.3 If the Author fails to deliver the typescript of the Work together with all other materials provided in this Agreement in accordance with the provisions of this Agreement or if following the Publisher's request pursuant to Clause 7.2 (b) the Author refuses or is unable to make such changes to the Work as are satisfactory to the Publisher or if the Publisher shall have given notice of rejection of the Work or if an event beyond the control of the Publisher shall prevent or in the opinion of the Publisher render difficult or impossible the publication of the Work the Publisher shall have the right to give notice in writing to the Author specifying such fact and the receipt of such notice by the Author shall release the Publisher from all further obligations under this Agreement.

7.4 Where the Publisher has given notice to the Author pursuant to Clause 7.3 on the grounds of failure or inability of the Author to make changes or rejection by the Publisher [the Author shall within [*number*] weeks repay to

Clause 7.1 The obligation on the Publisher to publish the Work in clause 3.1 is subject to the Work being accepted by the Publisher. This clause requires the Publisher to examine the typescript and any revisions delivered by the Author and advise the Author whether such material is suitable for publication or not. No fixed time-scale is required for the Publisher to give such notice, although it is submitted that the Publisher should behave reasonably in implementing this provision.

Clause 7.2 This clause sets out the Publisher's options if it is discovered that the Work contains material which might be actionable, or which might damage the Publisher's reputation or business interests. A Publisher might become aware of such fact after it has previously accepted the Work and the provision acknowledges this fact.

Clause 7.3 This clause permits the Publisher to give notice to the Author if the Author fails to deliver the Work in accordance with the agreement, or refuses or is unable to make changes, or events beyond the control of the Publisher make it difficult or impossible for publication of the Work. The effect of giving notice is to remove the Publisher from any further liability to the Author under the agreement.

the Publisher all sums previously paid to the Author under this Agreement] or [the Author shall be free to re-submit the Work to third party publishers and the Publisher shall reassign to the Author or any third party publisher the rights acquired by the Publisher pursuant to this Agreement upon the repayment to the Publisher of all sums previously paid to the Author under this Agreement].

8.   ACCOUNTS

8.1   The Publisher shall keep full books and records relating to the payment of sums due to the Author pursuant to this Agreement and shall prepare and submit to the Author within 90 days from 30 September and 31 December of each year a statement of account in relation to all sums payable to the Author during the preceding six-month period. Each such statement of account [shall be in the form recommended by the Society of Authors and] shall be accompanied by a cheque in favour of the Author in the amount shown to be due.

8.2   The Publisher shall have the right to deduct and retain from payments to the Author all sums required to be deducted or retained by way of withholding or other tax pursuant to the laws of any country. In the event that the remittance of royalties to the Author is prohibited by reason of exchange control restrictions in any part of the world the Publisher shall if requested by the Author deposit the amount of any sums due to the Author in an account in the name of the Author situate in the country in question subject to the payment or reimbursement by the Author to the Publisher of the administrative costs incurred in so doing.

8.3   If any bona fide claim shall be made in relation to the Work or any of the matters relating to the Author's warranties pursuant to this Agreement the Publisher shall be entitled without prejudice to any of its rights under this Agreement to suspend payment of the Advance and/or the Royalties or to retain such sums by way of reserve as the Publisher considers appropriate until the withdrawal or settlement to the satisfaction of the Publisher and its insurers of such claim.

Clause 7.4   Where a Publisher has given notice to the Author, as a result of failure or inability of the Author to deliver the Work, or make changes to it, or where a Publisher has rejected the Work this clause offers two alternatives. Either the Author is required to repay all sums previously paid within a stated period of weeks, or the Author is free to submit the Work to a third party Publisher, and the Publisher will release the rights to the third party publisher on repayment of sums previously paid to the Author. It will be noted that the giving of notice under clause 7.3 or clause 7.1 merely releases the Publisher from liability to the Author and does not reassign the rights assigned under clause 3.1.

Clause 8.1   An option is provided for the statement of account to be in the form recommended by the Society of Authors.

Clause 8.2   A number of countries require withholding taxes to be deducted from royalties and this provision enables the Publisher to deduct such sums from royalty payments to the Author. The second part of the clause provides a mechanism for effecting payment to an Author from any country which imposes exchange control restrictions, by permitting the appropriate sum to be deposited in a bank account in the Author's name in the territory.

Clause 8.3   This provision permits a Publisher to suspend payment obligations on the occurrence of any adverse claim in relation to the Work. It should be noted that the provision is not as onerous as an indemnity provision, since it applies only to sums payable by the Publisher to the Author, instead of requiring indemnity payments from the Author to the Publisher.

8.4   Value Added Tax shall to the extent applicable be payable in addition to the sums payable to the Author under this Agreement subject to the production and delivery by the Author to the Publisher of a full accurate and correct Value Added Tax invoice bearing the Author's Value Added Tax registration number and country prefix accompanied by sufficient proof of the veracity of such details as the Publisher may request.

9.   ALTERNATIVE DISPUTE RESOLUTION

9.1   If either party is of the opinion that the other party in this Agreement is in breach of any material condition or obligation pursuant to this Agreement including without prejudice any obligation to pay money (but excluding any matter referred to in Clause 9.4) such dispute shall be dealt with in accordance with the alternative dispute resolution procedure set out in this clause.

9.2   The Publisher and the Author undertake that they shall endeavour in good faith to resolve any dispute or claim arising in relation to the Work or this Agreement by means of good faith negotiations which shall take place between the Author and a senior executive of the Publisher who shall have authority to settle the dispute. If the dispute is not resolved within [14] days from commencement of good faith negotiations the Publisher and the Author shall endeavour in good faith to resolve the dispute through an alternative dispute resolution procedure carried out in accordance with the recommendations of the Centre for Dispute Resolution.

9.3   All negotiations in relation to the matters in dispute shall be strictly confidential and shall be without prejudice to the rights of the Author and the Publisher in any future proceedings. If the parties fail to reach an agreement which finally resolves all matters in dispute within 60 days of having commenced negotiations pursuant to the alternative dispute resolution procedure or if such negotiations fail to take place within 30 days from the date specified in Clause 9.2 then either party shall be entitled:

(a)   to refer the matter to a single arbiter agreed upon by the Publisher and the Author whose decision shall be final and binding on the parties; or

(b)   to seek such legal remedies as may be appropriate.

9.4   The provisions of Clauses 9.1 to 9.3 shall not apply in relation to the exercise by the Publisher of any of its rights pursuant to Clause 7 [or any matter relating to such rights or to any dispute or claim which involves a third party].

Clause 8.4   There are circumstances where provision should be made for Value Added Tax (see paragraph 11.28) and where it may be appropriate for self billing arrangements to be made (see paragraph 12.26).

Clause 9   Many publishing agreements provide for resolution of disputes by arbitration. Arbitration is slow, ineffective and costly. Recently some publishing agreements have provided for resolution by arbitration through the Publishers' Association. There may be circumstances where Authors or Publishers do not wish the Publishers' Association to become involved in (or even know about) certain disputes. Clauses 9.1 to 9.4 of this Document provide for a quick, effective, cheap and private means of resolution of disputes.

10. INTERPRETATION

10.1 Unless the context otherwise requires words denoting the singular shall include the plural and vice versa and words denoting any one gender shall include all genders and words denoting persons shall include bodies corporate unincorporated associations and partnerships.

10.2 The word "Work" shall include all literary dramatic musical and artistic material (including notes and other preparatory material drafts revisions revised rejected surplus and derivative material) written by the Author or selected by the Author pursuant to this Agreement.

10.3 The word "copyright" means the entire copyright and design right subsisting under the laws of the United Kingdom and any and all analogous rights subsisting under the laws of each and every jurisdiction throughout the world.

11. MISCELLANEOUS

11.1 Nothing contained in this Agreement shall constitute or shall be construed as constituting a partnership or contract of employment between the parties.

11.2 Neither party shall have any obligation to the other in the event of any act or omission on the part of such party where such act or omission results from the occurrence of any event which is outside the reasonable control of such party.

11.3 Nothing contained in this Agreement shall constitute an undertaking on the part of the Publisher to publish the Work unless and until notice of Acceptance is given by the Publisher pursuant to Clause 7 and such notice is not withdrawn pursuant to the provisions of this Agreement. If the Publisher elects not to publish the Work in no event shall the Author be entitled to compensation or remedy in respect of loss of opportunity to enhance the Author's reputation or loss of publicity or for any other reason whatever.

Clause 10.2 The effect of this provision (when construed together with the provisions of clause 3.1) is to assign to the Publisher the entire copyright in all material written by the Author in relation to the Work after the date of the agreement. This may not always be appropriate but it may be relevant in circumstances where the Author dies between the time of signing the contract and delivering the Work (see paragraph 7.3).

Clause 11.1 Under English law if two parties carry on business in common with a view to profit and share profit, the arrangement is capable of being considered a partnership. This provision ensures that no partnership is created inadvertently and also expressly excludes the possibility of an employment contract being created.

Clause 11.2 This is a short form of what is frequently referred to as a "force majeure" clause. It may not always be appropriate for this clause to be included, since it may permit an Author to argue against a Publisher that the Author is not liable in certain circumstances which are beyond the Author's reasonable control.

Clause 11.3 This clause expressly excludes the possibility of any claim by the Author for compensation for loss of opportunity to enhance the Author's reputation or any other reason (see paragraph 1.3).

11.4   This Agreement and all representations obligations undertakings and warranties contained in it shall enure for the benefit of and shall be binding on the personal representatives heirs and beneficiaries of the Author and their successors and assignees and shall be binding upon the successors licensees and assignees of the Publisher.

11.5   This Agreement contains the full and complete understanding between the parties and supersedes all prior arrangements and understandings whether written or oral appertaining to the subject matter of this Agreement and may not be varied except by an instrument in writing signed by all the parties to this Agreement. The Author acknowledges that no representations or promises not expressly contained in this Agreement have been made to the Author by the Publisher or any of its servants agents employees members or representatives.

11.6   This Agreement shall be governed and construed in accordance with the laws of England and Wales whose courts shall be courts of competent jurisdiction.

AS WITNESS the hand of the duly authorised representative of the Publisher and the hand of the Author the day month and year first above written

SIGNED by [*name of officer*]
for and on behalf of
[*name of Publisher*] LIMITED

SIGNED by [*Author*]
in the presence of:

Clause 11.4   This provision gives the Publisher's successors, licensees and assignees the benefit of rights obtained by the Publisher and confirms the liability of the Author's estate in relation to the warranties and obligations of the Author.

Clause 11.5   There are occasions where oral agreements or other understandings may be created in relation to a Work which may contain either additional obligations or obligations which conflict with those set out in subsequent written agreement. This provision makes it clear that all previous arrangements and understandings are at an end and the contract is the only document relevant to the obligations and rights of the parties in relation to its subject matter. The final part of the clause expressly excludes the possibility of any liability of the Publisher for misrepresentation on the part of any of its servants, agents, employees or representatives (see paragraph 2.17).

Clause 11.6   Where a contract is made between two entities in England and Wales, it will generally not be necessary to insert a provision of this nature, but where a contract is to be created with a foreign company (or a company situate in Scotland or Northern Ireland) this provision should always be included.

DOCUMENT 8

Short form copyright assignment

[IMPORTANT NOTE: Please read the section "About this book" on page v, before copying or using this Document]

Purpose of this Document

This Document provides a short form of copyright assignment which may be suitable for use in circumstances where publishers are acquiring rights of copyright from third parties who are not the original author. It will generally be necessary for the publisher to check the chain of title of the work (see paragraph 4.10).

Relevant text

- general matters relating to authors' agreements (paragraphs 7.2 to 7.4)
- copyright and moral rights (paragraphs 7.5 to 7.8)
- specific provisions in authors' agreements (paragraphs 7.9 to 7.19)
- minimum terms agreements (paragraphs 7.20 to 7.22)
- acquiring rights generally (paragraphs 1.13 to 1.16)
- factors to be considered in relation to acquiring rights (paragraphs 1.17 to 1.21)
- commercial terms of offers (paragraphs 1.22 and 1.23)
- the law of contract and agency (paragraphs 2.1 to 2.30)
- creation, existence and transfer of copyrights and trademarks (paragraphs 3.1 to 3.45)
- international copyright protection (paragraphs 4.1 to 4.17)
- moral rights (paragraphs 5.1 to 5.22)
- permissions, fair dealings and rights clearances (paragraphs 8.1 to 8.44)
- liability for content (paragraphs 9.1 to 9.49)
- buying and selling rights (paragraphs 11.1 to 11.29)
- infringement and enforcement (paragraphs 13.1 to 13.17)
- termination and recapture (paragraphs 14.1 to 14.10)
- competition law (paragraphs 16.1 to 16.28)
- multimedia (Chapter 19)

THIS ASSIGNMENT is made the   day of
BETWEEN:

(1)   [*Name*] of [*address*] ("Owner") and

(2)   [*name*] LIMITED of [*address*] ("Publisher")

IT IS AGREED as follows:

1.   ASSIGNMENT

1.1   The Owner assigns to the Publisher the entire copyright whether vested contingent or future in the Work and all rights of action and all other rights of whatever nature in and to the Work whether now known or in the future created to which the Owner is now or may at any time after the date of this Agreement be entitled by virtue of or pursuant to any of the laws in force in any part of the world TO HOLD the same to the Publisher its successors and assignees absolutely for the whole period of such rights for the time being capable of being assigned by the Owner together with any and all renewals reversions and extensions throughout the world.

1.2   The Owner undertakes to do any and all acts and execute any and all documents in such manner and at such locations as may be required by the Publisher in its sole discretion in order to protect perfect or enforce any of the rights granted or confirmed to the Publisher pursuant to this Agreement. As security for the performance by the Owner of the Owner's obligations under this Agreement if the Owner shall have failed following 14 days notice from the Publisher to execute any document or perform any act required pursuant to this Agreement the Publisher shall have the right to do so in the place and stead of the Owner as the lawfully appointed attorney of the Owner and the Owner undertakes and warrants that the Owner shall confirm and ratify and be bound by any and all of the actions of the Publisher pursuant to this Clause and such authority and appointment shall take effect as an irrevocable appointment pursuant to the Powers of Attorney Act 1971 Section 4.

2.   REMUNERATION

2.1   The Publisher undertakes to pay to the Owner the following sums subject to and conditional upon the full complete and timely performance

---

Clause 1.1   This clause provides for an assignment from the Owner to the Publisher of all rights of copyright in the Work. There will be some cases where it may be preferable for the Publisher to amend this provision to an assignment of publication rights for the reasons set out in Document 7 in the note under "Purpose of this Document". An assignment of publication rights may be found in Document 5 (b).

Clause 1.2   In the United Kingdom an exclusive licensee may commence court proceedings to prevent infringement without the consent of the copyright owner. In some overseas territories the consent of the copyright owner may be required. This provision permits the Publisher to act as the lawfully appointed attorney of the Author in such circumstances. Many documents contain references to powers of attorney being coupled with an interest and therefore being irrevocable. The fact is, however, that such powers are not irrevocable unless they are given by way of security, as in the case of this clause.

and observance by the Owner of all the Owner's undertakings and warranties under this Agreement [*insert remuneration details*]:

2.2   Value Added Tax shall to the extent applicable be payable in addition to the sums payable to the Owner under this Agreement subject to the production and delivery by the Author to the Publisher of a full accurate and correct Value Added Tax invoice bearing the Owner's Value Added Tax registration number and country prefix accompanied by sufficient proof of the veracity of such details as the Publisher may request.

3.   WARRANTIES

The Owner warrants undertakes and agrees with the Publisher that:

3.1   the Author is the sole author of the Work and was at all material times throughout the writing of the Work a "qualifying person" within the meaning of the Copyright, Designs and Patents Act 1988;

3.2   the Owner is the sole absolute and unincumbered legal and beneficial owner of all rights of copyright and all other rights whatever in and to the Work throughout the world and has not assigned or licensed any rights in the Work to any person;

3.3   there is no present or prospective claim proceeding or litigation in respect of the Work or any rights in the Work or the title to the Work or the working title or final title of the Work or the ownership of copyright in the Work which may in any way impair limit inhibit diminish or infringe upon any of the rights in the Work;

Clause 2.1   The remuneration provisions may need to be adjusted to reflect the circumstances for the reasons set out in the note under "Purpose of this Document" above. As to the amounts of advances payable and the percentages on which they are paid see paragraph 7.21 and clause 5 of Document 4 and accompanying notes.

For guidance as to prevailing commercial practice in relation to royalty rates reference should be made to paragraph 7.21 and to the provisions of clauses 6 and 7 of Document 4 and accompanying annotations. This clause may require further adjustment depending on the circumstances in order to provide for remuneration to the Author in relation to Subsidiary Rights.

Paragraph 7.21 sets out current prevailing commercial practice in relation to Subsidiary Rights and reference should be made to the schedule to Document 4 and to clauses 9.1 to 9.3 of Document 4 and accompanying annotations.

Clause 2.2   There are circumstances where provision should be made for Value Added Tax (see paragraph 11.28) and where it may be appropriate for self billing arrangements to be made (see paragraph 12.26).

Clause 3.1   The Author is defined in Clause 4.1. Although clause 3.1 protects the Publisher by ensuring that copyright subsists in the Work, it is also necessary to ensure that the rights of copyright are owned by the Author, which is what clause 3.2 provides. The warranty assures the Publisher that the Author has not incumbered the Work (by mortgaging it or charging it) or licensed rights in the Work to third parties.

The provision also assures the Publisher that the Author has not entered into any other agreement or arrangement which might interfere with the Publisher's rights under the agreement. An option granted by the Author to another Publisher would interfere with the Publisher's rights, for example. There may be circumstances where it will be appropriate for publishers to remind authors of the extent of matters covered by this warranty and other warranties in this agreement.

Clause 3.3   If the Owner is aware of any dispute in relation to the Work, the Owner will be in breach of this warranty. It is, however, possible to exclude from the scope of warranties matters which have been expressly disclosed. If an Owner discloses the existence of a dispute to a Publisher, the question of interference with contractual relations may need to be considered (see paragraph 13.10).

3.4   the Work is original to the Author and does not and shall not infringe any right of copyright moral right or right of privacy or right of publicity or personality or any other right whatever of any other person;

3.5   the Owner warrants that the Author has irrevocably and unconditionally waived all rights in respect of the Work to which the Author is now or may in future be entitled pursuant to the Copyright, Designs and Patents Act 1988 Sections 77 80 84 and 85 and any other moral rights to which the Author may be entitled under any legislation now existing or in future enacted in any part of the world;

3.6   the Publisher shall have the right to use the name and likeness and biography of the Author and the Owner in connection with the exploitation by the Publisher of the rights assigned to the Publisher pursuant to this Agreement;

3.7   copyright in the Work is valid and subsisting pursuant to the laws of the United Kingdom and the United States of America and the provisions of the Berne Convention and Universal Copyright Convention;

3.8   all published copies of the Work have borne a copyright notice in such form as shall secure protection for the Work pursuant to the provisions of the Universal Copyright Convention;

3.9   the Owner shall supply to the Publisher forthwith on demand and as a condition precedent to the liability of the Publisher to make any payment to the Owner full chain of title information and copies of executed originals of all documents which are in the opinion of the Publisher necessary to vest the right in the Work in the Publisher in such form as shall be satisfactory to the Publisher;

Clause 3.4   Infringement of copyright, moral rights, rights of privacy or rights of publicity or personality could lead to legal liability on the part of the Publisher, which this provision seeks to exclude. There may be occasions when it will be useful for Publishers to give guidance to Authors on matters relating to infringement. It is certainly good practice for Publishers themselves to double-check material and ensure non-infringement and non-violation, since the legal costs of prevention are generally less than those incurred in trying to remedy a situation.

Clause 3.5   The Publisher will wish assurance that the moral rights of the Author may not be exercised in such a way as to undermine the Publisher's rights, for the reasons explained in paragraph 7.8.

Clause 3.6   The use of a person's name or likeness or biography may constitute a criminal misdemeanour in some states of the United States of America and may be unlawful in other territories.

Clause 3.7   This warranty to an extent reinforces the warranty contained in clause 3.1. There may be circumstances where it may be appropriate for a Publisher to reduce the scope of a warranty by limiting it to the Berne Convention and to the Universal Copyright Convention only so far as concerns any initial period of copyright protection in the Universal Copyright Convention.

Clause 3.8   The importance of copyright notices is examined in paragraphs 4.9 and 4.10.

Clause 3.9   Before being liable to make any payment to the Owner the Publisher will wish to satisfy itself that the Owner actually does own the rights of copyright which it is purporting to sell. This provision requires the Owner to deliver documentary proof of its title (or ownership) of the rights. If satisfactory documentation is not delivered to the Publisher, the Publisher will have no liability to pay to the Owner any of the sums provided in clause 2. It will be noted that the operation of this provision will not suspend the assignment of rights effected pursuant to clause 1, which will remain vested in the Publisher who will not have any payment liability unless and until the condition in clause 3.8 is satisfied.

3.10   all statements purporting to be facts in the Work are true and correct and no advice recipe formula or instruction in the Work will if followed or implemented by any person cause loss damage or injury to them or any other person;

3.11   the Owner shall not disclose reveal or make public except to the professional advisers of the Owner any information whatever concerning the Work or the business of the Publisher or this Agreement all of which shall be strictly confidential nor shall the Owner make any public statement or press statement in connection with the foregoing or commit any act which might prejudice or damage the reputation of the Publisher or the successful exploitation of the Work;

3.12   the Owner undertakes to indemnify the Publisher and keep the Publisher at all times fully indemnified from and against all actions proceedings claims demands costs (including without prejudice to the generality of this provision the Publisher's legal costs on a solicitor and own client basis) awards damages however arising directly or indirectly as a result of any breach or non-performance by the Owner of any of the Owner's obligations undertakings or warranties in this Agreement

4.   DEFINITIONS AND INTERPRETATION

4.1   The following definitions apply in this Agreement:

"Author"
[*name*] of [*address*]

"Work"
The [literary or dramatic or musical or artistic] work written by the Author [tentatively] entitled "(*name*)" [a copy of which is annexed as Exhibit 1].

4.2   Any reference in this Agreement to any statute or statutory provision shall be construed as including a reference to that statute or statutory provision as from time to time amended modified extended or re-enacted whether before or after the date of this Agreement and to all statutory instruments orders and regulations for the time being made pursuant to it or deriving validity from it.

4.3   Unless the context otherwise requires words denoting the singular shall include the plural and vice versa and words denoting any one gender shall include all genders and words denoting persons shall include bodies corporate unincorporated associations and partnerships.

Clause 3.10   There are occasions where a Publisher and an Author will be liable for negligent misstatement (see paragraphs 9.34 and 9.35). An example of a matter which could give rise to liability for negligent misstatement would be the printing of an incorrect chemical formula in a school chemistry textbook (which could cause an explosion).

Clause 3.11   This provision imposes confidentiality obligations on the Owner – see paragraphs 1.5 to 1.12.

4.4 The word "copyright" means the entire copyright and design right subsisting under the laws of the United Kingdom and all analogous rights subsisting under the laws of each and every jurisdiction throughout the world.

5. MISCELLANEOUS

5.1 Nothing contained in this Agreement shall constitute or shall be construed as constituting a partnership or contract of employment between the parties.

5.2 Nothing contained in this Agreement shall constitute an undertaking on the part of the Publisher to publish the Work and if the Publisher elects not to publish the Work in no event shall the Author or the Owner be entitled to make any claim in respect of loss of opportunity to enhance the Author's or the Owner's reputation or loss of publicity or for any other reason whatever.

5.3 This Agreement and all representations obligations undertakings and warranties contained in it shall enure for the benefit of the successors and assignees of the parties.

5.4 This Agreement contains the full and complete understanding between the parties and supersedes all prior arrangements and understandings whether written or oral appertaining to the subject matter of this Agreement and may not be varied except by an instrument in writing signed by all the parties to this Agreement. The Owner acknowledges that no representations or promises not expressly contained in this Agreement have been made to the Owner by the Publisher or any of its servants agents employees members or representatives.

5.5 This Agreement shall be governed and construed in accordance with the laws of England and Wales whose courts shall be courts of competent jurisdiction.

Clause 5.1 Under English law if two parties carry on business in common with a view to profit and share profit, the arrangement is capable of being considered a partnership. This provision ensures that no partnership is created inadvertently, and also expressly excludes the possibility of an employment contract being created.

Clause 5.2 This clause expressly excludes the possibility of any claim by the Author for compensation for loss of opportunity to enhance the Author's reputation.

Clause 5.3 This provision gives the Publisher's successors, licensees and assignees the benefit of rights obtained by the Publisher and confirms the liability of the Author's estate in relation to the warranties and obligations of the Author.

Clause 5.4 There are occasions where oral agreements or other understandings may be created in relation to a Work which may contain either additional obligations or obligations which conflict with those set out in subsequent written agreement. This provision makes it clear that all previous arrangements and understandings are at an end and the contract is the only document relevant to the obligations and rights of the parties in relation to its subject matter. The final part of the clause expressly excludes the possibility of any liability of the Publisher for misrepresentation on the part of any of its servants, agents, employees or representatives (see paragraph 2.17).

Clause 5.5 Where a contract is made between two entities in England and Wales, it will generally not be necessary to insert a provision of this nature, but where a contract is to be created with a foreign company (or a company situate in Scotland or Northern Ireland) this provision should always be included.

IN WITNESS this Assignment has been duly executed as a Deed and is intended to be delivered and is delivered on the day month and year first above written.

EXECUTED AND DELIVERED
AS A DEED BY
[*Publisher*]
acting by [*a director and
its secretary*] [*two Directors*]

        Director
        Director/Secretary

SIGNED AND DELIVERED
AS A DEED BY
[*Author*]
in the presence of:

Witness' Signature _____
Name _____
Address _____
_____
Occupation _____

Testimonium Clause This clause begins with the words "IN WITNESS". This form of wording is appropriate for documents which are executed as deeds. The purpose of executing this Document as a deed is to ensure that the appointment by the Publisher as the attorney of the Author permits the Publisher to execute documents by way of deed.

Attestation clause This form of wording is appropriate for documents which are executed as deeds. The purpose of executing this Document as a deed is to ensure that the appointment by the Publisher as the attorney of the Author permits the Publisher to execute documents by way of deed. In practice, the execution of documents by way of deed is often not required.

EXHIBIT 1

Work

(Clause 4.1)

DOCUMENT 9

Assignment of reversionary copyright

[IMPORTANT NOTE: Please read the section "About this book" on page v, before copying or using this Document]

Purpose of this Document

The purpose of this Document is to permit a publisher to acquire from an author's estate any rights of copyright which may have reverted or may be liable to reversion pursuant to pre-June 1957 United Kingdom copyright legislation. If there are circumstances where this document appears to be relevant, specialist legal advice will probably be necessary.

Relevant text

The text of this Work contains a number of topics which are relevant to documents of this nature including:

- pre-June 1957 automatic recapture rights (paragraph 4.13)
- effect of recapture (paragraph 4.14)
- post-July 1912 partial reversions of copyright (paragraph 4.12)
- pre-1988 United Kingdom copyright legislation (paragraph 4.11)
- United States termination rights (paragraph 4.15)
- advice to publishers on reversion of copyright (paragraph 4.16)
- acquisition of copyright outside the United Kingdom (paragraph 4.17)
- directive 93/98 on the harmonisation of copyright (paragraph 17.11 and paragraphs 20.1 to 20.10)

From   :   *[Rights Owner(s)]*
                  of *[address]*

To   :   *[Publisher]*
                  of *[address]*

Dated   :   *[date]*

Dear Sir/Madam

"title" ("Work") by *"name"* ("Author")

In consideration of your undertaking of paragraph 2 I/We warrant confirm and agree with you as follows:

EITHER

1.1   By virtue of Clause *[number]* of the will of the Author dated *[date]* all rights of copyright in the Work and all moral rights conferred by Chapter IV of the Copyright, Designs and Patents Act 1988 ("Act") were by testamentary disposition bequeathed to me/us.

OR

1.1   The will of the Author made no provision for the testamentary disposition of the moral rights conferred by the Copyright, Designs and Patents Act 1988 ("Act") but pursuant to Clause *[number]* of the will of the Author dated *[date]* all rights of copyright in the Work were by testamentary disposition bequeathed to me/us and pursuant to the provisions of Section 95(1)(b) of the Act all moral rights in the Work vested in me/us.

OR

1.1   The Author died intestate and pursuant to Section 95 (1)(c) of the Copyright, Designs and Patents Act 1988 ("Act") all moral rights conferred by Chapter IV of the Act are exercisable by me/us as the personal representative(s) of the Author pursuant to *[specify method of appointment]* which vested in me/us all rights of copyright in the Work.

Clause 1.1 Publishers should obtain suitably qualified legal advice when producing and dealing with documents of this nature. The transmission of copyright by testamentary disposition or by operation of law sometimes creates intricate problems. Disregarding the fact that different rights of copyright may be owned by different persons, it is possible for one person to own the copyright in the Work, whilst another person owns the moral rights, and yet another person owns the actual manuscript. The alternative provisions merely constitute guidelines as to the possible alternatives.

1.2   I/We irrevocably and unconditionally waive all rights to which I/we are entitled pursuant to the Copyright, Designs and Patents Act 1988 Sections 77 80 84 and 85 and any other moral rights provided for under the laws now or in future in force in any part of the world and now assign to you your successors and assigns absolutely the whole of the reversionary interest in the copyright in the Work throughout the world for the full period of copyright protection including all renewals reversions and extensions now or in the future existing under the laws in force in any part of the world and warrant that I am/we are the sole absolute unincumbered legal and beneficial owner(s) of the same.

2.   [*Insert remuneration provisions*]

Yours faithfully

Signed by [*name of Rights Owner(s)*]

I/We confirm and agree the above and agree to be bound by it.

Signed by [*name of officer*]
for and on behalf of [*name of Publisher*]

Clause 1.2 This clause provides a waiver of moral rights and a warranty as to ownership. Moral rights are examined in paragraphs 5.1 to 5.22. The reasons why Publishers should obtain waivers of moral rights are set out in paragraph 7.8. An explanation of the legal meaning of the term "warranty" is provided in paragraph 7.15.

Clause 2 It is difficult to provide guidelines for the remuneration provisions which it might be appropriate to include in an assignment of reversionary copyright. If a publisher is securing the right to continue to exploit a work for its final 25 (or 45) year period of copyright protection, then it would presumably be appropriate for the publisher to offer to pay either whatever royalty was originally offered to the author during his or her lifetime, or the publisher's current standard royalty provisions, together with some advance payment. Where a publisher is dealing with the estate of an author, there will also be other matters which might advantageously be dealt with which might assist the publisher in increasing interest in an author's work, such as the availability of papers, authorisation of official biographies and other matters.

DOCUMENT 10

Contributor's agreement

[IMPORTANT NOTE: Please read the section "About this book" on page v, before copying or using this Document]

Purpose of this Document

The purpose of this Document is to provide a form of engagement for a contributor to a work of multi-contributorship.

Relevant text

The text of this Work covers a number of topics which are relevant to documents of this nature including:

- general matters relating to authors' agreements (paragraphs 7.2 to 7.4)
- copyright and moral rights (paragraphs 7.5 to 7.8)
- specific provisions in authors' agreements (paragraphs 7.9 to 7.19)
- minimum terms agreements (paragraphs 7.20 to 7.22)
- acquiring rights generally (paragraphs 1.13 to 1.16)
- factors to be considered in relation to acquiring rights (paragraphs 1.17 to 1.21)
- commercial terms of offers (paragraphs 1.22 and 1.23)
- the law of contract and agency (paragraphs 2.1 to 2.30)
- creation, existence and transfer of copyrights and trade marks (paragraphs 3.1 to 3.45)
- international copyright protection (paragraphs 4.1 to 4.17)
- moral rights (paragraphs 5.1 to 5.22)
- permissions, fair dealings and rights clearances (paragraphs 8.1 to 8.44)
- liability for content (paragraphs 9.1 to 9.49)
- buying and selling rights (paragraphs 11.1 to 11.29)
- infringement and enforcement (paragraphs 13.1 to 13.17)
- termination and recapture (paragraphs 14.1 to 14.10)
- competition law (paragraphs 16.1 to 16.28)
- multimedia (Chapter 19)

Document 10   *Contributor's agreement*

From   :   [*Publisher*]
                       of [*address*]
                       ("Publisher")

To   :   [*Contributor*]
                       of [*address*]
                       ("Contributor")

Dated [*date*]

Dear [*Name of Contributor*]

<u>"*Name of Work*" ("Work")</u>

This letter sets out the terms and conditions which have been agreed between the Publisher and the Contributor in relation to the inclusion by the Publisher in the Work of certain materials written by the Contributor for inclusion in the Work.

1.   CONTRIBUTION

1.1   The Contributor undertakes to write not less than [*number*] words on the subject of [*subject*] (the "Contribution") in accordance with the outline annexed as Exhibit 1.

1.2   The Contributor undertakes to deliver to the Publisher two copies of a clearly typed legible typescript of the Contribution by no later than [*date*] in accordance with the Publisher's Guidelines for Contributors attached as Exhibit 2.

1.3   The Contributor undertakes to obtain all necessary releases and permissions in a form satisfactory to the Publisher signed by all relevant persons in relation to any material included in the Contribution where rights of copyright or other rights are vested in third parties.

Preamble   The opening paragraph clarifies the fact that the material written by the Contributor has been specifically written for the purpose of inclusion in the Work. The significance of this is explained in the annotation to Clause 1.4.

Clause 1.1   This clause should identify the subject matter of the Contribution and the number of words. The clause also permits the Contribution to be more tightly defined by referring to previous correspondence between the Contributor and the Publisher which may contain an outline of the proposed Contribution.

Clause 1.2   This clause contains a provision for the delivery date of the Contribution. It should be noted that time is not of the essence for the performance of the Contributor's obligation (see paragraph 2.10). It is, however, possible for the Publisher to make time of the essence of the agreement if the Contributor fails to deliver the Contribution by the specified date on giving reasonable notice to the Contributor. This provision also allows for incorporation of Publisher's guidelines as to style etc which may be incorporated.

Clause 1.3   Although the obligation to obtain all necessary releases and permissions is imposed on the Contributor, the Publisher will be liable in the event that adequate release documentation is not obtained. For this reason the Publisher should instigate and follow rights clearance procedures – see paragraph 8.44 and Document 30.

430

1.4   The Contributor undertakes to co-operate and collaborate with [*name*] or such other person as the Publisher may from time to time nominate as the General Editor of the Work and undertakes that the Publisher and/or the General Editor shall have the right from time to time to amend the Contribution or require the Contribution to be amended by the Contributor so as to reflect the reasonable requirements of the Publisher and the General Editor.

2.   FEE

The Publisher undertakes to pay to the Contributor the sum of £[*amount*] which shall be payable:

(a)   As to £[*amount*] on signature of this Agreement;

(b)   As to £[*amount*] on delivery by the Contributor to the Publisher of the Contribution in accordance with this Agreement;

(c)   As to £[*amount*] within three months from publication of the Work.

3.   RIGHTS

3.1   The Contributor assigns to the Publisher the entire copyright whether vested contingent or future in the Contribution and all rights of action and all other rights of whatever nature in the Contribution whether now known or in the future created to which the Contributor is now or may at any time after the date of this Agreement be entitled by virtue of or pursuant to any of the laws in force in any part of the world excluding only the rights reserved by the Contributor pursuant to paragraph 3(b) TO HOLD the same to the Publisher its successors assignees and licensees absolutely for the whole period of such rights for the time being capable of being assigned by the Contributor together with any and all renewals reversions and extensions throughout the world.

3.2   The Contributor reserves the right to use reproduce and adapt the Contribution in the course of the Contributor's activities as a [*state profession*] and subject to the provisions of paragraph 3.3 reserves the non-exclusive right to authorise the use reproduction and adaptation of the Contribution by any third party.

3.3   The Contributor shall not make available or authorise any third party to make available the Contribution for publication in any work which is

---

Clause 1.4   This clause provides for the Contributor to co-operate and collaborate with the General Editor and other persons nominated by the Publisher. The clause specifically confirms that the General Editor and other persons may amend the Contribution. It will be noted that the Document does not provide for any waiver of moral rights on the part of the Contributor. This is not an omission. If the Contribution was written for the purpose of publication in a collective work, or made available for such purpose, the Contributor will have no statutory right to be identified or to object to derogatory treatment (see paragraphs 5.9 and 5.12).

Clause 3.1   This clause assigns to the Publisher the entire copyright in the Contribution throughout the world subject only to rights reserved to the Contributor pursuant to clause 3.2.

Clause 3.2   This reservation specifically permits the Contributor to use the Contribution in the course of the Contributor's professional activities and also gives the Contributor the non-exclusive rights to authorise reproduction and adaptation subject to compliance with the conditions set out in clause 3.3.

concerned with the same subject matter as the Work and which competes directly with the Work provided this restriction shall cease to apply if the Work is not first published for any reason on or before [*specify date*] or if the Work shall be out of print or fail to appear in the Publisher's catalogue for a continuous period of six months.

4.   PUBLICATION

4.1   It is the intention of the Publisher to publish the Contribution as part of the Work and if such publication takes place it shall be at the sole cost and expense of the Publisher. It is understood and agreed that nothing contained in this Agreement shall constitute an undertaking by the Publisher to publish either the Contribution or the Work and if the Publisher elects not to publish either the Contribution or the Work the Contributor shall not be entitled to make any claim in respect of loss of opportunity to enhance the reputation or loss of publicity or for any other reason whatever.

4.2   The Contributor undertakes to read check and correct all proofs of the Contribution sent to the Contributor by the Publisher and to return them to the Publisher within 14 days from receipt. If the Contributor does not within such time notify the Publisher of any corrections which may be required to be made the Publisher shall be entitled to proceed with publication of the Contribution in the Work and such non-notification shall be deemed to constitute further approval by the Contributor of the Contribution for the purposes of this Agreement.

4.3   Subject to the provisions of paragraphs 4.1 and 5.2 the Publisher undertakes that if the Contribution is published in the Work the Contributor shall receive an appropriate credit in accordance with the Publisher's current practice on the [contents page] of the Work [and at the beginning of the Contribution]. The Contributor acknowledges that the Contribution has been written and/or made available for the purpose of inclusion in the Work and that the Work is a collective work of reference which is intended to be updated on a continual and ongoing basis. For the avoidance of doubt the Contributor agrees with the Publisher that all updated contributions sections editions and revisions to the Work and/or the Contribution shall (together with all original material) be deemed to constitute one single collective work of reference.

Clause 3.3   Reference should be made to paragraph 7.2 for matters which should be considered in relation to restrictions on authors.

Clause 4.1   This provision clarifies the fact that if the Contribution is not published for any reason the Publisher will not incur any liability to the Contributor.

Clause 4.2   This clause provides for a shorter period of proofing than that normally required for a complete book. Additionally it provides for a default approval procedure. If a Publisher does not hear from the Contributor the Contribution is deemed approved.

Clause 4.3   This clause sets out the Contributor's contractual entitlement to a credit. It also contains wording clarifying the fact that the Contribution and any updated contributions or editions of the Work is considered by the parties to constitute one single collective work of reference. As has been noted above (see the note to clause 1.4) the right to be identified, and the right to object to derogatory treatment do not apply in relation to collective works.

4.4   The Publisher undertakes to provide to the Contributor [*number*] copies of the Work on first publication of the Work for the personal use of the Contributor and not for resale.

5.   UPDATING

5.1   The Contributor undertakes to advise the Publisher if any part of the Contribution is affected by technological or commercial or legislative developments which might make it necessary or advisable for the Contribution to be amended altered or updated. The Contributor undertakes to make all necessary alterations to the Contribution in accordance with such time schedule and in consideration of such updating fee as may be agreed between the Publisher and the Contributor.

5.2   If the Publisher and the Contributor fail to reach agreement as to the schedule for any updating or as to the amount of the appropriate fee or if the Contributor fails to update the material within such time as the Publisher considers reasonable then the Publisher shall have the right to engage another contributor to update revise and add to the Contribution and shall accord to such other person and the Contributor such respective authorship credits as the Publisher in its discretion considers appropriate.

6.   CONTRIBUTOR'S WARRANTIES

The Contributor represents warrants undertakes and agrees with the Publisher as follows:

6.1   the Contributor is the sole author of the Contribution and the sole unincumbered absolute legal and beneficial owner of all rights of copyright and all other rights whatever in the Contribution throughout the world and is and shall remain at all material times during the writing of the Contribution a "qualifying person" within the meaning of the Copyright, Designs and Patents Act 1988 Section 154;

6.2   the Contributor has not assigned or incumbered or licensed or transferred or otherwise disposed of any rights of copyright or any other rights in

---

Clause 5.1   This provision permits the Contributor to suggest updating and revision of the Work.

Clause 5.2   This clause protects the Publisher from having a section of the Work which is seriously out of date and which the original Contributor refuses or neglects to update. This clause permits the Publisher to engage another contributor to update any out-of-date contribution and permits the Publisher to adjust the credit provisions between the parties.

Clause 6.1   This provision is necessary to confirm that the Contributor is the sole Contributor of the Work and that no other persons own it (see paragraphs 3.14, 3.23 and 3.24) and that the Work qualifies for copyright protection. For further explanation of the purpose of this clause reference should be made to the notes to clause 10.1 of Document 4. Where the Contributor is an employee and the Contribution is written during the course of the Contributor's employment, the copyright will belong to the Contributor's employer (see paragraph 3.22) who will need to be made a party to the arrangement. It will be noted that the right to be identified and the right to object to derogatory treatment do not apply to works created in the course of employment (see paragraphs 5.9(d) and 5.12(d)).

or to the Contribution except pursuant to this Agreement and has not entered into any agreement or arrangement which might conflict with the Publisher's rights under this Agreement or might interfere with the performance by the Contributor of the Contributor's obligations under this Agreement;

6.3   the Contribution is original to the Contributor and does not and shall not infringe any right of copyright moral right or right of privacy or right of publicity or personality or any other right whatever of any person;

6.4   the Contribution is not under the laws of any jurisdiction obscene or blasphemous or offensive to religion or defamatory of any person and does not contain any material which has been obtained in violation of the Interception of Communications Act 1985 the Official Secrets Act 1989 or any analogous foreign legislation and nothing contained in the Contribution would if published constitute a contempt of court;

6.5   all statements purporting to be facts in the Contribution are true and correct and no advice recipe formula or instruction in the Contribution will if followed or implemented by any person cause loss damage or injury to them or any other person;

6.6   the Contributor undertakes to indemnify the Publisher and keep the Publisher at all times fully indemnified from and against all actions proceedings claims demands costs (including without prejudice to the generality of this provision the legal costs of the Publisher on a solicitor and own client basis) awards damages however arising directly or indirectly as a result of any breach or non-performance by the Contributor of any of the Contributor's undertakings warranties or obligations under this Agreement.

Clause 6.2   Although clause 6.1 protects the Publisher by ensuring that copyright subsists in the Work, it is also necessary to ensure that the rights of copyright are owned by the Contributor, which is what clause 6.2 provides. The warranty assures the Publisher that the Contributor has not incumbered the Work (by mortgaging it or charging it) or licensed rights in the Work to third parties.

The provision also assures the Publisher that the Contributor has not entered into any other agreement or arrangement which might interfere with the Publisher's rights under the agreement. An option granted by the Contributor to another publisher would interfere with the Publisher's rights, for example. There may be circumstances where it will be appropriate for publishers to remind authors of the extent of matters covered by this warranty and other warranties in this agreement.

Clause 6.3   Infringement of copyright, moral rights, rights of privacy or rights of publicity or personality could lead to legal liability on the part of the Publisher, which this provision seeks to exclude. There may be occasions when it will be useful for Publishers to give guidance to Contributors on matters relating to infringement. It is certainly good practice for Publishers themselves to double-check material and ensure non-infringement and non-violation, since the legal costs of prevention are generally less than those incurred in trying to remedy a situation.

Clause 6.4   This warranty is designed to eliminate any liability on the Publisher's part for the matters examined in Chapters 9 and 10.

Clause 6.5   There are occasions where a Publisher and an Author will be liable for negligent misstatement (see paragraphs 9.34 and 9.35).

Clause 6.6   The extent to which it is appropriate for a Publisher to impose indemnity obligations on Contributors is a matter which should be given very careful thought for the reasons set out in paragraph 7.15.

7.   MISCELLANEOUS

7.1   Nothing contained in this Agreement shall constitute or shall be construed as constituting a partnership or contract of employment between the parties.

7.2   This Agreement and all representations obligations undertakings and warranties contained in it shall enure for the benefit of and shall be binding on the personal representatives heirs and beneficiaries of the Contributor and their successors and assigns and shall be binding upon the successors and assigns of the Publisher.

7.3   This Agreement contains the full and complete understanding between the parties and supersedes all prior arrangements and understandings whether written or oral appertaining to the subject matter of this Agreement and may not be varied except by an instrument in writing signed by all the parties to this Agreement. The Contributor acknowledges that no representations or promises not expressly contained in this Agreement have been made to the Contributor by the Publisher or any of its servants agents employees members or representatives.

7.4   This Agreement shall be governed and construed in accordance with the laws of England and Wales whose courts shall be courts of competent jurisdiction.

SIGNED by [*name of officer*] ⎫
for and on behalf of   ⎬
[*name of Publisher*]   ⎭

I confirm and agree the above and agree to be bound by it.

SIGNED by [*Contributor*] ⎫
the Contributor   ⎬
                           ⎭

Clause 7.1   Under English law, if two parties carry on business in common with a view to profit and share profit, the arrangement is capable of being considered a partnership. This provision ensures that no partnership is created inadvertently and also expressly excludes the possibility of an employment contract being created.

Clause 7.2   This provision gives the Publisher's successors, licensees and assignees the benefit of rights obtained by the Publisher and confirms the liability of the Contributor's estate in relation to the warranties and obligations of the Contributor.

Clause 7.3   There are occasions where oral agreements or other understandings may be created in relation to a Work which may contain either additional obligations or obligations which conflict with those set out in subsequent written agreement. This provision makes it clear that all previous arrangements and understandings are at an end and the contract is the only document relevant to the obligations and rights of the parties in relation to its subject matter. The final part of the clause expressly excludes the possibility of any liability on the part of a Publisher for misrepresentation on the part of any of its servants, agents, employees or representatives.

Document 10 *Contributor's agreement*

EXHIBIT 1
Outline

EXHIBIT 2
Publisher's Guidelines for Contributors

DOCUMENT 11

General editor's agreement

Purpose of this Document

This Document provides a suitable form of engagement for a general editor of a collective work. The form provides for the general editor both to render consultation and editing services and to contribute a section of text to the work.

Relevant text

The text of this Work covers a number of topics which are relevant to documents of this nature including:

- general matters relating to authors' agreements (paragraphs 7.2 to 7.4)
- copyright and moral rights (paragraphs 7.5 to 7.8)
- specific provisions in authors' agreements (paragraphs 7.9 to 7.19)
- minimum terms agreements (paragraphs 7.20 to 7.22)
- acquiring rights generally (paragraphs 1.13 to 1.16)
- factors to be considered in relation to acquiring rights (paragraphs 1.17 to 1.21)
- commercial terms of offers (paragraphs 1.22 and 1.23)
- the law of contract and agency (paragraphs 2.1 to 2.30)
- creation, existence and transfer of copyrights and trade marks (paragraphs 3.1 to 3.45)
- international copyright protection (paragraphs 4.1 to 4.17)
- moral rights (paragraphs 5.1 to 5.22)
- permissions, fair dealings and rights clearances (paragraphs 8.1 to 8.44)
- liability for content (paragraphs 9.1 to 9.49)
- buying and selling rights (paragraphs 11.1 to 11.29)
- infringement and enforcement (paragraphs 13.1 to 13.17)
- termination and recapture (paragraphs 14.1 to 14.10)
- competition law (paragraphs 16.1 to 16.28)
- multimedia (Chapter 19)

From : [*Publisher*]
        of [*address*]
        ("Publisher")

To : [*General Editor*]
        of [*address*]
        ("General Editor")

Dated   [*date*]

Dear [*Name of General Editor*]

"Name of Work" ("Work")

This letter sets out the terms and conditions which have been agreed between the Publisher and the General Editor in relation to the inclusion by the Publisher in the Work of certain materials written by the General Editor for inclusion in the Work.

1.   CONTRIBUTION

1.1   The Publisher engages the General Editor to render in relation to the Work such services ("Services") as are required by the Publisher and are normally rendered by general editors of works of a similar nature to the Work. The General Editor accepts such engagement and undertakes to provide the Services to the Publisher in collaboration with such persons as shall be nominated by the Publisher and in accordance with such reasonable publication schedule for the Work as may be specified by the Publisher in consultation with the General Editor.

1.2   The General Editor acknowledges that the Publisher shall have sole control of all matters in relation to the production and publication of the Work including without limitation editorial production print runs numbers of reprints and editions marketing pricing advertising distribution and terms of sale.

1.3   The Services of the General Editor shall include but not be limited to:

(a)   the selection of topics which may be suitable for inclusion in the Work and the choice of Contributors ("Contributors") for such topics;

Preamble   The opening paragraph clarifies the fact that the material written by the General Editor has been specifically written for the purpose of inclusion in the Work. The significance of this is explained in the annotation to Clause 1.2.

Clause 1.1   This clause provides for the engagement of the services of the General Editor which are to be rendered in accordance with the directions of the Publisher in line with the production schedule for the Work.

Clause 1.2   It will be noted that the document does not provide for any waiver of moral rights on the part of the General Editor. This is not an omission. If the Text (as defined in Clause 1.7) was written for the purpose of publication in a collective work, the Contributor will have no statutory right to be identified or to object to derogatory treatment (see paragraphs 5.9 and 5.12)

(b)   advising on the content and quality of all contributions ("Contributions") made to the Work by Contributors and making recommendations as to updating and other matters relating to the Work;

(c)   advising and assisting the Contributors on their Contributions but without assuming any liability for their respective Contributions;

(d)   attending meetings of the editorial board;

(e)   co-ordinating the delivery of all Contributions;

(f)   supervising the correction of all proofs for the Work.

1.4   The General Editor undertakes to write not less than [*number*] words on the subject of [*subject*] ("General Editor's Contribution") in accordance with the outline annexed as Exhibit 1.

1.5   The General Editor undertakes to deliver to the Publisher two copies of a clearly typed legible typescript of the General Editor's Contribution by no later than [*date*] in accordance with the Publisher's Guidelines for Contributors attached as Exhibit 2.

1.6   The General Editor undertakes to obtain all necessary releases and permissions in a form satisfactory to the Publisher signed by all relevant persons in relation to any material included in the General Editor's Contribution where rights of copyright or other rights are vested in third parties.

1.7   For the purposes of this Agreement the General Editor's Contribution and the remaining product of the Services of the General Editor pursuant to this Agreement are together referred to as the "Text".

2.   REMUNERATION

The Publisher undertakes to pay to the General Editor:

2.1   an advance of £[*amount*] which shall be recoupable from royalties payable to the General Editor under this Agreement;

Clause 1.3   This clause itemises the services which may be required of a General Editor and will need to be reviewed or revised to take account of the appropriate circumstances.

Clause 1.4   This clause should identify the subject matter of the General Editor's Contribution and the number of words. The clause also permits the Contribution to be more tightly defined by referring to previous correspondence between the General Editor and the Publisher which may contain an outline of the proposed Contribution.

Clause 1.5   This clause contains a provision for the delivery date of the General Editor's Contribution. It should be noted that time is not of the essence for the performance of the General Editor's obligation (see paragraph 2.10). It is, however, possible for the Publisher to make time of the essence of the agreement if the General Editor fails to deliver the General Editor's Contribution by the specified date on giving reasonable notice to the General Editor. This provision also allows for incorporation of Publisher's guidelines as to style etc which may be incorporated.

Clause 1.6   Although the obligation to obtain all necessary releases and permissions is imposed on the General Editor, the Publisher will be liable in the event that adequate release documentation is not obtained. For this reason the Publisher should instigate and follow rights clearance procedures – see paragraph 8.44 and Document 30.

Clause 1.7   The Publisher needs to obtain rights of copyright in relation to the product of the services of the General Editor (improvements and alterations made to the Contributions of other Contributors) and also to the General Editor's Contribution itself. The definition of text is inserted for the sake of brevity in the copyright assignment clause and warranties later in the Document.

2.2   a royalty of [*percentage*]% of all sums received by the Publisher from copies of the Work sold by the Publisher or where the work is exploited by the Publisher's licensees [*percentage*]% of sums received by the Publisher from its licensees.

3.   RIGHTS

3.1   The General Editor assigns to the Publisher the entire copyright whether vested contingent or future in the Text and all rights of action and all other rights of whatever nature in the Text whether now known or in the future created to which the General Editor is now or may at any time after the date of this Agreement be entitled by virtue of or pursuant to any of the laws in force in any part of the world excluding only the rights reserved by the General Editor pursuant to paragraph 3.2 TO HOLD the same to the Publisher its successors assignees and licensees absolutely for the whole period of such rights for the time being capable of being assigned by the General Editor together with any and all renewals reversions and extensions throughout the world.

3.2   The General Editor reserves the right to use reproduce and adopt the Text in the course of the General Editor's activities as a [*state profession*] and subject to the provisions of paragraph 3.3 reserves the non-exclusive right to authorise the use reproduction and adaptation of the Text by any third party.

3.3   The General Editor shall not make available or authorise any third party to make available the Text for publication in any work which is concerned with the same subject matter as the Work and which competes directly with the Work provided this restriction shall cease to apply if the Work is not first published for any reason on or before [*specify date*] or if the Work shall be out of print or fail to appear in the Publisher's catalogue for a continuous period of six months.

4.   PUBLICATION

4.1   It is the intention of the Publisher to publish the Text as part of the Work and if such publication takes place it shall be at the sole cost and expense of the Publisher. It is understood and agreed that nothing contained in this Agreement shall constitute an undertaking by the Publisher to publish either the Text or the Work and if the Publisher elects not to publish either the Text or the Work the General Editor shall not be entitled to make any claim

---

Clause 3.1   This clause assigns to the Publisher the entire copyright in the text throughout the world subject only to rights reserved to the General Editor pursuant to clause 3.2.

Clause 3.2   This reservation specifically permits the General Editor to use the Contribution in the course of the General Editor's professional activities and also gives the General Editor the non-exclusive rights to authorise reproduction and adaptation subject to compliance with the conditions set out in clause 3.3.

Clause 3.3   Reference should be made to paragraph 7.2 for matters which should be considered in relation to restrictions on authors.

in respect of loss of opportunity to enhance the reputation or loss of publicity or for any other reason whatever.

4.2 The General Editor undertakes to read check and correct all proofs of the Text and all other Contributions to the Work which are sent to the General Editor by the Publisher and to return them to the Publisher within 14 days from receipt. If the General Editor does not within such time notify the Publisher of any corrections which may be required to be made the Publisher shall be entitled to proceed with publication of the Text in the Work and such non-notification shall be deemed to constitute further approval by the General Editor of the Text and other Contributions for the purposes of this Agreement.

4.3 Subject to the provisions of paragraph 4.1 the Publisher undertakes that if the Text is published in the Work the General Editor shall receive an appropriate credit in accordance with the Publisher's current practice on the cover and the title page of the Work [and at the beginning of the General Editor's Contribution]. The General Editor acknowledges that the Text has been written and/or made available for the purpose of inclusion in the Work and that the Work is a collective work of reference which is intended to be updated on a continual and ongoing basis. For the avoidance of doubt the General Editor agrees with the Publisher that all updated texts sections editions and revisions to the Work and/or the Text shall (together with all original material) be deemed to constitute one single collective work of reference.

4.4 The Publisher undertakes to provide to the General Editor [*number*] copies of the Work on first publication of the Work for the personal use of the General Editor and not for resale.

5. UPDATING

5.1 The General Editor undertakes to advise the Publisher if any part of the Text is affected by technological or commercial or legislative developments which might make it necessary or advisable for the Text or any other contributions to the Work to be amended altered or updated. The General Editor undertakes to make all necessary alterations to the Text and to procure that suitable persons update all other parts of the Work in accordance with such time schedule and in consideration of such updating fee as may be agreed between the Publisher and the General Editor.

Clause 4.1 This provision clarifies the fact that if the Contribution is not published for any reason the Publisher will not incur any liability to the General Editor.

Clause 4.2 This clause provides for a shorter period of proofing than that normally required for a complete book. Additionally it provides for a default approval procedure. If a Publisher does not hear from the General Editor the Contribution is deemed approved.

Clause 4.3 This clause sets out the General Editor's contractual entitlement to a credit. It also contains wording clarifying the fact that the Contribution and any updated Contributions or editions of the Work are considered by the parties to constitute one single collective work of reference. As has been noted above (see the note to clause 1.2) the right to be identified, and right to object to derogatory treatment, do not apply in relation to collective works.

Clause 5.1 This provision permits the General Editor to suggest updating and revision of the Work.

5.2   If the Publisher and the General Editor fail to reach agreement as to the schedule for any updating or as to the amount of the appropriate fee or if the General Editor fails to update or procure the updating of the Work within such time as the Publisher considers reasonable then the Publisher shall have the right to engage another General Editor to update revise and add to the Text and the Work and shall accord to such other person and the General Editor such respective authorship and editorship credits as the Publisher in its discretion considers appropriate.

6.   GENERAL EDITOR'S WARRANTIES

The General Editor represents warrants undertakes and agrees with the Publisher as follows:

6.1   the General Editor is the sole author of the Text and the sole unincumbered absolute legal and beneficial owner of all rights of copyright and all other rights whatever in the Text throughout the world and is and shall remain at all material times during the writing of the Text a "qualifying person" within the meaning of the Copyright, Designs and Patents Act 1988 Section 154;

6.2   the General Editor has not assigned or incumbered or licensed or transferred or otherwise disposed of any rights of copyright or any other rights in or to the Text except pursuant to this Agreement and has not entered into any agreement or arrangement which might conflict with the Publisher's rights under this Agreement or might interfere with the performance by the General Editor of the General Editor's obligations under this Agreement;

6.3   the Text is original to the General Editor and does not and shall not infringe any right of copyright moral right or right of privacy or right of publicity or personality or any other right whatever of any person;

Clause 5.2   This clause protects the Publisher from having a section of the Work which is seriously out of date and which the original General Editor refuses or neglects to update. This clause permits the Publisher to engage another General Editor to update any out-of-date Contribution and permits the Publisher to adjust the credit provisions between the parties.

Clause 6.1   This provision is necessary to confirm that the General Editor is the sole General Editor of the Work and that no other persons own it (see paragraphs 3.14, 3.23 and 3.24) and that the Work qualifies for copyright protection. For further explanation of the purpose of this clause reference should be made to the notes to clause 10.1 of Document 4. Reference should also be made to the annotation to Clause 6.1 of Document 10.

Clause 6.2   Although clause 6.1 protects the Publisher by ensuring that copyright subsists in the Work, it is also necessary to ensure that the rights of copyright are owned by the General Editor, which is what clause 6.2 provides. The warranty assures the Publisher that the General Editor has not incumbered the Work (by mortgaging it or charging it) or licensed rights in the Work to third parties.

The provision also assures the Publisher that the General Editor has not entered into any other agreement or arrangement which might interfere with the Publisher's rights under the agreement. An option granted by the General Editor to another Publisher would interfere with the Publisher's rights, for example. There may be circumstances where it will be appropriate for publishers to remind authors of the extent of matters covered by this warranty and other warranties in this agreement.

Clause 6.3   Infringement of copyright, moral rights, rights of privacy or rights of publicity could lead to legal liability on the part of the Publisher, which this provision seeks to exclude. There may be occasions when it will be useful for Publishers to give guidance to General Editors on matters relating to infringement. It is certainly good practice for Publishers themselves to double-check material and ensure non-infringement and non-violation, since the legal costs of prevention are generally less than those incurred in trying to remedy a situation.

6.4   the Text is not under the laws of any jurisdiction obscene or blasphemous or offensive to religion or defamatory of any person and does not contain any material which has been obtained in violation of the Interception of Communications Act 1985 the Official Secrets Act 1989 or any analogous foreign legislation and nothing contained in the Text would if published constitute a contempt of court;

6.5   all statements purporting to be facts in the Text are true and correct and no advice recipe formula or instruction in the Text will if followed or implemented by any person cause loss damage or injury to them or any other person;

6.6   the General Editor undertakes to indemnify the Publisher and keep the Publisher at all times fully indemnified from and against all actions proceedings claims demands costs (including without prejudice to the generality of this provision the legal costs of the Publisher on a solicitor and own client basis) awards damages howsoever arising directly or indirectly as a result of any breach or non-performance by the General Editor of any of the General Editor's undertakings warranties or obligations under this Agreement.

7.   ACCOUNTS

7.1   The Publisher shall keep full books and records relating to the payment of sums due to the General Editor pursuant to this Agreement and shall prepare and submit to the General Editor within 90 days from 30 June and 31 December of each year a statement of account in relation to all sums payable to the General Editor during the preceding six-month period. Each such statement of account shall be accompanied by a cheque in favour of the General Editor in the amount shown to be due.

7.2   The Publisher shall have the right to deduct and retain from payments to the General Editor all sums required to be deducted or retained by way of withholding or other tax pursuant to the laws of any country. In the event that the remittance of royalties to the General Editor is prohibited by reason of exchange control restrictions in any part of the world the Publisher shall if requested by the General Editor deposit the amount of any sums due to the General Editor in an account in the name of the General Editor situate in the country in question subject to the payment or reimbursement by the General Editor to the Publisher of the administrative costs incurred in so doing.

Clause 6.4   This warranty is designed to eliminate any liability on the Publisher's part for the matters examined in Chapters 9 and 10.

Clause 6.5   There are occasions where a Publisher and an Author will be liable for negligent misstatement (see paragraphs 9.34 and 9.35).

Clause 6.6   The extent to which it is appropriate for a Publisher to impose indemnity obligations on General Editors is a matter which should be given very careful thought for the reasons set out in paragraph 7.15.

Clause 7.2   A number of countries require withholding taxes to be deducted from royalties and this provision enables the Publisher to deduct such sums from royalty payments to the General Editor. The second part of the clause provides a mechanism for effecting payment to a General Editor from any country which imposes exchange control restrictions, by permitting the appropriate sum to be deposited in a bank account in the General Editor's name in the territory.

7.3   If any bona fide claim shall be made in relation to the Work or any of the matters relating to the General Editor's warranties pursuant to this Agreement the Publisher shall be entitled without prejudice to any of its rights under this Agreement to suspend payment of the advance and/or the royalties payable under this Agreement or to retain such sums by way of reserve as the Publisher considers appropriate until the withdrawal or settlement to the satisfaction of the Publisher and its insurers of such claim.

7.4   Value Added Tax shall to the extent applicable be payable in addition to the sums payable to the General Editor under this agreement subject to the production and delivery by the General Editor to the Publisher of a full accurate and correct Value Added Tax invoice bearing the General Editor's Value Added Tax registration number and country prefix accompanied by sufficient proof of the veracity of such details as the Publisher may request.

8.   TERMINATION AND SUSPENSION

The Publisher shall be entitled by giving notice to the General Editor to suspend this Agreement by notice in writing (or terminate this Agreement 30 days from notice of suspension) if:

8.1   the General Editor fails or refuses to perform any of the Services or is in breach of any obligations undertakings or warranties contained in this Agreement;

8.2   the General Editor has been prevented from performing the Services or is deemed by the Publisher unable to perform the Services by reason of any illness injury or otherwise.

9.   EFFECT OF SUSPENSION AND TERMINATION

9.1   The period of suspension shall be the remainder of the duration of the event in Clause 8 in relation to which notice was given plus any time required by the Publisher in order to resume the use of the Services.

9.2   During the period of suspension the Publisher will be relieved of any obligation to remunerate the General Editor and the dates for future payment obligations shall be extended by a period equivalent to the length of suspension.

Clause 7.3   This provision permits the Publisher to suspend payment obligations on the occurrence of any adverse claim in relation to the Work. It should be noted that the provision is not as onerous as an indemnity provision, since it applies only to sums payable by the Publisher to the General Editor, instead of requiring indemnity payments from the General Editor to the Publisher.

Clause 7.4   There are circumstances where provision should be made for Value Added Tax (see paragraph 11.28) and where it may be appropriate for self billing arrangements to be made (see paragraph 12.26).

Clause 8   Although the Publisher will have common law rights of rescission of a contract (see paragraph 14.4) this clause provides that the Publisher may suspend the engagement of the General Editor by notice in writing if the General Editor fails or refuses to perform the services or is otherwise in breach or is incapacitated.

Clause 9   The effect of suspension or subsequent termination of the Agreement is to relieve the Publisher from the obligations to use the General Editor's services, but not to relieve the Publisher of the assignment of the rights or the warranties given by the General Editor.

9.3   During a period of suspension or after termination the General Editor shall continue to comply with all obligations not affected by suspension or termination and the Publisher shall remain entitled to all rights granted or assigned to the Publisher by the General Editor and the entire product of the Services.

10.   DISPUTES RESOLUTION

10.1   If either party is of the opinion that the other party in this agreement is in breach of any material condition or obligation pursuant to this Agreement including without prejudice any obligation to pay money (but excluding any matter referred to in Clause 10.4) such dispute shall be dealt with in accordance with the alternative dispute resolution procedure set out in this clause.

10.2   The Publisher and the General Editor undertake that they shall endeavour in good faith to resolve any dispute or claim arising in relation to the Work or this Agreement by means of good faith negotiations which shall take place between the General Editor and a senior executive of the Publisher who shall have authority to settle the dispute. If the dispute is not resolved within [14] days from commencement of good faith negotiations the Publisher and the General Editor shall endeavour in good faith to resolve the dispute through an alternative dispute resolution procedure carried out in accordance with the recommendations of the Centre for Dispute Resolution.

10.3   All negotiations in relation to the matters in dispute shall be strictly confidential and shall be without prejudice to the rights of the General Editor and the Publisher in any future proceedings. If the parties fail to reach an agreement which finally resolves all matters in dispute within 60 days of having commenced negotiations pursuant to the alternative dispute resolution procedure or if such negotiations fail to take place within 30 days from the date specified in Clause 10.2 then either party shall be entitled:

(a)   to refer the matter to a single arbiter agreed upon by the Publisher and the General Editor whose decision shall be final and binding on the parties; or

(b)   to seek such legal remedies as may be appropriate.

10.4   [The provisions of Clauses 10.1 to 10.3 shall not apply in relation to the provisions of Clauses 5 or 8 or in relation to any dispute or claim which involves a third party.]

Clause 10   Many publishing agreements provide for resolution of disputes by arbitration. Arbitration is slow, ineffective and costly. Recently some publishing agreements have provided for resolution by arbitration through the Publishers' Association. There may be circumstances where General Editors or Publishers do not wish the Publishers' Association to become involved in (or even know about) certain disputes. Clauses 10.1 to 10.4 of this document provide for a quick, effective, cheap and private means of resolution of disputes.

11.   MISCELLANEOUS

11.1   Nothing contained in this Agreement shall constitute or shall be construed as constituting a partnership or contract of employment between the parties.

11.2   This Agreement and all representations obligations undertakings and warranties contained in it shall enure for the benefit of and shall be binding on the personal representatives heirs and beneficiaries of the General Editor and their successors and assigns and shall be binding upon the successors and assigns of the Publisher.

11.3   This Agreement contains the full and complete understanding between the parties and supersedes all prior arrangements and understandings whether written or oral appertaining to the subject matter of this Agreement and may not be varied except by an instrument in writing signed by all the parties to this Agreement. The General Editor acknowledges that no representations or promises not expressly contained in this Agreement have been made to the General Editor by the Publisher or any of its servants agents employees members or representatives.

11.4   This Agreement shall be governed and construed in accordance with the laws of England and Wales whose courts shall be courts of competent jurisdiction.

SIGNED by [*name of officer*]
for and on behalf of
[*name of Publisher*]

I confirm and agree the above and agree to be bound by it.

SIGNED by
[*name of General Editor*]

Clause 11.2   This provision gives the Publisher's successors, licensees and assignees the benefit of rights obtained by the Publisher and confirms the liability of the General Editor's estate in relation to the warranties and obligations of the General Editor.

Clause 11.3   There are occasions where oral agreements or other understandings may be created in relation to a Work which may contain either additional obligations or obligations which conflict with those set out in subsequent written agreement. This provision makes it clear that all previous arrangements and understandings are at an end and the contract is the only document relevant to the obligations and rights of the parties in relation to its subject matter. The final part of the clause expressly excludes the possibility of any liability of the Publisher for misrepresentation on the part of any of its servants, agents, employees or representatives.

EXHIBIT 1

The Outline

EXHIBIT 2

Publisher's Guidelines for Contributors

DOCUMENT 12

Artwork commissioning form

[IMPORTANT NOTE: Please read the section "About this book" on page v, before copying or using this Document]

Purpose of this Document

The purpose of this Document is to provide a simple form of commissioning agreement suitable for use by a Publisher for commissioning artwork, illustrations and other materials. The form is designed in such a way as to enable the insertion of relevant details for artwork, delivery materials, fee and other commissions. The Agreement incorporates a number of other standard provisions which might be suitable for incorporation on the reverse of a printed standard form of engagement. It will be noted that the copyright in the commissioned work remains with the Contributor. This retention of ownership of copyright is, however, subject to the grant of exclusive rights to the Publisher in the agreement.

Relevant text

The text of this Work contains a number of topics which are relevant to documents of this nature including:

- acquiring rights (paragraphs 1.17 to 1.21)
- copyright in artistic works (paragraph 3.6)
- transfers of copyright (paragraphs 3.38 to 3.40)
- moral rights (paragraphs 5.1 to 5.22)
- permissions and rights clearances (paragraphs 8.1 to 8.44)

Artwork commissioning form

[*name*]
of [*address*
              ]
(the "Publisher")

[*name*]
of [*address*
              ]
(the "Contributor")

Dated [*date*]

The Contributor agrees to produce the Commissioned Artwork and deliver to the Publisher the Materials by the Delivery Date and the Contributor grants the Publisher on an exclusive basis the Licensed Rights in the Commissioned Artwork upon the terms and conditions of the attached Artwork Commissioning Standard Provisions which are incorporated in this Commissioning Form.

The Publisher agrees to pay the Contributor the Fee and confirms that subject to the grant of Licensed Rights the copyright in the Commissioned Artwork shall remain with the Contributor.

1. COMMISSIONED ARTWORK:
   Description: [*insert details*]

2. DELIVERY DATE: [*insert date*]

3. MATERIALS: [*insert description*]

4. LICENSED RIGHTS:
   The [sole and exclusive] right to use publish and/or reproduce the Commissioned Artwork in any and all media.

5. FEE:
   [*amount*] payable [*instalment date*]

6. OTHER CONDITIONS: [See Exhibit 1] [OR None]

The Contributor confirms and agrees the Contributor's acceptance of the above terms and confirms the Contributor's agreement and acceptance of the attached Artwork Commissioning Standard Provisions which the Contributor has read and understood.

SIGNED by [*name of officer*]
for and on behalf of
[*name of Publisher*]

SIGNED by
[*name of Contributor*]

Artwork commissioning standard provisions

1.   PUBLISHER'S UNDERTAKINGS

1.1   The Publisher shall pay to the Contributor the Fee on the dates specified in the Commissioning Form subject to the delivery by the Contributor to the Publisher of the Commissioned Artwork and the Materials on the Delivery Date and subject to the performance and observance by the Contributor of the obligations and warranties on the part of the Contributor contained in these Standard Provisions.

1.2   The Fee shall be inclusive of all expenses incurred by the Contributor to enable the Contributor to produce or deliver the Commissioned Artwork and the Materials including without limitation the cost and expense of all transportation porterage duplication and hire of equipment facilities and personnel.

1.3   The Publisher shall pay Value Added Tax on the Fee (where appropriate) subject to the delivery to the Publisher of a full complete and accurate Value Added Tax invoice.

2.   CONTRIBUTOR'S UNDERTAKINGS

The Contributor warrants undertakes and agrees with the Publisher that:

2.1   the Commissioned Artwork shall be original to the Contributor and shall not have been previously published or exploited and shall not under the laws in force in any part of the world be obscene libellous blasphemous or offensive to religion and shall not infringe any right of copyright design right moral right right of privacy right of publicity or personality or any other right whatever of any third party;

2.2   the Contributor shall be the sole author of the Commissioned Artwork and the sole absolute unincumbered legal and beneficial owner of all rights of copyright and other rights in and to the Commissioned Artwork but the Publisher shall own all physical materials which this Agreement provides are to be delivered to the Publisher;

Clause 1.1   The obligation of the Publisher to pay the Contributor is conditional on delivery of the materials on the Delivery Date and subject to the performance and observance by the Contributor of its other obligations.

Clause 1.2   This provision prevents the Contributor from delivering the Publisher invoices for additional items of expenditure.

Clause 2   The legal meaning of the expression "warranty" is examined in paragraph 7.15.

Clause 2.1   The warranty as to originality extends also to prior publication or exploitation. A Publisher will normally wish to ensure that the commissioned material is new. The warranty also covers usual matters such as obscenity and libel etc. It will be noted that these matters are defined not under United Kingdom law (as many agreements provide) but under the laws in any part of the world.

Clause 2.2   This warranty extends not only to ownership of the rights of copyright and other rights in the artwork but also to ownership of physical materials which will pass to the Publisher.

2.3   property and title in and to all Materials shall pass to the Publisher automatically on their delivery to the Publisher;

2.4   unless expressly indicated to the contrary in the Artwork Commissioning Form the Licensed Rights granted to the Publisher in respect of the Commissioned Artwork shall be granted on a sole and exclusive basis and shall extend throughout the world for the full period of copyright including all renewals reversions and extensions and may be exercised on any number of occasions in any and all media by any manner or means without any restrictions or limitations by the Publisher and the Publisher's assignees or licensees;

2.5   all authors of any copyright works included in the Commissioned Artwork and/or the Materials or from which the same may directly or indirectly be derived have irrevocably and unconditionally waived all rights which they may now have or which they may in future be entitled to pursuant to the provisions of the Copyright Designs and Patents Act 1988 Sections 77 80 84 and 85 and any other moral rights legislation now existing or which may in future be enacted in any part of the world;

2.6   the Publisher its assignees and licensees shall have the right to cut transpose adapt add to delete from and/or alter in any way the Commissioned Artwork;

2.7   the Publisher shall not be under any obligation to use or exploit the Commissioned Artwork and if the Publisher in its sole discretion decides not to do so the Contributor shall not have any claim against the Publisher for loss of opportunity to enhance the Contributor's reputation or for any other reason whatever and shall not be entitled to payment of any sum other than the Fee to the extent the same falls to be paid;

2.8   the Fee shall be full and final consideration in respect of all rights granted to the Publisher and no further sums shall be payable in connection with the use of the Commissioned Artwork by the Publisher its assignees or licensees. If any part of the Fee is expressed to be conditional on acceptance of the Commissioned Artwork by the Publisher then such part shall not be payable if the Publisher in its entire discretion decides not to accept the Commissioned Artwork whether or not any reason for such decision is given by the Publisher;

Clause 2.4   This clause states the territorial extent and the duration of the Publisher's rights. It may be advisable to bring this to the attention of the Contributor in order to prevent any misunderstanding.

Clause 2.5   This provision is a waiver of moral rights. In those circumstances where an absolute waiver is not acceptable a compromise position may be found along the lines explained in paragraph 7.8 and set out in Document 4 clauses 2.3, 2.4 and 2.5.

Clause 2.6   There may be circumstances where a Contributor will seek to subject the Publisher's rights under this clause to an obligation not to infringe any moral right of the Contributor. If the Publisher accepts such an obligation, it might have the effect of severely limiting its ability to exploit the commissioned artwork.

Clause 2.7   The inclusion of this provision rebuts any suggestion that the Publisher has undertaken to publish the Commissioned Artwork irrespective of its quality (see paragraph 1.22).

2.9   the Contributor shall keep the terms of this Agreement the Fee and any information relating to the Publisher strictly confidential and shall not disclose the same to any third parties;

2.10   the Contributor undertakes to indemnify the Publisher and to keep the Publisher fully and effectively indemnified from and against all actions proceedings claims demands costs (including without prejudice the legal costs of the Publisher on a solicitor and own client basis) awards and damages however arising directly or indirectly as a result of any breach or non-performance by the Contributor of any of the Contributor's warranties obligations or undertakings.

3.   <u>MISCELLANEOUS</u>

3.1   Nothing contained in this Agreement shall constitute a partnership or contract of employment between the Publisher and the Contributor.

3.2   Words and phrases in these Standard Conditions shall be construed in accordance with the material particulars of the Commissioning Form to which they are attached and the word "Agreement" shall mean any such Commissioning Form in which these Standard Provisions are incorporated.

3.3   The provisions of the Agreement shall be governed by and construed in accordance with the laws of England and Wales whose courts shall be courts of competent jurisdiction.

Clause 2.10   The extent to which it is appropriate for a Publisher to impose indemnity obligations on Contributors is a matter which should be given very careful thought for the reasons set out in paragraph 7.15.

Clause 3.1   Under English law if two parties carry on business in common with a view to profit and share profit, the arrangement is capable of being considered a partnership. This provision ensures that no partnership is created inadvertently, and also expressly excludes the possibility of an employment contract being created.

Clause 3.3   Where a contract is made between two entities in England and Wales, it will generally not be necessary to insert a provision of this nature, but where a contract is to be created with a foreign company (or a company situate in Scotland or Northern Ireland) this provision should always be included.

DOCUMENT 13

Photograph commissioning form

[IMPORTANT NOTE: Please read the section "About this book" on page v, before copying or using this Document]

Purpose of this Document

The purpose of this Document is to provide a simple form of commissioning agreement suitable for use by a publisher for commissioning photographs. The form is designed in such a way as to enable the insertion of relevant details for photographs, delivery materials, fee and other commissions. The agreement incorporates a number of other standard provisions which might be suitable for incorporation on the reverse of a printed standard form of engagement. It will be noted that the copyright in the commissioned work shall remain with the contributor. This retention of ownership of copyright is, however, subject to the grant of exclusive rights to the publisher in the agreement.

Relevant text

The text of this Work contains a number of topics which are relevant to documents of this nature including:

- acquiring rights (paragraphs 1.17 to 1.21)
- copyright in photographs (paragraphs 3.26 and 3.27)
- copyright in artistic works (paragraph 3.6)
- transfers of copyright (paragraphs 3.38 to 3.40)
- moral rights (paragraphs 5.1 to 5.22)
- permissions and rights clearances (paragraphs 8.1 to 8.44)

Photograph commissioning form

[*name*]
of [*address*
             ]
(the "Publisher")

[*name*]
of [*address*
                  ]
(the "Photographer")

Dated [*date*]

The Photographer agrees to produce the Commissioned Photographic Work and deliver it to the Publisher together with the Materials by the Delivery Date and the Photographer grants to the Publisher on an exclusive basis the Licensed Rights in the Commissioned Photographic Work upon the terms and conditions of the attached Photograph Commissioning Standard Provisions which are incorporated in this Photograph Commissioning Form.

The Publisher agrees to pay the Photographer the Fee and confirms that subject to the grant of Licensed Rights the copyright in the Commissioned Photographic Work shall remain with the Photographer.

1. COMMISSIONED PHOTOGRAPHIC WORK:
   Description: [*insert details*]

2. DELIVERY DATE: [*insert date*]

3. MATERIALS: [*insert details*]

4. LICENSED RIGHTS:
   The [sole and exclusive] right to use publish and/or reproduce the Commissioned Photographic Work in any and all media.

5. FEE:
   [*amount*] payable [*instalment date*]

6. OTHER CONDITIONS: [See Exhibit 1] [OR None]

The Photographer confirms and agrees the Photographer's acceptance of the above terms and confirms the Photographer's agreement and acceptance of the attached Photograph Commissioning Standard Provisions which the Photographer has read and understood.

SIGNED by [*name of officer*]
for and on behalf of
[*name of Publisher*]

SIGNED by
[*name of Photographer*]

454

Photograph commissioning standard provisions

1. PUBLISHER'S UNDERTAKINGS

1.1 The Publisher shall pay to the Photographer the Fee on the dates specified in the Commissioning Form subject to the delivery by the Photographer to the Publisher of the Commissioned Photographic Work and the Materials on the Delivery Date and subject to the performance and observance by the Photographer of the obligations and warranties on the part of the Photographer contained in these Standard Provisions.

1.2 The Fee shall be inclusive unless otherwise agreed of all expenses incurred by the Photographer to enable the Photographer to produce or deliver the Commissioned Photographic Work and the Materials including without limitation the cost and expense of all photographic film development enlarging printing processing transportation porterage hire of equipment facilities and personnel.

1.3 The Publisher shall pay Value Added Tax on the Fee (where appropriate) subject to the delivery to the Publisher of a full complete and accurate Value Added Tax invoice.

2. PHOTOGRAPHER'S UNDERTAKINGS

The Photographer warrants undertakes and agrees with the Publisher that:

2.1 the Commissioned Photographic Work shall be original to the Photographer and shall not have been previously published or exploited in any part of the world and shall not be obscene libellous blasphemous or offensive to any religion and shall not infringe any right of copyright moral right right of privacy right of publicity or personality or any other right whatever of any third party;

2.2 the Photographer shall be the sole author of the Commissioned Photographic Work and the sole absolute unincumbered legal and beneficial owner of all rights of copyright and other rights in and to the Commissioned Photographic Work but the Publisher shall own all physical Materials which this Agreement provides are to be delivered to the Publisher;

Clause 1.1 The obligation of the Publisher to pay the Photographer is conditional on delivery of the materials on the Delivery Date and subject to the performance and observance by the Photographer of its other obligations.

Clause 1.2 This provision prevents the Photographer from delivering the Publisher invoices for additional items of expenditure.

Clause 2 The legal meaning of the expression "warranty" is examined in paragraph 7.15.

Clause 2.1 The warranty as to originality extends also to prior publication or exploitation. A Publisher will normally wish to ensure that the commissioned material is new. The warranty also covers usual matters such as obscenity and libel etc. It will be noted that these matters are defined not under United Kingdom law (as many agreements provide) but under the laws in any part of the world.

Clause 2.2 This warranty extends not only to ownership of the rights of copyright and other rights in the photographs but also to ownership of physical materials which will pass to the Publisher.

2.3   property and title in and to all Materials shall pass to the Publisher automatically on their delivery to the Publisher;

2.4   unless expressly indicated to the contrary in the Photograph Commissioning Form the Licensed Rights granted to the Publisher in respect of the Commissioned Photographic Work shall be granted on a sole and exclusive basis and shall extend throughout the world for the full period of copyright including all renewals reversions and extensions and may be exercised on any number of occasions in any and all media by any manner or means without any restrictions or limitations by the Publisher and the Publisher's assignees or licensees;

2.5   all authors of any copyright works included in the Commissioned Photographic Work and/or the Materials or any materials from which the same may directly or indirectly be derived and all persons who are featured in or may have commissioned the Commissioned Photographic Work and/or the Materials have irrevocably and unconditionally waived all rights which they may now have or which they may in future be entitled to pursuant to the provisions of the Copyright, Designs and Patents Act 1988 Sections 77 80 and 84 and any other moral rights legislation which may in future be enacted in any part of the world;

2.6   unless expressly indicated to the contrary in the Agreement the Publisher its assigns and licensees shall have the right to reprint the Commissioned Photographic Work in other publications in any language;

2.7   the Publisher shall not be under any obligation to use or exploit the Commissioned Photographic Work and if the Publisher in its sole discretion decides not to do so the Photographer shall not have any claim against the Publisher for loss of opportunity to enhance the Photographer's reputation or for any other reason whatever and shall not be entitled to payment of any part of the Fee which falls to be paid for the Commissioned Photographic Work;

2.8   where any part of the Commissioned Photographic Work or Materials consists of films or photographs their use by the Publisher shall not infringe or violate any right of privacy conferred by the Copyright, Designs and Patents Act 1988 Section 85 or any right of privacy or any right of publicity or any other right of any person whatever;

2.9   the Fee shall be full and final consideration in respect of all rights

Clause 2.4   This clause states the territorial extent and the duration of the Publisher's rights. It may be advisable to bring this to the attention of the Photographer in order to prevent any misunderstanding.

Clause 2.5   This provision is a waiver of moral rights. In those circumstances where an absolute waiver is not acceptable a compromise position may be found along the lines explained in paragraph 7.8 and set out in Document 4 clauses 2.3, 2.4 and 2.5.

Clause 2.7   The inclusion of this provision rebuts any suggestion that the Publisher undertook to publish the photographic works irrespective of its quality (see paragraph 1.22).

Clause 2.8   A right of privacy exists in favour of the commissioner of photographs or films taken for private and domestic purposes on or after 1 August 1989. The consent of such persons is required for the exploitation of such films or photographs (see paragraph 5.15).

granted to the Publisher and no further sums shall be payable in connection with the use of the Commissioned Photographic Work by the Publisher its assignees or licensees. If any part of the Fee is expressed to be conditional on acceptance of the Commissioned Photographic Work by the Publisher then such part shall not be payable if the Publisher in its entire discretion decides not to accept the Commissioned Photographic Work whether or not any reason for such decision is given by the Publisher;

2.10   the Photographer shall keep the terms of this Agreement the Fee and any information relating to the Publisher strictly confidential and shall not disclose the same to any third parties;

2.11   the Photographer shall deliver to the Publisher written consents from all persons featured in the Commissioned Photographic Work in such form as shall be approved by the Publisher;

2.12   the Photographer undertakes to indemnify the Publisher and to keep the Publisher fully and effectively indemnified from and against all actions proceedings claims demands costs (including without prejudice the legal costs of the Publisher on a solicitor and own client basis) awards and damages however arising directly or indirectly as a result of any breach or non-performance by the Photographer of any of the Photographer's warranties obligations or undertakings.

3.   MISCELLANEOUS

3.1   Nothing contained in the Agreement shall constitute a partnership or contract of employment between the Publisher and the Photographer.

3.2   Words and phrases in these Standard Conditions shall be construed in accordance with the material particulars of the Commissioning Form to which they are attached and the word "Agreement" shall mean any such Commissioning Form in which these Standard Provisions are incorporated.

3.3   The provisions of the Agreement shall be governed by and construed in accordance with the laws of England and Wales whose courts shall be courts of competent jurisdiction.

Clause 2.11   This provision requires the Photographer to obtain all necessary permissions and releases from persons featured in the Commissioned Photographic Work (see paragraphs 8.2 to 8.44 and Documents 16 to 30).

Clause 2.12   The extent to which it is appropriate for a Publisher to impose indemnity obligations on photographers is a matter which should be given very careful thought for the reasons set out in paragraph 7.15.

Clause 3.1   Under English law if two parties carry on business in common with a view to profit and share profit, the arrangement is capable of being considered a partnership. This provision ensures that no partnership is created inadvertently and also expressly excludes the possibility of an employment contract being created.

Clause 3.3   Where a contract is made between two entities in England and Wales, it will generally not be necessary to insert a provision of this nature, but where a contract is to be created with a foreign company (or a company situate in Scotland or Northern Ireland) this provision should always be included.

DOCUMENT 14

Picture researcher's agreement

[IMPORTANT NOTE: Please read the section "About this book" on page v, before copying or using this Document]

Purpose of this Document

The purpose of this Document is to provide a standard form letter of engagement between a publisher and a picture researcher. The form of the letter will, of course, require adjustment to reflect the precise nature of the services which the picture researcher is to perform but will provide a basic guideline.

Relevant text

The text of this Work contains a number of topics which are relevant to documents of this nature including:

- acquiring rights (paragraphs 1.17 to 1.21)
- copyright in photographs (paragraphs 3.26 and 3.27)
- copyright in artistic works (paragraph 3.6)
- transfers of copyright (paragraphs 3.38 to 3.40)
- moral rights (paragraphs 5.1 to 5.22)
- permissions and rights clearances (paragraphs 8.1 to 8.44)

From   :   [*Publisher*] of [*address*] ("Publisher")

To   :   [*Picture Researcher*] of [*address*] ("Picture Researcher")

Dated   :   [*date*]

Dear [*Name of Picture Researcher*]

"*Name of Work*" ("Work")

This letter sets out the terms and conditions which have been agreed between the Publisher and the Picture Researcher in relation to the inclusion in the Work of certain picture materials which are to be obtained by the Picture Researcher for inclusion in the Work.

1.   ENGAGEMENT OF SERVICES

1.1 The Publisher engages the Picture Researcher to render in relation to the Work such services ("Services") as are required by the Publisher and are normally rendered by Picture Researchers in relation to publications of a similar nature to the Work. The Picture Researcher accepts such engagement and undertakes to provide the Services to the Publisher in accordance with the Production Schedule for the Work specified by the Publisher.

1.2 The Services of the Picture Researcher shall include but not be limited to the performance by the Picture Researcher of the following services:

(a)   the Picture Researcher shall undertake all necessary research in order to identify and procure the supply by third parties of photographic materials complying with the Publisher's requirements and suitable for inclusion in the Work ("Picture Material") which shall be not less than [*minimum number*] and not more than [*maximum number*] pictures of [*specify description*] which are intended to comprise not less than [*minimum number*] and not more than [*maximum number*] pages of [*specify format*] which Picture Material shall be supplied to the Publisher on colour transparencies or in CD-ROM format;

(b)   the Picture Researcher shall check all Picture Material on receipt and ensure that it is undamaged and that it satisfies the Publisher's quality requirements for which purpose the Picture Researcher shall use all appropriate magnification means and processes;

Preliminary paragraph This engagement relates to one particular Work. There is no reason, however, why the form should not relate to a series of Works or where the period of the engagement should not be specified by reference to a particular period of time.

Clause 1.1 In this clause the Publisher engages the services of the Picture Researcher to provide services in accordance with the Publisher's production schedule. It should be noted that the letter agreement does not create a contract of employment (see clause 6.1).

(c)   the Picture Researcher shall ensure that all Picture Material received is safely stored and at all times adequately protected and shall ensure that the whereabouts of all such material is at all times recorded in writing and that where Picture Material is supplied to third parties who are not engaged by the Publisher adequate receipts are obtained by the Picture Researcher for all Picture Material supplied loaned or otherwise transferred;

(d)   the Picture Researcher shall provide full background information in relation to all Picture Material obtained by the Picture Researcher for the purpose of inclusion in the Work and shall if requested supply captions and descriptions for all such Picture Material;

(e)   the Picture Researcher shall ensure that all Picture Material is adequately identified and shall ensure that the identity of all owners of rights of copyright and/or moral rights and any other rights in relation to such Picture Material is established beyond doubt and recorded in writing in such manner as may be acceptable to the Publisher;

(f)   the Picture Researcher shall negotiate with all relevant third parties appropriate rights fees in relation to the use of the Picture Material in accordance with the Publisher's requirements and shall obtain from such parties executed clearances and permissions in relation to the use of the Picture Material which documents shall be in such form as may be acceptable to the Publisher;

(g)   the Picture Researcher shall keep a full and accurate record of all credit obligations which are required to be accorded to third parties in relation to Picture Material supplied to the Publisher;

(h)   the Picture Researcher shall agree with [*name*] or such other person as may be nominated by the Publisher the selection of all Picture Material to be used in the Work and shall return all surplus Picture Material to its owners taking all due care to ensure its safe and undamaged return to them;

(i)   the Picture Researcher shall supply all selected Picture Material to the Publisher's production department in accordance with the Publisher's Production Schedule and shall check and amend proofs of all such selected material and following the approval by the Publisher's production department shall return all surplus original photographic material to the relevant suppliers;

(j)   the Picture Researcher shall prior to publication of the Work assemble a full and comprehensive list of all Picture Material used in the Work together with captions and descriptions where appropriate and together with copies of all executed permissions and the Picture Researcher shall check all such Picture Material to ensure that all contractual obligations in relation to published Picture Material have been complied with by the Publisher and that adequate permissions and consents in accordance with the Publisher's requirements have been obtained in writing in relation to all Picture Material included in the Work.

2.   FEE

The Publisher undertakes to pay to the Picture Researcher the sum of £[*amount*] which shall be payable:

(a)   as to £[*amount*] on signature of this Agreement;

(b)   as to £[*amount*] on delivery by the Picture Researcher to the Publisher of all material and information required to be delivered or provided by the Picture Researcher pursuant to this Agreement.

3.   RIGHTS

The Picture Researcher assigns to the Publisher the entire copyright whether vested contingent or future in the product of the Services of the Picture Researcher and all rights of action and all other rights of whatever nature in the product to the Services of the Picture Researcher whether now known or in the future created to which the Picture Researcher is now or may at any time after the date of this Agreement be entitled by virtue of or pursuant to any of the laws in force in any part of the world TO HOLD the same to the Publisher its successors and assignees absolutely for the whole period of such rights for the time being together with any and all renewals reversions and extensions throughout the world.

4.   TERMINATION AND SUSPENSION

The Publisher shall be entitled by giving notice to the Picture Researcher to suspend this Agreement by notice in writing (or terminate this Agreement 14 days from notice of suspension) if:

4.1   the Picture Researcher fails or refuses to perform any of the Services or is in breach of any obligations undertakings or warranties contained in this Agreement;

4.2   the Picture Researcher has been prevented from performing the Services or is deemed by the Publisher unable to perform the Services by reason of any illness injury or otherwise.

Clause 1.2 A number of specific services are identified in this clause. It may not always be appropriate for such services to be included. There may be additional services which a Publisher may wish the Picture Researcher to render and this clause should therefore be reviewed carefully. In particular it will be noted that certain obligations are imposed on the Picture Researcher in relation to the identification of owners of rights and the obtaining of clearances and permissions. It will not be appropriate in every case for services of this nature to be performed by a Picture Researcher and the Publisher should in any event ensure that the Publisher's rights clearance procedures (see paragraph 8.44 and Documents 16 to 30) contain provisions for the review of all documentation obtained by the Picture Researcher.

Clause 3 This clause assigns to the Publisher the entire copyright in the services of the Picture Researcher throughout the world.

Clause 4 Although the Publisher will have common law rights of rescission of a contract (see paragraph 14.4) this clause provides that the Publisher may suspend the engagement of the Picture Researcher by notice in writing if the Picture Researcher fails or refuses to perform the services or is otherwise in breach or is incapacitated.

5. EFFECT OF SUSPENSION AND TERMINATION

5.1   The period of suspension shall be the remainder of the duration of the event in Clause 4 in relation to which notice was given plus any time required by the Publisher in order to resume the use of the Services.

5.2   During the period of suspension the Publisher shall be relieved of any obligation to remunerate the Picture Researcher and the dates for future payment obligations shall be extended by a period equivalent to the length of suspension.

5.3   During any period of suspension or after termination the Picture Researcher shall continue to comply with all obligations not affected by suspension or termination and the Publisher shall remain entitled to all rights granted or assigned to the Publisher by the Picture Researcher and the entire product of the Services.

6. MISCELLANEOUS

6.1   Nothing contained in this Agreement shall constitute or shall be construed as constituting a partnership or contract of employment between the parties.

6.2   Neither party shall have any obligation to the other in the event of any act or omission on the part of such party where such act or omission results from the occurrence of any event which is outside the reasonable control of such party.

6.3   Nothing contained in this Agreement shall constitute an undertaking on the part of the Publisher to publish the Picture Material and if the Publisher elects not to publish the Picture Material in no event shall the Picture Researcher be entitled to make any claim in respect of loss of opportunity to enhance the Picture Researcher's reputation or loss of publicity or any other for any other reason whatever.

6.4   This Agreement and all representations obligations undertakings and

---

Clause 5   The effect of suspension or subsequent termination of the agreement is to relieve the Publisher from the obligations to use the Picture Researcher's services, but not to relieve the Publisher of the assignment of the rights or the warranties given by the Picture Researcher.

Clause 6.1   Under English law if two parties carry on business in common with a view to profit and share profit, the arrangement is capable of being considered a partnership. This provision ensures that no partnership is created inadvertently and also expressly excludes the possibility of an employment contract being created.

Clause 6.2   This provision gives the Publisher's successors, licensees and assigns the benefit of rights obtained by the Publisher and confirms the liability of the Picture Researcher's estate in relation to the warranties and obligations of the Picture Researcher.

Clause 6.3   There are occasions where oral agreements or other understandings may be created in relation to a Work which may contain either additional obligations or obligations which conflict with those set out in subsequent written agreement. This provision makes it clear that all previous arrangements and understandings are at an end and the contract is the only document relevant to the obligations and rights of the parties in relation to its subject matter. The final part of the clause expressly excludes the possibility of any liability of the Publisher for misrepresentation on the part of any of its servants, agents, employees or representatives.

warranties contained in it shall enure for the benefit of and shall be binding on the personal representatives heirs and beneficiaries of the Picture Researcher and their successors and assigns and shall be binding upon the successors and assigns of the Publisher.

6.5   This Agreement contains the full and complete understanding between the parties and supersedes all prior arrangements and understandings whether written or oral appertaining to the subject matter of this Agreement and may not be varied except by an instrument in writing signed by all the parties to this Agreement. The Picture Researcher acknowledges that no representations or promises not expressly contained in this Agreement have been made to the Picture Researcher by the Publisher or any of its servants agents employees members or representatives.

6.6   This Agreement shall be governed and construed in accordance with the laws of England and Wales whose courts shall be courts of competent jurisdiction.

SIGNED by [*name of officer*] ⎫
for and on behalf of   ⎬
[*Publisher*]   ⎭

I confirm and agree the above and agree to be bound by it.

SIGNED by
[*Picture Researcher*]

DOCUMENT 15

Translator's agreement

[IMPORTANT NOTE: Please read the section "About this book" on page v, before copying or using this Document]

Purpose of this Document

The purpose of this Document is to acquire rights in a translation from a translator. The precise rights to be acquired from the translator, the method of acquisition (assignment or licence), any terms on which the rights are acquired including editing of the translator's work will need to be conformed to the publisher's standard practice in these areas.

Relevant text

The text of this Work contains a number of topics which are relevant to documents of this nature including:

- general matters relating to authors' agreements (paragraphs 7.2 to 7.4)
- copyright and moral rights (paragraphs 7.5 to 7.8)
- specific provisions in authors' agreements (paragraphs 7.9 to 7.19)
- minimum terms agreements (paragraphs 7.20 to 7.22)
- acquiring rights generally (paragraphs 1.13 to 1.16)
- factors to be considered in relation to acquiring rights (paragraphs 1.17 to 1.21)
- commercial terms of offers (paragraphs 1.22 and 1.23)
- the law of contract and agency (paragraphs 2.1 to 2.30)
- creation, existence and transfer of copyrights and trade marks (paragraphs 3.1 to 3.45)
- international copyright protection (paragraphs 4.1 to 4.17)
- moral rights (paragraphs 5.1 to 5.22)
- permissions, fair dealings and rights clearances (paragraphs 8.1 to 8.44)
- liability for content (paragraphs 9.1 to 9.49)
- buying and selling rights (paragraphs 11.1 to 11.29)
- infringement and enforcement (paragraphs 13.1 to 13.17)
- termination and recapture (paragraphs 14.1 to 14.10)
- competition law (paragraphs 16.1 to 16.28)
- multimedia (Chapter 19)

THIS AGREEMENT is made the day of 199

BETWEEN

(1) *[Name]* LIMITED of *[address]* ("Publisher"); and

(2) *[Name]* of *[address]* ("Translator")

IT IS AGREED as follows:

1. THE WORK

1.1 The Publisher engages the Translator to prepare an original English language translation ("Translation") of the *[identify language]* language work entitled *[name of work]* ("Work") by *[name of author]* ("Author"). The Translator accepts such engagement and undertakes to prepare a faithful and accurate Translation in good literary English in a style appropriate to the style of the Work in the original language.

1.2 The Translator shall collaborate with the Author in order to clarify any questions of meaning or stylistic intention in relation to the Work and shall prepare a suitable introduction and suitable textual notes for the Translation or shall recommend a suitably qualified person who shall be engaged by the Publisher for such purpose. The Translator shall collaborate with any person engaged by the Publisher for the purpose of preparing any introduction or notes to the Translation and shall collaborate with the Publisher's commissioning editor and any other person nominated by the Publisher in order to ensure the creation and publication of a translation of the highest possible quality.

1.3 The Translator shall complete and deliver to the Publisher two copies of a clearly typed legible typescript of the Translation by no later than *[date]*. It shall be the responsibility of the Translator to keep duplicate copies of all material submitted to the Publisher and whilst the Publisher undertakes to take all reasonable steps to safeguard copies of the Translation in the Publisher's possession the Publisher shall have no liability for loss or destruction of any material submitted to it.

1.4 The Translator shall obtain releases or permissions in a form satis-

---

Clause 1.1 This provision requires the Translator to reflect the style and tone of the original in the translation. Normally a Publisher will have seen a sample translation, but where this is not the case, it should be understood that the Publisher will not be able to copy-edit the Translator's translation to put it into what the Publisher may consider to be a more popular English form, since this could amount to a derogatory treatment of the translation as well as a derogatory treatment of the original work, and an infringement of the copyright in the original work.

Clause 1.2 Although the first part of this clause is not normally found in translation agreements, where the original Author is still alive, it is common for the Translator to have some contact with the Author and corroboration, if not collaboration, is obviously desirable for all concerned. The preparation of an introduction and text may not always be appropriate, although if the work has any literary standing an introduction and notes may be required.

Clause 1.3 The delivery date needs to be inserted. Although the document does not provide that time is of the essence of the contract (see paragraph 2.10) it would be possible for the Publisher to make time of the essence if the Translator failed to deliver by the specified date. The Publisher would need to give the Translator a reasonable period of notice requiring the Translator to perform his or her obligations by the end of such period.

465

factory to the Publisher signed by all relevant persons in relation to all quotations and other third party material used in the introduction or notes to the Translation and shall deliver original or certified copies to the Publisher on the date referred to in Clause 1.3. If the Work is out of copyright and the Translator intends to base the Translation on a published edition of the Work which is protected by copyright the Translator shall obtain a release in a form satisfactory to the Publisher signed by the owners of copyright in the relevant edition and shall deliver an original or certified copy to the Publisher on the date referred to in Clause 1.3.

2.   EDITING CORRECTIONS AND TRANSLATOR'S CREDIT

2.1   The Translator shall read check correct and approve all proofs of the Translation submitted to the Translator by the Publisher and shall return to the Publisher clearly marked corrected proofs within 21 days from receipt [time being of the essence of this Clause]. The Translator shall bear the cost of all corrections and alterations to proofs other than printer's errors in excess of 10% of the cost of composition or typesetting of the Translation and the Publisher shall have the right to deduct such costs from any sums which may be payable to the Translator pursuant to this Agreement without prejudice to the Publisher's rights. If the amount of such extra costs exceeds the amount of Advances payable to the Translator pursuant to this Agreement the Translator shall within 30 days from demand by the Publisher pay to the Publisher the amount by which such extra costs exceed the Advances.

2.2   All copies of the Translation published by the Publisher shall contain the following copyright notice:

[conform to reflect copyright position determined by Clause 3]

2.3   The Translator asserts the Translator's right to be identified in relation to the Translation on the title page and cover in the following form:

[state form of identification required]

and the Publisher undertakes to comply with such request and to require all sub-publishers and other licensees to honour this right. The Translator

---

Clause 2.1   Time is made of the essence of this clause (see paragraph 2.10) because time is frequently critical during production schedules. The level beyond which the cost of correction is borne by the Translator is fixed at the conventional level of 10% although it may be appropriate to change this where electronic delivery material is provided by the Translator (see paragraphs 7.12 and 7.13).

Clause 2.2   The copyright notice should state the identity of the copyright owner. If copyright is assigned to the Publisher, the copyright owner will be the Publisher. If copyright is reserved to the Translator and the Translator grants an exclusive licence to the Publisher, the copyright owner will be the Translator. It is possible for the copyright owner in one country to be different from the copyright owner in another country (see paragraph 1.20). There are a number of other notices which traditionally appear on publications (see paragraph 4.9) and there are legal advantages to ensuring that the copyright information on publications is correct (see paragraphs 4.9 and 4.10). In some countries – notably the United States – there are strong advantages to registering copyright works in the relevant foreign copyright registry (see paragraph 4.7).

acknowledges that no casual or inadvertent failure by the Publisher or by any third party to comply with this provision shall constitute a breach by the Publisher of this Agreement and in the event of any breach of this Clause the Translator shall not have the right to seek injunctive relief and the sole remedy of the Translator shall be a claim for damages.

3. RIGHTS

3.1 The Translator grants to the Publisher sole and exclusive licence to print and/or publish the Translation in volume or sheet form in paperback or hardback format and the right to authorise others to do so throughout the [world or territory of specify] for the full period of copyright from time to time existing under the laws in force in any part of the world including all renewals reversions and extensions [or for the period commencing on the date of this Agreement and termination [*number*] years from the date specified in Clause 1.3.

3.2 The Publisher confirms that the following rights are reserved to the Translator:

(a) all reprographic rights in relation to the Translation (other than reprographic rights subsisting in relation to the typographical arrangement of the published edition of the Translation)

(b) all rights of the Translator in relation to the Translation pursuant to the Public Lending Right Act 1979 and any analogous legislation in any part of the world.

3.3 The Translator warrants to the Publisher that the Translator is a member in good standing of the Author's Lending and Copyright Society and warrants that the Author's Lending and Copyright Society and its overseas affiliated bodies (together with such other bodies as may be approved by both the Translator and Publisher in writing) shall have the exclusive right to authorise the reprographic exploitation of the Translation.

Clause 3.1 If the grant of the licence (which should be expressed to be sole and exclusive) is not for the full period of copyright then the period will need to be specified. There are certain limitations on exclusivity implied by European Union legislation (see particularly paragraph 16.15) whose provisions have important implications for Publishers. It is necessary to define the territorial extent of the Publishers rights (see paragraph 11.4). The provisions of this clause will not be suitable for all acquisitions of translation rights and alternative clauses are contained in Document 5.

Clause 3.2 Reprographic rights in relation to works may be the subject of licences granted by the Copyright Licensing Agency (see paragraph 6.17). Clause 3.2 reserves reprographic rights of the Translation to the Translator – in other words they are excluded from the rights granted under clause 3.1 – but in view of the confirmation contained in clause 3.3 (that the Translator is a member of the ALCS) and in view of the fact that all ALCS-controlled works are licensed by the Copyright Licensing Agency, the end result is that although the reprographic rights are reserved to the Translator initially they are subsequently transmitted to the Copyright Licensing Agency. If the Publisher is a member of the Copyright Licensing Agency, all reprographic rights in works controlled by the Publisher will be capable of administration by the CLA which will account for money collected in such a way that the Publisher and the ALCS receive 50% each. The Translator will be entitled to collect his or her share from the ALCS after the deduction of their administration expenses.

The rights of the Translator in relation to the Public Lending Right Act 1979 are set out in paragraph 6.16, and the reservation of these rights does not conflict with any of the Publisher's interests.

Clause 3.3 The effect of this clause is that although the Translator reserves reprographic rights, they are transmitted to the Copyright Licensing Agency which will account between Translator and Publisher on a 50/50 basis in relation to income collected (see note to clause 3.2 of this Document).

4. REMUNERATION

The Publisher undertakes to pay to the Translator:

4.1 An advance of £[*amount*] which shall be recoupable from royalties payable to the Translator under this Agreement;

4.2 A royalty of [*percentage*]% of all sums received by the Publisher from copies of the Translation sold by the Publisher or where the Translation is exploited by the Publisher's licensees [*percentage*]% of sums received by the Publisher from its licensees.

5. PUBLICATION

5.1 Subject to the Acceptance by the Publisher of the Translation and subject to the remaining provisions of this Agreement the Publisher undertakes to publish the Translation to the customary standard of the Publisher at the cost and expense of the Publisher.

5.2 It is the intention of the Publisher to print [*number*] copies of the Translation in [hard][paper] back format with an anticipated retail price of [*amount*] but nothing contained in this Clause 5.2 shall constitute an obligation on the part of the Publisher in relation to print run or pricing of the first or any subsequent edition of the Translation and the Translator acknowledges that the Publisher shall have sole control of all matters in relation to the production and publication of the Translation including without limitation print runs numbers of reprints and editions.

5.3 The Publisher shall provide the Translator with 12 free copies of the Translation on first publication in hardback format [and in the case of any paperback edition up to 20 free copies] and the Translator shall have the right to purchase additional further copies at a discount of [*percentage*]% of the Publisher's list price for the personal use of the Translator but not for resale purposes.

Clause 4.1 The remuneration provisions may need to be adjusted to reflect the circumstances. As to the amounts of advances payable and the percentages on which they are paid see paragraph 7.21 and clause 5 and accompanying notes to Document 4.

Clause 4.2 For guidance as to prevailing commercial practice of royalty rates reference should be made to paragraph 7.21 and to the provisions of clauses 6 and 7 of Document 4 and accompanying annotations. This clause may require further adjustment depending on the circumstances in order to provide for remuneration to the Translator in relation to Subsidiary Rights.

Paragraph 7.21 sets out current prevailing commercial practice in relation to Subsidiary Rights and reference should be made to the schedule to Document 4 and to clauses 9.1 to 9.3 of Document 4 and accompanying annotations.

Clause 5.1 The Publisher's obligation to publish the Translation is subject to acceptance by the Publisher of the Translation (see clause 7).

Clause 5.2 This clause requires the Publisher to state the intended print run and publication price. The statements will not bind the Publisher for the future and the clause makes it clear that the Publisher retains sole control over production matters.

Clause 5.3 The number of free copies of the Translation and the provisions relating to purchase of additional copies are matters on which the practice varies from Publisher to Publisher.

6. TRANSLATOR'S WARRANTIES

The Translator represents warrants undertakes and agrees with the Publisher as follows:

6.1   the Translator is the sole author of the Translation and the sole unincumbered absolute legal and beneficial owner of all rights of copyright and all other rights whatever in the Translation throughout the world and is and shall remain at all material times during the writing of the Translation a "qualifying person" within the meaning of the Copyright, Designs and Patents Act 1988 Section 154;

6.2   the Translator has not assigned or incumbered or licensed or transferred or otherwise disposed of any rights of copyright or any other rights in or to the Translation except pursuant to this Agreement and has not entered into any agreement or arrangement which might conflict with the Publisher's rights under this Agreement or interfere with the performance by the Translator of the Translator's obligations under this Agreement;

6.3   the Translation is original to the Translator and does not and shall not infringe any right of copyright moral right or right of privacy or right of publicity or personality or any other right whatever of any person;

6.4   copyright in the Translation is and shall throughout the full period of copyright protection be valid and subsisting pursuant to the laws of the United Kingdom and the United States of America and the provisions of the Berne Convention and Universal Copyright Convention;

6.5   the Translator undertakes to indemnify the Publisher and keep the Publisher at all times fully indemnified from and against all actions proceedings claims demands costs (including without prejudice to the generality of this provision legal costs of the Publisher on a solicitor and own client basis)

Clause 6.1   This provision is necessary to confirm that the Translator is the sole author of the Translation and that no other persons own it (see paragraphs 3.14, 3.23 and 3.24) and that the Translation qualifies for copyright protection.

For further explanation of the purpose of this clause reference should be made to the notes to clause 10.1 of Document 4.

Clause 6.2   Although clause 6.1 protects the Publisher by ensuring that copyright subsists in the Translation, it is also necessary to ensure that the rights of copyright are owned by the Translator, which is what clause 6.2 provides. The warranty assures the Publisher that the Translator has not encumbered the Translation (by mortgaging it or charging it) or licensed rights in the Translation to third parties.

The provision also assures the Publisher that the Translator has not entered into any other agreement or arrangement which might interfere with the Publisher's rights under the Agreement. An option granted by the Translator to another Publisher would interfere with the Publisher's rights, for example. There may be circumstances where it will be appropriate for Publishers to remind Translators of the extent of matters covered by this warranty, and other warranties in this agreement.

Clause 6.3   Infringement of copyright, moral rights, rights of privacy and rights of publicity or personality could lead to legal liability on the part of the Publisher, which this provision seeks to exclude. There may be occasions when it will be useful for Publishers to give guidance to Translators on matters relating to infringement. It is certainly good practice for Publishers themselves to double check material and ensure non-infringement and non-violation, since the legal costs of prevention are generally less than those incurred in trying to remedy a situation.

Clause 6.4   This warranty is designed to eliminate any liability on the Publisher's part for the matters examined in Chapters 9 and 10.

awards damages however arising directly or indirectly as a result of any breach or non-performance by the Translator of any of the Translator's undertakings warranties or obligations under this Agreement.

7.   ACCEPTANCE AND REJECTION

7.1   Following receipt of the typescript of the Translation and any revisions requested the Publisher agrees within a reasonable time after delivery of the typescript and revisions (such period to be determined by the Publisher in the light of its publication schedule and the other commitments of the Publisher and the Translator) to examine or procure the examination of the Translation and to give the Translator notice of acceptance ("Acceptance") or rejection of the Translation or to request the Translator to make such changes to the Translation as the Publisher considers appropriate.

7.2   If following the Publisher's request the Translator refuses or is unable to make such changes to the Translation as are satisfactory to the Publisher or if the Publisher shall have given notice of rejection of the Translation or if notwithstanding any prior Acceptance of the Translation the Publisher gives notice to the Translator that the Publisher considers that any material contained in the Work or the Translation might be actionable at law or might damage the Publisher's reputation or business interests or if an event beyond the control of the Publisher shall prevent or in the opinion of the Publisher render difficult or impossible the publication of the Translation the Publisher shall be released from all further obligations under this Agreement.

8.   ACCOUNTS

8.1   The Publisher shall keep full books and records relating to the payment of sums due to the Translator pursuant to this agreement and shall prepare and submit to the Translator within 90 days from 30 September and 31 December of each year a statement of account in relation to all sums payable to the Translator during the preceding six-month period. Each such statement of account shall be accompanied by a cheque in favour of the Translator in the amount shown to be due.

8.2   The Publisher shall have the right to deduct and retain from payments to the Translator all sums required to be deducted or retained by way of withholding or other tax pursuant to the laws of any country. In the event that the remittance of royalties to the Translator is prohibited by reason of exchange control restrictions in any part of the world the Publisher shall if requested by the Translator deposit the amount of any sums due to the Translator in an account in the name of the Translator situate in the country

---

Clause 6.5   The extent to which it is appropriate for a Publisher to impose indemnity obligations on Translators is a matter which should be given very careful thought for the reasons set out in Paragraph 7.15.

Clause 7.1   The obligation on the Publisher to publish the Translation in clause 3.1 is subject to the Translation being accepted by the Publisher. This clause requires the Publisher to examine the typescript and any revisions delivered by the Translator and advise the Translator whether such material is suitable for publication or not. No fixed time scale is required for the Publisher to give such notice, although it is submitted that the Publisher should behave reasonably in implementing this provision.

in question and subject to the payment or reimbursement by the Translator to the Publisher of the administrative costs incurred in so doing.

8.3   If any bona fide claim shall be made in relation to the Translation or any of the matters relating to the Translator's warranties pursuant to this Agreement the Publisher shall be entitled without prejudice to any of its rights under this Agreement to suspend payment of the Advance and/or the Royalties or to retain such sums by way of reserve as the Publisher considers appropriate until the withdrawal or settlement to the satisfaction of the Publisher and its insurers of such claim.

8.4   Value Added Tax shall to the extent applicable be payable in addition to the sums payable to the Translator under this Agreement subject to the production and delivery by the Translator to the Publisher of a full accurate and correct Value Added Tax invoice bearing the Translator's Value Added Tax registration number and country prefix accompanied by sufficient proof of the veracity of such details as the Publisher may request.

9.   ALTERNATIVE DISPUTE RESOLUTION

9.1   If either party is of the opinion that the other party in this Agreement is in breach of any material condition or obligation pursuant to this Agreement including without prejudice any obligation to pay money (but excluding any matter referred to in Clause 9.4) such dispute shall be dealt with in accordance with the alternative dispute resolution procedure set out in this clause.

9.2   The Publisher and the Translator undertake that they shall endeavour in good faith to resolve any dispute or claim arising in relation to the Translation or this Agreement by means of good faith negotiations which shall take place between the Translator and a senior executive of the Publisher who shall have authority to settle the dispute. If the dispute is not resolved within [14] days from commencement of good faith negotiations the Publisher and the Translator shall endeavour in good faith to resolve the dispute through an alternative dispute resolution procedure carried out in accordance with the recommendations of the Centre for Dispute Resolution.

9.3   All negotiations in relation to the matters in dispute shall be strictly confidential and shall be without prejudice to the rights of the Translator and the Publisher in any future proceedings. If the parties fail to reach an

---

Clause 8.2   A number of countries require withholding taxes to be deducted from royalties and this provision enables the Publisher to deduct such sums from royalty payments to the Translator. The second part of the clause provides a mechanism for effecting payment to a Translator from any country which imposes exchange control restrictions, by permitting the appropriate sum to be deposited in a bank account in the Translator's name in the territory.

Clause 8.3   This provision permits a Publisher to suspend payment obligations on the occurrence of any adverse claim in relation to the Translation. It should be noted that the provision is not as onerous as an indemnity provision, since it applies only to sums payable by the Publisher to the Translator instead of requiring indemnity payments from the Translator to the Publisher.

Clause 9   Many publishing agreements provide for resolution of disputes by arbitration. Arbitration is slow, ineffective and costly. Recently some publishing agreements have provided for resolution by arbitration through the Publishers' Association. There may be circumstances where Translators or Publishers do not wish the Publishers' Association to become involved in (or even know about) certain disputes. Clauses 9.1 to 9.4 of this document provide for a quick, effective, cheap and private means of resolution of disputes.

agreement which finally resolves all matters in dispute within 60 days of having commenced negotiations pursuant to the alternative dispute resolution procedure or if such negotiations fail to take place within 30 days from the date specified in Clause 9.2 then either party shall be entitled:

(a) to refer the matter to a single arbiter agreed upon by the Publisher and the Translator whose decision shall be final and binding on the parties; or

(b) to seek such legal remedies as may be appropriate.

9.4   [The provisions of Clauses 9.1 to 9.3 shall not apply in relation to any dispute or claim which involves a third party.]

10.   MISCELLANEOUS

10.1   Nothing contained in this Agreement shall constitute or shall be construed as constituting a partnership or contract of employment between the parties.

10.2   Neither party shall have any obligation to the other in the event of any act or omission on the part of such party where such act or omission results from the occurrence of any event which is outside the reasonable control of such party.

10.3   Nothing contained in this Agreement shall constitute an undertaking on the part of the Publisher to publish the Translation unless and until notice of Acceptance is given by the Publisher pursuant to Clause 7 and such notice is not withdrawn pursuant to the provisions of this Agreement. If the Publisher elects not to publish the Translation in no event shall the Translator be entitled to make any claim in respect of loss of opportunity to enhance the Translator's reputation or loss of publicity or any other for any other reason whatever.

10.4   This Agreement and all representations obligations undertakings and warranties contained in it shall enure for the benefit of and shall be binding on the personal representatives heirs and beneficiaries of the Translator and their successors and assignees and shall be binding upon the successors and assignees of the Publisher.

Clause 10   Under English law if two parties carry on business in common with a view to profit and share profit, the arrangement is capable of being considered a partnership. This provision ensures that no partnership is created inadvertently, and also expressly excludes the possibility of an employment contract being created.

Clause 10.2   This is a short form of what is frequently referred to as a "force majeure" clause. It may not always be appropriate for this clause to be included, since it may permit a Translator to argue against a Publisher that the Translator is not liable in certain circumstances which are beyond the Translator's reasonable control.

Clause 10.3   This clause expressly excludes the possibility of any claim by the Translator for compensation for loss of opportunity to enhance the Translator's reputation or any other reason (see paragraph 1.23).

Clause 10.4   This provision gives the Publisher's successors, licensees and assignees the benefit of rights obtained by the Publisher and confirms the liability of the Translator's estate in relation to the warranties and obligations of the Translator.

10.5   This Agreement contains the full and complete understanding between the parties and supersedes all prior arrangements and understandings whether written or oral appertaining to the subject matter of this Agreement and may not be varied except by an instrument in writing signed by all the parties to this Agreement. The Translator acknowledges that no representations or promises not expressly contained in this Agreement have been made to the Translator by the Publisher or any of its servants agents employees members or representatives.

10.6   This Agreement shall be governed and construed in accordance with the laws of England and Wales whose courts shall be courts of competent jurisdiction.

AS WITNESS the hand of the duly authorised representative of the Publisher and the hand of the Translator the day month and year first above written

SIGNED by [*name of officer*]
for and on behalf of
[*name of Publisher*] LIMITED

SIGNED by [*Translator*]
in the presence of:-

Clause 10.5   There are occasions where oral agreements or other understandings may be created in relation to a work which may contain either additional obligations or obligations which conflict with those set out in subsequent written agreement. This provision makes it clear that all previous arrangements and understandings are at an end and the contract is the only document relevant to the obligations and rights of the parties in relation to its subject matter. The final part of the clause expressly excludes the possibility of any liability on the part of a Publisher for misrepresentation on the part of any of its servants, agents, employees or representatives (see paragraph 2.17).

C. Permissions, releases, reversionary assignments and waivers

DOCUMENT 16

Edition permission

[IMPORTANT NOTE: Please read the section "About this book" on page v, before copying or using this Document]

Purpose of this Document

This Document is intended to provide a release from the publisher of a published edition of a foreign work which is to be used as the basis of an English language translation of a work.

Relevant text

The text of this Work contains a number of topics which are relevant to documents of this nature including:

- clearance procedures for publishers (paragraph 8.44)
- permissions and fair dealing (paragraphs 8.2 to 8.5)
- reporting events, incidental inclusion etc (paragraphs 8.6 to 8.12)
- other permitted acts (paragraphs 8.24 to 8.39)
- educational establishments, libraries and archives (paragraphs 8.13 to 8.23)
- Crown and Parliamentary Copyright (paragraphs 8.40 to 8.43)
- multimedia (paragraphs 19.2 to 19.55)

The permission authorises use of the edition as the basis of a translation. It also authorises the translation being published and sold in volume and/or sheet form throughout the world.

This form of permission is likely to be suitable for the use of a modern text of (say) a medieval work where the original work will be in the public domain but the edition is in copyright (see paragraph 3.21). Where the original foreign language work is in copyright, it is likely that the foreign publisher will require payment of additional copyright royalties and may wish to enter into a contract which requires the payment of an advance and royalties along the lines of that contained in Document 38 or Document 39. If the English publisher intends to exploit the work otherwise than in volume or sheet form, the permission will need to be amended.

It will be noted that the consent is given in consideration of the English publisher's agreement to give an acknowledgment on all published copies of the work. It may be appropriate to include wording relating to accidental failure or omission along the lines included in clause 2.4 of Document 4. The reference to consideration in the third paragraph will (subject to the intention of the parties to create legal relations and other matters) in most cases be sufficient to establish a contract between the parties (see paragraph 2.7). Where a contract exists the foreign publisher will generally not be able to withdraw consent for exploitation on capricious grounds at a subsequent date.

From   :   [*Foreign Publisher*] of [*address*]

To   :   [*Publisher*] of [*address*]

Dated   :   [*date*]

Dear [*insert name*]

"*title*" by [*Author*] ("Work")

We refer to your recent enquiry in relation to the edition of the Work ("Edition") established by [*name of Editor*] ("Editor") and first published by us on [*date*] and confirm that we are the owners of the copyright in the Edition throughout the world.

We consent to your using the Edition as the basis of your English language translation of the Work and to you and your assignees and licensees and sub-licensees publishing and selling your translation in volume and/or sheet form throughout the world for the full period of copyright.

Such consent is granted in consideration of and conditional on an acknowledgment being given to us by you and your assignees licensees and sub-licensees on all published copies of your translation of the Work in the following form:

[*Specify form of identification required*]

You undertake to provide us with [*number*] copies of every hardback and paperback edition of your translation of the Work upon first publication of each such edition.

Yours faithfully

Signed by [*name of officer*]
for and on behalf of
[*name of Foreign Publisher*]

We confirm and agree the above
and agree to be bound by it.

Signed by [*name of officer*]
for and on behalf of
[*name of Publisher*]

DOCUMENT 17

Quotation permission

[IMPORTANT NOTE: Please read the section "About this book" on page v, before copying or using this Document]

Purpose of this Document

The purpose of this Document is to provide a form of permission for quotations which are used in books.

Relevant text

The text of this Work contains a number of topics which are relevant to documents of this nature including:

- clearance procedures for publishers (paragraph 8.44)
- permissions and fair dealing (paragraphs 8.2 to 8.5)
- reporting events, incidental inclusion etc (paragraphs 8.6 to 8.12)
- other permitted acts (paragraphs 8.24 to 8.39)
- educational establishments, libraries and archives (paragraphs 8.13 to 8.23)
- Crown and Parliamentary Copyright (paragraphs 8.40 to 8.43)
- multimedia (paragraphs 19.2 to 19.55)

The permission is addressed to the Author, although its benefit extends to the Author's successors, assignees and licensees. There is no reason, however, why the permission should not be addressed to the Publisher. The Publisher should, in any event, vet all permissions and releases for the reasons referred to in paragraph 8.44.

It may be appropriate for the Author to obtain a warranty from the Publisher of the quoted Work that the quoted section is not obscene or blasphemous or defamatory or offensive to religion and does not infringe any right of copyright or other right.

It will be noted that the consent is given in consideration of the English publisher's agreement to give an acknowledgment on all published copies of the work. It may be appropriate to include wording relating to accidental failure or omission along the lines included in clause 2.4 of Document 4. The reference to consideration in the third paragraph will (subject to the intention of the parties to create legal relations and other matters) in most cases be sufficient to establish a contract between the parties (see paragraph 2.7).

From   :   [*Name of Publisher of quoted work*]
                 of [*address*]

To   :   [*Author*]
                 of [*address*]

Dated   :   [*date*]

Dear [*name of Author*]

We refer to your letter dated [*date*] seeking our consent to quote from the works which you referred to in your letter – namely [*specify works*] – ("Works") in your forthcoming book tentatively called "*title*" ("Book").

We now confirm our consent to your quoting from the Works in your Book and publishing distributing and otherwise exploiting the Book in any and all media throughout the world for the full period of copyright in the Book and we confirm that this consent shall extend to your successors assignees licensees and sub-licensees.

Such consent is granted in consideration of and conditional on us receiving an acknowledgment in all published copies of the Work in the following form:

[*State form of acknowledgment required*]

Yours faithfully

Signed by [*name of officer*]
for and on behalf of
[*name of Publisher*]

I confirm and agree the above and agree to be bound by it.

Signed by
[*name of Author*]

DOCUMENT 18

Synopsis permission

[IMPORTANT NOTE: Please read the section "About this book" on page v, before copying or using this Document]

Purpose of this Document

The purpose of this Document is to provide a form of permission for the use of a synopsis in a book.

Relevant text

The text of this Work contains a number of topics which are relevant to documents of this nature including:

- clearance procedures for publishers (paragraph 8.44)
- permissions and fair dealing (paragraphs 8.2 to 8.5)
- reporting events, incidental inclusion etc (paragraphs 8.6 to 8.12)
- other permitted acts (paragraphs 8.24 to 8.39)
- educational establishments, libraries and archives (paragraphs 8.13 to 8.23)
- Crown and Parliamentary Copyright (paragraphs 8.40 to 8.43)
- multimedia (paragraphs 19.2 to 19.55)

The permission is addressed to the Author, although its benefit extends to the Author's successors, assignees and licensees. There is no reason, however, why the permission should not be addressed to the Publisher. The Publisher should in any event vet all permissions and releases for the reasons referred to in paragraph 8.44.

It may be appropriate to obtain a warranty from the Publisher that the Work is not obscene or blasphemous or defamatory or offensive to religion and does not infringe any right of copyright or other right.

The synopsis permission extends only to using the synopsis in the Book in volume form not in any other media. The reason for this is that the Publisher of the original work which is being used in synopsis form will wish to prevent the synopsis being used as the basis for (say) a television series.

From   :   *[Name of Publisher]*
               of *[address]*

To   :   *[Author]*
               of *[address]*

Dated :   *[date]*

Dear *[name of Author]*

"*[Title]*" ("Work") by *[name of Author]*

We refer to your letter dated *[date]* seeking our consent to you preparing a synopsis of the Work for publication in your forthcoming book tentatively entitled "*title*" ("Book").

We confirm our consent to you producing a synopsis of the Work and including it in the Book provided that such synopsis is an accurate summary of the Work and does not exceed *[number]* words in length.

Such consent shall cover exploitation of the synopsis in volume form for the full period of copyright in the Book and is conditional on us receiving an acknowledgment in all published copies of the Work in the following form:

[State form of acknowledgment required]

We warrant that we have the right to grant the consent above referred to the benefit of which shall extend to you your assignees licensees and sub-licensees and warrant that the Work is not obscene or defamatory and does not infringe any copyright moral right or any other right whatever of any person.

Yours faithfully

Signed by *[name of officer]*
for and on behalf of
[name of Publisher]

DOCUMENT 19

Author's release

[IMPORTANT NOTE: Please read the section "About this book" on page v, before copying or using this Document]

Purpose of this Document

This Document is intended to be used in circumstances where a publisher acquires rights of copyright in a work from a person who is not its author. There are many occasions where such a state of affairs is perfectly regular: equally, there are others where it is not. In such other circumstances, a release from the relevant author will be necessary or advisable. This release is intended to be signed by the author(s) of the relevant work, and is intended to provide documentary corroboration of the chain of title of the work, so as to establish that the person who sold it to the publisher actually owned it.

Relevant text

The text of this Work contains a number of topics which are relevant to documents of this nature including:

- clearance procedures for publishers (paragraph 8.44)
- permissions and fair dealing (paragraphs 8.2 to 8.5)
- reporting events, incidental inclusion etc (paragraphs 8.6 to 8.12)
- other permitted acts (paragraphs 8.24 to 8.39)
- educational establishments, libraries and archives (paragraphs 8.13 to 8.23)
- Crown and Parliamentary Copyright (paragraphs 8.40 to 8.43)
- multimedia (paragraphs 19.2 to 19.55)

The payment of consideration (see paragraph 2.7) establishes a contract (subject to the other matters referred to in paragraphs 2.1 to 2.30) between the author and the publisher.

From : [*Author*] of [*address*] ("Author")

To : [*Publisher*] of [*address*] ("Publisher")

Dated : [*date*]

Dear [*name of Publisher*]

"[*Title*]" ("Work")

In consideration of the payment by the Publisher to me of the sum of £1 (receipt of which I acknowledge) I warrant undertake and agree as follows:

1. I am the sole author of the Work.

2. All publication rights in the Work [*specify identity of rights if other*] were [*assigned*] [*licensed*] by me to [*name*] of [*address*] ("Owner") pursuant to the [*describe nature of agreement*] ("Original Agreement") dated [*specify date*].

3. All consideration payable to me up to this time under the Original Agreement has been paid by the Owner.

4. The rights were [*assigned*] [*licensed*] to the Owner for the full period of copyright protection including all renewals reversions and extensions throughout the world in the Work.

5. I understand that the Owner intends to enter into a [*describe nature of agreement*] ("Subsequent Agreement") with the Publisher and I warrant undertake and agree with the Publisher that:

(a) [I have consented to the [*assignment*] [*licence*] from the Owner to the Publisher of the rights in the Work] or [the Owner is entitled to [*assign*] [*license*] to the Publisher the Work pursuant to the Subsequent Agreement].

Clause 1 If the Author is not the sole Author, then a similar release will need to be obtained from all co-Authors, since they are likely to own rights of copyright in the original work. Alternatively they could be joined to this document. A Publisher may need to consider whether the work was written by any of the co-Authors during the course of their employment (see paragraphs 3.22 to 3.24) in which case the Authors may not be the first owners of copyright. This matter will normally form part of a Publisher's rights clearance procedures (see paragraph 8.44).

Clause 2 The background to this Document is that the Owner has sold to the Publisher the rights which the Owner originally acquired from the Author. The details to be inserted in this paragraph will relate to the Original Agreement between the Owner and the Author.

Clause 3 The purpose of this confirmation is to establish whether the Author has any claim against the Owner under the Original Agreement. In some circumstances the Author may be able to terminate the Original Agreement if all remuneration which is due has not been paid.

Clause 4 The provisions of this paragraph will need to be conformed to reflect the details of the Original Agreement.

Clause 5 (a) If the rights have been assigned to the Owner, it may be that no consent to the assignment is necessary from the Author. Similarly, if the rights were originally licensed to the Owner, the terms of the Original Agreement may have permitted the Owner to grant sub-licences in which case consent may be unnecessary.

481

(b)   I assign the whole of my reversionary interest and any and all rights in and to the Work to which I may be entitled on the termination of the Original Agreement including all rights of copyright and other rights and the right to exploit the Work in any and all media by any manner or means to the Publisher its successors assignees and licensees absolutely for the full period of copyright protection including all renewals and reversions and extensions throughout the world.

(c)   If for any reason the rights in respect of the Work licensed pursuant to the Original Agreement should revert to me or if the Original Agreement should terminate then in the event of such reversion or termination the Publisher shall automatically be deemed to be substituted as a party to the Original Agreement in the place of and in the stead of the Owner and all the Publisher's rights under the Supplemental Agreement shall remain in full force and effect subject to the performance by the Publisher of all the obligations of the Owner arising to be performed after the date of termination or repudiation of the Original Agreement and the payment by the Publisher to me of all sums which would have been payable to me after such date by the Owner under the Original Agreement.

(d)   I shall give you notice in writing of the termination of the Original Agreement and/or of my acceptance of the Owner's repudiation of the Original Agreement.

(e)   The warranties and agreements on my part contained in the Original Agreement shall be deemed to be repeated by me to the Publisher on the termination of the Original Agreement or my acceptance of the Owner's repudiation of the Original Agreement.

6.   This Agreement shall be governed and construed in accordance with the laws of England and Wales the courts of which shall be courts of competent jurisdiction.

Yours faithfully

Signed by
[*the Author*]

Clause 5 (b)   The effect of this clause is to transfer to the Publisher any rights which the Author is capable of reclaiming from the Owner.

Clause 5 (c)   This clause reinforces clause 5 (b). It provides that if the Original Agreement between the Owner and the Author is terminated a new agreement will be created between the Publisher and the Author and the Publisher will be liable to pay to the Author only those sums which the Owner would have been liable to pay to the Author under the Original Agreement after the relevant date.

Clause 5 (e)   The effect of this provision is to give the Publisher direct warranties from the Author, rather than warranties from the Owner, if the Original Agreement is terminated. There may, however, be circumstances in which a Publisher will wish to have the reassurance of warranties from the Author (as to non-infringement etc) and there is no reason why such warranties should not be inserted in a letter of this type.

Clause 6   Where a contract is made between two entities in England and Wales, it will generally not be necessary to insert a provision of this nature, but where a contract is to be created with a foreign company (or a company situate in Scotland or Northern Ireland) this provision should always be included.

DOCUMENT 20

Publisher's release

Purpose of this Document

This is a form of publisher's release which is commonly required by producers of films or television programmes.

Relevant text

The text of this Work contains a number of topics which are relevant to documents of this nature including:

- clearance procedures for publishers (paragraph 8.44)
- permissions and fair dealing (paragraphs 8.2 to 8.5)
- reporting events, incidental inclusion etc (paragraphs 8.6 to 8.12)
- other permitted acts (paragraphs 8.24 to 8.39)
- educational establishments, libraries and archives (paragraphs 8.13 to 8.23)
- Crown and Parliamentary Copyright (paragraphs 8.40 to 8.43)
- multimedia (paragraphs 19.2 to 19.55)

Document 20 *Publisher's release*

From   :   [*Publisher*] of [*address*]

To   :   [*Company*] of [*address*]

Dated   :   [*date*]

Dear [*insert name*]

"[*Title*]" ("Work")

In consideration of the payment by you to us of the sum of £1 (receipt of which we acknowledge) we warrant undertake and agree as follows:

1.   We have not now nor have we ever had any right title or interest in any radio live stage motion picture television or allied or ancillary rights in the Work [and so far as we are aware such rights have not been assigned or sub-licensed to any third party].

2.   The Work was published in [*specify territory*] [by us] [by [*specify name*]] on [*specify date*].

3.   We consent to the writing publishing and publication by you your licensees sub-licensees and/or assignees in any and all languages in any and all parts of the world and in any form or medium of synopses and excerpts of the Work and/or any cinema film and/or television film version of the Work provided that such excerpts shall not exceed 10,000 words in length and shall

---

Clause 1 The purpose of this confirmation is to provide the film, television or theatre company who wishes to exploit the work in non-printed publication media with reassurance that the Publisher has not acquired the film or television or live stage rights.

It is possible for a Publisher to own such rights if the copyright in the Work was originally assigned to the Publisher (see paragraphs 1.13 to 1.16).

The company acquiring the benefit of this release will normally have entered into an agreement directly with the Author of the Work in relation to the exploitation of the motion picture, television, live stage or radio rights etc.

Clause 2 The purpose of this clause is to give the company acquiring rights details as to copyright protection. Copyright will subsist in the Work either by virtue of its authorship (see paragraph 3.12) or by virtue of first publication (see paragraph 3.15).

Companies who obtain the benefit of releases of this type may also ask for information relating to United States copyright registration (see paragraphs 4.5 to 4.8). There are certain advantages to registration of copyright in the United States of America (see paragraph 4.7).

Clause 3 Film, television and theatre companies will frequently need to provide written synopses of the plot either to potential investors or by way of programme notes etc. Where these synopses are made available in printed form it is possible for these to infringe the rights granted to the Publisher, and this clause provides a consent for such use.

Where the work concerned is a short story it may be appropriate to reduce the number of words which may be used in synopsis form. Where, however, these rights are owned by the Publisher, it will obviously be inappropriate for a Publisher to enter into a release of this nature. Where the rights form part of the subsidiary rights controlled by the Publisher, and the Publisher is the agent of the author for the purpose of authorising exploitation by third parties, it is likely that the company acquiring the rights will wish the Publisher to be joined as a party to the Document in its own right (not merely as agent for the Author).

be used solely for the purposes of advertising any film motion picture television or other production based on the Work.

Yours faithfully

Signed by [*name of officer*]
for and on behalf of
[*name of Publisher*]

DOCUMENT 21

Interview release

[IMPORTANT NOTE: Please read the section "About this book" on page v, before copying or using this Document]

Purpose of this Document

This is a form of release to be obtained from individuals who are interviewed by authors and who provide material or information which is to be used in a work.

Relevant text

The text of this Work contains a number of topics which are relevant to documents of this nature including:

- clearance procedures for publishers (paragraph 8.44)
- permissions and fair dealing (paragraphs 8.2 to 8.5)
- reporting events, incidental inclusion etc (paragraphs 8.6 to 8.12)
- other permitted acts (paragraphs 8.24 to 8.39)
- educational establishments, libraries and archives (paragraphs 8.13 to 8.23)
- Crown and Parliamentary Copyright (paragraphs 8.40 to 8.43)
- multimedia (paragraphs 19.2 to 19.55)

From   :   Author

To   :   Individual

Dated   :   [   ]

Dear [*Insert name*]

I am writing to set out the terms which we have agreed relating to the information which you have kindly agreed to provide in [an interview] [a series of interviews] in relation to [*specify individual or events etc*] for publication in my forthcoming book currently entitled "[*Name of Work*]" ("Work").

I undertake to pay you the sum of £[*amount*] payable as to [*specify*] % on signature of this Agreement and as to [*specify*] % on publication of the Work. In consideration of my undertaking you warrant confirm and agree as follows:

1. I shall have the right to use the material and the information which you provided me with as well as the right to portray the events which you describe in the Work;

2. I shall have the right to refer to you and to use your name and likeness and biographical information and include in the Work and any ancillary advertising and publicity material any copies of photographs owned by or featuring you and any excerpts of any correspondence and documentation in which you own or control the copyright together with the right to use the same in any and all media throughout the world.

The benefit of this Agreement shall extend to my assignees licensees and

---

Preliminary paragraph   Relevant details relating to the information and material to be provided by the individual need to be inserted. The Agreement is between the individual and the Author and for the reasons set out in paragraph 8.44 it is advisable for the Publisher to verify and approve the terms of the Agreement which needs to be extended to the Publisher.

Clause 1.7 of the Author's Agreement (Document 4) automatically extends to the Publisher the benefit of any releases, consents and provisions which may have been obtained by the Author. If the contract between the Publisher and the Author does not contain a similar provision, then either all releases, consents and permissions should be in the name of the Publisher or a short letter agreement should be drawn up between the Publisher and the Author extending the benefit of the releases, consents and permissions to the Publisher along the lines set out in clause 1.7 of Document 4.

Clause 1   This provision protects the Author/Publisher from any claim by a person who is interviewed that the annotation and use of words spoken during the interview constitutes an infringement of the oral copyright of the person being interviewed (see paragraph 3.11).

Clause 2   This provision protects the Author/Publisher from any claim of infringement of rights of privacy (see paragraph 5.21) outside the United Kingdom. At the date of publication of this work no privacy rights (other than the right to privacy in relation to certain films and photographs commissioned for private and domestic purposes – see paragraph 5.15) exist in the United Kingdom. There are, however, current proposals for certain rights of privacy to be created in United Kingdom law and the document may need to be reviewed in the light of such proposals.

The provision also extends to the Author/Publisher the right to use certain material and include it in the Work. Publishers will need to ensure that the use of such material does not amount to derogatory treatment (see paragraph 5.11) or infringement of any privacy rights of persons featured or referred to in the material.

sub-licensees and shall be irrevocable and shall last for the full period of copyright or other protection in the Work and/or the material.

Would you please indicate your acceptance of the above by signing and returning the enclosed duplicate copy of this letter.

Yours faithfully

[*Signed by the Author*]

I confirm and agree the above and agree to be bound by it.

[*Signed by the Individual*]

DOCUMENT 22

Permission for photograph use

[IMPORTANT NOTE: Please read the section "About this book" on page v, before copying or using this Document]

Purpose of this Document

This is a form of release which entitles the publisher to use photographs.

Relevant text

The text of this Work contains a number of topics which are relevant to documents of this nature including:

- clearance procedures for publishers (paragraph 8.44)
- permissions and fair dealing (paragraphs 8.2 to 8.5)
- reporting events, incidental inclusion etc (paragraphs 8.6 to 8.12)
- other permitted acts (paragraphs 8.24 to 8.39)
- educational establishments, libraries and archives (paragraphs 8.13 to 8.23)
- Crown and Parliamentary Copyright (paragraphs 8.40 to 8.43)
- multimedia (paragraphs 19.2 to 19.55)

Document 22 *Permission for photograph use*

From : [*Owner*] of [*address*]

To : [*Publisher*] of [*address*]

Dated : [*date*]

Dear [*insert name*]

"[*Title*]" ("Work")

In consideration of the payment by you to me of the sum of £[*amount*] receipt of which is acknowledged I confirm and agree with you:

1. You your successors licensees sub-licensees and assignees shall have the right to use the photographs referred to in the Schedule ("Photographs") by including the same in the Work and shall have the right to publish and distribute the Work and any ancillary advertising and publicity material in any and all media throughout the world for the full period of copyright in the Photographs and the Work.

2. I am the owner of the copyright in the Photographs and have the right to enter into and perform this agreement and grant you the above rights.

3. Nothing contained in the Photographs is obscene libellous blasphemous or defamatory or infringes any moral right or right of copyright or right of privacy or right of publicity or any other right whatever.

4. Apart from the payment by you to me of the sum referred to above you shall incur no liability to make any payment to me or to any third party in relation to the use of the Photographs.

5. I undertake to deliver to you such transparency or negative and/or print material as you shall require to enable the use of the Photographs.

6. All material created by you shall at all times be and remain your sole property and save in respect of the fee above referred to I shall have no right title or interest in or to the Work or any part of it or any proceeds from it.

7. I undertake to indemnify and keep you fully indemnified from and against all actions proceedings costs claims damages and demands however arising in respect of any breach or non-performance by me of

---

Clause 1 The consent extends not just to use in the Work but use in and through advertising material in all media throughout the world.

Clause 2 The Agreement has been drafted on the basis that the owner is an individual. If the owner is a company references to the first person singular will need to be changed to the first person plural and the appropriate adjustment made to the signature line of the document.

Clause 5 A precise description of the material required by the Publisher should be inserted where appropriate.

490

any or all of the undertakings warranties or obligations under this Agreement.

8. This Agreement shall be governed and construed in accordance with the laws of England and Wales whose courts shall be courts of competent jurisdiction.

The Schedule

Photographs

[*Specify photographs*]

Yours faithfully

Signed by [*owner*]

We confirm and agree the above and agree to be bound by it.

Signed by [*name of officer*]
for and on behalf of
[*Publisher*]

Clause 7   For the significance of indemnities reference should be made to paragraph 7.15.

DOCUMENT 23

Release of right to privacy

[IMPORTANT NOTE: Please read the section "About this book" on page v, before copying or using this Document]

Purpose of this Document

This is a form of release to authorise the inclusion in works of photographs which have been commissioned for private and domestic purposes on or after 1 August 1989 in the United Kingdom.

Relevant text

The text of this Work contains a number of topics which are relevant to documents of this nature including:

- moral rights generally (paragraph 5.2)
- the right to privacy (paragraph 5.15)
- consent and waiver (paragraph 5.18)
- transitional provisions (paragraph 5.19)
- moral rights outside the United Kingdom (paragraph 5.20)
- rights of privacy and publicity (paragraph 5.21)
- how moral rights might affect publishers (paragraph 5.22)
- clearance procedures for publishers (paragraph 8.44)
- permissions and fair dealing (paragraphs 8.2 to 8.5)
- reporting events, incidental inclusion etc (paragraphs 8.6 to 8.12)
- other permitted acts (paragraphs 8.24 to 8.39)
- educational establishments, libraries and archives (paragraphs 8.13 to 8.23)
- Crown and Parliamentary Copyright (paragraphs 8.40 to 8.43)
- multimedia (paragraphs 19.2 to 19.55)

From   :   *[Individual]* of *[address]*

To   :   *[Publisher]* of *[address]*

Dated   :   *[date]*

Dear *[insert name]*

"*[Title]*" ("Work")

I understand that you have acquired from *[Name]* the right to include in the Work certain photographic material details of which are set out below ("Photographs") the copyrights in which being (so far as I am aware) owned and controlled by *[Name]*.

The material in question was commissioned by me for private and domestic purposes but I now confirm that in consideration of the payment by you to me of a fee of £*[amount]* receipt of which I acknowledge I consent to the Photographs being included in the Work and ancillary advertising material in relation to the Work all of which may be exploited in any and all media throughout the world for the full period of copyright protection of the Work and/or the Photographs. This consent extends to you your successors licensees sub-licensees and assignees for the full period of copyright in the Photographs and the Work.

The Photographs above referred to are *[insert details]*.

Yours faithfully

Signed by *[name of individual]*

Preliminary paragraph It will be noted that the owner of copyright in a Work may not necessarily own the moral rights in the Work. The reason for this is that it is possible by testamentary disposition to provide that the owner of copyright in any Work is different from the person who owns the moral rights.

Additionally, in the case of photographs, the copyright will belong to the Author of the photograph. In most cases the Author of a photograph will be the person who takes the photograph, but in some cases authorship could extend to persons who design or arrange the material included in the photograph and photographers' assistants might have claims as to co-authorship depending on the terms of their employment.

Where a person commissions a photographer to take a photograph for private and domestic purposes, that person has a right to privacy (see paragraph 5.15) in relation to photographs taken by the photographer, the copyright in which will belong to the photographer, unless assigned to the commissioner.

Second paragraph It will be noted that the consent extends to the use of the photographs in the Work but also in ancillary advertising material in any and all media throughout the world for the full period of copyright. The duration of the right to privacy is the same duration as the right of copyright in the photographs, and is calculated with reference to the life of the "Author" of the photograph (see paragraph 3.27).

DOCUMENT 24

Waiver of moral rights by individual

[IMPORTANT NOTE: Please read the section "About this book" on page v, before copying or using this Document]

Purpose of this Document

This is a form of waiver of moral rights which may be required if a publisher has obtained rights of copyright from an author pursuant to a contract which fails to make provision for moral rights. It will be noted that contracts entered into pursuant to minimum terms agreements in their form subsisting as at the date of publication of this book (see paragraphs 7.20 to 7.22) do not make provision for moral rights waivers. The consequences for publishers are explained in paragraphs 5.22, 7.8 and 7.22.

Relevant text

The text of this Work contains a number of topics which are relevant to documents of this nature including:

- moral rights generally (paragraph 5.2)
- the right to be identified (paragraphs 5.3 to 5.9)
- derogatory treatments (paragraphs 5.7 to 5.13)
- duration and transmission of moral rights (paragraphs 5.16 to 5.19)
- foreign moral rights (paragraphs 5.20 and 5.21)
- how moral rights might affect publishers (paragraph 5.22)
- publisher and minimum terms agreements (paragraphs 7.8 and 7.20 to 7.22)
- clearance procedures for publishers (paragraph 8.44)
- permissions and fair dealing (paragraphs 8.2 to 8.5)
- reporting events, incidental inclusion etc (paragraphs 8.6 to 8.12)
- other permitted acts (paragraphs 8.24 to 8.39)
- educational establishments, libraries and archives (paragraphs 8.13 to 8.23)
- Crown and Parliamentary Copyright (paragraphs 8.40 to 8.43)
- multimedia (paragraphs 19.2 to 19.55)

From   :   [*Individual*] of [*address*] ("Author")

To   :   [*Publisher*] of [*address*] ("Publisher")

Dated   :   [*date*]

Dear [*Name*]

"[*Title*]" ("Work")

1. The Author asserts the Author's right to be identified in relation to the Work on the title page and cover in the following form:

    [*State form of identification required*]

    and the Publisher undertakes to comply with such request and to require all sub-publishers and other licensees to honour this right. The Author acknowledges that no casual or inadvertent failure by the Publisher or by any third party to comply with this provision shall constitute an infringement of this right and in the event of any infringement the Author agrees that the Author shall not seek injunctive relief and the sole remedy of the Author shall be a claim for damages.

2. The Author acknowledges that it is necessary for the purposes of publication for the Publisher to have the right to make alterations of the text of the Work in order to make corrections and conform the text to the Publisher's house style and also for the purpose of authorising translations of the Work and for removing any material which might in the opinion of the Publisher be actionable at law or which might damage the Publisher's reputation or business interests and also for the purpose of complying with the advice of the Publisher's legal advisers and for other general copy-editing purposes and the Author consents to the exercise by the Publisher of such rights and agrees that the product of such exercise shall not be capable of being considered a distortion mutilation or derogatory treatment of the Work.

OR

The Author irrevocably and unconditionally waives all rights to which the Author may be entitled pursuant to Sections [77], 80, 84 and 85 of the Copyright, Designs and Patents Act 1988 and any other moral rights provided for under the laws now or in future in force in any part of the

---

Clause 2   This provision provides the Publisher with reassurance that the making of alterations to the text for the purpose of copy editing etc cannot be construed by the Author as amounting to derogatory treatment of the Author's work. The exercise or attempted exercise by an Author of rights to object to derogatory treatment could have serious consequences for Publishers (see paragraphs 5.22, 7.8 and 7.22). The effect of the clause in foreign territories will need to be considered.

The alternative provision provided in clause 2 is an irrevocable waiver of all statutory moral rights. If the Author's right to be identified has been asserted, it may be appropriate to omit the reference to Section 77 of the Copyright, Designs and Patents Act. If the reference is included it is possible that the Document will amount to a waiver of the statutory right to be identified (see paragraphs 5.3 to 5.9) in favour of a contractual provision giving the Author a similar right.

world in relation to the exploitation by the Publisher its successors assignees and licensees of the Work.

Yours faithfully

Signed by [*the Author*]

We confirm and agree the above and agree to be bound by it.

Signed by [*name of officer*]
for and on behalf of [*the Publisher*]

DOCUMENT 25

Waiver of moral rights by personal representatives

[IMPORTANT NOTE: Please read the section "About this book" on page v, before copying or using this Document]

Purpose of this Document

This is a form of waiver of moral rights which may be obtained from the personal representatives of a deceased author. The form of this Document is intended to provide a basic guide only. Suitably qualified legal advice will generally need to be obtained in dealing with the estates of deceased authors.

Relevant text

The text of this Work contains a number of topics which are relevant to documents of this nature including:

- moral rights generally (paragraph 5.2)
- the right to be identified (paragraphs 5.3 to 5.9)
- derogatory treatment (paragraphs 5.10 to 5.13)
- false attribution and privacy (paragraphs 5.14 and 5.15)
- duration and transmission of moral rights (paragraphs 5.16 to 5.19)
- foreign moral rights (paragraphs 5.20 and 5.21)
- how moral rights might affect publishers (paragraphs 5.22, 7.8 and 7.22)
- clearance procedures for publishers (paragraph 8.44)
- permissions and fair dealing (paragraphs 8.2 to 8.5)
- reporting events, incidental inclusion etc (paragraphs 8.6 to 8.12)
- other permitted acts (paragraphs 8.24 to 8.39)
- educational establishments, libraries and archives (paragraphs 8.13 to 8.23)
- Crown and Parliamentary Copyright (paragraphs 8.40 to 8.43)
- multimedia (paragraphs 19.2 to 19.55)

Document 25 *Waiver of moral rights by personal representatives*

From   :   [*Moral Rights Owner*] of [*address*]

To   :   [*Publisher*] of [*address*]

Date   :   [*date*]

Dear [*insert name*]

[*Name of Work*] ("Work")

By [*Name of author*] ("Author")

1.   In consideration of your undertaking in paragraph 2 I/we warrant confirm and agree as follows:

EITHER:

1.1   By virtue of Clause [*number*] of the will of the Author dated [*insert date*] all moral rights conferred by Chapter IV of the Copyright, Designs and Patents Act 1988 were by testamentary disposition bequeathed to me/us.

OR

1.1   The will of the Author made no provision for the testamentary disposition of the moral rights conferred by Chapter IV of the Copyright, Designs and Patents Act 1988 but pursuant to Clause [*number*] of the will of the Author dated [*insert date*] all rights of copyright in the Work were by testamentary disposition bequeathed to me/us and pursuant to the provisions of Section 95(1)(b) of the Copyright, Designs and Patents Act 1988 all moral rights in the work are vested in me/us.

OR

1.1   The Author died intestate and pursuant to Section 95(1)(c) of the Copyright, Designs and Patents Act 1988 all moral rights conferred by Chapter IV of such Act are exercisable by me/us as the Personal Representative(s) of the author pursuant to [*specify method of appointment*].

1.2   I/we irrevocably and unconditionally waive all rights to which I/we am/are entitled pursuant to Sections 77 80 84 and 85 of the Copyright, Designs and Patents Act 1988 and any other moral rights provided for under the laws now or in future in force in any part of the world in respect of the inclusion and exploitation by you your successors licensees and assignees of the Work.

Clause 1.1   Three possibilities exist in relation to the ownership of moral rights. Either the Will of the Author will make specific provision for them, in which case consent will need to be obtained from the designated persons. Alternatively, the Will of the Author may fail to make provision for moral rights, but may provide that certain copyrights are bequeathed to certain persons, who may be entitled to the moral rights in the Work. Alternatively the Author may die intestate (without a Will) and personal representatives of the Author may be appointed.

There will be occasions when the laws of foreign countries may be relevant, and suitably qualified legal advice will need to be obtained.

Clause 1.2   This provision is an irrevocable unconditional waiver of moral rights. It may be preferable to insert a provision along the lines of those contained in Document 24, since this provision protects the interests of Publishers without requiring a complete waiver of moral rights.

2. The Publisher undertakes to pay to the personal representative (s) the sum of £*insert amount*] [*or other*].

Yours faithfully

Signed by
[*Moral Rights Owners*]

We confirm and agree the above and agree to be bound by it.

Signed by
for and on behalf of
[*Publisher*]

Clause 2 United Kingdom legislation does not require consideration (see paragraph 2.7) for a waiver of moral rights, but there may be circumstances where it is appropriate to include it. Equally, there may be circumstances where it will be appropriate for a Publisher to present personal representatives with a form of waiver (possibly modelled along the lines of Document 24), and to explain to such persons that although the Publisher is not carrying out any activities which would amount to an infringement of moral rights, the Publisher has been advised that it would be good practice to obtain this consent.

Equally, however, there may be occasions where it is inappropriate for consent to be obtained, either because the persons entitled to give the consent would be estopped from denying that valid consent had already been given by an Author (see paragraph 5.22) or if a consent or waiver had not been given by the Author, the time period during which legal action might be commenced had expired (see paragraph 5.22).

DOCUMENT 26

Waiver of moral rights and assignment of reversionary copyright

[IMPORTANT NOTE: Please read the section "About this book" on page v, before copying or using this Document]

Purpose of this Document

This is a form of waiver of moral rights which may be obtained from the personal representatives of a deceased author. The form of this Document is intended to provide a basic guide only. Suitably qualified legal advice will generally need to be obtained in dealing with the estates of deceased authors.

Relevant text

The text of this Work contains a number of topics which are relevant to documents of this nature including:

- moral rights generally (paragraph 5.2)
- the right to be identified (paragraphs 5.3 to 5.9)
- derogatory treatment (paragraphs 5.10 to 5.13)
- false attribution and privacy (paragraphs 5.14 and 5.15)
- duration and transmission of moral rights (paragraphs 5.16 to 5.19)
- foreign moral rights (paragraphs 5.20 and 5.21)
- how moral rights might affect publishers (paragraphs 5.22, 7.8 and 7.22)
- clearance procedures for publishers (paragraph 8.44)
- permissions and fair dealing (paragraphs 8.2 to 8.5)
- reporting events, incidental inclusion etc (paragraphs 8.6 to 8.12)
- other permitted acts (paragraphs 8.24 to 8.39)
- educational establishments, libraries and archives (paragraphs 8.13 to 8.23)
- Crown and Parliamentary Copyright (paragraphs 8.40 to 8.43)
- multimedia (paragraphs 19.2 to 19.55)
- reversion and recapture of copyright (paragraphs 4.11 to 4.17)

From   :   [*Rights Owner*] of [*address*]

To   :   [*Publisher*] of [*address*]

Date   :   [*date*]

Dear [*insert name*]

[*Name*] ("Work")

By [*Name of Author*] ("Author")

1. In consideration of your undertaking in paragraph 2 I/we warrant confirm and agree as follows:

EITHER

1.1 By virtue of Clause [*number*] of the will of the Author dated [*insert date*] all rights of copyright in the Work and moral rights conferred by Chapter IV of the Copyright, Designs and Patents Act 1988 ("Act") were by testamentary disposition bequeathed to me/us.

OR

1.1 The will of the Author made no provision for the testamentary disposition of the moral rights conferred by Chapter IV of the Copyright, Designs and Patents Act 1988 ("Act") but pursuant to Clause [*number*] of the will of the Author dated [*insert date*] all rights of copyright in the Work were by testamentary disposition bequeathed to me/us and pursuant to the provisions of Section 95(1)(b) of the Act all moral rights in the Work are vested in me/us.

OR

1.1 The Author died intestate and pursuant to Section 95(1)(c) of the Copyright, Designs and Patents Act 1988 ("Act") all moral rights conferred by Chapter IV of the Act are exercisable by me/us as the Personal Representative(s) of the Author pursuant to [*specify method of appointment*] which vested in me/us all rights of Copyright in the Work.

1.2 I/we irrevocably and unconditionally waive all rights to which I/we am/are entitled pursuant to the Copyright, Designs and Patents Act 1988 Sections 77 80 84 and 85 and any other moral rights provided for under the laws now or in future in force in any part of the world in respect of the publication and expectation by you your successors assignees and licensees of the Work and I/we now assign to you your successors assignees and licensees

Clause 1.1 Three possibilities exist in relation to the ownership of moral rights. Either the Will of the Author will make specific provision for them, in which case consent will need to be obtained from the designated persons. Alternatively, the Will of the Author may fail to make provision for moral rights, but may provide that certain copyrights are bequeathed to certain persons, who may be entitled to the moral rights in the Work. Alternatively the Author may die intestate (without a Will) and personal representatives of the Author may be appointed.

There will be occasions when the laws of foreign countries may be relevant, and suitably qualified legal advice will need to be obtained.

absolutely the whole of the reversionary interests in the copyright in the Work throughout the world for the full period of copyright protection including all renewals reversions and extensions now or in the future existing under the laws in force in any part of the world and warrant that I am/we are the sole absolute unincumbered legal and beneficial owner(s) of the same.

2.   The Publisher undertakes to pay to [*the Rights Owner*] the sum of £[*insert amount*] [*or other*].

Yours faithfully

Signed by [*Owner/s*]

We confirm and agree the above and agree to be bound by it.

Signature on behalf of
[*Publisher*]

Clause 1.2 This provision is an irrevocable unconditional waiver of moral rights. It may be preferable to insert a provision along the lines of those contained in Document 24, since this provision protects the interests of Publishers without requiring a complete waiver of moral rights.

This provision also assigns to the Publisher the rights of reversion in relation to the Work. This right may exist in relation to copyrights which were first assigned to the Publisher before June 1957 (see paragraph 4.13).

Clause 2 United Kingdom legislation does not require consideration (see paragraph 2.7) for a waiver of moral rights, but there may be circumstances where it is appropriate to include it. Equally, there may be circumstances where it will be appropriate for a Publisher to present personal representatives with a form of waiver (possibly modelled along the lines of Document 24), and to explain to such persons that although the Publisher is not carrying out any activities which would amount to an infringement of moral rights, the Publisher has been advised that it would be good practice to obtain this consent.

Equally, however, there may be occasions where it is inappropriate for consent to be obtained, either because the persons entitled to give the consent would be estopped from denying that valid consent had already been given by an Author (see paragraph 5.22) or if a consent or waiver had not been given by the Author, the time period during which a legal action might be commenced had expired (see paragraph 5.22).

DOCUMENT 27

Performer's consent

[IMPORTANT NOTE: Please read the section "About this book" on page v, before copying or using this Document]

Purpose of this Document

This is a form of performer's consent which may be required for the exploitation of multimedia works.

Relevant text

The text of this Work contains a number of topics which are relevant to documents of this nature including:

- multimedia (paragraphs 19.2 to 19.55)
- performances (paragraphs 6.7 to 6.15)
- clearance procedures for publishers (paragraph 8.44)
- permissions and fair dealing (paragraphs 8.2 to 8.5)
- reporting events, incidental inclusion etc (paragraphs 8.6 to 8.12)
- other permitted acts (paragraphs 8.24 to 8.39)
- educational establishments, libraries and archives (paragraphs 8.13 to 8.23)
- Crown and Parliamentary Copyright (paragraphs 8.40 to 8.43)

Document 27 *Performer's consent*

From   :   *[Performer]* of *[address]*

To   :   *[Company]* whose registered office is at *[address]*

Dated   :   *[date]*

Dear *[insert name]*

"[name of work or album]"

In consideration of the payment to me of the sum of £*[amount]* (receipt of which I acknowledge) in respect of the recording my performance for you in connection with the above [work] [album] [record]:

1.   I irrevocably give and confirm to you in respect of my performance all consents required pursuant to Part II Copyright, Designs and Patents Act 1988 and any other laws now or in future in force in any part of the world for the sole and exclusive worldwide exploitation by you your successors assignees and licensees of my performance [of such work or on such albums] in any and all media by any and all means now known or developed in future and I assign to you the copyright and all other rights to and in the product of my services rendered in connection with such performance <u>TO HOLD</u> the same to you without reservation for your own use and benefit and that of your successors assignees and licensees absolutely throughout the world for the full period of copyright including all renewals reversions and any extensions created or provided by the law of any country and confirm the irrevocable and unconditional waiver of all rights which I may have pursuant to Sections 77 80 84 and 85 of the Copyright, Designs and Patents Act 1988 and any other moral rights provided for under the laws now or in future in force in any part of the world.

2.   I undertake warrant covenant and agree that I:

2.1   shall execute any and all deeds and documents and take such steps required by you as are necessary to secure to you the rights granted to you.

2.2   have attained the age of eighteen and am free to enter into this Agree-

---

Clause 1 This clause provides for an irrevocable Performer's consent authorising worldwide all-media exploitation, as well as an assignment of copyright in the product of the services of the Performer (since it is possible that the Performer may have created a copyright work) together with an irrevocable unconditional waiver of moral rights.

In circumstances where use is made of a pre-existing performance, the assignment of the copyright in the services of the Performer will be inappropriate. In cases where the Performer has not created any original copyright work, the assignment will also be inappropriate, as will the waiver of moral rights. There may be circumstances where it is arguable that the Performer has created an arrangement of the copyright works sufficiently original to entitle the Performer to rights of copyright, in which case the provision should be retained.

Clause 2.1 Provisions of this type are generally referred to as covenants for further assurance (see paragraph 4.17).

ment and have not and shall not enter into any arrangement which may conflict with it.

2.3   shall not for a period of five years from the date this Agreement directly or indirectly be involved in the recording of material which might lead to a competing recording.

2.4   shall keep confidential all matters connected with the [work] [album] [record] and this Agreement.

2.5   shall not be entitled to any credit in respect of my performance.

2.6   am and was at the time of the recording of my performance a member in good standing of [the Musicians Union] [Equity].

3.   There shall not be any obligation on you to produce records or other devices embodying my performance or for you to include my performance in them or for you to exploit or continue to exploit such records or other devices.

4.   You shall be free to assign sub-license or otherwise howsoever deal with the whole or any part of your rights in the [work] [album] [record].

5.   This Agreement shall be governed and construed in accordance with the laws of England and Wales the courts of which shall be courts of competent jurisdiction.

Signed by [*Performer*]
in the presence of: }

Name:

Address:

_____

Clause 2.2   Contracts with minors may not be enforceable (see paragraph 2.3) and where persons are aged less than 18 years a contract will generally need to be entered into with the person's parent or guardian.

Clause 2.3   This provision protects against the Performer re-recording of competing material.

Clause 2.5   This provision is designed to prevent the Company being under an obligation to accord credit to dozens of persons. There will be circumstances where it is inappropriate.

Clause 2.6   This provision may not always be relevant although facts surrounding the making of the recording and the membership of unions may need to be established.

Clause 3   This provision protects the Company from possible claims by the Performer that failure of the Company to exploit the performance has caused the Performer loss of an opportunity to enhance the Performer's reputation.

Clause 4   This provision clarifies the fact that the Company has the right to assign or licence the benefit of the Agreement.

Clause 5   Where a contract is made between two entities in England and Wales, it will generally not be necessary to insert a provision of this nature, but where a contract is to be created with a foreign company (or a company situate in Scotland or Northern Ireland) this provision should always be included.

DOCUMENT 28

Reassignment and release of rights

[IMPORTANT NOTE: Please read the section "About this book" on page v, before copying or using this Document]

Purpose of this Document

This is a form of reassignment and release of rights which a publisher may have obtained from an author. It transfers the rights to a new publisher, permitting an author to change publishers in circumstances where a publisher has decided not to publish a work (see Document 4 clause 12, and associated annotations).

Relevant text

The text of this Work contains a number of topics which are relevant to documents of this nature including:

- death of an author (paragraph 7.3)
- publication rights (paragraph 7.5)
- termination and reversion of rights (paragraph 7.18)

From   :   [*Publisher*] of [*address*]

To   :   [*New Publisher*] of [*address*]

Dated   :   [*date*]

Dear [*insert name*]

<u>"[*Title*]" ("Work") by "[*Name*]" ("Author")</u>

We refer to the agreement dated [*date*] ("Agreement") between ourselves and the Author pursuant to which [the Author assigned to us the entire copyright in the Work] [the Author licensed to us certain rights in respect of the Work].

We understand that you now wish to acquire the rights above referred to from the Author and we have agreed in principle to release the Author from the scope of the Agreement and assign to you the rights previously acquired by us subject to the payment to us of a sum equal to the advances paid by us to the Author pursuant to the Agreement.

Subject to and in consideration of the payment by you to us of the sum of £[*amount*] [plus Value Added Tax] on or before [*date*] we undertake that we shall enter into an agreement with you and the Author in the form annexed as Exhibit 1 pursuant to which we shall assign such works to you and release the Author from the Author's obligations pursuant to the Agreement.

Yours faithfully

SIGNED [   ]
for and on behalf of
[*The Publisher*]

Exhibit 1
<u>Quitclaim</u>
[*see text of Document 29*]

Preliminary paragraph Appropriate details relating to the original Publisher/Author Agreement need to be inserted.

Final paragraph This paragraph provides that when the Publisher has been repaid the amount of any advance previously paid by the Publisher to the Author (or whatever other consideration is appropriate) the Publisher will enter into a quitclaim in the form annexed as Exhibit 1. A suitable form of quitclaim is included as Document 29.

DOCUMENT 29

Publisher's quitclaim

[IMPORTANT NOTE: Please read the section "About this book" on page v, before copying or using this Document]

Purpose of this Document

This is a form of Document pursuant to which a publisher may assign rights without incurring liability for infringement of copyright and other matters.

Relevant text

The significance of quitclaims and their meaning is explained in paragraph 11.21.

From   :   [*Publisher*] of [*address*] ("Publisher")

To   :   [*Assignee*] of [*address*] ("Assignee")

Dated :   [*date*]

Dear [*insert name*]

We refer to the [*specify nature of agreement*] ("Agreement") dated [*date*] between the Publisher and the Author pursuant to which the Owner acquired [*specify rights*] ("Rights").

1.   In consideration of the payment by the Assignee to the Publisher of the sum of [US$] [£] [*amount*] receipt of which is acknowledged the Publisher assigns to the Assignee the whole of the Publisher's property right title and interest in and to the Rights [subject to the Disclosed Agreements listed in the Schedule].

2.   The Publisher warrants to the Assignee that it has not [except as disclosed in the Schedule] entered into any arrangement or agreement relating to the Rights or assigned charged sub-licensed or incumbered any of the Rights.

3.   The Assignee confirms and agrees that the Publisher has not made any representation or warranty relating to the Rights or the Agreement other than the warranty and representation contained in paragraph 2 and the Publisher shall not be liable to the Assignee or to any other person in respect of any other matter relating to the Rights or the Agreement.

4.   This letter agreement shall be governed and construed in accordance with the laws of England and Wales the courts of which shall be courts of competent jurisdiction.

[5.   (*Certificate of Value if appropriate*)]

Clause 1 If payment has not been made the assignment should be conditional on it being made.

Clause 2 There will be circumstances where a Publisher has entered into agreements or arrangements in relation to the rights previously assigned to it, and where this is the case they should be listed in the Schedule.

Clause 3 The only warranty given by the Publisher is that all agreements which the Publisher has entered into are listed in the Schedule. The Publisher will normally be prepared to provide copies of these agreements to the assignee.

Clause 4 Where a contract is made between two entities in England and Wales, it will generally not be necessary to insert a provision of this nature, but where a contract is to be created with a foreign company (or a company situate in Scotland or Northern Ireland) this provision should always be included.

Clause 5 If it is appropriate to insert a Certificate of Value, a form of certificate may be found in Document 6 (d). Reference should also be made to paragraph 11.29.

THE SCHEDULE
Disclosed Agreements

Yours faithfully

SIGNED BY
for and on behalf of
[*name of Publisher*]   }

We confirm and agree the above and agree to be bound by it.

SIGNED BY
for and behalf of
[*name of Assignee*]   }

DOCUMENT 30

Rights clearance checklist

[IMPORTANT NOTE: Please read the section "About this book" on page v, before copying or using this Document]

The following are some of the aspects which may need to be considered in relation to the obtaining of permissions and consents in relation to books. It is not intended to be a comprehensive list, but will indicate some of the principal requirements.

1. Check qualification for copyright of Work/Author in United Kingdom and Berne Union countries. Consider date and location of first publication, nationality of Author(s), domicile of Author(s) at the material time, dates of death, first ownership in the case of photographs, films and sound recordings, commissioned works and works of journalism. In the case of a play, establish dates of first performance and first publication of the text of the play.

2. Qualification for US copyright. Consider the factors referred to in paragraph 1 and see also Copyright Act 1909 (USA) and Copyright Act 1976 (USA).

3. Establish publication history and investigate possibility of simultaneous publication in UK (or Canada) and USA securing Berne/US copyright protection. Consider applicability of wartime extensions.

4. Establish whether all published copies of the Work contain notice in accordance with the Universal Copyright Convention Article III.

5. Carry out US Copyright Registry and title search on Work if appropriate and check renewal of copyright in the USA and all recorded transfers of copyright in the Work.

6. Check all reported facts of authorship and obtain clear bankruptcy searches on all listed Authors in all known name variants and pseudonyms. Check or obtain warranty that no community property or confidentiality right is involved.

7. Where appropriate check reversion of copyright pursuant to Copyright Act 1911 Sections 5 (2) and 24.

8. Establish date of death of Author(s) and consider testamentary chain of title and devolution of copyright and moral rights.

9. If rights are being acquired from a person other than an Author, check the validity of the assignment from the Author or other assignor and any events relating to termination or recapture, such as non-payment or breach of any other material term.

10. Identify any underlying rights which may be infringed. Is the Work based on another Work or does it use extracts from any other Work?

11. If events described in the Work are based on real occurrences consider evasions of privacy and rights of publicity of persons featured or referred to in the Work and obtain all necessary legal opinions and releases.

12. Check for any material which is defamatory, obscene, blasphemous, offensive to religion or which infringes any confidentiality right or official secrecy legislation.

13. Check that adequate releases have been obtained for Publishers and rights owners in relation to works used in the Work, and ensure that such releases extend to the Publisher and cover the territory of the Publisher's right, and the term of the Publisher's right, or the term of copyright in the Work.

14. Check the chain of title in relation to the Work, and carry out company searches on all UK companies appearing in the chain of title of the Work.

15. Check that the rights in the Work are unincumbered, searching for registered charges and obtaining appropriate warranties where necessary.

16. Check that the benefit of warranties in key areas is assignable, or obtain appropriate additional warranties and indemnities.

17. Check that no events of default such as would permit termination or recapture of rights have arisen, and that all options have been validly exercised in accordance with the provisions of relevant agreements within any requisite time period. Obtain confirmation or receipts in relation to all payments due.

18. Where any documents are executed pursuant to powers of attorney, or as agent, check the irrevocability/revocation and capacity of appointor. Where powers are enduring powers of attorney check that they have been registered.

19. Check that all Authors have executed contracts with the Publisher.

20. Check that where appropriate the typescript has been read for defamation/secrecy purposes, and necessary legal advice has been sought, and has been complied with. Check that the requirements of any insurers have been fully complied with.

21. Check that consents have been obtained from all persons portrayed in the Work or their estates if appropriate and all persons whose names likeness or biographies are referred to or whose rights of personality may be infringed.

22. Check that releases have been obtained from the Publisher or other rights owner of any literary material (published or unpublished) which is quoted anywhere, and check that such releases contain appropriate warranties.

23. Check that a consent in an appropriate form has been obtained from any foreign publisher or editor if the Work is based on a foreign edition.

24. Check that all illustrators have executed contracts with the publisher.

25. Check that an executed release in a form approved by the Publisher containing appropriate warranties has been obtained in relation to each illustration used in the Work.

26. Check that an executed release in a form approved by the Publisher containing appropriate warranties has been obtained in relation to each photograph used in the Work.

27. Check all photographs to establish if any were commissioned for private and domestic purposes on or after 1 August 1989, and obtain appropriate waiver of rights to privacy from the commissioner of such photographs.

28. Check that all consents, releases and permissions obtained authorise the exploitation of the Work for the full period of copyright in all territories and media where the Publisher intends to exploit the Work.

29. Where consents are given by the estate of any deceased person, obtain appropriate legal advice to check that the necessary rights are vested in the persons granting them.

30. If the Work is to be exploited in the multimedia format or by means of CD ROM or CD-I, a number of more extensive consents and permissions will need to be obtained for which it is advisable to seek legal advice.

D. Rights acquisition and licensing

DOCUMENT 31

Rights acquisition agreement

[IMPORTANT NOTE: Please read the section "About this book" on page v, before copying or using this Document]

Purpose of this Document

This is a form of agreement suitable for use by publishers when acquiring publication rights and subsidiary rights in Works from persons other than the authors of the works. This Document has been drafted from the point of view of the publisher acquiring rights, and should be contrasted with the provisions of Document 32 which is drafted from the point of view of a publisher licensing rights.

Relevant text

The text of this Work covers a number of topics which are relevant to documents of this nature including:

- buying and selling rights (paragraphs 11.2 to 11.9)
- remuneration provisions in rights agreements (paragraphs 11.22 to 11.26)
- taxation (paragraphs 11.27 to 11.29 and 12.22 to 12.30)
- commercial terms of offers (paragraphs 1.22 and 1.23)
- the law of contract and agency (paragraphs 2.1 to 2.30)
- creation, existence and transfer of copyrights (paragraphs 3.1 to 3.45)
- international copyright protection (paragraphs 4.1 to 4.17)
- moral rights (paragraphs 5.1 to 5.22)
- permissions, fair dealings and rights clearances (paragraphs 8.1 to 8.44)
- liability for content (paragraphs 9.1 to 9.49)
- buying and selling rights (paragraphs 11.1 to 11.29)
- infringement and enforcement (paragraphs 13.1 to 13.17)
- termination and recapture (paragraphs 14.1 to 14.10)
- competition law (paragraphs 16.1 to 16.28)
- multimedia (paragraphs 19.1 to 19.55)

THIS AGREEMENT is made the   day of   199

BETWEEN

(1) *[Name]* LIMITED of *[address]* ("Publisher"); and

(2) *[Name]* LIMITED of *[address]* ("Proprietor")

IT IS AGREED as follows:

1. GRANT OF RIGHTS

1.1 The Proprietor grants to the Publisher the sole and exclusive licence to exploit the Publication Rights in the original literary work entitled "*[title]*" ("Work") written by *[name of author]* ("Author") throughout the *[specify territory]* ("Territory") [in the *[specify]* language] for the full period of copyright from time to time existing under the laws in force in any part of the world including all reversions renewals and extensions.

1.2 The Proprietor undertakes to deliver to the Publisher within *[specify]* days from the date of this Agreement the following delivery materials ("Delivery Materials") *[specify materials required]* in respect of all text and illustrations contained in the Work and the Proprietor confirms and agrees that the licence granted pursuant to Clause 1.1 shall extend to all Delivery Materials and shall expressly include the typographical arrangement of the published edition of the Work published by the Proprietor and the jacket design of the Work and all associated publicity and advertising material produced by the Proprietor which shall form part of the Delivery Materials.

1.3 The Proprietor warrants and confirms to the Publisher that all permissions and consents required in order to enable exploitation of any illustrations or photographs contained in the Work and any other material the rights in which are owned or controlled by third parties have been obtained and that such consents and permissions extend to and authorise the

---

Clause 1.1 This provision grants the Publisher a sole and exclusive licence in relation to the publication rights (see paragraph 1.14). Details of the territory and the work need to be inserted. It should be noted that the licence extends to any renewals or extensions of copyright. It is submitted that many licences should be so framed in view of the European Union Directive 93/98 which extends the term of protection of copyright (see paragraph 17.11 and paragraphs 20.2 to 20.10). The Publisher may wish to acquire rights throughout the entire European Economic Area in the English language, so as to protect against parallel imports (see paragraph 11.3). Where the Work is itself a translation of a non-English language original, the wording of clause 1.1 should be amended to reflect this fact. The Publisher may also wish to vet the chain of title documentation under which the Proprietor has acquired rights from the Author (see paragraph 8.44 and Document 30).

Clause 1.2 In some cases, the Proprietor from whom the Publisher will be acquiring the rights, will be an individual. In other cases the Proprietor may be another Publisher, who may have published a previous edition of the Work. In such circumstances it is likely that the Proprietor may have materials such as jacket designs, publicity and advertising material and plates or sheets of the Work which could be acquired by the Publisher. This clause provides for such materials to be delivered to the Publisher.

exploitation by the Publisher of the rights granted to the Publisher in this Agreement.

2.   NOTICES AND CREDIT

2.1   All copies of the Work published by the Publisher shall contain the following copyright notice:

[*conform to reflect copyright position of the Work*]

2.2   The Proprietor confirms that the Author has asserted the Author's right to be identified in relation to the Work on the title page and cover in the following form:

[*state form of identification required*]

and the Publisher undertakes to comply with such request and to require all sub-publishers and other licensees to honour this right. The Proprietor acknowledges that no casual or inadvertent failure by the Publisher or by any third party to comply with this provision shall constitute a breach by the Publisher of this Agreement and in the event of any breach of this Clause the Proprietor warrants that the Author shall not have the right to seek injunctive relief and the sole remedy of the Author or the Proprietor shall be a claim for damages.

2.3   The Proprietor acknowledges that it is necessary for the purposes of publication for the Publisher to have the right to make alterations to the text of the Work in order to make corrections and conform the text to the Publisher's house style and also for the purpose of authorising translations of the Work or removing any material which might in the opinion of the Publisher be actionable at law or which might damage the Publisher's reputation or business interests and for the purpose of complying with the advice of the Publisher's legal advisers and for other general copy-editing purposes and the Proprietor warrants that the Author has consented to the exercise by the Publisher of such rights and warrants that the Author has agreed that the

Clause 1.3   Releases and permissions are of fundamental importance and should always be double-checked by Publishers. There are circumstances when permissions and releases may not be required (see paragraphs 8.2 to 8.39). Publishers should ensure that appropriate clearance procedures are followed (see paragraph 8.44 and Document 30).

Clause 2.1   The copyright notice should state the identity of the copyright owner. If copyright is assigned to the Publisher, the copyright owner will be the Publisher. If copyright is reserved to the Proprietor and the Proprietor grants an exclusive licence to the Publisher, the copyright owner will be the Proprietor. It is possible for the copyright owner in one country to be different from the copyright owner in another country (see paragraph 1.20). There are a number of other notices which traditionally appear on publications (see paragraph 4.9) and there are legal advantages to ensuring that the copyright information on publications is correct (see paragraphs 4.9 and 4.10). In some countries – notably the United States – there are strong advantages to registering copyright works in the relevant foreign copyright registry (see paragraph 4.7).

Clause 2.2   This clause contains confirmation that the Author's right to be identified (see paragraphs 5.3 to 5.9) has been asserted. The assertion is included for the reasons referred to in paragraph 7.8. There are circumstances in which a person who, for example, loses the opportunity to enhance their reputation can apply for injunctive relief (see paragraph 13.12) and restrain the publication or distribution of works which do not contain appropriate credit wording. The final sentence of the clause is intended to reduce the risk.

product of such exercise shall not be capable of being considered a distortion mutilation or derogatory treatment of the Work.

3. PUBLICATION AND PROMOTION

3.1   Subject to the provisions of this Agreement the Publisher undertakes to publish the Work to the customary standard of the Publisher at the cost and expense of the Publisher on or around such date as may be indicated by the Publisher pursuant to Clause 3.3.

3.2   It is the intention of the Publisher to print [*number*] copies of the Work in [hard][paper] back format with an anticipated retail price of [*price*] but nothing contained in this Clause 3.2 shall constitute an obligation on the part of the Publisher in relation to the print run or pricing of the first or any subsequent edition of the Work and the Proprietor acknowledges that the Publisher shall have sole control of all matters in relation to the production and publication of the Work including without limitation print runs numbers of reprints and editions marketing price advertising editorial production distribution and terms of sale.

3.3   The Publisher shall use all reasonable endeavours to give the Proprietor advance notice of the publication of the Work. The Publisher shall provide the Proprietor with 12 free copies of the Work on first publication in hard-back format [and in the case of any paperback edition up to 20 free copies] and the Proprietor shall have the right to purchase additional further copies at a discount of [*percentage*]% of the Publisher's list price for the personal use of the Proprietor but not for resale purposes.

3.4   The Proprietor shall supply the Publisher with details of suitable persons and other information relating to publicity and advertising of the Work and shall provide the Publisher with a list of suggested individuals and periodicals who might be suitable recipients for review copies of the Work.

4. ADVANCE AND ROYALTIES

4.1   Subject to and conditional upon the full performance and observance by the Proprietor of all the undertakings obligations and warranties on the part of the Proprietor contained in this Agreement the Publisher undertakes

---

Clause 2.3   This clause contains a warranty from the Proprietor that the Author has consented to certain acts being done without violating the Author's right to object to derogatory treatment of the Author's work (see paragraphs 5.10 to 5.13). The clause has been inserted for the reasons referred to in paragraph 7.8, being a more acceptable alternative (from an Author's point of view) to a complete waiver of moral rights. Although provisions of this nature are not generally found in minimum terms agreements (see paragraph 7.20), there are strong commercial arguments to support their inclusion (see paragraph 7.22).

Clause 3.1   Publication costs are generally borne by publishers, although in the area which is referred to as "vanity publishing" it is usual for authors to pay to have the privilege of seeing their names in print.

Clause 3.2   This clause requires the Publisher to state the intended print run and publication price. The statements will not bind the Publisher for the future, and the clause makes it clear that the Publisher retains sole control over production matters.

Clause 3.3   The number of free copies of any work and the provisions relating to purchase of additional copies are matters on which the practice varies from publisher to publisher.

Clause 3.4   This provision may not always be suitable for inclusion. It does not, however, impose an obligation on the Publisher to send all notified individuals copies of the Work.

to pay to the Proprietor the recoupable advance ("Advance") set out in Clause 4.2 which shall be paid on account of and be recoverable from the royalties ("Royalties") payable pursuant to Clause 4.3.

4.2   The Advance payable by the Publisher to the Proprietor shall be £[*amount*] payable:

(a)   as to £[*amount*] on the date of this Agreement receipt of which the Proprietor acknowledges;

(b)   as to £[*amount*] on delivery of the Delivery Material; and

(c)   as to £[*amount*] on publication of the Work.

4.3   The Royalties payable by the Publisher to the Proprietor shall be:

(a)   [*specify hardback royalty*]

(b)   [*specify paperback royalty*]

(c)   [*specify overseas royalty and from sub-licensing*]

5.   SPECIFIC ROYALTY PROVISIONS

5.1   Where the Proprietor has granted to the Publisher paperback rights in the Work in the United States of America the following provisions shall apply:

(a)   if the Publisher sub-licenses the paperback rights in the Work to a United States publisher the Publisher shall be entitled to a commission of [*percentage*]% of all sums paid by the United States publisher in relation to the Work and shall remit the balance of such sums to the Proprietor after the recovery of all sums to which the Publisher is entitled pursuant to this Agreement; and/or

(b)   if the Publisher sells sheets or bound copies of the Work to a publisher or sub-publisher in the United States of America the Proprietor shall be entitled to receive a royalty of [*percentage*]% of the Publisher's Receipts from such sale except in relation to sales discounted by more than [*percentage*] where the applicable percentage shall be [*percentage*]%.

Clause 4.1   The Proprietor's entitlement to receive the royalties is subject to and conditional upon the full performance and observance by the Proprietor of all the Proprietor's obligations in the Agreement.

Clause 4.2   The advance is expressed to be recoupable. In other words it is paid on account of royalties and recouped from future royalties paid to the Author. In other words the Proprietor will not receive any royalties until the total accrued royalty obligations amount to more than the amount paid by way of advance. It will be noted that the advance is not described as "non-returnable".
   The Proprietor's entitlement to receive the advance is subject to and conditional on full performance and observance by the Proprietor of the Proprietor's warranties and obligations under the Agreement.

Clause 4.3   For prevailing commercial practice in relation to royalty rates see paragraph 7.21.

Clause 5.1   Some agreements contain specific royalty provisions relating to sales of Works in the United States of America. It may not always be appropriate for these provisions to be included.

5.2   On reprints of less than [1500] copies of the Work the royalty percentages payable pursuant to Clauses [*specify*] shall be the same as those percentages specified in Clauses [*specify*].

5.3   No royalties shall be payable on copies of the Work given to the Proprietor or distributed for the purposes of publicity or advertising or distributed as review copies or on copies of the Work which are lost or destroyed or for which the Publisher has not received payment.

6.   RESERVED RIGHTS AND SUBSIDIARY RIGHTS

6.1   The Publisher confirms that the following rights are reserved to the Author:

(a)   all reprographic rights in relation to the Work (other than reprographic rights subsisting in relation to the typographical arrangement of the published edition of the Work)

(b)   all rights of the Author in relation to the Work pursuant to the Public Lending Right Act 1979 and any analogous legislation in any part of the world

(c)   all rights reserved by the Author shall be subject to the provisions of Clause 6.2.

6.2   The Proprietor appoints the Publisher as the sole and exclusive agent of the Proprietor during the [period referred to in Clause 1.1] [period of [*specify*] years from the date of this Agreement] to sell and exploit and enter into contracts and collect all income arising in relation to the exercise by third parties in the Territory of the Subsidiary Rights listed in the Schedule. In consideration of such appointment the Publisher undertakes to pay to the Proprietor the applicable percentages of Publisher's Receipts listed in Clause 6.3 arising in relation to each such Subsidiary Right.

Clause 5.2   This clause excludes the application of any royalty escalator in relation to reprints of a Work of less than a designated number. Whether it should be included will depend on what royalty terms are specified in clause 4.3.

Clause 5.3   It is normal for agreements to provide that royalties are not paid on copies of the Work which are given to the Author or given for publicity or advertising or are lost or destroyed.

Clause 6.1   Reprographic rights in relation to Works may be the subject of licences granted by the Copyright Licensing Agency (see paragraph 6.17). Clause 6.1 reserves reprographic rights of the Work to the Proprietor.

The rights of the Author in relation to the Public Lending Right Act 1979 are set out in paragraph 6.16. The reservation of these rights does not conflict with any of the Publisher's interests.

Clause 6.2   This clause deals with subsidiary rights (see paragraph 1.16). The clause appoints the Publisher as the Proprietor's agent for the purpose of licensing the subsidiary rights for the reasons set out in paragraph 2.30. The clause needs to be modified to contain specific reference to the period of the Publisher's rights. This clause has been drafted on the basis that the Publisher is appointed as agent for all subsidiary rights. It should be noted that the Advance (see the definition in clause 13.1) is payable from all other sums payable under the Agreement. If subsidiary rights income is generated and the Advance is unrecouped the Proprietor's share of the subsidiary rights income will be retained by the Publisher until recoupment. However, if some subsidiary rights are being retained by the Proprietor, then the Publisher should consider whether it is appropriate for the Publisher to obtain the agreement of the Proprietor not to exercise such right for an initial period, to avoid them being exploited in competition with the Publisher's rights. An example would be where, for example, CD-ROM rights were retained by the Proprietor and did not form part of the subsidiary rights. The sale of the Work in CD-ROM format might impact on other exploitation of the Work.

6.3   The applicable percentages of Publisher's Receipts referred to in Clause 6.2 are as follows:

(a)   Anthology and Quotation Rights: [*percentage*]% Publisher's Receipts

(b)   Book Club Rights: [*percentage*]% Publisher's Receipts

(c)   Braille Rights: [*percentage*]% Publisher's Receipts

(d)   Computer Game Rights: [*percentage*]% Publisher's Receipts

(e)   Digest Rights: [*percentage*]% Publisher's Receipts

(f)   Educational Rights: [*percentage*]% Publisher's Receipts

(g)   First Serial Rights: [*percentage*]% Publisher's Receipts

(h)   Information Storage and
      Retrieval Rights: [*percentage*]% Publisher's Receipts

(i)   Merchandising Rights: [*percentage*]% Publisher's Receipts

(j)   Motion Picture and
      Television Rights: [*percentage*]% Publisher's Receipts

(k)   Other Rights: [*percentage*]% Publisher's Receipts

(l)   Paperback Rights: [*percentage*]% Publisher's Receipts

(m)   Radio Rights   [*percentage*]% Publisher's Receipts

(n)   Reading Rights: [*percentage*]% Publisher's Receipts

(o)   Reprographic Rights: [*percentage*]% Publisher's Receipts

(p)   Reprint Rights: [*percentage*]% Publisher's Receipts

(q)   Second and Subsequent
      Serial Rights: [*percentage*]% Publisher's Receipts

(r)   Single Issue Rights: [*percentage*]% Publisher's Receipts

(s)   Sound Recording Rights: [*percentage*]% Publisher's Receipts

(t)   Translation Rights: [*percentage*]% Publisher's Receipts

(u)   US Rights: [*percentage*]% Publisher's Receipts

6.4   In authorising the exploitation of the Subsidiary Rights in the Territory the Publisher shall have the right to grant licences for periods up to and including the full period of copyright in the Work in the Territory and the

---

Clause 6.3 Prevailing commercial practice in relation to percentage payments of subsidiary rights is considered in paragraph 7.21. The provisions of the clause will need to be adjusted so that they conform with the definition of Publication Rights contained in clause 13.1. Publication Rights may well include book club rights, paperback rights, reprint rights and US rights. The provisions of this clause will require careful adjustment to fit the circumstances. It should be noted that the definition of Information Storage and Retrieval Rights (in the Schedule to Document 4) covers most forms of multimedia and electronic publishing. It may, however, be appropriate to refer to these in a separate category of subsidary rights. Alternatively, if the Publisher itself wishes to exploit these rights, it may be appropriate to include them within the definition of Publication Rights, and insert appropriate royalty provisions in clause 4.3.

Publisher's sole and exclusive rights and obligation to administer such licences and right to collect all income arising thereunder shall subsist for the full period of such licences irrespective of the expiry or termination of the licence contained in Clause 1.1 or the expiry or termination of the Publisher's appointment as agent.

7. PROPRIETOR'S WARRANTIES

The Proprietor represents warrants undertakes and agrees with the Publisher as follows:

7.1 the Author is the sole Author of the Work and was at all material times during the writing of the Work a "qualifying person" within the meaning of the Copyright, Design, and Patents Act 1988 Section 154 and the Proprietor is the sole unincumbered absolute legal and beneficial owner of all rights of copyright and all other rights whatever in the Work and the Delivery Materials throughout the world;

7.2 the Proprietor has not assigned or incumbered or licensed or transferred or otherwise disposed of any rights of copyright or any other rights in or to the Work or the Delivery Material except pursuant to this Agreement and has not entered into any agreement or arrangement which might conflict with the Publisher's rights under this Agreement or might interfere with the performance by the Proprietor of the Proprietor's obligations under this Agreement;

7.3 the Work is original to the Author and neither the Work nor the Delivery Materials infringe any right of copyright moral right or right of privacy or right of publicity or personality or any other right whatever of any person;

7.4 the Work is not under the laws of any jurisdiction obscene or blasphemous or offensive to religion or defamatory of any person and does not contain any material which has been obtained in violation of the Interception

Clause 6.4 This clause will be necessary where the period of the Publisher's appointment as agent under clause 6.2 is for a period of less than the full duration of copyright (see paragraphs 3.25 to 3.35 and paragraph 17.11 and paragraphs 20.2 to 20.10). The effect of this provision is to permit a Publisher who is appointed as agent for a term of (say) seven years, to grant licences to third parties during the seven-year term but to provide that the period of the licences granted can be for the full period of copyright (generally the life of the Author plus 50/70 years). At the end of the Publisher's seven-year appointment the licences will continue to remain in force and the Publisher will be entitled to receive all income from the licences.

Clause 7.1 This provision is necessary to confirm that the Author is the sole Author of the Work and that no other persons own the Work (see paragraphs 3.14, 3.23 and 3.24) and that the Work qualifies for copyright protection. A more detailed analysis of the clause may be found in the notes to clause 10.1 in Document 4.

Clause 7.2 Although clause 7.1 protects the Publisher by ensuring that copyright subsists in the Work, it is also necessary to ensure that the rights of copyright are owned by the Proprietor, which is what the provision in clause 7.2 provides. The warranty assures the Publisher that the Proprietor has not incumbered the Work (by mortgaging it or charging it) or licensed rights in the Work to third parties. The provision also assures the Publisher that the Proprietor has not entered into any other agreement or arrangement which might interfere with the Publisher's rights under the Agreement. An option which the Proprietor had granted to another Publisher would interfere with the Publisher's rights, for example, if it was enforceable – and many in the publishing world are not (see paragraph 7.17).

Clause 7.3 Infringement of copyright, moral rights, rights of privacy and rights of publicity or personality could lead to legal liability on the part of the Publisher, which this provision seeks to exclude.

of Communications Act 1985 the Official Secrets Act 1989 or any analogous foreign legislation and nothing contained in the Work or the Delivery Materials would if published constitute a contempt of court;

7.5 all statements purporting to be facts in the Work and the Delivery Materials are true and correct and no advice recipe formula or instruction in the Work or the Delivery Materials will if followed or implemented by any person cause loss damage or injury to them or any other person;

7.6 there is no present or prospective claim proceeding or litigation in respect of the Work or the Delivery Materials or the title to the Work or the Delivery Materials or the working title or final title of the Work or the ownership of the copyright in the Work or the Delivery Material which may in any way impair limit inhibit diminish or infringe upon any or all of the rights granted to the Publisher in this Agreement;

7.7 copyright in the Work is and shall throughout the full period of copyright protection be valid and subsisting pursuant to the laws of the United Kingdom and the United States of America and the provisions of the Berne Convention and Universal Copyright Convention;

7.8 the Proprietor shall not disclose reveal or make public except to the professional advisers of the Proprietor any information whatever concerning the Work or the business of the Publisher or this Agreement all of which shall be strictly confidential nor shall the Proprietor make any public statement or press statement in connection with the foregoing or commit any act which might prejudice or damage the reputation of the Publisher or the successful exploitation of the Work;

7.9 the Proprietor undertakes to indemnify the Publisher and keep the Publisher at all times fully indemnified from and against all actions proceedings claims demands costs (including without prejudice to the generality of this provision the legal costs of the Publisher on a solicitor and own client basis) awards damages however arising directly or indirectly as a result of any breach or non-performance by the Proprietor of any of the Proprietor's undertakings warranties or obligations under this Agreement.

Clause 7.4   This warranty is designed to eliminate any liability on the Publisher's part for the matters examined in Chapters 9 and 10.

Clause 7.5   There are occasions where a Publisher will be liable for negligent misstatement (see paragraphs 9.34 and 9.35). Examples of matters which could give rise to liability for negligent misstatement are referred to in the notes to clause 10.5 of Document 4.

Clause 7.6   If the Proprietor is aware of any dispute in relation to the Work, the Proprietor will be in breach of this warranty. It is, however, possible to exclude from the scope of warranties matters which have been expressly disclosed. If a Proprietor discloses the existence of a dispute to a Publisher, the question of interference with contractual relations may need to be considered (see paragraph 13.10).

Clause 7.7   This warranty to an extent reinforces the warranty contained in clause 10.1. There may be circumstances where it may be appropriate for a Publisher to reduce the scope of a warranty by limiting it to the Berne Convention and to the Universal Copyright Convention only so far as concerns any initial period of copyright protection in the Universal Copyright Convention.

Clause 7.8   This provision imposes confidentiality obligations on the Proprietor – see paragraphs 1.5 to 1.12.

Clause 7.9   For an explanation of the meaning of an indemnity clause, reference should be made to paragraph 7.15.

8.   ACCOUNTS

8.1   The Publisher shall keep full books and records relating to the payment of sums due to the Proprietor pursuant to this Agreement and shall prepare and submit to the Proprietor within 90 days from 30 September and 31 December of each year a statement of account in relation to all sums payable to the Proprietor during the preceding six-month period. Each such statement of account shall be accompanied by a cheque in favour of the Proprietor in the amount shown to be due.

8.2   The Publisher shall have the right to deduct and retain from payments due to the Proprietor up to [*percentage*]% of sums payable to the Proprietor in relation to the exploitation of Publishing Rights in paperback form as a reserve against returns in any accounting period. Each such reserve shall be liquidated (to the extent not applied against returns) in the [three/four] accounting periods following which the reserve is made and at the end of such period the balance remaining in such reserve shall be paid to the Proprietor in full.

8.3   The Publisher shall have the right to deduct and retain from payments to the Proprietor all sums required to be deducted or retained by way of withholding or other tax pursuant to the laws of any country. In the event that the remittance of royalties to the Proprietor is prohibited by reason of exchange control restrictions in any part of the world the Publisher shall if requested by the Proprietor deposit the amount of any sums due to the Proprietor in an account in the name of the Proprietor situate in the country in question and subject to the payment or reimbursement by the Proprietor to the Publisher of the administrative costs incurred in so doing.

8.4   If any bona fide claim shall be made in relation to the Work or any of the matters relating to the Proprietor's warranties pursuant to this Agreement the Publisher shall be entitled without prejudice to any of its rights under this Agreement to suspend payment of the Advance and/or the Royalties or to retain such sums by way of reserve as the Publisher considers appropriate until the withdrawal or settlement to the satisfaction of the Publisher and its insurers of such claim.

8.5   Value Added Tax shall to the extent applicable be payable in addition to the sums payable to the Proprietor under this Agreement subject to the production and delivery by the Proprietor to the Publisher of a full accurate

---

Clause 8.2   This provision permits the Publisher to make reserves from sums. The percentage permitted to be retained, and the accounting period over which it is required to be liquidated, are matters which need to be specified.

Clause 8.3   A number of countries require withholding taxes to be deducted from royalties, and this provision enables the Publisher to deduct such sums from royalty payments to the Proprietor. The second part of the clause provides a mechanism for effecting payment to a Proprietor from any country which imposes exchange control restrictions, by permitting the appropriate sum to be deposited in a bank account in the Proprietor's name in the territory.

Clause 8.4   This provision permits a Publisher to suspend payment obligations on the occurrence of any adverse claim in relation to the Work. It should be noted that the provision is not as onerous as an indemnity provision, since it applies only to sums payable by the Publisher to the Proprietor, instead of requiring indemnity payments from the Proprietor to the Publisher.

and correct Value Added Tax invoice bearing the Proprietor's Value Added Tax registration number and country prefix accompanied by sufficient proof of the veracity of such details as the Publisher may request.

9.   ACTIONS FOR INFRINGEMENT

9.1   If at any time during the period the Publication Rights in the Work are vested in the Publisher the copyright in the Work is infringed by any person or any person is in breach of any contract in relation to the Subsidiary Rights the Proprietor shall have the option of joining in with the Publisher in any action taken by the Publisher to prevent such infringement and of sharing costs and damages relating to such action in such proportion as may be agreed. Where any proceedings are instituted by the Publisher and no agreement exists between the Publisher and the Proprietor in relation to the costs of such proceedings then the Publisher shall have the right to take such action as the Publisher considers appropriate and the damages in relation to such action shall be applied by the Publisher first by way of repayment of any costs incurred by the Publisher (including a reasonable allowance for overhead costs of the Publisher) and the balance remaining shall be applied [as to [*percentage*]% to the Proprietor the remainder being retained and applied by the Publisher in accordance with the provisions of Clauses 4.3 and 6.3].

9.2   The Proprietor undertakes to do any and all acts and execute any and all documents in such manner and at such locations as may be required by the Publisher in its sole discretion in order to protect perfect or enforce any of the Subsidiary Rights or any of the other rights granted to the Publisher pursuant to this Agreement. As security for the performance by the Proprietor of the Proprietor's obligations under this Agreement if the Proprietor shall have failed following 14 days' notice from the Publisher to execute any document or perform any act required pursuant to this Agreement the Publisher shall have the right to do so in the place and stead of the Proprietor as the lawfully appointed attorney of the Proprietor and the Proprietor undertakes and warrants that the Proprietor shall confirm and ratify and be bound by any and all of the actions of the Publisher pursuant to this Clause and such Proprietority and appointment shall take effect as an irrevocable appointment pursuant to Section 4 of the Powers of Attorney Act 1971.

Clause 8.5   There are circumstances where provision should be made for Value Added Tax (see paragraph 11.28) and where it may be appropriate for self billing arrangements to be made (see paragraph 12.26).

Clause 9.1   The royalty provisions do not make any specific allowance for sums recovered by the Publisher through court actions against third parties who infringe copyright in the Work. This provision permits Publisher and Proprietor to agree upon how such sums are applied.

Clause 9.2   In the United Kingdom an exclusive licensee may commence court proceedings to prevent infringement without the consent of the copyright owner. In some overseas territories the consent of the copyright owner may be required. This provision permits the Publisher to act as the lawfully appointed attorney of the Proprietor in such circumstances. Many documents contain references to Powers of Attorney being coupled with an interest and therefore being irrevocable. The fact is, however, that such powers are not irrevocable unless they are given by way of security, as in the case of this clause.

10. ALTERNATIVE DISPUTE RESOLUTION

10.1 If either party is of the opinion that the other party to this Agreement is in breach of any material condition or obligation pursuant to this Agreement including without prejudice any obligation to pay money (but excluding any matter referred to in Clause 10.4) such dispute shall be dealt with in accordance with the alternative dispute resolution procedure set out in this Clause.

10.2 The Publisher and the Proprietor undertake that they shall endeavour in good faith to resolve any dispute or claim arising in relation to the Work or this Agreement by means of good faith negotiations which shall take place between the Proprietor and a senior executive of the Publisher who shall have authority to settle the dispute. If the dispute is not resolved within [14] days from commencement of good faith negotiations the Publisher and the Proprietor shall endeavour in good faith to resolve the dispute through an alternative dispute resolution procedure carried out in accordance with the recommendations of the Centre for Dispute Resolution.

10.3 All negotiations in relation to the matters in dispute shall be strictly confidential and shall be without prejudice to the rights of the Proprietor and the Publisher in any future proceedings. If the parties fail to reach an agreement which finally resolves all matters in dispute within 60 days of having commenced negotiations pursuant to the alternative dispute resolution procedure or if such negotiations fail to take place within 30 days from the date specified in Clause 10.2 then either party shall be entitled:

(a) to refer the matter to a single arbiter agreed upon by the Publisher and the Proprietor whose decision shall be final and binding on the parties; or

(b) to seek such legal remedies as may be appropriate.

10.4 [The provisions of Clauses 10.1 to 10.3 shall not apply in relation to any dispute or claim which involves a third party.]

11. TERMINATION

11.1 If pursuant to the provisions of Clause 10 any party to this Agreement is found to be in breach of any material obligation on its part pursuant to this Agreement and shall not have remedied such breach to the extent possible within 30 days of the date of such finding the other party may terminate this Agreement by notice in writing.

Clause 10 Many publishing agreements provide for resolution of disputes by arbitration. Arbitration is slow, ineffective and costly. Recently some publishing agreements have provided for resolution by arbitration through the Publishers' Association. There may be circumstances where Proprietors or Publishers do not wish the Publishers' Association to become involved in (or even know about) certain disputes. Clauses 10.1 to 10.4 of this Document provide for a quick, effective, cheap and private means of resolution of disputes.

Clause 11.1 This clause provides each party with a termination right if alternative dispute resolution has not been successful and if the party in breach has failed to remedy any breach of any material provision of the Agreement after a 30-day notice period.

11.2 The waiver by either party of any breach by the other of the terms of this Agreement shall not be deemed to be a continuing waiver or a waiver of any other breach or default on the part of the other of the terms of this Agreement.

11.3 Termination of the grant of rights pursuant to Clause 11.1 shall be without prejudice to:

(a) the continuation of any licence or sub-licence granted by the Publisher and the right of the Publisher to collect and account to the Proprietor in relation to all income due to the Proprietor under this Agreement arising pursuant to agreements entered into in relation to any subsidiary rights;

(b) the right of the Proprietor to receive remuneration from the Publisher;

(c) any claims by the Proprietor against the Publisher as at the date of termination.

12. <u>NOTICES</u>

12.1 Notice or other document required to be given under this Agreement or any communication between the parties with respect to any of the provisions of this Agreement shall be in writing in English and be deemed duly given if signed by or on behalf of a duly authorised officer of the party giving the notice and if left at or sent by pre-paid registered or recorded delivery post or by telex telegram cable facsimile transmission or other means of telecommunication in permanent written form to the address of the party receiving such notice as set out at the head of the Agreement or as notified between the parties for the purpose of this Clause.

12.2 Any such notice or other communication shall be deemed to be given to and received by the addressee:

(a) at the time the same is left at the address of or handed to a representative of the party to be served;

(b) by post on the day not being a Sunday or Public Holiday two days following the date of posting;

(c) in the case of a telex telegram cable facsimile transmission or other means of telecommunication on the next following day.

12.3 In proving the giving of a notice it should be sufficient to prove that the notice was left or that the envelope containing the notice was properly addressed and posted or that the applicable means of telecommunication was addressed and despatched and despatch of the transmission was confirmed and/or acknowledged as the case may be.

Clause 12.1 A number of clauses in the Document provide for a means of exercising rights and a notice provision is therefore necessary.

12.4   Communications addressed to the Publisher shall be marked for the attention of [*name*] with a copy to [*address*].

13.   DEFINITIONS AND INTERPRETATION

13.1   The following definitions apply in this Agreement:

"Advance"
The sum specified in Clause 4.1 which shall be recoupable from all other sums payable to the Proprietor under this Agreement.

"Publication Rights"
The sole and exclusive right to print and/or publish the Work [in the [*specify*] language] in volume or sheet form in paperback or hardback form and the right to authorise others to do so.

["Published Price"]
The price recommended by the Publisher in any country of sale of copies of the Work exclusive of any amount of sales or value added or other taxes (if applicable).

["Publisher's Receipts"]
100% of all sums directly and identifiably received by the Publisher in sterling in the United Kingdom (excluding any sums paid for the use of the typographical arrangement of the Work or paid for the supply of disks plates or other pre-print materials) in relation to the categories of Publication Rights and Subsidiary Rights referred to in Clauses 4.3 and 6.3 the Publisher's Receipts in each such category being computed on a separate basis.

13.2   The following terms are defined in this Agreement in the place indicated:

"Advance":	Clauses 4 and 13.1
"Delivery Materials":	Clause 1.1
"Royalties":	Clause 4.3
"Subsidiary Rights":	The Schedule
"Territory":	Clause 1.1
"Work":	Clause 1.1 and Clause 13.7

13.3   Any reference in this Agreement to any statute or statutory provision shall be construed as including a reference to that statute or statutory provision as from time to time amended modified extended or re-enacted whether before or after the date of this Agreement and to all statutory

Clause 13.1   The definitions contained in clause 13.1 will need review in order to fit the appropriate circumstances. The Publisher may wish the Publication Rights to contain express reference to the language of the Publisher's home market, in order to protect against parallel imports. (See the annotation to clause 1.1 of this document, and see also paragraph 11.3).

Clause 13.2   The references in this clause need to be adjusted to fit the appropriate circumstances. In particular, it may be appropriate to insert additional clauses (such as those contained in Documents 6 (a) and 6 (b)) which will necessitate consequential renumbering.

instruments orders and regulations for the time being made pursuant to it or deriving validity from it.

13.4   Unless the context otherwise requires words denoting the singular shall include the plural and vice versa and words denoting any one gender shall include all genders and words denoting persons shall include bodies corporate unincorporated associations and partnerships.

13.5   All warranties and obligations on the part of the Proprietor pursuant to this Agreement shall survive the expiry of any term of years specified in this Agreement whether by determination or by effluxion of time.

13.6   The word "copyright" means the entire copyright and design right subsisting under the laws of the United Kingdom and any and all analogous rights subsisting under the laws of each and every jurisdiction throughout the world.

13.7   The word "Work" shall include the typographical arrangement of any published edition of the Work printed by the Proprietor and all associated materials such as jacket design and publicity and advertising material.

14.   MISCELLANEOUS

14.1   Nothing contained in this Agreement shall constitute or shall be construed as constituting a partnership or contract of employment between the parties.

14.2   Neither party shall have any obligation to the other in the event of any act or omission on the part of such party where such act or omission results from the occurrence of any event which is outside the reasonable control of such party.

14.3   This Agreement contains the full and complete understanding between the parties and supersedes all prior arrangements and understandings whether written or oral appertaining to the subject matter of this Agreement and may not be varied except by an instrument in writing signed by all the parties to this Agreement. The Proprietor acknowledges that no representations or promises not expressly contained in this Agreement have been made to the Proprietor by the Publisher or any of its servants agents employees members or representatives.

Clause 14.1   Under English law if two parties carry on business in common with a view to profit and share profit, the arrangement is capable of being considered a partnership. This provision ensures that no partnership is created inadvertently, and also expressly excludes the possibility of an employment contract being created.

Clause 14.2   This is a short form of what is frequently referred to as a "force majeure" clause. It may not always be appropriate for this clause to be included, since it may permit a Proprietor to argue against a Publisher that the Proprietor is not liable in certain circumstances which are beyond the Proprietor's reasonable control.

Clause 14.3   There are occasions where oral agreements or other understandings may be created in relation to a Work which may contain either additional obligations or obligations which conflict with those set out in subsequent written agreement. This provision makes it clear that all previous arrangements and understandings are at an end and the contract is the only document relevant to the obligations and rights of the parties in relation to its subject matter. The final part of the clause expressly excludes the possibility of any liability of the Publisher for misrepresentation on the part of any of its servants, agents, employees or representatives (see paragraph 2.17).

14.4   This Agreement shall be governed and construed in accordance with the laws of England and Wales whose courts shall be courts of competent jurisdiction.

[certificate of value]

IN WITNESS this Agreement has been executed as a Deed and is intended to be delivered and is delivered on the day month and year first above written

THE SCHEDULE
Subsidiary Rights
(Clause 6.3)

The expression "Subsidiary Rights" means in relation to the Work the following sole and exclusive rights throughout the world:

(1)   "Anthology and Quotation Rights" namely the sole and exclusive right to authorise the reproduction of extracts and quotations from the Work (including illustrations diagrams and maps contained in the Work) in other publications.

(2)   "Book Club Rights" namely the sole and exclusive right to license the Work to book clubs and similar organisations [*these rights may form part of the Publication Rights*].

(3)   "Braille Rights" namely the sole and exclusive right to authorise the use of the Work in braille form or in "talking-book" form.

(4)   "Computer Game Rights" namely the sole and exclusive right to authorise the making of any computer game based on the Work.

(5)   "Digest Rights" namely the sole and exclusive right to authorise the publication of abridgments or condensations of the Work either in volume form or in magazines journals periodicals newspapers or other works.

Clause 14.4   Where a contract is made between two entities in England and Wales, it will generally not be necessary to insert a provision of this nature, but where a contract is to be created with a foreign company (or a company situate in Scotland or Northern Ireland) this provision should always be included.

Certificate of value   Although it had been intended to abolish stamp duty on assignments of intellectual property at the same time as the introduction of paperless share transfer, the failure of the Stock Exchange system TAURUS has delayed the abolition of stamp duty which is still technically payable in relation to assignments of copyright. The publishing industry has, traditionally, never made provision for the payment of stamp duty in assignments of copyright and for this reason no provision is included in this Document – although there are now many circumstances where it is advisable. A suitable form of wording may, however, be found in Document 6 (d) and a summary of the current legislation relating to stamp duty may be found in paragraph 11.29.

Testimonium clause   This clause begins with the words "IN WITNESS". This form of wording is appropriate for documents which are executed as deeds. The purpose of executing this document as a deed is to ensure that the appointment by the Proprietor of the Publisher as the attorney of the Proprietor permits the Publisher to execute documents by way of deed.

(6) "Educational Rights" namely the sole and exclusive right to authorise the publication of special editions of the Work which may contain additional material or limited vocabulary and which are suitable for educational use.

(7) "First Serial Rights" namely the sole and exclusive right to authorise the publication of extracts of the Work in one issue on more than one successive or non-successive issue of newspapers magazines or periodicals.

(8) "Information Storage and Retrieval Rights" namely the sole and exclusive right to authorise the use of the Work in electronic database by means of storage and retrieval systems and/or by any "on-line" or "off-line" and any other means in any format whatever including without limitation microfilm magnetic tape reprography magnetic and/or optical disk and other digital and/or mechanical and/or electronic means whether now known or in future invented.

(9) "Merchandising Rights" namely the sole and exclusive right to author- ise the use of characters or illustrations from the Work in or upon artifacts and/or articles other than books.

(10) "Motion Picture and Television Rights" namely the sole and exclusive right to authorise the making of any film or television production or video- gram based upon the Work.

(11) "Other Rights" namely any right of publication in the Work other than those referred to in this Schedule.

(12) "Paperback Rights" namely the sole and exclusive right to authorise the publication of the Work in paperback format [*these rights may form part of the Publication Rights*].

(13) "Radio Rights" namely the sole and exclusive right to authorise the making of any radio adaptation or dramatisation of the Work.

(14) "Reading Rights" namely the sole and exclusive right to authorise the non-dramatic reading of the Work on radio or television or upon the live stage including the making of videograms or records of such non-dramatic or "straight" reading.

(15) "Reprint Rights" namely the sole and exclusive right to authorise the use by foreign publishers of materials which have been produced by the Publisher so as to enable the foreign publishers to produce their own editions of the Work.

(16) "Reprographic Rights" namely the sole and exclusive right to author- ise the reprographic reproduction of the Work.

(17) "Second and Subsequent Serial Rights" namely the sole and exclusive right to authorise the issue or publication of the Work in newspapers or periodicals appearing subsequent to those publications first granted licences in relation to the First Serial Rights.

(18) "Single Issue Rights" namely the sole and exclusive right to authorise the single issue or "one-shot" publication of the complete work or a condensed version of it in a single issue of a periodical or newspaper.

(19) "Sound Recording Rights" namely the sole and exclusive right to authorise the reproduction distribution and other exploitation of the Work by means of sound recordings.

(20) "Translation Rights" namely the sole and exclusive right to authorise the making and exploitation of the Work in foreign languages.

(21) "US Rights" namely the sole and exclusive right to authorise the exploitation of the Work in hardback or paperback form in the United States of America [*these rights may form part of the Publication Rights*].

EXECUTED AND DELIVERED AS A DEED BY
[*Publisher*]
acting by [*a director*
and its secretary]
[*two directors*]

EXECUTED AND DELIVERED AS A DEED BY
[*Publisher*]
acting by [*a director*
and its secretary]
[*two directors*]

Schedule The Schedule needs to be modified to reflect the commercial circumstances in each case.

DOCUMENT 32

Rights licence

[IMPORTANT NOTE: Please read the section "About this book" on page v, before copying or using this Document]

Purpose of this Document

This is a form of agreement suitable for use by publishers when licensing rights. This Document is drafted from the point of view of the publisher granting rights and should be contrasted with the provisions of Document 31 which is drafted from the point of view of a publisher acquiring rights.

Relevant text

The text of this Work covers a number of topics which are relevant to documents of this nature including:

- buying and selling rights (paragraphs 11.2 to 11.9)
- remuneration provisions in rights agreements (paragraphs 11.22 to 11.26)
- taxation (paragraphs 11.27 to 11.29 and 12.22 to 12.30)
- commercial terms of offers (paragraphs 1.22 and 1.23)
- the law of contract and agency (paragraphs 2.1 to 2.30)
- creation, existence and transfer of copyrights (paragraphs 3.1 to 3.45)
- international copyright protection (paragraphs 4.1 to 4.17)
- moral rights (paragraphs 5.1 to 5.22)
- permissions, fair dealings and rights clearances (paragraphs 8.1 to 8.44)
- liability for content (paragraphs 9.1 to 9.49)
- buying and selling rights (paragraphs 11.1 to 11.29)
- infringement and enforcement (paragraphs 13.1 to 13.17)
- termination and recapture (paragraphs 14.1 to 14.10)
- competition law (paragraphs 16.1 to 16.28)
- multimedia (paragraphs 19.1 to 19.55)

THIS AGREEMENT is made the   day of

BETWEEN:

(1) [*Name*] LIMITED (registered number [*number*]) whose [registered office] [principal place of business] is at [*address*] ("Publisher") and

(2) [*Name*] LIMITED (registered number [*number*]) whose [registered office] [principal place of business] is at [*address*] ("Licensee" which expression shall include all Associates sub-licensees and assignees with the prior written consent of the Publisher deriving title through or from the Licensee)

IT IS AGREED as follows:

1. GRANT OF RIGHTS

1.1 In consideration of the obligations warranties and undertakings of the Licensee in this Agreement and subject to and conditional upon their full and timely performance and observance the Publisher grants to the Licensee the exclusive licence to exploit the Publication Rights in the work entitled "[*title*]" ("Work") written by [*name of author*] ("Author") throughout the [*specify territory*] ("Territory") for the period of [*specify*] years from the date of this Agreement ("Licence Period").

1.2 The Publisher undertakes to deliver to the Licensee within [*specify*] days from the date of this Agreement the following delivery materials ("Delivery Materials") [*specify materials required*] in respect of all text and illustrations contained in the Work and grants the Licensee the non-exclusive right in the Territory during the Licence Period to use such Delivery Materials subject to the provisions of Clause 1.3.

1.3 The Licensee agrees and undertakes with the Publisher to obtain and pay for all permissions and consents required in order to enable the exploitation of any illustrations or photographs contained in the Work and any other material in respect of which the Publisher notifies the Licensee that rights are owned or controlled by third parties.

2. PUBLISHER'S WARRANTIES

The Publisher warrants agrees and undertakes with the Licensee that:

2.1 the Publisher is free to enter into this Agreement and grant the Licensee the rights granted in it and is not under any disability restriction or prohibition which might prevent the Publisher from performing or observing any of the Publisher's obligations under this Agreement;

Clause 1.1 Relevant details need to be inserted. It will be noted that the grant of rights is conditional upon full and timely performance by the Licensee of its obligations under the Agreement.

Clause 1.2 The licence to use the Delivery Materials is non-exclusive. In other words the Publisher may itself use the Delivery Materials or permit third parties to use them.

Clause 1.3 This provision requires the Licensee to pay all fees relating to permissions, consents and use of third party rights.

2.2   the Publisher has not entered into and shall not enter into any arrangement which may conflict with this Agreement;

2.3   following the expiry of the Licence Period by effluxion of time the Licensee shall have the non-exclusive right subject to the terms and conditions of this Agreement for the further period of three calendar months to sell off copies of the Work previously printed by the Licensee during the Licence Period;

2.4   to the best of the Publisher's knowledge the Work is not obscene or defamatory and does not infringe any right of copyright.

3.   REMUNERATION

3.1   The Licensee agrees to pay or procure the payment to all relevant third parties in a timely manner of all sums required to be paid pursuant to the provisions of Clause 1.3 and undertakes to pay to the Publisher:

(a)   an advance ("Advance") of £[*amount*] as to [*percentage*]% on signature of this Agreement and [*percentage*]% on delivery of the Delivery Materials

(b)   the following royalties ("Royalties") on each Accounting Date in accordance with the provisions of this Agreement:

[*specify*]

[*specify*]

[*specify*]

(c)   such costs in respect of the manufacture and delivery to the Licensee of the Delivery Materials as may be notified by the Publisher in writing.

3.2   The Licensee shall not have the right to withhold any part of sums due to the Publisher as a reserve against returns and/or credits and in the event that the Licensee is required by law to make any withholding from sums to be remitted to the Publisher the Licensee shall prior to the making of any withholding furnish the Publisher with evidence satisfactory to the Publisher

---

Clause 2.3   The Licensee is entitled to a three-month non-exclusive sell-off period (see paragraphs 12.4 and 11.11).

Clause 2.4   The warranty is given to the best of the Publisher's belief. In other words it is not an absolute warranty that the Work is not obscene or defamatory etc.

Clause 3.1   The obligation to pay permission fees etc is passed on to the Licensee. The dates for payments of the instalments of the Advance are linked to signature of the Agreement and delivery of materials rather than publication of the Work. The Advance is not expressed to be recoupable from the royalties. The Licensee is required to pay the costs of provision of Delivery Material and there is no provision permitting the Licensee to recover such costs from the Royalty. If rights other than printed volume publication rights are to be granted to the Licensee provision will need to be made for payment based on the Licensee's receipts (or receivables – see paragraphs 11.24 and 1.16) possibly along the lines provided in Document 4 clauses 9.1 and 9.2.

in its entire discretion as to the Licensee's obligation to make such withholding of payment.

3.3   If exchange control or other restrictions prevent or threaten to prevent the remittance to the Publisher of any money payable under this Agreement the Licensee shall immediately advise the Publisher in writing and follow the Publisher's instructions in respect of the money to be remitted including if required depositing the same with any bank or other person designated by the Publisher at such location as may be designated by the Publisher.

3.4   If any withholding or other taxes are required to be deducted from any money provided to be remitted to the Publisher pursuant to this Agreement it shall be the responsibility of the Licensee to ensure that no improper deductions are made and that the Publisher is provided with all necessary receipts certificates and other documents and all information required in order to avail the Publisher of any tax credit or other fiscal advantage and the Licensee undertakes to account to the Publisher in relation to any tax credit or saving received by the Licensee in relation to royalty payments to the Publisher.

4.   LICENSEE'S UNDERTAKINGS

The Licensee warrants undertakes confirms and agrees with the Publisher:

4.1   all rights and title in and to the Work and the Delivery Materials are expressly reserved to the Publisher subject to the licence in Clause 1;

4.2   the Licensee shall publish the Work at the Licensee's sole cost and expense by no later than [*specify date*] and shall deliver to the Publisher not less than [*specify*] copies of each edition or publication of the Work published by the Licensee;

4.3   the Licensee shall not by any act or omission impair or prejudice the copyright in the Work or violate any moral right or deal with the Work or the Delivery Materials so that any third party might obtain any lien or other right of whatever nature incompatible with the rights of the Publisher and the Licensee shall ensure that all copies of the Work and artwork published and

---

Clause 3.2   This provision prevents the Licensee from deducting parts of the royalty payments to hold as reserves against returned books. If the Licensee is required by law to deduct withholding taxes on royalty payments it is required to produce documentary evidence satisfactory to the Publisher of its liability.

Clause 3.3   This provision protects the Publisher if exchange control restrictions are imposed in any territory, and permits the Publisher to receive income in that territory.

Clause 3.4   This clause not only requires the Licensee to provide the Publisher with all necessary receipts and information, but also provides that the Licensee is to bring into account any tax credits or savings achieved by the Licensee which are attributable to royalty payments under the Agreement.

Clause 4.1   This clause clarifies that the copyright remains vested in the Publisher, subject only to the licence granted to the Licensee.

Clause 4.2   This clause obliges the Licensee to publish by a certain date and clarifies the fact that all costs of publication are borne by the Licensee. It is also usual for a Publisher to request copies of editions published by the Licensee.

distributed by the Licensee shall contain full and accurate copyright notices credit attributions and acknowledgments;

4.4   the Licensee shall by no later than the date specified in Clause 4.2 or the determination of the Licence Period if sooner at the Licensee's cost and expense return to the Publisher the Delivery Materials and all other material supplied by the Publisher in the same condition as when supplied to the Licensee;

4.5   the Licensee shall not create any promotional material or artwork relating to the Work without the prior written consent of the Publisher and in respect of any material commissioned or manufactured by the Licensee the copyright shall be secured in the name of the Publisher and title to all physical material shall belong to and be dealt with as if such physical material had been supplied by the Publisher and the Publisher shall at all times have unrestricted access to the same for the purposes of the Publisher;

4.6   the Licensee shall give full particulars to the Publisher as soon as the Licensee becomes aware of any actual or threatened claim by any third party in connection with the Work;

4.7   the Licensee shall punctually pay to the Publisher all sums owing to the Publisher under this Agreement;

4.8   the Licensee shall not assign charge license sub-license or otherwise part with possession of the benefit or burden of this Agreement without the prior written consent of the Publisher;

4.9   the Licensee shall not copy or duplicate the Delivery Materials or any part of them otherwise than for the purpose of printing and publishing the Work in accordance with this Agreement;

Clause 4.3 This provision protects the Delivery Materials from being impounded by third parties, and protects the copyright in the Work from the consequences of failure to include correct copyright notices (see paragraphs 4.9 and 4.10). The clause also protects the Publisher from the Licensee violating any moral right in relation to the Work (see paragraphs 5.2 to 5.22).

Clause 4.4 When the Licensee has used the Delivery Materials to create its edition it will no longer need them and they should be returned to the Publisher.

Clause 4.5 The Publisher will in many circumstances wish to control the nature and type of publicity and advertising material. There are occasions where material produced by the Publisher's Licensee may be of value to the Publisher since it can be used by licensees in other territories. This provision passes all rights of copyright and other rights in such material to the Publisher in order to permit the Publisher to provide the benefit of this material to its other Licensees.

Clause 4.6 If there is any claim in relation to copyright infringement or invasion of privacy or any other matter in relation to the Work it is in the Publisher's interests to be apprised of such claim at the earliest possible moment.

Clause 4.7 In circumstances where the Agreement does not contain a provision making time of the essence such as that contained in clause 8.6 this provision requires the Licensee to make payments in a punctual manner.

Clause 4.8 Generally licences are considered to be personal, but there are some circumstances in which a licence may be sub-licensed. This provision expressly precludes the Licensee from entering into sub-licences or assigning the benefit of the Agreement.

Clause 4.9 Although the Licensee will not have the right to use copyright materials for purposes other than those consented to by their owner, this provision makes it clear that all materials provided under the Agreement can be used only to assist the Licensee to print and publish the Work.

4.10   the Licensee shall retain total control and actual possession at all times of the Delivery Materials and maintain the Delivery Materials safe and secure in appropriate storage facilities the risk in the Delivery Materials passing to the Licensee on the Publisher's appropriation in order to effect Delivery pursuant to this Agreement;

4.11   the Licensee shall maintain the Work in a prominent position in the Licensee's catalogue and ensure that the Work does not go out of print at any time during the Licence Period;

4.12   the Licensee shall advertise the Work throughout the Territory in the same manner as other books published by the Licensee in the Territory and the Licensee shall not alter or adapt the Work in any way or omit or remove any author's credits or acknowledgments from the Work or add any imprint or trade mark other than the Licensee's and such other imprint or trade mark as may be permitted by the Publisher;

4.13   the Licensee shall exploit the rights granted to the Licensee to the best of the Licensee's skill and ability with the utmost despatch and ensure the highest possible Royalties payable to the Publisher and ensure that the Work is given fair and equitable treatment and not discriminated in favour of any other books which the Licensee may publish or distribute in the Territory;

4.14   the Licensee shall at the end of the three month sell-off period referred to in Clause 2.3 at the discretion of the Publisher permit the Publisher to purchase from the Licensee all copies of the Work in the possession of or under the control of the Licensee which are then unsold at a unit cost equal to the actual cost of printing of the Licensee or if the Publisher shall direct the Licensee shall procure their destruction and provide certificates and affidavits of destruction in such form as may be satisfactory to the Publisher;

4.15   the Licensee shall indemnify and keep fully indemnified the Publisher from and against all actions proceedings claims demands costs (including without prejudice to the generality of this provision the legal costs of the Publisher on a solicitor and own client basis) awards and damages arising

---

Clause 4.10   This provision protects the Publisher's interests in the Delivery Materials and specifies the moment when risk in the Delivery Materials passes to the Licensee (see paragraph 12.11).

Clause 4.11   The Licensee is required to keep the Work in print and in the Licensee's catalogue during the Licence Period.

Clause 4.12   This provision ensures that the Work is given the same degree of prominence as that given by the Licensee to the Licensee's other works and prevents the addition of imprints or trade marks other than those of the Publisher and the Licensee. The clause also specifically prohibits the Licensee from making any alteration or adaptation to the Work or omitting any of the Author's credits or acknowledgments.

Clause 4.13   The Licensee is required to exploit the rights in a manner consistent with achieving the highest royalties and to ensure that the Work is not discriminated against in favour of other publications in which the Licensee may have an interest.

Clause 4.14   This provision permits the Publisher to eliminate or purchase the Licensee's unsold stock of books at the end of the Licence Period.

directly or indirectly as a result of any breach or non-performance by the Licensee of any of the Licensee's undertakings warranties or obligations under this Agreement.

5.   ROYALTY ACCOUNTING

5.1   The Licensee shall on each Accounting Date render to the Publisher a full and complete statement showing all money owing to the Publisher in respect of the preceding Accounting Period.

5.2   The statement of account in Clause 5.1 shall be in such form as the Publisher shall require and shall contain full details of all copies of the Work sold and each such statement shall be accompanied by payment of all amounts owing without reserve.

5.3   Pounds sterling shall be the currency of account and where any sums are received in a currency other than pounds sterling the same shall be converted at the [mid-market rate calculated using the "Financial Times" index on the date of receipt] [best obtainable rate of exchange on the date payment is due].

5.4   Value Added Tax shall be payable by the Licensee to the Publisher in respect of all payments made to or to the order of the Publisher pursuant to this Agreement.

5.5   The Licensee shall keep full and proper books of account relating to the exploitation of its rights under this Agreement and the Publisher or its representative at any time during the Licence Period and for six years afterwards shall have the right on giving reasonable prior notice to inspect audit and take copies of such books of account during normal business hours. In the event that such audit or inspection reveals any deficiency in money paid to the Publisher then the Licensee shall immediately pay the same to the Publisher together with interest from the date first due calculated with monthly rests at a rate of [*percentage*]% above prime or base rate charged by its bankers to the Publisher from time to time and shall pay all reasonable costs incurred by the Publisher directly as a result of such inspection.

5.6   The Licensee shall keep confidential and shall not disclose to any third parties (other than professional advisers where necessary) the results of any

---

Clause 4.15   An explanation of the significance of warranties and indemnities may be found in paragraph 7.15.

Clause 5.1   The Accounting Dates and Accounting Periods are defined in clause 8.1 in accordance with standard industry practice. There may be occasions, however, where it is appropriate to vary these.

Clause 5.2   This provision gives the Publisher the opportunity of determining the particulars which are to be contained in the statement of account. Each statement must be accompanied by payment of sums shown to be owing without deduction of any reserves.

Clause 5.3   It may or may not be appropriate for pounds sterling to be the currency of account. If the Licensee is situate in a foreign territory, exchange conversion provisions may be required.

Clause 5.4   It will be necessary to adjust this provision in the light of prevailing law. A short explanation of current Value Added Tax legislation may be found in paragraph 11.28 and paragraphs 12.22 to 12.30.

Clause 5.5   There may be occasions when a Publisher will wish to inspect and audit the books of account of the Licensee. Even if such audit rights are not exercised, an audit provision should always be included in licence agreements.

such inspection or audit or any of the terms of this Agreement or any matters incidental to it or relating to the business of the Publisher and shall indemnify the Publisher fully in respect of any breach of its obligations under this Clause 5.6.

6.   DETERMINATION

It shall constitute the repudiation by the Licensee of its obligations under this Agreement and at any time the Publisher may serve written notice on the Licensee accepting such repudiation and determining the Licence Period and the Licensee's rights under this Agreement if:

6.1   the Licensee fails to pay any amount due under this Agreement in full within three days of its due date and such failure is not remedied within seven days of receipt of written notice;

6.2   the Licensee is in breach of any other material term of this Agreement which is incapable of remedy or if capable of remedy is not remedied within fourteen days of the Licensee becoming aware of it;

6.3   any of the Licensee's representations shall prove to have been incorrect when made or become materially incorrect and the Publisher's rights and entitlements under this Agreement are materially and adversely affected;

6.4   the Licensee transfers disposes of or threatens to transfer or dispose of any part of its assets which is likely in the opinion of the Publisher to prevent or materially to inhibit the performance by the Licensee of its obligations under this Agreement;

6.5   any indebtedness guarantee or similar obligation of the Licensee or of any guarantor of the Licensee becomes due or capable of being declared due before its stated maturity or is not discharged at maturity or the Licensee or any guarantor of the Licensee defaults under or commits a breach of the provisions of any guarantee or other obligation (whether actual or contingent) of any agreement pursuant to which any such indebtedness guarantee or other obligation was incurred all or any of which shall in the reasonable opinion of the Publisher materially affect its rights and entitlements under this Agreement;

Clause 6   For an examination of the legal significance of the term "repudiation" reference should be made to paragraph 14.5 and to paragraphs 14.2 to 14.4.

Clause 6.1   This clause provides the Licensee with the opportunity of remedying a breach. The time period allowed to remedy pecuniary breaches is normally less than that allowed to remedy non-pecuniary breaches.

Clause 6.2   This clause permits the Licensee to remedy a non-pecuniary material breach. The time period allowed is longer than that for a pecuniary breach.

Clause 6.3   There may be circumstances where the Publisher has entered into the Agreement on the basis of representations made by the Licensee. This clause permits the Publisher to terminate the Agreement if the representations prove to have been incorrect or subsequently become incorrect.

Clause 6.4   There are occasions where a Licensee becomes less financially secure and disposes of its assets. Where a Publisher has entered into an agreement in reliance on the Licensee being an entity of substance, such occasions may cause concern to the Publisher, and this provision permits the Publisher to terminate the Agreement in such instances.

Clause 6.5   Financial default of the Licensee in relation to any guarantee or obligation is a further event normally permitting termination.

6.6   the Licensee is declared or becomes insolvent;

6.7   the Licensee convenes a meeting of its creditors or proposes or makes any arrangement or composition with or any assignment for the benefit of its creditors or a petition is presented or a meeting is convened for the purpose of considering a resolution or other steps are taken for the winding up of the Licensee (save for the purpose of and followed by a voluntary reconstruction or amalgamation previously approved in writing by the Publisher) or if an incumbrancer takes possession or a trustee administrator administrative receiver liquidator or similar officer is appointed in respect of all or any part of its business or assets or any distress execution or other legal process is levied threatened enforced upon or sued out against any of such assets;

6.8   the Licensee shall cease or abandon or announce that it intends to cease or abandon the business of publishing books;

6.9   the Work goes out of print or is deleted from the Licensee's catalogue.

7.   NOTICE

7.1   Any notice or other document required to be given under this Agreement or any communication between the parties with respect to any of the provisions of this Agreement shall be in writing in English and be deemed duly given if signed by or on behalf of a duly authorised officer of the party giving the notice and if left at or sent by pre-paid registered or recorded delivery post or by telex telegram cable facsimile transmission or other means of telecommunication in permanent written form to the address of the party receiving such notice as set out at the head of the Agreement or as notified between the parties for the purpose of this Clause.

7.2   Any such notice or other communication shall be deemed to be given to and received by the addressee:

(a)   at the time the same is left at the address of or handed to a representative of the party to be served;

(b)   by post on the day not being a Sunday or Public Holiday two days following the date of posting;

(c)   in the case of a telex telegram cable facsimile transmission or other means of telecommunication on the next following day.

Clause 6.6   For the consequences of insolvency, reference should be made to paragraphs 15.2 to 15.4.

Clause 6.7   There may be occasions when a Licensee does not actually become insolvent, but a creditor enforces security over the Licensee's business. This could have serious consequences for a Publisher and this clause protects the Publisher's interests by providing that such circumstances will entitle the Publisher to terminate the Agreement.

Clause 6.8   Where a Licensee ceases to carry on business or announces that it intends to cease its business, a Publisher will wish to recover its rights as soon as possible.

Clause 6.9   Although clause 4.11 imposes a specific obligation on the Licensee to keep the Work in print, this clause permits the Publisher to terminate if it does not do so.

Clause 7   A number of clauses in the document provide for a means of exercising rights, and a notice provision is therefore necessary.

7.3   In proving the giving of a notice it should be sufficient to prove that the notice was left or that the envelope containing the notice was properly addressed and posted or that the applicable means of telecommunication was addressed and despatched and despatch of the transmission was confirmed and/or acknowledged as the case may be.

7.4   Communications addressed to the Publisher shall be marked for the attention of [*name*] with a copy to [*name*] of [*address*].

8.   DEFINITIONS AND INTERPRETATION

8.1 The following definitions apply in this Agreement:

"Accounting Date"
90 days from the end of each Accounting Period

"Accounting Period"
successive periods ending on 30 June and 31 December in each year

"Associate"
in relation to the Licensee any associate or associated company within the meaning of Section 416 or 417 of the Income and Corporation Taxes Act 1988

"Publication Rights"
the sole and exclusive right to print and/or publish the Work only in volume form in [paperback or] hardback format

8.2   The following terms are defined in this Agreement in the place indicated:

"Advance":	Clause 3.1
"Author":	Clause 1.1
"Delivery Materials":	Clause 1.1
"Licence Period":	Clause 1.1
"Royalties":	Clause 3.1
"Territory":	Clause 1.1
"Work":	Clause 1.1

Clause 8.1   Depending on the royalty provisions which are inserted in clause 3.1(b), it may be necessary to insert definitions for terms such as "Published Price" or "Publisher's Receipts". Document 4, clause 18.1, contains definitions which may be appropriate. The definition of Publication Rights may also need adjustment (see annotation to Document 4, clause 9.2).

Clause 8.2   The references in this clause need to be adjusted to fit the appropriate circumstances. In particular, it may be appropriate to insert additional clauses (such as those contained in Documents 6 (a) and 6 (b)) which will necessitate consequential renumbering.

8.3   Any reference in this Agreement to any statute or statutory provision shall be construed as including a reference to that statute or statutory provision as from time to time amended modified extended or re-enacted whether before or after the date of this Agreement and to all statutory instruments orders and regulations for the time being made pursuant to it or deriving validity from it.

8.4   Unless the context otherwise requires words denoting the singular shall include the plural and vice versa and words denoting any one gender shall include all genders and words denoting persons shall include bodies corporate unincorporated associations and partnerships.

8.5   The word "copyright" means the entire copyright and design right subsisting under the laws of the United Kingdom and any and all analogous rights subsisting under the laws of each and every jurisdiction throughout the world.

8.6   Unless otherwise stated time shall be of the essence for the purpose of the performance of the Licensee's obligations under this Agreement.

8.7   Unless otherwise stated references to clauses sub-clauses sub-paragraphs schedules annexures and exhibits relate to this Agreement.

9.   MISCELLANEOUS

9.1   Nothing contained in this Agreement shall constitute or shall be construed as constituting a partnership or contract of employment between the parties.

9.2   The Publisher shall not be liable to the Licensee for failing to supply or procure the supply of the Delivery Materials and any other material to be supplied under this Agreement due to circumstances beyond its control and it shall not be liable for any expenses or consequential losses whatever suffered by the Licensee.

9.3   The Licensee warrants that it is not the nominee or agent of any undisclosed principal and warrants that it shall assume sole and complete responsibility for the performance of the obligations in this Agreement expressed to be performed by the Licensee.

Clause 8.6   For the significance of time being of the essence reference should be made to paragraph 2.10.

Clause 9.1   Under English law if two parties carry on business in common with a view to profit and share profit, the arrangement is capable of being considered a partnership. This provision ensures that no partnership is created inadvertently, and also expressly excludes the possibility of an employment contract being created.

Clause 9.2   This provision protects the Publisher from any claim by the Licensee in relation to failure to supply Delivery Materials, although there are likely to be circumstances in which the Publisher will incur some liability.

Clause 9.3   This provision protects the Publisher from the consequences of it contracting with a Licensee which has acted as the agent of an undisclosed company whom the Publisher may not consider to be a suitable person to be the Publisher's Licensee.

9.4   This Agreement contains the full and complete understanding between the parties and supersedes all prior arrangements and understandings whether written or oral appertaining to the subject matter of this Agreement and may not be varied except by an instrument in writing signed by all the parties to this Agreement. The Licensee acknowledges that no representations or promises not expressly contained in this Agreement have been made to the Licensee by the Publisher or any of its servants agents employees members or representatives.

9.5   This Agreement shall be governed and construed in accordance with the laws of England and Wales whose courts shall be courts of competent jurisdiction.

AS WITNESS the hands of the duly authorised representatives of the parties the day month and year first above written

SIGNED by [   ]
for and on behalf of
[*The Publisher*]

SIGNED by [   ]
for and on behalf of
[*The Licensee*]

Clause 9.4   There are occasions where oral agreements or other understandings may be created in relation to a Work which may contain either additional obligations or obligations which conflict with those set out in subsequent written agreement. This provision makes it clear that all previous arrangements and understandings are at an end and the contract is the only document relevant to the obligations and rights of the parties in relation to its subject matter. The final part of the clause expressly excludes the possibility of any liability on the part of a Publisher for misrepresentation on the part of any of its servants, agents, employees or representatives.

Clause 9.5   Where a contract is made between two entities in England and Wales, it will generally be necessary to insert a provision of this nature, but where a contract is to be created with a foreign company (or a company situate in Scotland or Northern Ireland) this provision should always be included.

Certificate of value   Although it had been intended to abolish stamp duty on assignments of intellectual property at the same time as the introduction of paperless share transfer, the failure of the Stock Exchange system TAURUS has delayed the abolition of stamp duty which is still technically payable in relation to assignments of copyright. The publishing industry has, traditionally, never made provision for the payment of stamp duty in assignments of copyright and for this reason no provision is included in this Document – although there are now many circumstances where it is advisable. A suitable form of wording may, however, be found in Document 6 (d) and a summary of the current legislation relating to stamp duty may be found in paragraph 11.29.

DOCUMENT 33

Reprint licence

[IMPORTANT NOTE: Please read the section "About this book" on page v, before copying or using this Document]

Purpose of this Document

This is a form of agreement suitable for use by a publisher when licensing reprint rights to a licensee. The Document is drafted from the point of view of a publisher licensing the rights and should be contrasted with the provisions of Document 31 which is drafted from the point of view of a publisher acquiring rights.

Relevant text

The text of this Work covers a number of topics which are relevant to documents of this nature including:

- buying and selling rights (paragraphs 11.2 to 11.9)
- remuneration provisions in rights agreements (paragraphs 11.22 to 11.26)
- taxation (paragraphs 11.27 to 11.29 and 12.22 to 12.30)
- commercial terms of offers (paragraphs 1.22 and 1.23)
- the law of contract and agency (paragraphs 2.1 to 2.30)
- creation, existence and transfer of copyrights (paragraphs 3.1 to 3.45)
- international copyright protection (paragraphs 4.1 to 4.17)
- moral rights (paragraphs 5.1 to 5.22)
- permissions, fair dealings and rights clearances (paragraphs 8.1 to 8.44)
- liability for content (paragraphs 9.1 to 9.49)
- buying and selling rights (paragraphs 11.1 to 11.29)
- infringement and enforcement (paragraphs 13.1 to 13.17)
- termination and recapture (paragraphs 14.1 to 14.10)
- competition law (paragraphs 16.1 to 16.28)
- multimedia (paragraphs 19.1 to 19.55)

THIS AGREEMENT is made the   day of   19

BETWEEN:

(1) *[Name]* LIMITED (registered number *[number]*) whose [registered office] [principal place of business] is at *[address]* ("Publisher") and

(2) *[Name]* LIMITED (registered number *[number]*) whose [registered office] [principal place of business] is at *[address]* ("Licensee" which expression shall include all Associates sub-licensees and assignees with the prior written consent of the Publisher deriving title through or from the Licensee)

WHEREAS

(A) Pursuant to a Licence Agreement dated *[date]* the Publisher granted to the Licensee the sole and exclusive licence to exploit the Publication Rights in the work entitled "*[title]*" ("Work") written by *[name of author]* ("Author") throughout the *[specify territory]* ("Territory") for the period of *[specify]* years ("Term").

(B) The Term has expired and the Licensee wishes to reprint the Work and the Publisher wishes to grant to the Licensee the right to reprint the Work.

NOW IT IS AGREED as follows:

1. GRANT OF RIGHTS

1.1 In consideration of the obligations warranties and undertakings of the Licensee in this Agreement and subject to and conditional upon their full and timely performance and observance the Publisher grants to the Licensee the exclusive licence [to exploit the Publication Rights in the work throughout the Territory for the period of *[specify]* years from the date of this Agreement ("Licence Period")] or [to print and publish an edition of up to *[specify]* numbers of copies of the Work and sell and distribute copies of the Work in the Territory for the period of *[specify]* years from the date of this Agreement ("Licence Period")].

1.2 The Licensee agrees and undertakes with the Publisher to obtain and pay for all permissions and consents required in order to enable the exploitation of any illustrations or photographs contained in the Work and any other material in respect of which the Publisher notifies the Licensee that rights are owned or controlled by third parties.

Recital A The relevant details need to be inserted into this paragraph.

Clause 1.1 Relevant details need to be inserted. It will be noted that the grant of rights is conditional upon full and timely performance by the Licensee of its obligations under the Agreement. This clause offers two alternatives: either the Licensee is granted publication rights for a period of years in the territory or the Licensee is granted the right to print and sell and distribute a specified number of copies of the Work. It will be noted that the Agreement does not provide for delivery of any materials to the Licensee, on the assumption that the Licensee already has these. If this assumption is not correct revisions will need to be made.

Clause 1.2 This provision requires the Licensee to pay all fees relating to permissions, consents and use of third party rights.

2.   PUBLISHER'S WARRANTIES

The Publisher warrants agrees and undertakes with the Licensee that:

2.1   the Publisher is free to enter into this Agreement and grant the Licensee the rights granted in it and is not under any disability restriction or prohibition which might prevent the Publisher from performing or observing any of the Publisher's obligations under this Agreement;

2.2   the Publisher has not entered into and shall not enter into any arrangement which may conflict with this Agreement;

2.3   following the expiry of the Licence Period by effluxion of time the Licensee shall have the non-exclusive right subject to the terms and conditions of this Agreement for the further period of three calendar months to sell off copies of the Work previously printed by the Licensee during the Licence Period;

2.4   to the best of the Publisher's knowledge the Work is not obscene or defamatory and does not infringe any right of copyright.

3.   REMUNERATION

3.1   The Licensee agrees to pay or procure the payment to all relevant third parties in a timely manner of all sums required to be paid pursuant to the provisions of Clause 1.2 and undertakes to pay to the Publisher:

(a)   an advance ("Advance") of £[amount] as to [percentage]% on signature of this Agreement and [percentage]% on [specify date]

(b)   the following royalties ("Royalties") on each Accounting Date in accordance with the provisions of this Agreement:

[specify]

[specify]

[specify]

Clause 2.3   The Licensee is entitled to a three-month non-exclusive sell-off period (see paragraphs 12.4 and 11.11).

Clause 3.1   The obligation to pay permission fees etc is passed on to the Licensee. The dates for payments of the instalments of the Advance are linked to signature of the Agreement and a pre-specified date rather than publication of the Work. The Advance is not expressed to be recoupable from the royalties. If rights other than printed volume publication rights are to be granted to the Licensee provision will need to be made for payment based on the Licensee's receipts (or receivables – see paragraphs 11.24 and 1.16) possibly along the lines provided in Document 4 clauses 9.1 and 9.2.

3.2   The Licensee shall not have the right to withhold any part of sums due to the Publisher as a reserve against returns and/or credits and in the event that the Licensee is required by law to make any withholding from sums to be remitted to the Publisher the Licensee shall prior to the making of any withholding of payment furnish the Publisher with evidence satisfactory to the Publisher in its entire discretion as to the Licensee's obligation to make such withholding of payment.

3.3   If exchange control or other restrictions prevent or threaten to prevent the remittance to the Publisher of any money payable under this Agreement the Licensee shall immediately advise the Publisher in writing and follow the Publisher's instructions in respect of the money to be remitted including if required depositing the same with any bank or other person designated by the Publisher at such location as may be designated by the Publisher.

3.4   If any withholding or other taxes are required to be deducted from any money provided to be remitted to the Publisher pursuant to this Agreement it shall be the responsibility of the Licensee to ensure that no improper deductions are made and that the Publisher is provided with all necessary receipts certificates and other documents and all information required in order to avail the Publisher of any tax credit or other fiscal advantage and the Licensee undertakes to account to the Publisher in relation to any tax credit or saving received by the Licensee in relation to royalty payments to the Publisher.

4.   LICENSEE'S UNDERTAKINGS

The Licensee warrants undertakes confirms and agrees with the Publisher:

4.1   all rights and title in and to the Work are expressly reserved to the Publisher subject to the licence in Clause 1;

4.2   the Licensee shall publish the Work at the Licensee's sole cost and expense by no later than [*specify date*] and shall deliver to the Publisher not less than [*specify*] copies of the edition or publication;

Clause 3.2   This provision prevents the Licensee from deducting parts of the royalty payments to hold as reserves against returned books. If a Licensee is required by law to deduct withholding taxes on royalty payments it is required to produce documentary evidence satisfactory to the Publisher of its liability.

Clause 3.3   This provision protects the Publisher if exchange control restrictions are imposed in any territory, and permits the Publisher to receive income in that territory.

Clause 3.4   This clause not only provides that the Licensee is to provide the Publisher with all necessary receipts and information, but also provides that the Licensee is to bring into account any tax credits or savings achieved by the Licensee which are attributable to royalty payments under the Agreement.

Clause 4.1   This clause clarifies that the copyright remains vested in the Publisher subject only to the licence granted to the Licensee.

Clause 4.2   This clause obliges the Licensee to publish by a certain date and clarifies the fact that full costs of publication are borne by the Licensee. It is also usual for a Publisher to request copies of editions published by the Licensee.

4.3   the Licensee shall not by any act or omission impair or prejudice the copyright in the Work or violate any moral right or deal with the Work so that any third party might obtain any lien or other right of whatever nature incompatible with the rights of the Publisher and the Licensee shall ensure that all copies of the Work and artwork published and distributed by the Licensee shall contain full and accurate copyright notices credit attributions and acknowledgments;

4.4   the Licensee shall not create any promotional material or artwork relating to the Work without the prior written consent of the Publisher and in respect of any material commissioned or manufactured by the Licensee the copyright shall be secured in the name of the Publisher and title to all physical material shall belong to and be dealt with as if such physical material had been supplied by the Publisher and the Publisher shall at all times have unrestricted access to the same for the purposes of the Publisher;

4.5   the Licensee shall give full particulars to the Publisher as soon as the Licensee becomes aware of any actual or threatened claim by any third party in connection with the Work;

4.6   the Licensee shall punctually pay to the Publisher all sums owing to the Publisher under this Agreement;

4.7   the Licensee shall not assign charge license sub-license or otherwise part with possession of the benefit or burden of this Agreement without the prior written consent of the Publisher;

4.8   the Licensee shall maintain the Work in a prominent position in the Licensee's catalogue and ensure that the Work does not go out of print at any time during the Licence Period;

4.9   the Licensee shall advertise the Work throughout the Territory in the same manner as other books advertised by the Licensee in the Territory and the Licensee shall not alter or adapt the Work in any way or omit or remove

Clause 4.3 This provision protects the Delivery Materials from being impounded by third parties and also protects the copyright in the work from the consequences of failure to include correct copyright notices (see paragraphs 4.9 and 4.10). The clause also protects the Publisher from the Licensee violating any moral right in relation to the Work (see paragraphs 5.2 to 5.22).

Clause 4.4 The Publisher will in many circumstances wish to control the nature and type of publicity and advertising material. There are occasions where material produced by the Publisher's Licensee may be of value to the Publisher since it can be used by Licensees in other territories and this provision passes all rights of copyright and other rights in such material to the Publisher in order to permit the Publisher to provide the benefit of this material to its other Licensees.

Clause 4.5 If there is any claim in relation to copyright infringement or invasion of privacy or any other matter in relation to the Work it is in the Publisher's interests to be apprised of such claim at the earliest possible moment.

Clause 4.6 In circumstances where the Agreement does not contain a provision making time of the essence (such as that contained in clause 8.6), this provision requires the Licensee to make payments in a punctual manner.

Clause 4.7 Generally licences are considered to be personal, but there are some circumstances in which a licence may be sub-licensed. This provision expressly precludes the Licensee from entering into sub-licences or assigning the benefit of the Agreement.

Clause 4.8 The Licensee is required to keep the Work in print and in the Licensee's catalogue during the licence period.

authors' credits or acknowledgments from the Work or add any imprint or trade mark other than the Licensee's and such other imprint or trade mark as may be permitted by the Publisher;

4.10   the Licensee shall exploit the rights granted to the Licensee to the best of the Licensee's skill and ability with the utmost despatch and ensure the highest possible Royalties payable to the Publisher and ensure that the Work is given fair and equitable treatment and not discriminated in favour of any other books which the Licensee may publish or distribute in the Territory;

4.11   the Licensee shall at the end of the three-month sell-off period referred to in Clause 2.3 at the discretion of the Publisher permit the Publisher to purchase from the Licensee all copies of the Work in the possession of or under the control of the Licensee which are then unsold at a unit cost equal to the actual cost of printing of the Licensee or if the Publisher shall direct the Licensee shall procure their destruction and provide certificates and affidavits of destruction in such form as may be satisfactory to the Publisher;

4.12   the Licensee shall indemnify and keep fully indemnified the Publisher from and against all actions proceedings claims demands costs (including without prejudice to the generality of this provision the legal costs of the Publisher on a solicitor and own client basis) awards and damages arising directly or indirectly as a result of any breach or non-performance by the Licensee of any of the Licensee's undertakings warranties or obligations under this Agreement.

5.   ROYALTY ACCOUNTING

5.1   The Licensee shall on each Accounting Date render to the Publisher a full and complete statement showing all money owing to the Publisher in respect of the preceding Accounting Period.

5.2   The statement of account in Clause 5.1 shall be in such form as the Publisher shall require and shall contain full details of all copies of the Work sold and each such statement shall be accompanied by payment of all amounts owing without reserve.

Clause 4.9   This provision ensures that the Work is given the same degree of prominence as that given by the Licensee to the Licensee's other works and prevents the addition of imprints or trade marks other than those of the Publisher and the Licensee. The clause also specifically prohibits the Licensee from making any alteration or adaptation to the work or omitting any of the author's credits or acknowledgments.

Clause 4.10   The Licensee is required to exploit the rights in a manner consistent with achieving the highest royalties and ensures that the Work is not discriminated against in favour of other publications in which the Licensee may have an interest.

Clause 4.11   This provision permits the Publisher to eliminate or purchase the Licensee's unsold stock of books at the end of the Licence Period.

Clause 4.12   An explanation of the significance of warranties and indemnities may be found in paragraph 7.15.

Clause 5.1   The Accounting Dates and Accounting Periods are defined in clause 8.1 in accordance with standard industry practice. There may be occasions, however, where it is appropriate to vary these.

Clause 5.2   This provision gives the Publisher the opportunity of determining the particulars which are to be contained in the statement of account. Each statement must be accompanied by payment of sums shown to be owing without deduction of any reserves.

5.3   Pounds sterling shall be the currency of account and where any sums are received in a currency other than pounds sterling the same shall be converted at the [mid-market rate calculated using the "Financial Times" index on the date of receipt] [best obtainable rate of exchange on the date payment is due].

5.4   Value Added Tax shall be payable by the Licensee to the Publisher in respect of all payments made to or to the order of the Publisher pursuant to this Agreement.

5.5   The Licensee shall keep full and proper books of account relating to the exploitation of its rights under this Agreement and the Publisher or its representative at any time during the Licence Period and for six years afterwards shall have the right on giving reasonable prior notice to inspect and audit and take copies of such books of account during normal business hours. In the event that such audit or inspection reveals any deficiency in money paid to the Publisher hereunder then the Licensee shall immediately pay the same to the Publisher together with interest from the date first due calculated with monthly rests at a rate of [*percentage*]% above prime or base rate charged by its bankers to the Publisher from time to time and shall pay all reasonable costs incurred by the Publisher directly as a result of such inspection.

5.6   The Licensee shall keep confidential and shall not disclose to any third parties (other than professional advisers where necessary) the results of any such inspection or audit or any of the terms of this Agreement or any matters incidental to it or relating to the business of the Publisher and shall indemnify the Publisher fully in respect of any breach of its obligations under this Clause 5.6.

6.   DETERMINATION

It shall constitute the repudiation by the Licensee of its obligations under this Agreement and at any time the Publisher may serve written notice on the Licensee accepting such repudiation and determining the Licence Period and the Licensee's rights under this Agreement if:

6.1   the Licensee fails to pay any amount due under this Agreement in full within three days of its due date and such failure is not remedied within seven business days of receipt of written notice;

Clause 5.3   It may or may not be appropriate for pounds sterling to be the currency of account. If the Licensee is situate in a foreign territory exchange conversion provisions will be required.

Clause 5.4   It will be necessary to adjust this provision in the light of prevailing law. A short explanation of the current Value Added Tax legislation may be found in paragraph 11.28 and paragraphs 12.22 to 12.29.

Clause 5.5   There may be occasions when a Publisher will wish to inspect and audit the books of account of the Licensee, and even if such audit rights are not exercised, an audit provision should always be included in licence Agreements.

Clause 6   For an examination of the legal significance of the term "repudiation", reference should be made to paragraph 14.5 and to paragraphs 14.2 to 14.4.

Clause 6.1   This clause provides the Licensee with the opportunity of remedying a breach through non-payment. The time period allowed to remedy pecuniary breaches is normally less than that allowed to remedy non-pecuniary breaches.

6.2 the Licensee is in breach of any other material term of this Agreement which is incapable of remedy or if capable of remedy is not remedied within fourteen days of the Licensee becoming aware of it;

6.3 any of the Licensee's representations shall prove to have been incorrect when made or become materially incorrect and the Publisher's rights and entitlements under this Agreement are materially and adversely affected;

6.4 the Licensee transfers disposes of or threatens to transfer or dispose of any part of its assets which is likely in the opinion of the Publisher to prevent or materially to inhibit the performance by the Licensee of its obligations under this Agreement;

6.5 any indebtedness guarantee or similar obligation of the Licensee or of any guarantor of the Licensee becomes due or capable of being declared due before its stated maturity or is not discharged at maturity or the Licensee or any guarantor of the Licensee defaults under or commits a breach of the provisions of any guarantee or other obligation (whether actual or contingent) of any agreement pursuant to which any such indebtedness guarantee or other obligation was incurred all or any of which shall in the reasonable opinion of the Publisher materially affect its rights and entitlements under this Agreement;

6.6 the Licensee is declared or becomes insolvent;

6.7 the Licensee convenes a meeting of its creditors or proposes or makes any arrangement or composition with or any assignment for the benefit of its creditors or a petition is presented or a meeting is convened for the purpose of considering a resolution or other steps are taken for the winding up of the Licensee (save for the purpose of and followed by a voluntary reconstruction or amalgamation previously approved in writing by the Publisher) or if an incumbrancer takes possession or a trustee administrator administrative receiver liquidator or similar officer is appointed in respect of all or any part of its business or assets or any distress execution or other legal process is levied threatened enforced upon or sued out against any of such assets;

Clause 6.2 This clause permits the Licensee to remedy a non-pecuniary material breach. The time period allowed is longer than that for a pecuniary breach.

Clause 6.3 There may be circumstances where the Publisher has entered into the Agreement on the basis of representations made by the Licensee. This clause permits the Publisher to terminate the Agreement if the representations prove to have been incorrect or subsequently become incorrect.

Clause 6.4 There are occasions where a Licensee becomes less financially secure and disposes its assets. Where a Publisher has entered into an Agreement in reliance on the Licensee being an entity of substance, such occasions may cause concern to the Publisher, and this provision permits the Publisher to terminate the Agreement in such instances.

Clause 6.5 Financial default of the Licensee in relation to any guarantee or obligation is a further event normally permitting termination.

Clause 6.6 For the consequences of insolvency reference should be made to paragraphs 15.2 to 15.4.

Clause 6.7 There may be occasions when a Licensee does not actually become insolvent but where a creditor enforces security over the Licensee's business. This could have serious consequences for a Publisher and this clause protects the Publisher's interests by providing that such circumstances will entitle the Publisher to terminate the Agreement.

6.8 the Licensee shall cease or abandon or announce that it intends to cease or abandon the business of publishing books;

6.9 the Work goes out of print or is deleted from the Licensee's catalogue.

7. NOTICE

7.1 Any notice or other document required to be given under this Agreement or any communication between the parties with respect to any of the provisions of this Agreement shall be in writing in English and be deemed duly given if signed by or on behalf of a duly authorised officer of the party giving the notice and if left at or sent by pre-paid registered or recorded delivery post or by telex telegram cable facsimile transmission or other means of telecommunication in permanent written form to the address of the party receiving such notice as set out at the head of the Agreement or as notified between the parties for the purpose of this Clause.

7.2 Any such notice or other communication shall be deemed to be given to and received by the addressee:

(a) at the time the same is left at the address of or handed to a representative of the party to be served;

(b) by post on the day not being a Sunday or Public Holiday two days following the date of posting;

(c) in the case of a telex telegram cable facsimile transmission or other means of telecommunication on the next following day.

7.3 In proving the giving of a notice it should be sufficient to prove that the notice was left or that the envelope containing the notice was properly addressed and posted or that the applicable means of telecommunication was addressed and despatched and despatch of the transmission was confirmed and/or acknowledged as the case may be.

7.4 Communications addressed to the Publisher shall be marked for the attention of [name] with a copy to [name] of [address].

8. DEFINITIONS AND INTERPRETATION

8.1 The following definitions apply in this Agreement:

"Accounting Date"
90 days from the end of each Accounting Period

Clause 6.8 Where a Licensee ceases to carry on business or announces that it intends to cease its business, a Publisher will wish to recover its rights as soon as possible.

Clause 6.9 Although clause 4.11 imposes a specific obligation on the Licensee to keep the Work in print, this clause permits the Publisher to terminate if it does not do so.

Clause 7 A number of clauses in the Document provide for a means of exercising rights and a notice provision is therefore necessary.

"Accounting Period"
successive periods ending on 30 June and 31 December during the Licence Period

"Associate"
in relation to the Licensee any associate or associated company within the meaning of Section 416 or 417 of the Income and Corporation Taxes Act 1988

"Publication Rights"
The sole and exclusive right to print and/or publish the Work only in volume form in [paperback or] hardback format

8.2   The following terms are defined in this Agreement in the place indicated:

"Advance":	Clause 3.1
"Author":	Clause 1.1
"Royalties":	Clause 3.1
"Territory":	Clause 1.1
"Work":	Clause 1.1

8.3   Any reference in this Agreement to any statute or statutory provision shall be construed as including a reference to that statute or statutory provision as from time to time amended modified extended or re-enacted whether before or after the date of this Agreement and to all statutory instruments orders and regulations for the time being made pursuant to it or deriving validity from it.

8.4   Unless the context otherwise requires words denoting the singular shall include the plural and vice versa and words denoting any one gender shall include all genders and words denoting persons shall include bodies corporate unincorporated associations and partnerships.

8.5   The word "copyright" means the entire copyright and design right subsisting under the laws of the United Kingdom and any and all analogous rights subsisting under the laws of each and every jurisdiction throughout the world.

Clause 8.1   The definitions contained in clause 8.1 will need review in order to fit the appropriate circumstances. Depending on the royalty provisions which are inserted in clause 3.1(b), it may be necessary to insert definitions for terms such as "Published Price" or "Publisher's Receipts". Document 4, clause 18.1, contains definitions which may be appropriate. The definition of Publication Rights may also need adjustment (see annotation to Document 4, clause 9.2).

Clause 8.2   The references in this clause need to be adjusted to fit the appropriate circumstances. In particular, it may be appropriate to insert additional clauses (such as those contained in Documents 6 (a) and 6 (b)) which will necessitate consequential renumbering.

8.6   Unless otherwise stated time shall be of the essence for the purpose of the performance of the Licensee's obligations under this Agreement.

8.7   Unless otherwise stated references to clauses sub-clauses sub-paragraphs schedules annexures and exhibits relate to this Agreement.

9.   MISCELLANEOUS

9.1   Nothing contained in this Agreement shall constitute or shall be construed as constituting a partnership or contract of employment between the parties.

9.2   The Licensee warrants that it is not the nominee or agent of any undisclosed principal and warrants that it shall assume sole and complete responsibility for the performance of the obligations in this Agreement expressed to be performed by the Licensee.

9.3   This Agreement contains the full and complete understanding between the parties and supersedes all prior arrangements and understandings whether written or oral appertaining to the subject matter of this Agreement and may not be varied except by an instrument in writing signed by all the parties to this Agreement. The Licensee acknowledges that no representations or promises not expressly contained in this Agreement have been made to the Licensee by the Publisher or any of its servants agents employees members or representatives.

9.4   This Agreement shall be governed and construed in accordance with the laws of England and Wales whose courts shall be courts of competent jurisdiction.

Clause 8.6   For the significance of time being of the essence reference should be made to paragraph 2.10.

Clause 9.1   Under English law if two parties carry on business in common with a view to profit and share profit, the arrangement is capable of being considered a partnership. This provision ensures that no partnership is created inadvertently and also expressly excludes the possibility of an employment contract being created.

Clause 9.2   This provision protects the Publisher from the consequences of it contracting with a Licensee which has acted as the agent of an undisclosed company whom the Publisher may not consider to be a suitable person to be the Publisher's Licensee.

Clause 9.3   There are occasions where oral agreements or other understandings may be created in relation to a Work which may contain either additional obligations or obligations which conflict with those set out in subsequent written agreement. This provision makes it clear that all previous arrangements and understandings are at an end and the contract is the only document relevant to the obligations and rights of the parties in relation to its subject matter. The final part of the clause expressly excludes the possibility of any liability on the part of a Publisher for misrepresentation on the part of any of its servants, agents, employees or representatives.

Clause 9.4   Where a contract is made between two entities in England and Wales, it will generally not be necessary to insert a provision of this nature, but where a contract is to be created with a foreign company (or a company situate in Scotland or Northern Ireland) this provision should always be included.

[Certificate of Value]

AS WITNESS the hands of the duly authorised representatives of the parties the day month and year first above written

SIGNED by [*insert name*]
for and on behalf of
[*The Publisher*]

SIGNED by [*insert name*]
for and on behalf of
[*The Licensee*]

Certificate of Value   Although it had been intended to abolish stamp duty on assignments of intellectual property at the same time as the introduction of paperless share transfer, the failure of the Stock Exchange system TAURUS has delayed the abolition of stamp duty which is still technically payable in relation to assignments of copyright. The publishing industry has, traditionally, never made provision for the payment of stamp duty in assignments of copyright and for this reason no provision is included in this document – although there are now many circumstances where it is advisable. A suitable form of wording may, however, be found in Document 6 (d) and a summary of the current legislation relating to stamp duty may be found in paragraph 11.29.

DOCUMENT 34

Book club licence

[IMPORTANT NOTE: Please read the section "About this book" on page v, before copying or using this Document]

Purpose of this Document

This is a form of agreement suitable for use by a publisher when licensing rights to book clubs. The Document is drafted from the point of view of the publisher licensing rights and should be contrasted with the provisions of Document 31 which is drafted from the point of view of the publisher acquiring rights. In practice many book clubs have standard documentation and comparison with this Document may prove useful.

Relevant text

The text of this Work contains a number of topics which are relevant to documents of this nature including:

- book clubs (paragraph 11.11)
- buying and selling rights (paragraphs 11.2 to 11.9)
- remuneration provisions in rights agreements (paragraphs 11.22 to 11.26)
- taxation (paragraphs 11.27 to 11.29 and 12.22 to 12.30)
- commercial terms of offers (paragraphs 1.22 and 1.23)
- the law of contract and agency (paragraphs 2.1 to 2.30)
- creation, existence and transfer of copyrights (paragraphs 3.1 to 3.45)
- international copyright protection (paragraphs 4.1 to 4.17)
- moral rights (paragraphs 5.1 to 5.22)
- permissions, fair dealings and rights clearances (paragraphs 8.1 to 8.44)
- liability for content (paragraphs 9.1 to 9.49)
- buying and selling rights (paragraphs 11.1 to 11.29)
- infringement and enforcement (paragraphs 13.1 to 13.17)
- termination and recapture (paragraphs 14.1 to 14.10)
- competition law (paragraphs 16.1 to 16.28)
- multimedia (paragraphs 19.1 to 19.55)

THIS AGREEMENT is made the   day of
BETWEEN:

(1) *[Name]* LIMITED (registered number *[number]*) whose [registered office] [principal place of business] is at *[address]* ("Publisher") and

(2) *[Name]* LIMITED (registered number *[number]*) whose [registered office] [principal place of business] is at *[address]* ("Book Club" which expression shall include all Associates sub-licensees and assignees with the prior written consent of the Publisher deriving title through or from the Book Club)

IT IS AGREED as follows:

1. GRANT OF RIGHTS

1.1 In consideration of the obligations warranties and undertakings of the Book Club in this Agreement and subject to and conditional upon their full and timely performance and observance the Publisher grants to the Book Club the exclusive licence to exploit the Publication Rights in the work entitled "*[title]*" ("Work") written by *[name of author]* ("Author") throughout the *[specify territory]* ("Territory") for the period of *[specify]* years from the date of this Agreement ("Licence Period").

1.2 The Publisher undertakes to deliver to the Book Club within *[specify]* days from the date of this Agreement the following delivery materials ("Delivery Materials") *[specify materials required]* in respect of all text and illustrations contained in the Work and grants the Book Club the non-exclusive right in the Territory during the Licence Period to use such Delivery Materials.

2. PUBLISHER'S OBLIGATIONS

The Publisher warrants agrees and undertakes with the Book Club that:

2.1 the Publisher confirms that the Work [has been] [will be] published at a price of £*[specify]* and the Publisher undertakes that it shall not alter the price or issue copies of the Work or license the issue of copies of the Work at less than this price during the period of *[specify]* months commencing from the date of this Agreement;

2.2 the Publisher undertakes not to issue or authorise the issue of a paper-

---

Clause 1.1 Relevant details need to be inserted. It will be noted that the grant of rights is conditional upon full and timely performance by the Licensee of its obligations under the Agreement. The exclusivity of the rights to be licensed and the extent of the Publication Rights require careful consideration. The Publisher's Association regulations for the conduct of book clubs and the concordat relating to competition between book clubs contain a number of provisions which are relevant to agreements of this nature. Reference should be made to these, in order to assist in determining the extent of exclusivity to be enjoyed by the Book Club, the number of copies to be sold, precisely what publication rights are granted and other matters.

Clause 1.2 The licence to use the Delivery Materials is non-exclusive. In other words the Publisher may itself use the Delivery Materials or commit third parties to use them.

Clause 2.1 This clause gives the Book Club the reassurance which it will need as to initial publication price and maintenance of the publication price. This provision would, were it not for the provisions of the Net Book Agreement (see paragraph 16.4), contravene the Resale Prices Act (see paragraph 16.3).

back version of the Work during the period of [*specify*] months from the date of this Agreement;

2.3   the Publisher shall not sell any copies of the Work as remainder copies during the period of [*specify*] months from the date of this Agreement;

2.4   the Publisher shall deliver to the Book Club copies of the jacket and illustrations and other publicity material in order to permit the Book Club to give advance notice of the availability of the Work to its members provided such notice is otherwise in accordance with the terms and conditions of this Agreement;

2.5   the Publisher shall if requested by the Book Club enter into negotiations with the Book Club in relation to any new edition of the Work or any new work by the Author;

2.6   the Publisher is free to enter into this Agreement and grant the Book Club the rights granted in it and is not under any disability restriction or prohibition which might prevent the Publisher from performing or observing any of the Publisher's obligations under this Agreement;

2.7   the Publisher has not entered into and shall not enter into any arrangement which may conflict with this Agreement;

2.8   following the expiry of the Licence Period by effluxion of time the Book Club shall have the non-exclusive right subject to the terms and conditions of this Agreement for the further period of three calendar months to sell off copies of the Work previously printed by the Book Club during the Licence Period;

2.9   to the best of the Publisher's knowledge the Work is not obscene or defamatory and does not infringe any right of copyright.

3.   IMPRINT ADVERTISING AND AVAILABILITY ANNOUNCEMENTS

3.1   Each copy of the Work shall bear an imprint crest or legend on the title page jacket and binding which indicates that the copy is a Book Club edition of the Work.

Clause 2.2   Book Clubs normally wish to hold back the issue of paperback versions of works, since these will compete with the Book Club hardback version of the Work.

Clause 2.3   Book Clubs normally wish to prevent Publishers from remaindering works during the period in which the Book Club will be exploiting their rights in the Work.

Clause 2.4   So far as possible Book Clubs will wish to avail themselves of the Publisher's advertising and publicity material.

Clause 2.5   Because a number of books have a "sequel" value, Book Clubs may wish to have a negotiation right in relation to new editions of works or new works by the same Author.

Clause 2.8   The Book Club is entitled to a three-month non-exclusive sell-off period (see paragraphs 12.4 and 11.11).

Clause 2.9   The warranty is given to the best of the Publisher's belief. In other words it is not an absolute warranty that the Work is not obscene or defamatory etc.

Clause 3.1   This provision is in accordance with the Publishers' Association regulations for the conduct of Book Clubs.

3.2 The Book Club undertakes and agrees with the Publisher that any comparison of price of the Publisher's trade edition with the Book Club edition shall be in the following form only:

"Publisher's Price   [   ]
Book Club Price   [   ]"

3.3 The Book Club undertakes and agrees that no advertising or publicity material will suggest in any way that copies of the Work supplied by the Book Club are identical to the Publisher's trade edition.

3.4 The Book Club undertakes that no announcement will be made to the public or to members of the Book Club that the Work is to be offered as a Book Club Choice or a Premium until three months before the intended date of issue of the Book Club Choice or Premium.

3.5 The Book Club undertakes that the Work shall not be offered as a Premium until at least six months after its first issue by the Publisher as a trade edition and then shall be so offered only with the prior written consent of the Publisher.

3.6 The Book Club undertakes and agrees that it shall at all times fully comply with the Publishers' Association Regulations for the conduct of Book Clubs as from time to time amended.

4.   REMUNERATION

4.1   The Book Club undertakes to pay to the Publisher:

(a)   an advance ("Advance") of £[*amount*] as to [*percentage*]% on signature of this Agreement and [*percentage*]% on delivery of the Delivery Materials

(b)   the following royalties ("Royalties") on each Accounting Date in accordance with the provisions of this Agreement:

[*specify*]

[*specify*]

[*specify*]

Clause 3.2 This provision is in accordance with the Publishers' Association regulations for the conduct of Book Clubs.

Clause 3.3 This provision is in accordance with the Publishers' Association regulations for the conduct of Book Clubs.

Clause 3.4 This provision is in accordance with the Publishers' Association regulations for the conduct of Book Clubs.

Clause 3.5 This provision is in accordance with the Publishers' Association regulations for the conduct of Book Clubs.

Clause 3.6 This provision ensures that if the Publishers' Association amends its code of conduct for Book Clubs during the term of the Licence Period the Publisher will have a contractual right to ensure that the Book Club complies with such regulations.

(c) such costs in respect of the manufacture and delivery to the Book Club of the Delivery Materials as may be notified by the Publisher in writing.

4.2   The Book Club undertakes that all receipts payable to the Publisher will be converted into sterling at the best obtainable rate of exchange on each Accounting Date provided that in the event of any continuous materially adverse currency movement of longer than seven days duration during any Accounting Period it shall be the responsibility of the Book Club to ensure that all receipts are converted into sterling as soon as practicable following receipt and the Book Club shall follow all directions to the Publisher from time to time relating to currency conversion.

4.3   If exchange control or other restrictions prevent or threaten to prevent the remittance to the Publisher of any money payable under this Agreement the Book Club shall immediately advise the Publisher in writing and follow the Publisher's instructions in respect of the money to be remitted including if required depositing the same with any bank or other person designated by the Publisher at such location as may be designated by the Publisher.

4.4   If any withholding or other taxes are required to be deducted from any money provided to be remitted to the Publisher pursuant to this Agreement it shall be the responsibility of the Book Club to ensure that no improper deductions are made and that the Publisher is provided with all necessary receipts certificates and other documents and all information required in order to avail the Publisher of any tax credit or other fiscal advantage and the Book Club undertakes to account to the Publisher in relation to any tax credit or saving received by the Book Club in relation to royalty payments to the Publisher.

5.   BOOK CLUB'S OBLIGATIONS

The Book Club warrants undertakes confirms and agrees with the Publisher:

5.1   all rights and title in and to the Work and the Delivery Materials are expressly reserved to the Publisher subject to the licence in Clause 1;

Clause 4.2 If the Book Club is in the United Kingdom the provisions of this clause may be deleted. This provision prevents the Licensee from deducting parts of the royalty payments to hold as reserves against returned books. If a Licensee is required by law to deduct withholding taxes on royalty payments it is required to produce documentary evidence satisfactory to the Publisher of its liability.

Clause 4.3 If the Book Club is in the United Kingdom the provisions of this clause may be deleted. This provision protects the Publisher if exchange control restrictions are imposed in any territory and permits the Publisher to receive income in that territory.

Clause 4.4 If the Book Club is in the United Kingdom the provisions of this clause may be deleted. This clause not only provides that the Book Club is to provide the Publisher with all necessary receipts and information but also provides that the Book Club is to bring into account any tax credits or savings achieved by the Book Club which are attributable to royalty payments under the Agreement.

Clause 5.1 This clause clarifies that the copyright remains vested in the Publisher subject only to the licence granted to the Book Club.

5.2   the Book Club shall publish the Work at the Book Club's sole cost and expense by no later than [*specify date*] and shall deliver to the Publisher not less than [*specify*] copies of the edition on publication;

5.3   the Book Club shall not remainder its stock of the Work within two years following first publication by the Book Club without the consent of the Publisher and shall offer to the Publisher all stocks of the Work which the Book Club intends to remainder at [75%] of the [cost of printing] and if the Publisher shall not have accepted the offer within [30] days from receipt in respect of any copies of the Work the Book Club shall be free to sell such copies elsewhere;

5.4   the Book Club shall not by any act or omission impair or prejudice the copyright in the Work or violate any moral right or deal with the Work or the Delivery Materials so that any third party might obtain any lien or other right of whatever nature incompatible with the rights of the Publisher and the Book Club shall ensure that all copies of the Work and artwork published and distributed by the Book Club contain full and accurate copyright notices credit attributions and acknowledgments;

5.5   the Book Club shall by no later than the date specified in Clause 5.2 or the determination of the Licence Period if sooner at the Book Club's cost and expense return to the Publisher the Delivery Materials and all other material supplied by the Publisher in the same condition as when supplied to the Book Club;

5.6   the Book Club shall not create any promotional material or artwork relating to the Work without the prior written consent of the Publisher and in respect of any material commissioned or manufactured by the Book Club the copyright shall be secured in the name of the Publisher and title to all physical material shall belong to and be dealt with as if such physical material had been supplied by the Publisher and the Publisher shall at all times have unrestricted access to the same for the purposes of the Publisher;

5.7   the Book Club shall give full particulars to the Publisher as soon as the

Clause 5.2   This clause obliges the Book Club to publish by a certain date and clarifies the fact that full costs of publication are borne by the Book Club. It is also usual for a Publisher to request copies of editions published by the Book Club.

Clause 5.3   The Publisher needs to protect itself from the Book Club remaindering stock which could depress the Publisher's own sales figures in the trade market. This provision permits the Publisher to buy out stocks which the Book Club intends to remainder.

Clause 5.4   This provision protects the Delivery Materials from being impounded by third parties and also protects the copyright in the Work from the consequences of failure to include correct copyright notices (see paragraphs 4.9 and 4.10). The clause also protects the Publisher from the Book Club violating any moral right in relation to the Work (see paragraphs 5.2 to 5.22).

Clause 5.5   When the Book Club has used the Delivery Materials to create its edition it will no longer have use for them and they should be returned to the Publisher.

Clause 5.6   The Publisher will in many circumstances wish to control the nature and type of publicity and advertising material. There are occasions where material produced by the Book Club may be of value to the Publisher since it can be used by licensees in other territories and this provision passes all rights of copyright and other rights in such material to the Publisher in order to permit the Publisher to provide the benefit of this material to its other licensees.

Book Club becomes aware of any actual or threatened claim by any third party in connection with the Work;

5.8   the Book Club shall punctually pay to the Publisher all sums owing to the Publisher under this Agreement;

5.9   the Book Club shall not assign charge license sub-license or otherwise part with possession of the benefit or burden of this Agreement without the prior written consent of the Publisher;

5.10   the Book Club shall not copy or duplicate the Delivery Materials or any part of them otherwise than for the purpose of printing and publishing the Work in accordance with this Agreement;

5.11   the Book Club shall retain total control and actual possession at all times of the Delivery Materials and maintain the Delivery Materials safe and secure in appropriate storage facilities the risk in the Delivery Materials passing to the Book Club on the Publisher's appropriation in order to effect Delivery pursuant to this Agreement;

5.12   the Book Club shall maintain the Work in a prominent position in the Book Club's catalogue and ensure that the Work does not go out of print at any time during the Licence Period;

5.13   the Book Club shall advertise the Work throughout the Territory in the same manner as other books advertised by the Book Club in the Territory and the Book Club shall not alter or adapt the Work in any way or omit or remove any authors' credits or acknowledgments from the Work or add any imprint or trade mark other than the Book Club's and such other imprint or trade mark as may be permitted by the Publisher;

5.14   the Book Club shall exploit the rights granted to the Book Club to the best of the Book Club's skill and ability with the utmost despatch and ensure the highest possible Royalties payable to the Publisher and ensure that the

Clause 5.7   If there is any claim in relation to copyright infringement or invasion of privacy or any other matter in relation to the Work it is in the Publisher's interests to be apprised of such claim at the earliest possible moment.

Clause 5.8   In circumstances where the Agreement does not contain a provision making time of the essence, this provision requires the Book Club to make payments in a punctual manner.

Clause 5.9   Generally licences are considered to be personal, but there are some circumstances in which a licence may be sub-licensed. This provision expressly precludes the Book Club from entering into sub-licences or assigning the benefit of the Agreement.

Clause 5.10   Although the Book Club will not have the right to use copyright material for the purposes other than those consented to by their owner, this provision makes it clear that all materials provided under the Agreement can be used only to assist the Book Club to print and publish the Work.

Clause 5.11   This provision protects the Publisher's interests in licence materials and specifies the moment when risk in the Delivery Materials passes to the Book Club (see paragraph 12.11).

Clause 5.12   The Licensee is required to keep the Work in print and in the Licensee's catalogue during the licence period.

Clause 5.13   This provision ensures that the Work is given the same degree of prominence as that given by the Book Club to the Book Club's other books and prevents the addition of imprints or trade marks other than those of the Publisher and the Book Club. The clause also specifically prohibits the Book Club from making any alteration or adaptation to the Work or omitting any of the Author's credits or acknowledgments.

Work is given fair and equitable treatment and not discriminated in favour of any other books which the Book Club may publish or distribute in the Territory;

5.15 the Book Club shall at the end of the three-month sell-off period referred to in Clause 2.8 at the discretion of the Publisher permit the Publisher to purchase from the Book Club all copies of the Work in the possession of or under the control of the Book Club which are then unsold at a unit cost equal to the actual cost of printing of the Book Club or if the Publisher shall direct the Book Club shall procure their destruction and provide certificates and affidavits of destruction in such form as may be satisfactory to the Publisher;

5.16 the Book Club shall indemnify and keep fully indemnified the Publisher from and against all actions proceedings claims demands costs (including without prejudice to the generality of this provision the legal costs of the Publisher on a solicitor and own client basis) awards and damages arising directly or indirectly as a result of any breach or non-performance by the Book Club of any of the Book Club's undertakings warranties or obligations under this Agreement.

6. ROYALTY ACCOUNTING

6.1 The Book Club shall on each Accounting Date render to the Publisher a full and complete statement showing all money owing to the Publisher in respect of the preceding Accounting Period.

6.2 The statement of account in Clause 6.1 shall be in such form as the Publisher shall require and shall contain full details of all copies of the Work sold and each such statement shall be accompanied by payment of all amounts owing without reserve.

6.3 Pounds sterling shall be the currency of account and where any sums are received in a currency other than pounds sterling the same shall be converted at the [mid-market rate calculated using the "Financial Times" index on the date of receipt] [best obtainable rate of exchange on the date payment is due].

6.4 Value Added Tax shall be payable by the Book Club to the Publisher in

---

Clause 5.14 The Book Club is required to exploit the rights in a manner consistent with achieving the highest royalties and ensures that the Work is not discriminated against in favour of other publications in which the Book Club may have an interest.

Clause 5.15 This provision permits the Publisher to eliminate or purchase the Book Club's unsold stock of books at the end of the licence period.

Clause 5.16 An explanation of the significance of warranties and indemnities may be found in paragraph 7.15.

Clause 6.1 The Accounting Dates and Accounting Periods are defined in clause 8.1 in accordance with standard industry practice. There may be occasions, however, where it is appropriate to vary these.

Clause 6.2 This provision gives the Publisher the opportunity of determining the particulars which are to be contained in the statement of account. Each statement must be accompanied by payment of sums shown to be owing without deduction of any reserves.

Clause 6.3 It may or may not be appropriate for pounds sterling to be the currency of account. If the Book Club is situate in a foreign territory, exchange conversion provisions will be required.

respect of all payments made to or to the order of the Publisher pursuant to this Agreement.

6.5   The Book Club shall keep full and proper books of account relating to the exploitation of its rights under this Agreement and the Publisher or its representative shall have the right on giving reasonable prior notice at any time during the Licence Period and for six years afterwards to inspect and audit and take copies of such books of account during normal business hours. In the event that such audit or inspection reveals any deficiency in money paid to the Publisher hereunder then the Book Club shall immediately pay the same to the Publisher together with interest from the date first due calculated with monthly rests at a rate of [*percentage*]% above prime or base rate charged by its bankers to the Publisher from time to time and shall pay all reasonable costs incurred by the Publisher directly as a result of such inspection.

6.6   The Book Club shall keep confidential and shall not disclose to any third parties (other than professional advisers where necessary) the results of any such inspection or audit or any of the terms of this Agreement or any matters incidental to it or relating to the business of the Publisher and shall indemnify the Publisher fully in respect of any breach of its obligations under this Clause 6.6.

7.   <u>DETERMINATION</u>

It shall constitute the repudiation by the Book Club of its obligations under this Agreement and at any time the Publisher may serve written notice on the Book Club accepting such repudiation and determining the Licence Period and the Club's rights under this Agreement if:

7.1   the Book Club fails to pay any amount due under this Agreement in full within three days of its due date and such failure is not remedied within seven days of receipt of written notice;

7.2   the Book Club is in breach of any other material term of this Agreement which is incapable of remedy or if capable of remedy is not remedied within fourteen days of the Book Club becoming aware of it;

7.3   any of the Book Club's representations shall prove to have been incorrect when made or become materially incorrect and the Publisher's

---

Clause 6.4 It will be necessary to adjust this provision in the light of prevailing law. A short explanation of the current Value Added Tax legislation may be found in paragraph 11.28 and paragraphs 12.22 to 12.29.

Clause 6.5 There may be occasions when a Publisher will wish to inspect and audit the books of account of the Book Club, and even if such audit rights are not exercised an audit provision should always be included in licence agreements.

Clause 7 For an examination of the legal significance of the term "repudiation" reference should be made to paragraph 14.5 and to paragraphs 14.2 to 14.4.

Clause 7.1 This clause provides the Book Club with the opportunity of remedying a breach through non-payment. The time period allowed to remedy pecuniary breaches is normally less than that allowed to remedy non-pecuniary breaches.

Clause 7.2 This clause permits the Book Club to remedy a non-pecuniary material breach. The time period allowed is longer than that for a pecuniary breach.

rights and entitlements under this Agreement are materially and adversely affected;

7.4   the Book Club transfers disposes of or threatens to transfer or dispose of any part of its assets which is likely in the opinion of the Publisher to prevent or materially to inhibit the performance by the Book Club of its obligations under this Agreement;

7.5   any indebtedness guarantee or similar obligation of the Book Club or of any guarantor of the Book Club becomes due or capable of being declared due before its stated maturity or is not discharged at maturity or the Book Club or any guarantor of the Book Club defaults under or commits a breach of the provisions of any guarantee or other obligation (whether actual or contingent) of any agreement pursuant to which any such indebtedness guarantee or other obligation was incurred all or any of which shall in the reasonable opinion of the Publisher materially affect its rights and entitlements under this Agreement;

7.6   the Book Club is declared or becomes insolvent;

7.7   the Book Club convenes a meeting of its creditors or proposes or makes any arrangement or composition with or any assignment for the benefit of its creditors or a petition is presented or a meeting is convened for the purpose of considering a resolution or other steps are taken for the winding up of the Book Club (save for the purpose of and followed by a voluntary reconstruction or amalgamation previously approved in writing by the Publisher) or if an incumbrancer takes possession of or a trustee administrator administrative receiver liquidator or similar officer is appointed in respect of all or any part of its business or assets or any distress execution or other legal process is levied threatened enforced upon or sued out against any of such assets;

7.8   the Work goes out of print or is deleted from the Book Club's catalogue;

7.9   the Book Club shall cease or abandon the business of publishing and/or distributing books or the Book Club or any associate shall announce that it is intended that the Book Club shall cease or abandon such business.

Clause 7.3   There may be circumstances where the Publisher has entered into the Agreement on the basis of representations made by the Book Club. This clause permits the Publisher to terminate the Agreement if the representations prove to have been incorrect or subsequently become incorrect.

Clause 7.4   There are occasions where a Book Club becomes less financially secure and disposes its assets. Where a Publisher has entered into an Agreement in reliance on the Book Club being an entity of substance, such occasions may cause concern to the Publisher, and this provision permits the Publisher to terminate the Agreement in such instances.

Clause 7.5   Financial default of the Book Club in relation to any guarantee or obligation is a further event normally permitting termination.

Clause 7.6   For the consequences of insolvency reference should be made to paragraphs 15.2 to 15.4.

Clause 7.7   There may be occasions when the Book Club does not actually become insolvent but where a creditor enforces security over the Book Club's business. This could have serious consequences for a Publisher and this clause protects the Publisher's interests by providing that such circumstances will entitle the Publisher to terminate the Agreement.

Clause 7.8   Where the Book Club ceases to carry on business or announces that it intends to cease its business, a Publisher will wish to recover its rights as soon as possible.

Clause 7.9   Although clause 5.11 imposes a specific obligation on the Book Club to keep the Work in print, this clause permits the Publisher to terminate if it does not do so.

8.   NOTICE

8.1   Any notice or other document required to be given under this Agreement or any communication between the parties with respect to any of the provisions of this Agreement shall be in writing in English and be deemed duly given if signed by or on behalf of a duly authorised officer of the party giving the notice and if left at or sent by pre-paid registered or recorded delivery post or by telex telegram cable facsimile transmission or other means of telecommunication in permanent written form to the address of the party receiving such notice as set out at the head of the Agreement or as notified between the parties for the purpose of this Clause.

8.2   Any such notice or other communication shall be deemed to be given to and received by the addressee:

(a)   at the time the same is left at the address of or handed to a representative of the party to be served;

(b)   by post on the day not being a Sunday or Public Holiday two days following the date of posting;

(c)   in the case of a telex telegram cable facsimile transmission or other means of telecommunication on the next following day.

8.3   In proving the giving of a notice it should be sufficient to prove that the notice was left or that the envelope containing the notice was properly addressed and posted or that the applicable means of telecommunication was addressed and despatched and despatch of the transmission was confirmed and/or acknowledged as the case may be.

8.4   Communications addressed to the Publisher shall be marked for the attention of [*name*] with a copy to [*name*] of [*address*].

9.   DEFINITIONS AND INTERPRETATION

9.1   The following definitions apply in this Agreement:

"Accounting Date"
90 days from the end of each Accounting Period

"Accounting Period"
successive periods ending on 30 June and 31 December during the Licence Period

"Associate"
in relation to the Book Club any associate or associated company within the meaning of Section 416 or 417 of the Income and Corporation Taxes Act 1988

Clause 8   A number of clauses in the Document provide for a means of exercising rights and a notice provision is therefore necessary.

"Book Club Choice"
any book offered by the Book Club as a main or alternative choice to its members

"Premium"
any book offered by the Book Club to its members as an inducement to join the Book Club

"Publication Rights"
the [sole and exclusive] right to print and/or publish the Work only in volume form in [paperback or] hardback format

9.2   The following terms are defined in this Agreement in the place indicated:

"Advance":   Clause 4.1

"Author":   Clause 1.1

"Royalties":   Clause 3.1

"Territory":   Clause 1.1

"Work":   Clause 1.1

9.3   Any reference in this Agreement to any statute or statutory provision shall be construed as including a reference to that statute or statutory provision as from time to time amended modified extended or re-enacted whether before or after the date of this Agreement and to all statutory instruments orders and regulations for the time being made pursuant to it or deriving validity from it.

9.4   Unless the context otherwise requires words denoting the singular shall include the plural and vice versa and words denoting any one gender shall include all genders and words denoting persons shall include bodies corporate unincorporated associations and partnerships.

9.5   The word "copyright" means the entire copyright and design right

---

Clause 9.1   The definitions contained in clause 9.1 will need review in order to fit the appropriate circumstances. Depending on the royalty provisions which are inserted in clause 3.1(b) it may be necessary to insert definitions for terms such as "Published Price" or "Publisher's Receipts". Document 4, clause 18.1, contains definitions which may be appropriate. The definitions of Publication Rights may also need adjustment and the extent of exclusivity should also be examined (see the annotations to clause 9.2 of Document 4 and clause 1.1 of this document).

Clause 9.2   The references in this clause need to be adjusted to fit the appropriate circumstances. In particular, it may be appropriate to insert additional clauses (such as those contained in Documents 6 (a) and 6 (b)) which will necessitate consequential renumbering.

Clause 9.4   For the significance of time being of the essence reference should be made to paragraph 2.10.

subsisting under the laws of the United Kingdom and any and all analogous rights subsisting under the laws of each and every jurisdiction throughout the world.

9.6 Unless otherwise stated time shall be of the essence for the purpose of the performance of the Book Club's obligations under this Agreement.

9.7 Unless otherwise stated references to clauses sub-clauses sub-paragraphs schedules annexures and exhibits relate to this Agreement.

10. MISCELLANEOUS

10.1 Nothing contained in this Agreement shall constitute or shall be construed as constituting a partnership or contract of employment between the parties.

10.2 The Publisher shall not be liable to the Book Club for failing to supply or procure the supply of the Delivery Materials and any other material to be supplied under this Agreement due to circumstances beyond its control and it shall not be liable for any expenses or consequential losses whatever suffered by the Book Club.

10.3 The Book Club warrants that it is not the nominee or agent of any undisclosed principal and warrants that it shall assume sole and complete responsibility for the performance of the obligations in this Agreement expressed to be performed by the Book Club.

10.4 This Agreement contains the full and complete understanding between the parties and supersedes all prior arrangements and understandings whether written or oral appertaining to the subject matter of this Agreement and may not be varied except by an instrument in writing signed by all the parties to this Agreement. The Book Club acknowledges that no representations or promises not expressly contained in this Agreement have been made to the Book Club by the Publisher or any of its servants agents employees members or representatives.

10.5 This Agreement shall be governed and construed in accordance with

---

Clause 10.1 Under English law if two parties carry on business in common with a view to profit and share profit, the arrangement is capable of being considered a partnership. This provision ensures that no partnership is created inadvertently, and also expressly excludes the possibility of an employment contract being created.

Clause 10.2 This provision protects the Publisher from any claim by the Book Club in relation to failure to supply Delivery Materials, although there are likely to be circumstances in which the Publisher will incur some liability.

Clause 10.3 This provision protects the Publisher from the consequences of it contracting with a Book Club which has acted as the agent of an undisclosed company whom the Publisher may not consider to be a suitable person to be the Publisher's licensee.

Clause 10.4 There are occasions where oral agreements or other understandings may be created in relation to a Work which may contain either additional obligations or obligations which conflict with those set out in subsequent written agreement. This provision makes it clear that all previous arrangements and understandings are at an end and the contract is the only Document relevant to the obligations and rights of the parties in relation to its subject matter. The final part of the clause expressly excludes the possibility of any liability of the Publisher for misrepresentation on the part of any of its servants, agents, employees or representatives (see paragraph 2.17).

the laws of England and Wales whose courts shall be courts of competent jurisdiction.

[certificate of value]

AS WITNESS the hands of the duly authorised representatives of the parties the day month and year first above written

SIGNED by [   ] }
for and on behalf of
[*The Publisher*]

SIGNED by [   ] }
for and on behalf of
[*The Book Club*]

Clause 10.5 Where a contract is made between two entities in England and Wales, it will generally not be necessary to insert a provision of this nature, but where a contract is to be created with a foreign company (or a company situate in Scotland or Northern Ireland) this provision should always be included.

Certificate of Value Although it had been intended to abolish stamp duty on assignments of intellectual property at the same time as the introduction of paperless share transfer, the failure of the Stock Exchange system TAURUS has delayed the abolition of stamp duty which is still technically payable in relation to assignments of copyright. The publishing industry has, traditionally, never made provision for the payment of stamp duty in assignments of copyright and for this reason no provision is included in this document – although there are now many circumstances where it is advisable. A suitable form of wording may, however, be found in Document 6 (d) and a summary of the current legislation relating to stamp duty may be found in paragraph 11.29.

DOCUMENT 35

Book club sale and licence agreement

[IMPORTANT NOTE: Please read the section "About this book" on page v, before copying or using this Document]

Purpose of this Agreement

This is a form of agreement which may be suitable for use by a publisher when licensing rights to a book club and supplying printed copies of books. Document 34 merely licenses rights to the book club. In this document the publisher agrees to print a pre-specified number of books and sell them to the book club. In practice many book clubs have standard documentation and comparison with this document may prove useful.

Relevant text

The text of this Work covers a number of topics which are relevant to documents of this nature including:

- book clubs (paragraph 11.11)
- buying and selling rights (paragraphs 11.2 to 11.9)
- remuneration provisions in rights agreements (paragraphs 11.22 to 11.26)
- taxation (paragraphs 11.27 to 11.29 and 12.22 to 12.30)
- commercial terms of offers (paragraphs 1.22 and 1.23)
- the law of contract and agency (paragraphs 2.1 to 2.30)
- creation, existence and transfer of copyrights (paragraphs 3.1 to 3.45)
- international copyright protection (paragraphs 4.1 to 4.17)
- moral rights (paragraphs 5.1 to 5.22)
- permissions, fair dealings and rights clearances (paragraphs 8.1 to 8.44)
- liability for content (paragraphs 9.1 to 9.49)
- buying and selling rights (paragraphs 11.1 to 11.29)
- infringement and enforcement (paragraphs 13.1 to 13.17)
- termination and recapture (paragraphs 14.1 to 14.10)
- competition law (paragraphs 16.1 to 16.28)
- multimedia (paragraphs 19.1 to 19.55)

THIS AGREEMENT is made the   day of

BETWEEN:

(1)   *[Name]* LIMITED (registered number *[number]*) whose [registered office] [principal place of business] is at *[address]* ("Publisher") and

(2)   *[Name]* LIMITED (registered number *[number]*) whose [registered office] [principal place of business] is at *[address]* ("Book Club" which expression shall include all Associates sub-licensees and assignees with the prior written consent of the Publisher deriving title through or from the Book Club)

IT IS AGREED as follows:

1.   GRANT OF RIGHTS

In consideration of the obligations warranties and undertakings of the Book Club in this Agreement and subject to and conditional upon their full and timely performance and observance the Publisher grants to the Book Club the exclusive licence to exploit the Publication Rights in the work entitled "*[title]*" ("Work") written by *[name of author]* ("Author") throughout the *[specify territory]* ("Territory") for the period of *[specify]* years from the date of this Agreement ("Licence Period").

2.   PUBLISHER'S OBLIGATIONS

The Publisher warrants agrees and undertakes with the Book Club that:

2.1   the Publisher confirms that the Work [has been] [will be] published at a price of £*[amount]* and the Publisher undertakes that it shall not alter the price or issue copies of the Work or license the issue of copies of the Work at less than this price during the period of *[specify]* months commencing from the date of this Agreement;

2.2   the Publisher undertakes not to issue or authorise the issue of a paper-back version of the Work during the period of *[specify]* months from the date of this Agreement;

2.3   the Publisher shall not sell any copies of the Work as remainder copies during the period of *[specify]* months from the date of this Agreement;

Clause 1   Relevant details need to be inserted. It will be noted that the grant of rights is conditional upon full and timely performance by the Licensee of its obligations under the Agreement. The exclusivity of the rights to be licensed and the extent of the Publication Rights require careful consideration. The Publisher's Association regulations for the conduct of book clubs and the concordat relating to competition between book clubs contain a number of provisions which are relevant to agreements of this nature. Reference should be made to these, in order to assist in determining the extent of exclusivity to be enjoyed by the Book Club, the number of copies to be sold, precisely what publication rights are granted, and other matters.

Clause 2.1   This clause gives the Book Club the reassurance which it will need as to initial publication price and maintenance of the publication price. This provision would, were it not for the provisions of the Net Book Agreement (see paragraph 16.4), contravene the Resale Prices Act (see paragraph 16.3).

Clause 2.2   Book Clubs normally wish to hold back the issue of paperback versions of works, since these will compete with the Book Club hardback version of the Work.

Clause 2.3   Book Clubs normally wish to prevent Publishers from remaindering works during the period in which the Book Club will be exploiting their rights in the Work.

2.4   the Publisher shall deliver to the Book Club copies of the jacket and illustrations and other publicity material in order to permit the Book Club to give advance notice of the availability of the Work to its members provided such notice is otherwise in accordance with the terms and conditions of this Agreement;

2.5   the Publisher shall if requested by the Book Club enter into negotiations with the Book Club in relation to any new edition of the Work or any new work by the Author;

2.6   the Publisher is free to enter into this Agreement and grant the Book Club the rights granted in it and is not under any disability restriction or prohibition which might prevent the Publisher from performing or observing any of the Publisher's obligations under this Agreement;

2.7   the Publisher has not entered into and shall not enter into any arrangement which may conflict with this Agreement;

2.8   following the expiry of the Licence Period by effluxion of time the Book Club shall have the non-exclusive right subject to the terms and conditions of this Agreement for the further period of three calendar months to sell off copies of the Work previously printed by the Book Club during the Licence Period;

2.9   to the best of the Publisher's knowledge the Work is not obscene or defamatory and does not infringe any right of copyright.

3.   PURCHASE OF COPIES OF THE WORK

3.1   The Publisher agrees to print [*specify*] [copies of the Work which shall be supplied in folded sewn and end-papered sheets with the Book Club's imprint on the title page] [bound and jacketed copies of the Work in a format identical to the Publisher's published trade edition of the Work other than the imprint on such copies which imprint shall be in the form annexed as Exhibit 1].

3.2   The Publisher shall deliver all copies of the Work produced in accordance with Clause 3.1 to the Book Club in the following quantities on the following dates:

Clause 2.4   So far as possible Book Clubs will wish to avail themselves of the Publisher's advertising and publicity material.

Clause 2.5   Because a number of books have a "sequel" value, Book Clubs may wish to have a negotiation right in relation to new editions of works or new works by the same author.

Clause 2.8   The Book Club is entitled to a three-month non-exclusive sell-off period (see paragraphs 12.4 and 11.11).

Clause 2.9   The warranty is given to the best of the Publisher's belief. In other words it is not an absolute warranty that the work is not obscene or defamatory etc.

Clause 3.1   This clause permits the Book Club to obtain from the Publisher a specified number of bound and jacketed copies of the Work or of sewn sheets of the Work. There are circumstances where it may be more economical for the Book Club to buy such copies or sheets from the Publisher. Depending on the terms of the transaction the copies can be supplied at cost plus a percentage or on terms which require the Book Club to pay a royalty when copies are sold. Alternatively the copies can be sold at a royalty inclusive price and appropriate adjustments may be made to the Agreement.

[*quantity*]   [*date*]

[*quantity*]   [*date*]

[*quantity*]   [*date*]

3.3 The Book Club shall pay to the Publisher the purchase price of £[*amount*] per copy (plus Value Added Tax) within [*specify*] days from delivery to the Book Club of each copy of the Work.

3.4 The Publisher acknowledges that any delay in delivery may cause the Book Club to incur costs and undertakes to pay to the Book Club the reasonable direct cost of any communication made by the Book Club to members which have placed orders for copies of the Work advising such members of delay in fulfilment of orders placed by them but the payment of such costs shall be the Publisher's sole liability in relation to such delay.

3.5 The Book Club acknowledges that sums paid by the Book Club pursuant to this Clause are payable solely in relation to the printing of copies of the Work and do not form part of any Advance paid by the Book Club to the Publisher under this Agreement and are not recoupable from Royalties.

4.   IMPRINT ADVERTISING AND AVAILABILITY ANNOUNCEMENTS

4.1 Each copy of the Work shall bear an imprint crest or legend on the title page jacket and binding which indicates that the copy is a Book Club edition of the Work provided that the Book Club acknowledges that:

(a)   where an inadequate supply of copies is available to the Publisher copies bearing the Publisher's imprint as used in the trade edition of the Work may be supplied to the Book Club up to a maximum number of copies equivalent to 20% of copies ordered bearing the Book Club imprint; and

(b)   where the Book Club is not granted exclusive rights in relation to the Work the Publisher may permit the use by the Book Club of not more than 5,000 copies of the Publisher's trade edition or 50% of the Publisher's print order of such trade edition whichever is lower.

Clause 3.2 The appropriate production and delivery schedule details will need to be inserted.

Clause 3.3 This clause provides for the purchase price for each copy of the Work delivered to be payable within a specified number of days from delivery. It will be necessary, of course, to vary the payment schedule to fit the circumstances. Although books are currently Value Added Tax exempt, there are European Union proposals to harmonise Value Added Tax on books.

Clause 3.4 Under this clause the Publisher agrees to reimburse the Book Club the cost of sending communications relating to the late delivery of the Work but the Publisher does not accept any consequential liability for loss arising from late delivery.

Clause 3.5 This provision is an acknowledgment from the Book Club that the price paid for copies of the book relates solely to the purchase of physical materials, and not to the purchase of intellectual property rights in them. This clause will need to be adjusted if the transaction is agreed on a royalty inclusive basis.

Clause 4.1 This provision is in accordance with the Publishers' Association regulations for the conduct of Book Clubs.

4.2 The Book Club undertakes and agrees with the Publisher that any comparison of price of the Publisher's trade edition with the Book Club edition shall be in the following form only:

"Publisher's Price   [   ]
Book Club Price   [   ]"

4.3 The Book Club undertakes and agrees that no advertising or publicity material will suggest in any way that copies of the Works supplied by the Book Club are identical to the Publisher's trade edition.

4.4 The Book Club undertakes that no announcement will be made to the public or to members of the Book Club that the Work is to be offered as a Book Club Choice or a Premium until three months before the intended date of issue of the Book Club Choice or Premium.

4.5 The Book Club undertakes that the Work shall not be offered as a Premium until at least six months after its first issue by the Publisher as a trade edition and then shall be so offered only with the prior written consent of the Publisher.

4.6 The Book Club undertakes and agrees that it shall at all times fully comply with the Publishers' Association Regulations for the Conduct of Book Clubs as from time to time amended.

5.   REMUNERATION

5.1 The Book Club undertakes to pay to the Publisher:

(a) an advance ("Advance") of £[*amount*] as to [*percentage*]% on signature of this Agreement and [*percentage*]% on [*specify date*]
(b) the following royalties ("Royalties") on each Accounting Date in accordance with the provisions of this Agreement:

[*specify*]

[*specify*]

[*specify*]

5.2 The Book Club shall not have the right to withhold any part of sums due

---

Clause 4.2 This provision is in accordance with the Publishers' Association regulations for the conduct of Book Clubs.

Clause 4.3 This provision is in accordance with the Publishers' Association regulations for the conduct of Book Clubs.

Clause 4.4 This provision is in accordance with the Publishers' Association regulations for the conduct of Book Clubs.

Clause 4.5 This provision is in accordance with the Publishers' Association regulations for the conduct of Book Clubs.

Clause 4.6 This provision ensures that if the Publishers' Association amends its code of conduct for Book Clubs during the term of the Licence Period the Publisher will have a contractual right to ensure that the Book Club complies with such regulations.

to the Publisher as a reserve against returns and/or credits and in the event that the Book Club is required by law to make any withholding from sums to be remitted to the Publisher the Book Club shall prior to the making of any withholding of payment furnish the Publisher with evidence satisfactory to the Publisher in its entire discretion as to the Book Club's obligation to make such withholding of payment.

5.3   If exchange control or other restrictions prevent or threaten to prevent the remittance to the Publisher of any money payable under this Agreement the Book Club shall immediately advise the Publisher in writing and follow the Publisher's instructions in respect of the money to be remitted including if required depositing the same with any bank or other person designated by the Publisher at such location as may be designated by the Publisher.

5.4   If any withholding or other taxes are required to be deducted from any money provided to be remitted to the Publisher pursuant to this Agreement it shall be the responsibility of the Book Club to ensure that no improper deductions are made and that the Publisher is provided with all necessary receipts certificates and other documents and all information required in order to avail the Publisher of any tax credit or other fiscal advantage and the Book Club undertakes to account to the Publisher in relation to any tax credit or saving received by the Book Club in relation to royalty payments to the Publisher.

6.   BOOK CLUB'S UNDERTAKINGS

The Book Club warrants undertakes confirms and agrees with the Publisher:

6.1   all rights and title in and to the Work are expressly reserved to the Publisher subject to the licence in Clause 1;

6.2   the Book Club shall publish the Work at the Book Club's sole cost and expense by no later than [*specify date*].

6.3   the Book Club shall not remainder its stock of the Work within two years following first publication by the Book Club without the consent of the Publisher and shall offer to the Publisher all stocks of the Work which the

---

Clause 5.2   This provision prevents the Book Club from deducting parts of the royalty payments to hold as reserves against returned books. If the Book Club is required by law to deduct withholding taxes on royalty payments it is required to produce documentary evidence satisfactory to the Publisher of its liability.

Clause 5.3   If the Book Club is in the United Kingdom the provisions of this clause may be deleted. This provision protects the Publisher if exchange control restrictions are imposed in any territory and permits the Publisher to receive income in that territory.

Clause 5.4   If the Book Club is in the United Kingdom the provisions of this clause may be deleted. This clause not only provides that the Book Club is to provide the Publisher with all necessary receipts and information but also provides that the Book Club is to bring into account any tax credits or savings achieved by the Book Club which are attributable to royalty payments under the Agreement.

Clause 6.1   This clause clarifies that the copyright remains vested in the Publisher subject only to the licence granted to the Book Club.

Clause 6.2   This clause obliges the Book Club to publish by a certain date and clarifies the fact that full costs of publication are borne by the Book Club. It is also usual for a Publisher to request copies of editions published by the Book Club.

Book Club intends to remainder at [75%] of the cost referred to in Clause 3.3 and if the Publisher shall not have accepted the offer within [30] days from receipt in respect of any copies of the Work the Book Club shall be free to sell such copies elsewhere;

6.4 the Book Club shall not by any act or omission impair or prejudice the copyright in the Work or violate any moral right or deal with the Work so that any third party might obtain any lien or other right of whatever nature incompatible with the rights of the Publisher and the Licensee shall ensure that all copies of the Work and artwork published and distributed by the Book Club contain full and accurate copyright notices credit attributions and acknowledgments;

6.5 the Book Club shall not create any promotional material or artwork relating to the Work without the prior written consent of the Publisher and in respect of any material commissioned or manufactured by the Book Club the copyright shall be secured in the name of the Publisher and title to all physical material shall belong to and be dealt with as if such physical material had been supplied by the Publisher and the Publisher shall at all times have unrestricted access to the same for the purposes of the Publisher;

6.6 the Book Club shall give full particulars to the Publisher as soon as the Book Club becomes aware of any actual or threatened claim by any third party in connection with the Work;

6.7 the Book Club shall punctually pay to the Publisher all sums owing to the Publisher under this Agreement;

6.8 the Book Club shall not assign charge license sub-license or otherwise part with possession of the benefit or burden of this Agreement without the prior written consent of the Publisher;

6.9 the Book Club shall maintain the Work in a prominent position in the Book Club's catalogue and ensure that the Work does not go out of print at any time during the Licence Period;

6.10 the Book Club shall advertise the Work throughout the Territory in

---

Clause 6.3 The Publisher needs to protect itself from the Book Club remaindering stock which could depress the Publisher's own sales figures in the trade market. This provision permits the Publisher to buy out stocks which the Book Club intends to remainder.

Clause 6.5 The Publisher will in many circumstances wish to control the nature and type of publicity and advertising material. There are occasions where material produced by the Book Club may be of value to the Publisher since it can be used by Book Clubs in other territories. This provision passes all rights of copyright and other rights in such material to the Publisher in order to permit the Publisher to provide the benefit of this material to its other Book Clubs.

Clause 6.6 If there is any claim in relation to copyright infringement or invasion of privacy or any other matter in relation to the work it is in the Publisher's interests to be apprised of such claim at the earliest possible moment.

Clause 6.7 In circumstances where the Agreement does not contain a provision making time of the essence (such as that contained in clause 10.6), this provision requires the Book Club to make payments in a punctual manner.

Clause 6.8 Generally licences are considered to be personal, but there are some circumstances in which a licence may be sub-licensed. This provision expressly precludes the Book Club from entering into sub-licences or assigning the benefit of the Agreement.

the same manner as other books advertised by the Book Club in the Territory and the Book Club shall not alter or adapt the Work in any way or omit or remove any authors' credits or acknowledgments from the Work or add any imprint or trade mark other than the Book Club's and such other imprint or trade mark as may be permitted by the Publisher;

6.11 the Book Club shall exploit the rights granted to the Book Club to the best of the Book Club's skill and ability with the utmost despatch and ensure the highest possible Royalties payable to the Publisher and ensure that the Work is given fair and equitable treatment and not discriminated in favour of any other books which the Book Club may publish or distribute in the Territory;

6.12 the Book Club shall at the end of the three-month sell-off period referred to in Clause 2.8 at the discretion of the Publisher permit the Publisher to purchase from the Book Club all stocks of the Work then unsold at a unit cost equal to the actual cost of printing of the Book Club or if the Publisher shall direct the Book Club shall procure their destruction and provide certificates and affidavits of destruction in such form as may be satisfactory to the Publisher;

6.13 the Book Club shall indemnify and keep fully indemnified the Publisher from and against all actions proceedings claims demands costs (including without prejudice to the generality of this provision the legal costs of the Publisher or a solicitor and own client basis) awards and damages arising directly or indirectly as a result of any breach or non-performance by the Book Club of any of the Book Club's undertakings warranties or obligations under this Agreement.

7. ROYALTY ACCOUNTING

7.1 The Book Club shall on each Accounting Date render to the Publisher a full and complete statement showing all money owing to the Publisher in respect of the preceding Accounting Period.

7.2 The statement of account in Clause 7.1 shall be in such form as the Publisher shall require and shall contain full details of all Books sold and each such statement shall be accompanied by payment of all amounts owing without reserve.

7.3 Pounds sterling shall be the currency of account and where any sums are

---

Clause 6.9 The Book Club is required to keep the work in print and in the Book Club's catalogue during the licence period.

Clause 6.10 This provision ensures that the Work is given the same degree of prominence as that given by the Book Club to the Book Club's other works and prevents the addition of imprints or trade marks other than those of the Publisher and the Book Club. The clause also specifically prohibits the Book Club from making any alteration or adaptation to the Work or omitting any of the Author's credits or acknowledgments.

Clause 7.1 The Accounting Dates and Accounting Periods are defined in clause 8.1 in accordance with standard industry practice. There may be occasions, however, where it is appropriate to vary these.

Clause 7.2 This provision gives the Publisher the opportunity of determining the particulars which are to be contained in the statement of account. Each statement must be accompanied by payment of sums shown to be owing without deduction of any reserves.

received in a currency other than pounds sterling the same shall be converted at the [mid-market rate calculated using the "Financial Times" index on the date of receipt] [best obtainable rate of exchange on the date payment is due].

7.4   Value Added Tax shall be payable by the Book Club to the Publisher in respect of all payments made to or to the order of the Publisher pursuant to this Agreement.

7.5   The Book Club shall keep full and proper books of account relating to the exploitation of its rights under this Agreement and the Publisher or its representative shall have the right on giving reasonable prior notice at any time during the Licence Period and for six years afterwards to inspect audit and take copies of such books of account during normal business hours. In the event that such audit or inspection reveals any deficiency in money paid to the Publisher hereunder then the Book Club shall immediately pay the same to the Publisher together with interest from the date first due calculated with monthly rests at a rate of [*percentage*]% above prime or base rate charged by its bankers to the Publisher from time to time and shall pay all reasonable costs incurred by the Publisher directly as a result of such inspection.

7.6   The Book Club shall keep confidential and shall not disclose to any third parties (other than professional advisers where necessary) the results of any such inspection or audit or any of the terms of this Agreement or any matters incidental to it or relating to the business of the Publisher and shall indemnify the Publisher fully in respect of any breach of its obligations under this Clause 7.6.

8.   DETERMINATION

It shall constitute the repudiation by the Book Club of its obligations under this Agreement and at any time the Publisher may serve written notice on the Book Club accepting such repudiation and determining the Book Club's rights under this Agreement if:

8.1   the Book Club fails to pay any amount due under this Agreement in full within three days of its due date and such failure is not remedied within seven days of receipt of written notice;

8.2   the Book Club is in breach of any other material term of this Agreement

---

Clause 7.3 It may or may not be appropriate for pounds sterling to be the currency of account. If the Book Club is situate in a foreign territory, exchange conversion provisions may be required.

Clause 7.4 It will be necessary to adjust this provision in the light of prevailing law. A short explanation of current Value Added Tax legislation may be found in paragraph 11.28 and paragraphs 12.22 to 12.30.

Clause 7.5 There may be occasions when a Publisher will wish to inspect and audit the books of account of the Book Club. Even if such audit rights are not exercised, an audit provision should always be included in licence agreements.

Clause 8 For an examination of the legal significance of the term "repudiation" reference should be made to paragraph 14.5 and to paragraphs 14.2 to 14.4.

Clause 8.1 This clause provides the Book Club with the opportunity of remedying a breach. The time period allowed to remedy pecuniary breaches is normally less than that allowed to remedy non-pecuniary breaches.

which is incapable of remedy or if capable of remedy is not remedied within fourteen days of the Book Club becoming aware of it;

8.3   any of the Book Club's representations shall prove to have been incorrect when made or become materially incorrect and the Publisher's rights and entitlements under this Agreement are materially and adversely affected;

8.4   the Book Club transfers disposes of or threatens to transfer or dispose of any part of its assets which is likely in the opinion of the Publisher to prevent or materially to inhibit the performance by the Book Club of its obligations under this Agreement;

8.5   any indebtedness guarantee or similar obligation of the Book Club or of any guarantor of the Book Club becomes due or capable of being declared due before its stated maturity or is not discharged at maturity or the Book Club or any guarantor of the Book Club defaults under or commits a breach of the provisions of any guarantee or other obligation (whether actual or contingent) of any agreement pursuant to which any such indebtedness guarantee or other obligation was incurred all or any of which shall in the reasonable opinion of the Publisher materially affect its rights and entitlements under this Agreement;

8.6   the Book Club is declared or becomes insolvent;

8.7   the Book Club convenes a meeting of its creditors or proposes or makes any arrangement or composition with or any assignment for the benefit of its creditors or a petition is presented or a meeting is convened for the purpose of considering a resolution or other steps are taken for the winding up of the Book Club (save for the purpose of and followed by a voluntary reconstruction or amalgamation previously approved in writing by the Publisher) or if an encumbrancer takes possession of or a trustee administrator administrative receiver liquidator or similar officer is appointed in respect of all or any part of its business or assets or any distress execution or other legal

---

Clause 8.2   This clause permits the Book Club to remedy a non-pecuniary material breach. The time period allowed is longer than that for a pecuniary breach.

Clause 8.3   There may be circumstances where the Publisher has entered into the Agreement on the basis of representations made by the Book Club. This clause permits the Publisher to terminate the Agreement if the representations prove to have been incorrect or subsequently become incorrect.

Clause 8.4   There are occasions where a Book Club becomes less financially secure and disposes of its assets. Where a Publisher has entered into an Agreement in reliance on the Book Club being an entity of substance, such occasions may cause concern to the Publisher, and this provision permits the Publisher to terminate the Agreement in such instances.

Clause 8.5   Financial default of the Book Club in relation to any guarantee or obligation is a further event normally permitting termination.

Clause 8.6   For the consequences of insolvency, reference should be made to paragraphs 15.2 to 15.4.

Clause 8.7   There may be occasions when a Book Club does not actually become insolvent but a creditor enforces security over the Book Club's business. This could have serious consequences for a Publisher and this clause protects the Publisher's interests by providing that such circumstances will entitle the Publisher to terminate the Agreement.

process is levied threatened enforced upon or sued out against any of such assets;

8.8 the Book Club shall cease or abandon the business of publishing and/or distributing books or the Book Club or any Associate shall announce that it is intended that the Book Club shall cease or abandon such business;

8.9 the Work goes out of print or is deleted from the Book Club's catalogue.

9. NOTICE

9.1 Any notice or other document required to be given under this Agreement or any communication between the parties with respect to any of the provisions of this Agreement shall be in writing in English and be deemed duly given if signed by or on behalf of a duly authorised officer of the party giving the notice and if left at or sent by pre-paid registered or recorded delivery post or by telex telegram cable facsimile transmission or other means of telecommunication in permanent written form to the address of the party receiving such notice as set out at the head of the Agreement or as notified between the parties for the purpose of this Clause.

9.2 Any such notice or other communication shall be deemed to be given to and received by the addressee:

(a) at the time the same is left at the address of or handed to a representative of the party to be served;

(b) by post on the day not being a Sunday or Public Holiday two days following the date of posting;

(c) in the case of a telex telegram cable facsimile transmission or other means of telecommunication on the next following day.

9.3 In proving the giving of a notice it should be sufficient to prove that the notice was left or that the envelope containing the notice was properly addressed and posted or that the applicable means of telecommunication was addressed and despatched and despatch of the transmission was confirmed and/or acknowledged as the case may be.

9.4 Communications addressed to the Publisher shall be marked for the attention of [*name*] with a copy to [*name*] of [*address*].

10. DEFINITIONS AND INTERPRETATION

10.1 The following definitions apply in this Agreement:

"Accounting Date"
90 days from the end of each Accounting Period

Clause 8.8 Where a Book Club ceases to carry on business or announces that it intends to cease its business, a Publisher will wish to recover its rights as soon as possible.

Clause 8.9 Although clause 4.11 imposes a specific obligation on the Book Club to keep the Work in print, this clause permits the Publisher to terminate if it does not do so.

Clause 9 A number of clauses in the document provide for a means of exercising rights, and a notice provision is therefore necessary.

"Accounting Period"
successive periods ending on 30 June and 31 December during the Licence Period

"Associate"
in relation to the Book Club any associate or associated company within the meaning of Section 416 or 417 of the Income and Corporation Taxes Act 1988

"Book Club Choice"
any book offered by the Book Club to its members as an inducement to join the Book Club

"Premium"
any book offered by the Book Club as a main or alternative choice to its members

"Publication Rights"
the [sole and exclusive] right to print and/or publish the Work only in volume form in [paperback or] hardback format

10.2   The following terms are defined in this Agreement in the place indicated:

"Advance":	Clause 5.1
"Author":	Clause 1.1
"Royalties":	Clause 3.1
"Territory":	Clause 1.1
"Work":	Clause 1.1

10.3   Any reference in this Agreement to any statute or statutory provision shall be construed as including a reference to that statute or statutory provision as from time to time amended modified extended or re-enacted whether before or after the date of this Agreement and to all statutory instruments orders and regulations for the time being made pursuant to it or deriving validity from it.

10.4   Unless the context otherwise requires words denoting the singular shall include the plural and vice versa and words denoting any one gender shall include all genders and words denoting persons shall include bodies corporate unincorporated associations and partnerships.

Clause 10.1   The definitions contained in clause 10.1 will need review in order to fit the appropriate circumstances. Depending on the royalty provisions which are inserted in clause 3.1 (b) it may be necessary to insert definitions for terms such as "Published Price" or "Publisher's Receipts". Document 4 clause 18.1 contains definitions which may be appropriate. The definition of Publication Rights may also need adjustment and the extent of exclusivity should also be examined (see the annotations to clause 9.2 of Document 4 and clause 1 of this Document).

Clause 10.2   The references in this clause need to be adjusted to fit the appropriate circumstances. In particular, it may be appropriate to insert additional clauses (such as those contained in Documents 6 (a) and 6 (b)) which will necessitate consequential renumbering.

Clause 10.4   For the significance of time being of the essence reference should be made to paragraph 2.10.

10.5   The word "copyright" means the entire copyright and design right subsisting under the laws of the United Kingdom and any and all analogous rights subsisting under the laws of each and every jurisdiction throughout the world.

10.6   Unless otherwise stated time shall be of the essence for the purpose of the performance of the Book Club's obligations under this Agreement.

10.7   Unless otherwise stated references to clauses sub-clauses sub-paragraphs schedules annexures and exhibits relate to this Agreement.

11.   MISCELLANEOUS

11.1   Nothing contained in this Agreement shall constitute or shall be construed as constituting a partnership or contract of employment between the parties.

11.2   The Publisher shall not be liable to the Book Club for failing to supply any material to be supplied under this Agreement due to circumstances beyond its control and it shall not be liable for any expenses or consequential losses whatever suffered by the Book Club.

11.3   The Book Club warrants that it is not the nominee or agent of any undisclosed principal and warrants that it shall assume sole and complete responsibility for the performance of the obligations in this Agreement expressed to be performed by the Book Club.

11.4   This Agreement contains the full and complete understanding between the parties and supersedes all prior arrangements and understandings whether written or oral appertaining to the subject matter of this Agreement and may not be varied except by an instrument in writing signed by all the parties to this Agreement. The Book Club acknowledges that no representations or promises not expressly contained in this Agreement have been made to the Book Club by the Publisher or any of its servants agents employees members or representatives.

11.5   This Agreement shall be governed and construed in accordance with

Clause 11.1   Under English law if two parties carry on business in common with a view to profit and share profit, the arrangement is capable of being considered a partnership. This provision ensures that no partnership is created inadvertently and also expressly excludes the possibility of an employment contract being created.

Clause 11.2   This provision protects the Publisher from any claim by the Book Club in relation to failure to supply, although there are likely to be circumstances in which the Publisher will incur some liability.

Clause 11.3   This provision protects the Publisher from the consequences of it contracting with a Book Club which has acted as the agent of an undisclosed company whom the Publisher may not consider to be a suitable person to be the Publisher's Book Club.

Clause 11.4   There are occasions where oral agreements or other understandings may be created in relation to a Work which may contain either additional obligations or obligations which conflict with those set out in subsequent written agreement. This provision makes it clear that all previous arrangements and understandings are at an end and the contract is the only document relevant to the obligations and rights of the parties in relation to its subject matter. The final part of the clause expressly excludes the possibility of any liability on the part of a Publisher for misrepresentation on the part of any of its servants, agents, employees or representatives.

the laws of England and Wales whose courts shall be courts of competent jurisdiction.

[Certificate of Value]

<u>AS WITNESS</u> the hands of the duly authorised representatives of the parties the day month and year first above written

<u>SIGNED</u> by [   ] }
for and on behalf of
[*The Publisher*]

<u>SIGNED</u> by [   ] }
for and on behalf of
[*The Book Club*]

Clause 11.5   Where a contract is made between two entities in England and Wales, it will generally not be necessary to insert a provision of this nature, but where a contract is to be created with a foreign company (or a company situate in Scotland or Northern Ireland) this provision should always be included.

Certificate of Value   Although it had been intended to abolish stamp duty on assignments of intellectual property at the same time as the introduction of paperless share transfer, the failure of the Stock Exchange system TAURUS has delayed the abolition of stamp duty which is still technically payable in relation to assignments of copyright. The publishing industry has, traditionally, never made provision for the payment of stamp duty in assignments of copyright and for this reason no provision is included in this document – although there are now many circumstances where it is advisable. A suitable form of wording may, however, be found in Document 6 (d) and a summary of the current legislation relating to stamp duty may be found in paragraph 11.29.

EXHIBIT 1

Book Club Imprint

(Clause 3.1)

DOCUMENT 36

Packaging agreement

[IMPORTANT NOTE: Please read the section "About this book" on page v, before copying or using this Document]

Purpose of this Document

This is a form of agreement suitable for use by a publisher when entering into a contract with a packager. The Document is drafted from the point of view of the publisher and should be contrasted with the provisions of Document 37 which is the Book Packagers' Association recommended guidelines.

Relevant text

The text of this Work contains a number of topics which are relevant to documents of this nature including:

- book packaging (paragraph 11.10)
- buying and selling rights (paragraphs 11.2 to 11.9)
- remuneration provisions in rights agreements (paragraphs 11.22 to 11.26)
- taxation (paragraphs 11.27 to 11.29 and 12.22 to 12.30)
- commercial terms of offers (paragraphs 1.22 and 1.23)
- the law of contract and agency (paragraphs 2.1 to 2.30)
- creation, existence and transfer of copyrights (paragraphs 3.1 to 3.45)
- international copyright protection (paragraphs 4.1 to 4.17)
- moral rights (paragraphs 5.1 to 5.22)
- permissions, fair dealing and rights clearances (paragraphs 8.1 to 8.44)
- liability for content (paragraphs 9.1 to 9.49)
- buying and selling rights (paragraphs 11.1 to 11.29)
- infringement and enforcement (paragraphs 13.1 to 13.17)
- termination and recapture (paragraphs 14.1 to 14.10)
- competition law (paragraphs 16.1 to 16.28)
- multimedia (paragraphs 19.1 to 19.55)

585

THIS AGREEMENT is made the   day of
BETWEEN

(1)   *[Name]* LIMITED of *[address]*
      ("Publisher"); and

(2)   *[Name]* LIMITED of *[address]*
      ("Packager")

IT IS AGREED as follows:

1.   THE WORK

1.1   The Publisher engages the Packager to commission *[name]* ("Author")
to write the original literary [dramatic] work entitled "*[title]*" of not less than
[number] words and to commission *[name]* ("Illustrator") to provide not less
than *[number]* pages of suitable illustrations (the illustrations and the text
together being referred to as the "Work") and the Packager undertakes to
produce and print the Work and deliver it to the Publisher in accordance with
the provisions of this Agreement.

1.2   The Work shall be [*state description of the Work ie original work of
fiction or biography or historical analysis of certain events etc*] and shall be
based on the original outline of the Work written by the Author [dated [*date*]
or submitted to the Publisher on [*date*]] and shall [*state additional requirements*]. The illustrations of the Work shall be [original to the Illustrator)]
[selected by the Packager in consultation with the Publisher from [*specify
sources*]].

1.3   The Packager shall consult with and obtain the approval of the Publisher in relation to all aspects of the printing of copies of the Work including
page size paper weight and quality binding and jacket design and shall
produce the Work in accordance with all the Publisher's reasonable requirements and undertakes to submit the following to the Publisher for approval
by no later than the following dates:

Design of jacket of Work	*[date]*
Text of Work	*[date]*
Proofs of all illustrations	*[date]*
Ozalids	*[date]*
Dummy copies	*[date]*
Samples of Work	*[date]*
[number] of bound copies of Work	*[date]*
[number] jackets of the Work for promotional purposes	*[date]*

Clause 1.1   Appropriate details should be inserted into this clause in relation to the Work, the Author, the
Illustrators. This clause comprises the engagement of the Packager to produce the Work and deliver it to
the Publisher.

Clause 1.2   A full description of the Work should be inserted and the clause should be adjusted to suit
appropriate circumstances.

Clause 1.3   The Packager is required not only to consult with the Publisher but to obtain the Publisher's
approval in relation to the list of matters. The timetable of dates and matters requiring approval should
be adjusted to suit appropriate circumstances.

1.4   The Packager undertakes to engage the Author the Illustrator and all other persons providing services in relation to the Work on terms and conditions which shall be pre-approved by the Publisher and undertakes to obtain all necessary permissions consents and releases in relation to the illustrations and/or text of the Work in a form acceptable to the Publisher and undertakes to provide the Publisher with copies of all such executed documentation as a condition precedent to any liability on the part of the Publisher pursuant to Clause 2. The Packager irrevocably confirms that the benefit of all consents releases and permissions obtained by the Packager shall extend to the Publisher throughout the territory and for the full duration for which the Publication Rights are granted to the Publisher pursuant to this Agreement.

1.5   The Packager shall make such changes to the typescript design content or illustrations of the Work or any other matter as may be reasonably required by the Publisher and shall ensure that the Work contains an adequate index if the Publisher considers an index appropriate.

1.6   The Packager shall take all steps which are necessary to ensure that the Work is produced to the very highest standard and that all copies of the Work which are printed shall be of high quality and shall conform with the Publisher's requirements. The Packager acknowledges that any failure by the Packager to comply with this provision shall be a fundamental breach by the Packager of its obligations under this Agreement which may lead to damage being caused to the Publisher's reputation.

1.7   The Packager undertakes not to engage any printer ("Printer") unless the identity of such person has been approved by the Publisher and the Packager has obtained and delivered to the Publisher an access agreement in the form contained in Exhibit 1 or such other form as may be required by the Publisher.

2.   DELIVERY AND PAYMENT

2.1   The Packager undertakes to deliver to the Publisher [*specify*] complete bound copies of the Work to the Publisher's warehouse at [*address*] time being of the essence for the purpose of this Clause.

Clause 1.4 The Publisher should formally approve the terms and conditions of engagement of all persons who are engaged by the Packager in order to ensure that all necessary rights are obtained by the Packager and transmitted to the Publisher.

Clause 1.5 This provision gives the Publisher the right to require the Packager to make changes to various aspects of the Work.

Clause 1.6 This provision requires the Work to be of the highest standard and to conform with all the Publisher's requirements.

Clause 1.7 The Publisher requires the Packager to engage a printer which has been approved by the Publisher. The Publisher will require the printer to execute and deliver to the Publisher a letter in the form contained in Exhibit 1. This letter guarantees the Publisher access to material deposited with the printer by the Packager in order to ensure that the Publisher will be able to procure completion of printing and delivery to the Publisher of copies of the Work notwithstanding any dispute with the Packager or breach by the Packager of its obligations or the insolvency of the Publisher.

Clause 2.1 This clause needs to be adjusted to suit the appropriate circumstances.

2.2   In consideration of the obligations warranties and undertakings of the Packager in this Agreement and subject to and conditional upon their full and timely performance and observance the Publisher undertakes to pay to the Packager the sum of £[*amount*] payable:

as to £[*amount*] on signature of this Agreement;

as to £[*amount*] on approval of the proofs of the Work by the Publisher;

as to £[*amount*] on delivery of the Work to the Printer;

as to £[*amount*] on delivery of copies of the Work for binding;

as to £[*amount*] on delivery to the Publisher of all bound jacketed copies of the Work required to be delivered under this Agreement;

as to [*specify*] on publication by the Publisher of the Work.

2.3   The payments specified pursuant to Clause 2.2 shall be inclusive of all royalties fees and permissions payable to authors illustrators designers rights owners and all other persons in relation to the exploitation by the Publisher of the rights granted to the Publisher in relation to the Work.

3.   RIGHTS

3.1   The Packager assigns to the Publisher the Publication Rights in the Work and all rights of action and other rights of whatever nature in relation to the Publication Rights in the Work throughout the territory of [*specify*] ("Territory") and all rights of action and all other rights of whatever nature in relation to the Publication Rights in the Work whether now known or in future created to which the Packager is now or may at any time after the date of this Agreement be entitled by virtue or pursuant to any of the laws in force in the Territory <u>TO HOLD</u> the same to the Publisher its successors assignees and licensees absolutely for the full period of copyright protection from time to time existing under the laws in force in any part of the world including all renewals reversions and extensions.

3.2   All copies of the Work published by the Publisher shall contain the following copyright notice:

Clause 2.2 It will be noted that the obligation on the part of the Publisher to pay the Packager is dependent on the full and timely performance and observance of the Packager of its obligations warranties and undertakings in the agreement. The appropriate stages of payment and the amounts of payments will need to be adjusted to suit the relevant circumstances.

Clause 2.3 The payments to the Packager will be inclusive of all payments which the Packager is required to make to persons providing rights or services in relation to the Work.

Clause 3.1 This clause provides for an assignment to the Publisher of all Publication Rights in the Work. Subsidiary rights are dealt with in clause 6.1. It may be appropriate to adjust this clause depending on the commercial circumstances in line with the provisions of clause 8.1 of Document 4 or the provisions of Documents 5 (a) to 5 (e).

[conform to reflect copyright position determined by Clause 3.1.]

3.3 The Publisher acknowledges that the Author [and Illustrator] has asserted the Author's [and Illustrator's] right to be identified in relation to the Work on the title page and cover in the following form:

[state form of identification required]

and the Publisher undertakes with the Packager to comply with such request and to require all sub-Publishers and other licensees to comply honour this right. The Packager confirms that [each of] the Author [and Illustrator] has acknowledged that no casual or inadvertent failure by the Publisher or by any third party to comply with this provision shall constitute a breach by the Publisher of this Agreement and in the event of any breach of this Clause the [Author shall not] [neither the Author nor the Illustrator shall] have the right to seek injunctive relief.

3.4 The Publisher confirms to the Packager that the Publisher agrees that all reprographic rights in relation to the Work (other than reprographic rights subsisting in relation to the typographical arrangement of the published edition of the Work) shall be reserved to the Author [and the Illustrator] together with all rights of the Author [and Illustrator] pursuant to the Public Lending Right Act 1979 and any analogous legislation in any part of the world.

3.5 The Packager warrants to the Publisher that [each of] the Author [and the Illustrator] is a member in good standing of the Author's Licensing and Collecting Society Limited and warrants that the Author's Licensing and Collecting Society Limited and its overseas affiliated bodies (together with such other bodies as may be approved by the Author [and the Illustrator] and

---

Clause 3.2 The copyright notice should state the identity of the copyright owner. If copyright is assigned to the Publisher, the copyright owner will be the Publisher. If copyright is reserved to the Packager who grants an exclusive licence to the Publisher, the copyright owner will be the Packager. It is possible for the copyright owner in one country to be different from the copyright owner in another country (see paragraph 1.20). There are a number of other notices which traditionally appear on publications (see paragraph 4.9) and there are legal advantages to ensuring that the copyright information on publications is correct (see paragraphs 4.9 and 4.10). In some countries – notably the United States – there are strong advantages to registering copyright works in the relevant foreign copyright registry (see paragraph 4.7).

Clause 3.3 This clause contains confirmation that the Author's [and Illustrator's] right to be identified (see paragraphs 5.3 to 5.9) has been asserted. The assertion is included for the reasons referred to in paragraph 7.8. There are circumstances in which a person who, for example, loses the opportunity to enhance their reputation can apply for injunctive relief (see paragraph 13.12) and restrain the publication or distribution of works which do not contain appropriate credit wording. The final sentence of the clause is intended to reduce the risk.

Clause 3.4 The rights of the Author [and Illustrator] in relation to the Public Lending Right Act 1979 are set out in paragraph 6.16, and the reservation of these rights does not conflict with any of the Publisher's interests.

the Publisher in writing shall have the exclusive right to authorise the reprographic reproduction of the Work.

4. PUBLICATION

4.1 Subject to the approval by the Publisher of the proofs of the Work and subject to the remaining provisions of this Agreement the Publisher undertakes to publish the Work to the customary standard of the Publisher at the cost and expense of the Publisher on or around such date as may be indicated by the Publisher pursuant to Clause 4.2.

4.2 The Publisher shall consult with the Packager in relation to the publication date of the Work and shall use all reasonable endeavours to give the Packager advance notice of such date.

4.3 The Publisher shall provide the Packager with 12 free copies of the Work on first publication in hardback format [and in the case of any paperback edition up to 20 free copies] and the Packager shall have the right to purchase additional further copies at a discount of [*percentage*]% of the Publisher's list price for the personal use of the Packager but not for resale purposes.

4.4 The Packager shall supply the Publisher with details of suitable persons and other information relating to publicity and advertising of the Work and shall provide the Publisher with a list of suggested individuals and periodicals who might be suitable recipients for review copies of the Work.

4.5 The Packager shall procure that the Author shall be available to the Publisher for promotional purposes within the [*specify*] week preceding the publication date for up to [*specify*] days subject to the payment by the Publisher to the Author of pre-agreed expenses and subject always to the Author's pre-existing contractual arrangements with third parties.

4.6 The Publisher shall have the right to use the name likeness and biog-

---

Clause 3.5 Reprographic rights in relation to works may be the subject of licences granted by the Copyright Licensing Agency (see paragraph 6.17). Clause 3.4 reserves reprographic rights of the Work to the Author (in other words they are excluded from the rights granted under clause 3.1) but in view of the confirmation contained in clause 3.4 (that the Author is a member of the ALCS) and in view of the fact that all ALCS-controlled works are licensed by the Copyright Licensing Agency, the end result is that although the reprographic rights are reserved to the Author initially they are subsequently transmitted to the Copyright Licensing Agency. If the Publisher is a member of the Copyright Licensing Agency, all reprographic rights in Works controlled by the Publisher will be capable of administration by the CLA which will account for money collected in such a way that the Publisher and the ALCS receive 50% each. The author will be entitled to collect his or her share from the ALCS after the deduction of their administration expenses.

Clause 4.2 The consultation obligation does not oblige the Publisher to follow the Packager's requirements.

Clause 4.3 The number of free copies of any Work and the provisions relating to purchase of additional copies are matters on which the practice varies from publisher to publisher.

Clause 4.4 This provision may not always be suitable for inclusion. It does not, however, impose an obligation on the Publisher to send all notified individuals copies of the Work.

Clause 4.5 There may be circumstances where the Publisher wishes to have the services of the Author or Packager for publicity purposes.

raphy of the Author and Illustrator and the name of the Packager in any advertising and publicity material relating to the Work but not for the purposes of product endorsement.

5. REPRINTS

5.1 The Packager shall if requested in writing before [*specify*] provide the Publisher with [*number*] of copies of the Work to the same quality and standard as those copies of the Work required to be delivered to the Publisher pursuant to Clause 2 for a price of [*amount*] ("Reprint Price"). The Reprint Price shall be payable by the Publisher:

as to £[*amount*] on [*date*]

as to £[*amount*] on [*date*]

as to £[*amount*] on [*date*]

5.2 If the Publisher wishes to obtain reprint copies of the Work after the date specified in Clause 5.1 the parties shall negotiate in good faith on the amount of the reprint price but if they are unable to reach agreement the Publisher shall have the right to call for delivery to the Publisher by the Printer of such films plates and other material relating to the Work as may be in the Printer's possession (or technically acceptable duplicate copies) and the Publisher shall have the right to use the same to produce a reprint or further editions of the Work in relation to which the Publisher shall pay to the Packager the following royalty which shall be inclusive of all other royalties costs fees expenses and charges which may be payable in relation to the exercise by the Publisher of its rights.

5.3 The royalty payable to the Packager shall be:

[*specify royalty amount and basis*]

6. SUBSIDIARY RIGHTS

6.1 The Packager appoints the Publisher as the sole and exclusive agent of the Packager during the [period referred to in Clause 3.1] [period of [*specify*] years from the date of this Agreement] to sell and exploit and enter into contracts and collect all income arising in relation to the exercise by third parties of the Subsidiary Rights listed in the Schedule. In consideration of such appointment the Publisher undertakes to pay to the Packager the

Clause 4.6 It is unlawful in certain jurisdictions to use the name or likeness or biography of a person without their consent.

Clause 5.1 This provision gives the Publisher the benefit of a fixed price reprint order which the Packager will normally place with the Packager's printers.

Clause 5.2 The fixed price reprint order in clause 5.1 is exercisable only before a specific date. Clause 5.2 therefore provides provisions for the parties to negotiate after the date has passed.

Clause 5.3 The terms of the arrangement with the Packager may be that the number of copies of the Work provided by the Packager under clause 2.1 are provided on a royalty inclusive basis under clause 2.2 and no royalty is payable. The terms relating to reprint offers may, however, require the Publisher to pay to the Packager a royalty for the subsequent order and the provisions may be inserted as appropriate.

applicable percentages of Publisher's Receipts listed in Clause 6.2 arising in relation to each such Subsidiary Right.

6.2   The applicable percentages of Publisher's Receipts referred to in Clause 6.1 are as follows:

(a)	Anthology and Quotation Rights:	[*percentage*]% Publisher's Receipts
(b)	Book Club Rights:	[*percentage*]% Publisher's Receipts
(c)	Braille Rights:	[*percentage*]% Publisher's Receipts
(d)	Computer Game Rights:	[*percentage*]% Publisher's Receipts
(e)	Digest Rights:	[*percentage*]% Publisher's Receipts
(f)	Educational Rights:	[*percentage*]% Publisher's Receipts
(g)	First Serial Rights:	[*percentage*]% Publisher's Receipts
(h)	Information Storage and Retrieval Rights:	[*percentage*]% Publisher's Receipts
(i)	Merchandising Rights:	[*percentage*]% Publisher's Receipts
(j)	Motion Picture and Television Rights:	[*percentage*]% Publisher's Receipts
(k)	Other Rights:	[*percentage*]% Publisher's Receipts
(l)	Paperback Rights:	[*percentage*]% Publisher's Receipts
(m)	Radio Rights:	[*percentage*]% Publisher's Receipts
(n)	Reading Rights:	[*percentage*]% Publisher's Receipts
(o)	Reprint Rights:	[*percentage*]% Publisher's Receipts
(p)	Second and Subsequent Serial Rights:	[*percentage*]% Publisher's Receipts
(q)	Single Issue Rights:	[*percentage*]% Publisher's Receipts
(r)	Sound Recording Rights:	[*percentage*]% Publisher's Receipts
(r)	Translation Rights:	[*percentage*]% Publisher's Receipts

Clause 6.1   This clause deals with subsidiary rights (see paragraph 1.16). It may not always be appropriate for this subsidiary rights provision to be included. There may be circumstances, however, where a Publisher may agree to pay remuneration in relation to Subsidiary Rights, particularly where the Packager is required to pay sums to the Author and/or Illustrator. It will be noted, however, that the Publisher has the right to approve the contracts between the Packager and the Author/Illustrator (see clause 1.4 and the annotation to clauses 10.1 to 10.3). The clause appoints the Publisher as the Packager's agent for the purpose of licensing the subsidiary rights for the reasons set out in paragraph 2.30. The clause needs to be modified to contain specific reference to the period of the Publisher's rights.

This clause has been drafted on the basis that the Publisher is appointed as agent for all subsidiary rights. However, if some subsidiary rights are being retained by the Packager, then the Publisher should consider whether it is appropriate for the Publisher to obtain the agreement of the Packager not to exercise such right for an initial period to avoid them being exploited in competition with the Publisher's rights.

An example would be where, for example, CD-ROM rights were retained by the Packager and did not form part of the subsidiary rights. The sale of the Work in CD-ROM format might impact on other exploitation of the Work.

(s)   US Rights: [*percentage*]% Publisher's Receipts

6.3   In authorising the exploitation of the Subsidiary Rights the Publisher shall have the right to grant licences for periods up to and including the full period of copyright in the Work and the Publisher's sole and exclusive rights and obligation to administer such licences and right to collect all income arising thereunder shall subsist for the full period of such licences irrespective of the expiry or termination of the licence contained in Clause 3.1 or the expiry or termination of the Publisher's appointment as agent.

7.   PACKAGER'S WARRANTIES

The Packager represents warrants undertakes and agrees with the Publisher as follows:

7.1   the Author and the Illustrator are the sole Authors of the Work and the Packager is the sole unincumbered absolute legal and beneficial owner of all rights of copyright and all other rights whatever in the Work throughout the world and each of the Author and the Illustrator is and shall remain at all material times during the writing of the Work a "qualifying person" within the meaning of the Copyright, Designs and Patents Act 1988 Section 154;

7.2   the Packager has not assigned or incumbered or licensed or transferred or otherwise disposed of any rights of copyright or any other rights in or to the Work except pursuant to this Agreement and has not entered into any agreement or arrangement which might conflict with the Publisher's rights under this Agreement or interfere with the performance by the Packager of the Packager's obligations under this Agreement;

7.3   the Work is original to the Author and the Illustrator and does not and shall not infringe any right of copyright moral right or right of privacy or right of publicity or personality or any other right whatever of any person;

Clause 6.2   Prevailing commercial practice in relation to percentage payments of subsidiary rights is considered in paragraph 7.21. The provisions of the clause will need to be adjusted so that they conform with the definition of Publication Rights contained in clause 16.1. Publication Rights may well include book club rights, paperback rights, reprint rights and US rights. The provisions of this clause will require careful adjustment to fit the circumstances.

It should be noted that the definition of Information Storage and Retrieval Rights (in the Schedule to Document 36) covers most forms of multimedia and electronic publishing. It may, however, be appropriate to refer to these in a separate category of subsidary rights. Alternatively, if the Publisher itself wishes to exploit these rights, it may be appropriate to include them within the definition of Publication Rights and provide a separate royalty in clause 5.4.

Clause 7.1   This provision is necessary to confirm that the Packager is the sole Packager of the Work and that no other persons own the Work (see paragraphs 3.14, 3.23 and 3.24) and that the Work qualifies for copyright protection. A more detailed analysis of the clause may be found in the notes to clause 10.1 of Document 4.

Clause 7.2   Although clause 7.1 protects the Publisher by ensuring that copyright subsists in the Work, it is also necessary to ensure that the rights of copyright are owned by the Packager, which is what the provision in clause 7.2 provides. The warranty assures the Publisher that the Packager has not incumbered the Work (by mortgaging it or charging it) or licensed rights in the Work to third parties. The provision also assures the Publisher that the Packager has not entered into any other agreement or arrangement which might interfere with the Publisher's rights under the agreement. An option which the Packager had granted to another publisher would interfere with the Publisher's rights, for example, if it is enforceable – and many in the publishing world are not (see paragraph 7.17).

Clause 7.3   Infringement of copyright, moral rights, rights of privacy and rights of publicity or personality could lead to legal liability on the part of the Publisher, which this provision seeks to exclude.

7.4   the Work is not under the laws of any jurisdiction obscene or blasphemous or offensive to religion or defamatory of any person and does not contain any material which has been obtained in violation of the Interception of Communications Act 1985 the Official Secrets Act 1989 or any analogous foreign legislation and nothing contained in the Work would if published constitute a contempt of court;

7.5   all statements purporting to be facts in the Work are true and correct and no advice recipe formula or instruction in the Work will if followed or implemented by any person cause loss damage or injury to them or any other person;

7.6   there is no present or prospective claim proceeding or litigation in respect of the Work or the title to the Work or the working title or final title of the Work or the ownership of the copyright in the Work which may in any way impair limit inhibit diminish or infringe upon any or all of the rights granted to the Publisher in this Agreement;

7.7   copyright in the Work is and shall throughout the full period of copyright protection be valid and subsisting pursuant to the laws of the United Kingdom and the United States of America and the provisions of the Berne Convention and Universal Copyright Convention;

7.8   the Packager shall not disclose reveal or make public except to the professional advisers of the Packager any information whatever concerning the Work or the business of the Publisher or this Agreement all of which shall be strictly confidential nor shall the Packager make any public statement or press statement in connection with the foregoing or commit any act which might prejudice or damage the reputation of the Publisher or the successful exploitation of the Work;

7.9   the Packager undertakes to indemnify the Publisher and keep the Publisher at all times fully indemnified from and against all actions proceedings claims demands costs (including without prejudice to the generality of this provision the legal costs of the Publisher on a solicitor and own client basis) awards damages however arising directly or indirectly as a result of any

Clause 7.4   This warranty is designed to eliminate any liability on the Publisher's part for the matters examined in Chapters 9 and 10.

Clause 7.5   There are occasions where a Publisher will be liable for negligent misstatement (see paragraphs 9.34 and 9.35). Examples of matters which could give rise to liability for negligent misstatement are referred to in the notes to clause 10.5 of Document 4.

Clause 7.6   If the Packager is aware of any dispute in relation to the Work, the Packager will be in breach of this warranty. It is, however, possible to exclude from the scope of warranties matters which have been expressly disclosed. If a Packager discloses the existence of a dispute to a Publisher, the question of interference with contractual relations may need to be considered (see paragraph 13.10).

Clause 7.7   This warranty to an extent reinforces the warranty contained in clause 10.1. There may be circumstances where it may be appropriate for a Publisher to reduce the scope of a warranty by limiting it to the Berne Convention and to the Universal Copyright Convention only so far as concerns any initial period of copyright protection in the Universal Copyright Convention countries.

Clause 7.8   This provision imposes confidentiality obligations on the Packager – see paragraphs 1.5 to 1.12.

breach or non-performance by the Packager of any of the Packager's under-takings warranties or obligations under this Agreement.

8. ACCOUNTS

8.1   The Publisher shall keep full books and records relating to the payment of sums due to the Packager pursuant to this Agreement and shall prepare and submit to the Packager within 90 days from 30 September and 31 December of each year a statement of account in relation to all sums payable to the Packager during the preceding six month period. Each such statement of account shall be accompanied by a cheque in favour of the Packager in the amount shown to be due.

8.2   The Publisher shall have the right to deduct and retain from payments due to the Packager up to [*percentage*]% of sums payable to the Packager in relation to the exploitation of Publishing Rights in paperback form as a reserve against returns in any accounting period. Each such reserve shall be liquidated (to the extent not applied against returns) in the [three/four] accounting periods following which the reserve is made and at the end of such period the balance remaining in such reserve shall be paid to the Packager in full.

8.3   The Publisher shall have the right to deduct and retain from payments to the Packager all sums required to be deducted or retained by way of withholding or other tax pursuant to the laws of any country. In the event that the remittance of royalties to the Packager is prohibited by reason of exchange control restrictions in any part of the world the Publisher shall if requested by the Packager deposit the amount of any sums due to the Packager in an account in the name of the Packager situate in the country in question and subject to the payment or reimbursement by the Packager to the Publisher of the administrative costs incurred in so doing.

8.4   If any bona fide claim shall be made in relation to the Work or any of the matters relating to the Packager's warranties pursuant to this Agreement the Publisher shall be entitled without prejudice to any of its rights under this Agreement to suspend payment of all sums payable under this Agreement or to retain such sums by way of reserve as the Publisher considers appropriate until the withdrawal or settlement to the satisfaction of the Publisher and its insurers of such claim.

Clause 7.9   For an explanation of the meaning of an indemnity clause, reference should be made to paragraph 7.15.

Clause 8.2   This provision permits the Publisher to make reserves from sums payable to the Packager. The percentage permitted to be retained and the accounting period over which it is required to be liquidated are matters which need to be specified.

Clause 8.3   A number of countries require withholding taxes to be deducted from royalties and this provision enables the Publisher to deduct such sums from royalty payments to the Packager. The second part of the clause provides a mechanism for effecting payment to a Packager from any country which imposes exchange control restrictions, by permitting the appropriate sum to be deposited in a bank account in the Packager's name in the territory.

Clause 8.4   This provision permits a Publisher to suspend payment obligations on the occurrence of any adverse claim in relation to the Work. It should be noted that the provision is not as onerous as an indemnity provision, since it applies only to sums payable by the Publisher to the Packager instead of requiring indemnity payments from the Packager to the Publisher.

8.5   Value Added Tax shall to the extent applicable be payable in addition to the sums payable to the Packager under this agreement subject to the production and delivery by the Packager to the Publisher of a full accurate and correct Value Added Tax invoice bearing the Packager's Value Added Tax registration number and country prefix accompanied by sufficient proof of the veracity of such details as the Publisher may request.

9.   PACKAGER'S WARRANTIES

9.1   Before publishing a new edition of the Work the Publisher shall be entitled but not obliged to request the Packager by giving not less than [three] months' notice in writing to require the Packager to procure that the Packager shall update the Work. The Packager undertakes (subject to Clause 9.2) to provide the Publisher by the specified date with a legible typescript indicating all additions and alterations required to bring the Work fully and comprehensively up to date which typescript shall clearly indicate the places where such additions and alterations are required to be inserted.

9.2   If following receipt of notice from the Publisher the Packager decides that the Packager does not wish to carry out the additional work referred to in Clause 9.1 or the Packager for any reason fails or neglects to do so the Packager shall notify the Publisher who shall be entitled to make such arrangements in relation to the Work as the Publisher considers appropriate including the engagement of other suitable persons on terms as may be acceptable to the Publisher in order to bring the Work up to date and in such event the amount of all expenditure incurred by the Publisher in so doing shall be recovered from sums payable by the Publisher to the Packager under this Agreement and the provisions of Clauses 3.2 and 3.3 shall be amended so as to provide that the Author and Illustrator shall be entitled to receive such credit and copyright notice as the Publisher considers appropriate. The Packager confirms to the Publisher that the Packager's contracts with the Author [and the Illustrator] provides that the assertion by the Packager of the right to be identified shall be construed in accordance with the foregoing and warrants that [the Author shall not] [neither the Author nor the Illustrator shall] have any right to object to derogatory treatment of the Author's [and/or the Illustrator's] work.

9.3   The Packager undertakes to procure that [the Author shall not] [neither the Author nor the Illustrator shall] during the period commencing on the date of this Agreement and ending five years from first publication of any Work or any subsequent reissue or new edition of the Work write any English language work which [deals with the same subject as the Work] [covers substantially the same subject matter as the Work] which might reasonably be regarded by the Publisher as competing with the Work or being likely to affect sales of the Work and the Packager agrees at the request of the Publisher to seek injunctive and other relief in order to prevent any breach by

---

Clause 8.5 There are circumstances where provision should be made for Value Added Tax (see paragraph 11.28) and where it may be appropriate for self billing arrangements to be made (see paragraph 12.26).

the Author [and/or the Illustrator] of this provision notwithstanding the provisions of Clause 13.

10.   SUBSEQUENT WORKS

10.1   The provisions of this Clause apply to any literary [or dramatic] work the rights in which are acquired by the Packager ("Subsequent Work") written by the Author [and/or the Illustrator] alone or in collaboration with others [after the date of this Agreement and prior to the expiry of [*number*] years from the date of this Agreement] [which covers the same field or subject matter as the Work] [which contains any of the principal characters portrayed or appearing in the Work or any derivative revised or rejected or surplus material written by the Author [and/or the Illustrator] in connection with the Work and which contains a story that is different from that contained in the Work or any literary or dramatic work which is a sequel to the Work (whether such work or sequel is temporally prior to or concurrent with or subsequent to the events portrayed or occurring in the Work)].

10.2   The Packager undertakes to deliver to the Publisher the completed manuscript or typescript of any Subsequent Work following its completion and as further consideration for the undertakings of the Publisher under this Agreement the Packager agrees to procure that the Publisher shall have the sole and exclusive right to negotiate and obtain from the Author [and/or the Illustrator] the same rights in relation to any Subsequent Work ("Subsequent Work Rights") as those obtained by the Publisher from the Packager pursuant to this Agreement upon the same terms and conditions (other than the amount of any Advance) as specified in this Agreement. The Publisher's right shall commence on the date of this Agreement and terminate in relation to each such Subsequent Work [three calendar months] after the manuscript or typescript of such Subsequent Work shall have been delivered to the Publisher. As soon as the financial terms relating to the acquisition of the Subsequent Work Rights in relation to any Subsequent Work have been agreed the Packager undertakes to enter into a written agreement with the Publisher in the form of this Agreement or such other form as the Publisher may reasonably require and to procure that the Packager shall enter into such agreement as the Publisher shall require.

10.3   If following the expiry of the period referred to in Clause 10.2 the

---

Clauses 9.1 to 9.3   These provisions entitle the Publisher to require the Packager to procure the Author to update the Work and create a new edition but does not oblige the Packager to do so. It does not provide the Packager to receive any advance for the additional work needed to produce a new edition. If the Packager refuses or fails or neglects to carry out additional work the Publisher is entitled to engage other suitable personnel and either recover the amount of expenditure from sums payable to the Packager or suspend payment to the Packager of royalties in relation to any new editions of the work.

These are provisions which obviously need to be negotiated and consequential amendments may need to be made to credit provisions and copyright notices provided in the agreement (see clauses 2.3 and 2.4 of Document 4). In general terms it is preferable for Publishers who are acquiring rights in works which they anticipate will be the subject of new editions, to acquire their rights by way of assignment of copyright so that they have acquired clear ownership of the original underlying work and are free to use it to create updated versions.

The final part of the clause contains an undertaking from the Packager to procure that the Author shall not write any other book which competes with the Work, in which regard the provisions of paragraph 7.2 will be relevant. The Publisher's right to seek an injunction (see paragraph 13.12) is expressly excluded from the alternative dispute resolution provisions contained in clause 13.

parties shall not have agreed terms in relation to any Subsequent Work the Packager shall be free to negotiate with third parties in respect of the Subsequent Work Rights in such Subsequent Work provided however that the Packager shall give immediate written notice to the Publisher of any offer ("Offer") received by the Packager in respect of the Subsequent Work Rights. The Publisher shall have the right to acquire the Subsequent Work Rights in such Subsequent Work from the Packager upon the same financial terms as the Offer pursuant to an agreement with the Packager in the form of this Agreement or such other form as the Publisher may reasonably require. If any Offer is not a bona fide arm's length offer made by a third party not directly or indirectly connected with the Packager ("Arm's Length Offer") the Publisher shall have the right to acquire such rights on the same terms as would in the opinion of the Publisher constitute an Arm's Length Offer.

10.4   The rights of the Publisher pursuant to Clause 10.3 shall be exercisable by notice in writing given to the Packager within [28] days following receipt by the Publisher of notice of the Offer and the Packager undertakes that the Packager shall immediately on the exercise by the Publisher of its rights under this Clause 10.4 enter into a written agreement in relation to the Subsequent Work Rights with the Publisher or its nominee in the form of this Agreement or such other form as the Publisher may require.

10.5   The Packager undertakes not to dispose of or transfer or in any way whatever incumber or agree to dispose of or transfer or in any way whatever incumber any of the Subsequent Work Rights in contravention with the terms of this Clause 10.

11.   ACTIONS FOR INFRINGEMENT

11.1   If at any time during the period the Publication Rights in the Work are vested in the Publisher the copyright in the Work is infringed by any person or any person is in breach of any contract in relation to the Subsidiary Rights the Packager shall have the option of joining in with the Publisher in any action taken by the Publisher to prevent such infringement and of sharing costs and damages relating to such action in such proportion as may be agreed. Where any proceedings are instituted by the Publisher and no agreement exists between the Publisher and the Packager in relation to the costs of such

---

Clauses 10.1 to 10.3 These clauses are designed to apply to subsequent works. Many options contained in authors' agreements do not constitute enforceable contractual obligations. The provisions in these clauses (which are enforceable) first define what constitutes a subsequent work. Different definitions are required for fictional works from technical works and the clause will need to be amended in the appropriate manner. The clause requires the Packager to deliver the typescript of any subsequent work to the Publisher and gives the Publisher a specified period of time during which the Publisher can renegotiate the financial terms (principally the advance and royalty) payable in relation to the subsequent work. If at the end of this period the parties have agreed terms then the Packager will enter into an agreement with the Publisher in such form as may be required by the Publisher. If, however, at the end of the designated period, agreement has not been reached the Packager is free to negotiate with third parties in relation to the acquisition of rights in the subsequent Work provided that before concluding an agreement with the third party the Packager notifies the Publisher of the proposed terms and gives the Publisher the right to match the proposed terms. The Publisher will need to ensure that provisions which mirror the terms of clauses 10.1 to 10.5 are included in any agreements between the Packager and the Author and/or Illustrator. These documents are required (pursuant to clause 1.4) to be approved by the Publisher. If they do not contain appropriate provisions the Packager will need to enter into additional agreements with the Author and the Illustrator.

proceedings then the Publisher shall have the right to take such action as the Publisher considers appropriate and the damages in relation to such action shall be applied by the Publisher first by way of repayment of any costs incurred by the Publisher (including a reasonable allowance for overhead costs of the Publisher) and the balance remaining shall be applied [as to [*percentage*]%] to the Packager the remainder being retained and applied by the Publisher for its own benefit.

11.2   The Packager undertakes to do any and all acts and execute any and all documents in such manner and at such locations as may be required by the Publisher in its sole discretion in order to protect perfect or enforce any of the Subsidiary Rights or any of the other rights granted to the Publisher pursuant to this Agreement. As security for the performance by the Packager of the Packager's obligations under this Agreement if the Packager shall have failed following 14 days' notice from the Publisher to execute any document or perform any act required pursuant to this Agreement the Publisher shall have the right to do so in the place and stead of the Packager as the lawfully appointed attorney of the Packager and the Packager undertakes and warrants that the Packager shall confirm and ratify and be bound by any and all of the actions of the Publisher pursuant to this Clause and such Packagerity and appointment shall take effect as an irrevocable appointment pursuant to Section 4 of the Powers of Attorney Act 1971.

12.   ALTERNATIVE DISPUTE RESOLUTION

12.1   If either party is of the opinion that the other party to this Agreement is in breach of any material condition or obligation pursuant to this Agreement including without prejudice any obligation to pay money (but excluding any matter referred to in Clause 12.4) such dispute shall be dealt with in accordance with the alternative dispute resolution procedure set out in this Clause.

12.2   The Publisher and the Packager undertake that they shall endeavour in good faith to resolve any dispute or claim arising in relation to the Work or this Agreement by means of good faith negotiations which shall take place between the Packager and a senior executive of the Publisher who shall have authority to settle the dispute. If the dispute is not resolved within [14] days from commencement of good faith negotiations the Publisher and the Packager shall endeavour in good faith to resolve the dispute through an alterna-

---

Clause 11.1   The royalty provisions do not make any specific allowance for sums recovered by the Publisher through court actions against third parties who infringe copyright in the Work. This provision permits Publisher and Packager to agree upon how such sums are applied.

Clause 11.2   In the United Kingdom an exclusive licensee may commence court proceedings to prevent infringement without the consent of the copyright owner. In some overseas territories the consent of the copyright owner may be required. This provision permits the Publisher to act as the lawfully appointed attorney of the Packager in such circumstances. Many documents contain references to powers of attorney being coupled with an interest and therefore being irrevocable. The fact is, however, that such powers are not irrevocable unless they are given by way of security, as in the case of this clause.

Clause 12   Many publishing agreements provide for resolution of disputes by arbitration. Arbitration is slow, ineffective and costly. Recently some publishing agreements have provided for resolution by arbitration through the Publishers' Association. There may be circumstances where Packagers or Publishers do not wish the Publishers' Association to become involved in (or even know about) certain disputes. Clauses 13.1 to 13.4 of this Document provide for a quick, effective, cheap and private means of resolution of disputes.

tive dispute resolution procedure carried out in accordance with the recommendations of the Centre for Dispute Resolution.

12.3   All negotiations in relation to the matters in dispute shall be strictly confidential and shall be without prejudice to the rights of the Packager and the Publisher in any future proceedings. If the parties fail to reach an agreement which finally resolves all matters in dispute within 60 days of having commenced negotiations pursuant to the alternative dispute resolution procedure or if such negotiations fail to take place within 30 days from the date specified in Clause 12.2 then either party shall be entitled:

(a)   to refer the matter to a single arbiter agreed upon by the Publisher and the Packager whose decision shall be final and binding on the parties; or

(b)   to seek such legal remedies as may be appropriate.

12.4   The provisions of Clause 12.1 to 12.3 shall not apply in relation to the exercise by the Publisher of any of its rights pursuant to Clauses 9 or 10 [or any matter relating to such rights or to any dispute or claim which involves a third party.]

13.   TERMINATION

13.1   If pursuant to the provisions of Clause 12 the Publisher is found to be in breach of any material obligation on its part pursuant to this Agreement and the Publisher shall not have remedied such breach to the extent possible within 30 days of the date of such finding or if the Publisher shall have been put into liquidation other than for the purposes of solvent reconstruction the Packager shall have the right to give notice to the Publisher in writing terminating the rights granted to the Publisher pursuant to Clause 3.1.

13.2   On receipt of notice of termination from the Packager all rights granted to the Publisher pursuant to Clause 3.1 shall revert to the Packager and the appointment by the Publisher as the Packager's agent pursuant to Clause 6 shall also terminate.

13.3   Termination of the grant of rights pursuant to Clauses 13.1 and 13.2 shall be without prejudice to the obligations of the parties contained in Clauses 9 and 10 which shall continue to bind the parties and shall be without prejudice to:

(a)   the continuation of any sub-licence granted by the Publisher and the right of the Publisher to collect and account to the Packager in relation

Clause 13.1   This clause provides the Packager with a termination right if alternative dispute resolution has not been successful and if the Publisher has still failed to remedy any breach of the Agreement after a 30-day remedy period. The clause applies only to Publication Rights.

Clause 13.2   This clause provides that the appointment of the Publisher as the Packager's agent for the purpose of exploiting the Subsidiary Rights will terminate on the exercise of the Packager's termination right under clause 13.1.

Clause 13.3   This clause provides that the exercise of termination rights will not affect the rights of the Publisher under additional clauses (such as those of the type contained in Documents 6(a) and 6(b)) or in relation to the exploitation of subsidiary rights pursuant to licences previously granted.

to all income due to the Packager under this Agreement arising pursuant to agreements entered into in relation to any Subsidiary Rights;

(b)   the right of the Packager to receive remuneration from the Publisher;

(c)   any claims by the Packager against the Publisher as at the date of termination.

14.   NOTICES

14.1   Notice or other document required to be given under this Agreement or any communication between the parties with respect to any of the provisions of this Agreement shall be in writing in English and be deemed duly given if signed by or on behalf of a duly authorised officer of the party giving the notice and if left at or sent by pre-paid registered or recorded delivery post or by telex telegram cable facsimile transmission or other means of telecommunication in permanent written form to the address of the party receiving such notice as set out at the head of the Agreement or as notified between the parties for the purpose of this Clause.

14.2   Any such notice or other communication shall be deemed to be given to and received by the addressee:

(a)   at the time the same is left at the address of or handed to a representative of the party to be served;

(b)   by post on the day not being a Sunday or Public Holiday two days following the date of posting;

(c)   in the case of a telex telegram cable facsimile transmission or other means of telecommunication on the next following day.

14.3   In proving the giving of a notice it should be sufficient to prove that the notice was left or that the envelope containing the notice was properly addressed and posted or that the applicable means of telecommunication was addressed and despatched and despatch of the transmission was confirmed and/or acknowledged as the case may be.

14.4   Communications addressed to the Publisher shall be marked for the attention of [*name*] with a copy to [*name*] of [*address*].

15.   DEFINITIONS AND INTERPRETATION

15.1   The following definitions apply in this Agreement:

"Book Club Sales"
the sale of copies or sheets of the Work or the licensing of the Work to any book club

---

Clause 14   A number of clauses in the Document provide for a means of exercising rights and a notice provision is therefore necessary.

"Out of Print"
not listed as available in any catalogue of the Publisher or any licensee

"Publication Rights"
the sole and exclusive right to print and/or publish the Work in volume or
sheet form in paperback or hardback form and the right to authorise others
to do so

"Published Price"
the price recommended by the Publisher in any county for sale of copies of the
Work exclusive of any amount of sales or value added or other taxes (if
applicable)

"Publisher's Receipts"
100% of all sums directly and identifiably received by the Publisher in sterling
in the United Kingdom (excluding any sums paid for the use of the typographical arrangement of the Work or paid for the supply of disks plates or
other pre-print materials) in relation to the categories of Publication Rights
and Subsidiary Rights referred to in Clause 6 the Publisher's Receipts in each
such category being computed on a separate basis.

15.2   The following terms are defined in this Agreement in the place
indicated:

"Advance":	Clause 5
"Arm's Length Offer":	Clause 10
"Author":	Clause 1.1
"Illustrator":	Clause 1.2
"Subsequent Work":	Clause 10
"Subsequent Work Rights":	Clause 10
"Offer":	Clause 10
"Printer":	Clause 1.7
"Reprint Price":	Clause 3.1
"Subsidiary Rights":	The Schedule
"Territory":	Clause 3.1
"Work":	Clause 1.1

15.3   Any reference in this Agreement to any statute or statutory provision
shall be construed as including a reference to that statute or statutory
provision as from time to time amended modified extended or re-enacted
whether before or after the date of this Agreement and to all statutory
instruments orders and regulations for the time being made pursuant to it or
deriving validity from it.

Clause 15.1   The definitions contained in clause 15.1 will need review in order to fit the appropriate
circumstances. In particular, careful attention should be paid to those clauses dealing with rights (see
notes to clause 9.2 of Document 4) and money.

Clause 15.2   The references in this clause need to be adjusted to fit the appropriate circumstances. In
particular, it may be appropriate to insert additional clauses (such as those contained in Documents 6 (a)
and 6 (b)) which will necessitate consequential renumbering.

15.4 Unless the context otherwise requires words denoting the singular shall include the plural and vice versa and words denoting any one gender shall include all genders and words denoting persons shall include bodies corporate unincorporated associations and partnerships.

15.5 All warranties and obligations on the part of the Packager pursuant to this Agreement shall survive the expiry of any term of years specified in this Agreement whether by determination or by effluxion of time.

15.6 The word "copyright" means the entire copyright and design right subsisting under the laws of the United Kingdom and any and all analogous rights subsisting under the laws of each and every jurisdiction throughout the world.

16. MISCELLANEOUS

16.1 Nothing contained in this Agreement shall constitute or shall be construed as constituting a partnership or contract of employment between the parties.

16.2 Neither party shall have any obligation to the other in the event of any act or omission on the part of such party where such act or omission results from the occurrence of any event which is outside the reasonable control of such party.

16.3 Nothing contained in this Agreement shall constitute an undertaking on the part of the Publisher to publish the Work. If the Publisher elects not to publish the Work in no event shall the Packager or the Author or the Illustrator be entitled to make any claim in respect of loss of opportunity to enhance the Packager's or the Author's or the Illustrator's reputation or loss of publicity or any other for any other reason whatever.

16.4 This Agreement and all representations obligations undertakings and warranties contained in it shall enure for the benefit of and shall be binding on the successors and assignees of the Packager and shall be binding upon the successors and assigns of the Publisher.

Clause 15.5 This provision ensures that any obligation on the Packager which was intended to remain in force after the term of rights expired will remain in force.

Clause 16.1 Under English law if two parties carry on business in common with a view to profit and share profit, the arrangement is capable of being considered a partnership. This provision ensures that no partnership is created inadvertently and also expressly excludes the possibility of an employment contract being created.

Clause 16.2 This is a short form of what is frequently referred to as a "force majeure" clause. It may not always be appropriate for this clause to be included, since it may permit a Packager to argue against a Publisher that the Packager is not liable in certain circumstances which are beyond the Packager's reasonable control.

Clause 16.3 This clause expressly excludes the possibility of any claim by the Packager for compensation for loss of opportunity to enhance the Packager's reputation or any other reason (see paragraph 1.23).

Clause 16.4 This provision gives the Publisher's successors, licensees and assigns the benefit of rights obtained by the Publisher and confirms the liability of the Packager's estate in relation to the warranties and obligations of the Packager.

16.5   This Agreement contains the full and complete understanding between the parties and supersedes all prior arrangements and understandings whether written or oral appertaining to the subject matter of this Agreement and may not be varied except by an instrument in writing signed by all the parties to this Agreement. The Packager acknowledges that no representations or promises not expressly contained in this Agreement have been made to the Packager by the Publisher or any of its servants agents employees members or representatives.

16.6   This Agreement shall be governed and construed in accordance with the laws of England and Wales whose courts shall be courts of competent jurisdiction.

[Certificate of Value]

<u>AS WITNESS</u> the hand of the duly authorised representative of the Publisher and the hand of the Packager the day month and year first above written

---

Clause 16.5   There are occasions where oral agreements or other understandings may be created in relation to a Work, which may contain either additional obligations, or obligations which conflict with those set out in subsequent written agreement. This provision makes it clear that all previous arrangements and understandings are at an end and the contract is the only document relevant to the obligations and rights of the parties in relation to its subject matter. The final part of the clause expressly excludes the possibility of any liability of the Publisher for misrepresentation on the part of any of its servants, agents, employees or representatives (see paragraph 2.7).

Certificate of Value   Although it had been intended to abolish stamp duty on assignments of intellectual property at the same time as the introduction of paperless share transfer, the failure of the Stock Exchange system TAURUS has delayed the abolition of stamp duty which is still technically payable in relation to assignments of copyright. The publishing industry has, traditionally, never made provision for the payment of stamp duty in assignments of copyright and for this reason no provision is included in this document – although there are now many circumstances where it is advisable. A suitable form of wording may, however, be found in Document 6(d) and a summary of the current legislation relating to stamp duty may be found in paragraph 11.29.

THE SCHEDULE

Subsidiary Rights

(*Clause 6.1*)

The expression "Subsidiary Rights" means in relation to the Work the following sole and exclusive rights throughout the world:

(1)   "Anthology and Quotation Rights" namely the sole and exclusive right to authorise the reproduction of extracts and quotations from the Work (including illustrations diagrams and maps contained in the Work) in other publications.

(2)   "Book Club Rights" namely the sole and exclusive right to license the Work to book clubs and similar organisations [*these rights may form part of the Publication Rights*].

(3)   "Braille Rights" namely the sole and exclusive right to authorise the use of the Work in braille form or in "talking-book" form.

(4)   "Computer Game Rights" namely the sole and exclusive right to authorise the making of any computer game based on the Work.

(5)   "Digest Rights" namely the sole and exclusive right to authorise the publication of abridgements or condensations of the Work either in volume form or in magazines journals periodicals newspapers or other works.

(6)   "Educational Rights" namely the sole and exclusive right to authorise the publication of special editions of the Work which may contain additional material or limited vocabulary and which are suitable for educational use.

(7)   "First Serial Rights" namely the sole and exclusive right to authorise the publication of extracts of the Work in one issue on more than one successive or non-successive issue of newspapers magazines or periodicals.

(8)   "Information Storage and Retrieval Rights" namely the sole and exclusive right to authorise the use of the Work in electronic database by means of storage and retrieval systems, microfilm, magnetic tape magnetic and/or optical disk reprography and other digital and/or mechanical and/or electronic means whether now known or in future invented.

(9)   "Merchandising Rights" namely the sole and exclusive right to authorise the use of characters or illustrations from the Work in or upon artifacts and/or articles other than books.

(10)   "Motion Picture and Television Rights" namely the sole and exclusive right to authorise the making of any film or television production or videogram based upon the Work.

(11)   "Other Rights" namely any rights of exploitation in the Work other than those referred to in this Schedule.

(12)   "Paperback Rights" namely the sole and exclusive right to authorise the publication of the Work in paperback format [*these rights may form part of the Publication Rights*].

The Schedule   The various types of Subsidiary Rights will require adjustment to reflect those which are retained by the Packager (with the Publisher acting as agent) and those which form part of the Publication Rights. Reference should be made to the annotations against clauses 8.1, 9.1 and 9.2 of Document 4. Particular attention should be paid to the treatment of Book Club Rights, Computer Game Rights, Information Storage and Retrieval Rights, Paperback Rights, US Rights, Multimedia and other electronic exploitation rights.

(13) "Radio Rights" namely the sole and exclusive right to authorise the making of any radio adaptation or dramatisation of the Work.

(14) "Reading Rights" namely the sole and exclusive right to authorise the non-dramatic reading of the Work on radio or television or upon the live stage including the making of videograms or records of such non-dramatic or "straight" reading.

(15) "Reprint Rights" namely the sole and exclusive right to authorise the use by foreign Publishers of materials which have been produced by the Publisher so as to enable the foreign Publishers to produce their own editions of the Work.

(16) "Second and Subsequent Serial Rights" namely the sole and exclusive right to authorise the issue or publication of the book in newspapers or periodicals appearing subsequent to those publications first granted licences in relation to the First Serial Rights.

(17) "Single Issue Rights" namely the sole and exclusive right to authorise the Single Issue or "one-shot" publication of the complete work or a condensed version of it in a single issue of a periodical or newspaper.

(18) "Sound Recording Rights" namely the sole and exclusive right to authorise the reproduction distribution and other exploitation of the Work by means of sound recordings.

(19) "Translation Rights" namely the sole and exclusive right to authorise the making and exploitation of the Work in foreign languages.

(20) "US Rights" namely the sole and exclusive right to authorise the exploitation of the Work in hardback or paperback form in the United States of America [*these rights may form part of the Publication Rights*].

SIGNED by [*name of officer*]
for and on behalf of
[*name of Publisher*] LIMITED

SIGNED by [*name of officer*]
for and on behalf of
[*name of Packager*] LIMITED

EXHIBIT 1

Printer's Letter

(Clause 1.7)

From: [*Printer*]

To: [*Publisher*]

Dated: [*date*]

Dear Sirs

"[*Name of Work*]" ("Work")

In accordance with the directions we have today received from [*Packager*] ("Packager") and in consideration of the payment we have received from you of the sum of £1 we undertake and agree with you that:-

1.   we will retain and hold to your order all films plates disks and other material delivered to or created by us in relation to the printing and publication of the Work ("Materials");

2.   we shall not part with possession of any Materials without your consent;

3.   we shall at your request make the Materials (or technically acceptable copies) available to you or as you direct.

The Packager by counter-signature agrees and consents to our entering into the terms of this Agreement.

Yours faithfully

Signature on behalf of [*the Printer*]

We confirm and agree the above and agree to be bound by it.

Signature on behalf of [*the Packager*]

DOCUMENT 37

Packaging Agreement
(Based on the Book Packagers' Association standard contract for Packager/Publisher Agreements)

[CAUTION: Legal advice should be taken before using this Document]

[This Document may not be used without the consent of the Book Packagers' Association which may be obtained for nominal consideration. The Book Packagers' Association may be contacted at 93A Bleinheim Crescent, London W11 2EQ, Telephone 071 221 9089.]

Purpose of this Document

This is the form of agreement recommended by the Book Packagers' Association for use by book packagers. The form of this Document should be contrasted with the provisions contained in Document 36.

Relevant text

The text of this Work covers a number of topics which are relevant to Documents of this nature including:

- book packaging (paragraph 11.10)
- buying and selling rights (paragraphs 11.2 to 11.9)
- remuneration provisions in rights agreements (paragraphs 11.22 to 11.26)
- taxation (paragraphs 11.27 to 11.29 and 12.22 to 12.30)
- commercial terms of offers (paragraphs 1.22 and 1.23)
- the law of contract and agency (paragraphs 2.1 to 2.30)
- creation, existence and transfer of copyrights (paragraphs 3.1 to 3.45)
- international copyright protection (paragraphs 4.1 to 4.17)
- moral rights (paragraphs 5.1 to 5.22)
- permissions, fair dealing and rights clearances (paragraphs 8.1 to 8.44)
- liability for content (paragraphs 9.1 to 9.49)
- buying and selling rights (paragraphs 11.1 to 11.29)
- infringement and enforcement (paragraphs 13.1 to 13.17)
- termination and recapture (paragraphs 14.1 to 14.10)
- competition law (paragraphs 16.1 to 16.28)
- multimedia (paragraphs 19.1 to 19.55)

THIS AGREEMENT is made the   day of
BETWEEN:

(1)   [*Publisher*] LIMITED of [*address*] ("the Publishers", which expression shall where the context admits include the Publishers' assigns or successors in business as the case may be) and

(2)   [*Distributor*] LIMITED [*address*] ("the Proprietors", which expression shall where the context admits include the Proprietors' assigns or successors in business as the case may be)

WHEREBY IT IS MUTUALLY AGREED as follows concerning a work to be written/edited by [*author's name*] ("the Author") provisionally entitled [*title of work*] ("the Work"), of which the Proprietors have the sole rights of manufacture and disposal of the licence to publish.

1.   QUANTITY OF COPIES

The Proprietors agree to sell and the Publishers agree to purchase [*amount*] copies of the Work in accordance with the specification set out in Appendix 1 attached to and forming part of this Agreement and subject to the terms and conditions set out herein.

*2.   PRICE PER COPY AND DATE OF DELIVERY

2.1   The Publishers shall pay the Proprietors the sum of £[*amount*] per copy and shall make such payment in the following instalments:

£[*amount*] on signature of this Agreement;

£[*amount*] on

£[*amount*] on

£[*amount*] on

£[*amount*] on delivery to the Publishers of the complete edition of [*amount*] copies of the Work.

2.2   The *price per copy is inclusive of royalty and the costs of bulk packing, shipping and insurance for delivery to the Publishers' warehouse, which delivery shall be made, unless prevented by circumstances beyond the Proprietors' control, on or before [*date*] 199*, in accordance with the Publishers' delivery and packing requirements set out in Appendix 2 attached to and forming part of this Agreement. A variation of *5 per cent over or under the quantity of copies shall constitute full delivery of the complete edition.

2.3   The Publishers may by giving notice to the Proprietors in adequate

---

Clause 1   This clause provides for a sale and purchase agreement of copies of the Work which, pursuant to the provisions of clause 2.2, are on a royalty inclusive basis and, consequently, no royalty would appear to be payable.

time to enable the Proprietors to notify the printer of the Work order additional run-on copies of the Work at the price of £[*amount*] per copy and such copies shall be subject to the terms of this Agreement.

*3.   RIGHTS AND TERRITORY

The Proprietors hereby grant to the Publishers during the term of this Agreement the sole exclusive licence to publish, distribute and sell the Work in hardback volume form in the English language in the territory set out in Appendix 3 attached to and forming part of this Agreement ("the Territory") and within the Territory to sub-license the rights set out in Clause 11 hereof subject to the terms therein contained. All rights in the Work other than those expressly granted to the Publishers under this Agreement are retained by the Proprietors.

*4.   COPYRIGHT

4.1   The Proprietors shall ensure that all copies of the Work delivered to the Publishers bear the following copyright notice:

(c)   [*name of Copyright owner*], 199*

(* represents year of first publication)

4.2   The Publishers shall ensure that all copies of the Work published by them or under licence from them in the United Kingdom and in any other part of the Territory to which the Copyright, Design and Patents Act 1988 extends shall include the above copyright notice on the reverse of the title page.

4.3
4.3.1   If at any time during the term of this Agreement the copyright of the Work shall in the reasonable opinion of the Publishers be infringed by a third party the Publishers shall at their own expense be entitled to take proceedings in the joint name of the Publishers and the Proprietors on giving the Proprietors a sufficient and reasonable indemnity against all and any liability for costs and expenses (whether of the Proprietors or of the defendants in any such proceedings) and

---

Clause 2.3   This clause gives the Publishers the right to acquire additional copies of the Work from the proprietors on giving notice.

Clause 3   The licence granted to the Publishers extends to publishing, distributing and selling the Work in hardback form. It does not expressly include printing the Work, and, in view of the provisions of clause 2.3, it would seem that the Publishers do not have the right to print copies of the Work themselves but are required to purchase copies from the Proprietors.
   The clause purports to give the Publishers the rights to sub-license the rights referred to in clause 11. The clause 11 rights are not actually licensed to the Publishers, although it would appear that it is the intention of the Agreement that the Publishers should have the power to deal with them. Whether the Publishers are empowered in the capacity as agent or as licensee is not clear (although the reference to sub-licence would appear to indicate the latter). The significance of the law of agency for Publishers is explained in paragraph 2.30.

Clause 4.2   For the reasons explained in paragraph 3.11, it is not necessary to include copyright notices on copies of works to procure copyright protection in the United Kingdom.

the Proprietors shall give the Publishers all reasonable co-operation in such proceedings.

4.3.2 The Publishers shall be entitled to nominate the solicitors through whom such proceedings may be carried on and shall have full power to abandon compromise or settle such proceedings at their own discretion but will first consult fully with the Proprietors.

4.3.3 Any sum recovered by way of damages and costs shall be applied first towards repayment of the costs incurred in such proceedings and any balance shall be divided equally between the parties.

4.3.4 Notwithstanding any other provisions of this Agreement the Publishers and their sub-licensees shall if they reasonably consider it necessary for the protection of the Work be entitled to take urgent proceedings in their sole name in any country of the world for interlocutory relief without prior notice to the Proprietors provided that the Publishers shall as soon as reasonably practicable afterwards give to the Proprietors notice of such proceedings.

4.3.5 The provisions of this clause apply only to an infringement of the copyright in the Work which affects the interest in it granted to the Publishers under the terms of this Agreement.

5. AUTHOR'S MORAL RIGHTS

The Publishers hereby recognise that the Author has asserted the Author's moral rights to be identified as the Author of the Work in relation to all such rights as are granted in the Agreement by the Author to the Proprietors. The Proprietors have undertaken and the Publishers undertake likewise:

5.0.1 to print or to require to have printed in such manner and with such prominence as to give reasonable notice in all copies manufactured by the Proprietors or licensed by the Publishers the words *"the right of the Author to be identified as the Author of this work has been asserted by the Author in accordance with the Copyright Design and Patents Act 1988"*;

5.0.2 to ensure that the name of the Author shall appear in its customary

---

Clause 4.3.1 This is not strictly necessary since a sole and exclusive Licensee has the right to take proceedings in its own name.

Clause 4.3.2 See the note against 4.3.2.

Clause 4.3.3 The parties may agree between themselves the respective entitlements for claims for damages, but the sole and exclusive Licensee of rights will regard itself as entitled to receive all damages, subject to an obligation to pay to the Proprietors an appropriate percentage by way of royalty, where a royalty commitment exists. It will be noted in this Agreement that a royalty commitment may not exist in view of the provisions of clause 2.2.

Clause 4.3.4 In many jurisdictions, sole and exclusive Licensees may commence proceedings in their own right, so the provisions of this clause may be redundant. There are likely to be, however, foreign jurisdictions which may require the Proprietors to join in legal proceedings.

Clause 5 This clause deals only with the Author's right to be identified. It does not deal with the right to object to derogatory treatment, the false attribution right and the right to privacy (see paragraphs 5.1 to 5.22). It is submitted that the publisher should not accept this provision for the reasons set out in paragraph 7.8.

form with due prominence on the title page and on the binding of every copy of the Work produced by the Proprietors or the Publishers or under licence from the Proprietors or the Publishers.

6. PROPRIETORS' WARRANTIES

6.1 The Proprietors are the sole owners of the rights granted under this Agreement and have full power to enter into this Agreement and to give the warranties and indemnity contained in the Agreement.

6.2 To the best of the Proprietors' knowledge and belief the Work contains nothing obscene, blasphemous, libellous or in breach of the Official Secrets Act or otherwise unlawful and the exploitation of the rights granted under this Agreement will not infringe the copyright or any other rights of any third party.

6.3 To the best of the Proprietors' knowledge and belief all statements in the Work purporting to be facts are true and any recipe, formula or instruction contained in it will not if followed accurately cause any injury, illness or damage to the user.

*6.4 The Proprietors shall keep the Publishers fully indemnified against all losses and all actions, claims, proceedings, costs and damages (including any damages or compensation paid by the Publishers on the advice of their legal advisers) and after written approval by the Proprietors the Publishers may compromise or settle any claim and all legal costs or other expenses arising out of any breach of any of the above warranties.

7. IMPERFECT COPIES

The Publishers shall have the right at any time within six calendar months of delivery to reject any imperfect copies of the Work and to be credited accordingly and shall if requested return such imperfect copies to the Proprietors.

*8. APPROVAL OF MATERIAL

The Proprietors shall provide for the Publishers' inspection and approval the typescript of the Work and proofs including text, illustration and jacket proofs with a reasonable opportunity to approve such proofs, such approval

---

Clause 5.0.2 It is submitted that the Publishers should not give an undertaking in the form suggested, for the reasons set out in paragraph 7.8.

Clause 6.1 It might be preferable to the Publishers if the Proprietors warranted that they were the sole unincumbered absolute and beneficial owners of all rights of copyright and all other rights in the Work.

Clause 6.2 From a Publisher's point of view, warranties which are qualified as being "to the best of knowledge and belief" are generally undesirable.

Clause 6.3 From a Publisher's point of view, warranties which are qualified as being "to the best of knowledge and belief" are generally undesirable.

Clause 6.4 Reference should be made to the warranties contained in clause 7 of Document 36.

It would seem that the indemnity (see paragraph 7.15) extends to all claims. The requirement for written approval by the Proprietors would appear to relate only to the costs of settling any claim. In other words, the Publishers would be entitled to recover their costs of defending claims on an indemnity basis.

not to be unreasonably withheld. Any costs incurred as a consequence of changes required to material previously approved shall be borne by the Publishers.

9.   UNDERTAKING TO PUBLISH

The Publishers shall publish the Work at their own risk and expense, unless prevented by circumstances beyond their control, within six months of the delivery to them of copies of the Work.

*10.   UNDERTAKING TO ADVERTISE AND PROMOTE

The Publishers agree actively to advertise and promote the sales of the work in accordance with the best commercial practice, to ensure its circulation and availability throughout the Territory, to discuss their plans for its promotion with the Proprietors and to allow the Proprietors a reasonable opportunity to check advertising and promotional copy for accuracy.

11.   SUBSIDIARY RIGHTS

11.1   The Publishers shall pay to the Proprietors the following percentages of all monies received by the Publishers in respect of all monies received by the Publishers in respect of the rights set out below:

*   percent
                                                                           percent
                                                                           percent
                                                                           percent

*11.2   The Publishers shall consult with the Proprietors over any sale of rights under this Clause. No agreement for the disposal of rights including illustrations contained in the Work shall be entered into by the Publishers without the Proprietors' prior agreement in writing. In the event that in respect of such rights additional fees are payable to sources of illustrations contained in the Work such fees shall be paid by the Publishers.

11.3   The Publishers agree to supply the Proprietors with photocopies of all sub-licences and agreements in connection with the sale of rights within 28 days of signature of such documents by the Publishers and copies of all statements received by them in connection with all such sales when accounting for such sales to the Proprietors. The Publishers shall pay to the Proprietors their share of any advance payments received by the Publishers in respect of sales of rights within 28 days of their receipt by the Publishers.

12.   ACCOUNTING FOR SALES

12.1   The Publishers shall keep accurate, detailed and up-to-date accounts of sales and income from sales of copies of and exploitation of rights in the Work.

Clause 9 Publishers are generally reluctant to accept undertakings to publish books which are still being written, and this provision may, therefore, require review.

Clause 11 The precise status of the grant of subsidiary rights, or the appointment of the Publisher as agent to deal with subsidiary rights (whichever is intended), would benefit from clarification.

12.2   Within 90 days of the expiry of their regular half-yearly accounting dates at [*date*] and [*date*] following first publication the Publishers shall submit to the Proprietors a statement showing the sales of copies and editions of the Work and of the rights therein as set out in Clause 11 of this Agreement during the relevant period and also the monies received by the Publishers in respect of such rights during that period and the relevant percentage applicable thereto and shall forthwith pay to the Proprietors such sums as are then due.

*13.   OWNERSHIP OF GOODS

13.1   The legal and beneficial ownership of all copies of the Work ("the Goods") supplied shall remain vested in the Proprietors until either:

13.1.1 all sums owed to the Proprietors by the Publishers have been paid, or

13.1.2 (if for any reason the provision in sub-clause 13.1(a) is held to be invalid) the Publishers have paid to the Proprietors all sums due to the Proprietors in respect of the Goods.

13.2   Until the ownership of the Goods passes to the Publishers under the provisions of Clause 13.1 of this Agreement the Publishers shall hold the Goods as agent for the Proprietors and shall deal with the Goods only in accordance with such instructions as the Proprietors may give from time to time and in particular:

13.2.1 the Publishers shall store the Goods in such a manner that they are separate and identifiable from all other goods and shall notify the Proprietors of the place of storage;

13.2.2 the Publishers shall insure the Goods against all normal insurable risks and on such other items as the Proprietors may require and shall on request provide the Proprietors with details of the insurance policy.

13.3.1 the Proprietors shall be informed in advance of the terms of any disposal and shall have approved the same in writing

13.3.2 the proceeds of sale of any disposal together with proceeds of any insurance claim relating to the Goods shall be held by the Publishers as trustee for the Proprietors until ownership of the Goods would have been transferred to the Publishers under Clause 13.1 of this Agreement and such proceeds shall be placed by the Publishers in a separate bank account which is clearly marked as a trust account

---

Clause 13.1 This clause purports to retain ownership of all copies in the Work supplied to the Publishers until payment of all sums due under the Agreement. Sums due under the Agreement may include (but see comments against clauses 3 and 11 above) payments in relation to subsidiary rights.

Clause 13.3 In practice this clause may be extremely difficult to enforce and may, in some circumstances, be unenforceable for the reasons set out in paragraphs 12.14 to 12.17.

13.3.3 the Publishers shall on request assign to the Proprietors all the Publishers' rights against any person who purchases the Goods from the Publishers

*14.   TERMS OF AGREEMENT

This Agreement, unless previously terminated as provided elsewhere in this Agreement shall automatically terminate [x] years after the date of first publication by the Publishers. This Agreement may be extended on the same terms by a period of a further [y] years following written agreement by the Proprietors, such agreement not to be unreasonably withheld.

15.   TERMINATION

15.1   The following are fundamental breaches of this Agreement which will automatically terminate immediately on the occurrence of any of them:

15.1.1 if the Publishers fail to publish the Work within the time stipulated in Clause 9 of this Agreement

15.1.2 if the Publishers are in breach of any of their other obligations under this Agreement and in the case of a breach capable of being remedied fail to remedy such breach within one month of being requested in writing by the Proprietors to do so

15.1.3 if the Publishers purport to assign the benefit of this Agreement without the prior written consent of the Proprietors

15.1.4 if the Publishers go into liquidation either compulsorily or voluntarily (except for the purpose of and immediately followed by a reconstruction or amalgamation) or if a receiver, administrative receiver, receiver and manager or administrator is appointed in respect of the whole or any part of their assets or if the Publishers make an assignment for the benefit of or composition with their creditors generally or threaten to do any of these things

15.2   The Proprietors may by summary written notice to the Publishers terminate this Agreement if:

15.2.1 the Publishers remainder the Work under the terms of Clause 18 of this Agreement

15.2.2 the Publishers allow the Work to go out of print so that it is not available in the home market in the English language PROVIDED THAT this Agreement shall not terminate if within [x] months of receipt of notice in writing from the Proprietors (time being of the essence) the Publishers agree to publish in the home market a reprint

---

Clause 14   If the Publishers are to extend the term of rights, the method and procedure pursuant to which they are capable of acquiring copies of the Work would benefit from clarification.

of not less than [y] copies or notify the Proprietors that they have licensed another Publisher to publish such a reprint which will be published within that period time being of the essence

15.3

15.3.1 On the expiry or termination of this Agreement all rights granted to the Publishers under its terms shall automatically and immediately revert to the Proprietors absolutely

15.3.2 The Publishers may for a period of six months on a non-exclusive basis continue to sell any copies of the Work that are on hand as at the date of expiry or termination of this Agreement

15.3.3 Termination shall not affect:

15.3.3.1 the subsidiary rights (if any) of any third party under a sub-licence validly entered into by the Publishers prior to termination

15.3.3.2 the rights of the Proprietors to money accrued due to the Proprietors in respect of the Publishers' sales and exploitation of the Work up to the date of termination

15.3.3.3 any claim which the Author may have against the Publishers for damages or otherwise

15.4   After termination or expiry of this Agreement the Publishers shall from time to time when so requested do all such things and sign and execute such documents and deeds as the Proprietors may reasonably require in order to confirm the reversion of rights to the Proprietors under the terms of this Agreement and in particular (but not by way of limitation) the Publishers shall give notice in the form specified by the Proprietors to all (if any) of the Publishers' sub-licensees of the termination of this Agreement and requesting such sub-licensees as from the date of termination to account to the Proprietors or as the Proprietors shall direct for money payable by such sub-licensees in respect of the Work.

*16.   PENALTIES

16.1   If the Publishers fail to pay to the Proprietors sums due under this Agreement within the times specified in this Agreement the Publishers agree to pay to the Proprietors interest on such sums overdue equal to [x] per cent above the current base rate at [Bank] from the due date until such payment is made.

16.2   If delivery of the Work is delayed by more than four weeks after the date provided for in Clause 2.2 of this Agreement unless the parties have agreed in writing upon a revised date of delivery the Publishers shall be entitled to postpone publication by a maximum of 16 weeks and the settlement of the final instalment of the purchase price herein provided for shall be

---

Clause 16   While it is possible to recover liquidated damages at law (see paragraph 13.13) penalties are generally not recoverable.

postponed by an equivalent period. If delivery of the Work is delayed by more than 24 weeks after the date provided for in Clause 2.2 of this Agreement the Publishers shall be entitled to cancel this Agreement and to be repaid all sums advanced to the Proprietors hereunder together with interest on such sums equal to [x] per cent above the current base rate at [Bank] from [date] up to the date of cancellation.

17.   PROPRIETORS' COPIES

17.1   The Proprietors shall retain twelve copies of the Work of which six copies shall be presented to the author.

*17.2   The Proprietors shall additionally be entitled to repurchase not more than 250 copies of the Work from the Publishers at the price paid for them and additional copies at the best UK trade discount for promotional purposes only and not for resale.

17.3   The Publishers shall supply to the Proprietors free of charge six copies of each and every edition of the Work sub-licensed by them to third parties under the terms of this Agreement.

*18.   REMAINDERS

The Publishers shall be entitled not sooner than 24 calendar months after first publication of any edition of the Work to dispose of surplus copies of that edition only as a remainder after first making an offer in writing to the Proprietors to sell such copies to the Proprietors at a price equal to the best written offer from any potential purchaser, such offer to be accepted or refused within three months of its receipt. In the event of the disposal of the Publishers' stock under this provision all rights contained herein shall revert to the Proprietors without prejudice to any monies due to the Proprietors from the Publishers. The Publishers hereby acknowledge that breach of the provisions of this Clause would jeopardise the interest of the Proprietors and that the Proprietors would be entitled to compensation in the event of such a breach.

19.   INSPECTION OF RECORDS

The Proprietors shall have the right on giving reasonable notice to the Publishers to inspect all books, vouchers and documents in the possession of the Publishers relating to the exploitation of rights in and sales of the Work.

*20.   PROVISION OF ADVANCE MATERIAL

The Proprietors shall provide the Publishers with the advance material and information specified in Appendix 4 attached to and forming part of this Agreement and shall at the Publishers' request supply additional sales material at cost price subject to reasonable notice from the Publishers.

21.   ASSIGNMENT

Rights and obligations under this Agreement may not be assigned in whole or in part by either party without the prior consent in writing of the other party.

22. JURISDICTION

This Agreement shall be governed by the law of England and the parties hereby submit to the jurisdiction of the English Courts.

AS WITNESS the hands of authorised representatives of the parties on the date first above written

....

for and on behalf of the Publishers

....

for and on behalf of the Proprietors

APPENDIX 1
SPECIFICATION

Title:

Author:

Order No:

Quantity:

Price per copy:

Royalty:

Aggregate price:

Delivery date:

Extent:

Approximate number of words:

Trimmed page size:

Illustrations:

Printing:

Binding:

Jacket:

Text paper:

Date for supply of Publishers' ISBN, barcode, etc:

*APPENDIX 2

Publishers' delivery and packing requirements (attached)

*APPENDIX 3

Territory

Exclusive in the Commonwealth as constituted at the date of this Agreement excluding Canada, Australia and New Zealand; non-exclusive throughout the rest of the world excluding the United States of America and its dependencies and the Philippine Islands

*APPENDIX 4

Advance Information and Material

1. Not less than [x] days before delivery: full title; author's name; description of contents and illustrations; biographical details of author; jacket copy.
2. Not less than [x] days before delivery: [y] sets of complete proofs of the text.
3. Not less than [x] days before delivery: [y] advance jackets.
4. Not less than [x] days before delivery: [y] advance sets of sewn sheets with jackets/advance bound and jacketed copies.

DOCUMENT 38

Acquisition of translation rights

[IMPORTANT NOTE: Please read the section "About this book" on page v, before copying or using this Document]

Purpose of this Document

This is a form of agreement suitable for use by a publisher for the acquisition of translation rights. The Document is drafted from the point of view of a publisher acquiring the rights and should be contrasted with the provisions of Document 39 which are drafted from the point of view of a publisher licensing translation rights.

Relevant text

The text of this Work contains a number of topics which are relevant to documents of this nature including:

- buying and selling rights (paragraphs 11.2 to 11.9)
- remuneration provisions in rights agreements (paragraphs 11.22 to 11.26)
- taxation (paragraphs 11.27 to 11.29 and 12.22 to 12.30)
- commercial terms of Publisher's offer (paragraphs 1.22 and 1.23)
- the law of contract and agency (paragraphs 2.1 to 2.30)
- creation, existence and transfer of copyrights (paragraphs 3.1 to 3.45)
- international copyright protection (paragraphs 4.1 to 4.17)
- moral rights (paragraphs 5.1 to 5.22)
- permissions, fair dealing and rights clearances (paragraphs 8.1 to 8.44)
- liability for content (paragraphs 9.1 to 9.49)
- buying and selling rights (paragraphs 11.1 to 11.29)
- infringement and enforcement (paragraphs 13.1 to 13.17)
- termination and recapture (paragraphs 14.1 to 14.10)
- competition law (paragraphs 16.1 to 16.28)
- multimedia (paragraphs 19.1 to 19.55)

THIS AGREEMENT is made   the day of

BETWEEN

(1) [*Name*] LIMITED of [*address*]
     ("Proprietor")

(2) [*Name*] LIMITED of [*address*]
     ("Publisher"); and

IT IS AGREED as follows:

1.   GRANT OF RIGHTS

1.1   The Proprietor grants to the Publisher the sole and exclusive licence to exploit commission print and publish an English language translation ("Translation") of the original literary work entitled "[*title*]" ("Work") written by [*name of author*] ("Author") throughout the [*specify territory*] ("Territory") and the sole and exclusive right to authorise others to do so for the full period of copyright from time to time existing under the laws in force in any part of the world including all reversions renewals and extensions.

1.2   The Proprietor undertakes to deliver to the Publisher within [*specify*] days from the date of this Agreement twelve copies of the original [*specify*] language version of the Work as published by the Proprietor. The Proprietor warrants that the original language version of the Work has been approved by the Author and the Proprietor confirms and agrees that the licence granted pursuant to Clause 1.1 shall extend to all associated publicity and advertising material produced by the Proprietor.

1.3   The Proprietor warrants and confirms to the Publisher that all permissions and consents required in order to enable the exploitation of any illustrations or photographs contained in the Work and any other material whose rights are owned or controlled by third parties have been obtained and that such consents and permissions extend to and authorise the exploitation by the Publisher of the rights granted to the Publisher in this Agreement.

1.4   The Proprietor undertakes to use all reasonable endeavours to procure that the Author shall collaborate with the person ("Translator") engaged by the Publisher to translate the Work and to give such assistance as the

---

Clause 1.1   This provision grants the Publisher a sole and exclusive licence in relation to the publication rights (see paragraph 1.14). Details of the territory in the work need to be inserted. It should be noted that the licence extends to any renewals or extensions of copyright. It is submitted that all licences should be so framed in view of the European Union Directive 93/98 which extends the term of protection of copyright (see paragraph 17.11 and paragraphs 20.2 to 20.10). The Publisher may wish to acquire rights throughout the entire European Economic Area in the English language, so as to protect against parallel imports (see paragraph 11.3). The Publisher will generally wish to vet the chain of title documentation under which the Proprietor has acquired rights from the Author (see paragraph 8.44 and Document 30).

Clause 1.2   This provides that the Publisher will deliver copies of the original language version of the Work and further confirms that the original language version of the Work has been approved by the Author in order to avoid any possible claim from the Author that the Publisher's English language translation is based on a text which infringe the Author's moral rights.

Translator and the Publisher may require in order to ensure the creation and publication of a Translation of the highest possible quality.

2.   NOTICES AND CREDIT

2.1   All copies of the Work published by the Publisher shall contain the following copyright notice:

[conform to reflect copyright position of the Work]

2.2   The Proprietor confirms that the Author has asserted the Author's right to be identified in relation to the Work on the title page and cover in the following form:

[state form of identification required]

and the Publisher undertakes to comply with such request and to require all sub-publishers and other licensees to honour this right. The Proprietor acknowledges that no casual or inadvertent failure by the Publisher or by any third party to comply with this provision shall constitute a breach by the Publisher of this Agreement and in the event of any breach of this Clause the Proprietor warrants that the Author shall not have the right to seek injunctive relief and the sole remedy of the Author or the Proprietor shall be a claim for damages.

2.3   The Proprietor acknowledges that it is necessary for the purposes of publication for the Publisher to have the right to make alterations to the text of the Work for the purpose of authorising translations and the Proprietor warrants that the Author has consented to the exercise by the Publisher of such rights and warrants that the Author has agreed that the product of such exercise shall not be capable of being considered a distortion mutilation or derogatory treatment of the Work.

Clause 1.4   The provisions of this clause will not be applicable if the original Author is dead. In practice many translators work with the foreign language Authors, but agreements for the acquisition of translation rights rarely provide for this contractual obligation.

Clause 2.1   The copyright notice should state the identity of the copyright owner. If copyright is assigned to the Publisher, the copyright owner will be the Publisher. If copyright is reserved to the Proprietor and the Proprietor grants an exclusive licence to the Publisher, the copyright owner will be the Proprietor. It is possible for the copyright owner in one country to be different from the copyright owner in another country (see paragraph 1.20). There are a number of other notices which traditionally appear on publications (see paragraph 4.9) and there are legal advantages to ensuring that the copyright information on publications is correct (see paragraphs 4.9 and 4.10). In some countries – notably the United States – there are strong advantages to registering copyright works in the relevant foreign copyright registry (see paragraph 4.7).

Clause 2.2   This clause contains confirmation that the Author's right to be identified (see paragraphs 5.3 to 5.9) has been asserted. The assertion is included for the reasons referred to in paragraph 7.8. There are circumstances in which a person who, for example, loses the opportunity to enhance their reputation can apply for injunctive relief (see paragraph 13.12) and restrain the publication or distribution of works which do not contain appropriate credit wording. The final sentence of the clause is intended to reduce the risk.

Clause 2.3   This clause contains a warranty from the Proprietor that the Author has consented to certain acts being done without violating the Author's right to object to derogatory treatment of the Author's Work (see paragraphs 5.10 to 5.13). The clause has been inserted for the reasons referred to in paragraph 7.8 being a more acceptable alternative (from an Author's point of view) to a complete waiver of moral rights. Although provisions of this nature are not generally found in minimum terms agreements (see paragraph 7.20), there are strong commercial arguments to support their inclusion (see paragraph 7.22).

3. PUBLICATION AND PROMOTION

3.1 Subject to the provisions of this Agreement and the acceptance and approval of the Publisher of the Translator's translation of the Work the Publisher undertakes to publish the Translation to the customary standard of the Publisher at the cost and expense of the Publisher on or around such date as may be indicated by the Publisher pursuant to Clause 3.3.

3.2 It is the intention of the Publisher to print [*number*] copies of the Work in [hard][paper] back format with an anticipated retail price of [*price*] but nothing contained in this Clause 3.2 shall constitute an obligation on the part of the Publisher in relation to the print run or pricing of the first or any subsequent edition of the Translation and the Proprietor acknowledges that the Publisher shall have sole control of all matters in relation to the production and publication of the Translation including without limitation print runs numbers of reprints and editions marketing price advertising editorial production distribution and terms of sale.

3.3 The Publisher shall use all reasonable endeavours to give the Proprietor advance notice of the publication of the Translation. The Publisher shall provide the Proprietor with 12 free copies of the Translation on first publication in hardback format [and in the case of any paperback edition up to 20 free copies] and the Proprietor shall have the right to purchase additional further copies at a discount of [*percentage*]% of the Publisher's list price for the personal use of the Proprietor but not for resale purposes.

3.4 The Proprietor shall supply the Publisher with details of suitable persons and other information relating to publicity and advertising of the Work and shall provide the Publisher with a list of suggested individuals and periodicals who might be suitable recipients for review copies of the Translation.

4. ADVANCE AND ROYALTIES

4.1 Subject to and conditional upon the full performance and observance by the Proprietor of all the undertakings obligations and warranties on the part of the Proprietor contained in this Agreement the Publisher undertakes to pay to the Proprietor the recoupable advance ("Advance") set out in

---

Clause 3.1 Publication costs are generally borne by publishers, although in the area which is referred to as "vanity publishing" it is usual for authors to pay to have the privilege of seeing their names in print.

Clause 3.2 This clause requires the Publisher to state the intended print run and publication price. The statements will not bind the Publisher for the future, and the clause makes it clear that the Publisher retains sole control over production matters.

Clause 3.3 The number of free copies of any work and the provisions relating to purchase of additional copies are matters on which the practice varies from publisher to publisher.

Clause 3.4 This provision may not always be suitable for inclusion. It does not, however, impose an obligation on the Publisher to send all notified individuals copies of the Work.

Clause 4.2 which shall be paid on account of and be recoverable from the royalties ("Royalties") payable pursuant to Clause 4.3.

4.2 The Advance payable by the Publisher to the Proprietor shall be £[*amount*] payable:

(a) as to £[*amount*] on the date of this Agreement receipt of which the Proprietor acknowledges

(b) as to £[*amount*] on publication of the Translation.

4.3 The Royalties payable by the Publisher to the Proprietor shall be:

(a) [*specify hardback royalty*] on copies of the Translation published or licensed by the Publisher

(b) [*specify paperback royalty*] on copies of the Translation published or licensed by the Publisher

(c) [*specify overseas royalty and royalty from sub-licensing of the Translation*]

5. PROPRIETOR'S WARRANTIES

The Proprietor represents warrants undertakes and agrees with the Publisher as follows:

5.1 the Author is the sole Author of the Work and was at all material times during the writing of the Work a "qualifying person" within the meaning of the Copyright, Designs and Patents Act 1988 Section 154 and the Proprietor is the sole unincumbered absolute legal and beneficial owner of all rights of copyright and all other rights whatever in the Work and the Delivery Materials throughout the world;

5.2 the Proprietor has not assigned or incumbered or licensed or transferred or otherwise disposed of any rights of copyright or any other rights in or to the Work except pursuant to this Agreement and has not entered into any agreement or arrangement which might conflict with the Publisher's rights

---

Clause 4.1 The Proprietor's entitlement to receive the royalties is subject to and conditional upon the full performance and observance by the Proprietor of all the Proprietor's obligations in the Agreement.

Clause 4.2 The advance is expressed to be recoupable. In other words it is paid on account of royalties and recouped from future royalties paid to the Proprietor.

The Proprietor's entitlement to receive the advance is subject to and conditional on full performance and observance by the Proprietor of the Proprietor's warranties and obligations under the Agreement.

Clause 4.3 For prevailing commercial practice in relation to royalty rates see paragraph 7.21.

Clause 5.1 This provision is necessary to confirm that the Author is the sole Author of the Work and that no other persons own the Work (see paragraphs 3.14, 3.23 and 3.24) and that the Work qualifies for copyright protection. A more detailed analysis of the clause may be found in the notes to clause 10.1 in Document 4.

under this Agreement or interfere with the performance by the Proprietor of the Proprietor's obligations under this Agreement;

5.3   the Work is original to the Author and the Work does not infringe any right of copyright moral right or right of privacy or right of publicity or any other right whatever of any person;

5.4   the Work is not under the laws of any jurisdiction obscene or blasphemous or offensive to religion or defamatory of any person and does not contain any material which has been obtained in violation of the Interception of Communications Act 1985 the Official Secrets Act 1989 or any analogous foreign legislation and nothing contained in the Work constitute a contempt of court;

5.5   all statements purporting to be facts in the Work are true and correct and no advice recipe formula or instruction in the Work will if followed or implemented by any person cause loss damage or injury to them or any other person;

5.6   there is no present or prospective claim proceeding or litigation in respect of the Work or the title to the Work or the working title or final title of the Work or the ownership of the copyright in the Work which may in any way impair limit inhibit diminish or infringe upon any or all of the rights granted to the Publisher in this Agreement;

5.7   copyright in the Translation shall at all times belong to and remain vested in the Publisher and the Translator in accordance with the provisions of those agreements between the Publisher and the Translator and copyright in the Work is and shall throughout the full period of copyright protection be valid and subsisting pursuant to the laws of the United Kingdom and the United States of America and the provisions of the Berne Convention and Universal Copyright Convention;

Clause 5.2   Although clause 5.1 protects the Publisher by ensuring that copyright subsists in the Work, it is also necessary to ensure that the rights of copyright are owned by the Proprietor, which is what the provision in clause 5.2 provides. The warranty assures the Publisher that the Proprietor has not incumbered the Work (by mortgaging it or charging it) or licensed rights in the Work to third parties. The provision also assures the Publisher that the Proprietor has not entered into any other agreement or arrangement which might interfere with the Publisher's rights under the Agreement. An option which the Proprietor had granted to another Publisher would interfere with the Publisher's rights, for example, if it was enforceable – and many in the publishing world are not (see paragraph 7.17).

Clause 5.3   Infringement of copyright, moral rights, rights of privacy and rights of publicity could lead to legal liability on the part of the Publisher, which this provision seeks to exclude.

Clause 5.4   This warranty is designed to eliminate any liability on the Publisher's part for the matters examined in Chapters 9 and 10.

Clause 5.5   There are occasions where a Publisher will be liable for negligent misstatement (see paragraphs 9.34 and 9.35). Examples of matters which could give rise to liability for negligent misstatement are referred to in the notes to clause 10.5 of Document 4.

Clause 5.6   If the Proprietor is aware of any dispute in relation to the Work, the Proprietor will be in breach of this warranty. It is, however, possible to exclude from the scope of warranties matters which have been expressly disclosed. If a Proprietor discloses the existence of a dispute to a Publisher, the question of interference with contractual relations may need to be considered (see paragraph 13.10).

Clause 5.7   This warranty to an extent reinforces the warranty contained in clause 5.1. There may be circumstances where it may be appropriate for a Publisher to reduce the scope of a warranty by limiting it to the Berne Convention and to the Universal Copyright Convention only so far as concerns any initial period of copyright protection in the Universal Copyright Convention countries.

5.8   the Proprietor shall not disclose reveal or make public except to the professional advisers of the Proprietor any information whatever concerning the Work or the business of the Publisher or this Agreement all of which shall be strictly confidential nor shall the Proprietor make any public statement or press statement in connection with the foregoing or commit any act which might prejudice or damage the reputation of the Publisher or the successful exploitation of the Work;

5.9   the Proprietor undertakes to indemnify the Publisher and keep the Publisher at all times fully indemnified from and against all actions proceedings claims demands costs (including without prejudice to the generality of this provision the legal costs of the Publisher on a solicitor and own client basis) awards damages however arising directly or indirectly as a result of any breach or non-performance by the Proprietor of any of the Proprietor's undertakings warranties or obligations under this Agreement.

6.   ACCOUNTS

6.1   The Publisher shall keep full books and records relating to the payment of sums due to the Proprietor pursuant to this Agreement and shall prepare and submit to the Proprietor within 90 days from 30 September and 31 December of each year a statement of account in relation to all sums payable to the Proprietor during the preceding six-month period. Each such statement of account [shall be in the form recommended by the Society of Proprietors and] shall be accompanied by a cheque in favour of the Proprietor in the amount shown to be due.

6.2   The Publisher shall have the right to deduct and retain from payments due to the Proprietor up to [*percentage*]% of sums payable to the Proprietor in relation to the exploitation of the Translation in paperback form as a reserve against returns in any accounting period. Each such reserve shall be liquidated (to the extent not applied against returns) in the [three/four] accounting periods following which the reserve is made and at the end of such period the balance remaining in such reserve shall be paid to the Proprietor in full.

6.3   The Publisher shall have the right to deduct and retain from payments to the Proprietor all sums required to be deducted or retained by way of withholding or other tax pursuant to the laws of any country. In the event that the remittance of royalties to the Proprietor is prohibited by reason of exchange control restrictions in any part of the world the Publisher shall if requested by the Proprietor deposit the amount of any sums due to the Proprietor in an account in the name of the Proprietor situate in the country

---

Clause 5.8   This provision imposes confidentiality obligations on the Proprietor – see paragraphs 1.5 to 1.12.

Clause 5.9   For an explanation of the meaning of an indemnity clause, reference should be made to paragraph 7.15.

Clause 6.2   This provision permits the Publisher to make reserves from sums payable to the Proprietor. The percentage permitted to be retained, and the accounting period over which it is required to be liquidated, are matters which need to be specified.

in question and subject to the payment or reimbursement by the Proprietor to the Publisher of the administrative costs incurred in so doing.

6.4   If any bona fide claim shall be made in relation to the Work or any of the matters relating to the Proprietor's warranties pursuant to this Agreement the Publisher shall be entitled without prejudice to any of its rights under this Agreement to suspend payment of the Advance and/or the Royalties or to retain such sums by way of reserve as the Publisher considers appropriate until the withdrawal or settlement to the satisfaction of the Publisher and its insurers of such claim.

6.5   Value Added Tax shall to the extent applicable be payable in addition to the sums payable to the Proprietor under this agreement subject to the production and delivery by the Proprietor to the Publisher of a full accurate and correct Value Added Tax invoice bearing the Proprietor's Value Added Tax registration number and country prefix accompanied by sufficient proof of the veracity of such details as the Publisher may request.

7.   ALTERNATIVE DISPUTE RESOLUTION

7.1   If either party is of the opinion that the other party to this Agreement is in breach of any material condition or obligation pursuant to this Agreement including without prejudice any obligation to pay money (but excluding any matter referred to in Clause 7.4) such dispute shall be dealt with in accordance with the alternative dispute resolution procedure set out in this Clause.

7.2   The Publisher and the Proprietor undertake that they shall endeavour in good faith to resolve any dispute or claim arising in relation to the Translation or this Agreement by means of good faith negotiations which shall take place between the Proprietor and a senior executive of the Publisher who shall have authority to settle the dispute. If the dispute is not resolved within [14] days from commencement of good faith negotiations the Publisher and the Proprietor shall endeavour in good faith to resolve the dispute through an alternative dispute resolution procedure carried out in accordance with the recommendations of the Centre for Dispute Resolution.

7.3   All negotiations in relation to the matters in dispute shall be strictly

---

Clause 6.3   A number of countries require withholding taxes to be deducted from royalties, and this provision enables the Publisher to deduct such sums from royalty payments to the Proprietor. The second part of the clause provides a mechanism for effecting payment to a Proprietor from any country which imposes exchange control restrictions, by permitting the appropriate sum to be deposited in a bank account in the Proprietor's name in the territory.

Clause 6.4   This provision permits a Publisher to suspend payment obligations on the occurrence of any adverse claim in relation to the Work. It should be noted that the provision is not as onerous as an indemnity provision, since it applies only to sums payable by the Publisher to the Proprietor, instead of requiring indemnity payments from the Proprietor to the Publisher.

Clause 6.5   There are circumstances where provision should be made for Value Added Tax (see paragraph 11.28) and where it may be appropriate for self billing arrangements to be made (see paragraph 12.26).

Clause 7.1   Many publishing agreements provide for resolution of disputes by arbitration. Arbitration is slow, ineffective and costly. Recently some publishing agreements have provided for resolution by arbitration through the Publishers' Association. There may be circumstances where Proprietors or Publishers do not wish the Publishers' Association to become involved in (or even know about) certain disputes. Clauses 7.1 to 7.4 of this Document provide for a quick, effective, cheap and private means of resolution of disputes.

confidential and shall be without prejudice to the rights of the Proprietor and the Publisher in any future proceedings. If the parties fail to reach an agreement which finally resolves all matters in dispute within 60 days of having commenced negotiations pursuant to the alternative dispute resolution procedure or if such negotiations fail to take place within 30 days from the date specified in Clause 7.2 then either party shall be entitled:

(a) to refer the matter to a single arbiter agreed upon by the Publisher and the Proprietor whose decision shall be final and binding on the parties; or

(b) to seek such legal remedies as may be appropriate.

7.4 [The provisions of Clause 7.1 to 7.3 shall not apply in relation to any dispute or claim which involves a third party.]

8. TERMINATION

8.1 If pursuant to the provisions of clause 7 any party to this Agreement is found to be in breach of any material obligation on its part pursuant to this Agreement and shall not have remedied such breach to the extent possible within 30 days of the date of such finding the other party may terminate this Agreement by notice in writing.

8.2 The waiver by either party of any breach by the other of the terms of this Agreement shall not be deemed to be a continuing waiver or a waiver of any other breach or default on the part of the other of the terms of this Agreement.

8.3 Termination of the grant of rights pursuant to clause 8.1 shall be without prejudice to:

(a) the continuation of any licence or sub-licence granted by the Publisher and the right of the Publisher to collect and account to the Proprietor in relation to all income due to the Proprietor under this Agreement;

(b) the right of the Proprietor to receive remuneration from the Publisher;

(c) any claims by the Proprietor against the Publisher as at the date of termination.

9. NOTICES

9.1 Notice or other document required to be given under this Agreement or any communication between the parties with respect to any of the provisions of this Agreement shall be in writing in English and be deemed duly given if signed by or on behalf of a duly authorised officer of the party giving the notice and if left at or sent by pre-paid registered or recorded delivery post or by telex telegram cable facsimile transmission or other means of telecom-

---

Clause 8 This clause provides each party with a termination right if alternative dispute resolution has not been successful and if the party in breach has failed to remedy any breach of any material provision of the Agreement after a 30-day notice period.

munication in permanent written form to the address of the party receiving such notice as set out at the head of the Agreement or as notified between the parties for the purpose of this Clause.

9.2   Any such notice or other communication shall be deemed to be given to and received by the addressee:

(a)   at the time the same is left at the address of or handed to a representative of the party to be served

(b)   by post on the day not being a Sunday or Public Holiday two days following the date of posting

(c)   in the case of a telex telegram cable facsimile transmission or other means of telecommunication on the next following day.

9.3   In proving the giving of a notice it should be sufficient to prove that the notice was left or that the envelope containing the notice was properly addressed and posted or that the applicable means of telecommunication was addressed and despatched and despatch of the transmission was confirmed and/or acknowledged as the case may be.

9.4   Communications addressed to the Publisher shall be marked for the attention of [*name*] with a copy to [*name*] of [*address*].

10.   DEFINITIONS AND INTERPRETATION

10.1   The following terms are defined in this Agreement in the place indicated:

"Advance":	Clause 4
"Royalties":	Clause 4
"Territory":	Clause 1.1
"Translation":	Clause 1.1
"Work":	Clause 1.1

10.2   Unless the context otherwise requires words denoting the singular shall include the plural and vice versa and words denoting any one gender shall include all genders and words denoting persons shall include bodies corporate unincorporated associations and partnerships.

10.3   All warranties and obligations on the part of the Proprietor pursuant to this Agreement shall survive the expiry of any term of years specified in this Agreement whether by determination or by effluxion of time.

10.4   The word "copyright" means the entire copyright and design right

---

Clause 9   A number of clauses in the document provide for a means of exercising rights and a notice provision is therefore necessary.

Clause 10.1   The references in this clause need to be adjusted to fit the appropriate circumstances. In particular, it may be appropriate to insert additional clauses (such as those contained in Documents 6 (a) and 6 (b)) which will necessitate consequential renumbering.

subsisting under the laws of the United Kingdom and any and all analogous rights subsisting under the laws of each and every jurisdiction throughout the world.

11. MISCELLANEOUS

11.1 Nothing contained in this Agreement shall constitute or shall be construed as constituting a partnership or contract of employment between the parties.

11.2 Neither party shall have any obligation to the other in the event of any act or omission on the part of such party where such act or omission results from the occurrence of any event which is outside the reasonable control of such party.

11.3 This Agreement contains the full and complete understanding between the parties and supersedes all prior arrangements and understandings whether written or oral appertaining to the subject matter of this Agreement and may not be varied except by an instrument in writing signed by all the parties to this Agreement. The Proprietor acknowledges that no representations or promises not expressly contained in this Agreement have been made to the Proprietor by the Publisher or any of its servants agents employees members or representatives.

11.4 This Agreement shall be governed and construed in accordance with the laws of England and Wales whose courts shall be courts of competent jurisdiction.

[Certificate of Value]

Clause 11.1 Under English law if two parties carry on business in common with a view to profit and share profit, the arrangement is capable of being considered a partnership. This provision ensures that no partnership is created inadvertently and also expressly excludes the possibility of an employment contract being created.

Clause 11.2 This is a short form of what is frequently referred to as a "force majeure" clause. It may not always be appropriate for this clause to be included, since it may permit a Proprietor to argue against a Publisher that the Proprietor is not liable in certain circumstances which are beyond the Proprietor's reasonable control.

Clause 11.3 There are occasions where oral agreements or other understandings may be created in relation to a Work which may contain either additional obligations or obligations which conflict with those set out in subsequent written agreement. This provision makes it clear that all previous arrangements and understandings are at an end and the contract is the only document relevant to the obligations and rights of the parties in relation to its subject matter. The final part of the clause expressly excludes the possibility of any liability of the Publisher for misrepresentation on the part of any of its servants, agents, employees or representatives (see paragraph 2.17).

Clause 11.4 Where a contract is made between two entitles in England and Wales, it will generally not be necessary to insert a provision of this nature, but where a contract is to be created with a foreign company (or a company situate in Scotland or Northern Ireland) this provision should always be included.

Certificate of Value Although it had been intended to abolish stamp duty on assignments of intellectual property at the same time as the introduction of paperless share transfer, the failure of the Stock Exchange system TAURUS has delayed the abolition of stamp duty which is still technically payable in relation to assignments of copyright. The publishing industry has, traditionally, never made provision for the payment of stamp duty in assignments of copyright and for this reason no provision is included in this document – although there are now many circumstances where it is advisable. A suitable form of wording may, however, be found in Document 6(d) and a summary of the current legislation relating to stamp duty may be found in paragraph 11.29.

Document 38 *Acquisition of translation rights*

AS WITNESS the hand of the duly authorised representative of the Publisher and the hand of the Proprietor the day month and year first above written

SIGNED by [*name of officer*]
for and on behalf of
[*name of Proprietor*] LIMITED

SIGNED by [*name of officer*]
for and on behalf of
[*name of Publisher*] LIMITED

DOCUMENT 39

Licence of translation rights

[IMPORTANT NOTE: Please read the section "About this book" on page v, before copying or using this Document]

Purpose of this Document

This is a form of agreement suitable for use by a publisher when licensing translation rights. The Document is drafted from the point of view of the publisher licensing rights and should be contrasted with the provisions of Document 38 which is drafted from the point of view of a publisher acquiring translation rights.

Relevant text

The text of this Work contains a number of topics which are relevant to documents of this nature including:

- buying and selling rights (paragraphs 11.2 to 11.9)
- remuneration provisions in rights agreements (paragraphs 11.22 to 11.26)
- taxation (paragraphs 11.27 to 11.29 and 12.22 to 12.30)
- commercial terms of offers (paragraphs 1.22 and 1.23)
- the law of contract and agency (paragraphs 2.1 to 2.30)
- creation, existence and transfer of copyrights (paragraphs 3.1 to 3.45)
- international copyright protection (paragraphs 4.1 to 4.17)
- moral rights (paragraphs 5.1 to 5.22)
- permissions, fair dealing and rights clearances (paragraphs 8.1 to 8.44)
- liability for content (paragraphs 9.1 to 9.49)
- buying and selling rights (paragraphs 11.1 to 11.29)
- infringement and enforcement (paragraphs 13.1 to 13.17)
- termination and recapture (paragraphs 14.1 to 14.10)
- competition law (paragraphs 16.1 to 16.28)
- multimedia (paragraphs 19.1 to 19.55)

THIS AGREEMENT is made the   day of
BETWEEN:

(1) [*Name*] LIMITED (registered number [*number*]) whose [registered office] [principal place of business] is at [*address*] ("Publisher") and

(2) [*Name*] LIMITED (registered number [*number*]) whose [registered office] [principal place of business] is at [*address*] ("Licensee" which expression shall include all Associates sub-licensees and assignees with the prior written consent of the Publisher deriving title through or from the Licensee)

IT IS AGREED as follows:

1. GRANT OF RIGHTS

1.1 In consideration of the obligations warranties and undertakings of the Licensee in this Agreement and subject to and conditional upon their full and timely performance and observance the Publisher grants to the Licensee the exclusive licence to exploit the Translation Rights in the Work entitled "[*title*]" ("Work") written by [*name of author*] ("Author") throughout the [*specify territory*] ("Territory") for the period of [*specify*] years from the date of this Agreement ("Licence Period"). The licence granted pursuant to this clause shall extend to any rights which the Publisher may acquire in the Translation.

1.2 The Licensee undertakes to engage a suitably qualified and competent person ("Translator") to prepare a translation of the Work ("Translation") and the Licensee undertakes to procure that the Translation shall be a faithful and accurate translation of the Work in good literary [*specify language*] in a style appropriate to the style of the Work in the original language with no alterations or abbreviations to the original text unless both the Author and the Publisher shall have approved such alterations or abbreviations in writing.

1.3 The Licensee shall procure that the Translator shall collaborate with the Author in order to clarify any questions of meaning a stylistic intention in relation to the Work and shall if the Publisher considers it appropriate prepare a suitable introduction and suitable textual notes for the Translation.

1.4 The Licensee shall deliver to the Publisher two copies of a clearly typed legible transcript of the Translation by no later than [*date*] and the Publisher

---

Clause 1.1 Relevant details need to be inserted. It will be noted that the grant of rights is conditional upon full and timely performance by the Licensee of its obligations under the Agreement.

Clause 1.2 This clause imposes on the Licensee an obligation to ensure that the translation is faithful and accurate and in a good literary style suitable to the style of the original text. The language into which the Work is to be translated needs to be specified.

Clause 1.3 Although in practice many original authors will collaborate with their translators it is useful to require any translator engaged by a foreign Publisher to collaborate unless the original author objects. Many authors will appreciate their Publishers inserting a separate provision in licences for the sale of translation rights.

shall submit one copy of the Translation to the Author for approval and shall notify the Licensee within [six] weeks from receipt of those amendments (if any) which are required to be made to the Translation by the Author and the Licensee undertakes to procure that the published text of the Translation shall fully comply with such amendments.

1.5   The Licensee undertakes to publish the Translation at the Licensee's sole cost and expense by no later than [*specify date*] and deliver to the Publisher not less than [*specify*] copies on publication. The Licensee warrants that all rights of copyright in the Translation shall be assigned to the Licensee by the Translator and the Licensee assigns to the Publisher the entire copyright whether vested contingent or future in the Translation and all rights of action and other rights of whatever nature in the Translation whether now known or in the future created to which the Translator or the Licensee are now or may at any time after the date of this Agreement be entitled by virtue of or pursuant to any of the laws in force in any part of the world TO HOLD the same to the Publisher its assignees and licensees absolutely for the whole period of such rights for the time being capable of being assigned together with any and all renewals reversions and extensions throughout the world subject only to the rights of the Licensee pursuant to the licence granted in Clause 1.1.

1.6   The Licensee undertakes that the Licensee's contract with the Translator shall contain such provisions as enable the Licensee to comply fully with its obligations under this Agreement.

2.   PUBLISHER'S WARRANTIES

The Publisher warrants agrees and undertakes with the Licensee that:

2.1   the Publisher is free to enter into this Agreement and grant the Licensee the rights granted in it and is not under any disability restriction or prohibition which might prevent the Publisher from performing or observing any of the Publisher's obligations under this Agreement;

2.2   the Publisher has not entered into and shall not enter into any arrangement which may conflict with this Agreement;

2.3   following the expiry of the Term by effluxion of time the Licensee

---

Clause 1.4   This provision permits both the Publisher and the Author to make known to the Licensee or the translator any objections they have to the translation. In view of the obligation imposed on the Licensee to ensure that the translation is faithful and accurate and in an appropriate literary style, there may be occasions when the Publisher and/or Author may wish to suggest changes which the Licensee will take into account.

Clause 1.5   This provision clarifies the fact that the costs of the translation are to be borne by the Licensee and not deducted from the royalty. The number of copies which a Publisher is to receive on publication should take into account the fact that a Publisher may wish to provide the Author with an additional number of free copies.

The clause also ensures that all rights of copyright in the new translation which are required by the Licensee are assigned to the Publisher subject to the right of the Licensee to use them for the licence period during the Licensee's territory. This permits the Publisher to license the translation in other countries where the language is spoken which are not included in the Licensee's territory.

Clause 1.6   This provision requires the Licensee to include in its contract with any translator, provisions which have the same effect as those provisions in clauses 1.2 to 1.5.

shall have the non-exclusive right subject to the terms and conditions of this Agreement for the further period of three calendar months to sell off copies of the Translation previously printed by the Licensee during the Licence Period;

2.4 to the best of the Publisher's knowledge the Translation is not obscene or defamatory and does not infringe any right of copyright.

3. REMUNERATION

3.1 The Licensee undertakes to pay to the Publisher:

(a) an advance ("Advance") of £[*amount*] on signature of this Agreement; and

(b) the following royalties ("Royalties") on each Accounting Date in accordance with the provisions of this Agreement:

[*specify*]

[*specify*]

[*specify*]

3.2 The Licensee shall not have the right to withhold any part of sums due to the Publisher as a reserve against returns and/or credits and in the event that the Licensee is required by law to make any withholding from sums to be remitted to the Publisher the Licensee shall prior to the making of any withholding of payment furnish the Publisher with evidence satisfactory to the Publisher in its entire discretion as to the Licensee's obligation to make such withholding of payment.

3.3 If exchange control or other restrictions prevent or threaten to prevent the remittance to the Publisher of any money payable under this Agreement the Licensee shall immediately advise the Publisher in writing and follow the Publisher's instructions in respect of the money to be remitted including if required depositing the same with any bank or other person designated by the Publisher at such location as may be designated by the Publisher.

Clause 2.3   The Licensee is entitled to a three-month non-exclusive sell-off period (see paragraphs 12.4 and 11.13).

Clause 2.4   The warranty is given to the best of the Publisher's belief. In other words it is not an absolute warranty that the Work is not obscene or defamatory etc.

Clause 3.1   The obligation to pay permission fees etc. is passed on to the Licensee. The dates for payments of the instalments of the advance are linked to signature of the Agreement and delivery of materials rather than publication of the Work. The advance is not expressed to be recoupable from the royalties. The Licensee is required to pay the costs of provision of delivery material and there is no provision permitting the Licensee to recover such costs from the royalty. If rights other than printed volume publication rights are to be granted to the Licensee provision will need to be made for payment based on the Licensee's receipts (or receivables – see paragraphs 11.24 and 1.15(b)) possibly along the lines provided in Document 4 clauses 9.1 and 9.2.

Clause 3.2   This provision prevents the Licensee from deducting parts of the royalty payments to hold as reserves against returned books. If the Licensee is required by law to deduct withholding taxes on royalty payments it is required to produce documentary evidence satisfactory to the Publisher of its liability.

Clause 3.3   This provision protects the Publisher if exchange control restrictions are imposed in any territory and permits the Publisher to receive income in that territory.

3.4 If any withholding or other taxes are required to be deducted from any money provided to be remitted to the Publisher pursuant to this Agreement it shall be the responsibility of the Licensee to ensure that no improper deductions are made and that the Publisher is provided with all necessary receipts certificates and other documents and all information required in order to avail the Publisher of any tax credit or other fiscal advantage and the Licensee undertakes to account to the Publisher in relation to any tax credit or saving received by the Licensee in relation to royalty payments to the Publisher.

4. LICENSEE'S UNDERTAKINGS

The Licensee warrants undertakes confirms and agrees with the Publisher:

4.1 all rights and title in and to the Work are expressly reserved to the Publisher subject to the licence in Clause 1;

4.2 The Licensee shall publish the Translation at the Licensee's sole cost and expense by no later than [*specify date*] and shall deliver to the Publisher not less than [*specify*] copies of each edition of the Translation published by the Licensee.

4.3 the Licensee shall not by any act or omission impair or prejudice the copyright in the Work or the Translation or violate any moral right and the Licensee shall ensure that all copies of the Work and all artwork published and distributed by the Licensee contain full and accurate copyright notices credit attributions and acknowledgments;

4.4 the Licensee shall not create any promotional material or artwork relating to the Work or the Translation without the prior written consent of the Publisher and in respect of any material commissioned or manufactured by the Licensee the copyright shall be secured in the name of the Publisher and title to all physical material shall belong to and be dealt with as if such physical material had been supplied by the Publisher and the Publisher shall at all times have unrestricted access to the same for the purposes of the Publisher;

Clause 3.4 This clause not only requires that the Licensee is to provide the Publisher with all necessary receipts and information but also provides that the Licensee is to bring into account any tax credits or savings achieved by the Licensee which are attributable to royalty payments under the Agreement.

Clause 4.1 This clause clarifies that the copyright remains vested in the Publisher subject only to the licence granted to the Licensee.

Clause 4.2 This clause obliges the Licensee to publish by a certain date, and clarifies the fact that all costs of publication are borne by the Licensee. It is also usual for a publisher to request copies of all editions published by the Licensee.

Clause 4.4 The Publisher will in many circumstances wish to control the nature and type of publicity and advertising material. There are occasions where material produced by the Publisher's licensee may be of value to the Publisher since it can be used by Licensees in other territories. This provision passes all rights of copyright and other rights in such material to the Publisher in order to permit the Publisher to provide the benefit of this material to its other Licensees.

4.5   the Licensee shall give full particulars to the Publisher as soon as the Licensee becomes aware of any actual or threatened claim by any third party in connection with the Work or the Translation;

4.6   the Licensee shall punctually pay to the Publisher all sums owing to the Publisher under this Agreement;

4.7   the Licensee shall not assign charge license sub-license or otherwise part with possession of the benefit or burden of this Agreement without the prior written consent of the Publisher;

4.8   the Licensee shall maintain the Translation in a prominent position in the Licensee's catalogue and shall ensure that the Translation does not go out of print at any time during the Licence Period;

4.9   the Licensee shall advertise the Translation throughout the Territory in the same manner as other books published by the Licensee in the Territory and the Licensee shall not alter or adapt the Work or the Translation in any way or omit or remove any authors' credits or acknowledgments from the Work or add any imprint or trade mark other than the Licensee's and such other imprint or trade mark as may be permitted by the Publisher;

4.10   the Licensee shall exploit the rights granted to the Licensee to the best of the Licensee's skill and ability with the utmost despatch and ensure the highest possible Royalties payable to the Publisher and ensure that the Translation is given fair and equitable treatment and not discriminated in favour of any other books which the Licensee may publish or distribute in the Territory;

4.11   the Licensee shall at the end of the three-month-sell-off period referred to in Clause 2.3 at the discretion of the Publisher to permit the Publisher to purchase from the Licensee all copies of the Translation in the possession of or under the control of the Licensee which are then unsold at a unit cost equal

Clause 4.5   If there is any claim in relation to copyright infringement or invasion of privacy or any other matter in relation to the Translation it is in the Publisher's interests to be apprised of such claim at the earliest possible moment.

Clause 4.6   In circumstances where the Agreement does not contain a provision making time of the essence (such as that contained in clause 8.6), this provision requires the Licensee to make payments in a punctual manner.

Clause 4.7   Generally licences are considered to be personal, but there are some circumstances in which a licence may be sub-licensed. This provision expressly precludes the Licensee from entering into sub-licences or assigning the benefit of the Agreement.

Clause 4.8   The Licensee is required to keep the Translation in print and in the Licensee's catalogue during the licence period.

Clause 4.9   This provision ensures that the Translation is given the same degree of prominence as that given by the Licensee to the Licensee's other works and prevents the addition of imprints or trade marks other than those of the Publisher and the Licensee. The clause also specifically prohibits the Licensee from making any alteration or adaptation to the Translation or omitting any of the author's credits or acknowledgments.

Clause 4.10   The Licensee is required to exploit the rights in a manner consistent with achieving the highest royalties and to ensure that the Translation is not discriminated against in favour of other publications in which the Licensee may have an interest.

to the actual cost of printing of the Licensee or if the Publisher shall direct the Licensee procure their destruction and provide certificates and affidavits of destruction in such form as may be satisfactory to the Publisher;

4.12 the Licensee shall indemnify and keep fully indemnified the Publisher from and against all actions proceedings claims demands costs (including without prejudice to the generality of this provision the legal costs of the Publisher on a solicitor and own client basis) awards and damages arising directly or indirectly as a result of any breach or non-performance by the Licensee of any of the Licensee's undertakings warranties or obligations under this Agreement.

5. ROYALTY ACCOUNTING

5.1 The Licensee shall on each Accounting Date render to the Publisher a full and complete statement showing all money owing to the Publisher in respect of the preceding Accounting Period.

5.2 The statement of account in Clause 5.1 shall be in such form as the Publisher shall require and shall contain full details of all copies of the Translation sold and each such statement shall be accompanied by payment of all amounts owing without reserve.

5.3 Pounds sterling shall be the currency of account and where any sums are received in a currency other than pounds sterling the same shall be converted at the [mid-market rate calculated using the "Financial Times" index on the date of receipt] [best obtainable rate of exchange on the date payment is due].

5.4 Value Added Tax shall be payable by the Licensee to the Publisher in respect of all payments made to or to the order of the Publisher pursuant to this Agreement.

5.5 The Licensee shall keep full and proper books of account relating to the exploitation of its rights under this Agreement and the Publisher or its representative at any time during the Licence Period and for six years afterwards shall have the right on giving reasonable prior notice to inspect and audit and take copies of such books of account during normal business hours. In the event that such audit or inspection reveals any deficiency in money paid to the Publisher then the Licensee shall pay the same to the

---

Clause 4.11 This provision permits the Publisher to eliminate or purchase the Licensee's unsold stock of books at the end of the licence period.

Clause 4.12 An explanation of the significance of warranties and indemnities may be found in paragraph 7.15.

Clause 5.1 The Accounting Dates and Accounting Periods are defined in clause 8.1 in accordance with standard industry practice. There may be occasions, however, where it is appropriate to vary these.

Clause 5.2 This provision gives the Publisher the opportunity of determining the particulars which are to be contained in the statement of account. Each statement must be accompanied by payment of sums shown to be owing without deduction of any reserves.

Clause 5.3 It may or may not be appropriate for pounds sterling to be the currency of account. If the Licensee is situate in a foreign territory, exchange conversion provisions may be required.

Clause 5.4 It will be necessary to adjust this provision in the light of prevailing law. A short explanation of current Value Added Tax legislation may be found in paragraph 11.28 and paragraphs 12.22 to 12.29.

Publisher together with interest from the date first due calculated with monthly rests at a rate of [*percentage*]% above prime or base rate charged by its bankers to the Publisher from time to time and shall pay all reasonable costs incurred by the Publisher directly as a result of such inspection.

5.6   The Licensee shall keep confidential and shall not disclose to any third parties (other than professional advisers where necessary) the results of any such inspection or audit or any of the terms of this Agreement or any matters incidental to it or relating to the business of the Publisher and shall indemnify the Publisher fully in respect of any breach of its obligations under this Clause 5.6.

6.   DETERMINATION

It shall constitute the repudiation by the Licensee of its obligations under this Agreement and at any time the Publisher may serve written notice on the Licensee accepting such repudiation and determining the Licence Period and the Licensee's rights under this Agreement if:

6.1   the Licensee fails to pay any amount due under this Agreement in full within three days of its due date and such failure is not remedied within seven days of receipt of written notice;

6.2   the Licensee is in breach of any other material term of this Agreement which is incapable of remedy or if capable of remedy is not remedied within fourteen days of the Licensee becoming aware of it;

6.3   any of the Licensee's representations shall prove to have been incorrect when made or become materially incorrect and the Publisher's rights and entitlements under this Agreement are materially and adversely affected;

6.4   the Licensee transfers disposes of or threatens to transfer or dispose of any part of its assets which is likely in the opinion of the Licensor to prevent or materially to inhibit the performance by the Licensee of its obligations under this Agreement;

6.5   any indebtedness guarantee or similar obligation of the Licensee or of

---

Clause 5.5   There may be occasions when a Publisher will wish to inspect and audit the books of account of the Licensee. Even if such audit rights are not exercised, an audit provision should always be included in licence agreements.

Clause 6   For an examination of the legal significance of the term "repudiation", reference should be made to paragraph 14.5 and to paragraphs 14.2 to 14.4.

Clause 6.1   This clause provides the Licensee with the opportunity of remedying a breach. The time period allowed to remedy pecuniary breaches is normally less than that allowed to remedy non-pecuniary breaches.

Clause 6.2   This clause permits the Licensee to remedy a non-pecuniary material breach. The time period allowed is longer than that for a pecuniary breach.

Clause 6.3   There may be circumstances where the Publisher has entered into the Agreement on the basis of representations made by the Licensee. This clause permits the Publisher to terminate the Agreement if the representations prove to have been incorrect or subsequently become incorrect.

Clause 6.4   There are occasions where a Licensee becomes less financially secure and disposes of its assets. Where a Publisher has entered into an Agreement in reliance on the Licensee being an entity of substance, such occasions may cause concern to the Publisher and this provision permits the Publisher to terminate the Agreement in such instances.

any guarantor of the Licensee becomes due or capable of being declared due before its stated maturity or is not discharged at maturity or the Licensee or any guarantor of the Licensee defaults under or commits a breach of the provisions of any guarantee or other obligation (whether actual or contingent) of any agreement pursuant to which any such indebtedness guarantee or other obligation was incurred all or any of which shall in the reasonable opinion of the Publisher materially affect its rights and entitlements under this Agreement;

6.6   the Licensee is declared or becomes insolvent;

6.7   the Licensee convenes a meeting of its creditors or proposes or makes any arrangement or composition with or any assignment for the benefit of its creditors or a petition is presented or a meeting is convened for the purpose of considering a resolution or other steps are taken for the winding up of the Licensee (save for the purpose of and followed by a voluntary reconstruction or amalgamation previously approved in writing by the Publisher) or if an incumbrancer takes possession of or a trustee administrator administrative receiver liquidator or similar officer is appointed in respect of all or any part of its business or assets or any distress execution or other legal process is levied threatened enforced upon or sued out against any of such assets;

6.8   the Licensee shall cease or abandon or announce that it intends to cease or abandon the business of publishing books;

6.9   the Translation goes out of print or is deleted from the Licensee's catalogue.

7.   NOTICE

7.1   Any notice or other document required to be given under this Agreement or any communication between the parties with respect to any of the provisions of this Agreement shall be in writing in English and be deemed duly given if signed by or on behalf of a duly authorised officer of the party giving the notice and if left at or sent by pre-paid registered or recorded delivery post or by telex telegram cable facsimile transmission or other means of telecommunication in permanent written form to the address of the party receiving such notice as set out at the head of the Agreement or as notified between the parties for the purpose of this Clause.

Clause 6.5   Financial default of the Licensee in relation to any guarantee or obligation is a further event normally permitting termination.

Clause 6.6   For the consequences of insolvency, reference should be made to paragraphs 15.2 to 15.4.

Clause 6.7   There may be occasions when a Licensee does not actually become insolvent, but a creditor enforces security over the Licensee's business. This could have serious consequences for a Publisher and this clause protects the Publisher's interests by providing that such circumstances will entitle the Publisher to terminate the Agreement.

Clause 6.8   Where a Licensee ceases to carry on business or announces that it intends to cease its business, a Publisher will wish to recover its rights as soon as possible.

Clause 6.9   Although clause 4.11 imposes a specific obligation on the Licensee to keep the Work in print, this clause permits the Publisher to terminate if it does not do so.

Clause 7   A number of clauses in the Document provide for a means of exercising rights, and a notice provision is therefore necessary.

7.2   Any such notice or other communication shall be deemed to be given to and received by the addressee:

(a)   at the time the same is left at the address of or handed to a representative of the party to be served;

(b)   by post on the day not being a Sunday or Public Holiday two days following the date of posting;

(c)   in the case of a telex telegram cable facsimile transmission or other means of telecommunication on the next following day.

7.3   In proving the giving of a notice it should be sufficient to prove that the notice was left or that the envelope containing the notice was properly addressed and posted or that the applicable means of telecommunication was addressed and despatched and despatch of the transmission was confirmed and/or acknowledged as the case may be.

7.4   Communications addressed to the Publisher shall be marked for the attention of [*name*] with a copy to [*name*] of [*address*].

8.   DEFINITIONS AND INTERPRETATION

8.1   The following definitions apply in this Agreement:

"Accounting Date":
90 days from the end of each Accounting Period.

"Accounting Period":
successive periods ending on 30 June and 31 December in each year.

"Associate"
in relation to the Licensee any associate or associated company within the meaning of Section 416 or 417 of the Income and Corporation Taxes Act 1988

"Translation Rights"
the exclusive right to commission print and publish a(n) [*specify*] language translation of the Work in volume form only [paperback or] hardback format.

8.2   The following terms are defined in this Agreement in the place indicated:

"Advance":   Clause 4
"Author":   Clause 1.1

Clause 8.1 The definitions contained in clause 8.1 will need review in order to fit the appropriate circumstances. Depending on the royalty provisions which are inserted in clause 3.1 (b), it may be necessary to insert definitions for terms such as "Published Price" or "Licensee's Receipts". Document 4 clause 8.1 contains definitions which may be appropriate. The definition of Translation Rights may also need adjustment.

"Licence Period":	Clause 1.1
"Royalties":	Clause 3
"Territory":	Clause 1.1
"Translation":	Clause 1.1
"Translator":	Clause 1.1
"Work":	Clause 1.1

8.3 Any reference in this Agreement to any statute or statutory provision shall be construed as including a reference to that statute or statutory provision as from time to time amended modified extended or re-enacted whether before or after the date of this Agreement and to all statutory instruments orders and regulations for the time being made pursuant to it or deriving validity from it.

8.4 Unless the context otherwise requires words denoting the singular shall include the plural and vice versa and words denoting any one gender shall include all genders and words denoting persons shall include bodies corporate unincorporated associations and partnerships.

8.5 The word "copyright" means the entire copyright and design right subsisting under the laws of the United Kingdom and any and all analogous rights subsisting under the laws of each and every jurisdiction throughout the world.

8.6 Unless otherwise stated time shall be of the essence for the purpose of the performance of the Licensee's obligations under this Agreement.

8.7 Unless otherwise stated references to clauses sub-clauses sub-paragraphs schedules annexures and exhibits relate to this Agreement.

9. MISCELLANEOUS

9.1 Nothing contained in this Agreement shall constitute or shall be construed as constituting a partnership or contract of employment between the parties.

9.2 The Publisher shall not be liable to the Licensee for failing to supply or procure the supply of the Delivery Materials and any other material to be supplied under this Agreement due to circumstances beyond its control and it shall not be liable for any expenses or consequential losses whatever suffered by the Licensee.

Clause 8.2 The references in this clause need to be adjusted to fit the appropriate circumstances. In particular, it may be appropriate to insert additional clauses (such as those contained in Documents 6 (a) and 6 (b)) which will necessitate consequential renumbering.

Clause 8.6 For the significance of time being of the essence reference should be made to paragraph 2.10.

Clause 9.1 Under English law if two parties carry on business in common with a view to profit and share profits, the arrangement is capable of being considered a partnership. This provision ensures that no partnership is created inadvertently, and also expressly excludes the possibility of an employment contract being created.

Clause 9.2 This provision protects the Publisher from any claim by the Licensee in relation to failure to supply Delivery Materials, although there are likely to be circumstances in which the Publisher will incur some liability.

9.3 The Licensee warrants that it is not the nominee or agent of any undisclosed principal and warrants that it shall assume sole and complete responsibility for the performance of the obligations in this Agreement expressed to be performed by the Licensee.

9.4 This Agreement contains the full and complete understanding between the parties and supersedes all prior arrangements and understandings whether written or oral appertaining to the subject matter of this Agreement and may not be varied except by an instrument in writing signed by all the parties to this Agreement. The Licensee acknowledges that no representations or promises not expressly contained in this Agreement have been made to the Licensee by the Publisher or any of its servants agents employees members or representatives.

9.5 This Agreement shall be governed and construed in accordance with the laws of England and Wales whose courts shall be courts of competent jurisdiction.

[Certificate of Value]

AS WITNESS the hands of the duly authorised representatives of the parties the day month and year first above written

SIGNED by [   ]

for and on behalf of
[*The Publisher*]

SIGNED by [   ]
for and on behalf of
[*The Licensee*]

Clause 9.3 This provision protects the Publisher from the consequences of it contracting with a Licensee which has acted as the agent of an undisclosed company whom the Publisher may not consider to be a suitable person to be the Publisher's Licensee.

Clause 9.4 There are occasions where oral agreements or other understandings may be created in relation to a Work which may contain either additional obligations or obligations which conflict with those set out in subsequent written agreement. This provision makes it clear that all previous arrangements and understandings are at an end and the contract is the only document relevant to the obligations and rights of the parties in relation to its subject matter. The final part of the clause expressly excludes the possibility of any liability of the Publisher for misrepresentation on the part of any of its servants, agents, employees or representatives (see paragraph 2.17).

Clause 9.5 Where a contract is made between two entities in England and Wales, it will generally not be necessary to insert a provision of this nature, but where a contract is to be created with a foreign company (or a company situate in Scotland or Northern Ireland) this provision should always be included.

Certificate of Value Although it had been intended to abolish stamp duty on assignments of intellectual property at the same time as the introduction of paperless share transfer, the failure of the Stock Exchange system TAURUS has delayed the abolition of stamp duty which is still technically payable in relation to assignments of copyright. The publishing industry has, traditionally, never made provision for the payment of stamp duty in assignments of copyright and for this reason no provision is included in this document – although there are now many circumstances where it is advisable. A suitable form of wording may, however, be found in Document 6 (d) and a summary of the current legislation relating to stamp duty may be found in paragraph 11.29.

E. Commercial and non-commercial licences

DOCUMENT 40

Excerpt/serial rights licence

[IMPORTANT NOTE: Please read the section "About this book" on page v, before copying or using this Document]

Purpose of this Document

This is a form of agreement which may be suitable for use by a publisher when licensing the publication of excerpts or serial rights from a work.

Relevant text

The text of this Work covers a number of topics which are relevant to documents of this nature including:

- buying and selling rights (paragraphs 7.2 to 11.9)
- remuneration provisions in rights agreements (paragraphs 11.22 to 11.26)
- taxation (paragraphs 11.27 to 11.29 and 12.22 to 12.30)
- the law of agency (paragraphs 2.26 to 2.30)
- the law of contract (paragraphs 2.1 to 2.23)
- moral rights (paragraphs 5.1 to 5.22)
- rights clearances (paragraph 8.44)

Document 40 *Excerpt/serial rights licence*

From	:	[*Name*]
		("Publisher")

To	:	[*Name*]
		("Licensee")

Date	:	[*date*]

Dear [*insert name*]

"[*Name of Work*]" ("Work") by [*name of author*] ("Author")

1. Licence

(a) In consideration of the payment by the Licensee to the Publisher of the fee referred to in Paragraph 2 and subject to and conditional on performance by the Licensee of its obligations under this Agreement the Publisher grants to the Licensee the exclusive right to print and publish in the English language in [*name of newspaper or magazine*] [2] instalments of the Work selected in accordance with the provisions of paragraph 3 ("Excerpts") each of up to [*number*] words provided that the total number of words does not exceed [*number*] in the aggregate. The Licensee's rights shall be exercisable solely between the dates specified in paragraph 1 (c) and shall expire on the sooner of publication of the last Excerpt or the occurrence of the last date specified in paragraph 1 (c).

(b) The Publisher undertakes not to license or authorise the publication of the Work in newspapers or magazines in [*specify country*] before [*specify date*].

(c) The Licensee undertakes to publish the Excerpts in [*name of newspaper or magazine*] between [*date*] and [*date*] time being of the essence.

2. Fee

The Licensee undertakes to pay to the Publisher the sum of £[*amount*] which shall be payable:

as to £[*amount*] on [*date*]

Clause 1 (a) It will be noted that the licence granted by this clause is conditional on payment being made. In other words if no payment is made the Licensee will not have been granted a valid licence and will be infringing copyright.

The rights granted to the Licensee are exercisable solely between the dates specified in paragraph 1(c).

Rights of the type being licensed are normally considered to be subsidiary rights (see paragraph 1.16). If the Publisher obtains a licence in relation to the subsidiary rights it will be appropriate for the Publisher to enter into this Agreement. If, however, the Publisher was appointed as the agent for the purpose of granting licences of subsidiary rights, then the Publisher should enter into the Agreement as the agent of and on behalf of the Author and the appropriate amendment should be made to the Document.

Clause 1 (b) This provision protects the Licensee from prior publication of the Excerpts.

Clause 1 (c) If the Excerpts are published on the stated date the Publisher and the Author may be able to benefit from the publicity by way of increased sales.

as to £[*amount*] on [*date*]

as to £[*amount*] on [*date*]

3. Publisher's Warranties

The Publisher warrants to the Licensee that to the best of the Publisher's knowledge nothing contained in the Work is obscene or defamatory or infringes any right of copyright or any third party.

4. Licensee's Obligations

The Licensee undertakes and agrees with the Publisher:

(a) the Excerpts shall be selected by the Licensee in consultation with the Publisher and the Author from those selected passages of the Work listed in the Schedule;

(b) the Publisher and the Author shall have the right to approve the beginning and end point of each Excerpt such approval not to be unreasonably withheld or delayed;

(c) the Licensee shall not amend alter abridge delete or in any other way change the text of the Work or the Excerpts without the consent of the Publisher;

(d) all illustrations and photographs accompanying the Excerpts shall be supplied by or approved by the Publisher;

(e) the Licensee undertakes to print at the end of each Excerpt the following copyright notice:

"[*specify copyright notice details*]"

(f) each Excerpt shall be accompanied by details of the Work including title author publisher publication date and price which shall be printed in a prominent position.

5. Law

This Agreement shall be governed and construed in accordance with the laws of England and Wales whose courts shall be courts of competent jurisdiction.

Clause 4 These provisions should be amended to fit the appropriate circumstances. Particularly important, however, are clause 4 (f) which obliges the newspaper or periodical to print publication rights in relation to the Work in a prominent position, and clause 4 (e) which obliges the newspaper or periodical to print a correct copyright notice in relation to the work.

THE SCHEDULE

[insert details of selected passages]

Yours faithfully

Signed by [   ]   }
for and on behalf of   }
the Publisher   }

We confirm and agree the above and agree to be bound by it.

Signed by [   ]   }
for and on behalf of   }
the Licensee   }

DOCUMENT 41

Talking book/braille licence

[IMPORTANT NOTE: Please read the section "About this book" on page v, before copying or using this Document]

Purpose of this Document

This is a form of agreement which may be suitable for use by a publisher which intends to grant talking book or braille rights to a third party. The licence is a non-commercial licence and should be contrasted with the fuller provisions normally contained in rights licences, such as those contained in Document 32.

Document 41 *Talking book/braille licence*

From   :   [*Name*]
                 ("Publisher")

To   :   [*Name*]
                 ("Licensee")

Date   :   [*date*]

Dear [*insert name*]

This letter confirms the Agreement between us in relation to the literary work or works published by the Publisher details of which are set out in Exhibit 1 ("Work").

1.   Licence

The Publisher grants the Licensee the following exclusive licence to reproduce the Work [in braille] [in talking book form in the English language] in the territory of [*specify*] during the period of [*specify*].

2.   Remuneration

In consideration of the grant of rights in paragraph 1 the Licensee undertakes to pay to the Publisher [*specify royalty and/or advance*].

3.   Publisher's Warranty

The Publisher warrants to the Licensee that to the best of the Publisher's knowledge nothing contained in the Work is obscene or defamatory or infringes any right of copyright or any third party.

4.   Licensee's Undertakings

The Licensee warrants undertakes and agrees with the Publisher that:

(a)   the Licensee shall produce the [braille] [talking book] version of the Work to the highest possible standard and undertakes not to amend alter abridge delete or otherwise in any way change the text of the Work without the consent of the Publisher;

(b)   all copies of the Work produced by the Licensee shall bear a copyright notice in the following form:

   "[*specify details of copyright notice*]"

(c)   at the end of the period referred to in paragraph 1 the Licensee shall have a further three months to sell off any [braille] [talking book] copies of the Work in the possession of the Licensee and following the expiry of such three-month period the Licensee shall at the election of the Publisher either deliver up to the Publisher the remaining stock of

650

[braille] [talking book] copies of the Work or destroy them and provide evidence to the Publisher of such destruction.

5.   Law

This Agreement shall be governed and construed in accordance with the laws of England and Wales whose courts shall be courts of competent jurisdiction.

Signed by [*name*]
for and on behalf of
[*Publisher*]

We confirm and agree the above and agree to be bound by it.

Signed by [*name*]
for and on behalf of
[*Licensee*]

EXHIBIT 1

The Work

[*insert details*]

DOCUMENT 42

Licence for the visually handicapped

[IMPORTANT NOTE: Please read the section "About this book" on page v, before copying or using this Document]

Purpose of this Document

This is a form of commercial licence suitable for use by a publisher wishing to consent to visually handicapped persons using the publisher's works for private and commercial purposes.

The Document contains the basic elements of a licence. It would be appropriate, however, for any publisher wishing to use the Document to recast it in a more gracious format in the publisher's house style.

From : [*Name*]
("Publisher")

To : [*Name*]
("Individual")

Date : [*date*]

Dear [*name*]

This letter sets out the terms of the licence which we are prepared to grant to you in respect of the works set out in the Schedule ("Works").

The licence is personal and non-transferrable and is granted to you on the basis that you have represented to us that you are a registered blind or partially sighted person. The licence shall continue unless and until revoked by us.

Pursuant to this licence you shall have the right to store and reproduce the Works electronically and to use them in any computer or wordprocessing system to enable you to carry on your business or profession.

The licence does not permit you to make copies of the Works available to others or permit others to copy the Works directly or indirectly.

This licence may be revoked or cancelled by us:

(a) at any time if the representations relating to your personal status prove to be incorrect or if you are in breach of the provisions of this licence; or

(b) by our giving you [*specify*] weeks' notice of termination.

Upon termination of this licence all copies of the Works made by you or in your possession or derived from any such copies shall be deemed to be infringing copies for the purpose of United Kingdom copyright legislation and shall immediately be erased or destroyed.

The Schedule

The Works

[specify]

Signed by *[name]*
for and on behalf of
[the Publisher]

I agree and confirm the above and agree to be bound by it.

Signed by *[individual]*

F. Multimedia

DOCUMENT 43

Multimedia development agreement

[IMPORTANT NOTE: Please read the section "About this book" on page v, before copying or using this Document]

Purpose of this Document

This is a form of agreement which may be suitable for use when a company is commissioning a producer to develop a multimedia work suitable for exploitation by the company. The document may be used in relation to the production of a computer game, a CD-ROM, a CD-I or other multimedia product, in which case references to 'CD-I' will need to be changed accordingly. The document is drafted from the point of view of the company commissioning the development work.

Relevant text

The text of this Work contains a number of topics which are relevant to documents of this nature:

- development and production of multimedia works (paragraphs 19.31 to 19.41)
- what is multimedia? (paragraphs 19.2 and 19.3)
- consents and permissions required for multimedia works (paragraphs 19.4 to 19.13)
- music in multimedia (paragraphs 19.14 to 19.20)
- collective licensing schemes (paragraphs 19.21 to 19.24)
- licensing distribution and joint ventures (paragraphs 19.42 to 19.44)
- databases and computers (paragraphs 19.45 to 19.52)
- software publishing and video publishing (paragraphs 19.53 to 19.55)
- buying and selling rights (paragraphs 11.2 to 11.9)
- remuneration provisions in rights agreements (paragraphs 11.22 to 11.26)
- taxation (paragraphs 11.27 to 11.29 and 12.22 to 12.30)
- commercial terms of offers (paragraphs 1.22 and 1.23)
- the law of contract and agency (paragraphs 2.1 to 2.30)
- creation, existence and transfer of copyrights (paragraphs 3.1 to 3.45)
- international copyright protection (paragraphs 4.1 to 4.17)
- moral rights (paragraphs 5.1 to 5.22)
- permissions, fair dealing and rights clearances (paragraphs 8.1 to 8.44)
- liability for content (paragraphs 9.1 to 9.49)
- buying and selling rights (paragraphs 11.1 to 11.29)
- infringement and enforcement (paragraphs 13.1 to 13.17)
- termination and recapture (paragraphs 14.1 to 14.10)
- competition law (paragraphs 16.1 to 16.28)

Document 43   *Multimedia development agreement*

From   :   [*name*]
                      of [*address*]
                      ("Company")

To   :   [*name*]
                      of [*address*]
                      ("Producer")

Dated   :   [*date*]

Dear Sirs

"[*name of project*]"

This Commissioning Letter sets out the terms and conditions of the agreement which we have reached in connection with the production of certain development material in connection with an interactive compact disc based upon the Outline attached as Exhibit 1 with the above tentative title ("CD-I") which the Company intends but does not undertake to produce.

1.   The Company engages the Producer upon the Company's Standard Development Terms and Conditions ("Standard Conditions") contained in the attached Schedule to produce and deliver to the Company by the relevant dates listed in Exhibit 2 ("Delivery Dates") the development material ("Development Material") listed in Exhibit 2.

2.   On delivery to the Company of the Development Material by the relevant Delivery Dates the Company undertakes to pay to the Producer a development fee of £[*amount*] plus VAT ("Development Fee") in the following instalments [*specify payments and dates*].

3.   The Producer undertakes with the Company to produce and deliver to the Company the Development Material by the Delivery Dates and warrants undertakes and agrees with the Company in the terms set out in the Standard Conditions. The Producer confirms that the Producer has read and understood the Standard Conditions which shall be deemed to be included in this Commissioning Letter as if they were set out in full.

Letter: Initial Paragraph   The Agreement is structured in the form of a short covering letter to which will be attached relevant exhibits and a schedule of standard terms and conditions. The preliminary paragraph should be amended to accord with the particular facts of the situation. It is envisaged that the multimedia work will be based on an agreed outline which is annexed. The outline may take the form of a proposal from the Producer which may be summarised in a few paragraphs or even lines. Alternatively, it may be a far more detailed analysis of the multimedia product.

Letter: Paragraph 1   In this paragraph the Company engages the Producer to produce certain development material defined in Exhibit 2 and deliver it to the Company by specified delivery dates in accordance with the standard terms and conditions of the Company.

Letter: Paragraph 2   This paragraph contains the remuneration provisions. In practice there may be a number of separate payment stages.

Letter: Paragraph 3   In this paragraph the Producer undertakes and agrees with the Company to produce and deliver the Development Material by the Delivery Dates and warrants and undertakes in the terms contained in the Standard Conditions.

656

4.   The Producer assigns to the Company the entire copyright and all other rights in and to the Development Material for the full period of copyright including all renewals reversions and extensions existing under the laws in force in any part of the world TO HOLD the same to the Company its successors assignees and licensees absolutely for the full period that such rights are capable of subsisting throughout the world.

5.   The Producer shall obtain releases permissions or licences in a form satisfactory to the Company signed by all relevant persons in relation to all quotations text illustrations pictures sound recordings films performances and other material in which rights are controlled by third parties if such material forms part of the Development Material or may be incorporated or copied directly or indirectly in the CD-I. The Producer undertakes to deliver original or certified copies of all relevant documentation to the Company by no later than the latest date specified in Exhibit 2. The Producer irrevocably confirms that the benefit of all assignments licences consents releases and permissions obtained by the Producer in relation to such material shall extend to the Company throughout the world for the full period of such rights.

Yours faithfully

SIGNED by
[*name*]
for and on behalf of
[*name of the Company*]

We confirm and agree to the above and agree to be bound by it.

SIGNED by
[*name*]
for and on behalf of
[*name of the Producer*]

Letter: Paragraph 4   This provision assigns to the Company the entire copyright and all other rights in the Development Material.

Letter: Paragraph 5   It is of vital importance that all necessary releases and permissions are obtained and that the appropriate clearance procedures are followed (see paragraph 8.44 and Document 30). There are circumstances when permissions and releases may not be required (see paragraphs 8.2 to 8.39). Where permissions and consents are obtained in the name of the Producer, this provision automatically extends such permission (subject to any terms to the contrary contained in them) to the Company.

EXHIBIT 1

Outline

EXHIBIT 2

Development Material and Delivery Dates

1. An assignment of copyright in the Outline in such form as the Company shall approve and executed agreements in such form as the Company shall approve with [*name*] ("Writer") and [*name*];

2. A budget and cashflow schedule for the CD-I in such form as may be approved by the Company by [*date*];

3. A production schedule for the production and delivery of the CD-I in such form as may be approved by the Company by [*date*];

4. [*specify other materials and dates*].

Exhibit 1   The Outline is referred to in the initial paragraph of the Commissioning Letter. Appropriate details should be inserted in relation to any work on which the Development Material is to be based, together with a short description of the project.

Exhibit 2   The precise details of the Development Material will vary according to the project. It would be normal to expect assignments of copyright, waivers of moral rights and written performers' consents in relation to all contributors of material. Additionally, the Producer will normally be required to produce a budget and cash-flow schedule production schedule relating to the production and delivery of the multimedia work, together with test material such as animatics or computer programs based on the outline, proving the concept and conveying the idea of what a fully developed multimedia production based on the project might look like.

Development standard conditions

1. PRODUCER'S OBLIGATIONS

1.1 The obligations of the Company under this Agreement are subject to and conditional on the Producer having shown to the satisfaction of the Company that the Producer has made reasonable progress with the commissioning of the Development Material and is further conditional on the full and timely performance and observance of the Producer's other obligations and warranties under the Agreement.

1.2 The Producer shall expend the Development Fee in the most cost-effective manner possible solely in connection with the production of the Development Material.

1.3 The Producer shall prepare and keep full and proper books and accounts in respect of all expenditure incurred on the Development Material and the Company shall be entitled to examine such books and accounts at any time and the Producer shall ensure that its personnel are available during business hours to discuss any queries raised by the Company with regard to such books and accounts.

1.4 The Producer shall be solely responsible for all costs incurred in connection with the Development Material including without limitation all fees payable to writers and any third parties engaged in connection with the Development Material which shall be met exclusively out of the Development Fee. The Company shall have no liability or obligation to pay the Producer any sums additional to or in excess of the Development Fee regardless of the nature of any expenditure or liability incurred by the Producer.

1.5 The Producer shall use all reasonable endeavours to keep all costs incurred in connection with the Development Material to a minimum without compromising the standard of the Development Material.

1.6 The Producer undertakes to follow all rights clearance procedures from time to time required by the Company and to obtain irrevocable

---

Clause 1.1 The principal obligation of the Company is to make payment to the Producer of the Development Fee. This clause makes it clear that such obligation is conditional on the Producer having made reasonable progress and fully complying with its obligations under the Agreement.

Clause 1.2 The Producer is obliged to spend money advanced by the Company solely in relation to the development of the project.

Clause 1.3 The Company will wish to inspect books of account in order not only to determine that the Producer has complied with its obligations under clause 1.2, but to judge the efficiency and effectiveness of the Producer and its personnel in controlling costs and to obtain a more precise idea of what the final cost of the fully developed product might be.

Clause 1.4 This clause clarifies the fact that the Development Fee is the sum total of the Company's liability to the Producer. Any additional costs or expenses incurred by the Producer are the sole responsibility of the Producer.

Clause 1.5 The obligation of the Producer to minimise costs must be balanced with the need to preserve quality and maintain standards.

unconditional waivers of moral rights from all relevant persons and to make full and fair disclosure to the Company of all information correspondence and documentation relating to all rights of copyright and other rights in the Development Material and/or relating to any prior dealings with third parties in respect of any part of the Development Material.

2. DEVELOPMENT OF THE CD-I

2.1 The Producer shall consult with the Company at all times during the development of the CD-I and the Producer shall follow the reasonable directions of the Company and implement the creative and artistic requirements of the Company in respect of the characters featured in the CD-I and the overall tone and direction of the CD-I.

2.2 The Producer undertakes that the CD-I shall be faithful to the basic conceptualisation of the underlying works and shall reflect the same high standards of quality and integrity and adhere to the same portrayal of the characters as in the underlying works.

2.3 The Company shall have the right to approve the basic qualities characterisation (including context of living habitat and type and format of dialogue) powers accessories and costumes of the characters featured in the CD-I. Such approval shall be a condition precedent to the exercise of the Producer's rights and shall not be unreasonably withheld or delayed if such matters are substantially consistent with their portrayal in the CD-I.

2.4 The Producer shall comply with all requirements of the Company relating to the use or appearance in the CD-I of any character and in particular their powers basic qualities characterisation accessories and costumes.

2.5 All approvals required pursuant to this Agreement shall be in writing and signed by a duly authorised representative of the Company.

Clause 1.6 Not only should the Producer be required to follow rights clearance procedures specified by the Company, but also the Producer should be required to make full and fair disclosure of any relevant information. Prior dealings with third parties in relation to the project or the material should always be disclosed in order to eliminate any potential problems.

Clause 2.1 Although the document refers to a CD-I, the terms and conditions are, of course, suitable for the development of any multimedia product and terminology should be changed where appropriate. The Producer is required to consult with the Company in relation to the development of the project and to follow all reasonable directions of the Company. This clause gives the Company control over the overall terms and direction of the multimedia product.

Clause 2.2 Where a Company is the owner of rights in an underlying work which it wishes to use for a multimedia project, it is most important that the execution of the multimedia work should be in a style and tone which is consistent with the underlying work.

Clause 2.3 Multimedia applications frequently offer the possibility of "opening-out" underlying works, by including music, graphics, background, voices, additional characters and a wide range of other possibilities. These are all matters over which approvals may be required.

Clause 2.4 Powers basic qualities, characterisation, accessories, apparel and costumes of characters may assume great importance in multimedia applications.

Clause 2.5 There will be occasions where it is prudent to require all or approvals to be obtained or confirmed in writing. This avoids unnecessary disputes.

3. PAYMENT

3.1 The Company undertakes to pay to the Producer the Development Fee in accordance with the schedule of payments specified in Exhibit [2] to the Commissioning Letter. Each payment shall be subject to and conditional on the Producer having shown to the satisfaction of the Company that it has made reasonable progress with the performance of its obligations under this Agreement and subject to and conditional upon the Producer submitting to the Company a formal invoice (or Value Added Tax invoice if Value Added Tax is claimed) together with all vouchers invoices and receipts which may be required by the Company to evidence relevant expenditure.

3.2 All costs associated with the performance of the Producer's obligations under this Agreement shall be the sole responsibility of the Producer and shall be met exclusively out of the Development Fee. The Company shall have no liability or obligation to pay the Producer any sums additional to or in excess of the Development Fee regardless of the nature of any expenditure or liability incurred by the Producer.

4. PRODUCER'S WARRANTIES

The Producer warrants undertakes and agrees with the Company that:

4.1 the Producer is free to enter into and perform the Agreement and has full right and power and authority to assign the rights assigned to the Company under this Agreement free from all incumbrances and/or restrictions of whatever nature;

4.2 the Producer is and shall be the sole absolute unincumbered legal and beneficial owner of all rights of copyright and all other rights in the Development Material and all rights assigned to the Company under the Agreement and the Producer has not entered into and shall not enter into any other arrangements which might inhibit or restrict the exercise by the Company of the rights assigned pursuant to the Agreement;

4.3 the Development Material and each part of it shall be original (except

---

Clause 3.1 This clause offers the possibility of paying the Development Fee in agreed instalments with reference to specified dates or the attainment of designated objectives. The submission of a Value Added Tax invoice is a prerequisite to obtaining payment, as is compliance with obligations under the Agreement.

Clause 3.2 The Company has no obligation to pay the Producer any sums in excess of the Development Fee. If the Producer incurs any liability above this amount, the Producer will need to discharge such liability from the Producer's own resources.

Clause 4.1 This provision is intended to prevent any possibility of a claim arising from a third party that such third party had an option to acquire the rights which the Producer has assigned to the Company. Other incumbrances or restrictions might include a mortgage or charge over intellectual property rights, and if a Producer is a limited liability company the Company commissioning the Producer may wish to investigate the register of charges on file against the Producer at Companies House.

Clause 4.2 It is necessary to confirm that the Producer is the sole absolute unincumbered legal and beneficial owner of the rights which are assigned to the Company, and that no other person owns or has any claim in relation to such rights.

661

to the extent based on existing materials approved by the Company or in the public domain) and shall not be published and do not and shall not infringe any copyright moral right right of privacy right of publicity or personality or any other right whatever of any person and shall not be defamatory of any person libellous obscene blasphemous or offensive to any religion;

4.4   the Producer shall not pledge the credit of the Company or hold the Producer out as the Company's agent in any of the Producer's dealings in connection with the Development Material or the CD-I;

4.5   the Producer shall retain in a safe and secure place the Development Material until it is delivered to the Company and shall ensure that all elements of the Development Material shall contain a copyright notice in accordance with the Universal Copyright Convention in such form as shall be acceptable to the Company;

4.6   the Company shall have the right to add to delete from take from use and/or alter in any way and/or cut transpose adapt and/or translate into all languages and/or change the Development Material or any part of it including the titles characters plots themes dialogues sequences and situations to any extent and in any manner as the Company may desire [provided however that the Company shall consult with the Producer and give good faith consideration to any recommendations made by the Producer];

4.7   the Producer shall comply with all applicable laws statutes rules regulations and requirements of all governmental agencies and regulatory bodies and all relevant unions in connection with the Development Material or otherwise in connection with rendering services or performing its obligations pursuant to this Agreement;

4.8   the Producer shall use its best endeavours to procure that the production of the Development Material is effected in a first-class manner consistent with the standards expected of a first-class CD-I production company;

4.9   the Producer shall advise the Company in writing of the names of all

---

Clause 4.3 Infringement of copyright, moral rights, rights of privacy, rights of publicity or personality could lead to legal liability on the part of the Company which this provision seeks to exclude.

Clause 4.4 The relationship of agent and principal (see paragraphs 2.24 to 2.30) could result in certain liabilities being imposed on the Company by the Producer.

Clause 4.5 The Company will not wish the Development Material to fall outside the possession of the Producer or be seen by third parties. There are certain advantages in relation to the inclusion of copyright notices (see paragraphs 4.9 and 4.10).

Clause 4.6 It is likely that the Development Material may include audio and audio-visual recordings which may be protected as films and sound recordings pursuant to United Kingdom copyright law (paragraphs 3.7 and 3.30). Moral rights exist in relation to a number of categories of copyright works (see paragraphs 5.1 to 5.22). The Producer is required to follow the Company's clearance procedures which will normally require obtaining waivers of moral rights. There may be circumstances where, however, it is appropriate for the Company to agree to give ongoing consultation rights to the Producer.

Clause 4.7 The production of audio-visual material may require compliance with certain laws and statutes (for example health and safety at work legislation). Additionally, where a Producer engages the services of actors, musicians or performers, such services may be engaged pursuant to standard agreements of guilds or unions which the Producer will be required to observe.

Clause 4.8 The level and standard of performance expected of the Producer should not be left to a common understanding between the parties, but should be specified.

proposed researchers consultants and other third parties prior to engaging any such persons in connection with the Development Material;

4.10   the Producer shall not without the Company's prior written consent enter into or conclude any agreement with any third party relating to production of the CD-I or development of the Development Material;

4.11   the Producer shall not without the Company's prior consent reveal or make public any financial or other confidential information in connection with the CD-I the Development Material the terms of this Agreement or the business of the Company or issue any publicity relating to the same;

4.12   the Producer undertakes to indemnify the Company and keep the Company at all times fully indemnified from and against all actions proceedings claims demands costs (including without prejudice to the generality of this provision the legal costs of the Company on a solicitor and own client basis) awards and damages however arising directly or indirectly as a result of any breach or non-performance by the Producer of any of the Producer's undertakings warranties or obligations under this Agreement.

5.   PRODUCTION

5.1   The Producer acknowledges that the Company shall not be under any obligation to commission the Producer to make the CD-I.

5.2   The Producer confirms that the Company shall have the right exercisable by notice in writing to the Producer to offer to commission the Producer to produce the CD-I. If such commission is offered it shall be in the form of the Company's Production Agreement subject to such amendments as the Company may require.

6.   NOTICE

6.1   Any notice or other document required to be given under this Agreement or any communication between the parties with respect to any of the provisions of this Agreement shall be in writing in English and be deemed duly given if signed by or on behalf of a duly authorised officer of the party giving the notice and if left at or sent by pre-paid registered or recorded delivery post or by telex telegram cable facsimile transmission or other means of telecommunication in permanent written form to the address of the party

---

Clause 4.9   The Company will need to know names of researchers, consultants, writers and other third parties in order to ensure that its rights clearance procedures are followed properly.

Clause 4.10   There may be circumstances when the Company wishes to monitor or control all persons involved in relation to the creation of the Development Material.

Clause 4.11   For issues in relation to confidentiality see paragraphs 1.4 to 1.12 and Document 1.

Clause 4.12   For an explanation of the meaning of an indemnity clause, reference should be made to paragraph 7.14.

Clause 5.1   The function of this provision is to make it clear that the sole obligation of the Company is to commission and pay the Producer for making Development Material. There is no obligation on the Company to commission the Producer to produce a CD-I or other multimedia product.

Clause 5.2   This clause permits the Company to offer to engage the Producer in relation to a multimedia project based on the Development Material. For the significance of offers see paragraphs 2.5 and 2.6.

receiving such notice as set out in the Commissioning Letter or as notified between the parties.

6.2   Any such notice or other communication shall be deemed to be given to and received by the addressee:

(a)   at the time the same is left at the address or handed to a representative of the party to be served;

(b)   by post on the day not being a Sunday or public holiday two days following the date of posting;

(c)   in the case of telex telegram cable facsimile transmission or other means of telecommunication on the next following day not being a Sunday or public holiday.

6.3   In proving the giving of a notice it shall be sufficient to prove that the notice was left or that the envelope containing the notice was properly addressed and posted or that the applicable means of telecommunication was addressed and despatched and despatch of the transmission was confirmed and/or acknowledged as the case may be.

7.   MISCELLANEOUS

7.1   This Agreement contains the full and complete understanding between the parties and supersedes all prior arrangements and understandings whether written or oral appertaining to the subject matter of this Agreement and may not be varied except by an instrument in writing signed by all of the parties to this Agreement. The Producer acknowledges that no representations or promises not expressly contained in this Agreement have been made to the Producer by the Company or any of its servants agents employees members or representatives.

7.2   The Company shall be entitled to assign charge license or sub-license the whole or any part of its rights under this Agreement including without limitation all rights in and to the Development Material and in such event all of the representations warranties and covenants on the part of the Producer contained in this Agreement shall enure for the benefit of any assignee licensee or sub-licensee of the Company.

7.3   No failure or delay on the part of any of the parties to this Agreement relating to the exercise of any right power privilege or remedy provided under this Agreement shall operate as a waiver of such right power privilege or

---

Clause 6   A number of clauses in the document provide for a means of exercising rights, and a notice provision is therefore necessary.

Clause 7.1   This clause clarifies the fact that the Agreement is the sole agreement relating to its subject matter and all previous arrangements are superseded. The clause also contains an acknowledgement on the part of the Producer that no representations have been made by the Company. This will protect the Company from any subsequent claim by the Producer that the Company made any representations as to the likelihood of being subsequently commissioned to produce a multimedia work based on the development material. As to representations generally see paragraphs 2.17 and 2.18.

Clause 7.2   This provision clarifies the extent of the Company's rights to assign and sub-license and transfer the benefit of warranties given on the part of the Producer.

remedy or as a waiver of any preceding or succeeding breach by the other party to this Agreement nor shall any single or partial exercise of any right power privilege or remedy preclude any other or further exercise of such or any other right power privilege or remedy provided in this Agreement all of which are several and cumulative and are not exclusive of each other or of any other rights or remedies otherwise available to a party at law or in equity.

7.4   The Producer undertakes to do any and all acts and execute any and all documents in such manner and at such locations as may be required by the Company in its sole discretion in order to protect perfect or enforce any of the rights granted or confirmed to the Company pursuant to this Agreement. As security for the performance by the Producer of the Producer's obligations under this Agreement if the Producer shall have failed following 14 days' notice from the Company to execute any document or perform any act required by the Company pursuant to this Agreement the Company shall have the right to do so in the place and stead of the Producer as the lawfully appointed attorney of the Producer and the Producer undertakes and warrants to confirm and ratify and be bound by any and all of the actions of the Company pursuant to this Clause and such authority and appointment shall take effect as an irrevocable appointment pursuant to the Powers of Attorney Act 1971 Section 4.

7.5   This Agreement shall not be deemed to constitute a partnership or joint venture or contract of employment between the parties.

7.6   This Agreement shall be governed by and construed in accordance with the laws of England and Wales the courts of which shall be courts of competent jurisdiction.

8.   INTERPRETATION AND DEFINITIONS

8.1   Any reference in this Agreement to any statute or statutory provision shall be construed as including a reference to that statute or statutory provision as from time to time amended modified extended or re-enacted whether before or after the date of this Agreement and to all statutory instruments orders and regulations for the time being made pursuant to it or deriving validity from it.

8.2   Unless the context otherwise requires words denoting the singular shall include the plural and vice versa and words denoting any one gender shall include all genders and words denoting persons shall include bodies corporate unincorporated associations and partnerships.

8.3   The word "copyright" means the entire copyright and design right

---

Clause 7.3   Under English law, if two parties carry on business in common with a view to profit and share profits, the arrangement is capable of being considered a partnership. This provision ensures that no partnership is created inadvertently, and also expressly excludes the possibility of an employment contract being created.

Clause 7.4   Where a contract is made between two entities in England and Wales, it will generally not be necessary to insert a provision of this nature, but where a contract is to be created with a foreign company (or a company situate in Scotland or Northern Ireland) this provision should always be included.

subsisting under the laws of the United Kingdom and all analogous rights subsisting under the laws of each and every jurisdiction throughout the world.

8.4   The word "CD-I" shall be deemed to include any and all literary dramatic musical and/or artistic works audio-visual material and sound recordings included in the CD-I.

8.5   Unless otherwise stated time shall be of the essence for the purpose of the performance of the Producer's obligations under this Agreement.

8.6   Unless otherwise stated references to clauses sub-clauses sub-paragraphs schedules annexures and exhibits relate to this Agreement.

8.7   Any words or phrases which are defined in the commissioning letter ("Commissioning Letter") to which the Standard Conditions are attached shall have the same meaning in the Standard Conditions and the following words and expressions shall have the following meanings:

"Agreement"
The Commissioning Letter the Standard Conditions and all attached exhibits.

"Development Material"
The Development Material specified in the exhibits to the Commissioning Letter and any other material in connection with the CD-I or the Work produced by the Producer and/or any person engaged by the Producer.

[certificate of value]

Certificate of Value   Although it had been intended to abolish stamp duty on assignments of intellectual property at the same time as the introduction of paperless share transfer, the failure of the Stock Exchange system TAURUS has delayed the abolition of stamp duty which is still technically payable in relation to assignments of copyright. The publishing industry has, traditionally, never made provision for the payment of stamp duty in assignments of copyright and for this reason no provision is included in this document – although there are now many circumstances where it is advisable. A suitable form of wording may, however, be found in Document 6 (d) and a summary of the current legislation relating to stamp duty may be found in paragraph 11.29.

DOCUMENT 44

Multimedia production agreement

[IMPORTANT NOTE: Please read the section "About this book" on page v, before copying or using this Document]

Purpose of this Document

This is a form of agreement suitable for use by a company where commissioning the production of a multimedia work. The document may be used in relation to the production of a computer game, a CD-ROM, a CD-I or other multimedia product, in which case references to CD-I will need to be changed accordingly. The document is drafted from the point of view of the company commissioning the producer to produce and deliver a multimedia work.

Relevant text

The text of this Work contains a number of topics which are relevant to documents of this nature:

- development and production of multimedia works (paragraphs 19.31 to 19.41)
- what is multimedia? (paragraphs 19.2 and 19.3)
- consents and permissions required for multimedia works (paragraphs 19.4 to 19.13)
- music in multimedia (paragraphs 19.14 to 19.20)
- collective licensing schemes (paragraphs 19.21 to 19.24)
- licensing distribution and joint ventures (paragraphs 19.42 to 19.44)
- databases and computers (paragraphs 19.45 to 19.52)
- software publishing and video publishing (paragraphs 19.53 to 19.55)
- buying and selling rights (paragraphs 11.2 to 11.9)
- remuneration provisions in rights agreements (paragraphs 11.22 to 11.26)
- taxation (paragraphs 11.27 to 11.29 and 12.22 to 12.30)
- commercial terms of offers (paragraphs 1.22 and 1.23)
- the law of contract and agency (paragraphs 2.1 to 2.30)
- creation, existence and transfer of copyrights (paragraphs 3.1 to 3.45)
- international copyright protection (paragraphs 4.1 to 4.17)
- moral rights (paragraphs 5.1 to 5.22)
- permissions, fair dealing and rights clearances (paragraphs 8.1 to 8.44)
- liability for content (paragraphs 9.1 to 9.49)
- buying and selling rights (paragraphs 11.1 to 11.29)
- infringement and enforcement (paragraphs 13.1 to 13.17)
- termination and recapture (paragraphs 14.1 to 14.10)
- competition law (paragraphs 16.1 to 16.28)

THIS AGREEMENT is made the   day of

BETWEEN:

(1)   [*Name*] LIMITED of [*address*]
       ("Company"); and

(2)   [*Name*] LIMITED of [*address*]
       ("Producer")

IT IS AGREED as follows:

1.   PRODUCTION, DELIVERY AND ESSENTIAL ELEMENTS

1.1   The Producer undertakes to produce the CD-I in accordance with the provisions of this Agreement for an amount not exceeding the Budget and in accordance with the Production Schedule. The Producer undertakes to deliver all Delivery Material to the Company at its address aforesaid by no later than the Delivery Date.

1.2   No substitution amendment or alteration or subtraction from any of the Essential Elements of the CD-I or any contract with any person designated as an Essential Element shall be made without the prior written consent of the Company and if any substitution amendment alteration or subtraction is made or is required or any of the Essential Elements is not fulfilled for any reason or if the consent of the Company is not retained in relation to any substitution amendment alteration or subtraction the CD-I shall be deemed not to contain the Essential Element. No contract in relation to any of the foregoing shall be terminated without the consent of the Company.

1.3   The CD-I shall incorporate the Essential Elements and be produced at the Studios and in accordance with the Technical Specifications.

1.4   The Producer undertakes in relation to the CD-I to co-operate with and follow all reasonable directions of the Company.

Clause 1.1 This clause contains the basic undertaking of the Producer to produce the multimedia product for an amount not exceeding the Budget in accordance with the Production Schedule and to deliver the various items of Delivery Material to the Company by no later than the date for delivery.

Clause 1.2 The Agreement requires the multimedia product to contain designated Essential Elements. In view of the possibility that the designated personnel may become unavailable or other elements may need to be altered, this clause requires the Producer to obtain the consent of the Company before making any substitution or amendment and before terminating any contract in relation to any of the Essential Elements.

Clause 1.3 As well as incorporating the Essential Elements this clause requires the multimedia product to be produced at designated studio locations (which may be required for special effects purposes) and to comply with stated technical specifications.

Clause 1.4 This provision requires the Producer to follow all reasonable directions of the Company. Such directions might include making changes to elements of the multimedia product.

1.5   No tie-in or sponsorship or product placement arrangement shall be entered into in relation to the CD-I without the prior written consent of the Company.

2.   COPYRIGHT

2.1   The Producer assigns to the Company the entire copyright including all vested contingent and future rights all rights of action and all other rights of whatever nature in and to the CD-I the Delivery Material and the product of the Services whether now known or in the future created to which the Producer is now or may at any time after the date of this Agreement be entitled by virtue of or pursuant to any of the laws in force in any part of the world TO HOLD the same unto the Company its successors assignees and licensees absolutely for the full period of copyright throughout the world including all renewals reversions and extensions. The Producer confirms that ownership of all material in relation to the CD-I produced or acquired by the Producer or the Personnel specified in the Production Contracts shall vest in the Company absolutely free from incumbrances with effect from the moment of production or acquisition.

2.2   The Producer confirms that all consents required pursuant to Part II of the Copyright, Designs and Patents Act 1988 and all other laws now or in future in force in any part of the world which may be required in respect of the exploitation by the Company its successors assignees and licensees of the CD-I and the Delivery Material in any and all media by any and all means now known or developed in future for the full duration of the rights in such material have been irrevocably and unconditionally granted to the Producer its successors assignees and licensees.

2.3   The Producer confirms the irrevocable and unconditional waiver by all relevant persons of all rights relating to the Services and the CD-I and the Delivery Material to which such persons are now or may in the future be entitled pursuant to the provisions of Sections 77 80 84 and 85 of the Copyright, Designs and Patents Act 1988 and any other moral rights to which such persons may be entitled under any legislation now existing or in future enacted in any part of the world.

2.4   All persons whose names likenesses or biographies appear in the CD-I

Clause 1.5   It is important for the Company to eliminate any possibility of the Producer making tie-in sponsorship or product placement arrangements in relation to the multimedia product. Such arrangements might result in the inclusion of identifiable brand names within the multimedia product. This would clearly have some value for an advertiser or sponsor, but from the Company's point of view, quite apart from the fact that the Company may wish to use any income derived from such an arrangement, to reduce the amount of its contribution, the question whether the Company wishes in any way to be associated with the sponsor remains also to be considered.

Clause 2.1   This clause passes copyright from the Producer to the Company. It also passes ownership of all physical material in relation to the multimedia product.

Clause 2.2   This clause deals with performers' consents in relation to any performances which may be included with the multimedia product.

Clause 2.3   This clause deals with the waiver of any moral rights in relation to the multimedia product.

or any material connected with it shall have consented to the exploitation of the CD-I and all subsidiary ancillary and merchandising material incorporated or derived from the CD-I throughout the world without restriction or limitation other than the payment of pre-approved residual and repeat fees and payments approved pursuant to Clause 3.5.

2.5   The Producer shall obtain releases permissions or licences in a form satisfactory to the Company signed by all relevant persons in relation to all quotations text illustrations pictures sound recordings films performances and other material in which rights are controlled by third parties if such material is included or incorporated in any way in the Delivery Material or is incorporated directly or indirectly in the CD-I. The Producer undertakes to deliver original or certified copies of all relevant documentation to the Company by the Delivery Date. The Producer irrevocably confirms that the benefit of all assignments licences consents releases and permissions obtained by the Producer shall extend to the Company throughout the world for the full period of such rights.

2.6   The Producer undertakes to follow all rights clearance procedures from time to time required by the Company and to make full and fair disclosure to the Company of all information correspondence and documentation relating to all rights of copyright and other rights in relation to the CD-I and/or the Delivery Material or relating to any prior dealings between the Producer and any relevant third parties.

2.7   The Producer undertakes to do any and all acts and execute any and all documents in such manner and at such location as may be required by the Company in its sole discretion to protect perfect or enforce any of the rights granted or confirmed to the Company pursuant to this Agreement. As security for the performance by the Producer of the Producer's obligations under this Agreement if the Producer shall have failed following fourteen days' notice from the Company to execute any document or perform any act required by the Company pursuant to this Agreement the Company shall have the right to do so in the place and stead of the Producer as the lawfully appointed attorney of the Producer. The Producer undertakes and warrants to confirm and ratify and be bound by any and all of the actions of the Company pursuant to this clause and such authority and appointment shall take effect as an irrevocable appointment pursuant to the Powers of Attorney Act 1971 Section 4.

Clause 2.4   This clause confirms the ability of the Company to exploit elements of the multimedia product by means of merchandising and other means of exploitation without payment other than those express provisions agreed to by the Company pursuant to clause 3.5.

Clause 2.5   This Clause requires the Producer to obtain all necessary releases, assignments, licences and consents and to deliver originals or copies to the Company.

Clause 2.6   From the Company's point of view it is important not only that the Producer follows all rights clearance procedures, but also makes full and fair disclosure of any relevant factors which may affect the Company's ability to exploit multimedia product.

Clause 2.7   This provision gives the Company the right to execute certain documentation on behalf of the Producer in certain circumstances. The clause may not always be necessary, but if it is, the Company will need to ensure that the attestation clause of the documentation is in an appropriate form for execution of a deed.

3.   PRODUCTION CONTRACTS

3.1   The Producer shall ensure that all Production Contracts are in a form previously approved by the Company and that only persons previously approved by the Company in writing shall perform in the CD-I or be engaged in respect of the CD-I and the Producer shall as a condition precedent to any liability on the part of the Company to the Producer deliver executed copies of the Production Contracts to the Company.

3.2   All Production Contracts shall be effected on the best reasonably obtainable arm's length commercial terms and shall contain a provision permitting the Company or its nominee to exercise all rights exercisable by the Producer pursuant to such Production Contracts.

3.3   The terms and conditions of the Production Contracts shall not be amended altered varied rescinded terminated cancelled or suspended nor shall any rights granted pursuant to the Production Contracts or any document or arrangement relating to the CD-I be waived without the prior approval of the Company.

3.4   The remuneration payable pursuant to the Production Contracts shall where applicable be not less than the minimum rates provided by any Relevant Union Agreement but shall not exceed the amounts allocated in the Budget except in accordance with any provision made in the Production Contracts and shall not be payable before the date specified in the Production Schedule.

3.5   The Producer shall not enter into any Production Contract where royalties or residual repeat rerun reuse or other fees and payments are payable unless such fees or payments are required to be paid pursuant to the provisions of any Relevant Union Agreement and are approved by the Company. Where any Relevant Union Agreement requires the payment of any residual repeat rerun or reuse fees such fees shall be calculated on the minimum fee payable and any additional remuneration shall be applied on a prepayment basis to buy-out all residual repeats reruns reuse or other fees or

---

Clause 3.1   The Company will wish to insure that all Production Contracts follow a form approved by the Company not only to avoid additional liability in relation to the multimedia product, but also to ensure that the Company obtains all necessary rights.

Clause 3.2   The reason the Company will wish Production Contracts to contain a provision permitting the Company to exercise all rights exercisable by the Producer, is to facilitate any takeover by the Company of production of the multimedia product (see clause 14 et seq) .

Clause 3.3   The Company needs to control the variation of the terms of the Production Contracts for the same reasons as set out in the note to clause 3.1. If any Production Contract is terminated or suspended, or any right which the Producer has in relation to any Production Contract is waived, this may impede the Company's ability to take over production.

Clause 3.4   The engagement by the Producer of actors and musicians and other personnel requires compliance with collective bargaining agreements in particularly in relation to the minimum scale fees payable.

payments to the maximum extent permissible under the Relevant Union Agreement.

3.6   If the Company requests executed copies of any Production Contract it shall be entitled to receive these within 14 days from request.

3.7   All agreements relating to the use of any copyright material which is owned by third parties and is to be used in or in relation to the CD-I shall be subject to the approval of the Company before execution and shall be on such terms as permit the exploitation of the CD-I in all media by any manner or means throughout the world for the full period of copyright without any further payment other than payment of such sums as have been approved by the Company and such sums as may be payable to the PRS and PPL in relation to the public performance and/or broadcast of music and sound recordings in the CD-I.

3.8   The Producer shall not pledge the credit of the Company or hold the Producer out as the Company's agent in any of its dealings in connection with the CD-I or otherwise.

3.9   The Producer undertakes to procure that the [*specify capacity*] and all other personnel nominated by the Company who are connected with the CD-I shall enter into an agreement with the Company in the form of an inducement letter approved by the Company.

4.   PRODUCER'S WARRANTIES

The Producer warrants agrees and undertakes that:

4.1   the Producer is free to enter into and perform this Agreement and has not and shall not make any arrangement which may conflict with it;

4.2   the Producer is or shall be the sole absolute unincumbered legal and

Clause 3.5   Depending upon the type of multimedia product, additional fees relating to use of the contributions of actors, musicians and other creative personnel may be payable. Depending on the relevant collective bargaining agreement, it is possible in some circumstances to pre-pay residual and reuse fees, and this clause provides that, to the extent that any initial payments exceed those required to be made under the relevant collective bargaining agreement, the excess is applied by way of such prepayment.

Clause 3.7   The Performing Right Society Limited and Photographic Performance Limited (and similar and affiliated organisations throughout the world) control public performance of music and sound recordings. The Company will wish so far as possible to ensure that the multimedia product may be exploited in any media by any means throughout the world without payment of fees other than those required to be paid to the PRS, PPL and similar organisations. In practice, the Company may not wish to clear and make prepayment for exploitation in all media throughout the world, but this provision will ensure that the Company will know the precise cost of exploitation of the CD-I in the relevant media.

Clause 3.8   The Company will not wish the Producer to have power to enter into binding contract on its behalf. For an explanation of the law of agency see paragraphs 2.26 to 2.30.

Clause 3.9   This provision may be required when the Company wishes a designated individual to be engaged in a designated capacity in relation to the production. An inducement letter will give the Company a contractual relationship with that individual and will, amongst other matters, confirm the assignment by the individual of all rights to the Company or to the Producer.

Clause 4.1   This provision is intended to prevent any possibility of a claim arising from a third party that such third party had an option to acquire the rights which the Producer has assigned to the Company. Other incumbrances or restrictions might include a mortgage or charge over intellectual property rights, and if a Producer is a limited liability company, the Company commissioning the Producer may wish to investigate the register of charges on file against the producer at Companies House.

beneficial owner of all rights of copyright and all other rights in the CD-I and the Delivery Material and all rights assigned to the Company pursuant to this Agreement and has not assigned charged sub-licensed or otherwise in any way incumbered any of the foregoing rights;

4.3   the Producer shall not reveal or make public any financial or other confidential information in connection with the CD-I and/or the Delivery Material or the terms of this Agreement or the business of the Company or issue any publicity relating to the same;

4.4   the Producer shall ensure that all copies of the CD-I and the Delivery Material shall contain a copyright notice in accordance with the Universal Copyright Convention in such form as shall be acceptable to the Company;

4.5   the Producer shall consult with the Company and follow the Company's directions in respect of the CD-I at all stages in the Production Schedule;

4.6   all Production Contracts (including all contracts relating to the incorporation use and exploitation of the musical works contained in the CD-I in synchronisation with or in timed relation to visual images) shall be in such form as shall have been approved by the Company in writing and shall be executed by the Producer prior to the commencement of production of the CD-I and shall be for such amounts as shall be specified in the Budget;

4.7   nothing contained in the CD-I or the Delivery Material shall infringe any right of copyright right of trade mark right of privacy right of publicity or personality or any other right of any other nature of any person or be obscene or libellous or blasphemous or defamatory and the CD-I shall not incorporate any Third Party Material without the consent of the Company;

4.8   the CD-I shall be produced in accordance with all relevant rules and regulations of trade unions guilds or other bodies applicable to the production of promotional videograms including without limitation the rules and regulations from time to time of the Musicians' Union and British Actors' Equity and the Association of Cinematograph and Television Technicians and British Entertainment Trades Alliance;

4.9   the Delivery Material shall be in first-class condition and of first-class

---

Clause 4.2 It is necessary to confirm that the Producer is the sole absolute unincumbered legal beneficial owner of the rights which are assigned to the Company, and that no other person owns or has any claim in relation to such rights.

Clause 4.3 For an explanation of the law relating to confidentiality, reference should be made to paragraphs 1.5 to 1.12.

Clause 4.4 The form and wording of the copyright notice to be contained on the multimedia product is of significant importance. Reference should be made to paragraph 4.10.

Clause 4.6 Synchronisation licences will be required not only in relation to musical works, but also in relation to the use of sound recordings. The form of such documentation varies widely, and for this reason the Company will wish to approve the documentation.

Clause 4.7 The Development Material and each part of it shall be original (except to the extent based on existing materials approved by the Company or in the public domain) and shall not be published and do not and shall not infringe any copyright, moral right, right of privacy, right of publicity or any other right whatever of any person and shall not be defamatory of any person, libellous, obscene, blasphemous or offensive to any religion.

technical quality suitable for and the manufacture of multimedia interactive compact discs and other digital carriers of commercially and artistically acceptable quality;

4.10   the Producer has acquired or shall on Delivery have acquired the irrevocable right to use the names professional names likenesses and biographies of all Production Personnel and to use their voices and any photographs or recordings of the Production Personnel throughout the world for the full period of copyright and all other rights in the same including all renewals reversions and extensions for the purpose of exploiting the CD-I under this Agreement together with the sole and exclusive merchandising rights in and to the services and the product of the services of the Production Personnel in connection with the CD-I including without limitation the right to manufacture distribute and sell articles of all descriptions being reproductions or representations of any characters or physical material used in or portrayed in or associated with or based upon or derived from the CD-I or the product of the services of the Production Personnel provided that the Producer may agree in the Production Contracts to pay such persons remuneration in connection with the exploitation of such rights in addition to the sums specified in the Budget;

4.11   the Producer shall deliver the Delivery Material to the Company free and clear of all recording synchronisation mechanical and/or distribution fees or payments of whatever nature and all fees relating to all personnel facilities equipment or otherwise in connection with the production of the CD-I shall have been paid for in full by the Producer on or before Delivery;

4.12   the CD-I and the Delivery Material shall contain only those credits and notices approved by the Company and shall when delivered comply with all contractual credit and other obligations whatever to third parties connected with it;

4.13   the Budget shall be a complete bona fide accurate estimate of the total cost of production of the CD-I and shall include adequate provision for all expenses relating to the CD-I including without limitation any and all costs relating to music and other licences pre-release publicity public relations expenses and interest charges;

Clause 4.9   It is important that the Delivery Material is in a state fit for its intended use.

Clause 4.10   Any limitations relating to the use of names, likenesses and biographies should be approved by the Company. For a short summary of the law relating to privacy and rights of personality, reference should be made to paragraph 5.21.

Clause 4.11   This clause may need to be altered to reflect circumstances, where the Company has consented to additional fees being payable (for example, in relation to mechanical reproduction of music) following delivery.

Clause 4.12   Failure to comply with credit obligations is one of the grounds on which an injunction might be obtained to restrain distribution of the multimedia product. Compliance is therefore most important.

Clause 4.13   The Company will probably be committing to fund the production of the multimedia product in reliance on the budget being a full, complete and bona fide estimate. If it is not the case, the Company may have rights against the Producer on grounds of misrepresentation (see paragraph 2.17) or on grounds of negligent misstatement (see paragraphs 9.34 and 9.35) and may be entitled to avoid the contract on the grounds of mistake in certain circumstances (see paragraph 2.18).

4.14 the Producer shall be the sole "author" of the CD-I within the meaning of the Copyright, Designs and Patents Act 1988 Section 9(2)(a) and shall at all material times during the production of the CD-I be a "qualifying person" within the meaning of the Copyright, Designs and Patents Act 1988 Section 154;

4.15 the Producer has acquired all rights of copyright and other rights necessary for the production distribution exhibition advertising and exploitation of the CD-I in any and all media by any manner or means throughout the world for the full period of copyright protection and all fees and payments of whatever nature required to procure full exploitation of the CD-I (other than fees permitted pursuant to Clause 3.5) have been paid save where expressly indicated in the Budget or where the approval of the Company has been given;

4.16 the Producer shall promptly advise the Company of the occurrence of any event or the existence of any condition which will or might adversely affect the CD-I or of any material claims or material proceedings threatened or commenced against the Producer and shall keep the Company regularly informed of the progress of such events claims and/or proceedings and shall immediately notify the Company of any judgment or settlement in respect of the same;

4.17 each part of the CD-I shall be protected under statutory and common law copyright in all countries adhering to the Berne Convention and the Universal Copyright Convention and any other relevant convention and the Company and the Producer shall be the sole and unincumbered legal and beneficial owner of the Delivery Material and all rights in the CD-I;

4.18 the CD-I shall at all times during production contain and comply with the Essential Elements and no material the rights in which are owned by third parties shall be included in the CD-I without the consent of the Company;

4.19 the Producer shall not otherwise than as required by the exigencies of production alter or permit the alteration of any screenplay or storyboard or other literary dramatic or artistic material which has been approved by the Company in any way which might materially alter the nature or character of the CD-I and shall not alter the title of the CD-I without the prior written consent of the Company;

4.20 the Producer shall make all payments due to any persons who are

---

Clause 4.14 The Company wishes to ensure that the Producer will be the sole author, and therefore owner of copyright in the multimedia work, and also that the Producer will be a qualifying person within the meaning of United Kingdom copyright legislation. Reference should be made to paragraphs 3.11 to 3.15 and 3.22 to 3.24.

Clause 4.16 It is not unknown for adverse claims to be made during production of films and television programmes and for this reason the Company will wish to be apprised of such claims so it may take appropriate action.

Clause 4.18 The provisions of this clause link in with the Company's rights clearance procedures.

Clause 4.19 Where a Company has approved all other matters on which the multimedia product is to be based, the Producer will be required to adhere to or incorporate the various elements.

entitled to any payment in respect of services or goods or facilities rendered or provided or rights granted in respect of the CD-I in a timely manner;

4.21   no fees shall be payable in respect of any music contained in the CD-I otherwise than to the PRS or its affiliated organisations in respect of the public performance and broadcasting and inclusion in a cable programme of the CD-I;

4.22   nothing shall be contained in the CD-I which might breach any duty of confidence or constitute a contempt of court or contravene the provision of any statute including any provisions of the Broadcasting Act 1990 or regulations made pursuant to such Act;

4.23   the Producer shall at all times before and after Delivery comply with the provisions of all Relevant Union Agreements relating to the CD-I;

4.24   the Producer shall not without the prior written consent of the Company disclose reveal or make public any information of whatever nature in connection with the business of the Company the CD-I or this Agreement all of which shall be treated by the Producer on a strictly confidential basis and the Producer shall procure the strict observance of this Clause 4.24 by the Production Personnel and all persons contracted by the Producer in relation to the CD-I;

4.25   following Delivery the Producer shall hold on trust for the Company all props plant machinery and other physical material of whatever nature acquired or created by the Producer in relation to the CD-I and undertakes that it shall on demand deliver up and/or make such material available to any third party nominated by the Company and undertakes to keep all such material in a safe and secure place and in good repair and condition and undertakes to permit any other person access to such material and agrees to keep all such material fully insured upon terms which provide that the Company shall be the sole loss payee it being understood that the approved cost of such insurance shall be borne by the Company;

4.26   the Producer undertakes to indemnify the Company and keep the Company at all times fully indemnified from and against all actions proceedings claims demands costs (including without prejudice to the generality of this provision the legal costs of the Company on a solicitor and own client basis) awards and damages however arising directly or indirectly as a result of any breach or non-performance by the Producer of any of the Producer's undertakings warranties or obligations under this Agreement.

Clause 4.20   Failure to make payment to persons providing services or goods might create difficulties in exploiting the multimedia product in future.

Clause 4.21   The Performing Right Society Limited and its affiliated organisations control the public performance and broadcasting of certain musical and literary works.

Clause 4.25   Where physical materials are created during the course of production, the Company may wish either to have these materials delivered to it for future use, or it may wish to sell them and apply the proceeds towards recovery of the cost of production.

Clause 4.26   For an explanation as to the difference between a warranty and an indemnity, reference should be made to paragraph 7.15.

5. PRODUCTION REPRESENTATIVES AND REPORTS

5.1 The Company shall have the right to designate persons as Production Representatives in relation to the CD-I. The Producer shall ensure that the Production Representatives shall be afforded access to all relevant personnel associated with the production of the CD-I and all Studios and shall be provided with all information requested by such Production Representative or the Company in relation to the production of the CD-I. All Production Personnel shall attend such reasonable number of meetings as the Company or its representative may request at such reasonable venues to discuss any matters in relation to the CD-I.

5.2 The Producer shall procure that each Production Representative is provided with copies of all documentation and information requested and shall provide details of all dates times and locations of screening of rushes rough cuts and previews of the CD-I and shall respond within 24 hours to any requests from the Production Representatives for information and shall within such period provide the Company with all information that is available and indicate what steps are being taken to obtain additional information.

5.3 Cost reports and cashflow schedules in such form as the Company or its Production Representative may require shall be delivered in support of each invoice which is submitted for payment to the Company or at such other time as the Company may request provided that the Producer shall have 5 days' notice to prepare and present cost reports to the Company in such form as may be notified to the Producer on or before request.

6. INSURANCE

6.1 The Producer undertakes to procure that adequate insurance cover shall be effected for the CD-I in relation to cast negative faulty stock/tape props sets wardrobe equipment extra expense third party property damage office contents errors and omissions and general liability in such amounts as shall be necessary to provide full cover to the Company for all sums advanced by the Company in relation to the CD-I.

Clause 5.1 This clause gives the Company the right to designate a person as Production Representative. The Production Representative will have the right to obtain information and to have access in relation to any studios in order to monitor the continued progress and cost of production of the multimedia product.

Clause 5.2 In order for the Production Representative to discharge its function (s)he will need access to original material. Whether it is appropriate for the representative to have access to screening the rushes, rough cuts and previews will depend on the precise nature of the multimedia product being produced. It may be more appropriate for the Production Representative to have rights of access to any demo routines.

Clause 6.1 The provisions of this clause will need to be amended to fit the circumstances. Whether or not insurance is placed in relation to the multimedia product will depend upon its precise nature. Similarly there may be no requirements to ensure faulty stock or to insure props, sets or wardrobe equipment. Whether errors and omissions insurance is required will also depend on the circumstances.

677

6.2   The Company's interest shall be noted as named assured and loss payee on all policies of insurance relating to the CD-I.

6.3   Copies of all insurance policy documentation shall be provided to the Company on request and all premiums in relation to insurance policies shall be paid by the Producer which shall notify the Company of any claim relating to any policy of insurance which claim shall not be settled without the consent in writing of the Company.

6.4   The Producer shall co-operate fully with the Company and take all such actions as may be required by the Company in relation to any insurance claim. No provision relating to any insurance policy may be varied or waived without the prior written consent of the Company.

7.   CREDIT CENSORSHIP AND CONTENT

7.1   The CD-I shall contain such form of screen credit as may be specified by the Company and any credit required by the Company in relation to any executive producer.

7.2   The audio-visual logo of the Company shall be inserted at the beginning of the opening credit sequence and at the end of the final credit sequence of the CD-I.

7.3   No other screen credits shall be permitted in relation to the CD-I other than a credit for the Producer and those expressly required pursuant to the Production Contracts.

7.4   The CD-I shall comply with all contractual credit obligations owed towards third parties and shall contain notice in accordance with the Universal Copyright Convention naming the Company as copyright owner.

7.5   The CD-I shall comply with all requirements and guidelines of the British Broadcasting Corporation the Independent Television Commission and the British Board of Film Classification as appropriate.

8.   BUDGET PRODUCTION FEE UNDERSPEND AND OVERSPEND

8.1   Subject to and conditional on the full and timely performance and observance by the Producer of its warranties and obligations under this Agreement and provided no Event of Default shall have occurred the Company undertakes to pay to the Producer the Budget in accordance with the Cashflow Schedule.

Clause 6.2   The Company's interest is noted as named assured and loss payee, the Company will be entitled in certain circumstances to receive the proceeds of insurance policies.

Clause 6.3   It may be appropriate for the Producer to be required also to produce to the Company evidence that relevant premiums have been paid. Alternatively the Company may wish to deduct the premium cost from any sums required to be advanced by it as part of the Budget. This would permit the Company to make payment of such sums direct to any relevant insurance company.

8.2   The Producer shall be entitled to deduct and retain the Production Fee out of sums forming part of the Budget which have been advanced by the Company on the dates and instalments specified in the Cashflow Schedule.

8.3   All money made available by the Company in relation to the CD-I shall be held by the Producer in the Production Account upon strict trust for such purpose by the Producer and shall be used solely in connection with the production of the CD-I. Any money facilities or services not applied in full accordance with this provision without prejudice to any rights of the Company at law or under this Agreement shall be repayable and/or returnable to the Company immediately on demand.

8.4   If at any stage in production it appears likely that the Cost of Production of the CD-I will be less than the Budget any unspent money ("Surplus Funds") including without limitation any money received from the sale of props or other physical materials shall be held on trust for the Company and be repaid to the Company on the date of Delivery or within 14 days from the date such Surplus Funds arise if later and the Company agrees that subject to any Maximum Share of Surplus in accordance with Clause 8.5 below and after application of the Underspend Guidelines set out in Exhibit 5 the Producer shall be entitled to receive 50% of any such Surplus Funds in cash.

8.5   The Company may designate a Maximum Share of Surplus in respect of the CD-I where the Company in its sole discretion is of the view that there is particular potential for Budget underspend on the CD-I. In such circumstances the amount of Surplus Funds remitted to the Producer after application of the Underspend Guidelines shall not exceed the amount designated as the Maximum Share of Surplus.

8.6   If at any stage in production it appears likely that the Cost of Production of the CD-I is likely to exceed the Budget or the production of the CD-I is or is likely to fall materially behind the Production Schedule the Producer shall give immediate notice in writing of all relevant particulars to the Company and shall prepare and submit to the Company full particulars of all costs incurred and all liabilities likely to be incurred in order to complete the CD-I together with detailed revisions to the Production Schedule and the Budget for the CD-I and shall meet with the Company and follow all instructions of the Company in relation to the production of the CD-I.

Clause 8.2   The Company will advance to the Producer sums up to the amount of the Budget. The sums will be advanced in instalments in accordance with the Cashflow Schedule. The Producer will be entitled to retain the Production Fee out of the sums advanced to it. Normally the Production Fee will be payable in instalments on dates specified in the Cashflow Schedule.

Clause 8.3   This clause contemplates the establishment of a production account by the Producer and requires the Producer to pay all money made available by the Company into this production account, and apply it solely in relation to the multimedia product.

Clause 8.4   The operation of this clause entitles the Producer to participate in any underspend, subject to complying with the guidelines contained in Exhibit 5 to the Agreement.

Clause 8.5   The provision permitting the Company to designate a Maximum Share of Surplus protects the Company in circumstances where underspend is likely.

Clause 8.6   It is obviously in the interests of the Company to be notified at the earliest moment if the production is likely to go over budget or fall behind the Production Schedule.

8.7 The Producer shall pay all costs and liabilities incurred in connection with production and delivery of the CD-I including without limitation the Cost of Production and if any costs are incurred in connection with the CD-I which are in excess of the Budget the Producer shall pay the same and the Producer and/or the Company shall have the right to apply the Production Fee in reduction of such excess.

8.8 If at any stage in production the Producer through no fault of the Producer finds itself in a potential overspend position the Company undertakes to meet with the Producer in order to examine how the situation might be resolved.

8.9 All sums payable under this Agreement shall be exclusive of Value Added Tax which shall be payable by the Company subject to the Producer rendering to the Company full and correct Value Added Tax invoices.

9. BANKING

9.1 In relation to the CD-I the Producer shall establish a Production Account which shall identify the CD-I to which it relates.

9.2 All withdrawals from the Production Account shall be made solely in connection with the production of the CD-I in accordance with production reports made by the Producer and shall be authorised by the Production Representative.

9.3 All sums maintained in the Production Account shall be held on trust for the Company and all payments from the Production Account shall be in accordance with the overall Budget and the Cashflow Schedule. No payment shall be made to any Associate of the Producer except as expressly provided in the Budget.

9.4 No money other than money to be applied towards the production of the CD-I shall be maintained in the Production Account and the Producer shall not permit money remitted to such account to be commingled with any other money belonging to the Producer or its Associates.

9.5 The Producer shall issue irrevocable directions in writing to all relevant banks requiring them to provide to the Company or its Production Representative copies of statements and all other documents and information requested by the Company or the Production Representative relating to the

---

Clause 8.7 This clause specifies that the Producer is liable for any overspend. Even though the Producer will be technically liable to pay any excess costs, an overspend situation may result in additional expenditure to the Company, if the Producer does not have sufficient assets to meet the additional expenditure. In such circumstances the Company will have to choose between the alternative of writing off all expenditure it has incurred to date, or advancing additional sums in order to have a completed product to sell to mitigate its loss.

Clause 9.2 This clause contemplates authorisation of each withdrawal by the production representative who is nominated by the Company. Depending on the circumstances it may also be advisable for the Company to procure that the bank mandate for the production account may not be operated without the signature of the authorised representative of the Company.

Production Account and undertakes to procure the execution by such banks of any letter required by the Company excluding the banks' exercise of any contractual right of set-off.

10. BOOKS AND RECORDS

10.1   The Producer undertakes and agrees to maintain full accurate and proper records and books of account relating to the production of the CD-I together with all invoices vouchers receipts and other records evidencing expenses and charges incurred in the production of the CD-I and undertakes to keep and maintain such records for the period of three years following delivery of the CD-I or such longer period as may be requested by the Company if such request is made before the expiry of such period.

10.2   The Company shall have the right at any time on reasonable prior notice to inspect audit and take copies of all books and records relating to the CD-I.

10.3   The Producer undertakes within 60 days of Delivery of the CD-I to submit to the Company a fully itemised detailed statement of the Cost of Production of the CD-I certified at the request of the Company by a firm of accountants approved by the Company and containing a detailed itemisation of all sums actually expended for the production of the CD-I. Where a CD-I is part of a series of CD-Is the period above referred to shall be calculated with effect from Delivery of the last CD-I in the series or such part of the series for which the Company shall have made any funds available.

11. ROYALTIES

11.1   Subject to the full and timely performance and observance by the Producer of all of the Producer's obligations warranties and undertakings in this Agreement the Company undertakes to pay or procure the payment to the Producer by way of Royalties:

(a)   [ ]% of the Royalty Base Price on Net Sales in the United Kingdom

(b)   [ ]% of the Royalty Base Price on Net Sales outside the United Kingdom.

11.2   In respect of Disks sold to any club operation or similar operation the Royalty Rate shall be 50% of the rate otherwise applicable under this Agreement and no Royalties shall be payable to the Producer in respect of any Disks received by members of any club operation as part of any introductory offer or as free or bonus Disks or on terms pursuant to which the record club or similar operation does not receive payment.

Clause 9.5   The Company may in some circumstances require the bank at which the production account is maintained to confirm to it in writing that it will not apply sums held in the production account towards satisfaction of debts owed by the Producer to the bank.

Clause 11.1   The royalty is payable subject to full and timely performance and observance by the Producer. The clause permits the establishment of two different royalty rates, one applying in the United Kingdom and the other outside the United Kingdom. For an explanation of royalty provisions reference should be made to paragraph 19.31.

Clause 11.2   The royalty reduction here is analogous to the reduction prevailing in the record business.

11.3   In respect of Disks distributed or licensed to third parties in connection with any promotional or advertising operation or for so-called "premium" use the Producer shall be entitled to Royalties of [   ]% of all net sums actually received by the Company from third parties in respect of such exploitation in lieu of any other payment.

11.4   In respect of Disks sold to libraries or educational institutions or to the armed forces the Royalty Rate shall be 50% of the rate otherwise applicable.

11.5   In respect of Disks which are promoted by television advertising or which are sold at less than the Company's top line label price the Royalty Rate shall be 50% of the rate otherwise applicable.

11.6   The Royalty payable in respect of sales of Disks to dealers traders wholesalers trading groups or multiple stores or chains at a discount shall be reduced in the same proportion as the discount bears to the usual price to such customers. Without limitation of any of the Company's rights under this Agreement the Company shall have the right to license Disks to other parties on a flat fee basis as opposed to a royalty basis and the Company shall pay to the Producer Royalties of [   ]% of all net sums received by the Company pursuant to any such flat fee arrangement.

11.7   In respect of Disks sold to any club operation the Royalty Base Price shall at the election of the Company be the amount received by the Company or such club operation.

11.8   In respect of Disks incorporating material that is not derived from the CD-I the Royalty Base Price and the Royalty Rate payable to the Producer shall be that proportion of the Royalty Base Price and the Royalty Rate otherwise applicable as shall be computed by a fraction the numerator of which is the total of all material derived from the Master Tapes and the denominator the total of all material contained on such Records.

11.9   No Royalty shall be payable in respect of Disks which are distributed

Clause 11.3   A premium is any item of goods which is available to members of the public free of charge or for a nominal payment.

Clause 11.4   The royalty reduction in this clause is analogous to that prevailing in the recording industry.

Clause 11.5   The royalty reduction in this clause is analogous to that prevailing in the recording industry.

Clause 11.6   This clause has two functions. First it reduces the royalty proportional to any discount given to dealers, traders, wholesalers, trading groups or multiple stores or chains. Second, it substitutes a percentage of any sums received by the Company from sales on a flat fee basis in place of the royalty obligation in Clause 11.1.

Clause 11.7   Clubs are likely to pay the Company on a royalty base price which is less than that specified in this Agreement.

Clause 11.8   Depending on the nature of the multimedia product, it is possible it may be sold or licensed or distributed with other third party products. In such instances provision needs to be made to apportion the royalty. This type of clause is common in the record industry.

to promote or stimulate the sale of Disks or are distributed free as samples or as "cut-outs" discontinued goods or deletions.

11.10 Where the Company's licensees lessees sub-licensees or sub-lessees apply further or greater reductions deductions decreases or negations of any kind to the Royalties or other sums payable to the Company then these shall be applied for the purposes of calculating the Royalties owed to the Producer under this Agreement and under no circumstances shall the Producer be entitled to receive more than [   ]% of the net sums received by the Company by way of royalty in respect of any country or territory.

11.11 Royalties shall not be payable until the Company has itself received payment in sterling in the United Kingdom and foreign currency shall be converted at the same rate of exchange as the Company was paid in.

11.12 In calculating the number of Net Sales of Disks sold under this Agreement the Company shall have the right to deduct returns credits and exchanges of any kind arising in the course of business and shall have the right to make reserves for the same from the Royalties which reserves shall be determined by the Company in its entire discretion.

11.13 The Company shall have the right to recoup the Cost of Production from all Royalties payable to the Producer.

11.14 The Royalties payable to the Producer are inclusive of all royalties or other payments to any individual rendering services or providing rights in respect of the CD-I and the Producer irrevocably authorises and directs the Company to make such payments on behalf of the Producer and to deduct and apply to any such producer or other person all sums which may become payable from the Royalties payable to the Producer under this Agreement.

12. ROYALTY ACCOUNTING

12.1 The Company will render to the Producer within 90 days after 30 June and 31 December in each year any positive statement of account relating to the preceding six-month period indicating all Royalties due to the Producer in accordance with the provisions of this Agreement and each statement shall be accompanied by the payment of the amount indicated by such statement to be owing.

12.2 The first of the accounting statements shall be rendered at the end of

---

Clause 11.10 This provision offers essential protection to the Company in circumstances where the Company licences the product to a third party whose royalty calculation provisions are different from those operated by the Company. In such circumstances a mis-match would occur giving rise to additional liability on the part of the Company.

Clause 11.12 Items of product which are returned as faulty or supplied in error are normally deducted from total sales figures. Where goods are provided on a sale or return basis, the right to make a reserve against subsequent returns is commonplace.

Clause 11.13 This clause provides that the Company will have the right to recover a sum equal to the cost of production from all royalties payable to the Producer. This type of clause is frequently found in entertainment contracts. Whether it is appropriate or not will depend on all the circumstances.

Clause 11.14 The Company will normally wish to provide that it is obliged to pay one person only. This clause makes it clear that the Producer is responsible for making all payments owed to third parties.

the first full period immediately following the first release of Disks and shall be deemed to be binding on the parties to this Agreement unless the Producer shall within 90 days from receipt of any statement request that it be certified by the auditors of the Company. Such certification shall be at the cost and expense of the Producer and shall be final and binding on the parties to this Agreement.

12.3   If the Company shall not have paid any Royalties to the Producer or shall have incorrectly calculated the amount due the Producer shall give notice in writing to the Company of this omission or error and the Company shall have a further 30 days following the receipt of such notice during which period the Company shall not be deemed to be in default of its obligations under this Agreement if the Company shall make payment of the Royalties due or make good any incorrect payment without interest.

12.4   The Producer expressly authorises the Company to deduct and withhold from all sums due to the Producer under this Agreement any sums which may be deductible in accordance with local laws or regulations from time to time.

13.   DETERMINATION

It shall constitute the repudiation by the Producer of its obligations under the Agreement and the Company shall be entitled to accept such repudiation determining the Company's obligations and Producer's rights under the Agreement by written notice if:

13.1   the Producer is in breach of any material term of the Agreement which is incapable of remedy or if capable of remedy is not remedied within 7 days of receipt by the Producer of notice in writing from the Company;

13.2   any of the Producer's representations in relation to the Agreement shall prove to have been incorrect when made or become materially incorrect if such representations would not have been made by any reasonable Producer with the same knowledge at that time;

13.3   the Producer transfers disposes of or threatens to transfer or dispose of any part of its assets which is likely in the reasonable opinion of the Company to prevent or materially to inhibit the performance by the Producer of its obligations under the Agreement;

13.4   any indebtedness guarantee or similar obligation of the Producer

---

Clause 13   The significance of repudiation and termination is examined in paragraphs 14.2 to 14.5.

Clause 13.1   This clause permits the Producer to remedy certain breaches of the Agreement.

Clause 13.2   There may be circumstances where the Company enters into an agreement on the basis of representations or statements made by the Producer. If these prove subsequently to be incorrect this provision permits the Company to terminate. A brief statement of the law relating to misrepresentation may be found in paragraphs 2.17 and 2.18.

Clause 13.3   This provision permits the Company to terminate the agreement if the Producer finds itself in straitened circumstances and disposes or attempts to dispose of a substantial part of its assets. In such circumstances the Company might find itself disadvantaged in having contracted with an entity of significantly lower financial standing than it would otherwise have been prepared to do.

or of any guarantor of the Producer becomes due or capable of being declared due before its stated maturity or is not discharged at maturity or the Producer or any guarantor of the Producer defaults under or commits a breach of the provisions of any guarantee or other obligation (whether actual or contingent) of any agreement pursuant to which any such indebtedness guarantee obligation or other obligation was incurred all or any of which shall in the reasonable opinion of the Company materially affect its rights and entitlements under the Agreement;

13.5   the Producer is declared or becomes insolvent;

13.6   the Producer convenes a meeting of its creditors or proposes or makes any arrangement or composition with or any assignation for the benefit of its creditors or a petition is presented or a meeting is convened for the purpose of considering a resolution or other steps are taken for the winding up of the Producer (save for the purpose of and followed by a voluntary reconstruction or amalgamation previously approved in writing by the Company) or if an incumbrancer takes possession of or a trustee receiver administrator administrative receiver liquidator or similar officer is appointed in respect of all or any part of its business or assets or any distress execution or other legal process is levied threatened enforced upon or sued out against any of such assets;

13.7   control as defined in the Insolvency Act 1986 Section 435(10) of the Producer shall change without the prior approval of the Company;

13.8   an Event of Force Majeure shall have occurred and shall have continued for such duration as would in the reasonable opinion of the Company determined after consultation with the Producer materially interfere with the production of the CD-I.

14.   <u>TAKEOVER</u>

The Company shall have the right to take over and complete the making of the CD-I without prejudice to any of the Company's rights against the Producer and exercise the Company's rights of takeover set out in Clause 15 by giving notice in writing to the Producer at any time after the occurrence of any of the following events:

14.1   the Company believes in good faith after consultation with the Producer but in the Company's sole discretion that the actual Cost of Production

---

Clause 13.4   Default or breach under any other guarantee or other agreement constitutes an event of default under this Agreement.

Clause 13.6   The commencement of winding up proceedings or the enforcement of any judgment against the Producer constitute events of default.

Clause 13.7   The Company may wish to terminate its Agreement if a competitor acquires control of the Producer by buying its shares.

Clause 13.8   A brief statement of law relating to force majeure may be found at paragraph 2.20. The definition of such a term in any agreement should always be examined closely.

Clause 14   This clause sets out the circumstances in which the Company can take over production of the multimedia product without actually terminating the Agreement.

of the CD-I is likely to exceed the Budget or the progress of production of the CD-I is likely to fall materially behind the Production Schedule;

14.2   the total of the expenditure and liabilities incurred in connection with the production of the CD-I at any time exceeds 110% of the budgeted cost (as specified in the Budget excluding the Production Fee) for the stage of production at which the CD-I then is or the production of the CD-I falls materially behind the Production Schedule;

14.3   the Producer fails to carry out any reasonable instructions given by the Company or its Production Representative;

14.4   an Event of Force Majeure occurs and has continued for 14 days either consecutive or in the aggregate or in the reasonable opinion of the Company is likely to continue for such period;

14.5   an Event of Default occurs or in the reasonable opinion of the Company is likely to occur.

15.   CONSEQUENCES OF TAKEOVER

15.1   Without prejudice to the legal rights of the parties (other than any which conflict with the following provisions) the consequences of the exercise by the Company of its rights of takeover shall be:

(a)   any sums held by the Producer for the purposes of the Agreement as at determination shall be repaid by the Producer to the Company on demand and the Producer shall supply to the Company forthwith a detailed statement of income and expenditure up to the date of takeover, with full details of all unpaid debts, and all outstanding commitments for which no invoices have been received;

(b)   all parts of the CD-I which have been completed and all documents and film and sound recordings props plant machinery and other physical material of whatever nature acquired or created by the Producer in relation to the CD-I up to the date of takeover shall be delivered by the Producer to the nominee of the Company on the Company's demand;

(c)   the Company or its nominee shall have the right to take over and complete the making of the CD-I and for that purpose to use all physical properties facilities supplies equipment documents and materials relating to the CD-I and in such event:

(d)   the Company or its nominee shall have the right to assume supervision and control of the making of the CD-I and/or to appoint and contract with any third party to complete the production of the CD-I;

(e)   the Company or any person it nominates shall be and is irrevocably appointed the agent of the Producer with absolute discretion and with power and on behalf of the Producer to exercise or assign any right of the Producer (whether under any contract or otherwise) which is relevant to the making of the CD-I;

(f)   upon request the Producer shall execute a formal assignment in favour of the Company or its nominee in respect of the benefit of any agreements made by the Producer and relevant to the making of the CD-I;

(g)   the Producer agrees to indemnify the Company against liability arising from any fraudulent or negligent act or omission by the Producer in the exercise of the Producer's rights.

15.2   In the event of determination following a breach by the Producer if the total cost of completing the CD-I in accordance with this Agreement is increased the additional cost shall be paid by the Producer to the Company either by deduction from any money payable by the Company to the Producer or as an ordinary debt payable on demand provided nothing contained in this Clause shall make the Producer liable to pay for any element in the Cost of Production of any CD-I if the cost of such element is excessive and such cost was incurred unreasonably by the Company or its nominee.

15.3   Unless otherwise provided termination of this Agreement shall be without prejudice to the grants of rights and the warranties and undertakings given by either party and all other obligations and indemnities that have arisen or been given prior to termination all of which shall continue in full force and effect after termination notwithstanding that termination has taken place.

16.   DEFINITIONS AND GENERAL INTERPRETATION

16.1   The following words and phrases shall have the following meanings:

"PPL"
Phonographic Performance Limited.

"PRS"
Performing Right Society Limited.

"Associate"
In relation to the Producer any associated company or person within the meaning of the Income and Corporation Taxes Act 1988 Section 416 or 417.

"Budget"
The Budget for the production of the CD-I which has been approved by the Company and which is annexed as Exhibit 1.

"Cashflow Schedule"
The cashflow schedule annexed to the Budget.

"CD-I"
One fully edited software multimedia program designed to permit the inter-

---

Clause 15   The provisions of this clause specify what is to happen after the exercise by the Company of its Takeover rights.

active multimedia presentation of the [Work or Outline] in digital stereo sound with [*specify*] colour [full motion] video comprising text graphics and animated sequences which CD-I shall be based upon the [Work or Outline] and shall be tentatively entitled "[*name*]".

"Contingency Items"

Possible adverse eventualities identified in the Budget including without limitation and by way of example only bad weather ill health and unplanned travel.

"Contingency Funds"

Money identified in the Budget as intended for use only in relation to Contingency Items.

"Cost of Production"

The total direct and indirect cost of the pre-production production post-production and delivery of the CD-I including without limitation the cost of all development work and the acquisition of all underlying rights.

"Delivery"

Delivery by the Producer of the CD-I in accordance with the provisions of this Agreement.

"Delivery Date"

[*Specify*].

"Delivery Material"

The material referred to in Exhibit 2.

"Disc"

Any compact disc interactive carrier manufactured by the Company or its licensees which is derived from the CD-I.

"Essential Elements"

[*Specify director editor producer artists performers scriptwriter or other*].

"Event of Default"

Any of the events specified in Clause 13.

"Event of Force Majeure"

Any act or event which is beyond the control of the Producer or the Company which interferes or in the opinion of the Company is likely to interfere with production of any CD-I.

"Maximum Share of Surplus"

Such maximum share of Surplus Funds designated by the Company pursuant to Clause 8.5.

"Net Sales"

100% of all Disks which have been sold and for which the Company has received payment less returns and credits of whatever nature.

"Outline"

[*Specify*].

688

"Packaging Deduction"
[*Specify*]% of the Retail Price.

"Production Account"
A separate bank account in the joint names of the Company and the Producer
established under a mandate which stipulates that all sums paid into the
account shall be held on trust for the Company.

Production Contracts"
Any and all agreements entered into by the Producer in relation to any of the
Essential Elements the Studio or in any other respect whatever in connection
with the CD-I.

"Production Fee"
The sum of £[*amount*] as specified in and payable out of the Budget in
accordance with the Cashflow Schedule.

"Production Personnel"
All principal artists and all personnel who render services or supply goods
facilities or finance in respect of the CD-I or the Delivery Material.

"Production Representative"
Such person or persons in relation to any CD-I as may be appointed by the
Company.

"Production Schedule"
The Schedule for the production of the CD-I which has been approved by the
Company and is annexed as Exhibit 3.

"Relevant Union Agreements"
Any union agreement which may be relevant to the production of any CD-I.

"Retail Price"
The retail selling price from time to time recommended by the Company for
Discs in any part of the world.

"Royalty Base Price"
The Retail Price after the deduction of the Packaging Deductions and all
Value Added Tax and similar taxes.

"Royalties"
All sums payable to the Producer pursuant to Clause 11.

"Royalty Rate"
The relevant Royalty Rate referred to and computed in accordance with
provisions of Clause 11.

"Services"
The services of the Producer and the personnel specified in the Production
Contracts to produce the CD-I.

"Studios"
[*Specify*].

"Surplus Funds"
Any underspend in relation to the Budget as provided in Clause 8.4.

"Technical Specifications"
The CD-I Standard Specifications agreed by NV Philips Gloeilampenfabrie-ken in co-operation with Sony Corporation of Japan as amended from time to time and the technical specifications of the Company annexed as Exhibit 4 as amended from time to time.

"Third Party Material"
Any and all material incorporated or proposed to be incorporated in the CD-I in respect of which any rights of copyright or any other rights of whatever nature are vested in or controlled by third parties.

"Underspend Guidelines"
The Guidelines annexed as Exhibit 5 for determining the amount of Surplus Funds, if any, to be remitted to the Producer.

"Work"
[*Specify*].

16.2   Any reference in the Agreement to any statute or statutory provision shall be construed as including a reference to that statute or statutory provision as from time to time amended modified extended or re-enacted whether before or after the date of the Agreement and to all statutory instruments orders and regulations for the time being made pursuant to it or deriving validity from it.

16.3   Unless the context otherwise requires words denoting the singular shall include the plural and vice versa.

16.4   The word "copyright" means the entire copyright and design right subsisting under the laws of the United Kingdom and all analogous rights subsisting under the laws of each and every jurisdiction throughout the world.

16.5   The word "CD-I" shall be deemed to include any and all literary dramatic musical and/or artistic works audio-visual material and sound recordings included in the soundtrack of the CD-I.

16.6   Unless otherwise stated time shall be of the essence for the purpose of the performance of the Producer's obligations under this Agreement.

Clause 16.1 The definitions contained in this Clause will need review in order to fit the appropriate circumstances.

16.7   Unless otherwise stated references to clauses sub-clauses sub-paragraphs schedules annexures and exhibits relate to this Agreement.

17.   GENERAL

17.1   Notice

(a)   Any notice or other document required to be given under this Agreement or any communication between the parties with respect to any of the provisions of the Agreement shall be in writing in English and be deemed duly given if signed by or on behalf of a duly authorised officer of the party giving the notice and if left at or sent by pre-paid registered or recorded delivery post or by telex telegram cable facsimile transmission or other means of telecommunication in permanent written form to the address of the party receiving such notice as set out at the head of the Agreement or as notified between the parties for the purpose of this Clause.

(b)   Any such notice or other communication shall be deemed to be given to and received by the addressee:

at the time the same is left at the address of or handed to a representative of the party to be served;

by post on the day not being a Sunday or Public Holiday in England and Scotland two days following the date of posting;

in the case of a telex telegram cable facsimile transmission or other means of telecommunication on the next following day.

(c)   In proving the giving of a notice it should be sufficient to prove that the notice was left or that the envelope containing the notice was properly addressed and posted or that the applicable means of telecommunication was addressed and despatched and despatch of the transmission was confirmed and/or acknowledged as the case may be.

(d)   Communications addressed to the Company shall be marked for the attention of [*specify*] with a copy to [*specify*].

17.2   Severability

If any provision of the Agreement shall be prohibited by or adjudged by a Court to be unlawful void or unenforceable such provision shall to the extent required be severed from the Agreement and rendered ineffective as far as possible without modifying the remaining provisions of the Agreement and shall not in any way affect any other circumstances or the validity or enforcement of the Agreement.

Clause 17   A number of clauses in this Agreement specify rights which are capable of being exercised and a notice provision is therefore necessary.

Clause 17.2   For an explanation as to the law relating to severance see paragraph 2.22.

691

17.3 Force Majeure

Neither party shall be liable to the other for any failure to perform any obligation pursuant to the Agreement which arises as a result of the occurrence of an Event of Force Majeure and neither party shall incur any liability for any expenses or losses direct or consequential or otherwise which may be suffered by the other party as a result of the occurrence of such event of Force Majeure.

17.4 Entire Agreement

The Agreement contains the full and complete understanding between the parties and supersedes all prior arrangements and understandings whether written or oral appertaining to the subject matter of the Agreement and may not be varied except by an instrument in writing signed by all the parties to the Agreement.

17.5 Waiver

No failure or delay on the part of any of the parties to the Agreement relating to the exercise of any right power privilege or remedy provided under the Agreement shall operate as a waiver of such right power privilege or remedy or as a waiver of any preceding or succeeding breach by the other party to the Agreement nor shall any single or partial exercise of any right power privilege or remedy preclude any other or further exercise of such or any other right power privilege or remedy provided in the Agreement all of which are several and cumulative and are not exclusive of each other or of any other rights or remedies otherwise available to a party at law.

17.6 No Partnership

The Agreement shall not be deemed to constitute a partnership or joint venture or contract of employment between the parties.

17.7 Governing Law

The Agreement shall be governed by and construed in accordance with the laws of England and Wales whose courts shall be courts of competent jurisdiction.

Clause 17.3 For an explanation as to the law relating to force majeure see paragraph 2.20.

Clause 17.4 There are occasions where oral agreements or other understandings may be created in relation to a Work which may contain either additional obligations or obligations which conflict with those set out in subsequent written agreement. This provision makes it clear that all previous arrangements and understandings are at an end and the contract is the only document relevant to the obligations and rights of the parties in relation to its subject matter. The final part of the clause expressly excludes the possibility of any liability on the part of the Company for misrepresentation on the part of any of its servants, agents, employees or representatives.

Clause 17.6 Under English law if two parties carry on business in common with a view to profit and share profit, the arrangement is capable of being considered a partnership. This provision ensures that no partnership is created inadvertently, and also expressly excludes the possibility of an employment contract being created.

Clause 17.7 Where a contract is made between two entities in England and Wales, it will generally not be necessary to insert a provision of this nature, but where a contract is to be created with a foreign company (or a company situate in Scotland or Northern Ireland) this provision should always be included.

[Certificate of Value]

SIGNED by [   ] }
for and on behalf of
[*The Producer*]
in the presence of:

SIGNED by [   ] }
for and on behalf of
[*The Company*]
in the presence of:

Certificate of Value Although it had been intended to abolish stamp duty on assignments of intellectual property at the same time as the introduction of paperless share transfer, the failure of the Stock Exchange system TAURUS has delayed the abolition of stamp duty which is still technically payable in relation to assignments of copyright. The publishing industry has, traditionally, never made provision for the payment of stamp duty in assignments of copyright and for this reason no provision is included in this document – although there are now many circumstances where it is advisable. A suitable form of wording may, however, be found in Document 6 (d) and a summary of the current legislation relating to stamp duty may be found in paragraph 11.29.

Attestation Clause and Testimonium Clause: See corresponding annotations in Document 4 and also the annotation against clause 2.7 of Document 44.

EXHIBIT 1
Budget and Cashflow Schedule

EXHIBIT 2
Delivery Material

EXHIBIT 3
Production Schedule

EXHIBIT 4
Technical Specifications

EXHIBIT 5

Underspend Guidelines

In determining the amount of Surplus Funds to be remitted to the Producer pursuant to Clause 8.4, the following criteria shall be applied:

1.   Contingency Funds shall if unused be retained as to 100% by the Company.

2.   Any surplus in the general Budget shall be applied towards any necessary expenditure on Contingency Items before the use of Contingency Funds.

3.   Where any Production Contract is identified in the Budget as providing for remuneration at rates applicable in any Relevant Union Agreement, any underspend arising as a result of the payment of lesser remuneration shall be retained as to 100% by the Company.

4.   Underspend arising from any or all of the following shall be retained as to 100% by the Company:

(a)   reduction in agreed numbers of Production Personnel;

(b)   over-estimates in respect of taxation or National Insurance;

(c)   non-use of particular items specified in the Budget;

(d)   substantial reduction in the Production Schedule;

(e)   alterations substitution amendment or subtraction of any of the Essential Elements.

DOCUMENT 45

Licence for multimedia work

[IMPORTANT NOTE: Please read the section "About this book" on page v, before copying or using this Document]

Purpose of this Document

This is a form of agreement suitable for use by the owner of a multimedia work to license the multimedia work to a third party. The document is drafted from the point of view of the rights owner and might usefully be contrasted with the provisions of Document 46 which licenses the right to develop and exploit a multimedia work rather than a pre-existing multimedia work.

Relevant text

The text of this Work covers a number of topics which are relevant to documents of this nature including:

- licensing distribution and joint ventures (paragraphs 19.42 to 19.44)
- development and production of multimedia works (paragraphs 19.31 to 19.41)
- what is multimedia? (paragraphs 19.2 and 19.3)
- consents and permissions required for multimedia works (paragraphs 19.4 to 19.13)
- music in multimedia (paragraphs 19.14 to 19.20)
- collective licensing schemes (paragraphs 19.21 to 19.24)
- databases and computers (paragraphs 19.45 to 19.52)
- software publishing and video publishing (paragraphs 19.53 to 19.55)
- buying and selling rights (paragraphs 11.2 to 11.9)
- remuneration provisions in rights agreements (paragraphs 11.22 to 11.26)
- taxation (paragraphs 11.27 to 11.29 and 12.22 to 12.30)
- commercial terms of offers (paragraphs 1.22 and 1.23)
- the law of contract and agency (paragraphs 2.1 to 2.30)
- creation, existence and transfer of copyrights (paragraphs 3.1 to 3.45)
- international copyright protection (paragraphs 4.1 to 4.17)
- moral rights (paragraphs 5.1 to 5.22)
- permissions, fair dealing and rights clearances (paragraphs 8.1 to 8.44)
- liability for content (paragraphs 9.1 to 9.49)
- buying and selling rights (paragraphs 11.1 to 11.29)
- infringement and enforcement (paragraphs 13.1 to 13.17)
- termination and recapture (paragraphs 14.1 to 14.10)
- competition law (paragraphs 16.1 to 16.28)

THIS AGREEMENT is made the   day of
BETWEEN:

(1) [*Name*] LIMITED (registered number [*number*]) whose [registered office] [principal place of business] is at [*address*] acting as the agent of [*name*] of [*address*] ("Proprietor") and

(2) [*Name*] LIMITED (registered number [*number*]) whose [registered office] [principal place of business] is at [*address*] ("Licensee" which expression shall include all Associates and other persons deriving title through or from the Licensee with the prior written consent of the Proprietor)

IT IS AGREED as follows:

1.   GRANT OF RIGHTS

1.1   In consideration of the obligations warranties and undertakings of the Licensee in this Agreement and subject to and conditional upon their full and timely performance and observance the Proprietor grants to the Licensee the exclusive licence to exploit the Rights in the Work throughout [*specify territory*] ("Territory") for the period of [*specify*] years from the date of this Agreement ("Term").

1.2   The Proprietor undertakes to deliver to the Licensee within [*specify*] days from the date of this Agreement the following delivery materials ("Delivery Materials") [*specify materials required*] in respect of the Work and grants the Licensee the non-exclusive right in the Territory during the Term to use such Delivery Materials.

1.3   The Rights granted to the Licensee under this Agreement expressly exclude the right to hire or rent Disks to members of the public and expressly exclude the right to make the Work available to any third party by any electronic delivery service or by any other means of data transmission. All other rights in relation to the Work with the excepton of those expressly licensed to the Licensee pursuant to Clause 1.1 are reserved to the Proprietor absolutely.

2.   PROPRIETOR'S WARRANTIES

The Proprietor warrants agrees and undertakes with the Licensee that:

2.1   the Proprietor is free to enter into this Agreement and grant the Licensee the rights granted in it and is not under any disability restriction or prohibition which might prevent the Proprietor from performing or observing any of the Proprietor's obligations under this Agreement;

Clause 1.1   Relevant details need to be inserted. It will be noted that the grant of rights is conditional upon full and timely performance by the Licensee of its obligations under the Agreement.

Clause 1.2   This provision expressly excludes the right of the Licensee to rent or hire Disks. A rental right exists in relation to sound recordings, films and computer programs (see paragraph 3.10) and an audio visual multimedia work falls into all three categories.

Clause 2.1   The Licensee is entitled to a three-month non-exclusive sell-off period (see paragraphs 12.4 and 11.11).

2.2   the Proprietor has not entered into and shall not enter into any arrangement which may conflict with this Agreement;

2.3   to the best of the Proprietor's knowledge the Work is not obscene or defamatory of any person and does not infringe any copyright;

2.4   following the expiry of the Term by effluxion of time the Licensee shall have the non-exclusive right subject to the terms and conditions of this Agreement for the further period of three calendar months to sell off Disks previously manufactured by the Licensee during the Term;

2.5   the Proprietor confirms that the Licensee shall be free to market the Disks at whatever price the Licensee elects.

3.   REMUNERATION

3.1   The Licensee agrees to pay or procure the payment to all relevant third parties in a timely manner all Copyright Liabilities notified by the Proprietor relating to the manufacture and exploitation of the Disks and undertakes to pay to the Proprietor:

(a)   the advance of [*specify*] ("Advance") on signature of this Agreement;

(b)   the Royalty on each Accounting Date in accordance with the provisions of this Agreement;

(c)   such costs in respect of the manufacture and delivery to the Licensee of the Delivery Materials as may be notified by the Proprietor in writing.

3.2   The Licensee shall not have the right to withhold any part of sums due to the Proprietor as a reserve against returns and/or credits and in the event that the Licensee is required by law to make any withholding from sums to be remitted to the Proprietor the Licensee shall prior to the making of any withholding of payment furnish the Proprietor with evidence satisfactory to the Proprietor in its entire discretion as to the Licensee's obligation to make such withholding of payment.

Clause 2.2   The warranty is given to the best of the Proprietor's belief. In other words it is not an absolute warranty that the Work is not obscene or defamatory etc.

Clause 2.5   Although in the case of books it is currently possible to specify a minimum resale price (see paragraph 16.4) it is not possible for a similar provision to apply in relation to multimedia works (see paragraph 16.3). Although the Agreement requires the Licensee to pay to the Proprietor a minimum royalty this provision clarifies the fact that the Licensee is free to sell the Disks at whatever price the Licensee considers appropriate.

Clause 3.1   The obligation to pay permission fees etc is passed on to the Licensee. The Advance is not expressed to be recoupable from the royalties. The Licensee is required to pay the costs of provision of Delivery Material and there is no provision permitting the Licensee to recover such costs from the Royalty.

Clause 3.2   This provision prevents the Licensee from deducting parts of the royalty payments to hold as reserves against returned Disks. If the Licensee is required by law to deduct withholding taxes on royalty payments it is required to produce documentary evidence satisfactory to the Proprietor of its liability.

3.3   If exchange control or other restrictions prevent or threaten to prevent the remittance to the Proprietor of any money payable under this Agreement the Licensee shall immediately advise the Proprietor in writing and follow the Proprietor's instructions in respect of the money to be remitted including if required depositing the same with any bank or other person designated by the Proprietor at such location as may be designated by the Proprietor.

3.4   If any withholding or other taxes are required to be deducted from any money provided to be remitted to the Proprietor pursuant to this Agreement it shall be the responsibility of the Licensee to ensure that no improper deductions are made and that the Proprietor is provided with all necessary receipts certificates and other documents and all information required in order to avail the Proprietor of any tax credit or other fiscal advantage and the Licensee undertakes to account to the Proprietor in relation to any tax credit or saving received by the Licensee in relation to royalty payments to the Proprietor.

4.   LICENSEE'S UNDERTAKINGS

The Licensee warrants undertakes confirms and agrees with the Proprietor:

4.1   all rights and title in and to the Work are expressly reserved to the Proprietor subject to the licence in Clause 1.1;

4.2   the Licensee shall market the Disks incorporating the Work at the Licensee's sole cost and expense by no later than [*specify date*] and shall deliver to the Proprietor not less than [*specify*] copies of each separate Disk format in which the Work is marketed on first publication or distribution;

4.3   the Licensee shall not by any act or omission impair or prejudice the copyright in the Work or violate any moral right or deal with the Work so that any third party might obtain any lien or other right of whatever nature incompatible with the rights of the Proprietor and the Licensee shall ensure that all copies of the Work and artwork published and distributed by the Licensee contain full and accurate copyright notices credit attributions and acknowledgments;

4.4   The Licensee shall by no later than the date specified in Clause 4.2 or the

---

Clause 3.3   This provision protects the Proprietor if exchange control restrictions are imposed in any territory and permits the Proprietor to receive income in that territory.

Clause 3.4   This clause not only requires the Licensee to provide the Proprietor with all necessary receipts and information but also provides that the Licensee is to bring into account any tax credits or savings achieved by the Licensee which are attributable to royalty payments under the agreement.

Claues 4.1   This clause clarifies that the copyright remains vested in the Proprietor subject only to the licence granted to the Licensee.

Clause 4.2   This provision gives the Proprietor the opportunity of determining the particulars which are to be contained in the statement of account. Each statement must be accompanied by payment of sums shown to be owing without deduction of any reserves. This provision acknowledges that it is possible that the Licensee might market the Disks in a number of separate formats and provides for the Proprietor to receive a copy of each of these formats.

determination of the Term if sooner at the Licensee's cost and expense return to the Proprietor the Delivery Material and all other material supplied by the Proprietor in the same condition as when supplied to the Licensee;

4.5 the Licensee shall not create any promotional material or artwork relating to the Work without the prior written consent of the Proprietor and in respect of any material commissioned or manufactured by the Licensee the copyright shall be secured in the name of the Proprietor and title to all physical material shall belong to and be dealt with as if such physical material had been supplied by the Proprietor and the Proprietor shall at all times have unrestricted access to the same for the purposes of the Proprietor;

4.6 the Licensee shall give full particulars to the Proprietor as soon as the Licensee becomes aware of any actual or threatened claim by any third party in connection with the Work;

4.7 the Licensee shall punctually pay to the Proprietor all sums owing to the Proprietor under this Agreement;

4.8 the Licensee shall not assign charge license sub-license or otherwise part with possession of the benefit or burden of this Agreement without the prior written consent of the Proprietor;

4.9 the Licensee shall release the Disks throughout the Territory on the dates specified in Clause 4.2 and shall maintain the Disks in distribution in the Territory throughout the Term;

4.10 the Licensee shall submit the Disks to every competent authority to which it is required to be submitted for censorship certification or other purposes and shall comply with all rules regulations and other formalities relating to the same in each country of the Territory prior to the exercise of the rights granted to the Licensee under this Agreement;

4.11 the Licensee shall prior to any exercise of the rights granted under this Agreement make all necessary returns and pay all Copyright Liabilities

---

Clause 4.5 The Proprietor will in many circumstances wish to control the nature and type of publicity and advertising material. There are occasions where material produced by the Proprietor's Licensee may be of value to the Proprietor since it can be used by licensees in other territories. This provision passes all rights of copyright and other rights in such material to the Proprietor in order to permit the Proprietor to provide the benefit of this material to its other licensees.

Clause 4.6 If there is any claim in relation to copyright infringement, or invasion of privacy, or any other matter in relation to the Work, it is in the Publisher's interests to be apprised of such claim at the earliest possible moment.

Clause 4.7 In circumstances where the Agreement does not contain a provision making time of the essence (such as that contained in clause 8.6), this provision requires the Licensee to make payments in a punctual manner.

Clause 4.8 Generally licences are considered to be personal, but there are some circumstances in which a licence may be sub-licensed. This provision expressly precludes the Licensee from entering into sub-licences or assigning the benefit of the Agreement.

Clause 4.9 Although some multimedia works are currently not required to be submitted for classification (see paragraph 19.54 and 19.55), it is possible that there are obligations which apply in other territories.

notified by the Proprietor required to exploit the rights granted under this Agreement;

4.12 the Licensee shall not permit the Work to be coupled or compiled on any Disk with any other multimedia work and shall not permit the Disks to be sold as part of a package with any other disks incorporating any other works or with any other material of any description;

4.13 the Licensee shall advertise the Disks throughout the Territory in the same manner as other disks advertised by the Licensee in the Territory and not remove any details or credits from the Work or add any trade mark other than the Licensee's and such other trade mark as may be permitted by the Proprietor;

4.14 the Licensee shall exploit the rights granted to the Licensee to the best of the Licensee's skill and ability with the utmost despatch and ensure the highest possible Royalties payable to the Proprietor and ensure that the Disks are given fair and equitable treatment and not discriminated in favour of any other multimedia works which the Licensee may publish or distribute in the Territory;

4.15 the Licensee shall at the end of the three-month sell-off period referred to in Clause 2.4 at the discretion of the Proprietor permit the Proprietor to purchase from the Licensee all Disks in the possession of or under the control of the Licensee which are then unsold at a unit cost equal to the actual cost of manufacture of the Licensee or if the Proprietor shall direct the Licensee shall procure their destruction and provide certificates and affidavits of destruction in such form as may be satisfactory to the Proprietor;

4.16 the Licensee shall indemnify and keep fully indemnified the Proprietor from and against all actions proceedings claims demands costs (including without prejudice to the generality of this provision the legal costs of the Proprietor on a solicitor and own client basis) awards and damages arising directly or indirectly as a result of any breach or non-performance by the Licensee of any of the Licensee's undertakings warranties or obligations under this Agreement.

Clause 4.11 The manufacture and distribution of multimedia works is likely to involve use of music and other elements in which third parties may control rights and the cost for using such copyright elements should be borne by the Licensee (see paragraphs 19.4 to 19.24).

Clause 4.12 This provision protects the Proprietor from the Disks being made available in compilation format with other disks or from being packaged and sold with other works which the Proprietor might not wish to be associated with.

Clause 4.13 This provision ensures that the Disks are given the same degree of prominence as that given by the Licensee to the Licensee's other product and prevents the addition of imprints or trade marks other than those of the Proprietor and the Licensee. The clause also specifically prohibits the Licensee from making any alteration or adaptation to the Disks or omitting any of the credits or acknowledgments.

Clause 4.14 The Licensee is required to exploit the rights in a manner consistent with achieving the highest royalties and to ensure that the Disks are not discriminated against in favour of other disks in which the Licensee may have an interest.

Clause 4.15 This provision permits the Proprietor to eliminate or purchase the Licensee's unsold stock at the end of the Term.

Clause 4.16 An explanation of the significance of warranties and indemnities may be found in paragraph 7.15.

5. ROYALTY ACCOUNTING

5.1   The Licensee shall on each Accounting Date render to the Proprietor a full and complete statement showing all moneys owing to the Proprietor in respect of the preceding Accounting Period.

5.2   The statement of account in Clause 5.1 shall be in such form as the Proprietor shall require and shall contain full details of all Disks sold and each such statement shall be accompanied by payment of all amounts owing without reserve.

5.3   Pounds sterling shall be the currency of account and where any sums are received in a currency other than pounds sterling the same shall be converted at the [mid-market rate calculated using the "Financial Times" index on the date of receipt] [best obtainable rate of exchange on the date payment is due].

5.4   Value Added Tax shall be payable by the Licensee to the Proprietor in respect of all payments made to or to the order of the Proprietor pursuant to this Agreement.

5.5   The Licensee shall keep full and proper books of account relating to the exploitation of its rights and the Proprietor or its representative at any time during the Term and for six years afterwards on giving reasonable prior notice shall have the right to inspect and audit and take copies of such books of account during normal business hours. In the event that such audit or inspection reveals any deficiency in money paid to the Proprietor then the Licensee shall immediately pay the same to the Proprietor together with interest from the date first due calculated with monthly rests at a rate of [*percentage*]% above prime or base rate charged by its bankers to the Proprietor from time to time and shall pay all reasonable costs incurred by the Proprietor directly as a result of such inspection.

5.6   The Licensee shall keep confidential and shall not disclose to any third parties (other than professional advisers where necessary) the results of any such inspection or audit or any of the terms of this Agreement or any matters incidental to it or relating to the business of the Proprietor and shall indemnify the Proprietor fully in respect of any breach of its obligations under this Clause 5.6.

Clause 5.1   The Accounting Dates and Accounting Periods are defined in clause 8.1 in accordance with standard industry practice. There may be occasions, however, where it is appropriate to vary these.

Clause 5.2   This provision gives the Proprietor the opportunity of determining the particulars which are to be contained in the statement of account. Each statement must be accompanied by payment of sums shown to be owing without deduction of any reserves.

Clause 5.3   It may or may not be appropriate for pounds sterling to be the currency of account. If the Licensee is situate in a foreign territory, exchange conversion provisions may be required.

Clause 5.4   It will be necessary to adjust this provision in the light of prevailing law. A short explanation of current Value Added Tax legislation may be found in paragraph 11.28 and paragraphs 12.22 to 12.30.

Clause 5.5   There may be occasions when a company will wish to inspect and audit the books of account of the Licensee. Even if such audit rights are not exercised, an audit provision should always be included in licence agreements.

6.   DETERMINATION

It shall constitute the repudiation by the Licensee of its obligations under this Agreement and at any time the Proprietor may serve written notice on the Licensee accepting such repudiation and determining the Term and the Licensee's rights under this Agreement if:

6.1   the Licensee fails to pay any amount due under this Agreement in full within three days of its due date and such failure is not remedied within seven days of receipt of written notice;

6.2   the Licensee is in breach of any other material term of this Agreement which is incapable of remedy or if capable of remedy is not remedied within fourteen days of the Licensee becoming aware of it;

6.3   any of the Licensee's representations shall prove to have been incorrect when made or become materially incorrect and the Proprietor's rights and entitlements under this Agreement are materially and adversely affected;

6.4   the Licensee transfers disposes of or threatens to transfer or dispose of any part of its assets which is likely in the opinion of the Proprietor to prevent or materially to inhibit the performance by the Licensee of its obligations under this Agreement;

6.5   any indebtedness guarantee or similar obligation of the Licensee or of any guarantor of the Licensee becomes due or capable of being declared due before its stated maturity or is not discharged at maturity or the Licensee or any guarantor of the Licensee defaults under or commits a breach of the provisions of any guarantee or other obligation (whether actual or contingent) of any agreement pursuant to which any such indebtedness guarantee or other obligation was incurred all or any of which shall in the reasonable opinion of the Proprietor materially affect its rights and entitlements under this Agreement;

6.6   the Licensee is declared or becomes insolvent;

Clause 6   For an examination of the legal significance of the term "repudiation" reference should be made to paragraph 14.5 and to paragraphs 14.2 to 14.4.

Clause 6.1   This clause provides the Licensee with the opportunity of remedying a breach. The time period allowed to remedy pecuniary breaches is normally less than that allowed to remedy non-pecuniary breaches.

Clause 6.2   This clause permits the Licensee to remedy a non-pecuniary material breach. The time period allowed is longer than that for a pecuniary breach.

Clause 6.3   There may be circumstances where the publisher has entered into the Agreement on the basis of representations made by the Licensee. This clause permits the Proprietor to terminate the agreement if the representations prove to have been incorrect or subsequently become incorrect.

Clause 6.4   There are occasions where a Licensee becomes less financially secure and disposes of its assets. Where a Proprietor has entered into an agreement in reliance on the Licensee being an entity of substance, such occasions may cause concern to the Proprietor, and this provision permits the Proprietor to terminate the agreement in such instances.

Clause 6.5   Financial default of the Licensee in relation to any guarantee or obligation is a further event normally permitting termination.

Clause 6.6   For the consequences of insolvency, reference should be made to paragraphs 15.2 to 15.4.

6.7 the Licensee convenes a meeting of its creditors or proposes or makes any arrangement or composition with or any assignment for the benefit of its creditors or a petition is presented or a meeting is convened for the purpose of considering a resolution or other steps are taken for the winding up of the Licensee (save for the purpose of and followed by a voluntary reconstruction or amalgamation previously approved in writing by the Proprietor) or if an incumbrancer takes possession of or a trustee administrator administrative receiver liquidator or similar officer is appointed in respect of all or any part of its business or assets or any distress execution or other legal process is levied threatened enforced upon or sued out against any of such assets;

6.8 the Licensee shall cease or abandon or announce that it intends to cease or abandon the business of producing and distributing multimedia works;

6.9 the Disks cease to be distributed or are deleted from the Licensee's catalogue.

7.   NOTICE

7.1 Any notice or other document required to be given under this Agreement or any communication between the parties with respect to any of the provisions of this Agreement shall be in writing in English and be deemed duly given if signed by or on behalf of a duly authorised officer of the party giving the notice and if left at or sent by pre-paid registered or recorded delivery post or by telex telegram cable facsimile transmission or other means of telecommunication in permanent written form to the address of the party receiving such notice as set out at the head of the Agreement or as notified between the parties for the purpose of this Clause.

7.2 Any such notice or other communication shall be deemed to be given to and received by the addressee:

(a)   at the time the same is left at the address of or handed to a representative of the party to be served;

(b)   by post on the day not being a Sunday or Public Holiday two days following the date of posting;

(c)   in the case of a telex telegram cable facsimile transmission or other means of telecommunication on the next following day.

7.3 In proving the giving of a notice it should be sufficient to prove that the

---

Clause 6.7   There may be occasions when a Licensee does not actually become insolvent, but a creditor enforces security over the Licensee's business. This could have serious consequences for a company and this clause protects the Proprietor's interests by providing that such circumstances will entitle the Proprietor to terminate the Agreement.

Clause 6.8   Where a Licensee ceases to carry on business or announces that it intends to cease its business, a Proprietor will wish to recover its rights as soon as possible.

Clause 6.9   Although clause 5.8 imposes a specific obligation on the Licensee to keep the Work in the Licensee's catalogue, this clause permits the Proprietor to terminate if it does not do so.

Clause 7   A number of clauses in the Document provide for a means of exercising rights and a notice provision is therefore necessary.

notice was left or that the envelope containing the notice was properly addressed and posted or that the applicable means of telecommunication was addressed and despatched and despatch of the transmission was confirmed and/or acknowledged as the case may be.

7.4 Communications addressed to the Proprietor shall be marked for the attention of [*name*] with a copy to [*name*] of [*address*].

8. DEFINITIONS AND INTERPRETATION

8.1 The following definitions apply in this Agreement:

"Accounting Date"
45 days from the end of each Accounting Period

"Accounting Period"
successive periods ending on 31 March 30 June 30 September and 31 December in each year

"Associate"
in relation to the Licensee any associate or associated company within the meaning of Section 416 or 417 of the Income and Corporation Taxes Act 1988

"Copyright Liabilities"
All sums arising on or as a result of the manufacture or exploitation of Disks or the Work which may be payable to the owners of any right of copyright performer's right moral right or any right whatever in relation to the Disks or the Work including expressly without limitation any form of synchronisation or mechanical or performance fee or royalty or other payment whatever to performers owners of copyright performer's rights moral rights publishers and other third parties in relation to material included on the Disks

"Disk"
any CD-I CD-ROM compact disk disk cassette [or other physical carrier whether digital optical mechanical or electrical] which contains the Work and does not contain any other literary dramatic musical or artistic material or audio or audio-visual material which has not been expressly approved by the Proprietor in writing

"Retail Price"
the nominal retail selling price from time to time approved or specified by the Licensee for the sale of Disks in the Territory

---

Clause 8.1 The definitions provided in this clause may need to be adjusted to reflect the appropriate relevant circumstances.
  The definition of Rights expressly excludes rental rights (see paragraph 3.10) or making the Work available by electronic transmission.
  The provisions of clauses 3.1 and 4.10 oblige the Licensee to pay Copyright Liabilities. This definition may need to be adjusted to reflect the circumstances.
  The definition of Disk is limited to physical carriers.
  The royalty specifies a minimum sum. Both the Royalty Rate and the Retail Price on which it is based will require adjustment to reflect the particular circumstances.

"Rights"
the sole and exclusive right to manufacture sell and exploit Disks in accordance with the terms of this Agreement but the Rights expressly exclude any right to hire or rent Disks to members of the public and expressly exclude the right to make the Work available to any person by any electronic delivery service or by any other means of electronic or data transmission

"Royalty"
in respect of each Disk sold in the Territory during the Term [*amount*]% of the Retail Price and in any event not less than [*specify*] per Disk sold in the Territory during the Term.

"Work"
[*Specify multimedia work which is licensed*]

8.2   The following terms are defined in this Agreement in the place indicated:

"Advance":	Clause 3.1 (a)
"Delivery Materials":	Clause 1.2
"Term":	Clause 1.1
"Territory":	Clause 1.1

8.3   Unless the context otherwise requires words denoting the singular shall include the plural and vice versa and words denoting any one gender shall include all genders and words denoting persons shall include bodies corporate unincorporated associations and partnerships but successors and assigns shall not be deemed to include licensees.

8.4   The word "copyright" means the entire copyright and design right subsisting under the laws of the United Kingdom and any and all analogous rights subsisting under the laws of each and every jurisdiction throughout the world.

8.5   Unless otherwise stated time shall be of the essence for the purpose of the performance of the Licensee's obligations under this Agreement.

8.6   Unless otherwise stated references to clauses sub-clauses sub-paragraphs schedules annexures and exhibits relate to this Agreement.

9.   MISCELLANEOUS

9.1   Nothing contained in this Agreement shall constitute or shall be construed as constituting a partnership or contract of employment between the parties.

9.2   The Proprietor shall not be liable to the Licensee for failing to supply or

Clause 9.1   Under English law if two parties carry on business in common with a view to profit and share profit, the arrangement is capable of being considered a partnership. This provision ensures that no partnership is created inadvertently and also expressly excludes the possibility of an employment contract being created.

procure the supply of the Delivery Materials and any other material to be supplied under this Agreement due to circumstances beyond its control and it shall not be liable for any expenses or consequential losses of whatever kind suffered by the Licensee.

9.3   The Licensee warrants that it is not the nominee or agent of any undisclosed principal and warrants that it shall assume sole and complete responsibility for the performance of the obligations in this Agreement expressed to be performed by the Licensee.

9.4   This Agreement contains the full and complete understanding between the parties and supersedes all prior arrangements and understandings whether written or oral appertaining to the subject matter of this Agreement and may not be varied except by an instrument in writing signed by all the parties to this Agreement. The Licensee acknowledges that no representations or promises not expressly contained in this Agreement have been made to the Licensee by the Proprietor or any of its servants agents employees members or representatives.

9.5   This Agreement shall be governed and construed in accordance with the laws of England and Wales whose courts shall be courts of competent jurisdiction.

AS WITNESS the hands of the duly authorised representatives of the parties the day month and year first above written

SIGNED by [   ]
for and on behalf of
[*The Proprietor*]

SIGNED by [   ]
for and on behalf of
[*The Licensee*]

Clause 9.2   This provision protects the Proprietor from any claim by the Licensee in relation to failure to supply Delivery Materials, although there are likely to be circumstances in which the Proprietor may incur some liability.

Clause 9.3   This provision protects the Proprietor from the consequences of it contracting with a Licensee which has acted as the agent of an undisclosed company whom the Proprietor may not consider to be a suitable person to be the Proprietor's Licensee.

Clause 9.4   There are occasions where oral agreements or other understandings may be created in relation to a work which may contain either additional obligations or obligations which conflict with those set out in subsequent written agreement. This provision makes it clear that all previous arrangements and understandings are at an end and the contract is the only document relevant to the obligations and rights of the parties in relation to its subject matter. The final part of the clause expressly excludes the possibility of any liability on the part of the Proprietor for misrepresentation on the part of any of its servants, agents, employees or representatives.

Clause 9.5   Where a contract is made between two entities in England and Wales, it will generally not be necessary to insert a provision of this nature, but where a contract is to be created with a foreign company (or a company situate in Scotland or Northern Ireland) this provision should always be included.

DOCUMENT 46

Licence of multimedia rights

[IMPORTANT NOTE: Please read the section "About this book" on page v, before copying or using this Document]

Purpose of this Document

This is a form of agreement suitable for use by a rights owner licensing the right to make a multimedia work which is to be based on an underlying work, the rights in which are owned by the person defined in the document as the proprietor. The Document is drafted from the point of view of the proprietor and might usefully be contrasted with the provisions of Document 31.

Relevant text

The text of this Work covers a number of topics which are relevant to documents of this nature including:

- licensing distribution and joint ventures (paragraphs 19.42 to 19.44)
- development and production of multimedia works (paragraphs 19.31 to 19.41)
- what is multimedia? (paragraphs 19.2 to 19.3)
- consents and permissions required for multimedia works (paragraphs 19.4 to 19.13)
- music in multimedia (paragraphs 19.14 to 19.20)
- collective licensing schemes (paragraphs 19.21 to 19.24)
- databases and computers (paragraphs 19.45 to 19.52)
- software publishing and video publishing (paragraph 19.53 to 19.55)
- buying and selling rights (paragraphs 11.2 to 11.9)
- remuneration provisions in rights agreements (paragraphs 11.22 to 11.26)
- taxation (paragraphs 11.27 to 11.29 and 12.22 to 12.30)
- commercial terms of offers (paragraphs 1.22 and 1.23)
- the law of contract and agency (paragraphs 2.1 to 2.30)
- creation, existence and transfer of copyrights (paragraphs 3.1 to 3.45)
- international copyright protection (paragraphs 4.1 to 4.17)
- moral rights (paragraphs 5.1 to 5.22)
- permissions, fair dealing and rights clearances (paragraphs 8.1 to 8.44)
- liability for content (paragraphs 9.1 to 9.49)
- buying and selling rights (paragraphs 11.1 to 11.29)
- infringement and enforcement (paragraphs 13.1 to 13.17)
- termination and recapture (paragraphs 14.1 to 14.10)
- competition law (paragraphs 16.1 to 16.28)

THIS AGREEMENT is made the   day of

BETWEEN:

(1) *[Name]* LIMITED (registered number *[number]*) whose [registered office] [principal place of business] is at *[address]* acting as the agent of *[name]* of *[address]* ("Proprietor") and

(2) *[Name]* LIMITED (registered number *[number]*) whose [registered office] [principal place of business] is at *[address]* ("Licensee" which expression shall include all Associates sub-licensees and assignees with the prior written consent of the Proprietor deriving title through or from the Licensee)

WHEREAS

(A) The Proprietor is the owner of the entire copyright in the work entitled "*[title]*" ("Underlying Work") written by *[name of author]*.

(B) The Licensee wishes to obtain a licence to develop a multimedia work based on the Underlying Work and the Proprietor wishes to grant a licence to the Licensee upon the following terms.

NOW IT IS AGREED as follows:

1.   GRANT OF RIGHTS

1.1   In consideration of the obligations warranties and undertakings of the Licensee in this Agreement and subject to and conditional upon their full and timely performance and observance the Proprietor grants to the Licensee the exclusive licence to exploit the Rights in the Underlying Work throughout *[specify territory]* ("Territory") for the period of *[specify]* years from the date of this Agreement ("Term").

1.2   The Licensee shall consult with the Proprietor at all times during the development of the Work in respect of the use of the Rights Material and the Licensee shall follow the reasonable directions of the Proprietor and the creative and artistic requirements of the Proprietor in respect of the Character and the Rights Material and the overall tone and directions of the Underlying Work.

1.3   The Licensee undertakes that the Work shall be faithful to the basic conceptualisation of the Rights Material and the Character as contained in the Underlying Work and shall reflect the same high standards of quality and integrity and adhere to the same portrayal of the Character as in the Underlying Work.

Clause 1.2 This provision permits the Proprietor to control the development of the Work in order to ensure that the overall tone and direction of the Work fits in with that of the Underlying Work.

Clause 1.3 It is important for the Proprietor to ensure that whatever Work is made by the Licensee is faithful to the conceptualisation of the Rights Material and the Character. It should be remembered that the Character may be a valuable commodity in its own right and its merchandising potential might be damaged by a Work which did not reflect the same standards of integrity or adhere to the same portrayal as the Character.

1.4   The Licensee's judgment in respect of all creative and business matters relating to the Work shall be final provided that the Proprietor shall have the right to approve the basic qualities characterisation (including context of living habitat and type and format of dialogue) powers accessories and costumes of the Character and the Subsidiary Characters which approval shall be a condition precedent to the exercise of the Licensee's rights and shall not be unreasonably withheld or delayed if such matters are substantially consistent with their portrayal in the Underlying Work.

1.5   The Licensee shall consult with and give good faith consideration to the views of the Proprietor relating to the use or appearance in the Work of any New Characters and in particular their powers basic qualities characterisation accessories and costumes. If in the opinion of the Proprietor the role or function of the New Characters might change the basic characterisation of the Character or the Rights Material the Licensee undertakes not to use such New Characters.

1.6   All approvals required pursuant to this Agreement shall be in writing and signed by a duly authorised representative of the Proprietor.

1.7   All rights in relation to the Underlying Work which are not licensed to the Licensee pursuant to Clause 1.1 are reserved to the Proprietor absolutely.

2.   PROPRIETOR'S WARRANTIES

The Proprietor warrants agrees and undertakes with the Licensee that:

2.1   the Proprietor is free to enter into this Agreement and grant the Licensee the rights granted in it and is not under any disability restriction or prohibition which might prevent the Proprietor from performing or observing any of the Proprietor's obligations under this Agreement;

2.2   the Proprietor has not entered into and shall not enter into any arrangement which may conflict with this Agreement;

2.3   to the best of the Proprietor's belief the Rights Material does not infringe the copyright trade mark right of privacy right of publicity or any other rights whatever of any person;

Clause 1.4   A Proprietor will generally wish to have control over a number of matters relating to the situation in which the Character is put for the reasons explained in the note to clause 2.2.

Clause 1.5   There may be occasions when it is beneficial to both parties for new characters or assets to be created, but a Proprietor will normally wish to have at least some control over these matters.

Clause 1.6   A requirement that approvals are evidenced in writing protects the Proprietor from uncertainty. In most cases the Proprietor will wish to consult with the relevant author or authors of the Underlying Work, and in some cases the Proprietor may have an express contractual obligation to do so. In all cases, however, the Proprietor should be aware of the potential difficulty in relation to the authors' moral rights.

2.4   to the best of the Proprietor's knowledge the Rights Material is not obscene or defamatory of any person;

2.5   the Proprietor confirms that the Licensee shall be free to market the Disks at whatever price the Licensee elects;

2.6   following the expiry of the Term by effluxion of time the Licensee shall have the non-exclusive right subject to the terms and conditions of this Agreement for the further period of three calendar months to sell off Disks previously manufactured by the Licensee during the Term.

3.   REMUNERATION

3.1   The Licensee agrees to pay or procure the payment to all relevant third parties in a timely manner all Copyright Liabilities relating to the Work and undertakes to pay to the Proprietor:

(a)   the Advance of [*specify*] ("Advance") on signature of this Agreement;

(b)   the Royalty on each Accounting Date in accordance with the provisions of this Agreement.

3.2   The Licensee shall not have the right to withhold any part of sums due to the Proprietor as a reserve against returns and/or credits and in the event that the Licensee is required by law to make any withholding from sums to be remitted to the Proprietor the Licensee shall prior to the making of any withholding of payment furnish the Proprietor with evidence satisfactory to the Proprietor in its entire discretion as to the Licensee's obligation to make such withholding of payment.

3.3   If exchange control or other restrictions prevent or threaten to prevent the remittance to the Proprietor of any money payable under this Agreement the Licensee shall immediately advise the Proprietor in writing and follow the Proprietor's instructions in respect of the money to be remitted including if required depositing the same with any bank or other person designated by the Proprietor at such location as may be designated by the Proprietor.

Clause 2.4   The warranty is given to the best of the Proprietor's belief. In other words it is not an absolute warranty that the Rights Material is not obscene or defamatory etc.

Clause 2.5   Although in the case of books it is currently possible to specify a minimum resale price (see paragraph 16.4) it is not possible for a similar provision to apply in relation to multimedia works (see paragraph 16.3). Although the Agreement requires the Licensee to pay to the Proprietor a minimum royalty, this provision clarifies the fact that the Licensee is free to sell the Disks at whatever price the Licensee considers appropriate.

Clause 2.6   The Licensee is entitled to a three-month non-exclusive sell-off period (see paragraphs 12.4 and 11.13).

Clause 3.1   The obligation to pay fees relating to other copyright elements included by the Licensee in the Work (such as music) obviously requires to be performed by the Licensee. The Advance is not expressed to be recoupable from the royalties.

Clause 3.2   This provision prevents the Licensee from deducting parts of the royalty payments to hold as reserves against returned Disks. If the Licensee is required by law to deduct withholding taxes on royalty payments it is required to produce documentary evidence satisfactory to the Proprietor of its liability.

Clause 3.3   This provision protects the Proprietor if exchange control restrictions are imposed in any territory and permits the Proprietor to receive income in that territory.

3.4   If any withholding or other taxes are required to be deducted from any moneys provided to be remitted to the Proprietor pursuant to this Agreement it shall be the responsibility of the Licensee to ensure that no improper deductions are made and that the Proprietor is provided with all necessary receipts certificates and other documents and all information required in order to avail the Proprietor of any tax credit or other fiscal advantage and the Licensee undertakes to account to the Proprietor in relation to any tax credit or saving received by the Licensee in relation to royalty payments to the Proprietor.

4.   LICENSEE'S UNDERTAKINGS

The Licensee warrants undertakes confirms and agrees with the Proprietor:

4.1   all rights and title in and to the Underlying Work are expressly reserved to the Proprietor subject to the licence in Clause 1.1;

4.2   the Licensee shall develop the Work and market the Work by releasing and distributing Disks at the Licensee's sole cost and expense by no later than [*specify date*] and shall deliver to the Proprietor not less than [*specify*] copies of each separate disk format in which the Work is marketed on first publication or distribution;

4.3   the Licensee shall not by any act or omission impair or prejudice the copyright in the Underlying Work or violate any moral right or deal with the Underlying Work so that any third party might obtain any lien or other right of whatever nature incompatible with the rights of the Proprietor and the Licensee shall ensure that all copies of the Work and artwork published and distributed by the Licensee contain full and accurate copyright notices credit attributions and acknowledgments;

4.4   the Licensee shall not create any promotional material or artwork relating to the Work without the prior written consent of the Proprietor and in respect of any material commissioned or manufactured by the Licensee the copyright shall be secured in the name of the Proprietor and title to all such physical material shall belong to and be dealt with as if such physical material

---

Clause 3.4   This clause not only requires the Licensee to provide the Proprietor with all necessary receipts and information but also provides that the Licensee is to bring into account any tax credits or savings achieved by the Licensee which are attributable to royalty payments under the agreement.

Clause 4.1   This clause clarifies that the copyright remains vested in the Proprietor subject only to the licence granted to the Licensee.

Clause 4.2   This provision gives the Proprietor the opportunity of determining the particulars which are to be contained in the statement of account. Each statement must be accompanied by payment of sums shown to be owing without deduction of any reserves. This provision acknowledges that it is possible that the Licensee might market the game in a number of separate formats and provides for the Proprietor to receive a copy of each of these formats.

had been supplied by the Proprietor and the Proprietor shall at all times have unrestricted access to the same for the purposes of the Proprietor;

4.5   the Licensee shall give full particulars to the Proprietor as soon as the Licensee becomes aware of any actual or threatened claim by any third party in connection with the Work;

4.6   the Licensee shall punctually pay to the Proprietor all sums owing to the Proprietor under this Agreement;

4.7   the Licensee shall not assign charge license sub-license or otherwise part with possession of the benefit or burden of this Agreement without the prior written consent of the Proprietor;

4.8   the Licensee shall release Disks throughout the Territory on the dates specified in Clause 4.2 and shall maintain the Disks in distribution in the Territory throughout the Term;

4.9   the Licensee shall submit the Work and all Disks to every competent authority to which it is required to be submitted for censorship certification or other purposes and shall comply with all rules regulations and other formalities relating to the same in each country of the Territory prior to the exercise of the rights granted to the Licensee under this Agreement;

4.10   the Licensee shall prior to any exercise of the rights granted under this Agreement make all necessary returns and pay all Copyright Liabilities and other payments whatever required to exploit the rights granted under this Agreement;

4.11   the Licensee shall not permit the Disks to be coupled or compiled on any disk with any other work and shall not permit the Disks to be sold as part

---

Clause 4.4   The Proprietor will in many circumstances wish to control the nature and type of publicity and advertising material. It would be possible for the Proprietor to limit the Territory granted to the Licensee, and to require the Licensee to grant the Proprietor rights in material produced by the Licensee. Since the provisions of this Agreement require the Licensee to develop a Multimedia Work based on the Proprietor's Underlying Work, such a provision would give the Proprietor the right to exploit the newly-developed Multimedia Work outside the Territory. Appropriate amendments would need to be made to clause 1.

Clause 4.5   If there is any claim in relation to copyright infringement or invasion of privacy or any other matter in relation to the Work it is in the Proprietor's interests to be apprised of such claim at the earliest possible moment.

Clause 4.6   In circumstances where the Agreement does not contain a provision making time of the essence, this provision requires the Licensee to make payments in a punctual manner.

Clause 4.7   Generally licences are considered to be personal, but there are some circumstances in which a licence may be sub-licensed. This provision expressly precludes the Licensee from entering into sub-licences or assigning the benefit of the Agreement.

Clause 4.8   Although some multimedia works are currently not required to be submitted for classification (see paragraphs 19.54 and 19.55) it is possible that there are obligations which apply in other territories.

Clause 4.10   The manufacture and distribution of multimedia works is likely to involve use of music and other elements in which third parties may control rights and the cost for using such copyright elements should be borne by the Licensee (see paragraphs 19.4 and 19.24).

of a package with any other disks incorporating any other disks or with any other material of any description;

4.12   the Licensee shall advertise the Disks throughout the Territory in the same manner as other disks advertised by the Licensee in the Territory and not remove any details or credits from the Disk or add any trade mark other than the Licensee's and such other trade mark as may be permitted by the Proprietor;

4.13   the Licensee shall exploit the rights granted to the Licensee to the best of the Licensee's skill and ability with the utmost despatch and ensure the highest possible Royalties payable to the Proprietor and ensure that the Disks are given fair and equitable treatment and not discriminated in favour of any other multimedia works which the Licensee may publish or distribute in the Territory;

4.14   the Licensee shall at the end of the three-month sell-off period re-ferred-to in Clause 2.6 at the direction of the Proprietor permit the Proprietor to purchase from the Licensee all Disks in the possession of or under the control of the Licensee which are then unsold at a unit cost equal to the actual cost of manufacture of the Licensee or if the Proprietor shall direct the Licensee shall procure their destruction and provide certificates and affidavits of destruction in such form as may be satisfactory to the Proprietor;

4.15   the Licensee shall indemnify and keep fully indemnified the Proprietor from and against all actions proceedings claims demands costs (including without prejudice to the generality of this provision the legal costs of the Proprietor on a solicitor and own client basis) awards and damages arising directly or indirectly as a result of any breach or non-performance by the Licensee of any of the Licensee's undertakings warranties or obligations under this Agreement.

5.   ROYALTY ACCOUNTING

5.1   The Licensee shall on each Accounting Date render to the Proprietor a full and complete statement showing all moneys owing to the Proprietor in respect of the preceding Accounting Period.

Clause 4.11   This provision protects the Proprietor from the Disks being made available in compilation format with other disks or from being packaged and sold with other works which the Proprietor might not wish the Character to be associated with.

Clause 4.12   This provision ensures that the Disks are given the same degree of prominence as that given by the Licensee to the Licensee's other product and prevents the addition of imprints or trade marks other than those of the Proprietor and the Licensee. The clause also specifically prohibits the Licensee from making any alteration or adaptation to the Disks or omitting any of the credits or acknowledgments.

Clause 4.13   The Licensee is required to exploit the rights in a manner consistent with achieving the highest royalties and to ensure that the Disks are not discriminated against in favour of other disks in which the Licensee may have an interest.

Clause 4.14   This provision permits the Proprietor to eliminate or purchase the Licensee's unsold stock of Disks at the end of the Term.

Clause 4.15   An explanation of the significance of warranties and indemnities may be found in paragraph 7.15.

Clause 5   The Accounting Dates and Accounting Periods are defined in clause 8.1 in accordance with standard industry practice. There may be occasions, however, where it is appropriate to vary these.

5.2 The statement of account in Clause 5.1 shall be in such form as the Proprietor shall require and shall contain full details of all Disks sold and each such statement shall be accompanied by payment of all amounts owing without reserve.

5.3 Pounds sterling shall be the currency of account and where any sums are received in a currency other than pounds sterling the same shall be converted at the [mid-market rate calculated using the "Financial Times" index on the date of receipt] [best obtainable rate of exchange on the date payment is due].

5.4 Value Added Tax shall be payable by the Licensee to the Proprietor in respect of all payments made to or to the order of the Proprietor pursuant to this Agreement.

5.5 The Licensee shall keep full and proper books of account relating to the exploitation of its rights under this Agreement and the Proprietor or its representative shall have the right at any time during the Term and for six years afterwards on giving reasonable prior notice to inspect and audit and take copies of such books of account during normal business hours. In the event that such audit or inspection reveals any deficiency in money paid to the Proprietor then the Licensee shall immediately pay the same to the Proprietor together with interest from the date first due calculated with monthly rests at a rate of [*percentage*]% above prime or base rate charged by its bankers to the Proprietor from time to time and shall pay all reasonable costs incurred by the Proprietor directly as a result of such inspection.

5.6 The Licensee shall keep confidential and shall not disclose to any third parties (other than professional advisers where necessary) the results of any such inspection or audit or any of the terms of this Agreement or any matters incidental to it or relating to the business of the Proprietor and shall indemnify the Proprietor fully in respect of any breach of its obligations under this Clause 5.6.

6. DETERMINATION

It shall constitute the repudiation by the Licensee of its obligations under this Agreement and at any time the Proprietor may serve written notice on the Licensee accepting such repudiation and determining the Term and the Licensee's rights under this Agreement if:

Clause 5.2 This provision gives the Proprietor the opportunity of determining the particulars which are to be contained in the statement of account. Each statement must be accompanied by payment of sums shown to be owing without deduction of any reserves.

Clause 5.3 It may or may not be appropriate for pounds sterling to be the currency of account. If the Licensee is situate in a foreign territory, exchange conversion provisions may be required.

Clause 5.4 It will be necessary to adjust this provision in the light of prevailing law. A short explanation of current Value Added Tax legislation may be found in paragraph 11.28 and paragraphs 12.22 to 12.30.

Clause 5.5 There may be occasions when a Proprietor will wish to inspect and audit the books of account of the Licensee. Even if such audit rights are·not exercised, an audit provision should always be included in licence agreements.

Clause 6 For an examination of the legal significance of the term "repudiation" reference should be made to paragraph 14.5 and to paragraphs 14.2 to 14.4.

6.1   the Licensee fails to pay any amount due under this Agreement in full within three days of its due date and such failure is not remedied within seven days of receipt of written notice;

6.2   the Licensee is in breach of any other material term of this Agreement which is incapable of remedy or if capable of remedy is not remedied within fourteen days of the Licensee becoming aware of it;

6.3   any of the Licensee's representations shall prove to have been incorrect when made or become materially incorrect and the Proprietor's rights and entitlements under this Agreement are materially and adversely affected;

6.4   the Licensee transfers disposes of or threatens to transfer or dispose of any part of its assets which is likely in the opinion of the Proprietor to prevent or materially to inhibit the performance by the Licensee of its obligations under this Agreement;

6.5   any indebtedness guarantee or similar obligation of the Licensee or of any guarantor of the Licensee becomes due or capable of being declared due before its stated maturity or is not discharged at maturity or the Licensee or any guarantor of the Licensee defaults under or commits a breach of the provisions of any guarantee or other obligation (whether actual or contingent) of any agreement pursuant to which any such indebtedness guarantee or other obligation was incurred all or any of which shall in the reasonable opinion of the Proprietor materially affect its rights and entitlements under this Agreement;

6.6   the Licensee is declared or becomes insolvent;

6.7   the Licensee convenes a meeting of its creditors or proposes or makes any arrangement or composition with or any assignment for the benefit of its creditors or a petition is presented or a meeting is convened for the purpose of considering a resolution or other steps are taken for the winding up of the Licensee (save for the purpose of and followed by a voluntary reconstruction or amalgamation previously approved in writing by the Proprietor) or if an

Clause 6.1 This clause provides the Licensee with the opportunity of remedying a breach. The time period allowed to remedy pecuniary breaches is normally less than that allowed to remedy non-pecuniary breaches.

Clause 6.2 This clause permits the Licensee to remedy a non-pecuniary material breach. The time period allowed is longer than that for a pecuniary breach.

Clause 6.3 There may be circumstances where the Proprietor has entered into the Agreement on the basis of representations made by the Licensee. This clause permits the Proprietor to terminate the Agreement if the representations prove to have been incorrect or subsequently become incorrect.

Clause 6.4 There are occasions where a Licensee becomes less financially secure and disposes of its assets. Where a Proprietor has entered into an agreement in reliance on the Licensee being an entity of substance, such occasions may cause concern to the Proprietor, and this provision permits the Proprietor to terminate the Agreement in such instances.

Clause 6.5 Financial default of the Licensee in relation to any guarantee or obligation is a further event normally permitting termination.

Clause 6.6 For the consequences of insolvency, reference should be made to paragraphs 15.2 to 15.4.

incumbrancer takes possession of or a trustee administrator administrative receiver liquidator or similar officer is appointed in respect of all or any part of its business or assets or any distress execution or other legal process is levied threatened enforced upon or sued out against any of such assets;

6.8 the Licensee shall cease or abandon or announce that it intends to cease or abandon the business of publishing and distributing multimedia works;

6.9 the Disks cease to be distributed or are deleted from the Licensee's catalogue.

7. NOTICE

7.1 Any notice or other document required to be given under this Agreement or any communication between the parties with respect to any of the provisions of this Agreement shall be in writing in English and be deemed duly given if signed by or on behalf of a duly authorised officer of the party giving the notice and if left at or sent by pre-paid registered or recorded delivery post or by telex telegram cable facsimile transmission or other means of telecommunication in permanent written form to the address of the party receiving such notice as set out at the head of the Agreement or as notified between the parties for the purpose of this Clause.

7.2 Any such notice or other communication shall be deemed to be given to and received by the addressee:

(a) at the time the same is left at the address of or handed to a representative of the party to be served;

(b) by post on the day not being a Sunday or Public Holiday two days following the date of posting;

(c) in the case of a telex telegram cable facsimile transmission or other means of telecommunication on the next following day.

7.3 In proving the giving of a notice it should be sufficient to prove that the notice was left or that the envelope containing the notice was properly addressed and posted or that the applicable means of telecommunication was addressed and despatched and despatch of the transmission was confirmed and/or acknowledged as the case may be.

7.4 Communications addressed to the Proprietor shall be marked for the attention of [name] with a copy to [name] of [address].

Clause 6.7 There may be occasions when a Licensee does not actually become insolvent but a creditor enforces security over the Licensee's business. This could have serious consequences for a Proprietor and this clause protects the Proprietor's interests by providing that such circumstances will entitle the Proprietor to terminate the Agreement.

Clause 6.8 Where a Licensee ceases to carry on business or announces that it intends to cease its business, the Proprietor will wish to recover its rights as soon as possible.

Clause 6.9 Although clause 4.8 imposes a specific obligation on the Licensee to keep the Disks in distribution, this clause permits the Proprietor to terminate if it does not do so.

Clause 7 A number of clauses in the document provide for a means of exercising rights, and a notice provision is therefore necessary.

8.   DEFINITIONS AND INTERPRETATION

8.1   The following definitions apply in this Agreement:

"Accounting Date"
45 days from the end of each Accounting Period

"Accounting Period"
successive periods ending on 31 March 30 June 30 September and 31 December in each year

"Associate"
in relation to the Licensee any associate or associated company within the meaning of Section 416 or 417 of the Income and Corporation Taxes Act 1988

"Character"
[*Name or names*]

"Copyright Liabilities"
all sums arising on or as a result of the manufacture or exploitation of Disks or the Rights which may be payable to the owners of any right of copyright performer's right moral right or any right whatever in the Work including expressly without limitation any form of synchronisation or mechanical or performance fee or royalty or other payment whatever to performers owners of copyright performer's rights moral rights publishers and other third parties in relation to material included on the Disks the Work or the Rights

"Disk"
any CD-I CD-ROM compact disk disk cassette [or other physical carrier whether digital optical mechanical or electrical] which contains the Work and does not contain any other literary dramatic musical or artistic material or audio or audio-visual material which has not been expressly approved by the Proprietor in writing.

"New Characters"
any characters or other material of whatever nature created for the purpose of the Work whether or not such material is directly or indirectly based on the Rights Material

"Retail Price"
the nominal retail selling price from time to time approved or specified by the Licensee for the sales of Disks in the Territory

"Rights"
the sole and exclusive right to make the Work and the sole and exclusive right to manufacture sell and exploit Disks in accordance with this Agreement but the rights shall expressly [exclude] [include] making the Work available in any interactive form and shall expressly [exclude] [include] hiring or renting the Work or Disks to members of the public or making the Work or the Disks available to any person by any electronic delivery service or by any means of electronic or data transmission

"Rights Material"
the Character the Subsidiary Characters all plots themes outlines stories drawings pictures sketches characters locations scenarios treatments and other literary dramatic and artistic material included in the Underlying Work

"Royalty"
in respect of each Disk sold in the Territory during the Term [*amount*]% of the Retail Price and in any event not less than [*specify*] per Disk sold in the Territory during the Term

"Subsidiary Characters"
[*names*] and any other characters in the Underlying Work than the Character

"Work"
the multimedia work to be created by the Licensee based on the Underlying Work.

8.2 The following terms are defined in this Agreement in the place indicated:

"Advance:"   Clause 3.1(a)

"Copyright:"   Clause 8.6
"Term:"   Clause 1.1
"Territory:"   Clause 1.1
"Underlying Work:":   Recital (A)

8.3   Any reference in this Agreement to any statute or statutory provision shall be construed as including a reference to that statute or statutory provision as from time to time amended modified extended or re-enacted whether before or after the date of this Agreement and to all statutory instruments orders and regulations for the time being made pursuant to it or deriving validity from it.

8.4   Unless the context otherwise requires words denoting the singular shall include the plural and vice versa and words denoting any one gender shall include all genders and words denoting persons shall include bodies corporate unincorporated associations and partnerships but successors and assigns shall not be deemed to include Licensees.

Clause 8.1 The definitions provided in this clause may need to be adjusted to reflect the appropriate relevant circumstances.

The definition of Rights expressly excludes rental rights (see paragraph 3.10) or making the Work available by electronic transmission.

The provisions of clauses 3.1 and 4.10 oblige the Licensee to pay Copyright Liabilities. This definition may need to be adjusted to reflect the circumstances.

The definition for Disk is limited to physical carriers.

The royalty specifies a minimum sum. Both the Royalty rate and the Retail Price on which it is based will require adjustment to reflect the particular circumstances.

8.5 The word "copyright" means the entire copyright and design right subsisting under the laws of the United Kingdom and any and all analogous rights subsisting under the laws of each and every jurisdiction throughout the world.

8.6 Unless otherwise stated time shall be of the essence for the purpose of the performance of the Licensee's obligations under this Agreement.

8.7 Unless otherwise stated references to clauses sub-clauses sub-paragraphs schedules annexures and exhibits relate to this Agreement.

9. MISCELLANEOUS

9.1 Nothing contained in this Agreement shall constitute or shall be construed as constituting a partnership or contract of employment between the parties.

9.2 The Proprietor shall not be liable to the Licensee for failing to supply or procure the supply of any material to be supplied under this Agreement due to circumstances beyond its control and it shall not be liable for any expenses or consequential losses whatsoever thereby suffered by the Licensee.

9.3 The Licensee warrants that it is not the nominee or agent of any undisclosed principal and warrants that it will assume sole and complete responsibility for the performance of the obligations in this Agreement expressed to be performed by the Licensee.

9.4 This Agreement contains the full and complete understanding between the parties and supersedes all prior arrangements and understandings whether written or oral appertaining to the subject matter of this Agreement and may not be varied except by an instrument in writing signed by all the parties to this Agreement. The Licensee acknowledges that no representations or promises not expressly contained in this Agreement have been made to the Licensee by the Proprietor or any of its servants agents employees members or representatives.

Clause 9.1 Under English law if two parties carry on business in common with a view to profit and share profit, the arrangement is capable of being considered a partnership. This provision ensures that no partnership is created inadvertently and also expressly excludes the possibility of an employment contract being created.

Clause 9.2 This provision protects the Proprietor from any claim by the Licensee in relation to failure to supply Delivery Materials, although there are likely to be circumstances in which the Proprietor may incur some liability.

Clause 9.3 This provision protects the Proprietor from the consequences of it contracting with a Licensee which has acted as the agent of an undisclosed company whom the Proprietor may not consider to be a suitable person to be the Proprietor's Licensee.

Clause 9.4 There are occasions where oral agreements or other understandings may be created in relation to a work which may contain either additional obligations or obligations which conflict with those set out in subsequent written agreement. This provision makes it clear that all previous arrangements and understandings are at an end and the contract is the only document relevant to the obligations and rights of the parties in relation to its subject matter. The final part of the clause expressly excludes the possibility of any liability on the part of the Proprietor for misrepresentation on the part of any of its servants, agents, employees or representatives.

9.5   This Agreement shall be governed and construed in accordance with the laws of England and Wales whose courts shall be courts of competent jurisdiction.

<u>AS WITNESS</u> the hands of the duly authorised representatives of the parties the day month and year first above written

<u>SIGNED</u> by [   ]
for and on behalf of
[*The Proprietor*]

<u>SIGNED</u> by [   ]
for and on behalf of
[*The Licensee*]

Clause 9.5   Where a contract is made between two entities in England and Wales, it will generally not be necessary to insert a provision of this nature, but where a contract is to be created with a foreign company (or a company situate in Scotland or Northern Ireland) this provision should always be included.

G. Distribution

DOCUMENT 47

Distribution agreement
(where the company's product is being distributed)

[IMPORTANT NOTE: Please read the section "About this book" on page v, before copying or using this Document]

Purpose of this Document

This is a form of agreement which might be suitable for use by a company in certain circumstances where a company's product is being distributed by a third party distributor. The negotiation of distribution arrangements is, however, inevitably complex and involves the consideration of a number of commercial matters on which legal advice should always be obtained. The provisions of this Document may be contrasted with the provisions of Document 48 which has been drafted from the point of view of the distributor.

Relevant text

The text of this Work covers a number of topics which are relevant to documents of this nature including:

- distribution agreements, their principal terms (paragraphs 12.1 to 12.9)
- delivery and risk (paragraphs 12.10 to 12.13)
- retention of title (paragraphs 12.14 to 12.17)
- sale or return (paragraphs 12.18 and 12.19)
- undertakings and obligations (paragraphs 12.20 and 12.21)
- Value Added Tax (paragraphs 12.22 to 12.30)
- distribution and sale of goods (paragraphs 12.31 to 12.44)
- United Kingdom competition law (paragraphs 16.2 to 16.8)
- European Union competition law (paragraphs 16.9 to 16.15)
- competition law and distribution agreements (paragraphs 16.16 to 16.21)
- the law of contract (paragraphs 2.1 to 2.30)

THIS AGREEMENT is made the   day of

BETWEEN:

(1)   *[Company]* LIMITED of *[address]* ("Company"); and

(2)   *[Distributor]* LIMITED of *[address]* ("Distributor" which expression shall include all Associates and permitted sub-licensees and assignees of the Distributor).

IT IS AGREED as follows:

1.   APPOINTMENT AND DELIVERY

1.1   The Company grants the Distributor an exclusive licence to distribute and sell the Books under the Trade Mark in the Territory during the Term.

1.2   Orders for Books may initially be placed orally but the Distributor undertakes that all orders for Books shall be confirmed in writing within 24 hours from being made. The Company undertakes that it shall effect the delivery of all orders of Books *[number]* working days from the date of receipt by the Company of written confirmation of the relevant order by the Distributor provided that the Distributor shall not have any obligation to accept any order from the Distributor if the Distributor is in breach of its obligations or to accept any part of any order to which the provisions of Clause 2.4 apply.

1.3   If the aggregate total of Books for which the Company receives orders confirmed in writing by the Distributor in any *[number]* day period equals or exceeds *[number]* Books the Company shall not be in breach of its obligations if it fails to effect delivery of such Books within the time stated in this Clause provided it shall have made every reasonable effort to do so.

1.4   The Company shall arrange at its own cost and expense delivery of the Books to the Distributor's warehouse at *[address]* or such other address in the United Kingdom local to London as shall be notified to the Company in writing at the time of confirmation of the relevant order.

1.5   Risk in the Books shall pass to the Distributor when delivered in accordance with this Clause and title shall pass when payment in full has been made to the Company of all sums owed to the Company by the Distributor under this Agreement.

Clause 1.1   The provisions of this Agreement are capable, with suitable modifications, of applying to records, video cassettes and other items of product. This provision gives the Distributor the exclusive licence to distribute books (defined in clause 14.1) published by the Company under a designated imprint in the Territory and throughout the Term defined in clause 14.1. The Term is a specified period for each title and applies to all titles published under a designated imprint, before a specified date.

Clause 1.2   This Distribution Agreement contemplates the Company supplying the Distributor with regular orders of books. The procedure for ordering books therefore needs to be established.

Clause 1.3   This provision protects the Company from being unable to supply the Distributor by reasons of a surge in demand over a particular period.

Clause 1.4   The arrangements for delivery of books need to be specified in the Agreement. This provision requires delivery to be made at the Company's cost and expense to the Distributor's warehouse.

Clause 1.5   For an explanation as to risk and title reference should be made to paragraphs 12.10 to 12.17.

1.6   If any part of an order for Books made and confirmed in writing by the Distributor is not capable of being fulfilled during the relevant Term of any Book or if the fulfilment of such order would amount to a breach by the Company of its obligations to any Licensor the Company shall give the Distributor notice of such fact as soon as practicable and shall have the right to sever the Books so affected from the order.

2.   ADVANCE

2.1   The Distributor undertakes to pay the Company the Advance as to £[*amount*] on signature of this Agreement and the balance on [*date*] at the election of the Company by telegraphic transfer to the Company's bank account nominated by the Company or by banker's draft which Advance shall be recoupable from the Net Receipts in accordance with Clause 2.3.

2.2   The Distributor shall pay to the Company the Net Receipts without any deduction other than as permitted by Clause 2.3 and 2.4 [*number*] days from the end of each month during the Term in respect of all Books which have been sold by the Distributor during such month.

2.3   The Advance shall be recoupable from the Net Receipts payable to the Company during the Recoupment Period by [*number*] equal monthly instalments of £[*amount*] and shall not be recoupable from any Net Receipts payable to the Company prior to or after such period.

2.4   In the event the amount of Net Receipts payable to the Company during any month in the Recoupment Period is less than £[*amount*] the Distributor shall have the right to recoup such shortfall from the Net Receipts arising in any subsequent month or months during the Recoupment Period.

3.   MINIMUM ORDER LEVEL

3.1   The Distributor guarantees as a material term of this Agreement that it shall order and purchase from the Company and pay for the following minimum quantities of Books:

(a)   during the Term not less than the Aggregate Minimum Order Level of Books specified in the Schedule; and

---

Clause 1.6   For an explanation of the doctrine of severance reference should be made to paragraph 2.22.

Clause 2.1   This provision requires payment of an advance which is recoupable from Net Receipts in accordance with clause 2.3. Bank details and payment details will need to be varied to fit the circumstances.

Clause 2.2   Net Receipts are defined in clause 14.1. Receipts and profits are considered in paragraphs 11.22 to 11.26. Distribution commissions are considered in paragraphs 12.5 to 12.9.

Clause 2.3   This clause determines the circumstances in which the Advance is recoupable. It is recoupable only during a specified period in monthly instalments up to a specified amount. The effect of this is to require the Distributor to exceed the amount required to recoup the advance during the Recoupment Period.

(b) in each Period not less than the Period Minimum Order Level specified in the Schedule;

in each case as may be reduced pursuant to this Agreement.

3.2 All payments in relation to the minimum order commitment specified in Clause 3.1 shall be made by no later than [*number*] days from the end of each Period or if orders are placed before the end of such Period the date specified in Clause 2.2. The Distributor shall confirm with the Company in writing all orders which are made by the Distributor during any Period no later than [*number*] working days prior to the end of each Period. For the avoidance of doubt it is agreed that the Distributor shall not incur any obligation to pay for Books which are not delivered.

3.3 Failure to place orders in accordance with Clause 3.2 shall not relieve the Distributor from its obligation to pay to the Company the Guaranteed Price in respect of the appropriate quantity of Books in each Period. The Guaranteed Price shall be calculated with reference to the average price of all Titles which are the subject of this Agreement and shall be payable no later than [*number*] days from the end of each Period.

4. STOCK

4.1 The Distributor shall until payment in full has been made of all sums owed to the Company store all Books under conditions which shall prevent deterioration.

4.2 The Company and/or its authorised representative shall have the right to inspect any premises used or owned by the Distributor to store Books under the control of the Distributor from time to time upon reasonable prior written notice and if such inspection reveals any loss of stock in excess of 1% over any 12-month period the Distributor shall pay to the Company the cost of replacement of such copies within [*14*] days from demand.

Clause 3.1 This provision requires the Distributor to order and pay for not less than the specified minimum order level of books throughout the term of the Agreement as a whole. Throughout each quarterly or monthly period. The choice of books is left at the discretion of the Distributor.

Clause 3.2 This provision specifies a minimum number of days notice which must be given to the Company in order to permit the Company to supply the books chosen by the Distributor.

Clause 3.3 This provision protects the Company from the consequences of the Distributor failing to order the minimum order level in any relevant period. The clause provides that if the Distributor does not order the relevant minimum number of books the Distributor will owe the Company a debt the amount of which will be the minimum order quantity multiplied by the average price of all Titles which are in the Company's catalogue and which are the subject of the Agreement. The clause also provides that the debt is payable by a certain date. Failure by a company to pay debts when due is one of the grounds on which a company may be wound up (see paragraph 15.3).

Clause 4.1 This clause provides that the books are stored in proper conditions until the Company has been paid.

Clause 4.2 This clause permits the Company to inspect premises and to carry out stock audits. The Distributor is permitted "shrinkage" of up to 1% over any 12-month period. Above this figure the Distributor is liable to pay the replacement cost of any missing copies.

4.3 The Distributor shall at all times throughout the Term carry sufficient stock of the Books so that all orders received by the Distributor can be supplied without delay and shall provide to the Company monthly reports relating to stock levels and movements together with such other agreed information as the Company may from time to time reasonably require.

4.4 The Distributor shall at all times throughout the Term carry at least [twelve] months' stock of Books so that all orders received by the Distributor can be supplied without delay and shall provide to the Company such reports relating to stock levels and movements as the Company may from time to time require.

4.5 The Distributor shall retain total control and actual possession at all times of the Books and maintain the Books safe and secure in appropriate storage facilities.

4.6 The Distributor shall effect and keep in place adequate insurance on a comprehensive basis against all risks relating to the Books for an amount not less than their replacement cost and shall hold all proceeds of insurance policies on trust for the Company and shall apply the same in accordance with the directions of the Company.

5. DISTRIBUTION

5.1 The Distributor shall during the Term faithfully and diligently serve the Company as its Distributor in the Territory and actively and diligently promote the sale of Books and shall promptly fulfil all orders for Books received by the Distributor.

5.2 The Distributor undertakes to use its best endeavours consistent with the business practice of a competent and efficient book distributor to exploit and sell the Books throughout the Territory during the Term.

5.3 The Distributor shall not do anything which may prevent the sale or interfere with the development of sales of the Books in the Territory.

Clause 4.3 This provision requires the Distributor to anticipate orders of books so far as possible, in order to keep appropriate levels of stock necessary to supply orders. Efficient fulfilment of orders is, of course, in the interests of the Distributor, since the Distributor receives a commission on sales.

Clause 4.4 The precise level of stock to be carried is negotiated and will depend on the circumstances of the transaction.

Clause 4.5 It is important to a Company that the Distributor retain possession and control of the books until they are sold.

Clause 4.6 A Company may in some circumstances wish to receive a copy of the Distributor's insurance policy and to be named on it as a named insured and loss payee, in order to ensure that if there is any claim on the policy the Company is reimbursed.

Clause 5.1 This provision contains one of the key obligations of the Distributor.

Clause 5.2 This provision links the Distributor's performance to the objective level of performance which might be achieved by a competent and efficient book Distributor.

Clause 5.3 The Distributor's key function is to develop the sale of the Company's books in the territory.

5.4   The Distributor shall (subject to the Company fulfilling its delivery obligations in respect of Books ordered by the Distributor) sell and distribute Books of each Title on the relevant Publication Date.

5.5   The Distributor shall maintain throughout the Term sufficient staff to sell distribute and promote the Books throughout the Territory and to perform in a timely and satisfactory manner the obligations of the Distributor pursuant to this Agreement including without limitation the creation and maintenance of a sales force of sufficient size to fulfil the Distributor's obligations under this Agreement in relation to the sale and marketing of the Books.

5.6   The Distributor shall sell and distribute the Books and deliver the Books to customers solely in accordance with the Distributor's terms and conditions annexed as Exhibit 1 which terms and conditions shall not be changed without the consent of the Company.

5.7   The Distributor undertakes to procure that the Distributor its staff and agents shall accord due prominence to the Company's catalogue of titles and shall not accord greater prominence to any other books distributed by the Distributor.

5.8   The Distributor shall not during the Term distribute or sell in the Territory or any country outside the Territory any books which compete directly with the Company's Titles and the Distributor undertakes that it shall not have any direct or indirect interest in the importation into the Territory of any books which directly compete with the Company's Titles without the Company's prior written consent.

5.9   The Distributor shall throughout the Term refer to the Company all enquiries it receives for sale or ultimate delivery outside the European Union.

5.10   The Distributor shall not during the Term outside the Territory advertise the Books or canvass or solicit for orders for the Books or open branches for the sale of the Books without the prior written consent of the Company.

Clause 5.4   A Company will normally wish books to be marketed actively from their publication date.

Clause 5.5   The staffing levels and sales force information relating to the Distributor are central to the performance of its obligations.

Clause 5.6   It is important for a Company to control the terms and conditions on which books are distributed (see paragraphs 12.14 to 12.17).

Clause 5.7   A Company will normally wish to ensure that its catalogue receives due prominence.

Clause 5.8   It is important for a Company to protect the interests of its Licensees and Distributors in other territories, although European Union law provisions must be borne fairly in mind (see paragraphs 16.9 to 16.28).

Clause 5.9   The United Kingdom competition law and European Union law implications of distribution agreements will generally need to be considered.

5.11   The Distributor shall not during the Term sell the Books outside the European Union.

6.   DISTRIBUTOR'S UNDERTAKINGS

The Distributor warrants agrees and undertakes with the Company as follows:

6.1   the Distributor shall at all times throughout the Term conform with all legislation rules regulations and statutory requirements existing in the Territory from time to time in relation to the Books;

6.2   the Distributor is free to enter into this Agreement and is not under any disability restriction or prohibition which might prevent the Distributor from performing or observing any of the Distributor's obligations under this Agreement;

6.3   all rights title and interest in the Titles are reserved to the Company absolutely and all rights and title in and to the Books are expressly reserved to the Company until the Company has received payment in full from the Distributor of all sums due under this Agreement;

6.4   the Distributor shall not infringe the copyright in the Books and/or the Titles or by any act or omission permit any third party to obtain any lien or other right of whatsoever nature incompatible with the rights of the Company;

6.5   the Distributor shall indemnify and keep fully indemnified the Company from and against all actions proceedings claims demands costs (including without prejudice to the generality of the provision the legal costs of the Company on a solicitor and own client basis) awards and damages arising directly or indirectly as a result of any breach or non-performance by the Distributor of any of the Distributor's undertakings warranties or obligations under this Agreement.

Clause 5.10   The United Kingdom competition law and European Union law implications of distribution agreements will generally need to be considered.

Clause 5.11   The United Kingdom competition law and European Union law implications of distribution agreements will generally need to be considered.

Clause 6.1   The Company will wish to ensure that the Distributor is validly incorporated and lawfully existing under the laws of the relevant jurisdiction and has effected all registrations and complied with all regulations necessary in order to enable it to carry on its business.

Clause 6.2   The Company will wish to ensure that the Distributor is not prevented by a contractual commitment to a third party from performing the obligations contemplated under the Agreement (see paragraph 13.10).

Clause 6.3   This provision is a retention of title clause in favour of the Company – see paragraphs 12.14 to 12.17.

Clause 6.4   The Company wishes to ensure that the Distributor will not permit a third party to obtain possession of the stock, since such third party may exercise its rights over the stock in a way which is not in the Company's interest.

Clause 6.5   For an examination of the legal distinction between warranty and indemnity refer to paragraph 7.15.

7.   COMPANY'S UNDERTAKINGS

The Company warrants agrees and undertakes with the Distributor as follows:

7.1   the Company has the right to enter into this Agreement and controls and shall throughout the Term control the rights in the Books licensed to the Distributor pursuant to Clause 1 and shall not enter into any arrangement or do any act which conflicts with its obligations under this Agreement;

7.2   to the best of the Company's knowledge the copyright in the Titles in the Territory is and shall be valid and subsisting during the Term and to the best of the Company's knowledge the Books do not and shall not infringe any right of copyright or other right of any person or do not contain any material which is obscene defamatory or constitutes a contempt of court;

7.3   the Company warrants that so far as it is aware the incorporation by the Company of the Company's logo on the Books and the packaging shall not create any liability on the part of the Distributor towards any third parties;

7.4   the Company shall at all times keep the Distributor informed of all changes to the Company's catalogue and the addition or deletion of Titles and shall supply the Distributor with such quantity of advertising and publicity material as the Company considers appropriate.

7.5   All Books shall at the time of delivery in accordance with Clause 1.3 be of merchantable quality. The Distributor shall have the right to reject all Books not conforming with this Clause the risk and property in any such rejected Books passing back to the Company upon re-delivery to the Company and the Company undertakes to issue credit notes in accordance with the provisions of Clause 8.4. The liability of the Company to the Distributor shall be limited to such credit notes and except as set out in this Clause no warranty or representation is given by the Company in respect of the Books.

7.6   The Company shall at all times throughout the Term conform with all legislation rules regulations and statutory requirements existing in the Territory from time to time in relation to the Books to the extent the same are required to be conformed to by the Company.

Clause 7.1   The Company warrants that it has the right to enter into the Agreement and that it will not do anything to conflict with its obligations.

Clause 7.2   The Company's warranties are limited to its knowledge.

Clause 7.3   It may be appropriate for the Distributor to instigate a trade mark search in relation to the Company's logo in the Distributor's territory.

Clause 7.4   The Company will normally advise the Distributor of additions to or deletions from its catalogue as a matter of good practice.

Clause 7.5   This provision sets out the liability of the Company towards the Distributor in relation to the supply of books. Liability for the distribution and sale of goods is examined in paragraphs 12.31 to 12.44.

Clause 7.6   If the Distributor is to be responsible for all distribution activities in the territory the requirements of this clause will not be onerous for the Company.

8.   FINANCIAL AND ACCOUNTING

8.1   The Distributor shall within [*number*] days from the end of each calendar month during the Term provide the Company with a report of all sales of Books made by the Distributor in the Territory during the preceding month together with such other reasonable information to assist with the marketing as the Company may require.

8.2   The Distributor shall keep full and proper records relating to the warehousing and storage and supply of Books by the Company to the Distributor and by the Distributor to its customers and shall (to the extent only the Company requires the same in order to comply with contractual obligations with third parties) allow the Company or its authorised representatives at all reasonable times subject to reasonable prior written notice the right to inspect audit and copy the same.

8.3   The price at which the Distributor shall re-sell the Books shall be established and revised from time to time by the Distributor who shall notify such prices and any changes to the Company in a prompt manner provided that in the case of Books which are designated by the Company as Net Books the Distributor shall not authorise the resale of such Books at less than the Company's specified retail price.

8.4   In respect of Books that are delivered to the Distributor in a damaged condition (which damage shall be evidenced in writing or otherwise in such manner as the Company may reasonably require) the Company shall within 15 working days of receipt of such damaged Books issue the Distributor a credit note provided that the Distributor shall have ordered the relevant quantity of Books specified in the Schedule within the Period in question except as otherwise provided in this Agreement.

8.5   The Distribution Fee shall not be deducted in the case of any consignment by the Distributor on a sale or return or conditional sale basis until the sale has become unconditional.

8.6   The Distributor shall invoice all purchases of Books promptly and shall use the Distributor's best endeavours to collect and receive all Gross Receipts

---

Clause 8.1   In order to assist the Company to carry out its marketing activities it will need to receive certain sale information from the Distributor on a regular basis.

Clause 8.2   The Company needs to have the right to inspect, audit and take copies of books of account.

Clause 8.3   This provision permits the Distributor to increase or decrease the sale price of books other than books which are the subject of the Net Book Agreement. The provision will need to be reviewed in the light of future developments in United Kingdom and European Union law and reference should be made to paragraphs 16.3 and 16.4.

Clause 8.4   This provision entitles the Distributor to a credit note in relation to damaged books, rather than reimbursement.

Clause 8.5   This provision protects the Company from paying commission on sales which are effected on a sale or return basis (see paragraphs 12.18 and 12.19).

and other sums owed to the Distributor in relation to the Books. The Distributor shall make no deductions whatever from Net Receipts.

8.7   All sums payable in this Agreement are exclusive of Value Added Tax which shall be payable on receipt of the relevant party's Value Added Tax Invoice.

9.   SUBSTITUTION

9.1   If the Company is advised to withdraw any of the Titles from distribution because of any proceedings or threat of proceedings or if the Company receives notice of any claim which is adverse to or might conflict with the Company's rights in the relevant Titles or if the distribution of the relevant Titles or the Books might in the reasonable opinion of the Company contravene any law or regulation or cause offence to any person or damage the reputation of the Company and the Company gives written notice to this effect the Distributor shall where appropriate withdraw the relevant Titles and all Books from distribution and the Company shall as soon as possible provide the Distributor with a suitable substitute title agreed on by the Company and the Distributor and/or such substitute book or books to be of similar commercial value to the relevant Book or Books withdrawn and/or notify the Distributor that the Minimum Order Level for the relevant period shall be deemed to have been reduced by the number of Books so affected.

9.2   It is expressly agreed and understood that the withdrawal by the Company of any Titles or Books or the provision by the Company to the Distributor of any substitute titles or books or the reduction of the Minimum Order Level shall not constitute a breach by the Company or the Distributor of its obligations or warranties in this Agreement and the Company shall have no further liability to the Distributor in respect of any Titles or Books so withdrawn which shall for the purposes of Clause 1 be deemed not to have been licensed to the Distributor.

9.3   If any orders of Books made by the Distributor are severed by the Company pursuant to the provisions of Clause 1.4 on the grounds that fulfilment by the Company would amount to a breach by the Company of its obligations to any Licensor such orders shall count for the purpose of

---

Clause 8.6   The Company will wish to control its cashflow. If a Distributor is permitted to recover commission only from received income (see paragraph 12.8) the Distributor's commercial interests will coincide.

Clause 8.7   The effect of Value Added Tax in distribution arrangements needs careful thought (see paragraphs 12.22 to 12.30).

Clause 9.1   There are occasions where books have to be withdrawn from circulation and this provision insulates the Company from claims from the Distributor in such circumstances.

Clause 9.2   The final part of this provision would provide protection to the Company in circumstances where it had given an absolute unqualified warranty in relation to the matters referred to in clause 7.2.

Clause 9.3   For the effect of severance in relation to contracts reference should be made to paragraph 2.22.

determining whether the Distributor has met its obligations to order Books up to the Minimum Order Level.

10. COPYRIGHT

10.1 All rights of copyright and all other rights in and to the Books the Trade Mark and each part of the same are and shall remain the exclusive property of the Company and the Distributor shall enter into such agreements (including without limitation registered user agreements) and at the cost and expense of the Company execute such documents and carry out such actions as may be requested by the Company and necessary to protect the rights of the Company and the Licensors in respect of the Trade Mark and the Books in the Territory.

10.2 The Distributor shall not knowingly use or knowingly authorise the use of the Trade Mark in any manner liable to invalidate its registration and the right to use the Trade Mark in connection with the Books is granted to the Distributor.

10.3 The Distributor shall notify the Company as soon as it becomes aware of any unauthorised use or infringement in the Territory of any rights of whatever nature in the Trade Mark or the Books or of any other intellectual or industrial property rights in the Books or owned by the Company and shall at the cost and expense of the Company take part in or give assistance in respect of any legal proceedings requested by the Company and execute any documents and do any things reasonably necessary to protect the Company's and the Licensor's intellectual and industrial property rights in the Books and the Trade Mark in the Territory.

11. UNSOLD STOCK

11.1 At the end of the Term in respect of each Title the Company shall be entitled by written notice to require the Distributor to sell to the Company any unsold Books in the possession or control of the Distributor for which the Company has been paid at a price for which the Company was paid and the Distributor undertakes to deliver to the Company all unsold Books in the possession or control of the Distributor at the end of the Term in respect of each Title within fourteen days from notice from the Distributor requiring such delivery. The Company shall pay the Distributor 30 days after it has accepted such delivery.

Clause 10.1 This provision protects the Company's rights in relation to trade marks in the territory. If there are trade marks which are registered in the territory the Company would generally require the Distributor to enter into a registered user agreement (see paragraphs 3.41 to 3.45).

Clause 10.2 This provision will provide protection to a Company until such time as a registered user agreement is entered into.

Clause 10.3 It is in the interests of both Distributor and Company that the Company should be made aware of any infringement of intellectual property rights in the territory.

Clause 11.1 This provision protects the Company by providing what will happen to the Distributor's unsold stock of books at the end of the term of the Distribution Agreement.

11.2   If the Company elects not to buy back any Books which have been sold by the Company to the Distributor and paid for by the Distributor and which remain unsold the Distributor shall have the non-exclusive right to sell off such Books in the Territory for the period of three months following the expiry of the Term of the Title from which such Books are derived. At the end of such sell-off period the Distributor shall destroy all such unsold Books and provide the Company with such certificate or affidavit of destruction or other evidence as the Company may reasonably require.

12.   DETERMINATION

It shall constitute the repudiation by the Distributor of its obligations under this Agreement and at any time the Company may serve written notice on the Distributor accepting such repudiation and determining the Term and the Distributor's rights under this Agreement if:

12.1   the Distributor fails to pay any amount due under this Agreement in full within three days from receiving written notice from the Company of non-payment; or

12.2   the Distributor shall fail to place orders with the Company [*number*] working days prior to the end of each Period or the Distributor is in breach of any other material term of this Agreement which is incapable of remedy or if capable of remedy is not remedied within fourteen days of the Distributor becoming aware of it; or

12.3   any of the Distributor's representations shall prove to have been incorrect when made and the Company's rights and entitlements under this Agreement are materially and adversely affected; or

12.4   the Distributor transfers disposes of or threatens to transfer or dispose of any part of its assets which is material in the opinion of the Company; or

12.5   any indebtedness guarantee or similar obligation of the Distributor or any guarantor becomes due or capable of being declared due before its stated maturity or is not discharged at maturity or the Distributor or any guarantor defaults under or commits a breach of the provisions of any guarantee or

---

Clause 11.2 For an examination of the commercial significance of sell-off periods reference should be made to paragraphs 12.4 and 11.13.

Clause 12.1 This clause provides the Distributor with the opportunity of remedying a breach through non-payment. The time period allowed to remedy pecuniary breaches is normally less than that allowed to remedy non-pecuniary breaches.

Clause 12.2 This clause permits the Distributor to remedy a non-pecuniary material breach. The time period allowed is longer than that for a pecuniary breach.

Clause 12.3 There may be circumstances where the Company has entered into the agreement on the basis of representations made by the Distributor. This clause permits the Company to terminate the Agreement if the representations prove to have been incorrect or subsequently become incorrect.

Clause 12.4 There are occasions where a Distributor becomes less financially secure and disposes its assets. Where a Company has entered into an Agreement in reliance on the Distributor being an entity of substance, such occasions may cause concern to the Company, and this provision permits the Company to terminate the Agreement in such instances.

other obligation (whether actual or contingent) of any agreement pursuant to which any such indebtedness guarantee or other obligation was incurred all or any of which shall materially affect its rights and entitlements under this Agreement; or

12.6   the Distributor is declared or becomes insolvent; or

12.7   the Distributor convenes a meeting of its creditors or proposes or makes any arrangement or composition with or any assignment for the benefit of its creditors or a petition is presented or a meeting is convened for the purpose of considering a resolution or other steps are taken for the winding up of the Distributor (save for the purpose of and followed by the voluntary reconstruction or amalgamation which shall have been previously approved in writing by the Company) or if an incumbrancer takes possession of or a trustee receiver administrative receiver administrator liquidator or similar officer is appointed in respect of all or any part of its business or assets or any distress execution or other legal process is levied threatened enforced upon or sued out against any of such assets; or

12.8   the Distributor shall cease or abandon or announce that it intends to cease or abandon the business of distributing Books; or

12.9   the Books are deleted from the Distributor's catalogue.

13.   NOTICE

13.1   Any notice or other document required to be given under this Agreement or any communication between the parties with respect to any of the provisions of this Agreement shall be in writing in English and be deemed duly given if signed by or on behalf of a duly authorised officer of the party giving the notice and if left at or sent by pre-paid registered or recorded delivery post or by telex telegram facsimile transmission or other means of telecommunication in permanent written form to the address of the party receiving such notice as set out at the head of the Agreement or as notified between the parties for the purpose of this Clause.

13.2   Any such notice or other communication shall be deemed to be given to and received by the addressee:

(a)   at the time the same is left at the address of or handed to a representative of the party to be served;

Clause 12.5   Financial default of the Distributor in relation to any guarantee or obligation is a further event normally permitting termination.

Clause 12.6   For the consequences of insolvency reference should be made to paragraphs 15.2 to 15.4.

Clause 12.7   There may be occasions when a Distributor does not actually become insolvent but where a creditor enforces security over the Distributor's business. This could have serious consequences for a Company and this clause protects the Company's interests by providing that such circumstances will entitle the Company to terminate the Agreement.

Clause 12.8   Where a Distributor ceases to carry on business or announces that it intends to cease its business, a Company will wish to recover its rights as soon as possible.

Clause 13   A number of clauses in the document provide for a means of exercising rights and a notice provision is therefore necessary.

(b)   by post on the day not being a Sunday or Public Holiday two days following the date of posting;

(c)   in the case of a telex telegram facsimile transmission or other means of telecommunication on the day of service.

13.3   In proving the giving of a notice it should be sufficient to prove that the notice was left or that the envelope containing the notice was properly addressed and posted or that the applicable means of telecommunication was addressed and despatched and despatch of the transmission was confirmed and/or acknowledged as the case may be.

13.4   Communications addressed to the Company shall be marked for the attention of [*name*] of [*address*] with a copy [*name*].

14.   DEFINITIONS AND INTERPRETATION

14.1   The following definitions apply in this Agreement:

"Advance"
The non-returnable advance of £[*amount*] which shall be recoupable in accordance with the provisions of Clause 2.

"Agreement"
This Agreement and any and all schedules annexures and exhibits attached to it or incorporated in it by reference.

"Associate"
In respect of the Distributor any associate or associated company within the meaning of Section 416 or 417 of the Income and Corporation Taxes Act 1988.

"Book"
Any paperback or hardback [or CD-Rom] copy of any Title.

"Distribution Fee"
The distribution fee of [*percentage*]% of the Company's relevant wholesale price for each Title in respect of all Books sold by the Distributor during the Term for which the Company shall have received payment which fee shall be inclusive of all surcharges discounts and additional costs whatever.

"Gross Receipts"
100% of the relevant wholesale price specified by the Company in respect of each Book sold by the Distributor in the Territory during the Term.

"Guaranteed Price"
[*Specify*]% of the Company's wholesale price in respect of each published Title.

"Licensor"
Any person from whom the Company acquires the right to publish and distribute any Title.

"Minimum Order Level"
In respect of all of the Titles the aggregate minimum order level specified in the Schedule which aggregate minimum order level shall in each Period be no less than the minimum order level for Books specified for such Period save that any orders in excess of each Period minimum order level shall be carried forward to be set off against the minimum order levels for subsequent Periods.

"Net Book"
Any Book designated by the Company as being a Net Book for the purposes of the Net Book Agreement.

"Net Receipts"
100% of the Gross Receipts less the Distribution Fee.

"Period"
Each quarterly or other period listed in the Schedule.

"Publication Date"
In respect of each Title such date as may be agreed between the Company and the Distributor or in default of agreement such date as may be specified by the Company.

"Recoupment Period"
The [*number*]-month period commencing on [*date*] and terminating on [*date*].

"Term"
In respect of each Title the period of [*number*] months commencing on the relevant Publication Date of such Title and terminating on 31 December in the calendar year following the year in which the relevant Publication Date occurs.

"Territory"
[*Specify*].

"Title"
Any publication published by the Company under the [*specify*] imprint before [*specify date*].

"Trade Mark"
Any trade mark of the Company contained in the Books.

14.2   Unless the context otherwise requires words denoting the singular shall include the plural and vice versa and words denoting any one gender

---

Clause 14 The definitions contained in clause 4.1 will need review in order to fit the appropriate circumstances.

shall include all genders and words denoting persons shall include bodies corporate unincorporated associations and partnerships.

14.3   Unless otherwise stated time shall be of the essence for the purpose of the performance of the obligations of the Distributor under this Agreement.

14.4   Unless otherwise stated references to clauses sub-clauses sub-paragraphs schedules annexures and exhibits relate to this Agreement.

15.   MISCELLANEOUS

15.1   This Agreement shall not be deemed to constitute a partnership or joint venture or contract of employment between the parties.

15.2   Neither party shall be liable to the other party for failing to supply or procure the supply of the Books and any other material to be supplied under this Agreement due to circumstances beyond its control and it shall not be liable for any expenses or consequential losses whatever suffered by the other party.

15.3   The Distributor warrants that it is not the nominee or agent of any undisclosed principal and warrants that it will assume sole and complete responsibility for the performance of the obligations in this Agreement expressed to be performed by the Distributor.

15.4   If any provision of this Agreement shall be prohibited by or adjudged by a court to be unlawful void or unenforceable such provision shall to the extent required be severed from this Agreement and rendered ineffective as far as possible without modifying the remaining provisions of this Agreement and shall not in any way affect any other circumstances or the validity or enforcement of this Agreement.

15.5   This Agreement contains the full and complete understanding between the parties and supersedes all prior arrangements and understandings whether written or oral appertaining to the subject matter of this Agreement and may not be varied except by an instrument in writing signed by all of the parties to this Agreement. Each party acknowledges that no representations

---

Clause 14.2   The references in this clause need to be adjusted to fit the appropriate circumstances. In particular, it may be appropriate to insert additional clauses.

Clause 14.3   For the significance of time being of the essence reference should be made to paragraph 2.10.

Clause 15.1   Under English law if two parties carry on business in common with a view to profit and share profit, the arrangement is capable of being considered a partnership. This provision ensures that no partnership is created inadvertently and also expressly excludes the possibility of an employment contract being created.

Clause 15.2   This provision protects the Company from any claim by the Distributor in relation to failure to supply Books, although there are likely to be circumstances in which the Company will incur some liability.

Clause 15.3   This provision protects the Company from the consequences of it contracting with a Distributor which has acted as the agent of an undisclosed company whom the Company may not consider to be a suitable person to be the Company's Distributor.

Clause 15.4   For an explanation of the doctrine of severance reference should be made to paragraph 2.22.

or promises not expressly contained in this Agreement have been made by the other party or any of its servants agents employees members or representatives.

15.6   No failure or delay on the part of any of the parties to this Agreement relating to the exercise of any right power privilege or remedy provided under this Agreement shall operate as a waiver of such right power privilege or remedy or as a waiver of any preceding or succeeding breach by the other party to this Agreement nor shall any single or partial exercise of any right power privilege or remedy preclude any other or further exercise of such or any other right power privilege or remedy provided in this Agreement all of which are several and cumulative and are not exclusive of each other or of any other rights or remedies otherwise available to a party at law or in equity.

15.7   Neither party to this Agreement shall disclose (except to their professional advisers) any information relating to the financial provisions of this Agreement which shall be kept strictly confidential provided that this Clause shall not apply to any disclosures made pursuant to any court order or to any disclosure made pursuant to the rules of the Stock Exchange of Great Britain and Northern Ireland Limited provided that such information shall be disclosed to the Stock Exchange on a confidential basis.

15.8   This Agreement shall be governed by and construed in accordance with the laws of England and Wales the courts of which shall be courts of competent jurisdiction.

AS WITNESS the hands of the duly authorised representatives of the parties the day month and year first above written.

Clause 15.5   There are occasions where oral agreements or other understandings may be created in relation to a Work which may contain either additional obligations or obligations which conflict with those set out in subsequent written agreement. This provision makes it clear that all previous arrangements and understandings are at an end and the contract is the only document relevant to the obligations and rights of the parties in relation to its subject matter. The final part of the clause expressly excludes the possibility of any liability on the part of a Company for misrepresentation on the part of any of its servants, agents, employees or representatives.

Clause 15.8   Where a contract is made between two entities in England and Wales, it will generally not be necessary to insert a provision of this nature, but where a contract is to be created with a foreign company (or a company situate in Scotland or Northern Ireland) this provision should always be included.

THE SCHEDULE

Aggregate Minimum Order Level   [*number*]

Period Minimum Order Level
Period   Number of Books

[*period*]   [*number*]

                    Total   [*number*]

SIGNED by [*name of officer*] ⎫
for and on behalf of   ⎬
[*Company*]   ⎭

SIGNED by [*name of officer*] ⎫
for and on behalf of   ⎬
[*Distributor*]   ⎭

EXHIBIT 1

Distributor's Terms and Conditions of Sale

(*Clause 5.6*)

DOCUMENT 48

Distribution agreement
(where the company is acting as the distributor)

[IMPORTANT NOTE: Please read the section "About this book" on page v, before copying or using this Document]

Purpose of this Document

This is a form of agreement which might be suitable for use by a company in circumstances where the company is acting as a distributor for another company. The negotiation of distribution arrangements is, however, inevitably complex and involves the consideration of a number of commercial matters on which legal advice should always be obtained. The provisions of this Document may be contrasted with the provisions of Document 47 which has been drafted from the point of view of the company whose product is being distributed.

Relevant text

The text of this Work covers a number of topics which are relevant to documents of this nature including:

- distribution agreements, their principal terms (paragraphs 12.1 to 12.9)
- delivery and risk (paragraphs 12.10 to 12.13)
- retention of title (paragraphs 12.14 to 12.17)
- sale or return (paragraphs 12.18 and 12.19)
- undertakings and obligations (paragraphs 12.20 and 12.21)
- Value Added Tax (paragraphs 12.22 to 12.30)
- distribution and sale of goods (paragraphs 12.30 to 12.44)
- United Kingdom competition law (paragraphs 16.2 to 16.8)
- European Union competition law (paragraphs 16.9 to 16.15)
- competition law and distribution agreements (paragraphs 16.16 to 16.21)
- the law of contract (paragraphs 2.1 to 2.30)

THIS AGREEMENT is made the   day of

BETWEEN:

(1)   [*Name*] LIMITED (Registered Number [*number*]) whose [registered office] [principal place of business] is at [*address*] ("Proprietor" which expression shall include any Associate); and

(2)   [*Name*] LIMITED (Registered Number [*number*]) whose [registered office] [principal place of business] is at [*address*] ("Company")

IT IS AGREED as follows:

1.   GRANT OF RIGHTS

1.1   The Proprietor grants to the Company the sole and exclusive right throughout the Territory to sell distribute and otherwise exploit the Books and the Titles during the Term and the non-exclusive licence to use the Trade Mark in the Territory in relation to the sale and promotion of the Titles.

1.2   In connection with the exercise of the rights granted to the Company under this Agreement the Company shall have the non-exclusive right to distribute use and reproduce the Publicity Material together with the right to use excerpts from the Books in any and all media for the purpose of advertising and promotion and the right to authorise others to exploit the rights granted to the Company pursuant to this Agreement throughout the Territory during the Term.

1.3   The Proprietor confirms and agrees that the Company shall have the right to use the name trade name logo trade mark biography and likeness of the Proprietor and of all persons connected with the Books and the Titles in connection with the rights granted in this Agreement together with the right to use excerpts from the Books in any and all media for the purpose of advertising and promotion.

1.4   The Proprietor undertakes to provide the Company with sample materials of all Existing Titles within 7 days from the date of this Agreement and to notify the Company and provide sample materials of all New Titles within [28] days of the acquisition by the Proprietor and shall from time to time deliver all Publicity Material reasonably requested by the Company.

Clause 1.1   Under this clause the Company obtains the sole and exclusive licence to distribute Existing Titles and Future Titles (as defined in clause 14.1) throughout the Term, which is also defined in clause 14.1. In addition to the exclusive distribution and sale right the Company also acquires the exclusive licence to use the Trademark in the Territory.

Clause 1.2   This provision entitles the Company to have the non-exclusive right to distribute, use and reproduce various publicity materials which may be created by or obtained by the Proprietor.

Clause 1.3   This provision permits the Company to use names, logos, biographies and likenesses connected with the Proprietor and persons connected with the Books and the Titles in any and all media for advertising and promotional purposes.

Clause 1.4   The Company will normally wish to obtain as much advance notice as possible of new Titles in order to maximise their distribution.

741

2.   DELIVERY

2.1   The Proprietor undertakes to deliver to the Company's warehouse at [*specify address*] within [*number*] days from the date of this Agreement sufficient copies of the Existing Titles as to comprise [*number*] months stock calculated at average sales levels over the preceding 12-month period.

2.2   The Proprietor undertakes to give the Company not less than [*specify*] months' notice of the intended publication date of any New Title and at such date supply the Company with advance publicity material and all information usually required by the Company in its [*specify*] form.

2.3   Not less than [*number*] months before the publication date of any New Title the Company and the Proprietor shall meet to agree upon a sales forecast and the Proprietor shall deliver to the Company the number of Books indicated in the sales forecast [*number*] months before the publication date and shall deliver to the Company such additional Books as the Company may require at less than [*number*] weeks following the publication date.

2.4   The Proprietor shall on receipt of the Company's stock list prepared each month during the Term check the stock level of Books held by the Company in order to ensure that stock held by the Company in relation to any Books shall be not less than:

(a)   in relation to Titles which have not been published or Titles which have been published within the last [*number*] weeks the level specified in Clause 2.3; or

(b)   in relation to all other Titles [*number*] months' supply of stock calculated at the average monthly rate of sales of all relevant Titles over the previous 12 months or since the date of publication if less.

3.   PRICES AND STOCK

3.1   The Company shall sell and distribute the Books at such prices as may be specified by the Proprietor from time to time in consultation with the Company. The Company shall in its sole discretion determine the level and amount of discount and return policy (if any) to be applied to such prices. The Proprietor agrees that the Proprietor shall not change the Proprietor's price in respect of any Book more than [once] in each calendar year.

Clause 2.1   The mechanics of delivery need to be adjusted to suit particular situations. This clause relates solely to existing titles not future titles. The level of stock is normally the subject of negotiation.

Clause 2.2   This provision is designed to cover new titles and the Company will generally wish to obtain the maximum advance notice period and will wish to receive advance publicity material as far forward as possible.

Clause 2.3   The function of this clause is to gear stock levels to anticipated sales forecasts for new titles.

Clause 2.4   This clause sets the procedure by which stock levels of the Company are to be monitored in relation to each title. Order levels and stock supply numbers are subject to negotiation depending on the circumstances.

Clause 3.1   The pricing provisions and commission bases in this Agreement need to be reviewed in the light of United Kingdom and European Union competition law (see paragraphs 16.2 to 16.21).

3.2   The Proprietor shall ensure that the level of stock in relation to any Title held by the Company shall not at any time during the Term exceed the relevant figure calculated in accordance with Clause 2.4 by more than [*percentage*]% and shall remove all such surplus stock within [14] days from the date on which the surplus stock first exceeded such percentage. If removal is not effected by such date the Company shall be entitled to charge the Proprietor a storage fee calculated in accordance with the Company's charges set out in Exhibit 1.

3.3   The Proprietor shall bear all costs and expenses in relation to the delivery of stock to the Company including but not limited to any and all import duties import levies or bonded warehouse fees and all items of stock delivered to the Company shall be delivered in accordance with the Company's delivery requirements annexed as Exhibit 2 and shall contain such bar-code information as the Company may require.

4.   ADVERTISING AND PROMOTION

4.1   The Proprietor undertakes in respect of each year of the Term to ensure that not less than [*number*] and not more than [*number*] of new Titles are acquired by the Proprietor at such intervals or periods as may be specified by the Company and in accordance with such release schedule as the Company shall require. In the case of any deletions of Titles for whatever reason all such deletions are to be replaced with new Titles approved by the Company and the Proprietor shall ensure that the Company shall at all times during the Term have an up-to-date list of the Proprietor's catalogue and that all deletions are promptly notified to the Company.

4.2   The Proprietor shall use all reasonable endeavours to promote the Books including but not limited to advertising the Books to members of the public and the Proprietor shall be responsible for and bear the cost and expense of all such advertising and promotion.

4.3   During [each] [the first] year of the Term the Proprietor shall incur expenditure of not less than £[*amount*] on advertising promotion and publicity of the Books and produce receipts and vouchers evidencing such expenditure at the request of the Company.

Clause 3.2   The function of this provision is to relieve the Company from the burden of carrying surplus stock if the Proprietor's sale figures fall.

Clause 3.3   The responsibility for costs of delivery and import of stock needs to be allocated to either Proprietor or Company.

Clause 4.1   The value of any distribution catalogue generally depends on how many new titles are acquired by the Proprietor during each year. This provision imposes certain obligations on the Proprietor in this regard.

Clause 4.2   The sales and marketing obligations in relation to the catalogue fall upon the Proprietor rather than the Company.

Clause 4.3   This clause establishes certain minimum advertising and promotion expenditure obligations which are to be performed by the Proprietor during either the first year or each year of the term.

4.4   The Proprietor undertakes to supply the Company free of charge not less than [*number*] book jackets of each New Title and [*number*] copies of the book itself no later than [*number*] months and [*number*] weeks respectively before publication.

5.   PUBLISHER'S OBLIGATIONS

The Company undertakes and agrees with the Proprietor:

5.1   to use all reasonable efforts to distribute and sell the Books in the Territory during the Term;

5.2   to use all reasonable endeavours to fulfil all orders for Books within [*number*] days from receipt;

5.3   not to advertise the Books or canvass or solicit for orders for Books outside the Territory (provided this shall not prevent the Company from carrying out normal business activities at trade fairs and exhibitions);

5.4   not to use the Trade Mark for any purpose other than permitted in this Agreement;

5.5   within [*specify*] days from the end of each month in the Term to supply to the Proprietor a computerised summary listing stock levels and sales of each Title in the previous month.

6.   DISTRIBUTION FEE AND APPLICATION OF RECEIPTS

6.1   The Company shall be entitled to deduct from the Gross Receipts and retain for its own use and benefit absolutely:

(a)   the Distribution Fee; and

(b)   the Distribution Expenses.

6.2   Subject to the full and timely performance and observance by the Proprietor of its obligations undertakings and warranties under this Agreement the Company undertakes that the balance of Gross Receipts remaining after the deduction of the items listed in Clause 7.1 shall be remitted to the Proprietor in accordance with the provisions of Clause 11.

Clause 4.4   The advance supply of book jackets is of use to the Company for advance sales purposes.

Clause 5.1   The obligations of the Proprietor should be contrasted to the comparable obligations under Document 47.

Clause 5.2   The obligation of the Proprietor should be contrasted to the comparable obligation under Document 47.

Clause 5.3   The effect of European Union legislation on distribution agreements is examined in paragraphs 16.16 to 16.21.

Clause 5.4   Where the use of a trade mark is licensed to the Company the Company may be required to enter into a trade mark user agreement. Reference in relation to trade marks should be made to paragraphs 3.41 to 3.45.

Clause 5.5   The purpose of this clause is to permit the Proprietor to monitor sales figures in relation to each title.

Clauses 6.1 and 6.2   Remuneration provisions in rights agreements are examined in paragraphs 11.22 to 11.26. The commission basis in distribution agreements is examined in paragraphs 12.5 to 12.9 and relevant taxation matters are set out in paragraphs 11.27 to 11.29 and 12.20 to 12.29.

7.   PROPRIETOR'S WARRANTIES

The Proprietor as a material inducement to the Company entering into and performing this Agreement warrants to and agrees and undertakes with the Company that:

7.1   the Proprietor has the right to enter into and perform this Agreement and grant to the Company all of the rights granted in this Agreement and has not entered into and shall not enter into any arrangement or understanding or do any act or thing which might in any way inhibit restrict or impair the free and unrestricted exercise by the Company of the rights granted in this Agreement;

7.2   the Proprietor controls and shall control throughout the Term as the sole exclusive absolute and unincumbered legal and beneficial owner all rights necessary to grant to the Company the rights granted in this Agreement and the Proprietor has no actual or constructive notice of any defect in or restriction applying to such rights;

7.3   nothing contained in the Books or the Titles or the Publicity Material is or will be obscene libellous blasphemous or offensive to religion or defamatory under the laws in force in any part of the world or constitutes a contempt of court;

7.4   the exercise by the Company of the rights granted under this Agreement shall not infringe the copyright right of privacy right of publicity performer's right moral right or other right whatever of any third party;

7.5   the Books are and shall when delivered to the Company be in perfect condition;

7.6   the Company shall not incur any liability to any person firm company or other organisation whatever in respect of the Books or the use or display by the Company of the name logo or trade mark of the Proprietor or the biography or likeness of any or all of the persons connected with the Titles and/or the Books;

Clause 7.1   The Company will require a warranty that the Proprietor has the right to enter into the Agreement and has not entered into any incompatible arrangement.

Clause 7.2   It is a fundamental requirement that the Proprietor actually controls the rights which it is purporting to give to the Company.

Clause 7.3   If anything contained in the books or the titles or the publicity material is obscene, libellous or defamatory etc the Company will incur liability.

Clause 7.4   The exercise of the rights granted to the Company in relation to certain publicity and advertising material is capable of infringing certain rights of privacy.

Clause 7.5   The Company should satisfy itself as to the quality and condition of books delivered to it.

Clause 7.6   Since the Company will be displaying and distributing various items of publicity material it requires assurance that such material will not infringe any rights of privacy or names, logos or trade marks of any persons.

7.7 neither the Books nor any packaging nor any Publicity Material shall contain any defect which might give rise to any liability on the part of the Company to any person in respect of loss or damage or injury nor shall any of them contain any false attribution of authorship or any misleading or incorrect information;

7.8 all Books Publicity Material and other material delivered to the Company shall contain full complete and accurate copyright notices in such form as may be required to afford protection pursuant to the provisions of the Berne Convention Rome Convention and Universal Copyright Convention as the same may from time to time be amended and any other relevant copyright convention;

7.9 the Proprietor undertakes that it shall not itself or permit any third party to distribute Books in the Territory except the Company;

7.10 the Books and the Publicity Material shall at all times comply with all contractual credit and contractual statutory and other obligations of whatever nature owed by the Proprietor and its licensors or any other person to third parties whatever;

7.11 the Proprietor shall refer to the Company all orders and enquiries for Books received by the Proprietor from persons firms or companies in the Territory;

7.12 all importation and other requirements of whatever nature relating to the Books and other materials to be delivered to the Company pursuant to this Agreement of HM Commissioners of Customs and Excise and any other relevant body shall be observed and performed by the Proprietor and all import fees and charges and levies shall be the responsibility of and be paid by the Proprietor;

7.13 all consents licences permissions and waivers of moral rights and all other authorisations and licences of whatever nature which may be necessary for the sale distribution and exploitation of the Titles and the Books and the Publicity Material under any code or statute whatever have been obtained by the Proprietor and the Books and the Publicity Material comply and will throughout the Term comply with all applicable relevant codes regulations and statutes whatever in the Territory;

Clause 7.7 There are numerous areas in relation to which the distribution and publication of books may give rise to a liability to a third party (such as those covered in Chapters 9 and 10) which are covered by this warranty.

Clause 7.8 The importance of copyright notices and material is examined in paragraph 4.9.

Clause 7.9 The Company wishes the rights to be exclusive. If there is any derogation from exclusivity such as through a previous distributor having sell-off rights, such matters will need to be disclosed.

Clause 7.10 The Company will wish to ensure that all books and publicity material distributed comply with all contractual and statutory and other obligations owed by the Proprietor to all persons.

Clause 7.11 If the Proprietor receives orders or enquiries from other persons, since these orders and enquiries may be commission-bearing the Company will wish them to be referred to the Company.

Clause 7.12 This provision is designed to eliminate any possibility of any claim brought against the Company by HM Commissioners of Customs and Excise and other relevant bodies.

Clause 7.13 The Company will wish to ensure that all necessary consents, licences and permissions of whatever nature which may be necessary for the sale and distribution of the books have been obtained by the Proprietor from all relevant persons.

7.14   the Proprietor shall indemnify the Company and keep the Company at all times fully indemnified from and against all actions proceedings claims demands costs (including without prejudice to the generality of this provision legal costs of the Company on a solicitor and own client basis) awards and damages howsoever arising directly or indirectly as a result of any breach or non-performance by the Proprietor of any of the Proprietor's undertakings warranties or obligations under this Agreement.

8.   PROPERTY AND RISK

8.1   Risk in the Books shall pass to the Company upon delivery to the Company provided that this provision shall not prejudice the Company's right to require the Proprietor to replace any Books which the Company reasonably believes to have been damaged or defective at the time of their delivery.

8.2   The Company shall insure all Books for such amount and upon such conditions as the Company considers appropriate against loss or damage caused by the flooding neglect or other risks and shall take all reasonable steps in relation to any claims and shall pay to the Proprietor in full and final satisfaction of any claim of the Proprietor all appropriate sums received from insurers to the extent the Company reasonably considers such claim to be justified up to the amount of the Proprietor's loss.

8.3   The Company shall cause to be checked not less than once in each year all Books held by the Company in stock against the Company's inventory and in the event such check reveals a loss of stock in excess of [*percentage*]% the Company shall pay to the Proprietor the actual cost of production in relation to such excess lost books.

8.4   Property in the Books shall pass to the Company when such Books are appropriated by the Company for the purpose of meeting any order or orders for Books.

8.5   If the Company refuses to take the credit risk on any orders made for Books consigned or shipped out for sale pursuant to this Agreement then the Proprietor agrees that it shall accept the credit risk on such transaction and before the shipment is made shall supply to the Company written confirmation of such acceptance giving authorisation to the Company to make the

---

Clause 7.14   For the significance of indemnities reference should be made to paragraph 7.15.

Clause 8.1   For the significance of risk in relation to distribution agreements reference should be made to paragraphs 12.10 to 12.13.

Clause 8.2   This provision provides that sums received by the Company from insurers in relation to books shall to the extent the Company reasonably considers any claim made by the Proprietor in relation to loss to be justified satisfy any liability which the Company may have towards the Proprietor.

Clause 8.3   This clause makes the Company liable to the Proprietor in relation to "shrinkage" and the relevant percentage figure needs to be inserted.

Clause 8.4   For the significance of property or title in relation to books and other possessions reference should be made to paragraphs 12.14 to 12.17.

shipment. In the event that the customer ordering such shipment defaults in payment then the amount of such moneys due from such customer shall be paid by the Proprietor to the Company on demand but without prejudice to its right to require payment by the Proprietor the Company shall have the right to deduct such amount from the Gross Receipts arising in respect of such order.

8.6   The Proprietor agrees that nothing contained in this Agreement shall compel the Company to sell and/or distribute Books to any person firm or company who does not have a trading account with the Company or whose trading account has been suspended or stopped by the Company.

9.   <u>DISTRIBUTION</u>

9.1   If the Company has reasonable grounds for believing that the distribution by the Company of any Book would constitute or give rise to a breach by the Proprietor of any of its warranties undertakings or obligations in this Agreement or the Company in its entire discretion believes such distribution may be in violation of any statute or regulation or may subject the Company to civil or criminal liability or infringe any right of copyright or performer's right or be obscene blasphemous offensive to religion or defamatory or may subject the Company to civil or criminal liability or may cause industrial or other unrest or disruption then without prejudice to any other rights which the Company may have under this Agreement the Company may at any time and without prior notice to the Proprietor suspend the Term of this Agreement or withhold or withdraw such Book from distribution and the Proprietor may at its sole cost and expense make other arrangements for the distribution of such Book provided it shall first reimburse the Company for all costs and expenses it may have incurred.

9.2   The Company shall not be liable to the Proprietor for any failure or delay in fulfilling its obligations under this Agreement if such failure or delay is due to weather conditions war fire strike lock out riot act of God legal act of any public or governmental authority delay or default on the part of any third party shortage of raw materials or labour or any other circumstances beyond the control of the Company and the initial period of the Term shall be extended by a period equal to that during which the circumstance or event preventing the fulfilment of those obligations exists together with such supplemental period as shall be required by the Company to resume the distribution of Books pursuant to this Agreement.

Clause 8.5   This provision relates to credit risks which are referred to in the text at paragraph 12.12.

Clause 8.6   This provision relates to credit risks which are referred to in the text at paragraph 12.12.

Clause 9.1   Distribution of books may expose the Company to various civil and criminal liabilities (see Chapters 9 and 10). The provisions of this clause permit the Company to withdraw problem books from distribution.

Clause 9.2   This clause is what is commonly referred to as a force majeure provision which permits the Company to extend the term of the arrangement by a period equal to the duration of any event of force majeure plus whatever period is required by the Company to resume normal business patterns.

10.   ACCOUNTS AND PAYMENTS

10.1   The Company shall within [*number*] days of the end of each calendar month of the Term render to the Proprietor a statement showing the balance of Gross Receipts in respect of that calendar month due to the Proprietor under this Agreement.

10.2   Upon receipt of such statement the Proprietor shall prepare and send to the Company a full and correct Value Added Tax invoice in respect of the balance of Gross Receipts due to the Proprietor and within [30] days from the end of the calendar month in which the Company receives such invoice from the Proprietor the Company shall pay to the Proprietor such sums shown to be owing and the banking by the Proprietor of such sums shall be deemed to be acceptance by the Proprietor of the amount due to it in respect of the period to which the invoice refers.

10.3   The Company shall be entitled to establish and retain from the balance of Gross Receipts payable to the Proprietor a reserve for potential Returns for such amounts and for such periods as it deems appropriate. In the event that after the expiry of the Term or earlier termination of this Agreement Returns are delivered to the Company for credit then the Company shall be entitled to deduct as Distribution Expenses the amount of any such credit from the balance of Gross Receipts payable to the Proprietor or invoice the Proprietor and the Proprietor shall pay to the Company within 14 days of the receipt by the Proprietor of such invoice a sum equal to the amount or amounts previously paid to the Company in respect of such Returns by the person making such Returns.

10.4   The Company shall keep books of account relating to the sale and distribution of the Books pursuant to this Agreement and the Proprietor or its representative being a chartered accountant not otherwise engaged on an audit of the Company or any of its Associates shall have the right not more than once a year during normal business hours at the cost and expense of the Proprietor and on not less than 30 days' prior written notice to inspect and take copies of such books of account. In the event that such audit or inspection reveals any deficiency in moneys paid to the Proprietor pursuant to this Agreement the Company shall not be in breach of its obligations pursuant to this Agreement unless having agreed in writing that such a deficiency exists and following 30 days' written notice from the Proprietor it shall have failed to make payment of such sums.

Clause 10.1   This clause provides for monthly statements of account to be rendered to the Proprietor but the parties may decide that other periods are relevant.

Clause 10.2   This clause establishes the payment obligations of the parties and may need to be adjusted to reflect the commercial circumstances of the particular transaction.

Clause 10.3   This provision permits the Company to establish and retain from sums payable to the Proprietor a reserve for potential returns.

Clause 10.4   This provision permits the Proprietor to have the right of access to books of account for audit purposes and establishes a procedure if any audit shows under-payment.

10.5 The Proprietor shall and shall procure that its representative shall keep confidential and shall not disclose to any third parties (other than professional advisers where necessary) the results of any such inspection or audit relating to the business of the Company and shall indemnify the Company fully in respect of any breach of the obligations of the Proprietor or its representative under this Clause 10.5.

10.6 All sums expressed in this Agreement to be paid by one party to the other or to be due to or recovered by one party shall be exclusive of any Value Added Tax or any similar or replacement tax which (if applicable) shall be added to such sums and be recoverable in addition to them.

10.7 In the event that any moneys payable or receivable pursuant to this Agreement are subject to exchange control restrictions the Company shall notify the Proprietor to such effect and the Company shall at the Proprietor's written request and at the Proprietor's cost and expense and upon the condition that the same be permitted by the authorities of such foreign country transfer in accordance with the Proprietor's instructions any sums payable to the Proprietor to an account in the name of the Proprietor in such country.

10.8 The Proprietor confirms and agrees that the Company shall have the sole and exclusive right to initiate and maintain any and all actions or proceedings which the Company in its sole discretion deems necessary in order to establish maintain or preserve any of the Company's rights together with the right to defend any action in the sole name of the Company without prejudice to the right of the Company to join the Proprietor as a plaintiff or defendant in any such action and the Proprietor confirms that any money recovered by the Company in respect of such actions or proceedings shall form part of the Gross Receipts.

11. BREACH AND WAIVER

11.1 Either party may terminate this Agreement by notice in writing to the other if the other party shall commit any material breach of its obligations under this Agreement unless such breach is remedied to the extent that remedy is possible by the offending party within 30 days following notice in writing from the other party specifying the breach and causing the same to be remedied or if such other party shall compound or make any arrangements

---

Clause 10.5 This clause establishes confidentiality obligations (see paragraphs 1.5 to 1.12).

Clause 10.6 The Value Added Tax implications in relation to distribution agreements are considered in paragraphs 12.22 to 12.30.

Clause 10.7 This provision will not be appropriate in the case of an agreement between two companies in the United Kingdom but for the benefit of the Proprietor and permits the Company to deposit at the Proprietor's account any funds which are blocked through its exchange control obligations.

Clause 10.8 This provision is for the benefit of the Company since it permits the Company to initiate and pursue legal actions in relation to copyright infringement and other matters. Depending on the territory for which rights are granted and the nature of the rights granted, it may be necessary for the Company to obtain additional confirmation from the Proprietor.

with its creditors or go into liquidation or have a receiver or administrative receiver or receiver and manager appointed of all its assets.

11.2   Any act which if it were an act of the Proprietor would be a breach of this Agreement on its part shall be deemed to be an act of the Proprietor for which the Proprietor is responsible if done by any person firm or company who is an Associate of the Proprietor.

11.3   The waiver by either party of any breach by the other of the terms of this Agreement shall not be deemed to be a continuing waiver or a waiver of any other breach or default on the part of the other of the terms hereof.

12.   CONSEQUENCES OF TERMINATION

12.1   Upon termination of this Agreement for any reason the Company shall be entitled to make a retention of a sum equal to [25]% of Gross Receipts of the previous accounting period and retain such sum in order to cover the liability of the Company in respect of any Returns which might arise for a further period of 12 months.

12.2   After the expiry of the Term the Company shall give notice to the Proprietor of the Company's existing stock of Books and following such notice if the Proprietor does not collect such stock at its sole cost and expense within [14] days of the date of such notice the Company shall be entitled to dispose of such stock as it shall in its entire discretion think fit and shall be entitled to recover the cost and expense of such disposal from the Proprietor.

12.3   The termination of this Agreement for whatever reason shall not affect the respective rights and liabilities of the Proprietor and the Company which have accrued prior to such termination.

13.   NOTICES

13.1   Any notice or other document required to be given under this Agreement or any communication between the parties with respect to any of the provisions of this Agreement shall be in writing in English and be deemed duly given if signed by or on behalf of a duly authorised officer of the party giving the notice and if sent by pre-paid registered or recorded delivery post or by telex telegram cable facsimile transmission or other means of telecommunication in permanent written form to or left at the address of the party

---

Clause 11.1   This provision permits either party to terminate for breach in certain circumstances in the event of insolvency.

Clause 11.2   This provision protects the Company in circumstances where the Proprietor is a member of a group of companies and the distribution rights of publications of that group are being "funnelled" through the Proprietor. There may be circumstances in which the Proprietor is acting in the honest belief that (for example) no liability will be incurred by the Company distributing books, yet unknown to the Proprietor circumstances may (to the knowledge of the Proprietor's group companies) exist which might expose the Company to liability.

Clause 12.1   This provision protects the Company from liability in relation to returned books following termination.

Clause 12.2   This clause makes provision for the disposal of stock.

receiving such notice as set out at the head of this Agreement or as notified between the parties for the purpose of this Clause.

13.2 Any such notice or other communication shall be deemed to be given to and received by the addressee:

(a) at the time the same is left at the address of or handed to a representative of the party to be served

(b) by post on the day (not being a Sunday or a public holiday) two days following the day of posting and

(c) in the case of a telex telegram cable facsimile transmission or other means of telecommunication on the next following day.

13.3 In proving the giving of a notice it shall be sufficient to prove that the notice was left or that the envelope containing the notice was properly addressed and posted or that the applicable means of telecommunication was addressed and despatched and despatch of the transmission was confirmed and/or acknowledged (as the case may be).

13.4 Communications addressed to the Company shall be marked for the attention of [*name*] with a copy to [*name*] of [*address*].

14. DEFINITIONS AND INTERPRETATION

14.1 The following definitions apply in this Agreement:

"Associate".
In respect of the Proprietor any associate or associated company within the meaning of Section 416 or 417 of the Income and Corporation Taxes Act 1988.

"Book".
Any paperback or hardback or other printed version of any Title including all packaging and associated material and any CD-I CD-ROM or other electronic means of communicating any Title.

"Distribution Expenses".
Any and all costs and expenses incurred by the Company in connection with the distribution of the Books and the advertising and promotion of the Books and all other costs and expenses of whatever nature in connection with the Books and/or the Titles.

"Distribution Fee".
[*percentage*]% of [Gross Receipts] [Invoice Value].

"Existing Titles".
Any and all publications the rights in which are licensed to and/or owned by

---

Clause 13 A number of clauses in the document provide for a means of exercising rights and a notice provision is therefore necessary.

the Proprietor in the Territory [or any part of the Territory] including without limitation those publications short particulars of which are listed in Exhibit 3.

["Gross Receipts"].
All gross receipts and revenues received or receivable by the Company from the sale distribution and exploitation of the Titles and/or the Books in the Territory pursuant to this Agreement.

["Invoice Value"].
The invoice value of any and all consignments of Books ordered from the Company excluding any Value Added Tax payable in respect of such consignments.

"New Titles".
Any and all publications the rights in which are after the date of this Agreement licensed to and/or owned by the Proprietor in the Territory [or any part of the Territory] and which are issued [by the Proprietor] on the "[*name*]" imprint prior to the expiry of the Term.

"Publicity Material".
All publicity advertising and promotional material relating to the Books and the Titles and the persons who are featured in them which may be in the possession of the Proprietor or to which the Proprietor may have access at any time during the Term.

"Returns".
All Books which are returned to the Company described or indicated as or reasonably presumed to be damaged or sent out by the Company in error.

"Term".
The initial period of [*period*] commencing on [the date of this Agreement] [(*date*)] and continuing after that unless or until terminated by either party giving to the other at least [*specify*] calendar months' notice in writing such notice to be given after the expiry of the initial period of the Term.

"Territory".
[*Specify*].

"Titles".
Any and all Existing Titles and New Titles.

"Trade Mark".
[*Specify*] and any other trade mark owned by or licensed to the Proprietor during the Term.

14.2   Unless the context otherwise requires words denoting the singular shall include the plural and vice versa and words denoting any one gender shall include all genders and words denoting persons shall include bodies corporate unincorporated associations and partnerships.

Clause 14.1   The definitions contained in clause 14.1 will need review in order to fit the appropriate circumstances.

14.3   The word "copyright" means the entire copyright and design right subsisting under the laws of the United Kingdom and all analogous rights subsisting under the laws of each and every jurisdiction throughout the world.

14.4   Unless otherwise stated time shall be of the essence for the purpose of the performance of the Proprietor's obligations under this Agreement.

14.5   Unless otherwise stated references to clauses sub-clauses sub-paragraphs schedules annexures and exhibits relate to this Agreement.

15.   MISCELLANEOUS

15.1   If any provision of this Agreement shall be prohibited by or adjudged by a court to be unlawful void or unenforceable such provision shall to the extent required be severed from this Agreement and rendered ineffective so far as is possible without modifying the remaining provisions of this Agreement and shall in no way affect any other circumstances or the validity or enforceability of this Agreement.

15.2   This Agreement contains the full and complete understanding between the parties and supersedes all prior agreements and understandings whether written or oral pertaining to the subject matter of this Agreement and may not be varied except by an instrument in writing signed by all of the parties to this Agreement. The Proprietor acknowledges that no representations or promises not expressly contained in this Agreement have been made by the Company or any of its agents employees members or representatives in respect of the amounts of Gross Receipts payable under this Agreement (if any) or in any other respect whatever.

15.3   This Agreement is not and shall not be deemed to constitute a partnership or a joint venture between the parties.

15.4   The Proprietor shall not assign transfer mortgage charge or otherwise incumber any or all of its rights under this Agreement. The Company shall have the right to assign mortgage charge or otherwise incumber or sub-license the whole of its rights under this Agreement provided it shall not be relieved of its obligations to the Proprietor.

Clause 15.1   An explanation of the contractual doctrine of severance may be found at paragraph 12.22.

Clause 15.2   There are occasions where oral agreements or other understandings may be created in relation to a Work which may contain either additional obligations or obligations which conflict with those set out in subsequent written agreement. This provision makes it clear that all previous arrangements and understandings are at an end and the contract is the only document relevant to the obligations and rights of the parties in relation to its subject matter. The final part of the clause expressly excludes the possibility of any liability of the Company for misrepresentation on the part of any of its servants, agents, employees or representatives (see paragraph 2.17).

Clause 15.3   Under English law if two parties carry on business in common with a view to profit and share profit, the arrangement is capable of being considered a partnership. This provision ensures that no partnership is created inadvertently and also expressly excludes the possibility of an employment contract being created.

Clause 15.4   This provision precludes the Proprietor from assigning or transferring any of its rights yet permits the Company to do so.

15.5　This Agreement shall be construed in accordance with and governed by the laws of England and Wales the courts of which shall be courts of competent jurisdiction.

AS WITNESS the hands of the duly authorised representatives of the parties the day month and year first above written

SIGNED BY [*name of Officer*]
for and on behalf of
[*name of Proprietor*]

SIGNED BY [*name of Officer*]
for and on behalf of
[*name of Company*]

EXHIBIT 1

Company's Charges

(*Clause 3.2*)

EXHIBIT 2

Company's Delivery Requirements

(*Clause 3.3*)

EXHIBIT 3

Existing Titles

(*Clause 14.1*)

Clause 15.5　Where a contract is made between two entities in England and Wales, it will generally not be necessary to insert a provision of this nature, but where a contract is to be created with a foreign company (or a company situate in Scotland or Northern Ireland) this provision should always be included.

H. Merchandising

DOCUMENT 49

Merchandising agency agreement

[IMPORTANT NOTE: Please read the section "About this book" on page v, before copying or using this Document]

Purpose of this Document

This is a form of agreement suitable for use by a company when appointing an agent to negotiate merchandising licences in relation to a property. The Document is drafted from the point of view of the company.

Relevant text

The text of this Work covers a number of topics which are relevant to documents of this nature including:

- merchandising rights (paragraphs 11.12 to 11.18)
- remuneration provisions in rights agreements (paragraphs 11.22 to 11.26)
- taxation (paragraphs 11.27 to 11.29)
- buying and selling rights (paragraphs 11.2 to 11.9)
- trade marks and service rights (paragraphs 3.41 to 3.45)
- European Union directive on trade marks (paragraph 17.6)
- Value Added Tax (paragraphs 12.22 to 12.30)
- distribution and sale of goods (paragraphs 12.31 to 12.44)
- the United Kingdom and European Union competition law (paragraphs 16.2 to 16.28)

THIS AGREEMENT is made the   day of

BETWEEN:

(1)   *[Name]* LIMITED of *[address]*
      ("Company") and

(2)   *[Name]* LIMITED of *[address]*
      ("Agent")

IT IS AGREED as follows:

1.   AGENCY APPOINTMENT

1.1   Subject to and in consideration of the full and timely performance and observance by the Agent of the undertakings warranties and obligations in this Agreement the Company appoints the Agent as the Company's Agent during the Term to negotiate on behalf of the Company Licence Agreements in respect of the Merchandising Rights in the Property throughout the Territory.

1.2   The Agent undertakes to liaise with all Licensees and provide all materials required pursuant to the Licence Agreements in such manner as to exploit the Merchandising Rights to the maximum effect.

1.3   The Company undertakes to deliver to the Agent all such items as the Company reasonably considers necessary to enable the Agent to perform its obligations under this Agreement and warrants to the Agent that the Company is authorised to enter into and perform this Agreement.

1.4   The Agent undertakes as a material obligation to make available to the Company during the Term the services of the Key Personnel and undertakes to use the best endeavours of the Agent to procure the exploitation of the Merchandising Rights in as wide a manner as possible throughout the Territory by the maximum number of Licensees.

1.5   The Agent undertakes to carry out such advertising publicity and other activities as the Company may reasonably require in accordance with such budget and schedule for such activities as may be approved by the Company.

Clause 1.1   The appointment of the Agent to negotiate licence agreements in relation to the merchandising rights is subject to full and timely performance and observance by the Agent of its obligations. The provisions of this appointment may need to be reviewed in the light of the European Union directive relating to commercial Agents and the United Kingdom implementing legislation not yet in force at the date this book goes to print (see paragraphs 16.26 and 16.27).

Clause 1.2   Part of the Agent's duties consist in liaising with all licensees and dealing with all practical matters relating to the merchandising rights. It will normally be on the Agent's expertise in such matters that the Company will have relied in effecting the appointment.

Clause 1.3   The precise nature of materials to be delivered to the Agent may need to be specified.

Clause 1.4   Normally a Company will be relying on the services of one or two key individuals whose identities should be specified.

Clause 1.5   Whether or not a budget for advertising and publicity activities is appropriate will depend on the circumstances.

1.6   The Agent undertakes to refer to the Company all enquiries relating to the Property from possible Licensees and undertakes to make a list of all potential Licensees and provide the Company with copies of such a list as from time to time amended during the Term together with full details of all actual Licensees.

1.7   The Agent undertakes at all times throughout the Term to act in good faith and not to make any secret profit out of this arrangement and to disclose to the Company any and all matters which the Company may consider relevant to this Agreement and/or the Property and/or the Licensed Product.

2.   AGENT'S UNDERTAKINGS

The Agent acknowledges and undertakes and agrees that:

2.1   all rights and title in and to the Property and to all constituent parts of it and to any material supplied by the Company under this Agreement are reserved absolutely to the Company;

2.2   the Agent shall not by any act or omission impair or prejudice the copyright the Trade Mark or any other right in respect of the Property or in any constituent parts of it or deal with the material supplied under this Agreement so that any third party would have any lien or right to possess the same;

2.3   on the expiry or earlier determination of the Term the Agent shall at the cost of the Agent return or place to the order of the Company all material supplied by the Company in the same condition as that in which the same was received by the Agent fair wear and tear excepted as well as all material acquired by the Agent in relation to the Property during the Term. The Agent shall pay the costs incurred by the Company or its Agents in making good or otherwise restoring such material to the condition in which it should have been surrendered or in replacing any parts lost or destroyed or stolen during the Term;

2.4   the Agent shall not create any promotional or artwork material relating to the Property without the prior written consent of the Company and in respect of any material whatever relating to the Property commissioned or manufactured by the Agent the copyright shall be secured in the name of the Company and the title to the physical material so manufactured shall belong to and be dealt with as if such physical material had been supplied by the

---

Clause 1.6   This provision permits the Company and the Agent to plan who potential licensees are and to monitor the interest shown in the property.

Clause 1.7   The general principles of the laws of agency are examined in paragraphs 2.26 to 2.30.

Clause 2.1   Under this Agreement the Agent mainly requires the right to negotiate licences. All rights such as copyright and other rights in the property remain vested in the Company.

Clause 2.2   This clause effectively requires the Agent to retain control of the property as well as preventing the Agent from using the trade mark.

Clause 2.3   The Agent can be expected to acquire a significant quantity of material relating to the property which this provision requires the Agent to return to the Company as well as all material originally supplied by the Company.

Company and the Company shall at all times have unrestricted access to the same for its own purposes;

2.5   that the form of the Licence Agreements shall be approved by the Company in writing and shall be executed by the Company and be the only form of Licence Agreement that the Agent uses in connection with this agreement;

2.6   each Licence Agreement shall contain an irrevocable undertaking on the part of the Licensee to remit all sums payable to the Company to the Collection Account which undertaking shall not be capable of waiver or variation otherwise than by the Company in writing;

2.7   the Agent shall not alter nor add to any of the credits titles copyright notices trade marks trade names or insignia relating to the Property;

2.8   throughout the Term the Agent shall supply all Licensees with all material required by the Licensees in connection with the Property at their own cost and expense whenever possible and shall provide the Company with monthly statements of all exploitation of the Property which have taken place;

2.9   the Agent shall give full particulars to the Company immediately on any claim or threatened claim by any third party arising out of any exploitation of the Merchandising Rights;

2.10   the Agent shall not copy or duplicate any material provided by the Company under this Agreement or any part of it except for the purpose of providing materials pursuant to any Licence Agreements;

2.11   the Agent shall retain total control and actual possession and maintain safe secure and provide appropriate storage of any material provided by the Company under this Agreement at all times the risk in such Material passing to the Agent on the Company's appropriation of it under this Agreement;

Clause 2.4   The Company will wish to protect the goodwill and the identity of the property and for this reason the ability of the Agent to create any promotion or artwork material should be restricted.

Clause 2.5   Some agency arrangements permit the Agent to negotiate and execute on behalf of its principal agreements which are binding on the principal. Under this Agreement only the Company can sign licence agreements which must be in a form approved by the Company (such as the form contained in Document 50).

Clause 2.6   There are a number of different alternative ways of structuring the remuneration provisions. In this Agreement all income from the property is directed to a collection account which is in the name of the Publisher.

Clause 2.7   Careful attention needs to be paid to credits, titles, trade mark notices and copyright notices in order to ensure that the various intellectual property rights remain protected.

Clause 2.8   It is likely that licensees will have ongoing requirements for materials pursuant to the licence agreement. This provision places the onus of meeting requirements on the Agent and places the obligation to pay for such materials on the licensees.

Clause 2.9   It is in the interests of the Company to receive notice of any action or threatened claim at the earliest moment.

Clause 2.10   This provision expressly restricts the Agent's right to duplicate or make copies of any material relating to the property.

Clause 2.11   This provision requires the Agent to keep the physical materials secure in order to prevent unauthorised reproduction.

2.12   if any part of any material provided by the Company pursuant to this Agreement is lost or damaged in whole or in part the Agent shall pay to the Company the cost of replacing the same as a contract debt and shall swear such statements as may be required by the Company as to the fact of such loss;

2.13   the Agent shall exploit the Property to the best of the Agent's skill and ability and with the utmost despatch in order to ensure the highest possible Gross Receipts and shall ensure that the Property is at all times given fair and equitable treatment and is not discriminated against in favour of any other property which the Agent and/or its associates may have an interest in the Territory;

2.14   the Agent shall take all steps that may be necessary to secure and protect the copyright and all other rights in the Property and the Licensed Product and the trade mark in the Territory during the term in accordance with the directions (if any) of the Company and at the expense of the Company as regards all items of expenditure pre-approved by the Company;

2.15   the Agent shall not harm misuse or bring into disrepute the Property or any part of it;

2.16   the Agent shall procure the prompt payment by all Licensees to the Company of all sums owing to the Company under the Licence Agreement so far as reasonably practicable;

2.17   the Agent is not the undisclosed agent of any third party;

2.18   the Agent shall not make any warranties or representations to any Licensees and shall not pledge or bind the credit of the Company and in particular but without limitation the Agent shall not have the right to enter into any contract to enter into Licence Agreements;

Clause 2.12 There may be circumstances when the Company will wish to inquire as to why materials have been lost or damaged and although in many circumstances the Agent will be entirely liable, this provision creates express liability on the part of the Agent.

Clause 2.13 It will be in the Agent's interest to generate the highest possible gross receipts. The provision also, however, prevents unfair discrimination by the Agent against the property in favour of other properties in which the Agent or its associates have an interest.

Clause 2.14 There may be occasions where the Company is relying on the expertise of the Agent in the laws of a foreign jurisdiction in which case this provision will be relevant.

Clause 2.15 The goodwill in properties may be damaged by insensitive licensing. When dealing with foreign territories there may be cultural or linguistic connotations of which the Company is unaware which may cause the property of the Company to be brought into disrepute.

Clause 2.16 There will be circumstances where the Agent has a relationship with licensees which may be used in order to deal with any slow payment or other problems of this nature.

Clause 2.17 The Company will generally wish to deal with the Agent, and not an undisclosed principal (see paragraphs 2.26 to 2.30).

Clause 2.18 This provision expressly prohibits the Agent creating any contractual arrangement or liability on behalf of the Company towards third parties (see paragraphs 2.26 to 2.30).

2.19 the Agent shall keep confidential and shall not disclose to any third parties (other than professional advisers where necessary) the results of any such inspection or any of the terms of this Agreement or the Property or any Licence Agreement or any matters incidental to it or relating to the business of the Company;

2.20 The Agent undertakes to indemnify the Company and keep the Company fully indemnified from and against all actions proceedings claims demands costs (including without prejudice to the generality of this provision the legal costs of the Company on a solicitor and own client basis) awards and damages arising directly or indirectly as a result of any breach or non-performance by the Agent of any of the Agent's undertakings warranties or obligations under this Agreement.

3. REMUNERATION

3.1 Subject to the full and timely performance and observance by the Agent of its undertakings warranties and obligations in this Agreement the Company shall on each Accounting Date during the Term:

(a) pay to the Agent the Commission; and

(b) reimburse the Agent the amount of the Expenses subject to the production and delivery to the Company of receipts and vouchers evidencing such expenditure has been incurred by the Agent solely in connection with the Property;

3.2 the Company shall on each Accounting Date render to the Agent a full and complete statement showing all moneys owning to the Agent hereunder in respect of the preceding Accounting Period.

4. FORCE MAJEURE

The Company shall not be liable to the Agent for any failure to supply or procure the supply of any material to be supplied pursuant to this Agreement as a result of any circumstance beyond the control of the Company or because of any proceedings or threat of proceedings by a third party the Company is advised to withdraw the Property from distribution and gives notice in writing to the Agent to this effect the Company shall not incur any liability for any expenses or losses direct or consequential or otherwise whatever which may be suffered by the Agent.

Clause 2.19 Although confidentiality may be implied in relation to most of the matters stated in this Agreement (see paragraphs 1.2 to 1.12), this provision imposes an express obligation.

Clause 3 The remuneration provisions will need to be adjusted to fit the appropriate circumstances of the transaction. In this case all gross receipts are paid into a collection account controlled by the Company which agrees on each accounting date to pay to the Agent the commission and expenses. There will be circumstances where this provision may not be acceptable to the Agent.

There will also be circumstances where the Company will not be able to accept the risk that all gross receipts are paid into an account controlled by the Agent. If the Agent becomes insolvent (see Chapter 15) the gross receipts to which the Company is entitled may be used for the purposes of paying the Agent's secured creditors. In some cases Agreements may provide for charges or security interests to be created by the Agent (see paragraph 12.17) or for the collection accounts to be administered by both parties or for a separate third party collection agent to be appointed.

Clause 4 For a brief explanation of force majeure provisions reference should be made to paragraph 2.20.

5.   DETERMINATION

It shall constitute the repudiation by the Agent of its obligations under this Agreement and the Company shall be entitled by notice to the Agent to accept such repudiation in termination of the Agent's rights pursuant to this Agreement if:

5.1   the Agent is in breach of any material term of this Agreement which is incapable of remedy or if capable of remedy is not remedied within seven days of the Agent becoming aware of it;

5.2   any of the Agent's representations shall prove to have been incorrect when made or become materially incorrect and the Company's rights and entitlements under this Agreement are materially and adversely affected;

5.3   the Agent transfers disposes of or threatens to transfer or dispose of any part of its assets which is in the reasonable opinion of the Company to prevent or materially to inhibit the performance by the Agent of its obligations under this Agreement;

5.4   any indebtedness guarantee or similar obligation of the Agent or of any guarantor of the Agent becomes due or capable of being declared due before its stated maturity or is not discharged at maturity or the Agent or any guarantor of the Agent defaults under or commits a breach of the provisions of any guarantee or other obligation (whether actual or contingent) of any agreement pursuant to which any such indebtedness guarantee or other obligation was incurred all or any of which shall in the reasonable opinion of the Company materially affect its rights and entitlements under this Agreement;

5.5   the Agent is declared or becomes insolvent;

5.6   the Agent convenes a meeting of its creditors or proposes or makes any arrangement or composition with or any assignment for the benefit of its creditors or a petition is presented or a meeting is convened for the purpose of considering a resolution or other steps are taken for the winding up of the Agent (save for the purpose of and followed by a voluntary reconstruction or amalgamation previously approved in writing by the Company) or if an

---

Clause 5.1   This clause permits the Agent to remedy a non-pecuniary material breach. The time period allowed is longer than that for a pecuniary breach.

Clause 5.2   There may be circumstances where the Company has entered into the Agreement on the basis of representations made by the Agent. This clause permits the Company to terminate the Agreement if the representations prove to have been incorrect or subsequently become incorrect.

Clause 5.3   There are occasions where an Agent becomes less financially secure and disposes of its assets. Where a Company has entered into an Agreement in reliance on the Agent being an entity of substance, such occasions may cause concern to the Company and this provision permits the Company to terminate the Agreement in such instances.

Clause 5.4   Financial default of the Agent in relation to any guarantee or obligation is a further event normally permitting termination.

Clause 5.5   For the consequences of insolvency reference should be made to paragraphs 15.2 to 15.4.

incumbrancer takes possession of or a trustee receiver administrator administrative receiver liquidator or similar officer is appointed in respect of all or any part of its business or assets or any distress execution or other legal process is levied threatened enforced upon or sued out against any of such assets

5.7   the Agent shall abandon or announce that it intends to abandon the business of exploiting merchandising rights.

6.   EFFECT OF DETERMINATION

6.1   Upon determination under Clause 5 of the Agent's rights under this Agreement:

(a)   the Company may without notice retake possession of all material delivered by the Company under this Agreement and for that purpose be entitled to enter upon any land or building in the possession power or control of the Agent where all material delivered by the Company under this Agreement may be situated or believed to be situated

(b)   all material delivered by the Company under this Agreement shall no longer be in the Agent's possession or control with the Company's consent.

6.2   Upon the termination of the Term by effluxion of time the Agent shall be responsible at its own risk for re-delivery of all material delivered by the Company under this Agreement and the Property to such address in the United Kingdom as the Company may direct in good and serviceable condition.

6.3   The Agent undertakes not for a period of [*specify*] years after the termination or expiry of this Agreement to solicit any current or former Licensee or customers of the Company or engage directly in any capacity in any business venture which competes with the Property and/or Licensed Products in the Territory.

7.   ASSIGNMENT

The rights granted in this Agreement are personal to the Agent who shall not have the right to assign license or sub-license the whole or any part of such rights. The Company shall have the right at any time to assign its obligations

---

Clause 5.6   There may be occasions when a licensee does not actually become insolvent but where a creditor enforces security over the licensee's business. This could have serious consequences for a Company and this clause protects the Company's interests by providing that such circumstances will entitle the Company to terminate the Agreement.

Clause 5.7   Where a licensee ceases to carry on business or announces that it intends to cease its business, a Company will wish to recover its rights as soon as possible.

Clause 6.1   The provisions of this clause apply if the Company terminates the Agreement.

Clause 6.2   The provisions of this clause apply if the Agreement expires through passage of time.

Clause 6.3   The obligations of the Agent under this clause need to be reviewed in the light of the European Union directive on commercial Agents and implementing legislation in the United Kingdom not yet in force at the date of going to print (see paragraphs 16.26 and 16.27). The provisions of the Restrictive Trade Practices Act 1976 may also be relevant.

pursuant to this Agreement and/or its right to receive income pursuant to this Agreement.

8.   NOTICE

8.1   Any notice or other document required to be given under this Agreement or any communication between the parties with respect to any of the provisions of this Agreement shall be in writing in English and be deemed duly given if signed by or on behalf of a duly authorised officer of the party giving the notice and if left at or sent by pre-paid registered or recorded delivery post or by telex telegram cable facsimile transmission or other means of telecommunication in permanent written form to the address of the party receiving such notice as set out at the head of the Agreement or as notified between the parties for the purpose of this Clause.

8.2   Any such notice or other communication shall be deemed to be given to and received by the addressee:

(a)   at the time the same is left at the address of or handed to a representative of the party to be served

(b)   by post on the day not being a Sunday or Public Holiday two days following the date of posting

(c)   in the case of a telex telegram cable facsimile transmission or other means of telecommunication on the next following day.

8.3   In proving the giving of a notice it should be sufficient to prove that the notice was left or that the envelope containing the notice was properly addressed and posted or that the applicable means of telecommunication was addressed and despatched and despatch of the transmission was confirmed and/or acknowledged as the case may be.

8.4   Communications addressed to the Company shall be marked for the attention of [*name*] with a copy to [*name*] of [*address*].

9.   DEFINITIONS AND INTERPRETATION

9.1   The following definitions apply in this Agreement:

"Accounting Date"
90 days from the end of each Accounting Period

"Accounting Period"
In respect of the first three years following the date of this Agreement consecutive periods of three months to 31 March 30 June 30 September and 31 December and thereafter periods of six months to 30 June and 31 December in each year during the Term

---

Clause 7   Although agency agreements are not normally personal this provision clarifies the rights of the Agent and the Company.

Clause 8   A number of clauses in the Document provide for a means of exercising rights and a notice provision is therefore necessary.

"Collection Account"
An interest bearing sterling account number [*number*] in the name of the
Company at [*name*] Bank plc of [*address*] designated Property Licence
Account

"Commission"
[*percentage*]% of Net Receipts

"Expenses"
Those costs and expenses actually incurred by the Agent pursuant to contractual relationships with third parties for which receipts and vouchers are
delivered by the Agent to the Company and which expended solely in
connection with the licensing of the Merchandising Rights and negotiation of
Licence Agreements not to exceed in the aggregate [US$] [£] [*specify*]

"Gross Receipts"
All gross receipts and revenue actually received by the Company into the
Collection Account directly and identifiably from the exploitation of the
Merchandising Rights in the Territory during the Term pursuant to any
Licence Agreement negotiated by the Agent and executed by the Company
pursuant to this Agreement

"Key Personnel"
[*Specify*]

"Licensee"
Any party or parties to any Licence Agreement

"Licence Agreement"
Any agreement which the Company shall enter into with a Licensee pursuant
to this Agreement relating to the exploitation of the Merchandising Rights in
the Territory

"Licensed Product"
Any Product produced packaged sold or marketed derived from or incorporating any part of the Property

"Merchandising Rights"
The right to manufacture package market sell and distribute the Licensed
Product and to authorise others to do so

"Net Receipts"
Gross Receipts after the deduction of the Expenses

"Property"
[*Specify*] and/or the Trade Mark

"Product"
[*Specify*]

"Term"
The period commencing on the date of this Agreement and ending [*specify*]
years from the date of this Agreement

"Territory"
[*Specify*]

"Trade Mark"
[*Specify*]

9.2   Unless the context otherwise requires words denoting the singular shall include the plural and vice versa and words denoting any one gender shall include all genders and words denoting persons shall include bodies corporate unincorporated associations and partnerships.

9.3   Unless otherwise stated time shall be of the essence for the purpose of the performance of the Agent's obligations pursuant to this Agreement.

9.4   Unless otherwise stated references to clauses sub-clauses paragraphs sub-paragraphs schedules annexures and exhibits relate to this Agreement.

10.   MISCELLANEOUS

10.1   This Agreement shall not be deemed to constitute a partnership or joint venture between the parties.

10.2   If any provision of this Agreement shall be prohibited by or adjudged by a Court to be unlawful void or unenforceable such provision shall to the extent required be severed from this Agreement and rendered ineffective as far as possible without modifying the remaining provisions of this Agreement and shall not in any way affect any other circumstances or the validity or enforcement of this Agreement.

10.3   This Agreement contains the full and complete understanding between the parties and supersedes all prior arrangements and understandings whether written or oral appertaining to the subject matter of this Agreement and may not be varied except by an instrument in writing signed by all of the parties to this Agreement. The Agent acknowledges that no representations or promises not expressly contained in this Agreement have been made by the Company or any of its servants agents employees members or representatives.

Clause 9   The provisions of this clause will need to be adjusted to reflect the relevant circumstances.

Clause 10.1   Under English law if two parties carry on business in common with a view to profit and share profit, the arrangement is capable of being considered a partnership. This provision ensures that no partnership is created inadvertently and also expressly excludes the possibility of an employment contract being created.

Clause 10.2   For an explanation of the doctrine of severance reference should be made to paragraph 2.22.

Clause 10.3   There are occasions where oral agreements or other understandings may be created in relation to a Work which may contain either additional obligations or obligations which conflict with those set out in subsequent written agreement. This provision makes it clear that all previous arrangements and understandings are at an end and the contract is the only document relevant to the obligations and rights of the parties in relation to its subject matter. The final part of the clause expressly excludes the possibility of any liability on the part of a Company for misrepresentation on the part of any of its servants, agents, employees or representatives.

10.4   No failure or delay on the part of any of the parties to this Agreement relating to the exercise of any right power privilege or remedy provided under this Agreement shall operate as a waiver of such right power privilege or remedy or as a waiver of any preceding or succeeding breach by the other party to this Agreement nor shall any single or partial exercise of any right power privilege or remedy preclude any other or further exercise of such or any other right power privilege or remedy provided in this Agreement all of which are several and cumulative and are not exclusive of each other or of any other rights or remedies otherwise available to a party at law or in equity.

10.5   This Agreement shall be governed by and construed in accordance with the laws of England and Wales the courts of which shall be courts of competent jurisdiction.

AS WITNESS the hands of the duly authorised representatives of the parties the day month and year first above written

SIGNED by [*name of Officer*]

[*name of Company*]

SIGNED by [*name of Officer*]
for and on behalf of
[*name of Agent*]

Clause 10.4   This provision preserves the Company's rights in circumstances where, for example, the Company wishes to negotiate to resolve a breach by the Agent rather than enforce its strict contractual rights.

Clause 10.5   Where a contract is made between two entities in England and Wales, it will generally not be necessary to insert a provision of this nature, but where a contract is to be created with a foreign company (or a company situate in Scotland or Northern Ireland) this provision should always be included.

DOCUMENT 50

Merchandising licence

[IMPORTANT NOTE: Please read the section "About this book" on page v, before copying or using this Document]

Purpose of this Document

This is a form of agreement suitable for use by a company when licensing merchandising rights to a licensee. The Document is drafted from the point of view of the company and is suitable for use in connection with a merchandising agency agreement along the lines of Document 49.

Relevant text

The text of this Work covers a number of topics which are relevant to documents of this nature including:

- merchandising rights (paragraphs 11.12 to 11.18)
- remuneration provisions in rights agreements (paragraphs 11.22 to 11.26)
- taxation (paragraphs 11.27 to 11.29)
- buying and selling rights (paragraphs 11.2 to 11.9)
- trade marks and service rights (paragraphs 3.41 to 3.45)
- European Union directive on trade marks (paragraph 17.6)
- Value Added Tax (paragraphs 12.22 to 12.30)
- distribution and sale of goods (paragraphs 12.31 to 12.44)
- the United Kingdom and European Union competition law (paragraphs 16.2 to 16.28)

THIS AGREEMENT is made the   day of

BETWEEN:

(1) [*Name*] LIMITED of [*address*]
     ("Company") and
(2) [*Name*] LIMITED of [*address*]
     ("Licensee")

IT IS AGREED as follows:

1. GRANT OF RIGHTS

In consideration of the obligations warranties and undertakings of the Licensee in this Agreement and subject to and conditional upon their full and timely performance and observance the Company:

1.1 grants to the Licensee the non-exclusive right to manufacture and the sole and exclusive right to package market sell and distribute the Licensed Product in the Territory during the Term;

1.2 undertakes to enter into a licence with the Licensee in respect of the Trademark in the form set out in Exhibit 1;

1.3 undertakes to effect Delivery by no later than the Delivery Date.

2. PUBLISHER'S WARRANTIES

The Company warrants agrees and undertakes with the Licensee that:

2.1 the Company is free to enter into this Agreement and grant the Licensee the rights granted in it and is not under any disability restriction or prohibition which might prevent the Company from performing or observing any of the Company's obligations under this Agreement;

2.2 the Company has not entered into and shall not enter into any arrangement which may conflict with this Agreement;

2.3 following the expiry of the Term by effluxion of time the Licensee shall have the non-exclusive right subject to the terms and conditions of this Agreement for the further period of three calendar months to sell off the Licensed Product previously manufactured by or on behalf of the Licensee during the Term provided that in the last two calendar quarters of the Term the Licensee shall not manufacture items of Licensed Product in excess of the average aggregate number of sales of the Licensed Product in the preceding Accounting Period.

Clause 1.1 The manufacturing right is non-exclusive but will permit other licensees to manufacture in the Territory.

Clause 1.2 It may be necessary for the Company to enter into a registered user agreement in relation to the Trademark.

Clause 2.3 For an explanation as to the commercial significance of sell-off periods, reference should be made to paragraphs 12.4 and 11.13.

3. REMUNERATION

The Licensee undertakes to pay to the Company:

3.1 the Advance as to [*percentage*]% on signature of this Agreement and [*percentage*]% on Delivery;

3.2 the Royalty on each Accounting Date in accordance with the provisions of this Agreement;

3.3 such costs in respect of the manufacture and delivery to the Licensee of the Delivery Material and the preparation and drafting and negotiation of this Agreement as may be notified by the Company in writing.

4. DISTRIBUTION

The Licensee warrants undertakes and agrees with the Company that:

4.1 the Licensee is free to enter into and fully perform this Agreement;

4.2 the Licensee shall not do or omit to do or permit there to be done any act which may denigrate the value of or render invalid the Trademark or any right of copyright or other rights licensed under this Agreement or in any way detract from the value of the Property;

4.3 the Licensee shall maintain at its own expense product liability insurance in such amount as may be adequate to protect the Licensee and the Company against any and all claims actions losses or damages arising out of any actual or alleged defects in the Licensed Product such product liability insurance being from a reputable recognised insurance company;

4.4 the Licensee shall at the sole cost and expense of the Licensee take all steps that may be necessary to secure and protect the copyright and all other rights in the Property and the Licensed Product and the Trade mark in the Territory and during the Term in accordance with the directions (if any) of the Company;

4.5 the Licensee shall not sell or consign for sale any Licensed Product on a sale or return or stock balancing basis or permit any Licensed Product to be sold or exported outside the Territory unless with the prior written consent of the Company;

Clause 3 The provisions of this clause will need to be adjusted to reflect the appropriate circumstances. As to advances and minimum guarantees and royalties generally see paragraphs 11.22 and 11.23.

Clause 4.2 This clause effectively requires the Licensee to retain control of the property as well as preventing the Agent from using the Trademark.

Clause 4.3 The Company must protect itself from third party claims in relation to defective products. There may be circumstances where the Company may wish to have sight of the policy of insurance and have its interest on the policy as named assured and loss payee.

Clause 4.4 There may be occasions where the Company is relying on the expertise of the Licensee in the laws of a foreign jurisdiction in which case this provision will be relevant.

Clause 4.5 This provision first prevents sale or return sales and second prevents sales outside the Territory.

4.6 the Licensee shall give full particulars to the Company on becoming aware of any actual or threatened claim by any third party in connection with the Licensed Product;

4.7 the Licensee shall market the Licensed Product throughout the Territory within [*six*] months of Delivery and diligently and continuously maintain the Licensed Product in manufacture and distribution in the Territory throughout the Term;

4.8 the Licensee shall advertise the Licensed Product throughout the Territory during the Term and shall expend in each year not less than the Minimum Advertising Expenditure;

4.9 the Licensee shall exploit the rights granted to the Licensee to the best of the Licensee's skill and ability in accordance with the pricing policies from time to time specified by the Company with the utmost despatch and ensure the highest possible Royalties payable to the Company and ensure that the Licensed Product is given fair and equitable treatment and not discriminated in favour of any other property which the Licensee may have for distribution in the Territory;

4.10 no costs incurred in the manufacture sale distribution or exploitation of the Licensed Product shall be deductible from any sums payable by the Licensee;

4.11 [the sale price of the Licensed Product shall be not less than [*specify*] or such other sum as may be approved in writing by the Company or the minimum Royalty payable by the Licensee to the Company in respect of each item of Licensed Product sold shall be not less than [*specify*]];

4.12 the Licensee shall not enter into any arrangements for the sale of Premiums in connection with the Licensed Product without the prior written consent of the Company;

Clause 4.6 It is in the interests of the Company to receive notice of any action or threatened claim at the earliest moment.

Clause 4.7 The Company will generally wish the licensed product to be on sale in the Territory at the earliest possible opportunity and maintained in distribution throughout the Term of the Agreement.

Clause 4.8 The amount of advertising expenditure (if any) to be committed by the Licensee during each year of the term or during the Agreement will depend on the circumstances.

Clause 4.9 It will be in the Licensee's interest to generate the highest possible gross receipts. The provision also, however, prevents unfair discrimination by the Licensee against the property in favour of other properties in which the Licensee or its associates have an interest.

Clause 4.10 This provision clarifies the financial aspects of the transaction. It is important from the Company's point of view that no costs are deducted from the royalty.

Clause 4.11 This provision needs to be reviewed carefully in the light of the matters referred to in paragraphs 16.9 to 16.15 and 16.24 and 16.25 and 16.2 to 16.8. Generally speaking the stipulations for minimum retail price is not permissible within the European Union although there may be some territories in which such arrangements are tolerated.

Clause 4.12 The licensing of the property for premium (ie give away or nominal sale) used generally reduces the revenue earning capacity of the property.

4.13   nothing in this Agreement shall or shall be deemed to prevent the Company from granting licences in respect of the Property for product other than the Product;

4.14   the Company reserves to itself absolutely the right to license and/or manufacture Premiums;

4.15   the Licensee shall not harm misuse or bring into disrepute the Property the Licensed Product or any part of them;

4.16   the Licensee shall not knowingly manufacture or distribute any defective or sub-standard items of Licensed Product and shall ensure that all items of Licensed Product are of the highest attainable quality;

4.17   the Licensee shall not assign charge license sub-license or otherwise part with possession of the benefit or burden of this Agreement without the prior written consent of the Company;

4.18   the Licensee shall indemnify and keep fully indemnified the Company from and against all actions proceedings claims demands costs (including without prejudice to the generality of this provision the legal costs of the Company on a solicitor and own client basis) awards and damages arising directly or indirectly as a result of any breach or non-performance by the Licensee of any of the Licensee's undertakings warranties or obligations under this Agreement.

5.   THIRD PARTY INFRINGEMENT

5.1   If either the Company or the Licensee shall become aware of any infringement in relation to the Licensed Product or the Property then such party shall promptly give written notice of such infringement to the other. The Licensee undertakes to assist the Company to the extent necessary in protecting any of the Company's rights in the Property or the Licensed Product and the Licensee shall of the Company's request and expense allow the Company to conduct any negotiations or litigation or settle any claim or action and the Licensee shall give the Company all reasonable assistance in connection with such negotiation litigation or settlement.

5.2   Subject to Clause 5.1 the Licensee shall have the right to bring and/or defend any civil action in respect of the Property or the Licensed Product

---

Clause 4.13   The generic type of product for which the licence will be granted will be specified in the definitions. This provision clarifies that the Company is free to license the property for other types of product.

Clause 4.14   The right to license and/or manufacture premiums is reserved to the Company.

Clause 4.15   The goodwill in properties may be damaged by insensitive licensing. When dealing with foreign territories there may be cultural or linguistic connotations of which the Company is unaware which may cause the Company to be brought into disrepute.

Clause 4.16   Quality control is important to the Company.

Clause 4.17   Although licences are generally personal and non-assignable this provision expressly provides that the Licensee cannot assign or sub-license.

Clause 5.1   Whether or not the Company and the Licensee have co-extensive rights of action to curtail infringement in the territory depends on the laws of the country concerned (see paragraphs 13.2 to 13.10).

provided that the Licensee shall not make any admission or statement in connection with such action without the prior written consent of the Company.

5.3   The Licensee shall pay one half and the Company shall pay one half of all reasonable legal costs in connection with any such action and any monetary recovery from litigation commenced by the Licensee in this clause shall first be applied against all reasonable legal fees and costs of the Company or the Licensee and the remainder shall be divided equally between the Company and the Licensee.

6.   QUALITY AND DESIGN OF LICENSED PRODUCT

The Licensee undertakes and agrees with the Company that:

6.1   the Licensed Product shall be of a high standard and of such style appearance and quality as to be adequate and suited to exploitation to the best advantage of the Property and to protect and enhance the value of the Property and the goodwill relating to it;

6.2   the Licensed Product shall be manufactured sold and distributed in accordance with all applicable laws in the Territory and the policy of sale distribution and exploitation by the Licensee shall be consistent with earning the highest possible royalties and making available Licensed Product of the highest possible standard so as not to reflect in any adverse manner on the good name of the Company or the Property;

6.3   the Licensee shall before selling or distributing any item of Licensed Product furnish the Company free of charge for the written approval of the Company a reasonable number of samples of such Licensed Product together with all cartons containers packaging and wrapping material;

6.4   the quality and style of all articles provided by the Licensee to the Company pursuant to Clause 6.3 as well as any carton container or packing or wrapping material shall be subject to the reasonable approval of the Company. Following approval of any sample or item the Licensee shall not depart in any material respect from the quality of such sample in manufacturing the Licensed Product without the prior written consent of the Company;

Clause 5.2 It is important for the Company to restrict the Licensee from making any admission or claim in proceedings, since there may be financial consequences for the Company.

Clause 5.3 The apportionment and responsibility of legal costs and the apportionment of money recovered are matters which under the laws of England and Wales may be dealt with between the parties.

Clause 6.1 Style, appearance, quality and high standard are all matters which the Company will wish to maintain.

Clause 6.2 The Company is reliant on the Licensee for compliance with local laws.

Clause 6.3 This provision permits the Company to approve of any sample before the item is manufactured.

Clause 6.4 This provision sets the standard of manufacturing once approval has been granted and permits the Company to approve or require changes to packaging and containers.

6.5   the Licensee shall from time to time as requested by the Company provide the Company at the expense of the Licensee with samples of the Licensed Product to enable the Company to inspect and test the same;

6.6   the Company through its authorised representative may upon reasonable notice at its own expense visit the premises of the Licensee during normal business hours to inspect the method of manufacture of the Licensed Product and the materials used and the packaging and storing of the Licensed Product provided that the Company undertakes to keep any information it acquires confidential;

6.7   the Licensee shall not alter the design or constitution of the Licensed Product without the prior written consent of the Company.

7.   LABELLING

7.1   The Licensee shall affix the following notice to the Licensed Product and all its packaging:

"© [*specify name*] [*year of manufacture*] All rights reserved"

In addition the Licensee shall affix to the Licensed Product and all packaging:

"[*name of Trademark*] is a Trademark used under licence from [*name of Licensor*] Limited"

together with any additional notices which may be required by law within the Territory in order to protect the Licensed Product and in particular all rights of Trademark and copyright in the Licensed Product and the Property.

7.2   The Licensee shall ensure that the Licensed Property and all packaging bears the Trademark and any appropriate notice required by the laws in the Territory or by the Company.

7.3   The Licensee shall not use any mark or name similar to the Trademark in respect of any goods similar to the Licensed Product.

7.4   The Licensee agrees to co-operate fully and in good faith with the Company for the purpose of securing or preserving the rights of the Company in and to the Licensed Product and the Property.

7.5   On the determination or expiry of this Agreement the ownership of all

---

Clause 6.5   This provision permits the Company from time to time to inspect the quality of items being manufactured.

Clause 6.6   This provision also aims at maintaining high standards.

Clause 6.7   There may be occasions where the parties wish to alter the design of manufactured goods either to reduce manufacturing costs or other reasons.

Clause 7.1   The importance of affixing correct copyright notices and Trademark notices is fundamental to the maintenance of the intellectual property rights in the property.

Clause 7.2   There will be occasions where local laws may require different notice provisions.

Clause 7.3   Use by the Licensee of a similar mark may, in fact, amount to competing use which would not be in the Company's interest.

Clause 7.4   This provision permits the Company to comply with local laws.

rights licensed pursuant to this Agreement shall automatically revert to the Company and the Licensee shall execute any instruments required by the Company to confirm the foregoing.

8. RESERVATION OF RIGHTS

8.1 Nothing contained in this Agreement shall be construed as an assignment or grant to the Licensee of any rights title or interest in or to the Property it being understood that all rights in and to the Property and the Trademark and the Licensed Property other than the licence granted to the Licensee pursuant to Clause 1 are reserved by the Company.

8.2 The Licensee agrees that on termination or expiry of this Agreement the Licensee shall be deemed to have assigned transferred and conveyed to the Company any and all rights of copyright trademark rights equity goodwill title or other right in and to the Property and the Licensed Product which may have been obtained by the Licensee or vested in the Licensee and the Licensee undertakes to execute any instruments requested by the Company to accomplish or confirm the foregoing.

8.3 The Licensee undertakes and agrees that the use by the Licensee of the Trademark shall not operate to transfer to the Licensee any right in respect of the Trademark and that the whole of such Trademark including any and all goodwill associated with it shall at all times remain vested in the Company absolutely.

9. PROMOTIONAL MATERIAL

9.1 The cost of all artwork to be used by the Licensee in connection with the Licensed Product shall be borne by the Licensee.

9.2 All artwork developed by the Licensee in connection with the Property shall be subject to the express prior written approval of the Company and shall be assigned to the Company absolutely and may not be used in connection with the Property or the Licensed Product without such approval.

9.3 The Company shall have the non-exclusive and irrevocable licence in respect of all artwork produced by the Licensee to use such artwork in any Territory reserved by the Company or to license the use of such artwork to other third party licensees of the Company and the Licensee acknowledges that it shall have no right in respect of the use of such artwork in any territories other than the Territory and the Company shall not be required to

---

Clause 7.5 This provision permits the Company to obtain written confirmation from the Licensee following expiry of the term that the Licensee has acquired no rights in the Property.

Clause 8.1 All rights in the Property other than the licence granted to the Licensee are reserved to the Company.

Clause 8.2 This provision transfers to the Company any property or intellectual property rights acquired by the Licensee.

Clause 8.3 If the Licensee enters into a separate registered user agreement for the Trademark, a similar provision may be contained in the registered user agreement.

Clause 9.2 The Company will wish to have control over artwork produced by the Licensee in order to protect the goodwill in the Property.

make any payments to the Licensee in respect of its use or the use by any third party of such artwork.

9.4   The Company shall have the right but not the obligation to use the name of the Licensee in any publicity or advertising relating to the Property or the Licensed Product.

10.   ENHANCEMENTS

10.1   The Licensee shall obtain the consent of the Company to use of any enhancement or improvement in or in connection with the Licensed Product.

10.2   Where the consent of the Company is given in respect of any enhancement the rights in respect of such enhancement shall be deemed to vest in the Company absolutely throughout the world subject to a licence in favour of the Licensee for a territory and term co-extensive to the rights granted to the Licensee pursuant to Clause 1.

10.3   The Licensee undertakes that it shall not during the Term market manufacture sell or distribute any item or product of the description of the Licensed Product or any other product which may be similar to the Licensed Product.

11.   GOODWILL

The Licensee acknowledges that all existing and/or future goodwill in and to the Property the Licensed Product and any artwork associated with the same belongs or shall belong to the Company absolutely and that the Licensee has not now nor shall at any time in the future have any right title or interest in or to such goodwill.

12.   CONFIDENTIALITY

The Licensee acknowledges that all information received by the Licensee in connection with the Licensed Product and the Property is of a confidential nature and has or will have been communicated to the Licensee in the strictest confidence on terms requiring the Licensee not to divulge or permit such information to be divulged to third parties nor to permit such information to be used by third parties and not to use such information so as to gain unfair advantage over or compete with the Company at any time whether before or after the expiry of the Term and the Licensee warrants and undertakes with the Company that it shall not do or omit to do anything which might result in a breach of such terms.

Clause 9.3   This provision permits the Company to use the artwork in other territories.

Clause 10.1   There will be circumstances in which improvements or enhancements to the Property are made to the Licensee.

Clause 10.2   A Company will normally wish to obtain the right to any enhancement or improvements created by a Licensee subject to the Licensee being able to use such improvements or enhancements in the territory during the term. This provision will need to be reviewed when used in the European Union in order to comply with European Union legislation (see paragraphs 16.9 to 16.28).

Clause 12   Although confidentiality of certain aspects of the Agreement will be implied, this clause imposes an express confidentiality obligation (see paragraphs 1.2 to 1.12).

13.   PAYMENT

13.1   The Licensee shall not have the right to withhold any part of sums due to the Company as a reserve against returns and/or credits and in the event that the Licensee is required by law to make any withholding from sums to be remitted to the Company the Licensee shall prior to the making of any withholding of payment furnish the Company with evidence satisfactory to the Company in its entire discretion as to the Licensee's obligation to make such withholding of payment.

13.2   The Licensee undertakes to make all payments required under this Agreement by bankers draft in pounds sterling drawn on an English bank or by telegraphic transfer to the account of the Company as follows:

Bank   :

Branch   :

Address   :

Account Number   :

Sort Code   :

Attention   :

13.3   The Licensee undertakes that all Net Sales Revenues shall be converted into sterling at the best obtainable rate of exchange on each Accounting Date provided that in the event of any continuous materially adverse currency movement of longer than seven days' duration during any Accounting Period it shall be the responsibility of the Licensee to ensure that all Net Sales Revenues are converted into sterling as soon as practicable following receipt and the Licensee shall follow all directions to the Company from time to time relating to currency conversion.

13.4   If exchange control or other restrictions prevent or threaten to prevent the remittance to the Company of any money payable under this Agreement the Licensee shall immediately advise the Company in writing and follow the Company's instructions in respect of the money to be remitted including if required depositing the same with any bank or other person designated by the Company at such location as may be designated by the Company.

Clause 13.1   The Company will normally wish to eliminate any possibility of the Licensee deducting reserves from sums due to the Company.

Clause 13.2   Whether or not payment is required to be made by telegraphic transfer will depend on the circumstances.

Clause 13.3   If the Licensee is a foreign country, currency conversion provisions may need to be inserted.

Clause 13.4   Depending on the territory for which rights are being licensed it may be advisable to insert an exchange control provision.

13.5   If any withholding or other taxes are required to be deducted from any moneys provided to be remitted to the Company pursuant to this Agreement it shall be the responsibility of the Licensee to ensure that no improper deductions are made and that the Company is provided with all necessary receipts certificates and other documents and all information required in order to avail the Company of any tax credit or other fiscal advantage.

14.   ROYALTY ACCOUNTING

14.1   The Licensee shall on each Accounting Date render to the Company a full and complete statement showing all money owing to the Company under this Agreement in respect of the preceding Accounting Period

14.2   The statement of account referred to in Clause 14.1 shall be in such form as the Company shall require and shall show Licensed Product manufactured and where stored Licensed Product shipped Licensed Product returned Licensed Product sold and the amount of Net Sales Revenue and each such statement shall be accompanied by payment of all amounts owing without reserve.

14.3   Value Added Tax shall be payable by the Licensee to the Company on receipt of the Company's Value Added Tax invoice in respect of all payments made to or to the order of the Company pursuant to this Agreement.

14.4   The Licensee shall keep full and proper books of account relating to the exploitation of its rights under this Agreement and the Company or its representative shall have the right on reasonable prior notice during the Term and for five years afterwards to inspect and take copies of such books of account during normal business hours. In the event that such audit or inspection reveals any deficiency in moneys paid to the Company under this Agreement then the Licensee shall forthwith pay the same to the Company together with interest from the date first due calculated with monthly rests at a rate of 5% above the prime or base rate from time to time charged to the Company by its bankers and shall pay all reasonable costs incurred by the Company directly as a result of such inspection.

15.   DETERMINATION

It shall constitute the repudiation by the Licensee of its obligations under this Agreement and at any time the Company may serve written notice on the

---

Clause 13.5   This clause will need to be adjusted to fit the appropriate circumstances. There will be occasions where the Company may wish to have the benefit of a "gross up" provision requiring the Licensee to pay additional sums so that the net amount received by the Company after deduction of withholdings will be equal to the gross sum which would have been received had withholdings not been applied.

Clause 14.1   Accounting dates and periods will need to be adjusted to fit the circumstances.

Clause 14.2   The Company may wish its own standard form of accounting statement to be used.

Clause 14.3   Value Added Tax will need to be considered in relation to this transaction and reference should be made to paragraphs 12.22 to 12.30 and 11.27 to 11.29.

Clause 14.4   The Company's right to audit the accounts of the Licensee is an important right.

Licensee accepting such repudiation and determining the Term and the Licensee's rights under this Agreement if:

15.1   the Licensee fails to pay any amount due under this Agreement in full within five days of its due date and such failure is not remedied within three days of receipt of written notice

15.2   the Licensee is in breach of any other material term of this Agreement which is incapable of remedy or if capable of remedy is not remedied within fourteen days of the Licensee becoming aware of it

15.3   any of the Licensee's representations shall prove to have been incorrect when made or become materially incorrect and the Company's rights and entitlements under this Agreement are materially and adversely affected

15.4   the Licensee transfers disposes of or threatens to transfer or dispose of any part of its assets which is likely in the reasonable opinion of the Company to prevent or materially to inhibit the performance by the Licensee of its obligations under this Agreement

15.5   any indebtedness guarantee or similar obligation of the Licensee or of any guarantor of the Licensee becomes due or capable of being declared due before its stated maturity or is not discharged at maturity or the Licensee or any guarantor of the Licensee defaults under or commits a breach of the provisions of any guarantee or other obligation (whether actual or contingent) of any agreement pursuant to which any such indebtedness guarantee or other obligation was incurred all or any of which shall in the reasonable opinion of the Company materially affect its rights and entitlements under this Agreement

15.6   the Licensee is declared or becomes insolvent

15.7   the Licensee convenes a meeting of its creditors or proposes or makes any arrangement or composition with or any assignment for the benefit of its creditors or a petition is presented or a meeting is convened for the purpose of considering a resolution or other steps are taken for the winding up of the Licensee (save for the purpose of and followed by a voluntary reconstruction

---

Clause 15.1   This clause permits the Licensee to remedy a non-pecuniary material breach. The time period allowed is longer than that for a pecuniary breach.

Clause 15.2   There may be circumstances where the Company has entered into the Agreement on the basis of representations made by the Licensee. This clause permits the Company to terminate the Agreement if the representations prove to have been incorrect or subsequently become incorrect.

Clause 15.3   There are occasions where a Licensee becomes less financially secure and disposes of its assets. Where a Company has entered into an Agreement in reliance on the Licensee being an entity of substance, such occasions may cause concern to the Company, and this provision permits the Company to terminate the Agreement in such instances.

Clause 15.4   Financial default of the Licensee in relation to any guarantee or obligation is a further event normally permitting termination.

Clause 15.5   For the consequences of insolvency, reference should be made to paragraphs 15.2 to 15.4.

Clause 15.6   There may be occasions when a Licensee does not actually become insolvent but where a creditor enforces security over the Licensee's business. This could have serious consequences for a Company and this clause protects the Company's interests by providing that such circumstances will entitle the Company to terminate the Agreement.

or amalgamation previously approved in writing by the Company) or if an incumbrancer takes possession of or a trustee receiver liquidator or similar officer is appointed in respect of all or any part of its business or assets or any distress execution or other legal process is levied threatened enforced upon or sued out against any of such assets

15.8   the Licensee shall abandon or announce that it intends to abandon the business of exploiting merchandise of the same generic type as the Licensed Product.

16.   EFFECT OF DETERMINATION

16.1   Upon determination under Clause 15 of the Licensee's rights under this Agreement:

(a)   the Company may without notice retake possession of the Delivery Material and all stocks of Licensed Product and for that purpose be entitled to enter upon any land or building in the possession power or control of the Licensee where the Delivery Material and all stocks of Licensed Product may be situated or believed to be situated

(b)   the Delivery Material and all stocks of Licensed Product in the possession power or control of the Licensee shall no longer be in the Licensee's possession or control with the Company's consent

(c)   without prejudice to any right to damages of the Company the Licensee shall forthwith pay to the Company all sums owing and whether or not then due under this Agreement

(d)   the Licensee shall assign to the Company all its right title benefit and interest in any agreements entered into by it in respect of the Delivery Material and the Licensed Product (including the right to receive any money payable pursuant to such agreements) on terms satisfactory to the Company and shall immediately thereafter give notice of such assignment to the other parties to such agreements in a form and manner approved by the Company.

16.2   Upon the termination of the Term by effluxion of time the Licensee shall be responsible at its own risk for re-delivery of the Delivery Material and all stocks of Licensed Product to such address in the United Kingdom as the Company may direct in good and serviceable condition (fair wear and tear excepted) and free of any advertising permitted in writing by the Company.

17.   NOTICE

17.1   Any notice or other document required to be given under this Agreement or any communication between the parties with respect to any of the provisions of this Agreement shall be in writing in English and be deemed duly given if signed by or on behalf of a duly authorised officer of the party

---

Clause 15.7   Where a Licensee ceases to carry on business or announces that it intends to cease its business, a Company will wish to recover its rights as soon as possible.

Clause 16.1   The provisions of this clause apply if the Company terminates the Agreement.

Clause 16.2   The provisions of this clause apply if the Agreement expires through passage of time.

giving the notice and if left at or sent by pre-paid registered or recorded delivery post or by telex telegram cable facsimile transmission or other means of telecommunication in permanent written form to the address of the party receiving such notice as set out at the head of the Agreement or as notified between the parties for the purpose of this clause.

17.2   Any such notice or other communication shall be deemed to be given to and received by the addressee:

(a)   at the time the same is left at the address of or handed to a representative of the party to be served
(b)   by post on the day not being a Sunday or Public Holiday two days following the date of posting
(c)   in the case of a telex telegram cable facsimile transmission or other means of telecommunication on the next following day.

17.3   In proving the giving of a notice it should be sufficient to prove that the notice was left or that the envelope containing the notice was properly addressed and posted or that the applicable means of telecommunication was addressed and despatched and despatch of the transmission was confirmed and/or acknowledged as the case may be.

17.4   Communications addressed to the Company shall be marked for the attention of [*name*] of [*address*] with a copy to [*name*] of [*address*].

18.   DEFINITIONS AND INTERPRETATION

18.1   The following definitions apply in this Agreement:

"Accounting Date"
30 days from the end of each Accounting Period

"Accounting Period"
Successive 3-month periods ending on 31 March 30 June 30 September and 31 December in each year during the Term

"Advance"
The non-returnable sum of £[*amount*]

"Agreement"
This Agreement and any and all schedules annexures and exhibits attached to it or incorporated in it by reference

"Annual Minimum Advertising Expenditure"
[*Specify*]

"Delivery"
Delivery by the Company to the Licensee of the Delivery Material or at the discretion of the Company a bill of lading airways bill or other note evidencing physical delivery of the Delivery Material to a carrier

---

Clause 17   A number of clauses in the Document provide for a means of exercising rights and a notice provision is therefore necessary.

"Delivery Date"
[*date*]

"Delivery Material"
Such material relating to the Property short particulars of which are set out in the Schedule

"Licensed Product"
Any Product manufactured produced packaged sold or marketed by the Licensee its permitted assigns and sub-licensees derived from or incorporating any part of the Property

"Net Sales Revenue"
100% of all income derived from the sale of the Licensed Product in the Territory during the Term excluding sales taxes and Value Added Taxes

"Product"
[*Specify*]

"Property"
[*Specify*] and/or the Trademark

"Premiums"
Any item of Product offered to the public in connection with the sale or promotion of another product or service in such a way as to promote publicise and/or sell such other products services or their manufacturer or advertiser

"Royalty"
[*percentage*] % of Net Sales Revenue [and in no event less than [*specify*] in respect of each item of Licensed Product sold during the Term]

"Term"
[*Specify*]

"Territory"
[*Specify*]

"Trade mark"
[*Specify*]

18.2   Unless the context otherwise requires words denoting the singular shall include the plural and vice versa and words denoting any one gender shall include all genders and words denoting persons shall include bodies corporate unincorporated associations and partnerships.

18.3   Unless otherwise stated time shall be of the essence for the purpose of the performance of the Licensee's obligations under this Agreement.

Clause 18   The provisions of this clause will need to be adjusted to reflect the relevant circumstances.

18.4   Unless otherwise stated references to clauses sub-clauses sub-paragraphs schedules annexures and exhibits relate to this Agreement.

19.   <u>MISCELLANEOUS</u>

19.1   The Company shall not be liable to the Licensee for failing to supply or procure the supply of the Delivery Material and any other material to be supplied under this Agreement due to circumstances beyond its control and it shall not be liable for any expenses or consequential losses whatever suffered by the Licensee.

19.2   The Licensee warrants that it is not the ominee or agent of any undisclosed principal and warrants that it will a_sume sole and complete responsibility for the performance of the obligations in this Agreement expressed to be performed by the Licensee.

19.3   If any provision of this Agreement shall be prohibited by or adjudged by a court to be unlawful void or unenforceable such provision shall to the extent required be severed from this Agreement and rendered ineffective as far as possible without modifying the remaining provisions of this Agreement and shall not in any way affect any other circumstances or the validity or enforcement of this Agreement.

19.4   This Agreement contains the full and complete understanding between the parties and supersedes all prior arrangements and understandings whether written or oral appertaining to the subject matter of this Agreement and may not be varied except by an instrument in writing signed by all of the parties to this Agreement. The Licensee acknowledges that no representations or promises not expressly contained in this Agreement have been made by the Company or any of its servants agents employees members or representatives.

19.5   No failure or delay on the part of any of the parties to this Agreement relating to the exercise of any right power privilege or remedy provided under this Agreement shall operate as a waiver of such right power privilege or remedy or as a waiver of any preceding or succeeding breach by the other party to this Agreement nor shall any single or partial exercise of any right power privilege or remedy preclude any other or further exercise of such or any other right power privilege or remedy provided in this Agreement all of

Clause 19.2   The Company will wish to ensure that the person it is dealing with is the principal and not the representative of a third party who may be in fact a competitor.

Clause 19.3   For an explanation of the doctrine of severance, reference should be made to paragraph 2.22.

Clause 19.4   There are occasions where oral agreements or other understandings may be created in relation to a Work which may contain either additional obligations or obligations which conflict with those set out in subsequent written agreement. This provision makes it clear that all previous arrangements and understandings are at an end and the contract is the only document relevant to the obligations and rights of the parties in relation to its subject matter. The final part of the clause expressly excludes the possibility of any liability on the part of a Company for misrepresentation on the part of any of its servants, agents, employees or representatives.

which are several and cumulative and are not exclusive of each other or of any other rights or remedies otherwise available to a party at law or in equity.

19.6   This Agreement shall not be deemed to constitute a partnership or joint venture or contract of employment between the parties.

19.7   This Agreement shall be governed by and construed in accordance with the laws of England and Wales the courts of which shall be courts of competent jurisdiction.

AS WITNESS the hands of the duly authorised representatives of the parties the day month and year first above written

THE SCHEDULE

Delivery Material

(Clause 18.1)

SIGNED by [*name of officer*]
for and on behalf of [*The Company*]   }
in the presence of:

SIGNED by [*name of officer*]
for and on behalf of [*The Licensee*]   }
in the presence of:

Clause 19.5   This provision preserves the Company's rights in circumstances where, for example, the Company wishes to negotiate to resolve a breach by the Licensee rather than enforce its strict contractual rights.

Clause 19.6   Under English law if two parties carry on business in common with a view to profit and share profit, the arrangement is capable of being considered a partnership. This provision ensures that no partnership is created inadvertently and also expressly excludes the possibility of an employment contract being created.

Clause 19.7   Where a contract is made between two entities in England and Wales, it will generally not be necessary to insert a provision of this nature, but where a contract is to be created with a foreign company (or a company situate in Scotland or Northern Ireland) this provision should always be included.

EXHIBIT I
Trademark Licence
(*Clause 1.2*)

I. Engagement of personnel

DOCUMENT 51

Statement of terms and conditions of employment
[part-time/full-time employees]

[IMPORTANT NOTE: Please read the section "About this book" on page v, before copying or using this Document]

Purpose of this Document

This is a form of agreement which may be suitable in certain circumstances for use by a publisher when engaging employees. Suitably qualified legal advice should always be taken in relation to the use of this document.

From   :   [*Company*] ("Company")

To   :   [*Name of Employee*]

This Statement sets out the particulars of the terms and conditions of your employment and is given to you pursuant to the Employment Protection (Consolidation) Act 1978 (as amended).

1.   COMMENCEMENT OF EMPLOYMENT

1.1   Your employment with the Company began on [*insert date*].

1.2   Your period of continuous employment (taking into account any service with a previous employer which counts as continuous employment) began on [*insert date*].

2.   DUTIES

2.1   You are employed as [*specify job or brief description of the work for which the employee is employed*] and will perform such obligations and duties and will comply with all such orders as may reasonably be given to you by the Company.

2.2   The Company reserves the right to vary your job duties or to assign you additional job duties which are within your capabilities. You are required to comply with all the Company's rules, regulations and policies from time to time in force.

3.   REMUNERATION

3.1   Your basic salary is £[*amount*] per annum (or such sum as the Company may subsequently determine). Payment is made [monthly/weekly] in arrears after deduction of Income Tax (PAYE) National Insurance and any other deduction required to be made by law.

3.2   In addition to the basic salary specified in Clause 3.1 you shall be entitled to receive further remuneration by way of commission calculated in accordance with and subject to the terms and conditions specified in Schedule A attached [*Schedule to be drafted if commission is payable*].

3.3   The Company reserves the right to deduct from your salary one day's pay for each day of unauthorised absence. Unauthorised absence shall include any absence from work unless due to:

(a)   genuine sickness which has been notified to the Company according to paragraph 10 below;

(b)   absence for which the Company has given prior permission;

(c)   genuine reasons outside the employee's control which are acceptable to the Company.

4.   HOURS OF WORK AND OVERTIME

4.1   Your normal hours of work are [*37*]/[*45*] per week Monday to Friday [*00.00*] am to [*00.00*] pm (with one hour for lunch to be taken at a mutually agreed time). However you may be required to work additional hours in order to meet the Company's business requirements or to ensure the satisfactory performance of your duties. You [are/are not] entitled to be paid additional remuneration for any overtime worked.

4.2   Overtime working where applicable must be agreed in advance by the Manager of your department. Overtime rates of pay are:

[Monday to Friday: Basic × 1.5
Sunday & Public Holidays   Basic × 2.0]

4.3   The Company reserves the right to change your normal working hours in order to meet its business requirements.

4.4   Where you are required to work on public holidays or at weekends you may request time off in lieu.]

5.   COMPANY CAR

You will be notified separately in writing if you are entitled to the use of a Company car. Such entitlement is subject to the terms of the Company's policy on cars from time to time in force. The Company reserves the right to amend its car policy at its sole discretion.

6.   BUSINESS EXPENSES

You will be reimbursed all reasonable expenses properly incurred by you in the performance of your duties on the production of appropriate receipts or other satisfactory documentation.

7.   HOLIDAY ENTITLEMENT AND PAY

7.1   The holiday year is the [calendar year].

7.2   You will be entitled to a maximum of 3 weeks' holiday in the first 12 months of your employment calculated in accordance with clause 7.6 below and thereafter you will be entitled to a maximum of 4 weeks' holiday with full pay in any holiday year in addition to the usual statutory and bank holidays.

7.3   All holiday dates are subject to the prior approval of the Company.

7.4   Holidays may not be carried forward into the following holiday year without special arrangement with the Company.

7.5   Entitlement to holiday will accrue with each completed calendar month worked at the appropriate yearly rate. You may take your holiday for the current holiday year before it has accrued [provided that no holiday can be taken during the first 6 months of your employment by the Company without special arrangement with the Company]. On termination of employment an adjustment will be made in the final payment of wages to you either by way of an additional payment of wages at your normal rate in respect of holidays accrued but not taken or by way of similar deduction in respect of holidays taken but not earned provided that no additional payment will be made if you are dismissed for misconduct.

7.6   [After three years of service, reckoned from the date of commencement with the Company, full-time staff are entitled to an additional day's holiday in the next calendar year and in each ensuing calendar year until the maximum of five weeks holiday has been earned. Part-time staff accrue the extra holiday pro rata to their hours of work.]

8.   PERMANENT HEALTH INSURANCE

8.1   The Company will implement a permanent health insurance scheme for all employees. The scheme will come into effect on or about [*date*] or as soon as possible thereafter.

8.2   Employees will be entitled to join the scheme upon the completion of 15 months' service with the Company. The Company will provide cover for the employee their spouse and any children under the age of 18.

9.   PLACE OF WORK

9.1   You will initially work from the Company's offices at [*specify location*]. However the Company reserves the right to require you to work from or at any office it [or any Associated Company] may have within reasonable travelling distance of that location.

9.2   You will be required to travel (whether or not in the United Kingdom) as necessary in the course of your work as the Company shall from time to time direct.

10.   ABSENCE AND SICKNESS

10.1   In case of sickness or other incapability for work you must notify [*name*] as early as is practicable on the first day of absence giving details of the reason for and the anticipated length of absence.

10.2   Where sickness lasts seven days or less you will be required to complete a Self Certification form immediately you return to work. On returning to work you must report to [*name*] before 10.00 am on your first day back.

10.3   Where sickness lasts for more than seven days you must forward a Doctor's Statement to [*name*] without delay covering all days of absence. On the expiry of such Statement you must notify the Company whether you are returning to work or whether you have a further Statement.

10.4   The Company reserves the right to require you to undergo a medical examination by a doctor or consultant nominated by it at any time during your employment in which event the Company will bear the costs of such medical examination.

10.5 The Company will be liable to pay you Statutory Sick Pay ("SSP") in accordance with the relevant statutory provision.

[10.6 After the completion of the probationary period in Clause 12.1 below you will be paid your normal salary ("Company Sick Pay") in respect of any period of unavoidable absence through sickness or injury up to a maximum period of [*no.*] weeks in any one calendar year ie no carry forward of unutilised periods.] [Company Sick Pay will be inclusive of any SSP to which you are entitled.]

10.7 During your probationary period you will only receive sickness benefits under the Statutory Sick Pay Scheme provided you are eligible for benefit under its rules.

10.8 You shall be allowed reasonable time off with pay to attend doctor hospital or dental appointments. Such absences will only be authorised on production of written evidence of the appointment.

11. PENSIONS

The Company does not at present operate a Pension Scheme. There is no contracting-out certificate in force for your employment.

[OR]

[You shall be eligible to participate in the [*please specify name of pension scheme*] subject to its rules from time to time in force. Details of the scheme can be obtained from [*name*]. The Company reserves the right to terminate its participation in the scheme or substitute another scheme or alter the benefits available to you under any scheme. There is a/is contracting-out certificate in force in relation to the State Earnings Related Pension Scheme.]

[OR]

[The Company does not have its own pension scheme and all employees must accordingly pay contracted-in National Insurance contributions. The Company will if requested by you contribute to your pension arrangements an amount equal to [*percentage*]% of your annual salary from time to time. The Company's contribution will be on the basis that you will contribute an equal amount (including increases) to your pension scheme. Further details can be obtained from [*name*].]

12. TERMINATION OF EMPLOYMENT

12.1 You will be on probationary status for the first three months of your employment during which period your employment may be terminated by either the Company or yourself on giving [one] week's written notice.

12.2   After the probationary period this period of notice will increase to four weeks and will thereafter increase by one additional week for each completed year of service.

12.3   The Company reserves the right to make payment in lieu of notice on the above scale or to require you not to attend your place of work during your notice period as it sees fit (whether you or the Company gave notice) and to terminate your service without notice if you are guilty of serious misconduct. Any payment in lieu of notice will have PAYE tax and National Insurance contributions deducted at source. Where the Company requires you not to attend your place of work during your notice period during that time so long as you are on full pay you will not be permitted to work for any other person firm or company or on your own behalf.

12.4   The Company reserves the right to require you not to attend work or to undertake any work or to vary your duties during any period of notice of termination which is given by you or the Company. However during this time you will continue to receive your normal salary and benefits of employment.

12.5   The Company reserves the right to summarily dismiss you if you are guilty of serious misconduct or gross negligence or any other serious breach of the Terms and Conditions. Examples of serious misconduct are set out in the Company Disciplinary Procedure referred to in Clause 14.

12.6   Unless your employment has terminated at any earlier date it will terminate without any further notice at the end of the month in which your [60th] birthday falls.

12.7   On termination of your employment, howsoever arising, you are required to return immediately to the Company in accordance with its instructions all correspondence, records, price lists, specifications, models, notes, formulations, lists, papers, reports and other documents and all copies thereof and other property belonging to the Company (including any Company car) or relating to its business affairs or dealings which are in your possession or under your control.

13.   EXCLUSIVITY OF SERVICE

You are required to devote your full-time attention and abilities to your job duties during working hours and to act in the best interests of the Company at all times. You must not without the written consent of the Company be in any way directly or indirectly actively engaged or concerned in any other business or activity where this is (or is likely to be) in conflict with the interests of the Company or where it may adversely affect the proper performance of your duties. However this does not preclude your holding 5% of any class of securities in any company which is quoted on a recognised Stock Exchange.

14.   DISCIPLINARY PROCEDURE

14.1   If you are unhappy about any aspect of your employment you may raise the matter at first instance with your immediate superior. If this does not produce a satisfactory resolution of your grievance you should take it up with the Chief Executive whose decision shall be final.

14.2   The Employee will comply with the Disciplinary Rules and Procedures laid down by the Company from time to time. A copy of the current Company Disciplinary Procedure dated [*date*] is attached. Modifications or revisions may be obtained from [*name*].

15.   INTELLECTUAL PROPERTY

15.1   The entire copyright and all other rights including without limitation design rights registered design rights patent rights trade mark rights rights of action and all other rights of whatever nature in and to any and all material invention or process of whatever description created or produced by you whether alone or in collaboration with others in the performance of your duties whether or not during the working hours specified in paragraph 1 and whether or not at the location referred to in paragraph 9.1 or at any other location shall vest in the Company absolutely from the moment of creation and the Company its successors assignees and licensees shall be the sole absolute unincumbered legal and beneficial owner throughout the world of all rights in all such material for the full period during which such rights may now or at any time in the future subsist under the laws in force in any part of the world.

15.2   You confirm and agree that to the extent that your services result in the creation of any typographical arrangement of a published edition or film or sound recording or broadcast or cable programme (as such expressions are defined in the Copyright, Designs and Patents Act 1988) all rights in all such material shall vest in the Company as sole absolute legal and beneficial owner absolutely from the moment of creation. Where the performance of your services involves your undertaking arrangements for the making of any sound recording or film you confirm and agree that all such arrangements shall be made by you on behalf of the Company and shall be treated in all aspects as if such arrangements had been made by the Company. All material created as a result of your services shall be treated in all respects as if the Company were its author and first owner for the purposes of Sections 9(2) and 11(2) of the Copyright, Designs and Patents Act 1988.

15.3   You warrant that the product of your services shall be original to you except to the extent base upon material which is in the public domain or which has been acquired by the Company and you warrant that the product of your services shall not infringe any right of copyright or any other right whatever of any third party and shall not be obscene libellous or defamatory or constitute a contempt of court or infringe any moral right or performer's right or right of privacy or right to privacy or personality right of any person.

15.4   You irrevocably and unconditionally grant and confirm all consents for the worldwide exploitation by the Company its successors assignees and licensees of all performances given by you in the course of your duties in any and all media by any and all means whether now known or developed in future.

15.5 You irrevocably and unconditionally grant waive any and all moral rights to which you may be entitled in relation to your services pursuant to the laws in force throughout the world to the extent you are permitted to do so and you agree to disclose to the Company and its insurers all matters which may result in liability in relation to any copyright work created by you and/or the Company and to follow all errors and omissions clearance procedures required by insurers and/or any third party with whom the Company contracts.

16. CONFIDENTIALITY

16.1 You shall not except as authorised or required by your duties here-under use for your own benefit or gain or reveal to any person(s) firm company or other organisation whatsoever any trade secrets or Confidential Information belonging to the Company or any Associated Company or relating to the affairs or dealings of the Company or any Associated Company which may come to your knowledge during your employment. You shall treat the same with complete secrecy. This restriction shall continue to apply after the termination of your employment without limitation in time, but shall cease to apply to any information or knowledge which may subsequently come into the public domain, other than by way of unauthorised disclosure.

16.2 "Confidential Information" shall include but shall not be limited to information relating to the business sales enquiries prices pricing policies technical processes and finances of the Company or any Associated Company or other matters connected with the products or services marketed provided or obtained by the Company or any Associated Company or any of its suppliers agents or customers; or documents or other information to which you may have access which are either marked confidential or secret or which have been passed to you under an express or implied obligation of confidence.

16.3 In this Agreement an "Associated Company" includes any firm company corporation or other organisation which:

(a)   is directly or indirectly controlled by the Company; or

(b)   directly or indirectly controls the Company; or

(c)   is directly or indirectly controlled by a third party who also directly or indirectly controls the Company.

17. GENERAL

Changes to any of the Terms or Conditions in this statement will be notified to you in writing within four weeks of such changes being made. Enquiries regarding any such change should be made in the first instance to your Supervisor within four weeks of that notification.

18. DEDUCTIONS

The Company shall be entitled to deduct from your salary any money due from you to the Company on the termination of your employment any advances by the Company owed by you the cost of any damage to the Company's property caused by you and any other monies owed by you to the Company (eg excess holiday taken etc).

[19.   POST-TERMINATION RESTRICTIONS

You undertake that for the period of six months following the termination of your employment however arising you will not directly or indirectly solicit in competition with the Company the custom of any person firm company or other organisation who at any time during the twelve months immediately preceding the date of termination of your employment:

(a)   was a customer or client of the Company; or

(b)   was a person firm company or other organisation with whom you had regular substantial or a series of business dealings on behalf of the Company.]

20.   SUBSTITUTION FOR ANY PREVIOUS AGREEMENT

This Agreement cancels and is in substitution of all previous letters of engagement agreements and arrangements whether oral or in writing relating to the subject matter hereof between the Company and yourself all of which shall be deemed to have been terminated by mutual consent.

[SCHEDULE A – Clause 3.2]

Signed _____   Date _____

For and on behalf of
[*the Company*]

I agree to the above conditions and acknowledge receipt of one copy of the Statement of Terms and Conditions and one copy of the Company's Disciplinary Procedure.

Signed _____   Date _____

DOCUMENT 52

Freelance letter of engagement

Purpose of this Document

This is a form of agreement which may be suitable in certain circumstances for use by a publisher when engaging employees. Suitably qualified legal advice should always be taken in relation to the use of this document.

795

From   :   *[Publisher]*
                 of *[address]*
                 ("Company")

To   :   *[Name]*
                 of *[address]*

Date   :   *[date]*

Dear *[Name]*

This letter is to confirm the agreement between you and the Company for the engagement of your services upon and subject to the following terms and conditions:

1.   ENGAGEMENT

The Company engages you and in consideration of the undertaking in paragraph 5 you agree to render to the Company your services as a *[specify capacity]* and your services in such other capacity as may from time to time be agreed between you and the Company ("Services") in accordance with the provisions set out in this letter on a sole exclusive basis for the period of *[specify]* commencing *[date]* at *[location]* or such other locations specified by the Company. During such period your normal working hours shall be *[00.00]* to *[00.00]* but you shall be required to work such additional hours as may be necessary to ensure the satisfactory completion of all tasks assigned to you.

2.   COPYRIGHT

2.1   You assign to the Company the entire copyright whether vested contingent or future and all rights of action and all other rights of whatever nature in and to the product of the Services whether now known or in the future created to which you are now or may at any time after the date of this Agreement be entitled by virtue of or pursuant to any of the laws in force in any part of the world TO HOLD the same to the Company its successors assigns and licensees absolutely for the full period of copyright throughout the world including all renewals reversions and extensions.

2.2   You confirm the unconditional and irrevocable waiver of all rights to which you are now or may in future be entitled pursuant to the provisions of the Copyright, Designs and Patents Act 1988 Sections 77 80 84 and 85 and any other moral rights to which you may be entitled under any legislation now existing or in future enacted in any part of the world in respect of the product of the Services.

OR

2.2   You confirm and agree that to the extent your Services result in the creation of any typographical arrangement of a published edition or film or sound recording or broadcast or cable programme (as such expressions are defined in the Copyright, Designs and Patents Act 1988) all rights in such

796

material shall vest in the Company as sole absolute legal and beneficial owner absolutely from the moment of creation and such material shall be treated in all respects as if the Company were the author and first owner of such material pursuant to Sections 9(2) and 11(2) of such Act.

3. OBLIGATIONS

You warrant undertake and agree with the Company that:

3.1   You shall render the Services to the best of your skill and ability in a professional and workmanlike manner at such locations and times and in co-operation with such persons as the Company may from time to time direct.

3.2   You shall not without the prior written consent of the Company incur any expenditure or costs on behalf of the Company.

3.3   You shall not in connection with your activities under this Agreement do or suggest the doing of any act which might be unlawful or infringe the rights of any third party or which might prejudice or damage the reputation of the Company.

3.4   No literary dramatic musical artistic work or film sound recording made by you (whether alone or jointly with others) as part of the Services shall under the laws in force in any part of the world be obscene or defamatory or offensive to religion or blasphemous or infringe any right of copyright moral right right of privacy right of publicity or any other right whatever of any person and all such works films sound recordings broadcast or cable programme shall comply in all respects with the law.

3.5   Except to the extent that any copyright work created by you during the rendering of the Services is made by you jointly with any employee of the Company you shall be the sole absolute and unincumbered legal and beneficial owner of all rights in and to such copyright work and you warrant that you have the right to grant to the Company the rights granted in this Agreement.

3.6   Any literary dramatic musical artistic work or film sound recording broadcast or cable programme made by you (whether alone or jointly with others) as part of the Services shall comply in all respects with the provisions of all relevant Codes of Practice and Professional Standards of the Company which have been notified to you and shall comply with the Company's house rules and style requirements.

3.7   You shall not disclose reveal or make public any information whatever concerning the business of the Company or this Agreement all of which shall be strictly confidential.

3.8   You agree to indemnify and keep fully indemnified the Company from and against any actions proceedings costs awards claims and damages however incurred or arising against the Company in respect of arising out of any breach or non-performance by you of any or all of your obligations warranties and undertakings.

4. REMUNERATION

Subject to the full and complete performance and observance by you of your obligations and warranties under this Agreement the Company undertakes to pay you:

4.1 £[*amount*] per [*week or month*].

4.2 Reimbursement of all expenditure necessarily incurred by you in the performance of your obligations under this Agreement with the prior approval of the Company subject to the production of receipts or vouchers provided such expenditure shall not exceed such amount reasonably specified by the Company in respect of any period.

4.3 Subject to the delivery to the Company of a full accurate and proper Value Added Tax invoice all relevant Value Added Tax payable in respect of the sums referred to in paragraphs 4.1 and 4.2.

5. MISCELLANEOUS

5.1 Nothing contained in this letter shall constitute a partnership or contract of employment between the parties.

5.2 This Agreement shall be governed by and construed in accordance with the laws of England and Wales whose courts shall be courts of competent jurisdiction.

If you accept the terms and conditions of this Agreement please sign and return the enclosed duplicate copy.

Yours faithfully

SIGNED by [   ]
for and on behalf of
[*Publisher*]

I confirm and agree the above and agree to be bound by it.

SIGNED by [   ]
[*Individual*]
in the presence of:

Index